1080 RECIPES

Simone and Inés Ortega

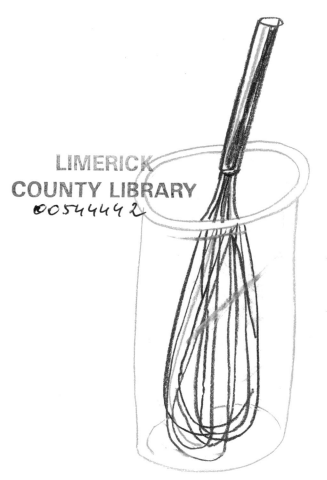

illustrations
Javier Mariscal

CONTENTS

PREFACES

From the Publisher

The popularity of Spanish food has grown exponentially throughout the world during the past decade. Tapas bars and Spanish restaurants are opening in every major city and, thanks to the growing reputations of the country's many fine chefs, including Ferran Adrià of El Bulli and others, gastronomic attention has been well and truly turned on the food of contemporary Spain. As *The New York Times* recently reported, Spanish cuisine currently enjoys a reputation for innovation and creativity previously only awarded to the food of France.

However, the imaginative recipes being developed by Spain's leading chefs are, despite their innovation, based on the solid traditions of Spanish food, which is unpretentious, healthy, simple and delicious.

As different cultures settled in various parts of Spain over the ages, each brought their own contribution to the development of its cuisine. The Greeks introduced the quintessentential Spanish ingredient, olive oil, while seasonings, spices and the many combinations of meat and fruit that we associate today with Spanish food are a legacy of the Moors. The diverse cultures of the country's history can be clearly traced through the variety and combination of ingredients in its dishes, the most famous of which is the surprising marriage of fish and meat in the country's national dish, paella.

1080 Recipes was written by Simone Ortega, who has been writing about food for over fifty years, and is the foremost authority on traditional Spanish cooking. It has been Spain's favourite cookery book since its first publication over thirty years ago, with millions of copies now sold. Over the years, Simone has been joined by her daughter Inés, also a respected food writer, and together, they have revised and updated the recipes to reflect modern methods without losing the traditional character of Spanish food.

This first edition in English has been further adapted for the English-speaking market, adding explanation and introduction to specialist ingredients and particular techniques of cooking. The great Spanish illustrator Javier Mariscal has filled the pages of *1080 Recipes* with hundreds of specially created colourful and evocative drawings depicting the food and atmosphere of Spain, and the recipes are also accompanied by more than 100 colour photographs showing the completed dishes.

With *1080 Recipes* on your table, you will quickly learn to love a cuisine that is filled with variety, subtlety and flavour.

Buen provecho!

From the authors

I am confident that this book has helped to improve the way people in Spain eat: it has made learning to cook easier for those who don't have much time to spend in the kitchen; the recipes are tasty and simple; and my readers have told me over the years that I have included clear and precise explanations that ensure my recipes always work, even in the hands of the most inexperienced of cooks.

Each recipe is numbered and the book is fully indexed, using the recipe numbers to direct you quickly and easily to the dish you are looking for. You will also see that the recipes do not have grandiose titles but, instead, I have given them names that describe the main ingredients in the dish – although there are just one or two exceptions to this rule, when I have used a name by which a dish is widely recognised, such as gazpacho.

Finally, I hope that this English edition will encourage a host of new readers to grab their saucepans with increasing enthusiasm.

Simone Ortega

My family has always regarded three things as important in our lives: reading, writing and cooking. I spent years watching my mother cook and later, as I grew up, I started to help her in the kitchen. As a result of constant nagging from her friends, my mother was eventually persuaded to collect her recipes together into a book. My father, being a publisher, then decided to publish this as *1080 Recipes*, a title that was taken from the number of recipes that the book contained. We never for a moment imagined that over the course of a little more than 3 decades this book would become a cookery classic and that we would soon be celebrating millions of copies sold!

Later, as I began writing and publishing my own cookery books, my mother began to ask me to update or modify recipes with her so that they were more in tune with contemporary styles of cooking and eating. Since then she and I have worked together to ensure that *1080 Recipes* is as relevant to contemporary lifestyles as it was when it was first published.

Over time, cooking habits may have changed, but *1080 Recipes* remains fresh. It is always up-to-date, always accessible, and its pages contain dishes that can be made successfully in any home and by any cook, thus ensuring the book's continuing success. Its aim has never changed: to offer the best of Spanish cuisine in a simple and accessible way, while maintaining an international and contemporary outlook. This was Simone Ortega's great secret when she created her classic first edition, and I am proud to follow in her footsteps.

Inés Ortega

From Ferran Adrià

I have great pleasure in writing a preface to this classic cookery book, which was written by one of the first people to raise food and cooks to their rightful places in society. *1080 Recipes* has now been translated into English, with Simone's daughter Inés helping to update and revise its recipes. This English edition proves that, for Simone Ortega, cooking has no borders.

The first time Simone came to El Bulli, I was very interested to know what she thought of my food, and I was pleased when I realised that she instinctively understood and enjoyed what we do in our restaurant. Simone is a sensitive and intuitive woman, traditional but at the same time evolutionary in her outlook. She has an instinctive feel for creating new flavours, demonstrating that she has the intuition necessary to be a great cook.

In this book, Simone and Inés offer us a wealth of gastronomic experience and wisdom and *1080 Recipes* will quickly transport you to the heart of Spain. This is a timeless book. When you read it, you suddenly realise the glories of the food in front of you, those that, until now, you have not fully appreciated. Ours is a splendid cuisine, born out of the pleasure of eating, and it is also one that is perfect for those who have little time to cook, but who don't want to give up the enjoyment of eating well and, thus, of feeding their souls as well as their stomachs.

In this book, we travel on a delicious journey through 1080 recipes with Simone and Inés, each recipe demonstrating its two authors' dedication to a job well done and their passion for creativity and good food.

One thousand and eighty thank yous!

APPETIZERS

Olives

How to cure

Fresh olives are inedible and must be cured to remove their bitterness. (Commercially available olives will already have been cured.) Put fresh olives into a container of caustic soda so that they are just covered. The proportions are 1 kg/2 ¼ lb olives to 30 g/1 oz caustic soda. Leave them for 24 hours. It does not matter if they are a little soft because the salt used for preserving them will make them firmer.

How to preserve

Wash the olives thoroughly, put them into containers and add enough water to cover them. Add salt to taste, a few sprigs of savory, some lemon rind and a few cloves of unpeeled garlic. Leave the olives in this mixture for a few days before eating them.

A dressing for black olives

Black olives preserved in brine can be eaten as they are or dressed with a little paprika, onion and olive oil.

1

Pastry for tartlets
MASA QUEBRADA PARA TARTALETAS

- **250 g/9 oz plain flour,**
  plus extra for dusting
- **½ teaspoon salt**
- **125 g/4¼ oz butter, margarine**
  or lard, or a mixture of equal
  quantities of any two of these,
  plus extra for greasing (optional)
- **2 teaspoons groundnut oil,**
  plus extra for greasing (optional)
- **1 egg, lightly beaten**

Makes 20

Sift the flour into a large bowl, add the salt and mix, lifting up the flour with a spoon and letting it fall back into the bowl to aerate it. Add the fat, oil and egg and quickly mix together with your fingertips until the mixture resembles breadcrumbs. Gradually add about 175 ml/6 fl oz water, a little at a time, and lightly bring the mixture together with your hands to form a smooth dough that comes away from the sides of the bowl. (The exact quantity of water required depends on the type of flour.) Leave the ball of dough in the bowl, cover with a clean tea towel and leave to rest in a cool place for 30 minutes. Preheat the oven to 200°C/400°F/Gas Mark 6 and grease 20 tartlet tins, 4 cm/ 1½ inches in diameter, with butter or oil. (You could also use boat-shaped barquette tins.) Roll out the dough on a lightly floured surface until it is quite thin (about 3 mm/⅛ inch). Stamp out 20 rounds with a 4-cm/1½-inch fluted cutter, re-rolling the dough as necessary, and use to line the prepared tins. Prick the base of each with a fork, line with greaseproof paper and fill with baking beans, dried chickpeas or dried beans. Bake for 15 minutes. Remove the paper and beans, return the tartlets to the oven and bake for a further 5 minutes, until golden brown. (This process of pre-cooking pastry before adding the filling is called 'baking blind', and it is done to prevent a wet filling causing the pastry to go soggy.) Transfer the tartlets to wire racks and leave to cool completely. If you are not using them immediately, store in an airtight container.

2

French pastry for tartlets
MASA FRANCESA PARA TARTALETAS

- 20 g/¾ oz fresh yeast
- 3 tablespoons lukewarm milk
- 2 egg yolks
- 100 g/3½ oz butter,
  plus extra for greasing
- 250 g/9 oz plain flour,
  plus extra for dusting
- pinch of salt

Makes 25

Mash the yeast with the milk in a cup or small bowl until smooth, then leave to stand for about 10 minutes, until the mixture is frothy. Transfer the yeast mixture to a mixing bowl and add the egg yolks and butter. Sift in the flour and salt and bring the mixture together with your hands. Roll out the dough on a lightly floured surface until very thin (about 3 mm/1/8 inch). Stamp out 25 rounds with a 4-cm/1½-inch fluted cutter, re-rolling the dough as necessary. Grease 25 tartlet tins, 4 cm/1½ inches, with butter and line with the dough rounds. Cover with a clean tea towel, leave to rise for 30 minutes. Preheat the oven to 200°C/400°F/Gas Mark 6. Prick the base of the tartlets with a fork, line with greaseproof paper and fill with baking beans or dried chickpeas or dried beans. Bake blind for 15 minutes. Remove the paper and beans, return the tartlets to the oven and bake for a further 5 minutes, until golden brown. Transfer the tartlets to wire racks and leave to cool completely. Once cold, they are ready to use. If not using immediately, store them in an airtight container.

3

Muffins with chopped ham
MUFFINS CON JAMÓN PICADO

- 10 muffins
- 50 g/2 oz butter, softened
- 150 g/5 oz ham, chopped

Makes 30

Cut the muffins into thirds. Spread them with a little butter and top with the chopped ham. Use the back of a spoon to press the ham down to prevent it falling off the muffin when it is picked up.

4

Muffins with foie gras and gelatine
MUFFINS CON FOIE-GRAS Y GELATINA

- 10 muffins
- 200 g/7 oz fresh or canned
  foie gras
- set gelatine (see recipe 42),
  finely chopped

Makes 30

Cut the muffins into thirds and spread generously with fresh or canned foie gras. Cover with the chopped gelatine and press down with the back of a spoon to prevent the gelatine falling off the muffin when it is picked up.

5

Little ham turnovers

EMPANADILLAS DE JAMÓN

- **1 quantity Pastry for Turnovers (see recipe 43)**
- **200 g/7 oz Serrano ham, chopped**
- **sunflower oil, for deep-frying**
  Makes 30

Fill the turnovers with the chopped ham. Heat the oil in a deep-fryer or deep saucepan to 180–190°C/350–375°F or until a cube of day-old bread browns in 30 seconds. Add the turnovers, in batches, and cook for 6–8 minutes, turning to brown both sides, then serve immediately.

6

Ham and pineapple canapés

CANAPÉS DE JAMÓN Y PIÑA

- **5 slices of bread, each cut into 4 x 4 cm rounds and toasted**
- **50 g/2 oz butter**
- **5 slices ham, each cut into 4 pieces**
- **20 pieces canned pineapple**
- **60 g/2 ¼ oz grated cheese**
  Makes 20

Preheat the oven to 180°C/350°F/Gas Mark 4. Spread the rounds of toasted bread with a little butter. Place a slice of ham on each, top with a piece of drained canned pineapple and sprinkle with grated cheese. Place on a baking sheet and bake for 5 minutes. Serve hot.

7

Foie gras canapés

CANAPÉS DE FOIE-GRAS

- **100 g/3 ½ oz fresh or canned foie gras**
- **1 tablespoon evaporated milk or lightly beaten double cream**
- **1 tablespoon brandy**
- **¼ teaspoon paprika**
- **5 slices of bread, each cut into 4 x 4 cm rounds and toasted**
- **20 capers**
  Makes 20

Mix together the foie gras, evaporated milk or double cream, brandy and paprika in a bowl until thoroughly combined. Spoon the mixture into a piping bag and pipe on to the rounds of toasted bread. Garnish each canapé with a caper, rinsed if salted.

8

Ham and cream cheese rolls
ROLLITOS DE JAMÓN Y QUESO BLANCO

• 2–3 medium-thick slices of ham
• lightly salted cream cheese,
  such as Philadelphia

Makes approx. 12

Spread each slice of ham with cream cheese. Roll up the slices of ham, wrap in foil and place in the freezer for 30 minutes. Unwrap the foil and cut the rolled ham into 1 ½ cm/½ inch slices before serving.

9

Prawn barquettes
BARQUITAS DE GAMBAS

• 20 pastry barquettes
  (see recipe 1)
• 100 g/3 ½ oz Classic Mayonnaise
  (see recipe 105)
• 40 medium sized,
  cooked, peeled prawns
• set gelatine (see recipe 42),
  finely chopped (optional)

Makes 20

Spread the base of the pastry barquettes with mayonnaise. For each one, put two prawns on top of the mayonnaise, then cover with the chopped gelatine. Chill for at least 30 minutes before serving.

10

Tuna canapés
CANAPÉS DE ATÚN

• 1 x 200 g/7 oz can tuna
• 2 tablespoons Thick Mayonnaise
  (see recipe 106)
• 5 slices of bread, each cut into
  4 x 4 cm rounds and toasted

Makes 20

Drain the tuna, place in a bowl and mash well with a fork. Stir in the mayonnaise until thoroughly combined, then spread the mixture on the rounds of toasted bread.

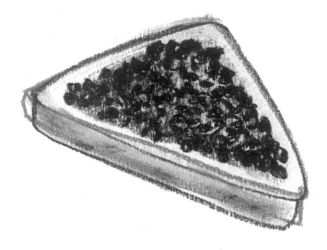

11

Caviar canapés
CANAPÉS DE CAVIAR

- **5 slices of bread, each cut into
  4 x 4 cm rounds and toasted**
- **50 g/2 oz butter**
- **100 g/3½ oz caviar**
- **1 lemon**
- **2 hardboiled eggs, chopped**
  Makes 20

Spread the rounds of toasted bread with butter and spoon a little caviar on top. Squeeze 2 drops of lemon juice on to each canapé and top with the hard-boiled eggs. Halved quail's eggs may be used for this recipe.

12

Smoked salmon canapés
CANAPÉS DE SALMÓN AHUMADO

- **5 slices of bread, each cut into
  4 x 4 cm rounds and toasted**
- **50 g/2 oz butter**
- **200 g/7 oz smoked salmon,
  thinly sliced**
- **1 lemon (optional)**
  Makes 20

Spread the rounds of toasted bread with butter and place the sliced smoked salmon on top. If you like, sprinkle each canapé with a few drops of lemon juice.

Note: You can also sprinkle the canapés with a little finely chopped spring onion on the butter before adding the smoked salmon.

13

Smoked trout or smoked eel canapés
CANAPÉS DE TRUCHA O ANGUILA AHUMADA

- **5 slices of bread, each cut into
  4 x 4 cm rounds and toasted**
- **50 g/2 oz butter**
- **200 g/7 oz smoked trout or
  smoked eel fillet, finely chopped**
- **1 lemon**
  Makes 20

Spread the rounds of toasted bread with butter and top with the smoked trout or smoked eel fillet. Sprinkle 2 drops of lemon juice on each canapé.

Snails

Snails gathered in the wild should be fed only flour for 5–6 days to eliminate any toxins. Live cultivated snails should be cooked on the day of purchase. You can also use freshly cooked, frozen or canned snails. If using live snails wash them well in plenty of salted water mixed with a little white-wine vinegar before cooking.

14

Snails (first version)

- 700 g/1 lb 5 oz snails
- 2 tablespoons olive oil
- 1 onion, chopped
- 1 red or green pepper,
  seeded and chopped
- 3 tomatoes,
  finely chopped and seeded
- 2 tablespoons plain flour
- pinch of paprika
- 1 bay leaf
- 50 g/2 oz Serrano ham, diced
- 2 cloves garlic, finely chopped
- 5 sprigs fresh parsley, chopped
- salt and pepper
- 1 hard boiled egg, chopped
  (optional)

Serves 6

If you are using fresh snails, put them snails in a large saucepan and pour in just enough lukewarm water to cover. Heat gently until the snails emerge from their shells, then increase the heat to high and cook for 30 minutes. Drain well, discard the shells and return the snails to the pan. Set aside. If you are using canned snails, drain and set aside. Heat the oil in another saucepan. Add the onion and pepper. Cook over a low heat, stirring occasionally, for about 10 minutes, until the onion begins to brown. Add the tomato and cook, stirring occasionally, for a further 10 minutes. Sprinkle the flour over the mixture, stir in, then remove the pan from the heat and season with paprika to taste. Stir in sufficient water to make a fairly thick sauce and add a bay leaf. Season with salt and pepper to taste. (The mixture should be quite spicy.) Stir in the Serrano ham, then add the garlic and parsley. Pour the sauce into the pan with the snails and heat through. If you are using canned snails, just add them to the sauce and heat through. If you like, you can add chopped hard-boiled egg.

15

Snails (second version)

- 700 g/1 lb 5 oz snails
- 1 onion, cut into wedges
- 1 bay leaf
- 2 tablespoons olive oil
- 1 onion, chopped
- 1 chilli, chopped
- 50 g/2 oz bacon, chopped
- 50 g/2 oz chorizo, thinly sliced
- 2 tablespoons plain flour
- 1 meat stock cube

Serves 6

If using fresh snails, put them, the onion wedges and bay leaf in a saucepan, pour in just enough water to cover and bring to the boil. Cook for 15 minutes. If using canned snails, skip this step. Meanwhile, heat a little olive oil in another saucepan. Add the chopped onion and chilli to taste (seeded if you prefer a milder flavour), bacon and chorizo. Sprinkle with the flour, crumble in the meat stock cube and cook over a low heat, stirring frequently, for about 10 minutes, until lightly browned. Add the onion and chilli mixture to the snails, which should now be in just a little water, and simmer for about 20 minutes.

Fish croquettes

CROQUETAS DE PESCADO

- **½ quantity Croquettes (see recipe 62)**
- **sunflower oil, for deep frying**

Makes 20

Make a half quantity of croquettes according to recipe 62. Shape the mixture into small croquettes. Heat the oil in a deep-fryer or deep saucepan to 180–190°C/350–375°F or until a cube of day-old bread browns in 30 seconds. Place several croquettes in the oil, being careful not to overcrowd the pan, and cook for 2 minutes, or until golden brown. Remove with a slotted spoon and keep warm while you quickly cook the remaining croquettes. Serve immediately.

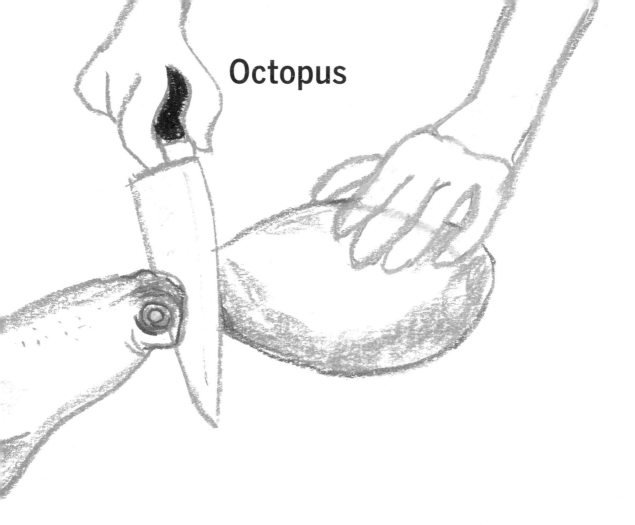

Octopus

How to cook

The easiest way to ensure that octopus will be tender is to freeze it for up to 2 weeks. On removing it from the freezer, put it straight into boiling water and cook for about 35 minutes, until tender. The time will depend on the size and tenderness of the octopus. Alternatively, pour plenty of water into a pressure cooker, add a bay leaf and a piece of onion and bring to the boil. Add the octopus, cover, bring to high pressure and cook for 15 minutes. Leave the pressure cooker to cool completely before opening it.

Here is a more classic way of cooking octopus. Clean and rinse the octopus and prick it all over with a fork. Bring a large saucepan of water to the boil with a bay leaf and a piece of onion. Add the octopus and cook for 1 minute, then remove it from the pan. When the water comes back to the boil, add the octopus again for 1 minute. Do this three times in a row, leaving the octopus to cook for 45 minutes the last time. Drain the octopus and rinse under cold running water.

17 📷 Octopus with paprika
PULPO CON PIMENTÓN

- **1 kg/2¼ lb octopus**
- **175 ml/6 fl oz olive oil**
- **pinch of hot paprika**
- **salt (optional)**

Serves 6

Prepare and cook the octopus (see page 21). Drain well and rinse under cold running water. Remove and discard any remaining dark skin and cut the meat into small pieces with kitchen scissors. Place the pieces in a bowl, pour the oil over them, season with salt if necessary and sprinkle with hot paprika to taste. Mix well to ensure the octopus is thoroughly coated and serve immediately. If this is not possible, transfer the octopus and oil to a heatproof bowl, cover with foil and keep warm in the oven.

- **175 ml/6 fl oz olive oil**
- **¼ small onion**
  (about 25 g/1 oz), chopped
- **1 clove garlic, finely chopped**
- **pinch of sweet paprika**
- **1 kg/2¼ lb octopus**

Serves 6

Variation

Heat the oil in a saucepan. Add the onion and garlic and cook over a low heat, stirring occasionally, for 10 minutes, until lightly browned. Remove the onion and garlic with a slotted spoon and discard. Remove the pan from the heat and stir in sweet paprika to taste. Add the flavoured oil to the octopus pieces, mix well and serve immediately

18 Octopus in vinaigrette
PULPO EN VINAGRETA

- **1 kg/2¼ lb octopus**
- **150 ml/¼ pint olive oil**
- **1½ tablespoons white-wine vinegar**
- **1 onion, finely chopped**
- **1 green pepper, halved, seeded and diced**
- **250 g/9 oz cooked or drained canned peas**
- **salt and pepper**

Serves 6

Prepare and cook the octopus (see page 21). Meanwhile, prepare the vinaigrette. Whisk together the oil and vinegar in a bowl and season to taste with salt and pepper. Stir in the onion and green pepper and set aside. Drain the octopus well and rinse under cold running water. Remove and discard any remaining dark skin and cut the meat into medium-sized pieces with kitchen scissors. Put the octopus pieces in a bowl, pour the vinaigrette over them and add the peas. Taste and adjust the marinade if necessary. Cover the bowl and leave to marinate in the refrigerator, stirring occasionally, for 2 hours before serving.

19

Little Pavian Soldiers
SOLDADITOS DE PAVÍA

- 500 g/1 lb 2 oz skinless salt
  cod fillet, cut into strips
- 2 teaspoons paprika
- pinch of freshly ground
  black pepper
- juice of 1 lemon
- about 500 ml/18 fl oz olive oil
- plain flour, for dusting
- 1 egg

Serves 4

Put the cod strips in a bowl and add water to cover. Leave to soak, changing the water once, for 24–48 hours. Drain well and pat dry thoroughly with kitchen paper. Mix together the paprika, pepper and lemon juice in a large bowl and stir in 175 ml/6 fl oz of the oil. Add the cod strips and mix well. Cover and leave to marinate, stirring occasionally, for at least 2 hours. Drain the cod and pat dry with kitchen paper. Heat the remaining oil in a deep-fryer or deep frying pan to 180–190°C/350–375°F or until a cube of day-old bread browns in 30 seconds. Spread out the flour on a shallow dish and lightly beat the egg in another shallow dish. Roll each strip of fish in the flour, shaking off any excess, then roll in the beaten egg. When the oil is hot, add the cod, in batches, and cook for 5 minutes until golden brown. Remove with a slotted spoon, drain on kitchen paper, then transfer to a warm oven while you cook the remaining strips. Serve immediately.

20

Stuffed mushrooms
CHAMPIÑONES RELLENOS

- 80 g/3 oz butter,
  plus extra for greasing
- 25 g/1 oz breadcrumbs
  (made from day-old bread)
- 3–4 tablespoons warm milk
- 12 large, fresh mushrooms
- juice of ½ lemon
- 50 g/2 oz Serrano ham, chopped
- 1 tablespoon chopped
  fresh parsley
- salt and pepper

Makes 12

Preheat the oven to 180°C/350°F/Gas Mark 4. Generously grease an ovenproof dish with butter. Put the breadcrumbs in a bowl, add the milk and leave to soak. Remove the stalks from the mushrooms and chop them. Reserve the caps. Put the stalks in a saucepan with 25 g/1 oz of the butter and the lemon juice and season with salt. Place the pan over a low heat and cook gently for 10 minutes. Put the mushroom caps, gill sides up, in a single layer in the prepared dish and dot with the remaining butter. Bake for 10 minutes. Meanwhile, drain the breadcrumbs if they have not absorbed all the milk. Mix together the mushroom stalks, breadcrumbs, ham and parsley in a bowl. Season with salt and pepper. Divide the mixture among the mushroom caps and return them to the oven for about 30 minutes. If the tops have not lightly browned, place the mushrooms under a preheated grill for the last 10 minutes. Serve immediately, straight from the dish.

Russian salad

ENSALADILLA RUSA

- 250 g/9 oz potatoes,
  diced and boiled
- 500 g/1 lb 2 oz carrots,
  diced and boiled
- 1 kg/2¼ lb fresh peas, boiled
- 250 g/7 oz Classic Mayonnaise
  (see recipe 105)

Serves 6

Drain the vegetables, transfer to a bowl and allow to cool. Add the mayonnaise and toss to combine thoroughly. Refrigerate until ready to serve.

Note: The base for this salad is a thick mayonnaise, which is mixed with a combination of vegetables and the above is the classic version. Delicious variations include adding pieces of tart eating apple, walnut or celery to the vegetables. Cooked, peeled prawns may also be added, and give an exquisite flavour to a simple Russian salad.

22

Watercress salad
ENSALADILLA DE BERROS

- **500 g/1 lb 2 oz potatoes diced**
- **500 g/1 lb 2 oz eating apples**
- **250 g/9 oz celery, sliced**
- **2 bunches watercress, leaves picked and coarsely chopped**
- **175 ml/6 fl oz Thick Mayonnaise (see recipe 106)**
- **1 quantity tartlet cases (see recipe 1), optional**

Serves 6

Cook the potato in salted water for 15–20 minutes, until tender but still firm to the bite. Drain and leave to cool completely. When the potato is cold, peel, core and dice the apples then mix them with the potato. Add the celery and watercress. Stir in the mayonnaise, cover and chill in the refrigerator for at least 1 hour. Serve the salad in a large bowl, or in individual round tartlet cases for a special occasion.

23

Fried canapés
CANAPÉS FRITOS

- **100 ml/3 ½ fl oz milk**
- **25 g/1 oz butter, plus extra for spreading**
- **25 g/1 oz plain flour**
- **50 g/2 oz gruyere cheese, grated**
- **1 egg**
- **5 slices of bread**
- **olive oil, for frying**
- **salt and pepper**

Makes 10

Put the milk and butter in a small saucepan, season and bring to the boil. Add the flour and cook, stirring constantly to prevent lumps. When the mixture is thick and smooth, remove the pan from the heat and leave to cool slightly, then stir in the gruyere. Leave to cool until the mixture is only just warm, then stir in the egg until incorporated. Season to taste. Spread the slices of bread with a little butter and a thick layer of the cheese mixture. Cut off the crusts and cut each slice diagonally to form two triangles. Heat the oil in a heavy-based frying pan. Add several of the bread triangles, topping sides down, and cook until golden brown. Remove with a fish slice and transfer to a warm oven while you cook the remaining bread triangles. Serve hot.

24

Hot cheese and mayonnaise canapés
CANAPÉS DE MAYONESA Y QUESO, CALIENTES

- **5 slices of bread, each cut into 4 x 4 cm rounds and toasted**
- **1 quantity Thick Mayonnaise (see recipe 106)**
- **120 g/4 oz grated cheese**
- **2 onions**

Makes 20

Preheat the oven to 180°C/350°F/Gas Mark 4. Combine the mayonnaise with the cheese in a bowl. Spread the mixture generously on the toasted bread rounds, reserving a little. Slice the centres of the onions very thinly and sprinkle them over the toasts. Top each toast with a small knob of the reserved cheese mixture. Place the toasts on a baking sheet and bake for a few minutes, until they are golden brown. (Take care as they burn very easily.) Serve hot.

25 Cheese, tomato and bacon canapés
CANAPÉS DE QUESO, TOMATE Y BACON

- 5 slices of bread, each cut into
  4 x 4 cm rounds and toasted
- 50 g/2 oz butter
- 100 g/3½ oz cheese triangles,
  sliced
- 3 ripe tomatoes,
  very thinly sliced
- 10 rashers bacon,
  halved widthwise

Makes 20

Preheat the oven to 200°C/400°F/Gas Mark 6. Spread the bread rounds lightly and evenly with a little softened butter. Place a slice of cheese on each, then add a slice of tomato. Place a rasher of bacon (or half a rasher if the rashers are very long) doubled over on top of each. Put the canapés on a baking sheet and bake for about 15 minutes, until the cheese has melted and the bacon is crisp. Serve hot.

26 Soft cheese and paprika canapés
CANAPÉS DE QUESO BLANDO Y PIMENTÓN

- 5 slices of bread, each cut into
  4 x 4 cm rounds and toasted
- 100 g / 3½ oz ricotta,
  or other soft white cheese
- pinch of paprika

Makes 20

Preheat the oven to 180°C/350°F/Gas Mark 4. Spread the toasted bread rounds with a generous layer of ricotta. Sprinkle with a little paprika, place on a baking sheet and bake for about 5 minutes, until the cheese has melted.

27 Soft cheese sandwiches
EMPAREDADOS DE QUESO BLANDO

- 100 g / 3½ oz ricotta
- 100 g / 3½ oz mascarpone
- 2 tablespoons double cream,
  or unsweetened evaporated milk
- 1 teaspoon finely chopped
  chives, shallot or spring onion
- 10 slices white bread,
  crusts removed
- 10 slices rye bread,
  crusts removed

Makes 20

Beat together the cheeses until combined, then beat in the double cream or unsweetened evaporated milk. Stir in the chives, shallot or spring onion. Spread the mixture on the slices of white bread and top each with a slice of rye bread. Cut each sandwich diagonally in half to form two triangles. The sandwiches may be kept in the refrigerator for a short time before serving.

28 Baked cheese sticks
PALITOS DE QUESO AL HORNO

- 100 g/3½ oz butter
- 80 g/3 oz plain flour
- 100 g/3½ oz Parmesan cheese, grated
- 50 g/2 oz breadcrumbs (made from day-old bread)
- salt (optional)

Makes about 20

Preheat the oven to 200°C/400°F/Gas Mark 6. Put the butter in a saucepan and melt it over a low heat but do not allow it to brown, then remove the pan from the heat. Stir in the flour, then stir in the Parmesan. Season with salt if necessary. Spread out the breadcrumbs in a shallow dish. Shape scoops of the cheese mixture into long, fat sticks, about the size of your little finger. Roll the cheese sticks in the breadcrumbs and place on a baking sheet. Bake for 8–10 minutes, until golden brown. Carefully transfer the cheese sticks to a wire rack (they will break easily) and leave to cool completely before serving.

29 Fried gruyere cheese
FRITOS DE QUESO GRUYÈRE

- 150 g/5 oz gruyere cheese
- 300 ml/½ pint milk
- plain flour, for dusting
- 1 egg, lightly beaten
- 50 g/2 oz breadcrumbs
- sunflower oil, for deep frying

Makes about 15

Cut the gruyere into 1 x 1½ x 3-cm/½ x ¾ x 1¼-inch pieces. Place in a bowl, add the milk and leave to soak for 2 hours. Drain the cheese and pat dry with kitchen roll. Roll each piece of cheese lightly in the plain flour, then in the beaten egg and finally in the breadcrumbs. Heat the sunflower oil in a deep-fryer or deep saucepan to 180–190°C/350–375°F or until a cube of day-old bread browns in 30 seconds. Add the cheese pieces, in batches, and cook for about 2 minutes, until golden. Drain well and serve immediately.

30 Fried gruyere cheese and bacon
FRITOS DE QUESO GRUYÈRE Y BACON

- 200 g/7 oz gruyere cheese
- 10 rashers thin rindless bacon
- 2–3 tablespoons oil

Makes about 15

Cut the gruyere into strips about 1 cm/½ inch thick and a little longer than the width of the rashers of bacon. Cut the rashers in half. Place a piece of cheese on each half, roll up the bacon and run a cocktail stick through, to secure the roll. Heat the oil in a frying pan. Add the bacon rolls and cook, turning frequently, for 10–15 minutes, until the bacon is browned and cooked through. Drain well and serve immediately, leaving the cocktail sticks in place.

31

Choux puffs with Roquefort or foie gras

PETITS-CHOUX AL ROQUEFORT O AL FOIE-GRAS

Choux pastry:
- **300 ml/½ pint milk**
- **50 g/2 oz butter,**
  plus extra for greasing
- **50 g/2 oz lard**
- **150 g/5 oz plain flour**
- **3 eggs**
- **2 egg whites**
- **salt**

Filling:
- **100 g/3½ oz foie gras combined**
  with 4 tablespoons lightly
  whipped cream or
  100 g/3½ oz Roquefort cheese
  combined with 100 g/3½ oz
  softened butter

Makes approx. 65

Pour the milk into a saucepan and add the butter, lard and a pinch of salt. Melt over a low heat, stir the mixture with a wooden spoon and bring to the boil. Immediately tip in all the flour and cook, stirring constantly, for 3 minutes. Remove the pan from the heat and leave to cool. Meanwhile, preheat the oven to 180°C/350°C/Gas Mark 4. Lightly grease one or two baking sheets with butter. When the milk mixture is nearly cold, beat in the eggs, one at a time, making sure that each one has been fully incorporated before adding the next. Whisk the egg whites in a clean, dry bowl until they form soft peaks, then fold them into the mixture. Using a teaspoon, make small mounds of the mixture on the prepared baking sheet, spacing them well apart as they spread during cooking. Bake for 8–10 minutes, until puffed up and golden brown. Transfer to wire racks and leave to cool. Slit the puffs on one side with kitchen scissors and open them with your fingers, choose your preferred filling, combine the ingredients, then use a small spoon to fill the puffs with the filling.

32

Celery with Roquefort

APIO CON ROQUEFORT

- **1 head celery,**
  trimmed and washed
- **50 g/2 oz Roquefort cheese**
- **50 g/2 oz butter, softened**

Makes approx. 25

Cut the celery sticks into 3-cm/1¼-inch lengths. Beat the Roquefort and butter in a bowl. Fill each piece of celery with the mixture, spreading it out evenly. Put the filled celery on a plate, cover and chill in the refrigerator for at least 1 hour before serving.

33

Fried date and bacon rolls
PINCHOS DE DÁTILES Y BACON FRITOS

• **20 dried dates**

• **20 rashers thin rindless bacon**

• **2–3 tablespoons groundnut oil**

Makes 20

Slit the dates along the longest sides and carefully remove and discard the stones. Wrap each date in a strip of bacon. Heat the oil in a frying pan, add the bacon rolls and cook, turning occasionally, for about 10 minutes, until the bacon is cooked through and lightly browned. Drain well and serve immediately.

34

Prunes stuffed with Roquefort, raisins and pine nuts
CIRUELAS RELLENAS DE ROQUEFORT, PASAS Y PIÑONES

• **100 g / 3½ oz Roquefort cheese**

• **12 pine nuts**

• **1/4 cup raisins**

• **1 tablespoon wine from Malaga or sweet sherry**

• **4 tablespoons single cream**

• **12 ready-to-eat prunes**

Makes 12

Crumble the Roquefort into a bowl and mash lightly with a fork. Add the pine nuts, raisins, wine or sherry and cream and mix to a paste. Remove the stones from the prunes and fill the cavities with the Roquefort paste. Close the prunes and secure with a wooden cocktail stick. Put the prunes on a plate, cover and chill in the refrigerator for at least 2 hours before serving.

Note: To use standard prunes, soak them in warm water to rehydrate, following the instructions on the packet, then remove the stones.

35

Mushroom tartlets
TARTALETAS DE CHAMPIÑON

- 1 quantity tartlet cases
  (see recipe 1)
- 120 g/4 oz button mushrooms,
  sliced
- 50 g/2 oz butter
- juice of ½ lemon
- 1 tablespoon sunflower oil
- 1 tablespoon plain flour
- 250 ml/7 fl oz milk
- pinch of curry powder
- salt

Makes 20

Put the mushrooms in a saucepan with half the butter and the lemon juice. Cover and cook over a low heat for 10–15 minutes, until tender. Heat the remaining butter with the sunflower oil. Stir in the flour, then gradually stir in the milk. Cook, stirring constantly, for about 8 minutes, until thickened and smooth. Season with salt and stir in a very small pinch of curry powder. Mix the sauce with the mushrooms and their cooking juices, then spoon the mixture into the tartlet cases and serve hot.

36

Asparagus éclairs
ÉCLAIRS DE ESPÁRRAGOS

- 1 quantity choux pastry
  (see recipe 31)
- butter, for greasing
- 1 quantity Thick Mayonnaise
  (see recipe 106)
- 1 jar asparagus tips, drained

Makes 20

Preheat the oven to 180°C/350°C/Gas Mark 4. Lightly grease 2 baking sheets with butter. Make the choux pastry as per recipe 31, but instead of making small balls, pipe finger shapes onto the baking sheets. Cook for 8–10 minutes until puffed up. Remove from the oven and allow to cool on the baking sheets. When the baked éclairs are cold, slit each one along one side with kitchen scissors. Fill with mayonnaise and asparagus tip, before gently closing. Serve reasonably soon after making, or the pastry will go soggy.

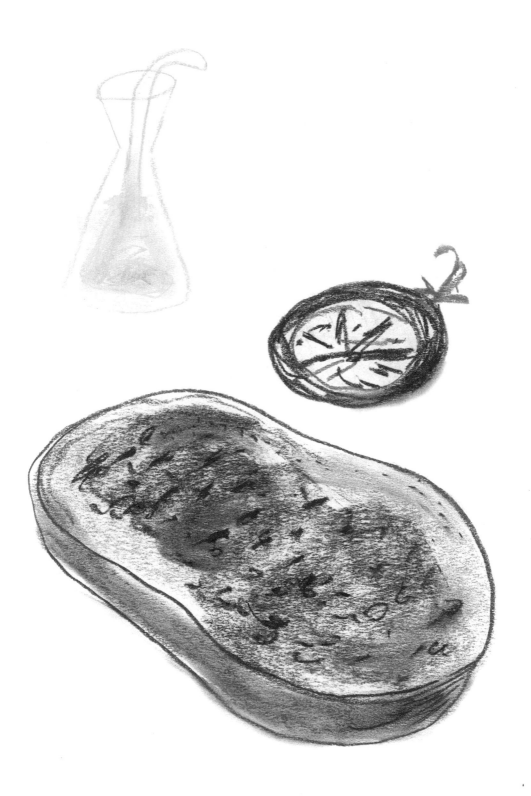

COLD PLATE SUGGESTIONS

37 Salad with yogurt dressing

ENSALADA CON SALSA DE YOGUR

- 150 ml/¼ pint natural yogurt
- juice of ½ lemon
- 1 head lettuce,
  cored and trimmed
- 1 tart eating apple
- 50 g/2 oz hazelnuts,
  coarsely chopped
- 1 tablespoon chopped
  fresh parsley
- salt and pepper

Serves 4

Mix together the yogurt and lemon juice in a small bowl and season to taste with salt and pepper. Line a salad bowl with the lettuce. Core the apple, cut into very thin slices and add to the bowl. Sprinkle the hazelnuts over the top. Pour the dressing over the salad and toss lightly. Sprinkle with the parsley before serving.

Note: When in season, green asparagus may be added to this recipe. It should be cooked (see page 309), cooled and cut into 5 cm/2-inch lengths.

38 Salad with asparagus, ham and mayonnaise

ENSALADA DE ESPÁRRAGOS, JAMÓN DE YORK Y MAYONESA

- 1 bunch white asparagus or
  400 g/14 oz canned
  white asparagus
- 3 firm tomatoes
- 1 cucumber
- 3 hard-boiled eggs
- 200 g/7 oz York or other
  dry-cured ham, diced
- 1 tablespoon chopped onion
- 1 tablespoon chopped
  fresh parsley
- salt

Mayonnaise
- 1 egg
- 300 ml/½ pint olive oil
- 1 tablespoon white-wine vinegar
  or lemon juice

Serves 6

Make the mayonnaise as described in recipe 105. If using fresh asparagus, trim, peel and cook (see page 309). Drain the cooked (or canned) asparagus well and leave on a clean tea towel to dry. Dice the tomatoes, put them in a colander, sprinkle with a little salt and leave to drain. Peel and dice the cucumber, put it in another colander, sprinkle with salt and leave to drain. Rinse both ingredients and pat dry. Cut the asparagus spears into 2.5-cm/1-inch lengths. Chop 1½ of the hard-boiled eggs and slice the remaining eggs. Mix together the asparagus, tomato, cucumber, chopped eggs, ham, onion and half the parsley in a bowl. Stir in the mayonnaise, cover and chill in the refrigerator for 1 hour. To serve, garnish the salad with the sliced eggs and sprinkle with the remaining parsley.

Roasted mixed vegetables
ESCALIBADA

- **2 large green peppers**
- **1 large red pepper**
- **3 aubergines,**
  about 800 g/1¾ lb total weight
- **1 large onion**
- **4 potatoes,**
  about 800 g/1¾ lb total weight
- **350 ml/12 fl oz olive oil**
- **2 tomatoes**
- **6 tablespoons white-wine**
  vinegar
- **1 clove garlic, finely chopped**
- **salt and pepper**

Serves 4

Preheat the oven to 200°C/400°F/Gas Mark 6. Put the peppers, aubergines, onion and potatoes (unpeeled) into a roasting tin. Pour in half the oil and toss to coat. Roast for 25 minutes. Stir gently, add the tomatoes and roast for a further 20 minutes. Remove the roasting tin from the oven and leave the vegetables to cool enough to handle. Peel, halve and seed the peppers, then cut them into strips. Peel the aubergines and cut them into strips. Cut the onion into wedges. Peel the tomatoes and cut them into pieces. Place in a bowl. Whisk together the remaining oil and the vinegar to make a vinaigrette. Season each vegetable separately with salt and pepper and sprinkle with the vinaigrette. Cut the potatoes in half and scoop out the flesh with a teaspoon, taking care not to pierce the skins. Chop the flesh, season to taste with salt and pepper and return it to the potato skins. The escalibada may be served in one large dish or four individual dishes. Put the potatoes in the centre and arrange the other vegetables around them. Stir the garlic into the vinaigrette remaining after the vegetables have been dressed and pour it over the salad.

Note: It may be better to use fresh vinaigrette for pouring over the salad at the end, as the vinaigrette used with the vegetables can take on a strong flavour, particularly from the peppers.

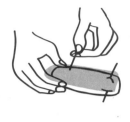

40

Rolls of ham with Russian salad and gelatine

CANUTILLOS DE JAMÓN DE YORK CON ENSALADA RUSA Y GELATINA

- 2 carrots
- 1 sachet (11 g/⅓ oz) powdered gelatine
- 100 g/3½ oz canned peas, drained
- 6 slices of York or other dry-cured ham
- 500 g/1 lb 2 oz Russian Salad (see recipe 21)
- lettuce leaves, sliced tomato and sliced hard-boiled egg (optional)
- salt

Serves 6

Cook the carrots in a saucepan of salted boiling water for about 15 minutes, until tender. Drain and slice thinly, then leave to cool. Pour 600 ml/1 pint water into a heatproof bowl. Sprinkle the gelatine over the surface and leave to stand for 5 minutes, until spongy. Set the bowl over a pan of barely simmering water and heat until the gelatine has dissolved and the mixture is clear. Do not stir. Remove the bowl from the heat. Pour a thin layer of gelatine into the base of a round cake tin, 23 cm/9 inches in diameter and 4 cm/1½ inches deep. Put the tin in the refrigerator and leave until the gelatine has set, then arrange the carrot slices and peas decoratively over the base. Place a slice of ham on a plate and put 1½ tablespoons of the Russian salad on top, then roll up the ham and secure it with a wooden cocktail stick. Repeat with the remaining slices of ham and Russian salad. Place the ham rolls in the tin, arranging them like the spokes of a wheel with the cocktail sticks sticking up. Pour in the remaining gelatine and put the tin in the refrigerator for 3–4 hours, until set. To serve, carefully remove and discard the cocktail sticks. Warm a palette knife in hot water and run it around the edge of the tin and turn the salad out on to a round plate. A typical Spanish garnish for this dish would include lettuce leaves, tomato slices and slices of hard-boiled egg.

41

Rolls of ham with asparagus and mayonnaise
ROLLOS DE JAMÓN DE YORK CON ESPÁRRAGOS Y MAYONESA

- 1 tablespoon capers,
  rinsed, drained and chopped
- 1 quantity Classic Mayonnaise
  (see recipe 105)
- 6 slices of York or other
  dry-cured ham
- 6 fat, canned asparagus spears
  or 18 thin, canned asparagus
  spears, drained
- 1 hard-boiled egg, chopped
- 1 tablespoon chopped
  fresh parsley
- 6 dried dates, stoned
- 3 tablespoons sunflower oil
- 1 tablespoon white-wine vinegar
  or lemon juice
- 3 carrots, cut into julienne strips
- salt

Serves 6

Stir the capers into the mayonnaise. Spread out a slice of ham and place 1 tablespoon mayonnaise mixture in the middle. Place 1 fat asparagus spear or 3 thin asparagus spears on top of the mayonnaise. Roll up the ham carefully with the asparagus in the middle, its tip poking out of the end. Repeat with the remaining ham and asparagus. Place the rolls on a serving dish. Set a little egg white to one side, then mix together the remaining chopped egg and the parsley. Sprinkle the mixture over the ham rolls. Place a date on the middle of each roll. Whisk together the oil and vinegar or lemon juice in a bowl and season to taste with salt. Add the carrot strips and toss, then decorate the serving dish with four mounds of carrot strips. If you are not serving the dish immediately, cover with foil and store in the refrigerator.

42

Foie-gras aspic mousse
ASPIC-MOUSSE DE FOIE-GRAS

- ½ sachet (11 g/⅓ oz) powdered
  gelatine
- 1 black truffle, sliced (optional)
- 50 g/2 oz goose or duck
  foie gras, fresh or canned
- 175 ml/6 fl oz double cream,
  whipped, until slightly thickened
- iceberg lettuce leaves
  or watercress (optional)

Serves 4

Pour 300 ml/½ pint water into a heatproof bowl. Sprinkle the gelatine over the surface and leave to stand for 5 minutes. Set the bowl over a pan of barely simmering water and heat until the gela-tine has dissolved and the mixture is clear. Do not stir. Remove the bowl from the heat and leave until the gelatine is almost cold but still liquid. Pour a thin layer over the base of a flan dish. Arrange slices of truffle, if using, on top and put in the refrigerator until the gelatine has set. Put the foie gras in a bowl and mash with a fork, then stir in about one-third of the whipped cream. When this has been fully incorporated, stir in half the remaining cream and when that has been fully incorporated, stir in the rest. Gradually, add the remaining gelatine, whisking con-stantly. Pour the mixture into the tin or flan dish with the gelatine and chill in the refrigerator for at least 3 hours, longer if time allows. To serve, warm a palette knife in hot water and run it around the edge of the tin or flan dish and turn out the mousse on to a round plate. Garnish with iceberg lettuce leaves or watercress.

For more dishes that could be served as cold plates,
see the following recipes:

Soups

Gazpacho (recipe 168)
Chunky gazpacho (recipe 169)
Chilled gazpachuelo (recipe 170)
Tomato juice soup (recipe 138)
Vichyssoise (recipe 172)

Fish and seafood

Tuna, mayonnaise and potato roll (recipe 239)
Cold bonito pie (recipe 564)
Fisherman's cold spider crab (recipe 651)
Bonito in aspic with mayonnaise (recipe 565)
Prawn cocktail (recipe 658)
Glasses of fish and shellfish with vegetable sauce (recipe 679)

Chicken

Chicken supremes (recipe 822)

Eggs

Eggs mimosa (recipe 483)
Hard-boiled eggs with salad (recipe 486)
Poached eggs in jelly (recipe 494)

Vegetables

Red peppers with hard-boiled eggs (recipe 431)
Tomatoes filled with sardines, green peppers and olives
 (recipe 455)

Vegetables and potatoes

Cold rice with vegetables and vinaigrette (recipe 186)
Cold rice with tuna and mayonnaise (recipe 183)
Lentil salad (recipe 229)
Potatoes with mayonnaise, tomato and anchovies (recipe 268)
Potato salad with tuna and hard-boiled egg (recipe 266)

Aspic mousses

Bonito in aspic with mayonnaise (recipe 565)

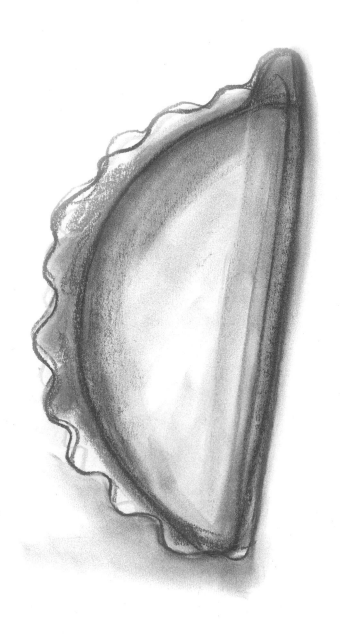

FRIED DISHES, SAVOURY TARTLETS, LITTLE TURNOVERS AND MOUSSES

43 📷 Pastry for little turnovers (first version)

MASA DE EMPANADILLAS

- **120 ml / 4 fl oz dry white wine**
- **25 g / 1 oz butter**
- **25 g / 1 oz lard**
- **300 g / 11 oz plain flour,**
  plus extra for dusting
- **vegetable oil, for deep frying**
- **salt**

Makes 30–36

Pour the wine into a saucepan and add 120 ml / 4 fl oz water, the butter and lard. Heat gently, stirring, until the fat has melted. Once the mixture is warm but not boiling, remove the pan from the heat, sift in the flour and a pinch of salt and stir well with a wooden spoon. Turn out the dough on to a floured surface and knead well until smooth. Form the dough into a ball, put it on a plate, cover with a clean tea towel and leave to rest for about 2 hours. To make the turnovers, roll out the dough on a floured surface until it is 3 mm / ⅛ inch thick. Place mounds of your chosen filling (see recipe 45) on half the dough and fold the other half over to cover them. Cut the filled mounds into half-moon shapes, leaving a small margin around the filling. To do this, you can use a crescent-shaped cutter, a pastry wheel or a fine-edged glass. Press the pastry edges securely together with your fingers to prevent the filling leaking out when the turnovers are deep-fried. Heat the oil in a deep-fryer or deep saucepan to 180–190°C/350–375°F or until a cube of day-old bread browns in 30 seconds. Carefully add the empanadas, in batches, and deep-fry for 6–8 minutes, until golden brown. Drain on kitchen paper. Season lightly with salt and serve the turnovers hot.

44 Pastry for little turnovers (second version)

MASA DE EMPANADILLAS

- **25 g / 1 oz butter**
- **3 tablespoons sunflower oil**
- **300 g / 11 oz plain flour,**
  plus extra for dusting
- **1 egg**
- **vegetable oil, for deep frying**
- **salt**

Makes about 30–36

Pour 250 ml / 8 fl oz water into a saucepan, add a pinch of salt, the butter and oil and heat gently to melt the butter. Once the mixture is warm but not boiling, remove the pan from the heat, tip in the flour and stir well with a wooden spoon. Stir in the egg. Bring the mixture together in the pan and then turn it out on to a floured surface and knead well (more flour can be added to the mixture if necessary). Cover the dough with a clean tea towel and leave to rest for at least 30 minutes. Make the turnovers as described in the previous recipe.

  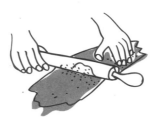 

45

Fillings for little turnovers

RELLENOS PARA LAS EMPANADILLAS

Filling suggestions:
- 1 onion, chopped and sautéed in olive oil for 5 minutes until softened and translucent
- 3 tablespoons tomato purée
- about 200 g/7 oz leftover cooked mince, or ham (York or Serrano), or cooked chicken, or cooked fish or canned, drained tuna
- 1 slice bread, crusts removed, soaked in warm milk and drained slightly, or a chopped hard-boiled egg
- 1 anchovy (optional)
- pepper, chopped fresh parsley or grated nutmeg

The principle for preparing the filling for the turnovers is almost always the same. Choose your preferred filling and combine the ingredients thoroughly. Use about 2 generous teaspoons of filling per turnover and fill turnovers (see recipe 43).

Note: Some people prefer to mix the meat or fish with a thick béchamel sauce (see recipe 77) instead of onion and tomato. The taste is also good, but will be milder in flavour.

46

Puff pastry for pies

EMPANADAS DE HOJALDRE.

- 200 g/7 oz plain flour, plus extra for dusting
- 120 g/4 oz lard, softened
- 120 g/4 oz margarine, softened
- juice of 1 lemon
- 1 egg, lightly beaten
- salt

Makes 1 pie

Make the puff pastry dough as described in recipe 968. Divide the pastry into 2 equal pieces. Roll each piece into a circle 25 cm/10 inches wide, ½ cm/¼ inch thick. Preheat the oven to 180°C/350°F/ Gas Mark 4. Arrange the filling (see recipes 47–49) on one circle of dough, carefully leaving a 2-cm/¾-inch margin around the edge so that the dough can be sealed around the filling. When you are happy with the filling, gently lay the second circle of dough over the top, pressing down around the edge to seal the pastry. Transfer to the oven and cook until lightly browned on top.

Note: You can vary the filling as much you like, although the classic recipe is a thick tomato sauce with strips of fresh, roasted or preserved red pepper.

47

- 1 quantity Puff Pastry Dough
  (see recipe 968)
- 1 quantity Classic Tomato Sauce
  (see recipe 73)
- 1 x 200 g/7 oz can tuna in brine,
  drained
- 2 canned or bottled peppers,
  cut into strips

Makes 1 pie

Tuna puff-pastry pie
EMPANADA DE HOJALDRE CON BONITO EN ESCABECHE

Prepare the dough as described in recipe 46. Spread the tomato sauce over the dough. Coarsely flake the tuna. Scatter it evenly over the dough and add the peppers. Proceed as in recipe 46.

48

- 1 quantity Puff Pastry Dough
  (see recipe 968)
- 1 quantity Classic Tomato Sauce
  (see recipe 73)
- 400 g/14 oz lean pork,
  cut into cubes
- 1 black pudding,
  cut into 2cm/¾ inch thick slices

Makes 1 pie

Lean pork and black pudding puff-pastry pie
EMPANADA DE HOJALDRE CON MAGRO DE CERDO Y MORCILLA

Prepare the dough as described in recipe 46. Spread the tomato sauce over the dough. Heat a little oil in a frying pan and add the pork. Cook for 5 minutes, or until cooked through and lightly browned. Scatter the pork and black pudding on the top. Proceed as in recipe 46.

49

- 1 quantity Puff Pastry Dough
  (see recipe 968)
- 1 quantity Classic Tomato Sauce
  (see recipe 73)
- 2 roasted chicken breasts, or
  other leftover cooked chicken,
  chopped
- 2 canned or bottled peppers,
  cut into strips

Makes 1 pie

Chicken puff-pastry pie
EMPANADA DE HOJALDRE CON POLLO

Prepare the dough as described in recipe 46. Spread the tomato sauce over the dough. Arrange the chicken and pepper evenly on the top. Proceed as described in recipe 46.

Galician pie

EMPANADA GALLEGA

- **10 g/¼ oz dried yeast**
- **175 ml/6 fl oz lukewarm water**
- **3 eggs**
- **400 g/14 oz plain flour,**
  plus extra for dusting
- **15 g/½ oz margarine,**
  at room temperature
- **2 tablespoons sunflower oil,**
  plus extra for brushing
- **400 g/14 oz pork fillet**
  or skinless, boneless chicken
  breasts, cut into strips
- **2 canned or bottled peppers,**
  or roasted peppers, drained
  and cut into strips
- **salt**

'Rustido':
- **2 tablespoons olive oil**
- **3 onions, coarsely chopped**
- **1 garlic clove, crushed**
- **1 tablespoon chopped**
  fresh parsley
- **1 chorizo sausage, sliced**

Serves 4–5

Mash the yeast with a pinch of salt and the lukewarm water in a cup or small bowl until smooth, then leave to stand for about 10 minutes, until the mixture is frothy. Beat two of the eggs in a bowl. Sift the flour with a pinch of salt on to a work surface. Make a well in the centre and pour in the beaten egg and yeast mixture. Gradually incorporate the flour into the liquid, then knead well for 10 minutes. Dust the work surface lightly with flour to prevent the dough sticking. Add the margarine and knead for a further 10 minutes, banging the dough on to the work surface. Add a little water to the dough if necessary. Once the dough is smooth and elastic, form it into a ball, place it in a bowl and cover with a clean tea towel. Leave to rise in a warm place for 1–2 hours, until doubled in volume. Meanwhile, make the 'rustido'. Heat the olive oil in a frying pan. Add the onion and cook over a low heat, stirring occasionally, for 10 minutes, until softened and translucent. Add the garlic and parsley and cook for a further 5 minutes. Stir in the chorizo and cook for 2 minutes more. Remove the pan from the heat and set aside. Heat the sunflower oil in a frying pan. Add the strips of meat and cook over a medium-low heat, stirring frequently, for about 8 minutes, until golden brown. Remove from the pan with a slotted spoon and set aside. Preheat the oven to 180°C/350°F/Gas Mark 4. Brush a 30-cm/12-inch baking tin or ovenproof baking dish with oil. Divide the dough into two pieces, one slightly bigger than the other. Roll out the larger piece on a lightly floured surface and use to line the tin or dish. Spread half the rustido over the dough. Lay the strips of meat on the rustido and add the strips of pepper. Spoon the remaining rustido over the top. Roll out the remaining dough and use it to cover the mixture. Seal the edges of the dough carefully, pressing them together and rolling them slightly. Pinch the dough in the centre of the pie with two fingers to create a chimney to allow the steam to escape. Beat the remaining egg and brush it over the dough to glaze. Bake for 15 minutes, then increase the oven temperature to 190°C/375°F/Gas Mark 5 and bake for 15 minutes longer. Increase the oven temperature to 200°C/400°F/Gas Mark 6 and bake for 15 more minutes, until golden brown. Remove the pie from the oven. Serve hot or warm, straight from the dish if preferred.

Note: You can vary the filling as much as you like. Try fresh sardines (scaled, cleaned and the heads, tails and backbones removed) or salt cod (soaked and blanched). Raisins can be added to a cod pie. Squid can also be used for the filling; fry it with the rustido.

51

Puff-pastry pie with curd cheese and mushrooms

EMPANADA DE HOJALDRE CONGELADO, QUESO DE BURGOS Y CHAMPIÑONES

- 150 g/5 oz mushrooms, thickly sliced
- 20 g/¾ oz margarine
- 2 tablespoons lemon juice
- 400 g/14 oz frozen puff pastry dough, thawed
- plain flour, for dusting
- 200 g/7 oz curd cheese
- 1 tablespoon chopped fresh parsley
- 1 large egg or 2 small eggs, lightly beaten
- salt (optional)

Serves 4

Preheat the oven to 200°C/400°F/Gas Mark 6. Put the mushrooms, margarine and lemon juice into a saucepan and cook over a low heat, stirring occasionally, for about 6 minutes. Remove the pan from the heat and set aside. Gently roll the thawed dough with a rolling pin, first in one direction and then the other (across and down) to make it thinner. Roll out on a lightly floured surface to 3 mm/⅛ inch thick. Cut a 23-cm/9-inch round from the dough and use it to line the base and sides of a 20-cm/8-inch loose-based baking tin. Reserve the remaining dough. Lightly prick the base with a fork and bake for about 10 minutes. Meanwhile, mash the cheese in a bowl with a fork. Drain the mushrooms and add them to the cheese with the parsley and most of the beaten egg, leaving just enough egg to glaze the pastry. Season lightly with salt if necessary. Remove the pastry case from the oven and spread the filling over the base. Roll out the remaining dough and place it on top of the filling, carefully sealing the sides. Make a hole in the centre of the lid with a knife to allow the steam to escape during cooking. Brush the remaining beaten egg over the pastry and bake for 15–20 minutes, until golden brown. (It may be necessary to put the pie under the grill for a short time to brown the top.) Leave the pie to stand for 10 minutes before transferring it to a serving dish. Serve warm.

52

Prawn and béchamel toasts

PAN DE MOLDE CON GAMBAS Y BECHAMEL

- 500 g/1 lb 2 oz raw prawns, shelled and deveined
- 25 g/1 oz butter
- 3 tablespoons olive oil
- 1 heaped tablespoon plain flour
- 500 ml/18 fl oz milk
- pinch of curry powder (optional)
- 12 slices of bread
- 50 g/2 oz gruyere cheese, grated
- salt

Serves 6

If the prawns are quite large, cut them in half. Set aside. Preheat the oven to 180°C/350°F/Gas Mark 4. Melt the butter with the oil in a saucepan over a low heat. Add the prawns and cook, stirring occasionally, for 3–4 minutes, until pink and cooked through. Using a slotted spoon, transfer the prawns to a plate. Stir the flour into the pan, then gradually add the milk, a little at a time, stirring constantly with a whisk or wooden spoon. Simmer gently for 10 minutes, then stir in the curry powder, if using, and season to taste with salt. Add the prawns and mix well before spreading the mixture on the slices of bread. Sprinkle the gruyere on top, place on a baking sheet and bake for about 5 minutes, until golden brown. Transfer to a large dish and serve immediately.

53

Mushroom, béchamel and cheese toasts

PAN DE MOLDE CON CHAMPIÑONES, BECHAMEL Y QUESO RALLADO

- 400 g/14 oz mushrooms
- 50 g/2 oz butter
- juice of 1 lemon
- 2 tablespoons sunflower oil
- 1 heaped tablespoon plain flour
- 500 ml/18 fl oz milk
- 12 slices of bread
- 50 g/2 oz gruyere or
  Parmesan cheese, grated
- salt and pepper

Serves 6

Prepare the mushrooms (see page 379), cutting them into thick slices and using 20 g/¾ oz of the butter and the lemon juice. Preheat the oven to 180°C/350°F/Gas Mark 4. Melt the remaining butter with the oil in a saucepan over a low heat. Stir in the flour, then gradually add the milk, a little at a time, stirring constantly with a whisk. Season with salt and a little pepper. Simmer gently for about 10 minutes, then add the mushrooms and their cooking juices. Stir well, remove the pan from the heat and leave to cool slightly. Spread the mixture on the slices of bread and sprinkle with the gruyere or Parmesan. Place on a baking sheet and bake for about 5 minutes, until golden brown. Transfer to a large dish and serve immediately.

54

Cheese toasts

PAN DE MOLDE CON QUESO RALLADO

- 275 ml/9 fl oz milk
- 75 g/2 ¾ oz butter
- 3 tablespoons plain flour
- 3 eggs
- 150 g/5 oz gruyere cheese,
  grated
- 12 slices of bread
- vegetable oil, for deep-frying
- salt and pepper

Serves 6

Pour the milk into a saucepan, add the butter, season with salt and pepper and bring to a rolling boil. Add the flour and cook, stirring constantly with a wooden spoon, until the mixture thickens and comes away from the sides of the pan. Remove the pan from the heat and leave to cool slightly. Stir in the eggs (unbeaten), one at a time, making sure each one is fully incorporated before adding the next. Stir in the gruyere. Spread the mixture on the slices of bread, covering them generously, and leave to stand in a cool place for 30 minutes. Heat the oil in a deep-fryer or frying pan to 180–190°C/350–375°F or until a cube of day-old bread browns in 30 seconds. Working in batches, carefully add the slices of bread, coated sides down, and cook for a few minutes, until golden brown. Remove with a fish slice, drain well and keep warm in the oven until all the toasts are cooked. Serve warm.

Note: These toasts can also be cooked in the oven. They taste equally good but do not look as attractive as the fried version. If cooking in the oven, sprinkle some extra gruyere on each slice, as this cheese melts well in the oven.

Pizza

PIZZA

Dough:
- **25g/1oz fresh yeast**
- **300ml/½ pint lukewarm water**
- **250g/9oz plain flour,**
  plus extra for dusting
- **1 teaspoon salt**
- **2 tablespoons olive oil,**
  plus extra for greasing

Serves 4

Mash the yeast with the lukewarm water in a cup or small bowl until smooth, then leave to stand for about 10 minutes, until the mixture is frothy. Sift the flour and salt on to a work surface and make a well in the centre. Pour in the oil and gradually add the yeast mixture. Using your fingers, gradually incorporate the flour into the liquid then knead the dough until it is smooth and elastic. Dust the work surface lightly with flour to prevent the dough sticking. Form the dough into a ball, place it in a china or glass bowl, cover with a clean tea towel and leave to rise in a warm place for 1–2 hours, until doubled in volume. Lightly grease a baking sheet with a little oil. Roll out the dough into a round and transfer it to the baking sheet. Add the topping (see Note), cover the pizza with foil and leave it to stand for about 30 minutes before baking in a preheated oven at 200°C/400°F/Gas Mark 6. It will take 20–30 minutes to cook.

Note: It is usual to cover the dough base with a thick tomato sauce (see recipe 73). On top of this place slices of mozzarella, or other cheeses that will melt easily. Add some anchovies, if you wish, and stoned olives (usually black) and slices of tomato. Use ripe tomatoes and slice them in advance to give them time to drain. Additional ingredients, such as bacon, mussels, etc. are a matter of personal taste. Sprinkle oregano over the pizza and season .

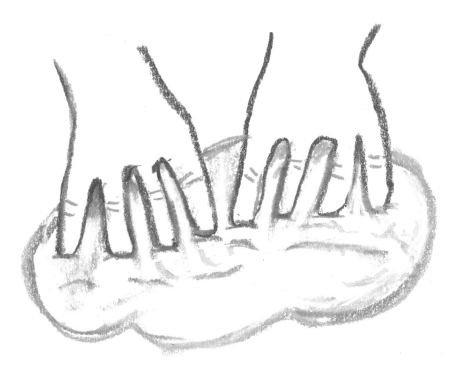

Bacon and cheese tart: quiche

TARTA DE BACON Y QUESO: QUICHE

Pastry:
- **200 g/7 oz plain flour,**
  plus extra for dusting
- **90 g/3¼ oz butter,**
  cut into small pieces,
  plus extra for greasing
- **1 egg yolk**
- **1 tablespoon sunflower oil**
- **salt**

Filling:
- **90 g/3¼ oz gruyere cheese**
- **2 rashers bacon or**
  slices of ham, diced
- **4 eggs, beaten**
- **250 ml/8 fl oz double cream**
- **175 ml/6 fl oz milk**
- **salt**

Serves 6–8

Make the pastry dough at least 2 hours before preparing the quiche. Sift the flour and a pinch of salt into a bowl, add the butter and rub it into the flour with your fingertips. Try to handle the ingredients as little as possible. Add the egg yolk and oil and work the mixture until it has the texture of fine breadcrumbs. Gradually stir in 300 ml/½ pint water, a little at a time. Turn out on to a lightly floured work surface and knead gently to form a dough. Roll it into a ball, put on a plate, cover and leave to rest in a cool place. Preheat the oven to 180°C/350°F/Gas Mark 4. Lightly grease with butter a loose-based quiche tin, 25 cm/10 inches in diameter and about 4 cm/1½ inches deep. Roll out the dough to a round on a lightly floured work surface. Lift the dough on the rolling pin into the prepared tin and press down with your fingers to make sure it is even over the base. Trim the excess dough with a sharp knife and lightly prick the base all over with a fork. For the filling, thinly slice 40 g/1½ oz of the gruyere and grate the remainder. Place the bacon or ham and the cheese slices in the pastry case and bake for about 20 minutes, until the pastry is cooked but not browned. Meanwhile, beat the eggs with the cream and milk in a bowl and season with salt. Remove the pastry case from the oven and increase the oven temperature to 220°C/425°F/Gas Mark 7. Pour the egg mixture into the pastry case, sprinkle the remaining grated cheese on top and return the quiche to the oven. Bake for 15 minutes, then lower the oven temperature to 180°C/350°F/Gas Mark 4 and bake for a further 25 minutes, until golden brown. Remove the quiche from the oven and leave to cool slightly. Transfer it to a serving dish and serve warm.

Onion tart

TARTA DE CEBOLLA

Pastry:
- 200 g/7 oz plain flour,
  plus extra for dusting
- 80 g/3 oz butter, cut into small
  pieces, plus extra for greasing
- 1 egg, separated
- 1 tablespoon olive oil
- salt

Filling:
- 6 tablespoons olive oil
- 25 g/1 oz margarine
- 1 kg/2¼ lb onions, thinly sliced
- 1 heaped tablespoon plain flour
- 200 ml/7 fl oz single cream
- 50 g/2 oz gruyere cheese, grated
- salt and pepper

Serves 6–8

Make the pastry dough as described in recipe 56, using the egg yolk but reserving the white. Leave to rest in a cool place for at least 2 hours. Preheat the oven to 180°C/450°F/Gas Mark 4. Lightly grease with butter a loose-based quiche tin, 28 cm/11 inches in diameter and about 4cm/1½ inches deep. Roll out the dough to a round on a lightly floured surface. Lift the dough on the rolling pin into the prepared tin and press down with your fingers to make sure it is even over the base. Trim the excess dough with a sharp knife and lightly prick the base all over with a fork. Bake for 15 minutes. Meanwhile, lightly whisk the egg white in a small, clean, dry bowl until it is frothy but not stiff. Brush the egg white over the base of the pastry case, then return the tin to the oven for a further 5 minutes. To make the filling, heat the oil in a large saucepan and, when it is hot, add the margarine. Add the onion and cook over a low heat, stirring occasionally, for about 5 minutes, until softened and translucent. Drain off the fat, return the pan to the heat, sprinkle in the flour and season with salt and pepper. Stir well, then stir in the cream. Spoon the mixture into the pastry case and spread it evenly over the base. Sprinkle the gruyere on top and bake for about 25 minutes, until golden brown. Remove the tart from the oven and leave to cool slightly. Serve warm.

58

Fritter batter (first version)
MASA PARA BUÑUELOS

- 300 g/11 oz plain flour
- 3 tablespoons white wine
- 3 tablespoons sunflower oil
- 300 ml/½ pint milk
- ½ teaspoon baking powder
- vegetable oil, for deep-frying
- salt

Serves 4–6

Sift the flour and a pinch of salt into a bowl. Make a well in the centre and pour in the wine and sunflower oil. Stir with a wooden spoon, then stir in the milk. Leave the mixture to rest for at least 30 minutes. Mix the baking powder into the batter. Heat the vegetable oil in a deep-fryer or deep saucepan to 180–190°C/350–375°F or until a cube of day old bread browns in 30 seconds. Working quickly but carefully, add some filling of your choice to one heaped teaspoon of fritter batter at a time and cook in batches, for 3–5 minutes or until golden brown. Drain on kitchen paper and season lightly with salt.

59

Fritter batter (second version)
MASA PARA BUÑUELOS

- 150 g/5 oz plain flour
- 1 egg, separated
- 1 tablespoon sunflower oil
- 250 ml/8 fl oz beer
- salt

Serves 4

This batter is good for frying fish, courgette, apple, etc. Sift the flour and a pinch of salt into a bowl. Make a well in the centre and pour in the egg yolk and oil. Stir well, then gradually stir in the beer, a little at a time, until a thick batter forms. Just before cooking, whisk the egg white with a pinch of salt in a clean, dry bowl until soft peaks form. Fold the egg white into the batter. Form the batter into fritters, add your chosen filling and cook as described in recipe 58.

60

Fritter batter (third version)
MASA PARA BUÑUELOS

- 150 g/5 oz plain flour
- 250 ml/8 fl oz soda water
- very small amount of baking
  powder (just enough to cover
  the tip of a knife)
- pinch of powdered saffron
- salt

Serves 4

This batter can be used for brains, squid, onions, etc. Mix all the ingredients to form a thick batter. Shape into fritters, add your chosen filling and cook as described in recipe 58.

Cheese fritters with tomato sauce
BUÑUELOS DE QUESO CON SALSA DE TOMATE

- **25 g/1 oz butter**
- **120 g/4 oz plain flour**
- **4 eggs**
- **150 g/5 oz gruyere cheese, grated**
- **vegetable oil, for deep-frying**
- **1 quantity Classic Tomato Sauce (see recipe 73)**
- **salt**

Serves 6

Pour 375 ml/13 fl oz water into a saucepan, add the butter and a pinch of salt and heat gently until the fat has melted. Bring to the boil, tip in the flour and stir vigorously with a wooden spoon until the mixture comes together and leaves the sides of the pan. Remove the pan from the heat and stir for about 5 minutes, until the mixture is cool. Stir in the eggs (unbeaten), one at a time, making sure each one is fully incorporated before adding the next. Stir in the gruyere and leave the mixture to stand for 2 hours. Heat the oil in a large deep saucepan. While it is still heating, scoop up a little of the cheese mixture on a teaspoon and use your finger to push it off the spoon into the oil. It should sink to the bottom of the pan. Repeat the process, but don't add too many fritters to the pan at the same time, as they expand considerably during cooking and it is better to fry them with plenty of space. As the oil heats up, the fritters will begin to rise to the surface. When they are golden brown remove them from the oil with a slotted spoon and place them in a large colander set over a baking pan in a warm oven until all the fritters are fried. Remove the pan from the heat between each batch of fritters to allow the oil to cool until it is just warm. Then repeat the cooking process again. Serve the fritters in a napkin-lined dish and offer the warmed tomato sauce separately.

Croquettes

CROQUETAS

- 2 tablespoons sunflower oil
- 40 g/1½ oz butter
- 4 tablespoons plain flour
- 750 ml/1¼ pints milk
- 2 eggs
- 175 g/6 oz breadcrumbs
- vegetable oil, for deep-frying
- salt
- fresh or deep-fried parsley
  sprigs (see recipe 918), optional

Filling:
- 500 g/1 lb 2 oz cooked,
  peeled and deveined prawns or
  350 g/12 oz cooked white fish,
  such as hake or
  2 chopped hard-boiled eggs or
  200 g/7 oz diced Serrano ham or
  1 diced cooked chicken breast or
  200 g/7 oz diced leftover roast
  chicken

Serves 6

Make a béchamel sauce by heating the sunflower oil in a saucepan. Add the butter and when it has melted, stir in the flour with a wooden spoon. Gradually stir in the milk, a little at a time, and cook, stirring constantly, until the béchamel sauce thickens. Season with salt and stir in your chosen filling, then spread the mixture out in a fish kettle or large dish to cool for at least 2 hours. Using two tablespoons, shape scoops of the mixture into croquettes. Finish forming the croquettes with your hands. Beat the eggs in a shallow dish. Spread out the breadcrumbs in another shallow dish. Roll each croquette lightly in the breadcrumbs, then in the beaten egg and finally in the breadcrumbs again, making sure that each one is evenly covered. If the croquettes are being prepared in advance, cover them with a damp tea towel to prevent them drying out. Heat the vegetable oil in a deep-fryer or deep saucepan to 180–190°C/350–375°F or until a cube of day-old bread browns in 30 seconds. Add the croquettes, in batches of about six at a time, and cook until crisp and golden brown. Using a slotted spoon, transfer them to a large colander set over a baking pan and place in a warm oven until all the croquettes have been cooked. Serve immediately on a dish garnished with sprigs of fresh or deep-fried parsley.

63

Cheese and egg croquettes

CROQUETAS DE QUESO RALLADO Y HUEVO

- **2 tablespoons sunflower oil**
- **40 g / 1½ oz butter**
- **4 tablespoons plain flour**
- **750 ml / 1¼ pints milk**
- **2 eggs**
- **200 g / 7 oz gruyere cheese, grated**

Serves 6

Make a thick béchamel sauce as described in recipe 77. Remove the pan from the heat and leave to cool slightly. Stir in the eggs (unbeaten), one at a time, making sure each one is fully incorporated before adding the next. Stir in the gruyere. Spread the mixture out in a fish kettle or large dish to cool for at least 2 hours, then proceed with the recipe as directed in recipe 62.

64

Salt cod and potato croquettes

CROQUETAS DE PATATA Y BACALAO

- **250 g / 9 oz salt cod fillet**
- **1.5 kg / 3¼ lb potatoes**
- **1–2 tablespoons olive oil**
- **1 garlic clove**
- **2 eggs, separated**
- **plain flour, for dusting**
- **vegetable oil, for deep-frying**
- **1 quantity Classic Tomato Sauce (see recipe 73)**
- **salt**

Serves 6

If the salt cod is dried, place it in a bowl, add water to cover and leave to soak for about 2 hours without changing the water, then drain. If it is vacuum packed, this is not necessary. Put the potatoes (unpeeled) and cod in a saucepan and add enough water to cover generously. Bring to the boil, then lower the heat and simmer for about 30 minutes, until the potatoes are tender. Drain well. Peel the potatoes, place in a bowl and mash well. Lift out the cod with a fish slice and remove any remaining skin and bones, then finely flake the flesh with your fingers and add to the mashed potato. Heat the olive oil in a small pan. Add the garlic and cook, stirring frequently, until lightly browned. Transfer the garlic to a mortar, add a pinch of salt and pound. Stir the garlic mixture into the mashed potato. Beat in the egg yolks, one at a time, making sure that each is fully incorporated before adding the next. Whisk the egg whites with a pinch of salt in a clean, dry bowl until soft peaks form. Fold the egg whites into the mashed potato. Shape the mixture into croquettes with your hands and roll lightly in flour. Heat the vegetable oil in a deep-fryer or deep saucepan to 180–190°C/350–375°F or until a cube of day-old bread browns in 30 seconds. Add the croquettes, in batches if necessary, and cook until crisp and golden brown. Using a slotted spoon, transfer them to a large colander set over a baking pan and place in a warm oven until all the croquettes have been cooked. Drain well and serve immediately, offering the tomato sauce separately.

65 Portuguese salt cod fritters
BUÑUELOS DE BACALAO PORTUGUESES

- **675 g/1½ lb salt cod**
- **1.5 kg/3¼ lb potatoes**
- **1 garlic clove, finely chopped**
- **1 teaspoon finely chopped**
  fresh parsley
- **3 egg yolks**
- **vegetable oil for deep-frying**
- **1 quantity Classic Tomato Sauce**
  (see recipe 73), optional

Serves 6

Put the salt cod in a bowl, add water to cover and leave to soak for a few hours, changing the water only once, then drain. Put the potatoes (unpeeled) and cod in a saucepan and add enough water to cover generously. Bring to the boil, then lower the heat and simmer for about 30 minutes, until the potatoes are tender. Drain well. Peel the potatoes, place in a bowl and mash well. Lift out the cod with a fish slice and remove any remaining skin and bones, then finely flake the flesh with your fingers. Add to the mashed potato, then stir in the garlic and parsley. Beat in the egg yolks, one at a time, making sure that each is incorporated before adding the next. Heat the vegetable oil in a deep-fryer or deep saucepan to 180–190°C/350–375°F or until a cube of day-old bread browns in 30 seconds. Drop tablespoons of the fish mixture into the hot oil and cook until crisp and golden brown. You will need to do this in batches. Remove with a slotted spoon, transfer to a large colander set over a baking pan and place in a warm oven until all the fritters have been cooked. Serve the fritters hot, offering the tomato sauce separately, if using.

Mushroom tart

TARTA DE CHAMPIÑONES

Pastry:
- **200 g/7 oz plain flour,**
  plus extra for dusting
- **90 g/3¼ oz butter,**
  cut into small pieces,
  plus extra for greasing
- **1 egg, separated**
- **1 tablespoon sunflower oil**
- **salt**

Filling:
- **500 g/1 lb 2 oz chestnut**
  mushrooms, thickly sliced
- **40 g/1½ oz butter**
- **few drops of lemon juice**
- **1 tablespoon sunflower oil**
- **1 heaped tablespoon plain flour**
- **300 ml/½ pint milk**
- **1 egg yolk**
- **salt**

Serves 6–8

First make the pastry dough as described in recipe 56, using the egg yolk but reserving the white. Leave to rest in a cool plac e for at least 2 hours. Preheat the oven to 180°C/350°F/Gas Mark 4. Grease a loose-based quiche tin, 25 cm/10 inches in diameter and about 4 cm/1½ inches deep, with butter. Roll out the dough to a round on a lightly floured work surface. Lift the dough on the rolling pin into the prepared tin and press down with your fingers to make sure it is even over the base. Trim the excess dough with a sharp knife and lightly prick the base all over with a fork. Lightly whisk the egg white in a clean, dry bowl until frothy but not stiff. Brush it over the inside of the pastry case. Bake for about 25 minutes, until firm and golden brown. Meanwhile, put the mushrooms in a saucepan, add 15 g/½ oz of the butter and the lemon juice and season lightly with salt. Cover and cook over a low heat for about 6 minutes. Make a béchamel sauce, by melting the remaining butter with the oil in another saucepan. Stir in the flour, then gradually whisk in the milk, a little at a time. Season with salt and cook, stirring constantly, for about 6 minutes. Lightly beat the egg yolk in a heatproof bowl, then very carefully stir in the béchamel sauce, a little at a time to prevent it separating. Pour the mixture back into the saucepan and stir well before adding the cooked mushrooms. When the pastry case is golden brown, remove from the oven and turn out on to a serving dish. Fill with the mushroom and béchamel mixture and serve immediately.

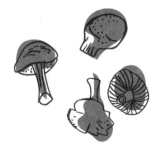

Green asparagus and béchamel tart

TARTA DE BECHAMEL Y ESPÁRRAGOS VERDES

Pastry:
- **200 g/7 oz plain flour,**
  plus extra for dusting
- **90 g/3¼ oz butter,**
  cut into small pieces,
  plus extra for greasing
- **1 tablespoon groundnut oil**
- **1 egg yolk**
- **salt**

Filling:
- **500 ml/18 fl oz milk**
- **1 heaped tablespoon cornflour**
- **100 g/3½ oz gruyere cheese,**
  grated
- **3 eggs, lightly beaten**
- **½ bunch of green asparagus,**
  cooked and cut into 4-cm/
  1½-inch pieces
- **salt**

Serves 6–8

First make the pastry dough as described in recipe 56. Leave to rest in a cool place for at least 2 hours. Preheat the oven to 180°C/350°F/Gas Mark 4. Grease with butter a loose-based quiche tin, 27 cm/10 ½ inches in diameter and about 4cm/1 ½ inches deep. Roll out the dough to a round on a lightly floured work surface. Lift the dough on the rolling pin into the prepared tin and press down with your fingers to make sure it is even over the base. Trim the excess dough with a sharp knife and lightly prick the base all over with a fork. Bake for about 15 minutes, until set but not browned. Meanwhile, make the filling. Pour the milk into a saucepan and bring to just below boiling point. Add the cornflour and cook, stirring constantly, for 3 minutes. Remove the pan from the heat and stir in nearly all the gruyere, leaving just enough to sprinkle over the top of the tart. Remove the pastry case from the oven and brush a little of the beaten egg around the edges. Do not switch off the oven. Gradually stir the remaining eggs into the filling mixture, season to taste with salt and pour the mixture into the pastry case. Gently press the pieces of asparagus deeper into the filling mixture to prevent them drying out during cooking. Sprinkle the remaining cheese over the top and bake for 15 minutes until golden. Remove the tart from the oven, transfer to a serving dish and serve immediately.

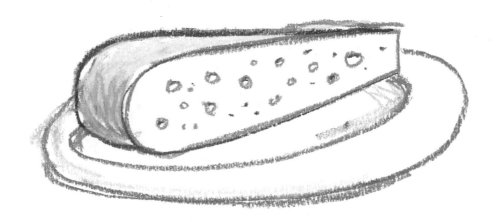

68

Hot asparagus mousse
MOUSSE CALIENTE DE ESPÁRRAGOS

- butter, for greasing
- 250 g/9 oz canned green or white asparagus, drained
- 165 g/5½ oz breadcrumbs (made from day-old bread)
- 175 ml/6 fl oz warm milk
- 2 egg yolks
- 1 large egg, lightly beaten
- salt and pepper

Sauce:
- ½ quantity Classic Béchamel Sauce (see recipe 77)
- 100 g/3½ oz cooked, drained spinach or green asparagus

Serves 4

Preheat the oven to 150°C/300°F/Gas Mark 2. Line the base and ends of a loaf tin 24 x 10 cm/9 ½ x 4 inches with foil and grease generously with butter. Pat the asparagus dry with kitchen paper. Put the breadcrumbs in a bowl, add the warm milk and leave to soak for 10 minutes. Put the asparagus in a food processor and process briefly to chop, then add the breadcrumbs. Scrape the mixture into a bowl and beat in the egg yolks, one at a time, making sure that the first is fully incorporated before adding the second. Beat in the whole egg and season to taste with salt and pepper, bearing in mind that the asparagus is already salted. Pour the mousse mixture into the prepared tin and smooth the top. Place the tin in a roasting tin and pour in boiling water to come about halfway up the sides. Place in the oven and bake for about 1 ¼ hours, until set. Meanwhile, pour the béchamel sauce into a food processor. Add the cooked spinach or asparagus and process until combined. Remove the mousse from the tin, using the foil to help you, and serve immediately with the green béchamel sauce.

69

Cold asparagus mousse
MOUSSE DE ESPÁRRAGOS FRÍA

- 350 g/12 oz canned white
  asparagus, drained
- 6 tablespoons powdered
  gelatine
- 350 ml/12 fl oz boiling water
- 4 heaped tablespoons
  Thick Mayonnaise
  (see recipe 106)
- escarole or lettuce, hard-boiled
  egg and tomato (optional)
- salt and pepper

Serves 6

Pat the asparagus dry with kitchen paper. Put the gelatine in a food processor, add the boiling water and process for 10 seconds. Immediately add the asparagus and process until finely chopped. Add the mayonnaise and process briefly again, until it has been incorporated. Taste and season with salt and pepper if necessary. Line the base and ends of a loaf tin 24 x 10 cm/9 ½ x 4 inches with foil and pour in the mixture. Cover and chill in the refrigerator for 5–6 hours, until set. To serve, turn out using the foil to help you. A typical Spanish garnish would include escarole or chopped lettuce, slices of hard-boiled egg and pieces of tomato.

70

Leek mousse
MOUSSE DE PUERROS

- 6 leeks, about 250 g/9 oz total
  weight, trimmed and rinsed well
- 50 g/2 oz breadcrumbs
- 275 ml/9 fl oz warm milk
- butter, for greasing
- 3 large eggs
- 175 ml/6 fl oz whipping cream,
  whipped until slightly thickened
- ½ quantity Classic Béchamel
  Sauce (see recipe 77)
- 100 g/3 ½ oz cooked, drained
  spinach
- salt

Serves 4

Cook the leeks in a saucepan of salted boiling water for 20–30 minutes, until tender. Drain well and pat dry with kitchen paper. Meanwhile, put the breadcrumbs in a bowl, add the warm milk and leave to soak. Preheat the oven to 160°C/325°F/Gas Mark 3. Line the base and ends of a 20-cm/8-inch long tin with foil and grease generously with butter. Cut off and reserve the bulbs and tops of the leeks and cut the remainder into 2-cm/¾-inch lengths. Put the reserved bulbs and tops in a food processor and add the breadcrumb and milk mixture. Process briefly, then with the motor running, add the eggs one at a time. When the mixture is smooth and thoroughly combined, pour it into a glass or china bowl and stir in the cream. Stir in the remaining leek. Pour the mixture into the prepared tin. Place the tin in a roasting tin and pour in boiling water to come about halfway up the sides. Place in the oven and bake for about 1 hour, until set. Meanwhile, pour the béchamel sauce into a food processor. Add the cooked spinach and process until combined. Serve the mousse hot and offer the sauce separately.

71 Individual fish mousses
PEQUEÑAS MOUSSES DE PESCADO

- 500 g/1 lb 2 oz white fish fillets, skinned
- 5 tablespoons lemon juice
- 3 tablespoons olive oil, plus extra for brushing
- 200 g/7 oz smoked salmon or smoked trout, thinly sliced
- 400 g/14 oz curd cheese
- 1 tablespoon chopped fresh parsley
- salt
- lettuce or escarole leaves (optional)

Serves 6

Cut the white fish fillets into cubes, put in a shallow bowl and pour the lemon juice over them. Leave to marinate, stirring occasionally, for about 3 hours. Brush 6 ramekins or individual glass or china dishes with a little oil. Line the base and the sides of the dishes with the slices of smoked fish, letting them overhang the rims. Drain the white fish, reserving the lemon juice. Put half the white fish in a food processor with half the cheese, 1 tablespoon of the reserved lemon juice and half the oil. Process briefly and scrape into a bowl. Put the remaining white fish, the remaining cheese, 1 tablespoon of the reserved lemon juice and the remaining oil in the food processor and process until smooth. Stir into the first batch of white fish, add the parsley and season to taste with salt. Spoon the mixture into the prepared dishes and fold over the overhanging smoked fish. Put the dishes on a tray, cover completely with foil and chill in the refrigerator for 5–6 hours, until set. (The mousses can be prepared up to a day in advance.) To serve, turn out the mousses on to individual plates and garnish with lettuce or escarole leaves.

72 Tomato jelly
GELATINA DE TOMATE

- 1 kg/2 ¼ lb ripe, fleshy tomatoes
- 1 large canned or bottled red pepper, chopped
- 1 tablespoon coarsely chopped fresh mint
- 80 g/3 oz gelatine powder
- 350 ml/12 fl oz double cream
- salt
- lettuce or escarole leaves

Serves 8

Cut a cross in the stalk end of each tomato with a sharp knife, put the tomatoes in a heatproof bowl and pour in boiling water to cover. Leave to stand for 1–2 minutes, then drain and peel off the skins. Cut the tomatoes in half, scoop out the seeds with a teaspoon and coarsely chop the flesh. Put in a food processor, together with any juice remaining on the chopping board, and add the pepper and mint. Process briefly to combine then transfer to a large heatproof bowl. Pour 350 ml/12 fl oz water into a saucepan, bring to the boil and stir in the gelatine powder with a wooden spoon. Remove the pan from the heat and pour the jelly into the tomato mixture. Lightly whisk the cream and fold it into the tomato mixture. Season to taste with salt. Pour the mixture into a mould 24 x 10 cm/9 ½ x 4 inches and chill in the refrigerator for at least 4 hours. Turn out the jelly and garnish with lettuce or escarole leaves. (It's easier to turn out the jelly from a plastic rather than a metal mould.)

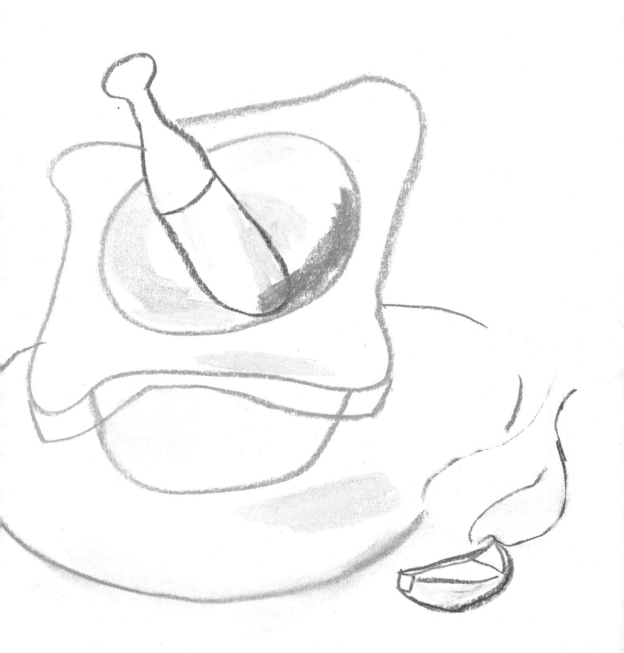

SAUCES

Hot sauces

73 📷

Classic tomato sauce
SALSA DE TOMATE CLÁSICA

- 3 tablespoons sunflower oil
- 1 onion, chopped (optional)
- 1 kg/2¼ lb ripe tomatoes,
  seeded and chopped
- 1 teaspoon sugar
- salt

Serves 6

Heat the oil in a frying pan. Add the onion, if using, and cook over a low heat, stirring occasionally, for about 5 minutes, until softened but not browned. (If you're not using the onion, add the tomato immediately.) Add the tomato and cook over a low heat, breaking the flesh up with the edge of a skimmer or slotted spoon, for about 15 minutes. Allow the mixture to cool slightly, then transfer to a food processor and process. Add the sugar, season to taste with salt and process briefly again. Serve the sauce in a sauce boat or poured directly over a dish.

74

Canned tomato sauce
SALSA DE TOMATE EN CONSERVA

- 3 tablespoons sunflower oil
- 1 onion, chopped
- 500 g/1 lb 2 oz canned tomatoes
- 1 teaspoon sugar
- salt

Serves 6

The sauce may also be made using canned tomatoes. To do this, follow the method described in recipe 73 but use the quantities of ingredients listed here.

Note: Making the tomato sauce with either fresh or canned tomatoes in a cast-iron frying pan will cause the pan to lose its 'seasoning' and turn a metallic, almost silver colour. If you have done so and want to use the frying pan for other dishes (omelettes, fried food, etc.), set it over the heat with nothing in it until the base turns black again. This re-seasons it and you can use it without ingredients sticking.

75

Tomato sauce with onion and wine
SALSA DE TOMATE CON CEBOLLA Y VINO

- 3 tablespoons sunflower oil
- 1 onion, chopped
- 1 kg/2 ¼ lb ripe tomatoes, chopped
- bouquet garni (1 sprig fresh parsley, 1 clove garlic and 1 bay leaf tied together in muslin)
- 3 tablespoons dry white wine
- 1 teaspoon sugar
- salt

Serves 6

Heat the oil in a frying pan. Add the onion and cook over a low heat, stirring occasionally, for 7–8 minutes, until lightly browned. Increase the heat to medium, add the tomato, bouquet garni and wine and cook, breaking up the tomato flesh with the side of a skimmer or slotted spoon, for about 15 minutes. Remove and discard the bouquet garni. Transfer the contents of the pan to a food processor and process. Add the sugar, season to taste with salt and process briefly to mix. The sauce is now ready to be served. If you prefer a thicker texture, return the sauce to the pan and cook over a high heat until some of the liquid has evaporated.

76

Chinese sweet-and-sour sauce
SALSA AGRIDULCE CHINA

- 1½ tablespoons sugar
- 2 tablespoons vinegar
- 1 tablespoon tomato purée
- 1 tablespoon soy sauce
- 3 tablespoons orange juice
- 1 teaspoon cornflour

Serves 4

Put the sugar, vinegar, tomato purée, soy sauce and orange juice in a saucepan. Mix the cornflour with 4 tablespoons water to a paste in a cup, then pour it into the pan. Bring the sauce to the boil over a low heat, stirring constantly, and serve hot. This sauce makes a good accompaniment for roast pork, chops, etc.

Béchamel

Tricks

- To prevent lumps forming with making béchamel, remove the saucepan from the heat when stirring in the flour. Stir briefly with a wooden spoon, return the pan to the heat and proceed as normal.
- To avoid a skin forming on top of a béchamel sauce prepared in advance, cover the surface with a disc of greaseproof paper lightly greased with butter.
- Béchamel sauce can be stored in the refrigerator for a few days or frozen. To reheat, put it into a heatproof bowl set over a pan of barely simmering water.

77

Classic béchamel sauce

SALSA BECHAMEL CORRIENTE

- **50 g/2 oz butter**
- **2 tablespoons sunflower oil**
- **2 tablespoons plain flour**
- **750 ml/1¼ pints milk**
- **salt**

Serves 6

Melt the butter with the oil in a saucepan and stir in the flour. Gradually stir in the milk, a little at a time, and bring to the boil, stirring constantly. Add salt to taste and simmer over a medium heat, stirring constantly, for 8–10 minutes. If a thinner sauce is required, add more milk. If the béchamel needs to be thicker, simmer the sauce longer, until it reaches the required consistency.

78

Béchamel sauce with tomato

SALSA BECHAMEL CON TOMATE

- **1 quantity Classic Béchamel Sauce (see recipe 77)**
- **1 tablespoon tomato purée**

Serves 6

Spoon a little of the béchamel sauce into a bowl and stir in the tomato purée. Pour the mixture back into the saucepan and mix well.

79

Béchamel sauce with egg yolks
SALSA BECHAMEL CON YEMAS

- 2 egg yolks
- 1 quantity Classic Béchamel
  Sauce (see recipe 77)

Serves 6

Put 2 egg yolks in a bowl and gradually add a little of the béchamel sauce, stirring constantly to prevent the eggs curdling. Then return the mixture to the sauce in the pan and reheat gently but do not boil.

80

Béchamel sauce with capers
SALSA BECHAMEL CON ALCAPARRAS

- 50 g/2 oz butter
- 2 tablespoons sunflower oil
- 2 tablespoons plain flour
- 375 ml/13 fl oz milk
- 375 ml/13 fl oz fish stock
  (use the cooking liquid left
  over after poaching fish)
- 1–2 tablespoons capers,
  rinsed and drained

Serves 6

Make the béchamel sauce as described in recipe 77, adding the stock at the same time you add the milk. When the sauce is ready, stir in the capers. This sauce is usually made to accompany poached fish.

Note: For added flavour, add 1–2 egg yolks as described in recipe 79.

81

Béchamel sauce with stock
SALSA BECHAMEL CON CALDO

- 25 g/1 oz butter
- 2 tablespoons sunflower oil
- 2 tablespoons plain flour
- 450 ml/¾ pint milk
- 450 ml/¾ pint chicken stock
  (home-made or made
  with a stock cube)
- salt

Serves 6

Make the béchamel sauce as described in recipe 77 but using the ingredients listed here. Both home-made stock and stock made from a cube contain salt, so bear this in mind when seasoning the sauce. This sauce is clearer and lighter than the previous recipes and is good for cannelloni, vegetables or baked fish dishes.

Spanish sauce

SALSA ESPAÑOLA

- **500 g/1 lb 2 oz boneless veal or beef, trimmed of visible fat**
- **3 tablespoons sunflower oil**
- **1 onion, chopped**
- **3 carrots, diced**
- **1 tablespoon plain flour**
- **bouquet garni (1 sprig fresh parsley, 1 clove garlic and 1 bay leaf tied together in muslin)**
- **1 clove**
- **1 small veal knuckle**
- **salt**

Serves 6

Dice the veal or beef very finely. Heat the oil in a saucepan. Add the onion and cook over a low heat, stirring occasionally, for about 10 minutes, until golden brown. Add the meat and cook, stirring frequently, for 8–10 minutes, until evenly browned. Stir in the carrot, then stir in the flour. Cook, stirring constantly, for about 5 minutes, then gradually stir in 1 litre/1 ¾ pints water. Add the bouquet garni, clove and veal knuckle and simmer gently for 30 minutes. Remove and discard the veal knuckle, clove and bouquet garni and pour the sauce through a fine sieve into a bowl, pressing it with a wooden spoon to get all the liquid. Return the sauce to the pan and stir well. Season to taste with salt and simmer until the sauce reaches the required consistency.

83

Bolognese sauce

SALSA BOLOÑESA

- **2 tablespoons olive oil**
- **50 g/2 oz bacon, finely chopped**
- **150 g/5 oz lean steak, finely chopped**
- **1 small onion, finely chopped**
- **1 carrot, finely chopped**
- **1–2 celery sticks, finely chopped**
- **1 clove**
- **6 tablespoons passata**
- **2 tablespoons white wine**
- **salt**

Serves 6

Heat the oil in a deep saucepan. Add the bacon and cook over a low heat, stirring occasionally, for 5 minutes. Add the steak, onion, carrot, celery and clove, season with salt and cook, stirring frequently, for about 10 minutes, until the meat is browned and the vegetables have softened. Stir in the passata and wine, cover and simmer gently for 10 minutes.

Note: This sauce is enough for 300 g/11 oz spaghetti. Toss the freshly cooked pasta in 275 ml/9 fl oz single cream and the bolognaise sauce, and serve with freshly grated Parmesan cheese.

84

Béarnaise sauce

SALSA BEARNESA

- **1 tablespoon finely chopped spring onion or shallot**
- **2 tablespoons white-wine vinegar**
- **150 g/5 oz butter**
- **juice of ½ lemon**
- **4 egg yolks**
- **pinch of potato flour**
- **1 tablespoon chopped fresh parsley**
- **salt and pepper**

Serves 6

Put the onion or shallot in a small saucepan, pour in the vinegar and cook for a few minutes until the liquid has reduced by half. Remove the pan from the heat and leave to cool. Melt the butter in another pan, but do not allow to brown. Stir 2 tablespoons water and the lemon juice into the cooled vinegar mixture. Make a bain-marie with a roasting tin or frying pan large enough to hold the saucepan. Half-fill the roasting tin with water and bring to just below boiling point. Lower the heat so that the water is barely simmering. Add the egg yolks to the vinegar mixture and, using the tip of a knife, add a pinch of potato flour. Whisk well, then place the pan in the simmering water and cook, whisking constantly, until the sauce thickens. Remove from the heat and take the pan out of the bain-marie. Gradually whisk in the butter, a little at a time. When all the butter has been fully incorporated, add the parsley and season to taste with salt and pepper. Serve in a warmed sauce boat with fillet, sirloin or rump steak or with grilled fish.

Note: This sauce is somewhere between a mayonnaise and a hollandaise, and is always served hot. It is delicious but a little fiddly to make as it curdles easily. If the butter seems to be separating in the sauce, whisk it well just before serving. To make a hollandaise sauce, follow the method above but leave out the shallots, vinegar, potato flour and parsley, and use 3 egg yolks, 1 cup butter and the juice of ½ lemon.

Cumberland sauce
SALSA CUMBERLAND

- **thinly pared rind of ½ orange**
- **juice and thinly pared rind of 1 lemon**
- **3 tablespoons redcurrant jelly**
- **½ teaspoon Dijon mustard**
- **1½ teaspoons Worcestershire sauce**

Serves 4

Cut the orange and lemon rind into very fine julienne strips. Bring a small saucepan of water to the boil. Add the orange and lemon rind and blanch for 2 minutes. Drain and reserve. Melt the jelly in the saucepan and add the lemon juice. Stir in the mustard and the Worcestershire sauce. Stir in the reserved citrus rind just before serving. The sauce may be served hot or cold and is good with fish or roasted meat.

Savoury lemon sauce
SALSA CON ZUMO DE LIMÓN

- **60 g / 2 ¼ oz butter**
- **1 heaped tablespoon plain flour**
- **1 chicken stock cube**
- **2 egg yolks**
- **juice of 1 lemon**
- **pinch of freshly grated nutmeg**
- **1 tablespoon chopped fresh parsley**
- **salt**

Serves 4

Melt the butter in a saucepan, then stir in the flour. Gradually stir in 450 ml / ¾ pint water, a little at a time, then cook, stirring constantly, for 5 minutes. Crumble in the stock cube and remove the pan from the heat. Put the egg yolks and lemon juice in a bowl, spoon in a little of the hot sauce and stir immediately to prevent the yolks curdling. Stir in a little more sauce and then tip the mixture back into the pan. The sauce does not require further cooking but should be kept warm. Season to taste with salt and stir in the nutmeg and parsley. Serve in a warmed sauce boat. This sauce goes well with fried or roasted meat and baked fish. It is similar to Béarnaise sauce but easier to make.

Note: You can also make this sauce using half stock and half milk.

87

Mousseline sauce for fish
SALSA MOUSSELINA PARA PESCADO

- 50 g/2 oz butter
- 2 tablespoons plain flour
- 750 ml/1¼ pints fish stock
- 1 egg white
- 2 egg yolks
- salt

Serves 6

Melt the butter in a saucepan, then stir in the flour. Gradually whisk in the fish stock, a little at a time, then remove the pan from the heat and continue to whisk until the sauce is smooth. Return the pan to the heat and cook, stirring constantly, for 4 minutes. Season to taste with salt. Transfer the sauce to a heatproof bowl and place over a pan of barely simmering water to keep warm. Just before serving, whisk the egg white in a clean, dry bowl until soft peaks form. Gently fold the egg yolks into the whites, then gradually fold in the hot sauce, a little at a time. Serve immediately in a warmed sauce boat.

88

Red wine sauce
SALSA DE VINO TINTO

- 1½ tablespoons olive oil
- 2 large shallots, chopped
- 500 ml/18 fl oz red wine
- 40 g/1½ oz butter
- 1 tablespoon plain flour
- 1 tablespoon chopped
  fresh parsley
- salt and pepper

Serves 6

Heat the oil in a frying pan. Add the shallots and cook over a low heat, stirring occasionally, for about 7 minutes, until beginning to brown. Add the wine and 175 ml/6 fl oz water and simmer gently for 10 minutes. Blend the butter and flour in a bowl with a fork to form a paste. Gradually stir the paste into the frying pan a small amount at a time. When the meat is ready, pour any cooking juices into the sauce. Stir in the parsley and season to taste with salt and pepper. Pour the sauce over the meat. This sauce goes well with sirloin or rump steak.

89

Madeira sauce
SALSA DE VINO DE MADEIRA

- 3 tablespoons olive oil
- 1 small onion, thinly sliced
- 1 tablespoon plain flour
- 250 ml/8 fl oz water mixed
  with ½ teaspoon meat extract
- 150 ml/¼ pint Madeira wine
- 20 g/¾ oz butter
- salt

Serves 4

Heat the oil in a saucepan. Add the onion and cook over a low heat, stirring occasionally, for about 7 minutes, until lightly browned. Stir in the flour, then gradually stir in the water with the meat extract, a little at a time. When incorporated, gradually stir in the Madeira. Simmer gently for 10 minutes. Strain through a coarse sieve into a clean pan and reheat. Season with salt if necessary (bearing in mind that the meat extract is salty). Just before serving, remove the pan from the heat and whisk in the butter. Serve with ham and spinach.

90

- **120 g / 4 oz mushrooms, sliced**
- **60 g / 2¼ oz butter**
- **juice of ½ lemon**
- **1 tablespoon sunflower oil**
- **1 tablespoon plain flour**
- **5 tablespoons sherry**
- **½ teaspoon meat extract**
- **1 tablespoon chopped fresh parsley (optional)**
- **salt**

Serves 4–6

Sherry and mushroom sauce

SALSA DE JEREZ Y CHAMPIÑONES

Put the mushrooms into a small saucepan. Add 25 g / 1 oz of the butter, the lemon juice and a pinch of salt. Cover and cook over a low heat for 10 minutes. Remove the pan from the heat and set aside. Melt the remaining butter with the oil in another saucepan. Stir in the flour and cook, stirring constantly, for a few minutes, until lightly browned. Gradually stir in the sherry and 300 ml / ½ pint water. Cook over a medium heat for 8 minutes, then strain the mixture into a clean pan to remove any lumps. Add the mushrooms with their cooking juices and the meat extract and parsley, if using, and reheat gently. Season with salt, if necessary, and serve in a warmed sauce boat. This sauce is a good one to serve with meat, sweetbreads, and poached or lightly boiled eggs.

91

- **2 tablespoons sunflower oil**
- **1 onion, chopped**
- **1 tablespoon plain flour**
- **1 tablespoon tomato purée**
- **5 tablespoons sherry**
- **50 g / 2 oz olives, stoned and sliced**
- **½ teaspoon meat extract**
- **salt**

Sserves 6

Sherry and olive sauce

SALSA DE JEREZ Y ACEITUNAS

Heat the oil in a small saucepan. Add the onion and cook over a low heat, stirring occasionally, for about 7 minutes, until beginning to brown. Stir in the flour and cook, stirring constantly, for 2 minutes. Stir in the tomato purée, then gradually stir in 450 ml / ¾ pint water, a little at a time. Stir in the sherry and olives. Simmer gently for about 5 minutes, then stir in the meat extract and season with salt if necessary (bearing in mind that the meat extract and the olives are salty). Serve in a warmed sauce boat. This sauce goes well with meat, sweetbreads and poached eggs.

92 White wine sauce
SALSA DE VINO BLANCO

- 3 tablespoons olive oil
- 1 onion, chopped
- 1 tablespoon plain flour
- 2 tomatoes,
  peeled, seeded and chopped
- 175 ml/6 fl oz white wine
- 100 g/3½ oz Serrano ham,
  chopped
- ½ teaspoon meat extract
- salt and pepper
Serves 6

Heat the oil in a saucepan. Add the onion and cook over a low heat, stirring occasionally, for about 7 minutes, until beginning to brown. Stir in the flour and cook, stirring constantly, for 2 minutes. Add the tomato and cook for 5 minutes, then add 300 ml/½ pint water and the wine. Simmer gently for about 10 minutes, then remove from the heat and allow to cool a little. Transfer the mixture to a food processor and process until smooth. Return the sauce to the pan, add the ham and cook over a low heat for 3 minutes. Add a little cold or hot water if the sauce is too thick, then keep warm until ready to serve. Just before serving, stir in the meat extract and season with salt, if necessary, and pepper (bearing in mind that the meat extract and ham are salty). This sauce goes well with lightly boiled or poached eggs and omelettes and should be served immediately after pouring.

93 Shallot sauce for fried meat
SALSA DE CHALOTAS PARA LA CARNE

- 2 shallots, finely chopped
- 1 teaspoon chopped
  fresh parsley
- 175 ml/6 fl oz dry white wine
- salt
Serves 4

Fry steaks or other cuts of meat in a frying pan, then transfer them to a plate and set aside in a warm place. Add the shallots, parsley and wine to the cooking juices in the frying pan. Add 150 ml/¼ pint water and cook over a high heat for 5 minutes, then lower the heat to medium and cook for a further 5 minutes. Season to taste with salt. To serve, pour the sauce over the meat.

94 Cream and meat extract sauce
SALSA DE NATA LÍQUIDA Y EXTRACTO DE CARNE

- 250 ml/8 fl oz single cream
- ½ teaspoon meat extract
Serves 4–6

Mix together the cream and meat extract in a heatproof bowl. Set the bowl over a pan of barely simmering water to heat the sauce, but do not allow it to boil. Serve in a warmed sauce boat. This sauce is a good one to serve with leftover meat.

Note: Meat extract is a seasoning that can add a meaty, salty flavour to sauces, soups and stews. One popular brand is Bovril. If you can't find it, use Maggi Seasoning or some crumbled beef stock cube.

95

Butter and anchovy sauce

SALSA DE MANTEQUILLA Y ANCHOAS

- **6 canned anchovy fillets, drained**
- **100 g/3½ oz butter, softened**
- **juice of 1 lemon**
- **1 tablespoon chopped**
  fresh parsley

Serves 4

Mash the anchovies with half the butter in a mortar. When the mixture is smooth, beat in the remaining butter. Put the mixture in a saucepan and heat gently, but do not allow to colour. Stir in the lemon juice and parsley. Pour the sauce over the dish you're serving or serve in a warmed sauce boat. This sauce goes well with fillets of meat, roasted fish such as grouper, fried fish such as sole or oven cooked fish such as turbot.

96 Black butter and caper sauce
SALSA DE MANTEQUILLA NEGRA Y ALCAPARRAS

- **150 g/5 oz butter**
- **½ teaspoon white-wine vinegar**
- **2 tablespoons capers,**
  rinsed and drained
- **salt**

Serves 4

Melt the butter in a saucepan over a low heat until it begins to colour but not burn, then remove from the heat and add the vinegar, capers and a pinch of salt. Return to the heat and cook, stirring constantly, for 1–2 minutes. Serve in a warmed sauce boat. This sauce is usually served with skate and turbot.

97 Redcurrant sauce for venison
SALSA DE GROSELLA PARA VENADO, CORZO O CIERVO

- **4 tablespoons olive oil**
- **2 shallots, chopped**
- **1 small celery stick, chopped**
- **200 g/7 oz boneless venison,**
  chopped
- **750 ml/1¼ pints red wine**
  (such as Burdeos)
- **bouquet garni (1 bay leaf,**
  1 sprig fresh thyme, 1 sprig
  fresh parsley and 1 clove garlic
  tied together in muslin)
- **5 tablespoons brandy**
- **250 g/9 oz redcurrant jelly**
- **1 tablespoon potato flour**
- **3–4 drops of red food colouring**
  (optional)
- **salt and pepper**

Serves 8

Heat the oil in a saucepan. Add the shallots, celery and venison and cook over a low heat, stirring occasionally, for 5 minutes, until the shallots are softened but not browned. Pour in the wine, add the bouquet garni and cook until the liquid has reduced by half. Pass the sauce through a sieve into a bowl, pressing down well, then return the sauce to the pan and place over the heat. Stir in the brandy and redcurrant jelly and season to taste with salt and pepper. Mix the potato flour to a paste with a little water in a bowl, then stir into the pan and cook, stirring constantly, for 2 minutes. Add the food colouring, if using, and serve in a warmed sauce boat. If you need to keep the sauce warm while you prepare the rest of the meal, pour it into a heatproof bowl, put a knob of butter on top to prevent a skin forming and set the bowl over a pan of barely simmering water.

Note: The thickness of the sauce will depend on the type of redcurrant jelly. If the sauce is too thick, add a little water. If it is too thin, add a little more potato flour mixed to a paste with water.

Cold sauces

Vinaigrette

The ideal proportions for a vinaigrette are 3 tablespoons oil to 1 tablespoon vinegar, but if the vinaigrette is too strong, add more lemon juice to the mixture.

Tricks
- If too much vinegar has been used, put a large piece of bread into the dish to absorb the sauce. Discard the bread and make a fresh vinaigrette. The salad will still be useable.
- Personalize the vinaigrette by adding chopped onion, chopped hard-boiled egg, a pinch of curry powder or saffron, capers, etc.
- See the glossary (page 964) for information on different types of vinegar.

98

- **pinch of salt**
- **1 tablespoon white- or red-wine vinegar**
- **3 tablespoons olive oil or other oil**

Serves 2–4

Vinaigrette
SALSA VINAGRETA

Dissolve the salt in the vinegar in a bowl, then add the oil, whisking well with a fork until all the ingredients are amalgamated.

Note: The vinaigrette can be varied in many ways: adding mustard, a little finely chopped onion and parsley, chopped capers or chopped hard-boiled egg, for example.

99

Special vinaigrette (first version)
SALSA VINAGRETA HISTORIADA

- **2 hard-boiled eggs**
- **1 teaspoon Dijon mustard**
- **1 tablespoon white-wine vinegar**
- **300 ml/½ pint sunflower oil**
- **1 tablespoon chopped fresh parsley**
- **salt**

Serves 4

Cut the hard-boiled eggs in half and scoop out the yolks with a teaspoon into a bowl. Finely chop and reserve the whites. Add the mustard to the bowl and mash into the egg yolks using the back of a spoon. Add the vinegar, then gradually whisk in the oil, a little at a time, as if making mayonnaise. When the oil has been fully incorporated, season to taste with salt. Just before serving, stir in the parsley and egg whites. Serve the vinaigrette in a sauce boat. This dressing is an excellent accompaniment to hot or cold fish, chickpeas and hot or cold asparagus.

100

Special vinaigrette (second version)
SALSA VINAGRETA HISTORIADA

- **3 tablespoons white-wine vinegar**
- **135 ml/4½ fl oz sunflower oil**
- **175 ml/6 fl oz vegetable stock**
- **1 hard-boiled egg**
- **1 tablespoon chopped fresh parsley**
- **1 tablespoon finely chopped spring onion (optional)**
- **salt**

Serves 4

Put the vinegar in a bowl and stir in a pinch of salt. Gradually whisk in the oil, a little at a time, followed by the stock. Chop the hard-boiled egg and add it to the vinaigrette with the parsley and spring onion, if using, just before serving in a sauce boat. This dressing is an excellent accompaniment to hot or cold fish, chickpeas and hot or cold asparagus.

101

Vinaigrette with garlic
SALSA VINAGRETA CON AJO

- **1 clove garlic**
- **2 tablespoons white-wine vinegar**
- **6 tablespoons sunflower oil**
- **1 tablespoon finely chopped fresh parsley**
- **salt**

Serves 4

Pound the garlic with a pinch of salt to a paste in a mortar. Transfer to a bowl and gradually whisk in the vinegar with a fork, then gradually whisk in the oil. Finally, add the parsley. Leave to stand in a cool place for 30 minutes before serving in a sauce boat. This sauce goes well with cold fish.

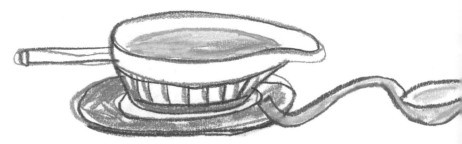

102

Roquefort sauce with cream
SALSA ROQUEFORT CON CREMA

- 80 g/3 oz Roquefort cheese
- 1 tablespoon olive oil
- 1 teaspoon white-wine vinegar
- salt
- 100 g/ 3 ½ oz single cream
  (optional)

Serves 2–4

Mash the Roquefort with the oil in a bowl, then add the vinegar and season with salt. Transfer to a food processor and process briefly. Return to the bowl and chill in the refrigerator for 30 minutes. Just before serving, if the sauce is too thick, add a little single cream. Serve the sauce with poultry, cooked ham, and other cold meats.

103

Roquefort sauce with yogurt
SALSA ROQUEFORT CON YOGUR

- 80 g/3 oz Roquefort cheese
- 1 tablespoon olive oil
- 1 teaspoon lemon juice
- 2 teaspoons natural yogurt
- salt and pepper

Serves 2–4

Mash the Roquefort with the oil in a bowl, then add the lemon juice. Season to taste with salt and pepper, then gradually stir in the yogurt. This sauce goes well with poultry, cooked ham, and endive salad, amongst other things.

104

Little butter mountains
MONTONCITOS DE MANTEQUILLA

- 1 tablespoon very finely
  chopped, fresh parsley
- 50g/2 oz butter, softened
- 1 teaspoon lemon juice
- 6 very thin slices lemon

- 50g/2 oz butter, softened
- 3 teaspoons white-wine vinegar
- ½ teaspoon dried tarragon
- 6 very thin slices lemon
- salt
- 6 small sprigs fresh parsley

Makes 6

First version
Mix together the parsley, butter and lemon juice in a bowl. Divide the mixture into six small mounds and place each one on a very slice of lemon. Store in the refrigerator or a cool place until required. Place a lemon slice, topped with butter, on each steak just before serving

Second version
Put the butter into a bowl and gradually add the vinegar, a little at a time, whisking as if making mayonnaise. Season with salt and stir the tarragon. Divide the mixture into six small mounds and place each one on a slice of lemon, then top each with a sprig of parsley. Store in the refrigerator until required. Place a lemon slice topped with butter on each steak before serving.

Note: To serve the butters with roasts and fried foods, make three times the quantity shown, melt over a low heat and serve separately in a warmed sauce boat.

Mayonnaise

Tricks

- For successful mayonnaise, make sure all the ingredients are at room temperature. If any are usually stored in the refrigerator, re-move them at least 1 hour before they are needed.
- If there is no wine vinegar available, you can use lemon juice instead.
- When the mayonnaise is finished, add 1 teaspoon hot water. This makes it lighter and prevents it curdling. If the mayonnaise needs to be lighter still, use unsweetened condensed milk instead of oil.
- To change the colour, add tomato sauce or chopped parsley.
- For mayonnaise intended to accompany seafood, add 1 tablespoon tomato sauce and 1 tablespoon brandy.
- If, even after you have carefully followed the instructions, the mayonnaise does not 'come together', mix it with a little egg white in a separate bowl.
- If the mayonnaise separates, transfer it to a chilled bowl and gradually beat in an egg yolk or 1 teaspoon vinegar.
- If the mayonnaise is too thick, add a little cold water or 1 table-spoon chilled single cream.
- Give the mayonnaise a special touch by adding a little chopped fresh parsley or tarragon.

105

Classic mayonnaise
SALSA MAYONESA CLÁSICA

- 2 egg yolks, at room temperature
- 2 tablespoons white-wine vinegar or lemon juice
- 500 ml/18 fl oz sunflower oil
- salt

Serves 4

Put the egg yolks in a bowl with 1½ teaspoons of the vinegar or lemon juice and a small pinch of salt. Stir lightly with a whisk or fork and then gradually whisk in the oil, 1–2 teaspoons at a time, until about a quarter has been added. Whisk in the remaining oil in a slow, steady stream. Add the remaining vinegar or lemon juice, then taste and adjust the seasoning. It is a good idea to make the mayonnaise in a cool place and store it in the refrigerator.

106

Thick mayonnaise
SALSA MAYONESA

- 1 egg, at room temperature
- juice of ½ lemon
- ¼ teaspoon Dijon mustard
  (optional)
- 500 ml/18 fl oz sunflower oil
- salt

Serves 4

Put the egg, lemon juice, mustard, if using, a pinch of salt and a dash of oil in a food processor. (These ingredients should not quite cover its blades.) Gently combine the ingredients with a spatula or the handle of a spoon, then process for 20 seconds. Add the remaining oil, combine again with a spatula or the handle of a spoon, then process for about 35 seconds, until the mayonnaise is thick and creamy. Taste and add more salt, mustard or lemon juice to taste. Store it in the refrigerator.

Note: Instead of adding all the remaining oil at once, pour it gradually through the feeder hole of the food processor with the motor running.

107

Green mayonnaise
SALSA MAYONESA VERDE

- 1 egg, at room temperature
- juice of ½ lemon
- 250 ml/8 fl oz sunflower oil
- ½ bunch fresh parsley,
  leaves only
- 2 tablespoons coarsely chopped,
  rinsed and drained capers
- 2 gherkins, coarsely chopped
- a few drops of green food
  colouring (optional)
- salt

Serves 4

Make the mayonnaise as described in recipe 106, omitting the mustard, and transfer to a bowl. Pound the parsley leaves in a mortar, then add 1 tablespoon of the mayonnaise. Mix well, then stir into the rest of the mayonnaise until thoroughly and evenly combined. Stir in the capers and gherkins and add the green food colouring, if using. Store the green mayonnaise in the refrigerator until required.

108

Mayonnaise with tomato and brandy
SALSA MAYONESA CON TOMATE Y COÑAC

- 1 egg, at room temperature
- juice of ½ lemon
- 250 ml/8 fl oz sunflower oil
- 1 tablespoon brandy
- 1 teaspoon Dijon mustard
- 1 teaspoon tomato purée
- a few drops of Worcestershire sauce
- salt

Serves 4

Make the mayonnaise as described in recipe 106, omitting the mustard, and transfer to a bowl. Gradually stir in the brandy, a little at a time, then the mustard, tomato purée and Worcestershire sauce. Mix well, then store in the refrigerator until required.

109

Egg-free mayonnaise with tomato
SALSA TIPO MAYONESA CON TOMATE, SIN HUEVO

- 2 celery sticks, with leaves
- 1 tablespoon tomato purée
- 175 ml/6 fl oz milk
- 175 ml/6 fl oz sunflower oil
- juice of ½ lemon
- 10 blanched almonds
- 4 black peppercorns, crushed
- salt

Serves 4

Cut the celery sticks into 2-cm/¾-inch lengths and coarsely chop the leaves. Place all the ingredients in a food processor and process until thoroughly combined. Pour into a sauce boat and chill in the refrigerator for at least 1 hour.

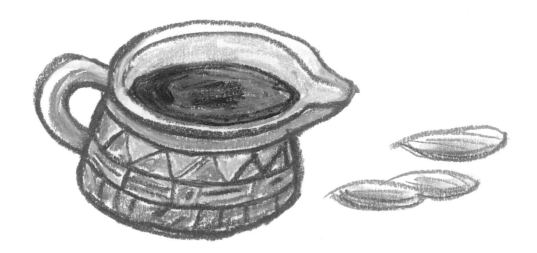

110 Garlic mayonnaise
ALIOLI

3 cloves garlic
- 1–2 egg yolks
- 500ml/18 fl oz sunflower oil
- 2 tablespoons white-wine
  vinegar or lemon juice

Serves 4

Crush 3 garlic with a little salt to a paste in a mortar. Transfer to a bowl, add the egg yolks, then gradually add the oil as described in recipe 105. Finally, add the vinegar or lemon juice and 1–2 tablespoons warm water, then serve. This garlic mayonnaise can be served with all kinds of cold meat. It also makes a good accompaniment to poached salt cod or a dish of potatoes and vegetables such as artichokes, leeks, turnips or carrots.

111 Quick garlic mayonnaise
ALIOLI RÁPIDO

- 3 cloves garlic
- 1 quantity Classic Mayonnaise
  (see recipe 105)
- salt

Serves 4

Crush the garlic with a little salt to a paste in a mortar; the salt absorbs the aroma of the garlic. Gradually stir the garlic paste into the mayonnaise, then serve.

112 Romesco sauce

SALSA ROMESCU

- 2 romesco or other
  hot dried red peppers
- 200 g/7 oz almonds
- 100 g/3½ oz hazelnuts
- 3 tomatoes
- 250 ml/8 fl oz light olive oil,
  plus extra for drizzling
- 2 Marie biscuits
- 1 tablespoon white-wine vinegar
- 1 tablespoon chopped
  fresh parsley
- 1 tablespoon chopped fresh mint
- salt and pepper

Serves 6

Preheat the oven to 200°C/400°F/Gas Mark 6. Put the peppers in a bowl, pour in warm water to cover and leave to soak for 30 minutes, then drain and peel. Place the almonds, hazelnuts and tomatoes on a baking sheet, drizzle with oil and roast in the oven for 10 minutes. Transfer the nuts to a bowl and return the tomatoes to the oven for a further 30 minutes. Pound the almonds, hazelnuts and biscuits together in a mortar or process in a food processor. Remove the tomatoes from the oven and, when cool enough to handle, peel and add them to the nut mixture. Add the peppers and pound or process. Gradually add the oil, a little at a time, as if making mayonnaise (see recipe 105). Finally, add the vinegar, parsley and mint. Season to taste with salt and pepper and stir in a little water if the sauce is too thick. This sauce goes very well with seafood, especially if grilled or barbecued. It has a strong flavour so it should be used in moderation.

113 Vegetable sauce

SALSA DE HORTALIZAS – PIPIRRANA

- 2 large, ripe tomatoes,
  seeded and finely chopped
- 1 cucumber, finely chopped
- 1 green pepper,
  seeded and finely chopped
- 1 small onion, finely chopped
- 3 tablespoons white wine
  vinegar
- 6 tablespoons sunflower oil
- salt and pepper

Serves 6

This sauce should be made 30 minutes prior to being served. This gives it enough time to marinate but not enough time for the tomato to break down and become very watery. Mix together the tomato, cucumber, green pepper and onion in a bowl. Whisk the vinegar with a pinch of salt and pepper in a separate bowl and whisk in the oil. Pour the dressing over the vegetables and mix well. Leave to stand in a cool place for about 30 minutes before serving. To serve, pour the sauce over fish or shellfish. If the sauce is to be served with meat, offer it separately in a china or glass bowl. More than just a sauce, this recipe is like a very finely chopped salad and goes very well with fish, shellfish and cold meat.

Guacamole

GUACAMOLE

- **1 large, very ripe avocado**
- **1 tablespoon finely chopped onion**
- **1 piece green pepper, finely chopped**
- **2 slices green chilli or 3 small green chillies**
- **½ tomato, finely chopped**
- **4 coriander seeds, crushed**
- **a few drops of lemon juice**
- **salt**

Serves 3

Halve the avocado and remove and reserve the stone. Scoop out the flesh with a spoon into a bowl. Mash with a fork until smooth. Add the onion, green pepper, chilli, tomato and coriander seeds, season with salt and stir in the lemon juice to prevent discolouration. Mix together well, spoon into a serving bowl and place the reserved avocado stone in the middle. Cover tightly with cling film and place in the refrigerator until ready to serve. Remove the chilli just before serving. Serve this spicy avocado sauce as an accompaniment to cold meat or as an appetizer on savoury crackers.

115

Sauce for seafood salad
SALSA PARA SALPICÓN DE MARISCOS

- 1 onion, very finely chopped
- oil
- 300 ml/ ½ pint white-wine vinegar
- 1 hard-boiled egg, chopped
- ½ red pepper, very finely chopped
- 1 tablespoon brandy
- salt

Serves 4

Place the onion and oil in a bowl and set aside for 5 minutes to infuse. Make a vinaigrette with white-wine vinegar, salt and the oil and onion mixture. Add the egg and pepper and brandy.

116

Marinade for game
ADOBO PARA CAZA

- 1 bottle red wine, to cover meat
- 1 thinly sliced onion
- 2 sliced carrots
- 3 sprigs fresh parsley
- 2 bay leaves or sprigs thyme
- 12 black peppercorns
- 2 ground cloves
- dash of olive oil
- salt

Makes enough for 1 joint

Mix together all the ingredients in an earthenware, glass or china dish; a metal dish will affect the flavour. Add the meat, turning well to coat. Cover the dish to prevent the aroma of the ingredients escaping and place in the refrigerator. The meat should be left to marinate for at least 5 hours and up to 24 hours. Turn the meat in the marinade from time to time, then re-cover. When the meat is ready to be cooked, remove it from the marinade and discard the marinade. Cook the meat as desired. This type of marinade is used to make meat more tender and improve flavour. Use it for strong meats such as venison or hare, for example.

Sweet sauces

117

Caramel sauce

CARAMELO LÍQUIDO

- 1 tablespoon caster sugar
- a few drops of lemon juice
- 175 ml / 6 fl oz hot water

Serves 4

Put the sugar, lemon juice and 2 tablespoons cold water into a saucepan. Cook over a high heat, whisking constantly, until golden brown. Remove from the heat and add the hot water very carefully as there will be a lot of steam. Return the pan to the heat and cook for about 5 minutes, until the sauce thickens a little. Remove from the heat and leave to cool before serving in a small jug.

118

Chocolate sauce
SALSA DE CHOCOLATE

• 200 g/7 oz plain chocolate, broken into squares
• 1 teaspoon potato flour
• 600 ml/1 pint milk
• 4 tablespoons caster sugar

Serves 4

Put the chocolate in a saucepan, add 4 tablespoons water and heat gently, stirring occasionally, until the chocolate has melted and the mixture is smooth. Mix the potato flour to a paste with 1 tablespoon of the milk in a cup. Gradually stir the remaining milk into the chocolate and add the sugar and the potato flour mixture. Cook, stirring constantly, for 2 minutes, then remove the pan from the heat. Leave the sauce to cool, then strain it through a coarse sieve into a sauce boat. This sauce goes well with baked desserts, vanilla ice cream and poached pears.

119

Jam sauce
SALSA DE MERMELADA

• 2 tablespoons caster sugar
• 3 tablespoons jam (such as redcurrant, raspberry or apricot)
• 2 teaspoons potato flour
• a few drops of lemon juice

Serves 4

Put the sugar and jam into a saucepan, pour in 450 ml/¾ pint water and cook over a medium heat, stirring constantly, for 10 minutes. Stir the potato flour to a paste with 2 tablespoons water in a cup, then stir into the jam mixture. Cook, stirring constantly, for a further 5 minutes. Add the lemon juice, strain and serve. This sauce goes well with steamed desserts and ice cream.

120

Orange sauce
SALSA DE ZUMO DE NARANJA

• juice of 4 large oranges
• 1 thinly pared strip lemon rind
• 200 g/7 oz caster sugar
• 1 teaspoon potato flour or rice flour
• 2 tablespoons Curaçao or Cointreau (optional)

Serves 6

Extract the orange juice using a juicer or a food processor, as both methods produce a thicker juice. Otherwise, squeeze the fruit in the usual way and use a little extra potato flour to thicken the sauce. Pour the orange juice into a saucepan, add the lemon rind and sugar and heat gently, stirring until the sugar has dissolved. Stir the potato flour to a thin paste with 3 tablespoons water in a cup. (If using rice flour, stir it with 1 tablespoon water.) Stir into the juice mixture and cook, stirring constantly, for 2 minutes. Remove from the heat, add the liqueur, if using, strain into a jug and leave to cool. Store in the refrigerator until required. This sauce can be served with baked desserts and ice cream.

STEWS & SOUPS

121

Swiss chard, potato, haricot beans and rice stew

POTAJE CON ACELGAS, PATATAS, JUDÍAS BLANCAS Y ARROZ

- 350 g/12 oz dried haricot beans,
  soaked overnight in cold water
  and drained
- 4 Swiss chard leaves,
  finely chopped
- 250 g/9 oz lean pork, diced
- 250 g/9 oz turnips, diced
- 3 tablespoons olive oil
- 1 small onion, finely chopped
- 1 tomato, peeled and seeded
- pinch of saffron threads
- 3 potatoes, diced
- 100 g/3½ oz rice
- salt

Serves 6

Put the beans in a saucepan and add cold water to cover. Bring to the boil and drain. Add fresh cold water to cover and bring back to the boil, then lower the heat and simmer for 25–30 minutes. Drain well. Put the Swiss chard leaves, pork and turnips into another saucepan and add water to cover and a pinch of salt. Bring to the boil, then lower the heat and simmer for about 1 hour, until quite tender. Add the beans, stir well and continue to simmer for a further 30 minutes, until very tender. Heat the oil in a frying pan. Add the onion and cook over a low heat, stirring occasionally, for about 7 minutes, until lightly browned. Add the tomato and cook for a further 5 minutes. Transfer the contents of the pan to the stew. Put the saffron in a mortar, add a spoonful of stock from the stew and crush with a pestle. Add to the stew. About 30 minutes before serving, add the potatoes to the stew and 15 minutes after adding the potatoes, add the rice. Serve the stew in a soup tureen.

122

Simple stew

POTAJE SENCILLO

- 250 g/9 oz dried haricot beans,
  soaked overnight in cold water
  and drained
- 1 bay leaf
- ½ onion, halved
- 2 cloves garlic
- 25 g/1 oz lard
- 120 g/4 oz lean ham in a single
  piece
- 120 g/4 oz bacon in a single piece
- 1 litre/1¾ pints warm water
- 1 kg/2¼ lb cabbage,
  preferably Savoy, shredded
- 500 g/1 lb 2 oz potatoes, diced
- salt

Serves 6

Put the beans, bay leaf, onion, garlic, lard, ham and bacon into a large saucepan and pour in 1 litre/1¾ pints cold water. Bring to the boil, then lower the heat and simmer for 15 minutes. Add 250 ml/8 fl oz fresh cold water, bring back to the boil and simmer for a further 15 minutes. Do this twice more at 15-minute intervals, then simmer for a further 15 minutes (making a total cooking time of about 1¼ hours.) Using a slotted spoon, remove the beans from the pan. Put about half the beans in a bowl, add some of the stock from the stew and set aside. Put the remaining beans in a food processor and process to a purée. Scrape the bean purée into the stew. Add the warm water and when the stew comes back to simmering point, stir in the cabbage. Continue to simmer for 1 hour, then add the potatoes and season with salt. Cook for a further 45 minutes, until the potato and cabbage are tender. Add the reserved beans. Remove the pieces of ham and bacon, cut them into small cubes and return them to the stew. Taste and adjust the seasoning, if necessary. Serve in a soup tureen.

123 Galician stew

POTE GALLEGO

- 250 g/9 oz dried haricot beans, soaked overnight in cold water and drained
- 150 g/5 oz ham
- 2 beef shin bones
- 500 g/1 lb 2 oz lean beef
- 4 potatoes
- 500 g/1 lb 2 oz turnip tops or Savoy cabbage
- 1 tablespoon lard
- salt

Serves 6

Put the beans in a saucepan and add cold water to cover. Bring to the boil and drain. Add fresh cold water to cover and bring back to the boil, then lower the heat and simmer for 25–30 minutes. Drain well. Put the ham, shin bones, beef, potatoes, turnip tops or Savoy cabbage and lard into a large stockpot. Add enough water to cover. Bring to a simmer and simmer for 1 hour. Add the beans, simmer for 30 minutes more and serve hot.

124 Thick chickpea soup

PURÉ DE GARBANZOS

- 2 tablespoons olive oil
- 2 leeks, chopped and rinsed well
- 1.5 litres/2 ½ pints beef or veal stock (home-made or made with a stock cube)
- 750 g/1 lb 10 oz canned cooked chickpeas
- 1 tablespoon cornflour
- croûtons
- salt

Serves 6

Heat the oil in a large saucepan. Add the leek and cook over a low heat, stirring occasionally, for about 15 minutes, until beginning to brown. Add 300 ml/½ pint of the stock and simmer for 5 minutes, then remove the pan from the heat. Pour the leek mixture back into the rest of the stock. Process the chickpeas, in batches, in a food processor with all but 2 tablespoons of the leeks and stock. Pour the processed chickpeas into a saucepan and heat gently. Mix the cornflour to a paste with the reserved leek and stock mixture in a cup and stir into the soup. Simmer gently for about 5 minutes. Season to taste with salt and serve in a soup tureen with the croûtons.

125

Thick bean soup

PURÉ DE JUDÍAS BLANCAS

- **300 g/11 oz dried haricot beans, soaked for 3–5 hours in cold water and drained**
- **2 cloves garlic**
- **1 bay leaf**
- **1 tablespoon olive oil**
- **2 tablespoons plain flour**
- **25 g/1 oz butter**
- **croûtons**
- **salt**

Serves 6

Put the beans in a large saucepan, pour in water to cover and bring to the boil. Drain well and add 2 litres/3 ½ pints fresh cold water, the garlic cloves, bay leaf and oil. Bring to the boil, then lower the heat and simmer for 1–1 ½ hours, until tender. (The cooking time depends on the type and age of the beans and the type of water, so the best way to check is by testing a few beans.) Remove the pan from the heat and leave to cool slightly. Remove and discard the garlic and bay leaf. Process the beans, in batches, in a food processor, then push through a fine sieve into a clean pan. Mix the flour to a paste with a little of the cold puréed beans in a bowl. Add this to the rest of the bean purée in the pan and simmer, stirring constantly, for about 8 minutes. Season to taste with salt and, just before serving, add the butter to the hot soup so that it melts without cooking. Serve in a soup tureen with croûtons

Note: This soup can also be made with leftover cooked beans or stew. The method you use is the same as for the thick chickpea soup (see recipe 124).

126

Thick lentil soup

PURÉ DE LENTEJAS

- **120 g/4 oz rice**
- **500 g/1 lb 2 oz cooked lentils, drained and the cooking stock reserved**
- **salt**

Serves 6

Bring a large saucepan of water to the boil, but do not add salt. Add the rice, bring back to the boil and cook for about 15 minutes, until tender. Drain well, refresh under cold running water and drain again. Set half the rice aside. Process the rest of the rice with the lentils and some of the cooking stock, in batches, in a food processor to form a thick soup. Pour into a clean saucepan. Add more stock if necessary. Heat the soup well and season to taste with salt. Season the reserved rice and place small mounds on top of the soup. Do this just before serving so that the rice does not have time to sink.

Note: A chicken stock cube dissolved in a little hot water will provide added flavour. Add it at the end, just before serving.

127 Thick pea soup
PURÉ DE GUISANTES SECOS

- 150 g/5 oz bacon in a single piece
- 500 g/1 lb 2 oz dried peas,
  soaked for 6–8 hours in cold
  water and drained
- 120 g/4 oz carrots
- 1 onion, coarsely chopped
- salt

Serves 6

Separate the fatty part of the bacon from the leaner part. Pour 2.5 litres/4 ¼ pints water into a large saucepan and add the peas. Bring to the boil and skim off the froth that rises to the surface with a skimmer or slotted spoon. Add the carrots, onion and the fattier part of the bacon. Lower the heat and simmer gently for 1 ½–2 hours, until the peas are very tender. Remove the pan from the heat and leave to cool slightly. Remove the bacon. Process the mixture, in batches, in a food processor and return to a clean pan. Dice the remaining bacon and put it into a separate saucepan. Add hot water to cover, bring to the boil and simmer for 5 minutes. Meanwhile, gently reheat the soup and season to taste with salt. Drain the bacon, add to the soup and simmer for 10 minutes. Serve in a soup tureen.

128 Thick pea soup with milk
PURÉ DE GUISANTES SECOS CON LECHE

- 350 g/12 oz dried peas,
  soaked for 12 hours in
  cold water and drained
- 1 small onion, halved
- 1 veal knuckle
- 1 bouquet garni (1 bay leaf,
  1 clove garlic and 1 sprig fresh
  parsley tied together in muslin)
- 300 ml/ ½ pint hot milk
- 40 g/1 ½ oz butter
- croûtons
- salt

Serves 6

Pour 2 litres/3 ½ pints water into a large saucepan and add the peas, onion, veal knuckle and bouquet garni. Bring to the boil over a medium heat, then lower the heat and simmer for 2 ½–3 hours. Remove the onion, veal knuckle and bouquet garni and reserve most of the cooking stock. Process the peas with some of the stock in a food processor and return to a clean pan. Season to taste with salt, stir in the hot milk and, if necessary, a little more of the stock. Reheat and stir in the butter. Serve in a soup tureen and offer the croûtons separately.

129

Thin onion soup
SOPA DE CEBOLLA CLARA

- **3 tablespoons olive oil**
- **2 onions, thinly sliced**
- **2 tablespoons plain flour**
- **2 litres/3½ pints chicken stock
  (home-made or made
  with a stock cube)**
- **1 tablespoon finely chopped
  fresh parsley**
- **100 g/3½ oz Parmesan cheese,
  grated (optional)**
- **salt**

Serves 6

Heat the oil in a large saucepan. Add the onion and cook over a low heat, stirring occasionally, for about 10 minutes, until browned. Using a slotted spoon, transfer the onion to a plate and set aside. Add the flour to the pan and cook, stirring constantly, for about 2 minutes, until lightly coloured. Gradually stir in the stock. Return the onion to the pan and simmer for 20 minutes. Remove the pan from the heat, season to taste with salt and add the parsley. Serve in a soup tureen and hand the Parmesan separately, if using.

130

Garlic soup with eggs
SOPA DE AJO CON HUEVOS

- **250 ml/8 fl oz olive oil**
- **150 g/5 oz day-old bread,
  thinly sliced**
- **5 cloves garlic**
- **1 tablespoon chopped onion**
- **1 teaspoon paprika**
- **1.5 litres/2½ pints boiling water**
- **1 sprig fresh parsley**
- **6 eggs**
- **salt**

Serves 6

Heat the oil in a frying pan over a medium heat. Add the bread slices, in batches, and fry for 2 minutes until golden brown on both sides. Remove with a fish slice and drain on kitchen paper. Drain off all but 4 tablespoons of the oil in the frying pan and return the pan to the heat. Add the garlic and onion and cook over a low heat, stirring occasionally, for 5 minutes, until softened. Remove the pan from the heat and stir in the paprika. Preheat the oven to 180°C/350°F/Gas Mark 4. Put the fried bread in a flameproof casserole. Remove and discard the garlic and pour the onion and paprika mixture on to the fried bread. Add the boiling water and season with salt. Stir well, add the parsley and bring to the boil, then lower the heat and simmer for 5 minutes. Transfer the casserole to the oven and bake for 7 minutes, until it forms a crust. Crack the eggs on to the crust, season each with a little salt and return the casserole to the oven. Bake until the whites are set. Serve immediately.

131   Creamy carrot soup
CREMA DE ZANAHORIAS

- **500 g/1 lb 2 oz potatoes,**
  cut into large pieces
- **500 g/1 lb 2 oz carrots, sliced**
- **½ onion, coarsely chopped**
- **2 t omatoes, peeled and seeded**
  or ½ teaspoon tomato purée
- **1 sprig fresh parsley**
- **3 tablespoons sunflower oil**
- **croûtons**
- **salt**

Serves 6

Pour 2 litres/3 ½ pints water into a large saucepan. Add the potato, carrot, onion, tomato, parsley and oil and season with salt. Bring to the boil, then lower the heat and simmer for about 1 hour, until the carrots and potatoes are tender. Check the liquid in the pan during cooking and top up with cold water if necessary. Remove the pan from the heat and discard the parsley. Leave the mixture to cool slightly, then process, in batches, in a food processor. Return to a clean pan and reheat. Serve hot and offer the croûtons separately.

Note: This soup can be made in advance but it is important to process the mixture in a food processor before it gets cold. Once it has been processed, this soup can be allowed to cool completely and then reheated before serving.

132   Pumpkin soup
SOPA DE CALABAZA

- **3 tablespoons olive oil**
- **2 leeks, chopped and rinsed well**
- **250 g/9 oz potatoes, diced**
- **750 g/1 lb 10 oz pumpkin, peeled,**
  seeded and diced
- **500 ml/18 fl oz hot milk**
- **½ teaspoon meat extract**
- **salt**

Serves 6

Heat the oil in a large saucepan. Add the leek and cook over a low heat, stirring occasionally, for about 5 minutes, until softened. Add the potato and pumpkin, pour in 1.5 litres/2 ½ pints water and season lightly with salt (remember that the meat extract will be salty). Bring to the boil, lower the heat and simmer for about 45 minutes. Remove the pan from the heat and leave to cool slightly. Process the mixture, in batches, in a food processor. Return to a clean pan and add the milk. Reheat gently and stir in the meat extract. Serve in a soup tureen.

Note: If you prefer, you can omit the potatoes from the soup and use 1.5 kg/3 ¼ lb pumpkin instead.

Porrusalda

PORRUSALDA

- **250 g / 9 oz salt cod fillet**
- **4 tablespoons olive oil**
- **6 leeks, chopped and rinsed well**
- **750 g / 1 lb 10 oz potatoes, diced**
- **salt**

Serves 6

Put the cod in a bowl and add water to cover. Leave to soak for up to 24 hours, changing the water several times. Drain well. Put the fish in a saucepan, pour in 500 ml / 18 fl oz water and bring to the boil. Remove the pan from the heat and lift out the cod with a fish slice. Remove any remaining bones and skin, flake the flesh with a fork and return it to the water in which it has been cooked. Heat the oil in a separate large saucepan. Add the leek and cook over a low heat, stirring occasionally, for about 5 minutes, until beginning to brown. Add the potato and cook for a further 5 minutes. Pour in 2 litres / 3 ½ pints water, bring to the boil and simmer for about 35 minutes, until the potatoes are tender but not disintegrating. Add the cod and its cooking water and simmer for a further 10 minutes. Season with salt, if necessary, and serve in a soup tureen.

Note: Porrusalda is a traditional soup from the Basque region.

134 Leek and potato soup

SOPA DE PUERROS Y PATATAS

- 3 large leeks, rinsed well
- 3 tablespoons olive oil
- 6 potatoes, diced
- 1 chicken stock cube
- salt

Serves 6

Trim the leeks, halve lengthways and cut into 2cm/¾ inch lengths. Rinse well and drain. Heat the oil in a large saucepan. Add the leek and cook over a low heat, stirring occasionally, for about 10 minutes, until beginning to brown. Pour in 2 litres/3½ pints water and season lightly with salt (bearing in mind that the stock cube will be salty). Bring to the boil and simmer for 5 minutes, then add the potato and simmer for a further 30 minutes, until the potato is tender. Crumble the stock cube into a jug and stir in a ladleful of soup, then pour back into the soup. Serve immediately.

135 Minestrone soup

MINESTRONE

- 100 g/3½ oz haricot beans, soaked overnight in cold water and drained
- 250 g/9 oz green beans, cut into short lengths
- 150 g/5 oz shelled peas
- 300 g/11 oz courgettes, diced
- 200 g/7 oz carrots, diced
- 250 g/9 oz pumpkin, peeled, deseeded and diced
- 1 leek, cut into 5 mm/¼ inch slices and rinsed well
- 2 tomatoes, diced
- 2 sticks celery, sliced
- 100 g/3½ oz small pasta shapes (such as shells, spirals or tubes), cooked
- 3 tablespoons olive oil
- 1 onion, chopped
- 1 clove garlic
- 1 sprig fresh mint
- 2 tablespoons chopped fresh mint
- freshly grated Parmesan cheese

Serves 6

Put the haricot beans in a saucepan, pour in water to cover and bring to the boil. Lower the heat and simmer for 1–1½ hours, until tender. (Top up the pan with cold water a couple of times during cooking, as this will make the beans softer.) Drain and set aside. Pour 2 litres/3½ pints water into a large saucepan and bring to the boil. Add the green beans, peas, courgette, carrot, pumpkin, leek, tomato and celery and bring back to the boil. Lower the heat and simmer gently for about 30 minutes, until all the vegetables are tender but not disintegrating. Stir in the cooked haricot beans and the pasta shapes. Heat 2 tablespoons of the oil in a frying pan. Add the onion and cook over a medium heat, stirring occasionally, for 5–6 minutes, until just beginning to brown. Add the contents of the frying pan to the soup. Crush the garlic and mint sprig in a mortar with a pestle, stir in the remaining oil to make a paste and add to the soup. Serve in a soup tureen, sprinkled with the chopped mint. Offer the Parmesan separately.

136

Leek soup with milk
SOPA DE PUERROS CON LECHE

- 2 tablespoons olive oil
- 4 leeks, sliced and rinsed well
- 5 potatoes, cut into pieces
- 500 ml/18 fl oz hot milk
- ½ teaspoon meat extract
- salt

Serves 6

Heat the oil in a large saucepan. Add the leek and cook over a low heat, stirring occasionally, for about 5 minutes, until softened but not coloured. Pour in 1.5 litres/2½ pints water and add the potato and a pinch of salt. Bring to the boil, then lower the heat and simmer for 1 hour. Remove the pan from the heat and leave to cool slightly, then process in a food processor. Stir in the hot milk and meat extract and serve in a soup tureen.

137

Green bean and tomato soup
SOPA DE TOMATE Y JUDÍAS VERDES

- 250 g/9 oz potatoes, cut into large pieces
- 1.5 kg/3¼ lb very ripe tomatoes, peeled, seeded and chopped
- 2 tablespoons olive oil
- 1 sprig fresh parsley
- 1 bay leaf
- pinch of bicarbonate of soda
- 250 g/9 oz green beans, trimmed and cut into 2-cm/¾-inch lengths
- salt

Serves 6

Put the potato, tomato, oil, parsley, bay leaf and a pinch of salt into a large saucepan, pour in 2 litres/3½ pints water and bring to the boil, then lower the heat and simmer for 45 minutes. Remove the pan from the heat and leave to cool slightly. Remove and discard the parsley and bay leaf, then process in a food processor, in batches if necessary. Bring a small pan of lightly salted water to the boil and add the bicarbonate of soda. Add the beans and cook for about 15 minutes, until tender. Drain well. Reheat the soup, if necessary, then pour into a soup tureen and sprinkle the green beans on top. Serve immediately.

138

Tomato juice soup
SOPA DE JUGO DE TOMATE

- 500 ml/18 fl oz chicken stock
  (home-made or made
  with a stock cube)
- 1 heaped tablespoon cornflour
  or 1 tablespoon potato flour
- 500 ml/18 fl oz tomato juice
- 2 tablespoons dry sherry
- 4 tablespoons single cream
- 1 tablespoon chopped
  fresh parsley
- salt

Serves 4

Pour the stock into a large saucepan and heat gently. Mix the corn-flour or potato flour to a paste with 2 tablespoons water in a cup or small bowl and stir into the stock. Cook, stirring constantly, for 2 minutes. Shake the tomato juice well and add to the pan, then stir in the sherry and season to taste with salt. Heat through gently but do not allow to boil. If serving the soup hot, ladle it into warm bowls. Swirl 1 tablespoon of cream into each bowl and sprinkle with the chopped parsley. If serving the soup cold, use a little less cornflour or potato flour in the stock. Leave the soup to cool, then chill in the refrigerator. Garnish with the cream and parsley before serving.

139

Courgette soup with cheese triangles
SOPA DE CALABACINES CON QUESITOS

- 4 courgettes
- 4 cheese triangles (Laughing
  Cow or similar) or other cheese,
  cut into 4 bite-size pieces
- salt

Serves 4

Peel half of each courgette and slice each whole courgette thinly. Put the slices in a saucepan and pour in just enough water to cover. Add a pinch of salt and bring to the boil, then lower the heat and simmer for about 20 minutes, until tender. Remove from the heat and leave to cool, then process, in batches, in a food processor. Taste and adjust the seasoning. Place a cheese triangle in each of 4 individual serving bowls and ladle in the hot soup. Serve immediately.

Note: Do not leave more than half the peel on the courgettes as this can make the soup bitter. This soup is also very good if a crumbled chicken stock cube is added to the cooking water.

140

Cream of asparagus soup

SOPA-CREMA DE ESPÁRRAGOS

- 30 asparagus spears
- about 750 ml/1¼ pints milk
  (see method)
- 50 g/2 oz butter
- 3 tablespoons plain flour
- 3 egg yolks
- 1 teaspoon finely chopped
  fresh parsley
- salt

Serves 6

Trim and, if necessary, peel the asparagus spears. Wash well, then cook in a saucepan of salted boiling water for about 20 minutes, until tender. (Test by piercing one of the spears with the point of a knife.) Remove the asparagus from the pan, reserving the cooking liquid. Cut off and reserve the tips. Cut the remaining stalks into two or three pieces and process to a purée in a food processor with a little of the reserved cooking liquid. Push the purée through a coarse sieve into a bowl. Measure the remaining cooking liquid and make up to 1 litre/1¾ pints with milk. Melt the butter in a saucepan, stir in the flour and cook, stirring constantly, for 2 minutes. Gradually stir in the milk and stock mixture, a little at a time. Add the asparagus purée, season to taste with salt and cook, stirring, until thickened to the required consistency. (Bear in mind that the egg yolks will thin the soup slightly.) Just before serving, put the egg yolks into a soup tureen and, very gradually to prevent them curdling, add the hot soup. Finally, add the reserved asparagus tips to the soup and sprinkle with the parsley.

141

Watercress soup

CREMA DE BERROS

- 3 tablespoons olive oil
- 1 thick leek, halved lengthways,
  sliced and rinsed well
- 1 onion, coarsely chopped
- 1 kg/2¼ lb potatoes,
  cut into pieces
- 2 bunches watercress,
  coarse stalks removed
- 1.5 litres/2½ pints hot water
- 250 ml/8 fl oz milk
- ½ teaspoon meat extract
- salt and pepper

Serves 6

Heat the oil in a large saucepan. Add the leek and onion and cook over a low heat, stirring occasionally, for 4–6 minutes, until softened. Add the potato and 1½ bunches of the watercress. Pour in the hot water, stir in 1 teaspoon salt and bring to the boil, then lower the heat, cover and simmer for 1 hour. Meanwhile, finely chop the remaining watercress. Remove the pan from the heat and leave to cool slightly, then process in a food processor. Return the soup to a clean pan and reheat gently. Just before serving, stir together the milk and meat extract and add to the soup. Simmer for a further 6 minutes. Season with salt and pepper to taste and pour into a soup tureen. Add the chopped watercress and serve immediately.

142

Rice and mint soup

SOPA DE ARROZ CON MENTA

- 1 litre/1¾ pints chicken stock
  (home-made or made
  with a stock cube)
- 2 tablespoons rice
- 150 ml/¼ pint natural yogurt
- 1 egg yolk, lightly beaten
- 1 heaped tablespoon plain flour
- 40 g/1½ oz butter
- 1 tablespoon chopped fresh mint
- salt and pepper

Serves 4

Pour the stock into a saucepan and bring to the boil. Add the rice, bring back to the boil and cook over a medium–high heat for 15 minutes. Season with salt (bearing in mind that the stock is salty). Mix together the yogurt, egg yolk and flour in a separate, large saucepan, then gradually stir in 250 ml/8 fl oz water, a little at a time. Simmer gently for 5 minutes, then stir in the rice and stock mixture and cook for a further 5 minutes. Melt the butter in a small pan, remove from the heat and stir in the mint. Add this mixture to the soup just before serving.

143

Celery and potato soup

SOPA DE APIO COY PATATAS

- 4 tablespoons olive oil
- 2 heads celery,
  cut into 5 cm/2 inch lengths
- 3 onions, coarsely chopped
- 750 g/1 lb 10 oz potatoes,
  cut into pieces
- 2 veal knuckles
- 1 tablespoon finely chopped
  celery leaves or fresh parsley
- salt

Serves 6

Heat the oil in a large saucepan. Add the celery and onion and cook over a low heat, stirring occasionally, for about 10 minutes, until beginning to soften. Add the potato, veal knuckles and 2.5 litres/ 4¼ pints water. Bring to the boil, then lower the heat and simmer for 1 hour. Remove the pan from the heat and leave to cool slightly. Remove the veal knuckles and process the soup, in batches, in a food processor. Return the soup to a clean pan, season to taste with salt and reheat gently. Serve hot in a soup tureen, garnished with the celery leaves or parsley.

144

Mushroom soup

CREMA DE CHAMPIÑONES

- **250 g/9 oz chestnut mushrooms,**
  finely chopped
- **25 g/1 oz butter**
- **a few drops of lemon juice**
- **4 tablespoons plain flour**
- **1.5 litres/2½ pints chicken stock**
  (home-made or made
  with a stock cube)
- **1 egg yolk**
- **salt**

Serves 6

Put the mushrooms, butter, lemon juice and a pinch of salt in a saucepan, cover and cook over a low heat for about 6 minutes. Put the flour in a separate, large saucepan over a low heat and cook, stirring constantly, for about 5–7 minutes, until lightly coloured. Gradually stir in the stock, a little at a time. Simmer, stirring constantly with a whisk, for 10 minutes. Add the mushrooms and their cooking juices and simmer for a further 5 minutes. Put the egg yolk into a soup tureen and gradually pour in the hot soup. Stir with a wooden spoon and serve immediately.

145

Soup with rice, hard-boiled egg and chopped parsley

CALDO DE COCIDO CON ARROZ, HUEVO DURO Y PEREJIL PICADO

- **2 litres/3½ pints**
  vegetable stock
- **4 tablespoons rice**
- **2 hard-boiled eggs**
- **1 tablespoon chopped**
  fresh parsley
- **salt**

Serves 6

Pour the stock into a saucepan and bring to the boil. Add the rice, bring back to the boil and cook over a medium–high heat for about 15 minutes, until tender. Meanwhile, chop the egg yolks and 1½ of the egg whites (all the egg whites would be too much). Pour the stock and rice into a soup tureen, season to taste with salt, add the parsley and eggs and serve immediately.

146

Consommé

CONSOMÉ

- 1 beef shin bone
- 500 g/1 lb 2 oz lean beef, cut into small pieces
- 200 g/7 oz carrots, thickly sliced
- 200 g/7 oz turnips,
- thickly sliced
- 1 small onion, halved
- 1 leek, halved lengthways, and rinsed well
- 1 stick celery
- 1 clove
- 2 egg whites
- salt

Makes 1.5 litres/2 ½ pints

Put the shin bone and beef into a large saucepan, pour in 2 litres/3 ½ pints water and bring to the boil. Lower the heat and simmer for 30 minutes, then skim off the froth that has risen to the surface with a skimmer or slotted spoon. Add the carrot, turnip, onion, leek, celery and clove and season to taste with salt. Bring back to the boil, then simmer over a low heat, stirring occasionally, for 1 ½ hours. Twice during this cooking time, add 5 tablespoons cold water to help any froth rise to the surface. In a clean, dry bowl, whisk the egg whites until they form soft peaks, then transfer them to a saucepan. Carefully and slowly pour the stock (including the vegetables) on to the egg whites, stirring constantly with a wooden spoon. Simmer for about 20 minutes. Strain the stock into a bowl; then strain again through a fine muslin-lined sieve into another bowl. Season to taste with salt. Serve in individual soup bowls with your choice of garnish (see recipes 147–150).

Note: if the consommé is very pale, you can use a little meat extract to darken the colour or a little caramel made with a teaspoon of sugar and a few drops of water heated in a pan until the sugar browns. (Be careful not to burn it as this will give the stock a bitter flavour.) Add a few spoonfuls of the consommé to the caramel and then return the mixture to the consommé and it will take on a good golden colour.

147

- **2 egg yolks**
- **250 ml/8 fl oz stock or milk**
- **salt**

Serves 2–4

Egg squares
FLAN

Preheat the oven to 160°C/325°F/Gas Mark 3. Lightly beat the egg yolks with the stock or milk, season with salt and pour into a lightly greased cast-iron egg dish or small gratin dish. Put the dish in a roasting tin and pour in hot water to come about halfway up the sides. Bake for 10–15 minutes, until the mixture has set. Remove the dish from the roasting tin and leave to cool and set. Turn out, cut into small squares and add to the soup just before serving.

148

- **butter, for greasing**
- **1 egg, plus 3 egg yolks**
- **200 ml/7 fl oz hot stock**
- **salt**

Serves 2–4

Egg cubes
FLAN

Preheat the oven to 160°C/325°F/Gas Mark 3. Grease a gratin dish with butter. Beat the egg and egg yolks in a bowl and gradually beat in the hot stock, a little at a time (taking care that it does not curdle them). Season with salt and pour into the prepared dish. Put the dish in a roasting tin and pour in hot water to come about halfway up the sides. Bake for 1 hour but do not allow to boil as this will cause small holes to form in the mixture. Remove the dish from the tin and leave to cool completely, then cut into cubes to serve.

149

- **100 g/3½ oz very lean York or other dry-cured ham**
- **2 hard-boiled eggs**

Serves 2–4

Chopped York ham and hard-boiled egg
PICADO DE JAMON DE YORK Y HUEVO DURO

Cut the ham into very thin strips about 2 cm/¾ inch long and chop the hard-boiled eggs. Put a little of each ingredient into each soup bowl before pouring in the consommé.

150

- **1 thick slice bread**
- **1 egg, beaten**
- **1 clove garlic, finely chopped**
- **2 sprigs fresh parsley, finely chopped**

Serves 2–4

Dumplings
BOLITAS

Cut the crusts off the bread, leaving a piece about the size of a large egg. Crumble it into a bowl and add the egg, garlic and parsley. Mix well to make a dough. Form the dough into small balls or one large sausage shape. Add the dumplings to the soup 5 minutes before the end of the cooking time. Or roll in breadcrumbs and fry in olive oil until golden brown all over, then add to the soup just before serving.

151

Simple noodle soup
SOPA DE FIDEOS SIMPLE

• 2 litres/3½ pints chicken stock
  (home-made or made
  with a stock cube)
• 120 g/4 oz fine noodles
• salt

Serves 6

Pour the stock into a saucepan and bring to the boil. Gradually add the noodles in batches and cook for about 15 minutes. (The cooking time will depend on the type of noodles. To test whether they are ready, bite a piece between your teeth.) Make sure the noodles don't begin to disintegrate, as this will turn the liquid cloudy and the soup will not taste as good. Skim off the froth that rises to the surface with a skimmer or slotted spoon. Season to taste with salt and serve immediately. This soup should not be made in advance.

152

Toasted flour soup
SOPA DE HARINA TOSTADA

• 6 tablespoons plain flour
• 1.75 litres/3 pints cold chicken
  stock (home-made or made with
  a stock cube)
• 2 egg yolks
• 25 g/1 oz butter
• croûtons
• salt

Serves 6

Put the flour into a saucepan and cook over a low heat, stirring constantly with a wooden spoon, for 5–7 minutes, until lightly toasted. Gradually stir in the cold stock, a little at a time. Bring to the boil, stirring constantly, then lower the heat and simmer for about 8 minutes. Season to taste with salt. Put the egg yolks into a soup tureen and, very slowly to prevent the eggs curdling, pour in the hot soup. Add the butter and when it has melted, stir the soup and serve, adding the croûtons at the last minute.

153

Chilled cucumber soup
SOPA DE PEPINOS FRÍA

• 4 cucumbers,
  each about 200 g/7 oz
• 300 ml/½ pint natural yogurt
• 1 small clove garlic
• 3 tablespoons white-wine
  vinegar
• 3 sprigs fresh mint
• 250 ml/8 fl oz single cream
• 2 tablespoons chopped
  fresh mint
• salt and pepper

Serves 6

Peel two of the cucumbers and coarsely dice all of them. Put the cucumber, yogurt, garlic, vinegar and mint sprigs into a food processor and process until smooth. Pour the soup into a china or glass bowl and gradually add the cream. Season to taste with salt and pepper. Cover and chill in the refrigerator until required. Serve chilled, sprinkled with the chopped mint.

154 Chicken soup

CREMA DE GALLINA

- **400 g/14 oz skinless chicken breasts**
- **250 g/9 oz beef shin bone**
- **2 carrots, thickly sliced**
- **1 onion, halved**
- **1 stick celery, including leaves**
- **bouquet garni (1 sprig fresh parsley, 1 clove garlic and ½ bay leaf tied together in muslin)**
- **20 g/¾ oz butter**
- **1 tablespoon sunflower oil**
- **2 tablespoons plain flour**
- **300 ml/½ pint milk**
- **1 egg yolk**
- **salt and pepper**

Serves 6

Put the chicken, shin bone, carrot, onion, celery, bouquet garni and a pinch of salt in a saucepan and pour in 2 litres/3 ½ pints water. Bring to the boil over a medium–low heat, then lower the heat and simmer for 1–1 ½ hours, until the chicken is tender and cooked through. Lift the chicken out of the pan and cut the meat into bite-size pieces and set aside. Remove and discard the beef bone and bouquet garni. Reserve the stock and vegetables. Melt the butter with the oil in another saucepan. Stir in the flour, then gradually add the milk, a little at a time, stirring constantly with a wooden spoon. Simmer for about 4 minutes and then stir in 1.2 litres/2 pints of the reserved stock. Remove the pan from the heat and leave to cool slightly, then process in a food processor with the carrot, celery and onion from the stock. Lightly beat the egg yolk with a little of the remaining stock in a cup and add to the soup. Reheat the soup but do not allow to boil. Put the chicken pieces into a soup tureen and pour in the soup through a coarse sieve. Serve immediately.

155 Belgian chicken soup

SOPA DE POLLO A LA BELGA

- 3 carrots
- 1 beef shin bone
- 1.5 kg/3¼ lb chicken
- 2 leeks, trimmed and rinsed well
- 1 head celery, including leaves
- 5 tablespoons olive oil
- pinch of dried aromatic herbs
  or 1 bouquet garni
  (1 sprig fresh thyme, 1 bay leaf
  and 1 sprig fresh parsley tied
  together in muslin)
- 25 g/1 oz butter
- 1 heaped tablespoon plain flour
- 2 egg yolks
- juice of ½ lemon
- fried bread (see recipe 130) or
  toasted bread
- salt and pepper

Serves 8

Slice 1 carrot. Put the shin bone, chicken, 1 leek, half the celery including the leaves, the sliced carrot and a pinch of salt into a saucepan and pour in 2.5 litres/4¼ pints water. Bring to the boil, then lower the heat and simmer for 1 hour. Remove the pan from the heat and strain the stock into a bowl. Reserve the chicken and, when it is cool enough to handle, remove and discard the skin and cut the meat off the bones. Chop the remaining uncooked carrots, leek and celery. Heat 3 tablespoons of the oil in another saucepan. Add the chopped carrots, leek and celery and cook over a low heat, stirring occasionally, for about 5 minutes, until the vegetables are softened but not coloured. Add the chicken meat and aromatic herbs or bouquet garni and season with a pinch of pepper. Pour in the stock and simmer gently for about 20 minutes. Melt the butter with the remaining oil in another saucepan. Stir in the flour, then gradually add 500 ml/18 fl oz of the chicken stock, a little at a time, stirring constantly. Cook for about 8 minutes, then stir back into the soup. Simmer for a further 10 minutes. Lightly beat the egg yolks with the lemon juice in a bowl and then, very slowly to prevent the eggs curdling, stir in a little chicken stock. Pour into the soup and transfer to a soup tureen. Serve immediately, offering the fried or toasted bread separately.

156 Chicken liver soup

SOPA DE HIGADITOS

- 3 tablespoons sunflower oil
- 1 clove garlic
- 60 g/2¼ oz blanched almonds
- 6 chicken livers
- a few saffron threads
- 1.5 litres/2½ pints chicken
  stock
- 1 tablespoon potato flour
- 1 egg yolk
- fried bread (see recipe 130) or
  toasted bread
- salt

Serves 6

Heat the oil in a frying pan. Add the garlic and cook for a few minutes, until just coloured. Remove with a slotted spoon and discard. Add the almonds to the pan and cook, stirring frequently, for 2–3 minutes, until golden brown. Remove with a slotted spoon and set aside. Add the chicken livers, season with salt, cover and cook over a low heat, stirring occasionally, for about 5 minutes, until evenly browned. Crush the saffron in a mortar and stir in a little of the stock. Remove the chicken livers from the pan with a fish slice. Put the livers, almonds and saffron mixture in a food processor, add a little stock and process until smooth. Scrape the purée into a saucepan and stir in the remaining stock. Simmer over a low heat for 10 minutes. Mix the potato flour to a paste with 3 tablespoons water in a small bowl and add to the soup. Bring the soup to the boil. Lightly beat the egg yolk in a bowl and gradually whisk in a few spoonfuls of hot soup, then stir into the soup. Serve in a soup tureen, offering the fried or toasted bread separately.

157

Vegetable soup

SOPA DE VERDURAS

- **500 g/1 lb 2 oz mixed, pre-cut fresh vegetables (such as carrots, celery, parsnip, green beans, etc)**
- **1 veal knuckle**
- **1 tablespoon olive oil**
- **1 tablespoon cornflour**
- **½ teaspoon meat extract**
- **salt**

Serves 6

Put 2 litres/3 ½ pints water into a saucepan and add the vegetables, veal knuckle, oil and a pinch of salt. Bring to the boil, then lower the heat and simmer for about 30 minutes, until the vegetables are tender. Mix the cornflour to a paste with 2 tablespoons water in a small bowl, then stir in a little soup. Pour back into the soup and stir well with a wooden spoon. Simmer for a further 5 minutes. Remove the veal knuckle, stir in the meat extract and serve in a soup tureen.

158

Cabbage soup

SOPA DE REPOLLO

- **3 tablespoons olive oil**
- **120 g/4 oz streaky bacon, diced**
- **1 large onion, finely chopped**
- **500 g/1 lb 2 oz Savoy cabbage, shredded**
- **2 litres/3 ½ pints boiling water**
- **4 tablespoons rice**
- **½ teaspoon meat extract**
- **salt**

Serves 6

Heat the oil in a large saucepan. Add the bacon and onion and cook over a low heat, stirring occasionally, for 8–10 minutes, until the onion is beginning to brown. Add the cabbage, cover and cook, stirring occasionally, for about 15 minutes. Pour in the boiling water and simmer for 10 minutes, then add the rice and cook for a further 30 minutes. Stir in the meat extract and serve in a soup tureen.

159

Russian beetroot soup
SOPA RUSA DE REMOLACHA

- 25 g/1 oz margarine
- 500 g/1 lb 2 oz cooked beetroot, peeled and sliced, or canned beetroot, sliced
- 1 litre/1¾ pints hot chicken stock (home-made or made with a stock cube)
- 1 tablespoon red-wine vinegar
- 6 tablespoons single cream
- salt and pepper

Garnish (optional):
- 2 tablespoons finely chopped red cabbage
- 1 tablespoon red-wine vinegar
Serves 6

If making the garnish, put the red cabbage in a china or glass bowl, add the vinegar and toss lightly. Set aside until ready to serve. Melt the margarine in a large saucepan. Add the beetroot and cook over a low heat, stirring occasionally, for 10 minutes. Pour in the hot stock, add the vinegar and season with salt and pepper and simmer over a low heat for 15 minutes. Remove the pan from the heat and leave the mixture to cool slightly, then process in a food processor. If serving chilled, pour the soup into a bowl, cover and chill in the refrigerator for at least 3 hours. Serve in individual bowls, adding a swirl of cream to each. If serving hot, pour the processed soup into a soup tureen, add the cream and mix lightly to create a marbled effect. Strain the red cabbage garnish, if using, and add to the soup.

Note: Versions of this hearty soup are popular throughout Eastern and Central Europe.

160

Grouper soup
SOPA DE MERO

- 3 tablespoons olive oil
- 2 leeks, thickly sliced and rinsed well
- 2 onions, thickly sliced
- 250 ml/8 fl oz white wine
- 1 white fish head, such as hake or whiting, gills removed
- 1 x 400 g/14 oz grouper fillet
- bouquet garni (1 sprig fresh parsley, 1 clove garlic and 1 bay leaf tied together in muslin)
- 1 kg/2¼ lb potatoes, cut into large pieces
- 175 ml/6 fl oz hot milk
- 2 egg yolks
- 1 teaspoon chopped fresh parsley
- croûtons
- salt
Serves 8

Heat the oil in a large saucepan. Add the leek and onion and cook over a low heat, stirring occasionally, for about 10 minutes, until beginning to brown. Pour in 1 litre/1¾ pints water and the wine and bring to the boil. Add the fish head, grouper and bouquet garni. Bring back to the boil, add the potato and a pinch of salt and cook for a further 30 minutes. Remove and discard the fish head and leave the mixture to cool slightly. Lift out the grouper with a fish slice and remove the skin and bones, if any. Flake the flesh with a fork, put in a food processor with the potatoes and stock and process until smooth and combined. Add the hot milk and process briefly again to combine. Lightly beat the egg yolks in a bowl and stir in a few spoonfuls of the soup, then add to the hot soup. Serve in a soup tureen, sprinkled with the parsley, and offer the croûtons separately.

Sailor's Soup
SOPA MARINERA

- 2 tablespoons olive oil
- 2 leeks, sliced and rinsed well
- ½ onion, chopped
- 2 tomatoes, seeded and chopped
- ½ bay leaf
- 2 cloves garlic, lightly crushed
- 500 g/1 lb 2 oz unpeeled
  raw prawns
- 250 g/9 oz monkfish tail
- a few saffron threads
- 120 g/4 oz fine noodles
- salt and pepper

Serves 6

Heat the oil in a large saucepan. Add the leek and onion and cook over a low heat, stirring occasionally, for 5 minutes, until softened. Stir in the tomato, add the bay leaf and garlic and pour in 2 litres/3 ½ pints water. Season with salt, add the prawns and monkfish and bring to the boil. Cook over a medium-high heat for 15 minutes, then remove the pan from the heat and strain the stock into a clean pan. Cut out the monkfish bone and discard. Peel the prawns, reserving the heads. Put the heads in a mortar and pound with a pestle, straining the liquid produced into the stock. Put the monkfish and prawns into a food processor, add some of the stock and process until thoroughly combined. Push the mixture through a fine sieve into the stock, pressing down hard with a spoon to make sure all the liquid is extracted. Crush the saffron with 2 tablespoons of the stock in a mortar and add to the soup. Reheat the soup over a low heat. Add the noodles and simmer for 15–20 minutes. Season with salt and pepper to taste and serve in a soup tureen.

📷

Cream of shellfish soup
CREMA DE CARABINEROS, GAMBAS O CANGREJOS

- 500 g/1 lb 2 oz raw unpeeled crevettes (large red Mediterranean prawns) or crayfish
- 500 g/1 lb 2 oz raw unpeeled large prawns
- 100 g/3 ½ oz butter
- 100 g/3 ½ oz rice flour
- 2 tablespoons brandy
- 100 ml/3 ½ fl oz single cream
- salt and pepper

Concentrated stock:
- 200 ml/7 fl oz white wine
- 2 carrots, sliced
- 1 onion, cut into 4 wedges
- 1 sprig fresh parsley
- 1 bay leaf
- pinch of salt

Serves 6–8

First make the concentrated stock. Put all the stock ingredients into a saucepan, add 2 litres/3 ½ pints water and bring to the boil. Lower the heat and simmer for 30 minutes, then remove from the heat and leave to cool completely. (This step can be done several hours in advance.) Put the crevettes or crayfish and the prawns in the cooled concentrated stock. Bring to the boil, then lower the heat and cook for about 5 minutes, depending on the size of the shellfish. Remove the shellfish with a slotted spoon and reserve the stock. Preheat the oven to 150°C/300°F/Gas Mark 2. Peel some of the prawns for the garnish and remove their heads. Reserve the heads and shells. Cut the tails in half, put in a bowl and cover with a plate to prevent them drying out. Remove and discard the crevette heads, as they have a very strong flavour. Use all the remaining shellfish and all the reserved shells and heads to prepare a flavoured butter. To do this, mash them with the butter, in batches, in a mortar with a pestle, or pulse in a food processor, to a purée. Transfer the purée to an ovenproof dish and bake for 25 minutes. Strain the concentrated stock into a measuring jug and, if necessary, make up to 1.5 litres/2 ½ pints with water. Line a colander with muslin, set it over a bowl and tip in the shellfish purée and some of the concentrated stock. Squeeze the muslin tightly to extract as much liquid as possible, then add the liquid to the concentrated stock. Mix the rice flour with a little of the concentrated stock or water in a bowl. Pour the stock into a saucepan, add the brandy and heat gently. When the stock is hot, stir in the rice flour mixture and simmer, stirring constantly, for 5–10 minutes. Season to taste with salt and pepper. Put the cream into a soup tureen and stir in a little hot soup to prevent it curdling. Gradually add the remaining soup and the reserved prawn tails. Serve immediately.

Note: This recipe can also be made using only crayfish or only prawns and the results are equally delicious.

163

Prawn soup
CREMA DE GAMBAS

- 500 g/1 lb 2 oz raw unpeeled prawns
- 50 g/2 oz butter or 4 tablespoons sunflower oil
- 3 tablespoons plain flour
- 2 tablespoons passata
- 2 litres/3½ pints warm fish stock (home-made or made with a stock cube)
- 2 tablespoons brandy
- 100 ml/3½ fl oz single cream
- salt and pepper

Serves 6

Remove the heads from all the prawns and peel 100 g/3½ oz of them. Reserve the heads. Set the peeled tails aside for the garnish. Mash the remaining prawns with the prawn heads in a mortar with a pestle. Alternatively, process them in a food processor in two or three batches, adding 2 tablespoons water to each batch. Heat the butter or oil in a saucepan. Stir in the flour and cook for a few minutes, stirring constantly, until lightly coloured. Add the prawn purée and the passata, then stir in the warm stock. Simmer over a low heat for 30 minutes, occasionally skimming off the froth that rises to the surface. Strain the soup into a clean pan and season to taste with salt and pepper. Reheat gently, and add the brandy and reserved prawn tails and reheat gently, ensuring that the prawn tails turn pink and are cooked through. Put the cream in a soup tureen and gradually add the hot soup, very slowly. Serve immediately.

164

Fish soup with cream and curry
CREMA DE PESCADO CON NATA Y CURRY

- 2 tablespoons rice
- 1 kg/2¼ lb white fish fillets
- 4 tablespoons olive oil
- 1 onion, chopped
- 1 carrot, chopped
- 1 turnip, chopped
- 1½ tablespoons plain flour
- ½ teaspoon curry powder
- juice of ½ lemon
- 120 ml/4 fl oz single cream
- 2 sprigs chopped fresh parsley
- salt

Concentrated stock:
- 1 carrot, thickly sliced
- 1 turnip, thickly sliced
- 1 onion, halved
- 175 ml/6 fl oz dry white wine
- 1 bay leaf
- pinch of salt

Serves 6

Cook the rice (see recipe 173) but do not fry it. Refresh under cold water and set aside. Cut the fish into pieces, put in a saucepan, pour in water to cover and add all the ingredients for the concentrated stock. Bring to the boil over a high heat, then lower the heat and simmer for 10 minutes. Remove the pan from the heat and leave to cool. Reserve some of the fish in a bowl with a little of the stock to prevent it drying out and set aside. Remove and discard the bay leaf. Heat the oil in a saucepan. Add the chopped onion, carrot and turnip and cook over a low heat, stirring occasionally, for about 8 minutes, until softened. Stir in the flour and curry powder, then gradually add the concentrated stock (including the fish and vegetables), a little at a time, stirring constantly. Cook over a low heat for 30 minutes, then remove the pan from the heat and leave to cool slightly before processing in a food processor. Return the soup to a clean pan and reheat gently. Stir in the lemon juice and season to taste with salt, then add the rice. Just before serving, stir in the cream and the reserved fish. Pour the soup into a soup tureen, sprinkle with the parsley and serve immediately.

Fish soup

SOPA DE PESCADO DESMENUZADO

- 100 g/3½ oz salt cod fillet
- 5 tablespoons olive oil
- 1 small onion, chopped
- 500 g/1 lb 2 oz tomatoes, seeded and chopped
- 500 g/1 lb 2 oz mixed fish fillets
- 500 g/1 lb 2 oz raw large unpeeled prawns or crayfish
- 1 bay leaf
- 100 g/3½ oz bread
- 1 teaspoon paprika
- salt and pepper

Serves 6

Put the salt cod in a bowl, add water to cover and leave to soak for several hours without changing the water. Heat the oil in a saucepan. Add the onion and cook over a low heat, stirring occasionally, for 6–8 minutes, until beginning to brown. Add the tomato and cook for a further 15 minutes, occasionally mashing them with the side of a skimmer or slotted spoon. Allow the mixture to cool slightly, then transfer to a food processor and blend. Pour into a bowl and set aside. Put the mixed fish and the prawns or crayfish into a saucepan, pour in water to cover and add the bay leaf and a pinch of salt. Bring to the boil over a high heat and boil for 2 minutes, then remove the pan from the heat. Lift out the fish with a fish slice and transfer to a plate. Remove and discard the bay leaf and reserve the stock. Tear the bread into pieces, place in a bowl, add a ladleful of the stock and leave to soak. Drain the salt cod. Remove the skin and any remaining bones from the mixed fish and the salt cod. Pass all the fish, together with the soaked bread, through a food mill fitted with a coarse disc into a bowl, or process briefly in a food processor. Lift out the prawns or crayfish from the stock with a slotted spoon. Remove and discard the heads and shells. Pass the shellfish through the food mill, then pour through a little stock to make sure that all the flavour has been extracted, or process in the food processor. Put the reserved tomato mixture into a saucepan. Add the paprika and cook over a low heat, stirring constantly, for 2 minutes. Add the cod, mixed fish, bread and shellfish and pour in 1.5–2 litres/2 ½–3 ½ pints of the stock. Season to taste with salt and pepper and simmer for 5–10 minutes. Serve in a soup tureen.

166

Mussel soup
SOPA DE MEJILLONES

- 1.5 kg/3¼ lb mussels
- 100 ml/3½ fl oz dry white wine
- 1 sprig fresh thyme
- ½ bay leaf
- 3 tablespoons olive oil
- 150 g/5 oz onions, chopped
- 1 clove garlic, lightly crushed
- 3 tablespoons potato flour
- 500 ml/18 fl oz hot milk
- 2 egg yolks
- 1 teaspoon chopped
  fresh parsley
- salt and pepper

Serves 6

Scrape the mussel shells with the blade of a knife and remove the 'beards', then scrub under cold running water. Discard any mussels with broken shells or any that do not shut immediately when sharply tapped. Put the mussels in a saucepan, pour in the wine and add the thyme, bay leaf and a pinch of salt. Cover tightly and cook over a high heat, shaking the pan occasionally, for about 6 minutes, until all the shells have opened. Remove the mussels with a slotted spoon and discard any that remain closed. Strain the cooking liquid through a muslin-lined sieve and reserve. Remove the mussels from their shells, put them on a plate and cover with a damp tea towel to prevent them drying out. Heat the oil in another saucepan. Add the onion and garlic and cook over a low heat, stirring occasionally, for 5 minutes, until softened. Pour in 1.5 litres/2 ½ pints water and the mussel cooking liquid and simmer for about 10 minutes. Mix the potato flour with 6 tablespoons water in a small bowl, then stir into the soup. Simmer for a further 5 minutes, then add the hot milk. Season to taste with salt and pepper. Put the egg yolks into a soup tureen and add the soup very slowly to prevent the yolks curdling. Add the mussels (cut in half with kitchen scissors if they are very large), sprinkle with the parsley and serve.

Fish soup with noodles

SOPA DE PESCADO BARATA CON FIDEOS GORDOS

- **1 large onion**
- **5 tablespoons white wine**
- **1 bay leaf**
- **backbone of a white fish**
- **1 hake or other white fish head, gills removed**
- **3 tablespoons olive oil**
- **2 tablespoons plain flour**
- **1 tablespoon passata**
- **a few saffron threads**
- **½ clove garlic**
- **120 g / 4 oz noodles**
- **salt**

Serves 6

Cut a thick slice from the onion and finely chop the remainder. Pour 2 litres / 3 ½ pints water into a saucepan and add the wine, onion slice, bay leaf and a pinch of salt. Add and submerge the fish backbone and head and bring to the boil, then lower the heat and simmer for 10 minutes. Remove the pan from the heat and strain the stock through a fine sieve into a bowl. Heat the oil in another saucepan. Add the chopped onion and cook over a low heat, stirring occasionally, for 8 minutes. Stir in the flour and cook, stirring constantly, for 2–4 minutes, until lightly coloured. Stir in the passata and pour in the strained fish stock. Pound the saffron with the garlic and a pinch of salt in a mortar with a pestle. Stir in a little of the fish stock, then pour into the pan. Bring to the boil, then lower the heat and simmer for 15 minutes. Strain the soup through a coarse sieve into another pan. Add the noodles and cook for about 15 minutes, until tender. Serve in a soup tureen.

Note: some of the water in this recipe can be replaced with seafood stock (or cooking liquid). This will give the soup added flavour.

Gazpacho with goats' cheese balls coated in chopped olives

GAZPACHO CON BOLAS DE QUESO DE CABRA ENVUELTAS
EN ACEITUNAS PICADAS

- 1 kg/2¼ lb ripe tomatoes,
  peeled, seeded and coarsely
  chopped
- ¼ onion, coarsely chopped
- 1 small cucumber,
  peeled and coarsely chopped
- ½ small green pepper,
  seeded and coarsely chopped
- 250 g/9 oz breadcrumbs
- 175 ml/6 fl oz olive oil
- 2 tablespoons white-wine
  vinegar
- 100 g/3/12 oz fresh goats'
  cheese
- 6 black olives,
  stoned and chopped
- chopped fresh basil
- salt

Serves 4–6

Working in batches, put the tomato, onion, cucumber, pepper, breadcrumbs, oil and vinegar into a food processor and process until smooth. Transfer to a bowl and if the mixture is too thick, add a little cold water. (This is not usually necessary as the tomatoes usually provide enough liquid.) Cover the bowl with cling film and chill in the refrigerator for at least 2 hours before serving. Just before serving, shape the goats' cheese into little balls using a melon baller or with your hands. Roll the balls in the chopped olives. Season the soup with salt to taste, stir well and garnish with the basil. Serve with the cheese balls.

Notes: To give the gazpacho a special touch, use sherry vinegar instead of white-wine vinegar. If the soup is not cold enough when it is time to serve, add a few ice cubes. You can add a little freshly ground black pepper at the last minute, if you like.

169 Chunky gazpacho
GAZPACHO EN TROZOS

- 1½ tablespoons white-wine vinegar
- 3 tablespoons sunflower oil
- 2 tablespoons breadcrumbs
- ½ clove garlic
- 1 sprig fresh parsley
- 3 plump ripe tomatoes, peeled, seeded and chopped
- 2 tablespoons finely chopped onion
- 1 small cucumber, peeled and finely chopped
- 1 small green pepper, seeded and finely chopped
- salt

Serves 4–5

Stir the vinegar and a pinch of salt in a jug until the salt has dissolved, then whisk in the oil with a fork. Pour into a soup tureen and gradually whisk in 1.2 litres/2 pints water, a little at a time. Add the breadcrumbs. Pound the garlic with the parsley and 1 tablespoon of the mixture from the soup tureen in a mortar with a pestle, then add to the tureen. Cover and chill in the refrigerator for at least 1 hour. Add the tomato, onion, cucumber and pepper to the tureen. If the soup is not sufficiently chilled when you're ready to serve, add a few ice cubes.

170 Chilled gazpachuelo
GAZPACHUELO FRÍO

- 3 egg yolks or 2 eggs, at room temperature
- 1½ tablespoons white-wine vinegar
- 500 ml/18 fl oz sunflower oil
- 1 litre/1¾ pints iced water
- 100 g/3½ oz olives, stoned and chopped
- 2 tomatoes, peeled, seeded and chopped
- salt and pepper

Serves 4–5

Make a classic mayonnaise with the egg yolks, vinegar and oil as described in recipe 105 and season with salt and pepper. Alternatively, make the mayonnaise with the whole eggs in a food processor as described in recipe 106. In either case, the mayonnaise should be very thick. Put the mayonnaise into a soup tureen and gradually stir in the iced water, a little at a time. Add the olives and tomato and serve immediately.

Note: Gazpachuelo is another traditional Spanish soup. It is usually served chilled. It is similar to gazpacho but has a mayonnaise base.

Hot fish gazpachuelo

GAZPACHUELO CALIENTE DE PESCADO

- ½ small onion, halved
- 1 bay leaf
- 2 tablespoons white wine
- 500 g/1 lb 2 oz white fish, such as monkfish or grouper
- 250 g/9 oz live carpetshell or Venus clams (optional)
- 2 egg yolks, at room temperature
- 1½ tablespoons white-wine vinegar
- 250 ml/8 fl oz sunflower oil
- 750 g/1 lb 10 oz waxy potatoes, cut into 5 mm/¼ inch slices
- thinly sliced and toasted or fried (see recipe 130) day-old bread
- salt and pepper

Serves 6

Pour 1.5 litres/2 ½ pints water into a saucepan and add the onion, bay leaf, wine, fish and a pinch of salt. Bring to the boil and cook for 2 minutes, then remove the pan from the heat, cover and set aside. Wash the clams under cold running water, if using. Discard any with broken shells or that do not shut immediately when sharply tapped. Put them in a saucepan, add 100 ml/3 ½ fl oz water, cover and cook over a high heat, shaking the pan occasionally, for about 5 minutes, until they have opened. Remove the clams with a slotted spoon and discard any that have not opened. Strain the cooking liquid through a muslin-lined sieve and add to the pan with the fish. Remove the clams from their shells, cover with a damp tea towel and set aside. Make a mayonnaise with the egg yolks, vinegar and oil (see recipe 105) and season with salt and pepper. Pour most of the fish stock into another saucepan, leaving just enough in the original pan to cover the fish and prevent it drying out. Add the potato and bring to the boil, then lower the heat and cook for about 30 minutes, until tender. Add more water if necessary to make sure there is enough soup. Remove any skin and bones from the fish and cut the flesh into pieces. Put the mayonnaise into a soup tureen and gradually pour in the hot soup, a little at a time, stirring constantly to prevent the mayonnaise separating. Add the potato and fish, and the clams, if using. Serve the bread separately or add it to the soup just before serving.

Vichyssoise

VICHYSSOISE FRÍA

- **40 g/1½ oz butter**
- **1 large onion, finely chopped**
- **4 large leeks,**
  finely chopped and rinsed well
- **1 kg/2¼ lb potatoes,**
  thinly sliced
- **750 ml/1¼ pints chicken stock**
  (home-made or made
  with a stock cube)
- **500 ml/18 fl oz milk**
- **250 ml/8 fl oz single cream**
- **2 teaspoons chopped**
  fresh parsley
- **salt**

Serves 8

Melt the butter in a saucepan. Add the onion and cook over a low heat, stirring occasionally, for 5 minutes, until softened. Add the leek and cook, stirring occasionally, for a further 5 minutes, until beginning to brown. Add the potato, pour in the stock and bring to the boil. (If using a stock cube, add 750 ml/1¼ pints water to the pan and when it comes to the boil, stir in the stock cube.) Simmer for about 40 minutes. Remove the pan from the heat and leave to cool slightly before processing in a food processor. Add the milk and process briefly again to mix. Pour the soup into a glass or china bowl, season to taste with salt and stir in the cream. Cover and chill in the refrigerator for at least 12 hours, 24 if possible. Serve in individual soup bowls, sprinkled with the parsley.

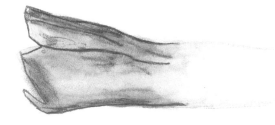

RICE, PULSES, POTATOES AND PASTA

Rice

Rice is a rich source of vitamins B and E and also contains useful amounts of phosphorus, potassium, sodium, iron, copper, zinc, magnesium and silicon. Refined white rice, that is, rice that has been husked, does not contain any vitamin B. Rice contains more carbohydrates than wheat but has fewer proteins and minerals. Rice is easily digested and is absorbed by the body almost in its entirety. It is widely used as a baby food and is useful for those suffering from diarrhoea and gastrointestinal problems. Rice goes well with most other foods and, given its high calorie and carbohydrate contents, it is best when partnered by foods that provide proteins, minerals and vitamins.

Tricks

- Each type of rice has its own cooking time. Follow the instructions on the packet to obtain perfect rice.
- When cooking white rice, add a few drops of lemon juice to the cooking water to ensure that the grains are separated and sparkling white.
- Never stir rice with a fork while it is cooking as this will make it stick.
- Always wait until the water is boiling before adding the rice, otherwise it will stick.
- For perfect rice pilaf, cook the grains in a little hot oil, stirring constantly, until they turn transparent, then add all the water or stock at once. The proportions are twice as much liquid as rice. Cover the saucepan and cook for 15 minutes without stirring. When the liquid has evaporated, remove the lid and leave the rice to finish cooking over a very low heat.
- For perfect paella, leave the cooked dish to stand for 5 minutes on a folded damp tea towel before serving.
- When serving rice as an accompaniment, make it more interesting by putting a little food colouring or a pinch of saffron in the cooking water. This will turn it yellow.

173

White rice

ARROZ BLANCO

- **500 g / 1 lb 2 oz long-grain rice**
- **50 g / 2 oz butter**
- **salt**

Serves 6

Bring a saucepan of unsalted water to the boil. Add the rice, stir with a wooden spoon to prevent the grains clumping together and cook over a high heat for 12–15 minutes, until tender. (The cooking time depends on the type of rice.) Drain the rice in a large colander and rinse well under cold running water, stirring to ensure that it is well washed. Leave the rice draining in the colander until required. Melt the butter in another saucepan. Add the rice, season with salt and heat through, stirring with a wooden spoon. Serve immediately.

Note: When reheating the rice you could add 100 g / 3 ½ oz canned peas, drained.

174

White rice with garlic

ARROZ BLANCO CON AJO

- **500 g / 1 lb 2 oz long-grain rice**
- **5 tablespoons olive oil**
- **1 clove garlic, lightly crushed**
- **salt**

Serves 4–6

Cook the rice in boiling water and rinse under cold running water as described in recipe 173. Heat the oil in a large frying pan, add the garlic and cook over a low heat for about 5 minutes. Remove and discard the garlic, then add the rice and heat through.

175

Rice with prawns, monkfish and mussels
ARROZ BLANCO CON GAMBAS, RAPE Y MEJILLONES

- 500 g/1 lb 2 oz long-grain rice
- 1 kg/2 ¼ lb mussels
- 5 tablespoons white wine
- 1 bay leaf or 1 sprig fresh parsley
- 250 g/9 oz raw unpeeled prawns
- 65 g/2 ½ oz butter
- 2 tablespoons sunflower oil
- 1 tablespoon chopped onion
- 2 tablespoons plain flour
- 450 ml/¾ pint milk
- 1 tablespoon tomato purée
- 250 g/9 oz boneless monkfish fillet, cut into pieces
- 1 tablespoon chopped fresh parsley
- salt

Serves 6

Cook the rice in boiling water and rinse under cold running water as described in recipe 173. Drain well and set aside. Scrape the mussel shells with the blade of a knife and remove the 'beards', then scrub under cold running water. Discard any mussels with broken shells or any that do not shut immediately when sharply tapped. Put them in a heavy-based saucepan with the wine and bay leaf or parsley. Cover and cook over a low heat for about 10 minutes, until the shells have opened. Remove the mussels with a slotted spoon, reserving the cooking liquid, and discard any that remain closed. Remove the mussels from their shells and if they are very large, cut them in half with kitchen scissors. Put on a plate, cover with another plate to prevent them drying out and set aside. Strain the reserved cooking liquid through a muslin-lined sieve into a bowl and set aside. Peel the prawns, reserving the heads and shells, and set the whole tails aside. Put the heads and shells in a saucepan, add water to cover and a pinch of salt and bring to the boil. Lower the heat and simmer for 10 minutes, then strain the prawn stock into the bowl of strained mussel stock. Make a béchamel sauce by melting 25 g/1 oz of the butter with the oil in a saucepan. Add the onion and cook over a low heat, stirring occasionally, for a few minutes, until softened. Stir in the flour and cook, stirring constantly, for 1 minute, then gradually stir in the milk, alternating with 450 ml/¾ pint of the shellfish stock. Simmer for 10 minutes, season to taste with salt and stir in the tomato purée. The sauce should be quite thick. Add the monkfish and reserved prawn tails to the sauce and cook for 6 minutes, then add the mussels to reheat briefly. Melt the remaining butter in another saucepan. Add the rice, season with salt and heat through, stirring with a wooden spoon. To serve, spoon the rice into a ring mould, then turn it out on to a warm serving dish. Fill the centre with the fish and sauce and sprinkle with the parsley. Alternatively, serve the rice on the side.

Rice with fish and seafood

ARROZ A BANDA

- 175 ml/6 fl oz olive oil
- 150 g/5 oz onions, chopped
- 300 g/11 oz tomatoes,
  peeled and chopped
- 1 bay leaf
- 1 sprig fresh parsley
- 1 sprig fresh thyme
- 1 clove garlic
- pinch of saffron threads
- 150 g/5 oz monkfish fillet,
  cut into chunks
- 150 g/5 oz conger eel steak, cut
  into chunks and bones removed
- 150 g/5 oz gurnard fillet,
  cut into chunks
- 200 g/7 oz scorpion fish
  (Aus: latchet) fillet,
  cut into chunks
- 150 g/5 oz raw Mediterranean
  prawns, peeled
- 675 g/1 ½ lb long-grain rice
- salt and pepper

Serves 4

Heat the oil in a saucepan. Add the onion and cook over a low heat, stirring occasionally, for about 8 minutes, until beginning to brown. Add the tomato, bay leaf, parsley and thyme and pour in 1.5 litres/2 ½ pints water. Pound the garlic with the saffron in a mortar and add to the pan. Bring to the boil and add the fish and prawns. Season with salt and pepper and cook over a high or medium–high heat for 15 minutes. Using a slotted spoon, transfer the fish and prawns to a serving dish and keep warm. Strain the fish stock into a flameproof casserole and bring to the boil. Add the rice, cover and cook for 20 minutes. Remove the casserole from the heat and leave to stand, still covered, for 5 minutes. Lightly stir with a fork to separate the grains. Serve the rice in the casserole with the fish and prawns served separately on a serving dish.

177

Murcian rice and fish hotpot
ARROZ CALDERO

- 1.5 kg/3 ¼ lb 1 grey mullet
  (sea mullet), cleaned
  and filleted, head reserved
- 500 g/1 lb 2 oz gurnard, cleaned
  and filleted, head reserved
- 500 g/1 lb 2 oz grouper or sea
  bream, cleaned and filleted,
  head reserved, or monkfish tail
- 200 ml/7 fl oz olive oil
- 2 ñoras or other small dried
  red chillies
- 2 ripe tomatoes,
  peeled and chopped
- 2 cloves garlic
- 400 g/14 oz long-grain rice
- 200 g/7 oz raw Mediterranean
  prawns, peeled
- salt

Serves 4

Cut out and discard the gills from the reserved fish heads, then set aside. Cut the fish into thick slices. Heat the oil in a large flameproof casserole or cocotte. Add the chillies and cook over a low heat, stirring frequently, for 2–4 minutes. Remove with a slotted spoon and set aside. Add the fish heads to the pan and cook, turning occasionally, for 10 minutes. Remove and discard, then add the tomato and cook, stirring occasionally, for 5 minutes. Pour in 2 litres/3 ½ pints water and bring to the boil. Meanwhile, pound the chillies with 1 garlic clove in a mortar, then add to the pan and simmer for 5 minutes. Season the slices of fish with salt, add to the pan and simmer gently for 5–10 minutes, until the flesh is opaque and flakes easily. Carefully remove the fish from the pan using a fish slice, put on a serving dish and keep warm. Strain the stock and return to a clean pan. Pound the remaining garlic in a mortar and stir in 250 ml/8 fl oz of the fish stock. Set aside. Taste the remaining stock, season with salt, if necessary, and bring to the boil. Add the rice and bring back to the boil, then lower the heat, cover and cook for 15 minutes. Put the prawns on top of the rice, re-cover the pan and cook for a further 5 minutes, until the rice is tender and the prawns are cooked through. The rice is served first and the fish is eaten afterwards with the garlic and stock mixture poured over it just before serving.

Note: The rice may be served with alioli, garlic mayonnaise (see recipe 110) or ajoaceite, garlic oil. To make this, mix 2 crushed garlic cloves with olive oil and salt, stirring until smooth.

One of the most famous restaurants in Madrid for Murcian cooking is El Caldero, run by Antonio Valero and his son Alfredo. Their style of cooking is very precise and individual, with very little influence from the cuisines of other regions of Spain. In general, Murcian dishes are strongly flavoured. Sauces, such as tártara sauce and alioli are a speciality. The region of Murcia in the south-east of the country is richly supplied with fish. Among the most important are mullet, gilthead bream, 'lobarro' and crevettes. Crevettes are available only at certain times of the year, making them one of Murcia's most expensive products.It is a long-standing local tradition to serve certain fish with rice, especially with caldero rice, literally 'cauldron rice'. The dish has traditional roots in the fishing villages of the region. The fishermen made a tripod with three canes stuck in the sand, hung an iron cooking pot from the top and lit a fire using dry seaweed. Sea water was used as stock to cook the fish and once they were cooked, they were removed and eaten while the rice cooked in the pot. The most important characteristics of caldero rice are its aroma, colour and flavour, all produced by 'ñora' chillies, an essential ingredient. The rice is always cooked in the same stock as the fish, creating a very intense partnership. The caldero is an iron pot still made today by specialist ironmongers. It is seasoned with heat to give caldero rice its special flavour. A cocotte, also known as a Dutch oven, is a fairly good substitute.

Sailors' rice
ARROZ CALDOSO A LA MARINERA

- **250 g/9 oz clams**
- **5 tablespoons olive oil**
- **1 large onion, chopped**
- **1 clove garlic, chopped**
- **250 g/9 oz tomatoes,**
  peeled and chopped
- **1 teaspoon paprika**
- **250 g/9 oz raw prawns, peeled**
- **400 g/14 oz long-grain rice**
- **1 bay leaf**
- **150 g/5 oz shelled peas**
- **6 young globe artichokes,**
  halved lengthways
- **salt**

Serves 4

Scrub the clams under cold running water and discard any with broken shells or any that do not shut immediately when sharply tapped. Pour about 5 tablespoons water into a frying pan, add a pinch of salt and the clams, cover and cook over a high heat, shaking the pan occasionally, for 5–7 minutes, until the clams have opened. Remove with a slotted spoon and discard the empty half shells and any clams that remain closed. Put the clams on the half shell into a dish and keep warm. Strain the cooking liquid into a bowl through a muslin-lined sieve and make up to 1 litre/1 ¾ pints with water. Heat the oil in a flameproof casserole. Add the onion and cook over a low heat, stirring occasionally, for about 10 minutes, until lightly browned. Add the garlic and tomatoes and cook, stirring occasionally, for 10 minutes. Stir in the paprika and add the prawns, rice and bay leaf. Stir well, pour in the diluted cooking liquid and bring to the boil. Simmer for 5 minutes, then add the peas and artichokes and cook for a further 20 minutes. Remove the casserole from the heat, remove the bay leaf, place the clams on top and serve immediately.

179

Castilian rice
ARROZ CASTIZO

- 4 tablespoons olive oil
- 2 onions, very finely chopped
- 1 green pepper,
  seeded and diced
- 2 cloves garlic, finely chopped
- 1 tablespoon finely chopped
  fresh parsley
- 2 tomatoes,
  peeled, seeded and chopped
- 4 dozen carpetshell clams
  (Aus: pipis) or warty Venus clams
- 500 g/1 lb 2 oz long-grain rice
- 1 teaspoon paprika
- pinch of saffron threads,
  toasted and crushed
- salt

Serves 6

Heat the oil in a flameproof casserole. Add the onion and green pepper and cook over a low heat, stirring occasionally, for 5 minutes, until softened. Add the garlic and parsley and cook, stirring occasionally, for a further 3 minutes. Add the tomato and stir well. Meanwhile, scrub the clams under cold running water and discard any with broken shells or any that do not shut immediately when sharply tapped. Pour 150 ml/¼ pint water into a frying pan, add the clams, cover and cook over a high heat, shaking the pan occasionally, for 3–5 minutes, until the clams have opened. Remove the clams with a slotted spoon and discard the empty half shells and any clams that remain closed. Put the clams on the half shell into a dish and keep warm. Strain the cooking liquid into a bowl through a muslin-lined sieve and make up to 1 litre/1 ¾ pints with water. Add the rice to the casserole, stir in the paprika and season with salt. Cook, stirring constantly, for 2 minutes, then pour in the diluted cooking liquid. Bring to the boil and cook for about 12 minutes, until the rice is tender. Stir in the saffron and add the clams. Remove the casserole from the heat and leave to stand for 5 minutes before serving.

Rice with cauliflower and cuttlefish

ARROZ CON COLIFLOR Y SEPIA

- **4 tablespoons olive oil**
- **150 g/5 oz onion, finely chopped**
- **2 cloves garlic, finely chopped**
- **500 g/1 lb 2 oz cuttlefish**
  or squid, cleaned (see page 468)
  and cut into strips
- **1 teaspoon paprika**
- **pinch of ground cinnamon**
- **1.5 kg/3 ¼ lb cauliflower,**
  separated into florets
- **500 g/1 lb 2 oz long-grain rice**
- **pinch of saffron threads**
- **pepper**

Serves 6

Heat the oil in a flameproof casserole. Add the onion and garlic and cook over a low heat, stirring occasionally, for about 10 minutes, until lightly browned. Increase the heat to medium, add the cuttlefish or squid and cook, stirring constantly, for 2–3 minutes, until lightly browned. Stir in the paprika, cinnamon and a pinch of pepper. Pour in water to cover and cook, stirring constantly, for 5 minutes, until the seafood is tender. Add the cauliflower and rice. Crush the saffron in a mortar and stir in a little water, then add to the pan. Add a little more water to cover the rice, if necessary, and bring to the boil. Lower the heat and cook, uncovered, for 20–25 minutes, until the rice is tender and the liquid has been absorbed. Serve immediately.

Black rice

ARROZ NEGRO

- **400 g/14 oz small squid ,
  cleaned with their ink sacs
  reserved (see page 468)**
- **275 ml/9 fl oz olive oil**
- **2 cloves garlic, finely chopped**
- **3 tomatoes,
  peeled, seeded and chopped**
- **1.5 litres/2 ½ pints fish stock
  (home-made or made
  with a stock cube)**
- **500 g/1 lb 2 oz long-grain rice**
- **1 canned or bottled red pepper,
  drained and cut into strips**
- **salt**

Serves 6

Put the ink sacs into a bowl of water. Using a sharp knife, cut the sac into thin rings. Heat the oil in a flameproof earthenware pot, a paella pan or a large heavy-based frying pan. Add the squid rings, and the tentacles if you like, and cook over a medium–high heat, stirring frequently, for 5 minutes. Stir in the garlic, add the tomato and pour in 150 ml/¼ pint of the stock. Lower the heat, cover and cook for 20 minutes. Meanwhile, carefully remove the ink pouches from the bowl of water and break them into a measuring jug. Add enough of the remaining stock to make the quantity up to 1.2 litres/2 pints. Stir the rice into the pan, then add the squid ink and stock mixture. Season with salt, mix well, cover and cook over a high heat for 10 minutes, then lower the heat to medium, stir in the pepper strips, re-cover and cook for a further 10 minutes. Remove the pan from the heat and leave to stand, still covered, for 5 minutes before serving.

182

Rice with chicken, mushrooms and truffles

ARROZ BLANCO CON PECHUGA DE GALLINA, CHAPIÑONES Y TRUFAS

- 1 skinless chicken breast
- 1 small leek,
  halved and rinsed well
- 1 carrot, sliced
- ½ bay leaf
- 500 g/1 lb 2 oz long-grain rice
- 500 g/1 lb 2 oz mushrooms,
  trimmed
- 120 g/4 oz butter
- a few drops of lemon juice
- 2 tablespoons olive oil
- 2 tablespoons plain flour
- 2 truffles, sliced
- 450 ml/¾ pint milk
- 2 egg yolks
- salt

Serves 6

Put the chicken breast (a quarter of a good chicken), leek, carrot and bay leaf into a saucepan and pour in water to cover. Add a pinch of salt and bring to the boil, then lower the heat to medium and cook for 20–30 minutes, until the chicken is cooked through. (Check by cutting into the thickest part with the point of a knife. If the juices run clear and the meat is no longer pink, the chicken is ready.) Remove the chicken from the pan and reserve 250 ml/8 fl oz of the stock. When the chicken is cool enough to handle, cut into bite-size pieces. Cook the rice in boiling water and rinse under cold running water as described in recipe 173. Drain well and set aside. Remove the mushroom stalks from the caps and cut both into fairly thick slices. Put into a saucepan with 25 g/1 oz of the butter, the lemon juice and a pinch of salt. Cover and cook over a low heat for 5 minutes. Meanwhile, make a béchamel sauce by melting 25 g/1 oz of the remaining butter with the oil in a saucepan. Stir in the flour and cook, stirring constantly, for 2 minutes. Gradually stir in the milk, alternating with the reserved chicken stock. Season with salt and cook, stirring constantly, for 10 minutes. Add the mushrooms and their cooking juices, then add the truffles and chicken. Melt the remaining butter in another saucepan. Add the rice, season with salt and heat through, stirring with a wooden spoon. Spoon it into a ring mould, then turn it out on to a warm serving dish. Whisk the egg yolks with a little of the béchamel sauce in a bowl, then stir into the pan with the chicken mixture. Remove the pan from the heat and spoon the mixture into the centre of the rice. Serve immediately

Note: In Spain, this dish is made with hen instead of chicken. If you are cooking it with hen, you will need to increase the cooking time for the meat to 45–60 minutes.

183 Cold rice with tuna and mayonnaise

ARROZ BLANCO FRÍO CON MAYONESA Y ATÚN

- 500 g/1 lb 2 oz long-grain rice
- 250 g/9 oz canned tuna, drained and flaked
- sunflower oil, for brushing
- salt

Garnish:
- baby lettuce leaves
- 3 tomatoes, sliced
- 1 hard-boiled egg, sliced

Mayonnaise:
- 2 eggs
- 2 tablespoons white-wine vinegar or lemon juice
- 750 ml/1 ¼ pints sunflower oil
- salt

Serves 6

Make the mayonnaise in a blender as described in recipe 105, as it will be thicker. Cook the rice in boiling water and rinse under cold running water as described in recipe 173. Drain well, tip into a large bowl, add a little salt and mix. Reserve a little of the tuna for the garnish. Stir the remainder into the rice with a little more than half the mayonnaise. Brush the inside of a mould with sunflower oil. Spoon the rice mixture into it, pressing down well to make sure there are no holes. Cover with cling film and chill in the refrigerator for at least 1 hour. To serve, run a round-bladed knife around the edge of the mould and invert the rice mixture on to a round serving dish. Top with the remaining mayonnaise and garnish with lettuce, tomatoes, hard-boiled egg and the reserved tuna. Serve immediately.

Notes: If you like, season the tomato slices with salt and put a little tuna and mayonnaise on the lettuce leaves. As an alternative, the hard-boiled egg may be chopped and put on top of the rice.

184

Rice with tomato sauce, green beans and omelette

ARROZ BLANCO CON SALSA DE TOMATE, JUDÍAS VERDES Y TORTILLA

- 2 tablespoons sunflower oil
- 1 kg/2 ¼ lb tomatoes, seeded and chopped
- 1 teaspoon sugar
- 500 g/1 lb 2 oz long-grain rice
- 750 g/1 lb 10 oz green beans, trimmed
- pinch of bicarbonate of soda
- 80 g/3 oz butter
- 3 tablespoons olive oil
- 3 eggs, beaten
- salt

Serves 6

Make a thick tomato sauce with the sunflower oil, tomato and sugar as described in recipe 73. Cook the rice in boiling water and rinse under cold running water as described in recipe 173. Drain well and set aside. If the beans are very fat, cut them into small cubes; otherwise cut into short lengths. Bring a saucepan of water to the boil and add a pinch of salt and the bicarbonate of soda. Add the beans and cook for about 20 minutes, until tender. (The cooking time will depend on the type and freshness of the beans.) Drain the beans well. Melt half the butter in a frying pan. Add the beans and cook for a few minutes. Heat the olive oil in another frying pan. Season the eggs with salt, tip them into the pan and tilt the pan to cover the base evenly. Cook until the underside has set, flip over the omelette, using the lid of the pan or a fish slice, and leave it in the pan over a low heat. Melt the remaining butter in a saucepan. Add the rice, season with salt and heat through, stirring with a wooden spoon. Spoon the rice along the centre of a warm oval serving dish and spoon the tomato sauce around it. Put the green beans on top of the rice and at either end. Cut the omelette into 2-cm/¾-inch wide strips and sprinkle over the beans, to garnish. Serve immediately.

185

Rice with Swiss chard

ARROZ CON ACELGAS

- 4 tablespoons olive oil
- 750 g/1 lb 10 oz Swiss chard, chopped
- 100 g/3 ½ oz bacon, cut into strips
- 200 g/7 oz long-grain rice
- 475 ml/16 fl oz beef stock (home-made or made with a stock cube)
- grated Parmesan cheese

Serves 4

Heat the oil in a saucepan. Add the Swiss chard and bacon and cook over a medium–low heat, stirring occasionally, for 5 minutes. Add the rice, pour in the stock and bring to the boil. Lower the heat, cover and cook for about 20 minutes, until the rice is tender and the stock has been absorbed. Serve the rice immediately, offering the Parmesan separately.

186

Cold rice with vegetables and vinaigrette
ARROZ BLANCO FRÍO CON VERDURAS Y VINAGRETA

- 400 g/14 oz long-grain rice
- 750 g/1 lb 10 oz green beans,
  cut into short lengths or
  1.5 kg/3 ¼ lb peas, shelled
- pinch of bicarbonate of soda
  (optional)
- salt

Vinaigrette:
- 2 tablespoons white-wine
  vinegar
- 6 tablespoons olive oil
- 1 teaspoon chopped
  fresh parsley
- 1 hard-boiled egg, finely chopped
- salt

Garnish:
- iceberg lettuce leaves
- 500 g/1 lb 2 oz ripe tomatoes,
  sliced
- 3 hard-boiled eggs,
  cut into segments

Serves 6

Cook the rice in boiling water and rinse under cold running water as described in recipe 173. Drain well and season with salt while it is still in the colander. Spoon the rice into a ring mould and set aside. Make the vinaigrette as described in recipe 98 and pour into a sauce boat. Set aside. If using the green beans, cook them in a large saucepan of salted boiling water for 20–30 minutes, until tender. (The cooking time will depend on the type and freshness of the beans.) If you like, add a pinch of bicarbonate of soda to the water to make the beans greener. Drain the beans and leave to cool. If using the peas, cook them in a large saucepan of salted boiling water for 15–30 minutes. (The cooking time will depend on the size and freshness of the peas.) Drain well and leave to cool. Turn the rice out on to a serving dish. Spoon the green beans or peas into the centre of the ring. Arrange alternating lettuce leaves and tomato slices around the outside of the ring. Garnish with the hard-boiled egg segments and serve, offering the vinaigrette separately.

Note: The dish may be kept in the refrigerator without its deteriorating for up to 1 hour before serving.

Cold rice salad

ENSALADA FRÍA DE ARROZ

- 500 g/1 lb 2 oz long-grain rice
- 750 g/1 lb 10 oz tomatoes, peeled, seeded and chopped
- 250 g/9 oz mushrooms, thinly sliced
- juice of ½ lemon
- 1 canned or bottled red pepper, drained and diced
- 2 tablespoons chopped fresh parsley
- 2 tablespoons white-wine vinegar
- 6 tablespoons olive oil
- 1 hard-boiled egg, chopped
- salt

Serves 6

Cook the rice in boiling water and rinse under cold running water as described in recipe 173. Drain well and set aside. Put the tomato in a colander, sprinkle with salt and leave to drain. Put the mushrooms in a bowl, add the lemon juice and mix well. Put the rice in a large salad bowl and add the tomato, mushrooms, red pepper and parsley. Whisk together the vinegar and oil in a jug and season with salt. Pour the dressing over the salad and mix well. Sprinkle the chopped hard-boiled egg over the salad just before serving. The salad can be served in the salad bowl or in a serving dish garnished with lettuce leaves around the edge.

Rice with chicken

ARROZ BLANCO CON GALLINA

- **1 chicken,
  weighing about 1.5 kg/3 ¼ lb**
- **1 onion**
- **2 cloves**
- **2 carrots, thickly sliced**
- **1 bay leaf**
- **175 ml/6 fl oz white wine**
- **500 g/1 lb 2 oz long-grain rice**
- **80 g/3 oz butter**
- **2 tablespoons sunflower oil**
- **2 tablespoons plain flour**
- **2 egg yolks, lightly beaten**
- **¼ teaspoon meat extract**
- **1 teaspoon chopped parsley**
- **salt**

Serves 6

Put the chicken into a saucepan, pour in enough water to cover and add a pinch of salt. Stud the onion with the cloves and add to the pan along with the carrots, bay leaf and white wine. Cover and bring to the boil, then lower the heat and simmer gently for 1 ½–2 hours, until tender. While the chicken is cooking, occasionally skim off the froth that rises to the surface with a skimmer or slotted spoon. (Check to see whether the chicken is done by cutting into the thickest part of the thigh with the tip of a knife. If the juices run clear and the meat is no longer pink, the chicken is ready.) Meanwhile, cook the rice in boiling water and rinse under cold running water as described in recipe 173. Drain well and set aside. Lift the chicken out of the pan and carve the meat. Put the meat in a dish and ladle some of the stock over it to keep it warm. Strain and reserve the remaining stock. To make the sauce, melt half the butter with the oil in a saucepan. Gradually stir in the flour and cook, stirring constantly, for 2 minutes. Stir in 750 ml/1 ¼ pints of the reserved chicken stock and cook, whisking constantly to prevent lumps forming. Gradually stir a little of the stock into the egg yolks in a bowl, taking care that the yolks do not curdle. Add to the sauce, together with the meat extract and parsley. Season with salt if necessary. Add the chicken meat and keep the sauce warm but do not allow it to cook any more. Melt the remaining butter in another saucepan. Add the rice, season with salt and heat through, stirring with a wooden spoon. Spoon the rice into a ring mould, then turn out on to a warm serving dish. Spoon the chicken mixture into the centre of the ring. Serve immediately.

Note: In Spain, this dish is made with hen instead of chicken. If you are cooking it with hen, you will need to increase the cooking time for the meat to 1 ½–3 hours.

189

Rice with mince

ARROZ CON CARNE PICADA

- 4 tablespoons olive oil
- 1 onion, thinly sliced
- 1 green pepper,
  seeded and cut into strips
- 2 tomatoes,
  peeled, seeded and chopped
- 400 g/14 oz minced meat
- pinch of paprika
- 250 g/9 oz long-grain rice
- 500 ml/18 fl oz boiling meat
  stock (home-made or made
  with a stock cube)
- salt and pepper

Serves 4–6

Heat the oil in a saucepan. Add the onion and green pepper and cook over a low heat, stirring occasionally, for 5 minutes, until softened. Add the tomato and mince and cook, breaking up the meat with a wooden spoon, for 5 minutes, until lightly browned. Add the paprika, season with salt and pepper and mix well, then stir in the rice and cook, stirring constantly, for 2 minutes. Pour in the stock, cover and cook for about 15 minutes, until the rice is tender and all the liquid has been absorbed. Serve immediately.

190

Rice with kidneys
ARROZ BLANCO CON RIÑONES

- 1 ox kidney,
  about 500 g/1 lb 2 oz
- 500 g/1 lb 2 oz long-grain rice
- 5 tablespoons olive oil
- 2 tablespoons plain flour
- 175 ml/6 fl oz sherry
- 40 g/1 ½ oz butter
- salt

Serves 6

Prepare the kidney as described on page 768. Cook the rice in boiling water and rinse under cold running water as described in recipe 173. Drain well and set aside. To make the sauce, heat the oil in a saucepan. Stir in the flour and cook, stirring constantly with a whisk, for 4–5 minutes, until beginning to brown. Gradually stir in the sherry and 600 ml/1 pint water and season with salt. Simmer for 5 minutes, then add the pieces of kidney and cook for a further 4 minutes. Melt the butter in another saucepan. Add the rice, season with salt and heat through, stirring with a wooden spoon. Spoon into a ring mould, then turn out on to a warm serving dish. Spoon the kidney mixture into the centre and serve immediately.

191

Yellow rice with peas
ARROZ DE ADORNO, AMARILLO Y CON GUISANTES

- pinch of saffron threads
- 500 g/1 lb 2 oz long-grain rice
- 100 g/3 ½ oz fresh or frozen peas
- 40 g/1 ½ oz butter
- salt

Serves 6

Crush the saffron threads in a mortar, then stir in 2 tablespoons water. Cook the rice in boiling water, adding the saffron mixture to the water, and rinse under cold running water as described in recipe 173. Drain well and set aside. If using fresh peas, cook in a saucepan of salted boiling water for 15–30 minutes, until tender. (Cook frozen peas according to the instructions on the packet.) Melt the butter in another saucepan. Add the rice, season with salt and heat through, stirring with a wooden spoon. Drain the peas and stir into the rice. Serve immediately.

192

Yellow rice with scrambled eggs
ARROZ AMARILLO CON HUEVOS REVUELTOS

- 500 g/1 lb 2 oz long-grain rice
- 100 g/3 ½ oz petits pois, cooked
- pinch of saffron threads
- 40 g/1 ½ oz butter
- salt

Eggs:
- 8 eggs, beaten
- 20 g/¾ oz butter
- 3 tablespoons milk
- 250 g/9 oz raw prawns,
  peeled and halved, or 2 truffles,
  thinly sliced
- salt

Serves 6

Prepare the rice and peas as described in recipe 191 and keep warm. It needs to be ready as the eggs must be served as soon as they are cooked. Half fill a large, deep pan or roasting tin with water and bring to the boil, then lower the heat so that the water is just simmering. Put the eggs, butter, milk and prawns, if using, into a saucepan and season with salt. Put the saucepan in the simmering water and cook, stirring constantly with a fork especially around the edge of the pan as this is where the eggs will set first. When the egg mixture begins to turn creamy, remove the pan from the simmering water, stir in the truffles, if using, and continue to stir well until the eggs have set. The total cooking time required depends on how firm you like your scrambled eggs; it is usually about 10 minutes. Spoon the rice into a ring mould and turn out on to a warm serving dish. Spoon the scrambled eggs into the centre and serve immediately.

193

Milanese rice
ARROZ MILANESA

- 500 g/1 lb 2 oz long-grain rice
- 3 tablespoons olive oil
- 1 onion, finely chopped
- 100 g/3 ½ oz Serrano or
  other dry-cured ham, diced
- 100 g/3 ½ oz chorizo, diced
- 250 g/9 oz canned peas, drained
- 100 g/3 ½ oz Parmesan cheese,
  grated
- salt

Serves 6

Cook the rice in boiling water and rinse under cold running water as described in recipe 173. Drain well and set aside. Heat the oil in a large saucepan. Add the onion and cook over a low heat, stirring occasionally, for 5–8 minutes, until lightly browned. Stir in the ham and chorizo, then add the rice and cook for 5 minutes, stirring constantly with a wooden spoon. Season to taste with salt and stir in the peas. Cook, stirring, for a few minutes more. Serve immediately, offering the Parmesan separately.

194

Indian rice with raisins and pine nuts
ARROZ HINDÚ CON PASAS Y PIÑONES

- **2 tablespoons raisins**
- **300 g/11 oz long-grain rice**
- **25 g/1 oz butter**
- **2 tablespoons pine nuts**
- **curry powder or soy sauce,**
  to taste
- **salt**

Serves 4

Put the raisins in a bowl, add warm water to cover and leave to soak for 15–30 minutes. Meanwhile, cook the rice in boiling water and rinse under cold running water as described in recipe 173. Drain well and set aside. Drain the raisins and pat dry with a tea towel. Melt the butter in a saucepan. Add the pine nuts and cook, stirring frequently, for 2–3 minutes, until light golden brown. Add the raisins and the rice and cook over a low heat, stirring constantly, for 10 minutes. If using curry powder, stir it in and season with salt. If using soy sauce, stir it in but do not add salt. Serve immediately.

Note: This dish is usually served as an accompaniment and the quantities shown reflect this. You can multiply them to serve more.

195

Rice with sausages and bacon
ARROZ CON SALCHICHAS Y BACON

- **225 g/8 oz long-grain rice**
- **5 tablespoons olive oil**
- **150 g/5 oz bacon, cut into strips**
- **4 frankfurter sausages,**
  each cut into 4 pieces
- **1 green pepper,**
  seeded and diced
- **2 sticks celery, thinly sliced**
- **1 large onion, diced**
- **50 g/2 oz olives,**
  stoned and halved
- **soy sauce, to taste**
- **salt**

Serves 4

Cook the rice in boiling water and rinse under cold running water as described in recipe 173. Drain well and set aside. Heat the oil in a large frying pan. Add the bacon and frankfurters and cook, stirring occasionally, for 5–6 minutes, until lightly browned. Remove from the pan and set aside. Add the pepper, celery and onion to the pan and cook, stirring occasionally, for 5–8 minutes, until crisp-tender. Add the olives and return the bacon and frankfurters to the pan. Stir in the rice. Mix well, add soy sauce to taste and heat through. Season with salt, if necessary, remembering that the soy sauce is salty. Serve immediately.

Rice with rabbit

ARROZ CON CONEJO

- 175 ml/6 fl oz olive oil
- 1 small onion, chopped
- 1 clove garlic, chopped
- 1 tomato, chopped
- 1 sprig fresh parsley, chopped
- 400 g/14 oz boned, diced rabbit
- 2 artichokes,
  cut lengthways into quarters
- pinch of ground cinnamon
- pinch of paprika
- 500 g/1 lb 2 oz long-grain rice
- salt

Serves 6

Heat the oil in a flameproof casserole. Add the onion, garlic, tomato and parsley and cook over a low heat, stirring occasionally, for 10 minutes. Add the rabbit and artichokes, sprinkle with the cinnamon and paprika, cover and cook, stirring occasionally, for 10 minutes, until the meat is browned. Pour in 1 litre/1 ¾ pints water, add a pinch of salt and bring to the boil. Add the rice, cover and cook for 15–20 minutes, until the rice is tender and the liquid has been absorbed. Serve immediately straight from the casserole.

Rice with a crust

ARROZ CON COSTRA

- 250 g/9 oz black pudding
- 250 g/9 oz chicken
- 120 g/4 oz chorizo
- 50 g/2 oz bacon
- 50 g/2 oz chickpeas,
  soaked overnight in
  cold water and drained
- 175 ml/6 fl oz sunflower oil
- 200 g/7 oz long-grain rice
- 2 eggs, lightly beaten
- salt

Serves 4

Put the black pudding, chicken, chorizo, bacon and chickpeas in a large saucepan. Pour in 1.5 litres/2 ½ pints water and bring to the boil, then lower the heat, cover and simmer for 1 ½–2 hours, until the meat and chickpeas are tender. Remove the pan from the heat. Remove all the meat and the chickpeas from the pan and reserve the stock. Leave to cool. Remove and discard any skin and bones and cut the meat into small pieces. Heat the oil in a flameproof casserole. Add the meat and chickpeas and cook over a low heat, stirring occasionally, for 8–10 minutes, until lightly browned. Stir in the rice and cook, stirring constantly, for 2 minutes. Pour in 475 ml/16 fl oz of the reserved stock, bring to the boil, cover and cook for 15 minutes, until the rice is tender and almost all the liquid has been absorbed. Meanwhile, preheat the oven to 180°C/350°F/Gas Mark 4. Remove the pan from the heat. Season the eggs with a pinch of salt and pour over the surface of the rice. Transfer to the oven and bake until the topping is golden brown. Serve the dish immediately straight from the casserole.

Note: It is best to use a fairly shallow casserole to ensure that this dish has a golden crust.

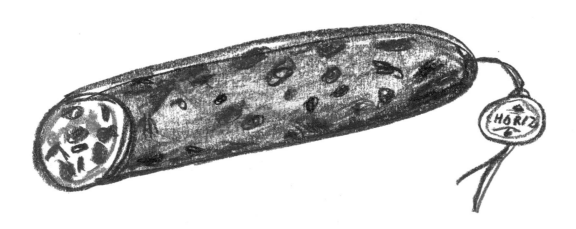

Curried rice
ARROZ AL CURRY

- 500 g/1 lb 2 oz long-grain rice
- 250 g/9 oz chestnut
  mushrooms, chopped
- 50 g/2 oz butter
- juice of ½ lemon
- 2 tablespoons sunflower oil
- ½ teaspoon curry powder
- 100 g/3 ½ oz canned peas,
  drained
- 100 g/3 ½ oz canned red
  peppers, drained and cut
  into 1-cm/½-inch squares
- salt
- 2 sliced hard-boiled eggs
  or strips of fried bacon

Serves 6

Cook the rice in boiling water and rinse under cold running water as described in recipe 173. Drain well and set aside. Meanwhile, put the mushrooms into a saucepan with 15 g/½ oz of the butter, a few drops of lemon juice and a pinch of salt. Cover and cook over a low heat, stirring occasionally, for 15 minutes. Melt the remaining butter with the oil in another saucepan. Stir in the rice, curry powder, the mushrooms with their cooking juices, peas and red peppers, season to taste with salt and heat through, stirring constantly. Transfer the rice mixture to a warm serving dish and garnish with slices of hard-boiled egg or bacon strips. Serve immediately.

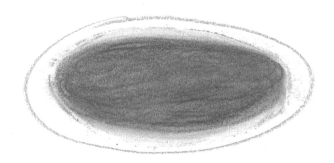

Chinese-style rice
ARROZ ESTILO CHINO

- 500 g/1 lb 2 oz long-grain rice
- 4–5 tablespoons groundnut
  (Aus: peanut) oil
- 250 g/9 oz carrots, diced
- 1 large green pepper,
  seeded and diced
- 225 g/8 oz bean sprouts,
  cut into short lengths
- 100 g/3 ½ oz lean pork, diced
- 5 tablespoons soy sauce
- salt

Serves 6

Cook the rice in boiling water and rinse under cold running water as described in recipe 173. Drain well and set aside. Heat the oil in a large frying pan. Add the carrot, pepper and bean sprouts and stir-fry for 10 minutes. Add the pork and stir-fry for a further 5 minutes, then stir in the rice. Pour in the soy sauce and season with salt, if necessary, remembering that the soy sauce is salty. Serve immediately.

200

Kidney bean, bacon and red pepper rice

GUISO CON ARROZ, JUDÍAS ROJAS, BACON Y PIMIENTO

- **250 g/9 oz dried kidney beans, soaked overnight in cold water and drained**
- **8–9 tablespoons olive oil**
- **100 g/3 ½ oz bacon, cut into strips**
- **1 large red pepper, seeded and cut into 4 strips**
- **2 onions, thinly sliced**
- **1 clove garlic, halved and green shoot removed, if necessary**
- **pinch of ground cumin**
- **pinch of dried oregano**
- **1 bay leaf**
- **500 g/1 lb 2 oz long-grain rice**
- **salt**

Serves 6

Put the beans in a saucepan, add water to cover and bring to the boil. Boil vigorously for 15 minutes, then remove from the heat and drain. Return the beans to the pan, add fresh cold water to cover and bring to the boil over a high heat. Lower the heat and simmer for 1 ½ – 2 hours, until tender. Alternatively, put the precooked beans in a pressure cooker, add water to cover, bring to high pressure and cook for 25 minutes. In both cases, drain the beans and reserve the cooking liquid. Meanwhile, heat 4–5 tablespoons of the oil in a frying pan. Add the bacon and cook, stirring occasionally, for 5–6 minutes, until lightly browned. Remove from the pan and set aside. Add the strips of pepper to the pan and cook, turning occasionally, for about 10 minutes, until tender. Remove the pan from the heat and when cool enough to handle, remove the pepper and peel off the skin, then set aside. Reserve the oil in the pan. Heat the remaining oil in a large sauté pan. Add the onion and cook over a low heat, stirring occasionally, for about 6 minutes, until softened and translucent. Add the garlic and cook, stirring occasionally, for a further 2 minutes. Stir in the cumin and oregano, add the bay leaf and season to taste with salt. Pour in 1 litre/1 ¾ pints of the reserved cooking liquid and bring to the boil. Add the rice, beans, bacon, red pepper and reserved oil. Cook, uncovered, over a high heat until the liquid has been absorbed. Then lower the heat, cover and cook for a further 6–8 minutes, until the rice is tender and the grains are separated. Remove the pan from the heat and leave to stand, still covered, for 2 minutes, then serve.

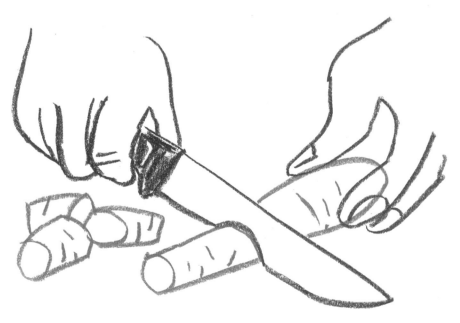

)

201

Simple paella
PAELLA SENCILLA

- **250 g/9 oz monkfish tail**
- **250 g/9 oz raw unpeeled prawns**
- **200 ml/7 fl oz olive oil**
- **1 small onion, chopped**
- **2 tomatoes,**
  peeled, seeded and chopped
- **500 g/1 lb 2 oz live warty Venus**
  clams or 1 kg/2 ¼ lb mussels
- **1 green pepper, seeded and cut**
  into 2.5 cm/1 inch squares
- **1 squid, cleaned (see page 468)**
  and cut into thin strips or rings
- **600 g/1 lb 5 oz long-grain rice**
- **1 thick slice garlic**
- **1 sprig fresh parsley**
- **pinch of saffron threads**
- **2 tablespoons warm water**
- **1 red pepper,**
  seeded and cut into strips
- **100 g/3 ½ oz canned peas,**
  drained
- **½ chorizo sausage,**
  skinned and sliced
- **salt**
- **lemon wedges**

Serves 8

If necessary, remove and discard the grey membrane from the monkfish tail. Using a sharp knife, cut along either side of the backbone, remove the two fillets, cut into chunks and set aside. Reserve the bone. Peel the prawns and reserve the heads and shells. Set the prawn tails aside. Put the monkfish bone and prawn heads and shells into a saucepan. Pour in plenty of water, add a pinch of salt and simmer for 15 minutes. Meanwhile, heat half the oil in a frying pan. Add the onion and cook over a low heat, stirring occasionally, for 5 minutes, until softened and translucent. Add the tomato and cook, stirring and breaking up the tomato with the side of the spoon, for a further 5 minutes. Allow to cool slightly, then transfer the mixture to a food processor and process to a purée. Scrape the purée into a paella pan or large, heavy-based frying pan. If using the clams, scrub under cold running water. If using mussels, scrape the shells with the blade of a knife and remove the 'beards', then scrub under cold running water. Discard any shellfish with broken shells or any that do not shut immediately when sharply tapped. Put the shellfish into a saucepan, pour in 50 ml/2 fl oz water and bring to the boil. Cover and cook over a high heat for 3–6 minutes, until the shells have opened. Remove the pan from the heat and lift out the shellfish with a slotted spoon, reserving the cooking liquid. Remove and discard any shellfish that have not opened and the empty half shells. Set aside the clams or mussels on the half shell. Strain the reserved cooking liquid through a muslin-lined sieve into a bowl. Strain the fish and prawn stock into the same bowl. Measure and make up to 1.75 litres/3 pints with water, if necessary. Pour the stock into a saucepan and heat gently, but do not allow to boil. Pour the remaining oil into the paella pan. Add the green pepper and cook over a medium heat, stirring occasionally, for 3–4 minutes. Add the squid, monkfish and rice and cook, stirring constantly, for a few minutes but do not allow to brown. Season with a pinch of salt and pour in the hot stock. Gently shake the pan to make sure that the liquid is evenly distributed. Pound the garlic, parsley and saffron in a mortar with a little salt, stir in the warm water and add to the pan. Gently shake the pan or stir with a spoon so the mixture is evenly incorporated. Stir in the prawn tails.

When about half the stock has been absorbed, arrange the red pepper strips, reserved shellfish, peas and chorizo attractively in the pan. Continue to cook until the rice is tender and all the stock has been absorbed. (The paella usually takes a total of about 20 minutes from the time the stock is added, but this depends on the type of rice.) Spread out a dampened tea towel on a work surface. Remove the paella pan from the heat, place it on the tea towel and leave to stand for 5 minutes. Serve the paella with lemon wedges hung over the side of the pan.

Note: Some people like to squeeze a little lemon juice over their paella once it has been served. Others prefer to add a few drops of lemon juice to the rice and stock during cooking, as the lemon helps to keep the rice grains separate.

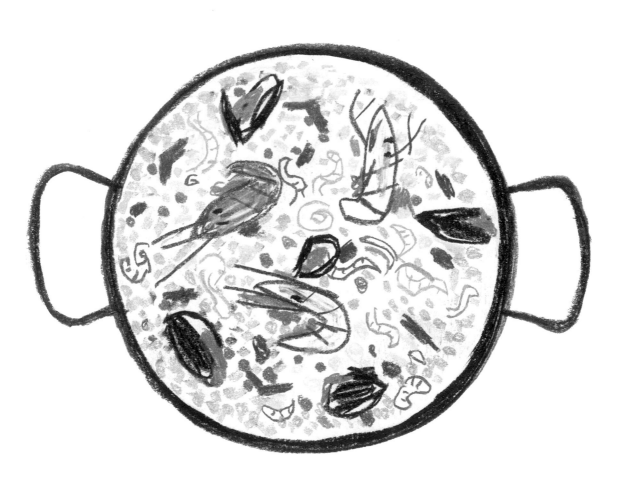

My paella

PAELLA A MI ESTILO

- 300 g/11 oz raw unpeeled prawns
- 1 kg/2 ¼ lb mussels or
  500 g/1 lb 2 lb carpetshell,
  Venus or warty Venus clams
- 175 ml/6 fl oz olive oil
- 1 small onion, finely chopped
- 1 clove garlic, finely chopped
- 3 tablespoons tomato sauce or
  1 large, ripe tomato, chopped
- 2 small squid, cleaned
  (see page 468) and cut into
  5-mm/¼-inch thick rings
- 500 g/1 lb 2 oz long-grain rice
- 3 sprigs fresh parsley
- pinch of saffron threads
- 2 chicken stock cubes
- 100 g/3 ½ oz canned peas,
  drained
- 1 red pepper,
  seeded and cut into strips
- salt
- lemon wedges

Serves 6–8

Peel the prawns and set the tails aside. Put the heads and shells into a saucepan, pour in plenty of water and simmer for about 10 minutes. Remove the pan from the heat and strain the stock into a bowl. If using the mussels, scrape the shells with the blade of a knife and remove the 'beards', then scrub under cold running water. If using the clams, scrub under cold running water. Discard any shellfish with broken shells or any that do not shut immediately when sharply tapped. Put the shellfish in a saucepan or frying pan, add 50 ml/2 fl oz water, cover and cook over a high heat for 3–6 minutes, until the shells have opened. Lift out the shellfish with a slotted spoon, discarding any that remain closed. Reserve the cooking liquid. Remove nearly all the shellfish from their shells but leave a few in the shell or half shell for the garnish. Strain the reserved cooking liquid through a muslin-lined sieve into the prawn stock. Measure and make up to 1.75 litres/3 pints with water, if necessary. Pour into a saucepan and heat gently, but do not allow to boil. Preheat the oven to 180°C/350°F/Gas Mark 4. Put just enough of the oil into a paella pan or large, heavy-based frying pan with a metal handle to cover the base and heat it. Add the onion and garlic and cook over a medium heat, stirring occasionally, for 7 minutes, until lightly browned. Add the tomato sauce or fresh tomato and cook, stirring constantly, for a few minutes. Reserve a few prawns for the garnish and add the remainder to the pan with the squid rings and rice. Cook, stirring constantly, until the squid becomes opaque. Add the shelled mussels or clams. Season with a pinch of salt and pour in the hot stock. Gently shake the pan to make sure the liquid is evenly distributed. Pound the parsley with the saffron in a mortar, then stir in 2 tablespoons water and add to the paella pan. Crumble in the stock cubes. Gently shake the pan or stir with a wooden spoon. Add the peas to the paella and cook for a few minutes more. Garnish the paella with the strips of red pepper, the reserved prawns and the reserved shellfish in the shell. Transfer the pan to the oven and bake for about 25 minutes. Spread out a dampened tea towel on a work surface. Remove the paella pan from the oven, place it on the tea towel and leave to stand for 5 minutes. Serve the paella with lemon wedges hung over the side of the pan.

203

Chicken paella
PAELLA DE POLLO

Additional ingredients:
• 1 skinless boneless chicken
breast

Serves 6–8

Make the paella as described in recipe 202, but first cut a skinless boneless chicken breast into bite-size pieces. Heat half the oil listed in the ingredients, in a frying pan, add the chicken and cook, stirring occasionally, for about 10 minutes, until light golden brown. Remove with a slotted spoon and set aside. Proceed with the paella as described, adding the chicken at the same time as the prawns.

204

Paella with stew ingredients
PAELLA CON TROPEZONES DE COCIDO

• 250 ml/8 fl oz olive oil
• 1 small onion, chopped
• 1 large ripe tomato,
   seeded and chopped
• 150 g/5 oz cooked bacon, diced
• 1 cooked chicken breast,
   cut into bite-size pieces
• 1 cooked black pudding, sliced
• 1 cooked chorizo, sliced
• 80 g/3 oz cooked or canned
   chickpeas
• 600 g/1 lb 5 oz long-grain rice
• 1.5 litres/2 ½ pints hot stock
   (home-made or made
   with a stock cube)
• 1 thick slice garlic
• 1 sprig fresh parsley
• pinch of saffron threads
• 2 tablespoons warm water
• 100 g/3 ½ oz canned peas,
   drained
• 1 roasted or canned red pepper,
   seeded and cut into strips
• salt

Serves 6

Heat half the oil in a saucepan. Add the onion and cook over a low heat, stirring occasionally, for about 5 minutes, until softened and translucent. Add the tomato and cook, stirring and breaking it up with the side of the spoon, for 5–10 minutes. Allow to cool slightly, then transfer the mixture to a food processor and process to a purée. Scrape the purée into a paella pan or large, heavy-based frying pan, add the remaining oil and set over a medium heat. Add the bacon, chicken, half the black pudding, half the chorizo and half the chickpeas. Stir in the rice and pour in the hot stock. Gently shake the pan to make sure that everything is evenly distributed. Pound the garlic, parsley and saffron in a mortar with a little salt and stir in the warm water, then stir into the paella pan. Cook for 15 minutes, then add the peas, the remaining black pudding, chorizo and chickpeas and the strips of red pepper. Cook for a further 5 minutes or until all the stock has been absorbed and the rice is tender. Spread out a dampened tea towel on a work surface. Remove the paella pan from the heat, place it on the tea towel and leave to stand for 5 minutes. Serve immediately.

Note: This paella is designed to be made with leftover ingredients from a stew made the previous day, but if you haven't made a stew, you can still make the paella using cooked ingredients that you have on hand or that you buy from the shop.

Salt cod paella

PAELLA DE BACALAO

- **350 g/12 oz salt cod fillet**
- **plain flour, for dusting**
- **275 ml/9 fl oz olive oil**
- **2 cloves garlic**
- **1 large onion, finely chopped**
- **1 teaspoon paprika**
- **500 g/1 lb 2 oz ripe tomatoes, peeled, seeded and chopped**
- **600 g/1 lb 5 oz long-grain rice**
- **1.5 litres/2 ½ pints hot chicken stock (home-made or made with stock cubes)**
- **pinch of saffron threads**
- **2 tablespoons warm water**
- **100 g/3 ½ oz canned peas, drained**
- **1 teaspoon chopped fresh parsley**
- **100 g/3 ½ oz canned red peppers, drained and cut into strips**
- **salt**

Serves 6

Put the salt cod into a bowl, and add water to cover. Leave to soak for at least 12 hours or overnight, changing the water at least four times. (Each time you change the water rinse out the bowl as the salt tends to deposit on the base.) Drain the fish and pat dry, then cut into bite-size pieces. Roll the pieces in the flour, shaking off any excess. Heat 175 ml/6 fl oz of the oil in a frying pan over a high heat. Add the pieces of cod and cook, turning occasionally, until golden brown all over. Remove with a slotted spoon and set aside. Heat the remaining oil in a paella pan or large, heavy-based frying pan. Meanwhile, finely chop one of the garlic cloves. Add the onion and chopped garlic to the pan and cook over a low heat, stirring occasionally, for 5 minutes until softened and translucent. Stir in the paprika and tomato and cook, stirring and breaking up the tomatoes with the side of the spoon, for 10 minutes. Stir in the rice and cook, stirring constantly, for 1–2 minutes but do not allow it to brown. Add the cod, season with a pinch of salt and pour in the hot stock. Pound the saffron with the remaining garlic clove and a pinch of salt in a mortar and stir in the warm water. Stir into the rice and gently shake the pan to make sure everything is evenly distributed. Cook for 15 minutes, until the rice is beginning to dry a little, then add the peas and parsley and place the strips of pepper on top to garnish. Cook for a further 5 minutes, or until all the stock has been absorbed and the rice is tender. Spread out a dampened tea towel on a work surface. Remove the paella pan from the heat, place it on the tea towel and leave to stand for 5 minutes. Serve immediately.

Canned fish paella

PAELLA DE PESCADOS DE LATA

- 175 ml/6 fl oz olive oil
- 1 onion, chopped
- small piece garlic,
  finely chopped
- 2 tomatoes,
  peeled, seeded and chopped
- 70 g/2 ¾ oz canned squid,
  drained
- 120 g/4 oz canned cockles,
  drained
- 90 g/3 ¼ oz canned tuna,
  drained and flaked
- 600 g/1 lb 5 oz long-grain rice
- 1.75 litres/3 pints fish stock
  (home-made or made
  with stock cubes)
- 70 g/2 ¾ oz canned mussels,
  drained [1 can]
- pinch of saffron threads
- 65 g/2 ½ oz canned sardines
  in oil, drained
- 1 canned or bottled red pepper,
  drained and cut into strips
- 1 sprig fresh parsley
- salt

Serves 6

Heat half the oil in a frying pan. Add the onion and garlic and cook over a low heat, stirring occasionally, for 5 minutes, until softened and translucent. Add the tomato and cook, stirring occasionally and breaking it up with the side of the spoon, for 5 minutes. Allow to cool slightly, then transfer the mixture to a food processor and process until smooth. Pour into a paella pan or large heavy-based frying pan. Add the remaining oil, the squid and half the cockles and cook over a low heat for a few minutes, then add the tuna and stir in the rice. Pour in the fish stock, add the mussels and the remaining cockles and bring to the boil. Add the saffron and cook for about 15 minutes, until the rice is tender and the stock has been absorbed. Season to taste with salt. Spread out a dampened tea towel on a work surface. Remove the paella pan from the heat and place it on the tea towel. Garnish the paella with the sardines, red pepper strips and parsley and leave to stand for 5 minutes before serving.

Rice with aubergine and courgettes

ARROZ CON BERENJENAS Y CALABACINES

- **2 tablespoons olive oil**
- **2 onions, chopped**
- **1 clove garlic, chopped**
- **2 courgettes, diced**
- **1 aubergine, diced**
- **400 g/14 oz long-grain rice**
- **1.2 litres/2 pints boiling vegetable stock (home-made or made with stock cubes)**
- **100 g/3 ½ oz Parmesan cheese, grated**
- **1 tablespoon chopped fresh parsley**
- **salt**

Serves 6

Heat the oil in a paella pan or large, heavy-based frying pan. Add the onion and garlic and cook over a low heat, stirring occasionally, for 5 minutes, until softened and translucent. Add the courgette and aubergine and cook, stirring occasionally, for a further 5 minutes. Stir in the rice and cook, stirring constantly, for 2 minutes, then pour in half the boiling stock. Cook until almost all the stock has been absorbed, then pour in the remaining stock and cook until it has been absorbed and the rice is tender. This will take 15–20 minutes. Season to taste with salt. Sprinkle the Parmesan and parsley over the rice and serve immediately.

Chicken risotto

RISOTTO DE POLLO

- 1 chicken, about 1 kg/2 ¼ lb
- 1 stick celery
- 1 carrot
- 1 onion, plus 1 small onion,
  very finely chopped
- 100 g/3 ½ oz butter
- 200 ml/7 fl oz dry white wine
- 200 g/7 oz risotto (arborio) rice
- 50 g/2 oz Parmesan cheese,
  grated
- salt and pepper

Serves 6

Ask the butcher to bone the chicken and give you the bones. Dice the chicken meat. Put the chicken bones, celery, carrot and whole onion into a saucepan, pour in 1.5 litres/2 ½ pints water, season with salt and pepper and bring to the boil. Lower the heat and simmer for 30 minutes. Strain the stock and pour 500 ml/18 fl oz into a clean saucepan. Return this to the heat and bring to simmering point. Melt 65 g/2 ½ oz of the butter in another saucepan. Add the chopped onion and the chicken meat and cook over a low heat, stirring frequently, for about 10 minutes, until lightly browned. Season with salt and pepper and pour in the wine. Simmer for 12–15 minutes, until the liquid has evaporated. Stir in the rice and cook, stirring constantly, for about 2 minutes, until translucent. Add a ladleful of the stock and cook, stirring constantly, until all the liquid has been absorbed. Continue adding the stock, a ladleful at a time, stirring constantly. Do not add more stock until the previous addition has been absorbed. When all the stock has been absorbed and the risotto is creamy – this will take about 20 minutes – remove the pan from the heat and stir in the remaining butter and the Parmesan. Cover and leave to stand for a few minutes before serving.

209

Baked rice

ARROZ AL HORNO

- 5 tablespoons olive oil
- 2 cloves garlic, chopped
- 250 g/9 oz tomatoes, peeled, seeded and finely chopped
- 500 g/1 lb 2 oz potatoes, sliced
- 500 g/1 lb 2 oz long-grain rice
- salt

Serves 6

Preheat the oven to 200°C/400°F/Gas Mark 6. Heat the oil in a flameproof casserole. Add the garlic and cook, stirring frequently, for 2 minutes. Add the tomato and cook, stirring occasionally, for 8 minutes, then add the potato. Season with salt, add the rice and pour in 1.2 litres/2 pints water. Bring to the boil, then cover and transfer the casserole to the oven. Bake for about 20 minutes, until the rice is dry and lightly browned. Serve immediately straight from the casserole.

210

Rice with sherry

ARROZ AL JEREZ

- 5 tablespoons olive oil
- 150 g/5 oz onion, finely chopped
- 175 ml/6 fl oz sherry
- 500 g/1 lb 2 oz long-grain rice
- 1.2 litres/2 pints boiling chicken stock (home-made or made with stock cubes)
- 25 g/1 oz butter, softened
- salt

Serves 4–6

Preheat the oven to 200°C/400°F/Gas Mark 6. Heat the oil in a flameproof casserole. Add the onion and cook over a low heat, stirring occasionally, for 6–8 minutes, until beginning to brown. Stir in the sherry and rice, then pour in the boiling stock and season with salt. Cover the casserole, transfer to the oven and bake for about 20 minutes, until the rice is tender. Just before serving, stir in the butter until melted. Serve straight from the casserole.

Pulses

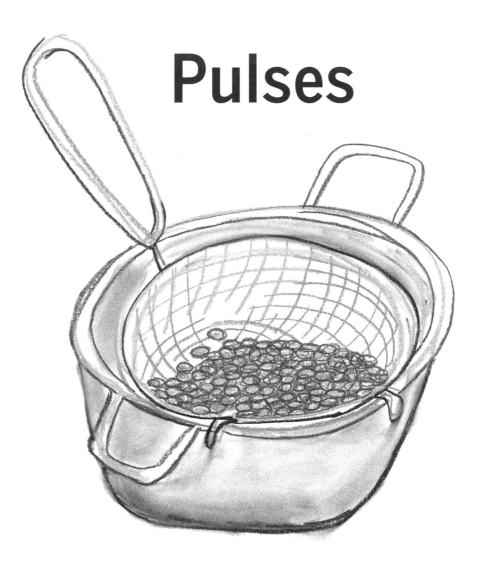

Tradition has it that soaking most dried beans for several hours or overnight makes them easier to digest and reduces the possibility of flatullence, as the water leeches out the indigestible substances they contain. Recent research has sparked debate on the topic of soaking, nevertheless I like to soak my beans.

Tricks

- It is important not to add salt to pulses before cooking them, as it will make them tough. For the same reason, it is important to put them in a saucepan of cold water and cook them over a low heat.
- Cooking in hard water prolongs the cooking time. You can add a pinch of bicarbonate of soda to counteract this, but it changes the flavour slightly and destroys the vitamin B.
- Pulses are enhanced if you add an onion, carrot, bouquet garni, garlic clove or other fla-vouring when they are cooking.
- Do not discard the cooking water as mineral salts and other nutrients will be dissolved in it.

Chickpeas

Tricks

- When soaking chickpeas, add a pinch of bicarbonate of soda. This helps to soften them and improves their digestibility.
- To avoid chick-peas becoming tough, do not add salt until they have been cooking for some time.
- For tender results, add warm rather than cold water to chickpeas, and if it is necessary to top them up with stock during the cooking time heat it first.

211

Baked leftover stew
RESTO DE COCIDO EN FORMA DE BUDÍN

- **sunflower oil, for brushing**
- **breadcrumbs, for sprinkling**
- **1–1.5 litres/1 ¾–2 ½ pints leftover stew**
- **3 eggs, separated**
- **1 quantity Classic Tomato Sauce (see recipe 73)**

Serves 6

Preheat the oven to 180°C/350°F/Gas Mark 4. Brush a loaf tin with the oil and sprinkle with the breadcrumbs, tipping out any excess. Put all the leftover stew through a mincer or process very briefly in a food processor. Lightly beat the egg yolks in a bowl, then stir them into the stew. Whisk the egg whites in a clean, dry bowl until they form soft peaks. Gently fold them into the mixture. Turn the mixture into the prepared tin. Place the tin in a roasting tin and pour in boiling water to come halfway up the sides. Bake for 20–30 minutes, until set. Remove the tin and turn out on to a warm serving dish. Serve immediately, offering the tomato sauce separately.

212

Dressed chickpeas

GARBANZOS ALIÑADOS

- 750 g/1 lb 10 oz dried chickpeas
- pinch of bicarbonate of soda
- 1 veal knuckle, preferably fatty
- 2 leeks, halved lengthways and rinsed well
- 250 g/9 oz carrots, halved lengthways
- 3 tomatoes, sliced
- salt

Dressing:
- 3 tablespoons white-wine vinegar
- 9 tablespoons sunflower oil
- 2 hard-boiled eggs, chopped
- 1 teaspoon very finely chopped fresh parsley
- 1 teaspoon chopped onion (optional)
- salt

Serves 6

Put the chickpeas in a bowl, pour in warm water to cover and add the bicarbonate of soda and a pinch of salt. Leave to soak for at least 12 hours, then drain and rinse well. Put the chickpeas in a saucepan and pour in hot, but not boiling, water to cover. Add a pinch of salt, the veal knuckle, leeks and carrots and bring to the boil. Lower the heat to medium or medium–low and cook for 2–3 hours, until the chickpeas are tender. (The time depends on the type and age of the chickpeas and the softness of the water.) Drain the chickpeas, reserving 2 tablespoons of the cooking liquid. Spoon the chickpeas into a mound on a round serving dish. Arrange the tomato slices around them and put the carrots on top of them in the shape of a star. Top with one-quarter of the chopped hard-boiled eggs (see dressing ingredients). To make the dressing, whisk the vinegar with a pinch of salt in a bowl, then gradually whisk in the oil. Stir in the reserved cooking liquid, the remaining chopped hard-boiled eggs, the parsley, and the onion if using. Pour into a sauce boat and serve with the chickpeas.

Note: The cooking liquid from the chickpeas is very good and can be used to cook rice, make soup, etc.

213

Fried chickpeas

GARBANZOS REFRITOS

- **500 g/1 lb 2 oz dried chickpeas**
- **pinch of bicarbonate of soda**
- **100 g/3 ½ oz lard**
- **1 onion, finely chopped**
- **3 ripe tomatoes,**
  seeded and chopped
- **1 teaspoon paprika**
- **½ cantimpalo chorizo**
  (finger-sized dried pork
  sausage with garlic and paprika),
  skinned and thinly sliced
- **salt**

Serves 4

Put the chickpeas in a bowl, pour in warm water to cover and add the bicarbonate of soda and a pinch of salt. Leave to soak for at least 12 hours, then drain and rinse well. Bring a saucepan of salted water to just below boiling point. Add the chickpeas, cover the pan and cook over a medium heat for about 2 hours, until tender but not falling apart. (The time depends on the type and age of the chickpeas and the softness of the water.) Meanwhile, melt the lard in a frying pan. Add the onion and cook over a low heat, stirring occasionally, for about 5 minutes, until softened and translucent. Add the tomato and cook, stirring and breaking it up with the side of a spoon, for 10 minutes. Stir in the paprika and chorizo, then remove the pan from the heat. Drain the chickpeas, add them to the frying pan and cook over a high heat, stirring constantly, for 5 minutes. Serve immediately.

Note: This recipe can be made with chickpeas left over from a stew made the day before, in which case they will need to be heated for a little longer.

Poor man's chickpeas

GARBANZOS A LO POBRE

- 500 g/1 lb 2 oz dried chickpeas
- pinch of bicarbonate of soda
- 2 beef shin bones
- 1 ham bone
- 500 g/1 lb 2 oz potatoes, diced
- 3–4 tablespoons olive oil
- 1 large onion, chopped
- 2 cloves garlic, finely chopped
- 1 tablespoon plain flour
- 1 teaspoon paprika
- 5 tablespoons white wine
- 1 ½ tablespoons chopped
  fresh parsley
- salt

Serves 4

Put the chickpeas in a bowl, pour in warm water to cover and add the bicarbonate of soda and a pinch of salt. Leave to soak for at least 12 hours, then drain and rinse well. Put the chickpeas in a large saucepan, pour in hot, but not boiling, water to cover and add the beef bones, ham bone and a pinch of salt. (Remember that the ham bone will probably be quite salty.) Cook for 1 ½ hours. (Alternatively, cook the chickpeas and bones in a pressure cooker on high for 25 minutes.) Add the potato and cook for a further 15–20 minutes, until the potato is tender. Meanwhile, heat the oil in a frying pan. Add the onion and cook over a low heat, stirring occasionally, for about 6 minutes, until softened but not coloured. Add the garlic, stir in the flour and cook for a further 4 minutes. Remove the pan from the heat and add the paprika, then return the pan to the heat. Pour in the wine, add about 300 ml / ½ pint of the cooking liquid from the chickpeas and cook for a further 5 minutes. Meanwhile, remove the bones from the pan containing the chickpeas and drain off most of the remaining cooking liquid, depending on how soupy you like the dish. Add the onion and tomato mixture to the chickpeas and cook for 10 minutes. Taste and adjust the seasoning, sprinkle with the parsley and serve.

Chickpea stew with spinach
POTAJE CON ESPINACAS

- **500 g/1 lb 2 oz dried chickpeas**
- **pinch of bicarbonate of soda**
- **200 g/7 oz salt cod fillet**
- **½ bulb garlic**
- **1 bay leaf**
- **2 small onions**
- **1 kg/2 ¼ lb spinach,**
  coarse stalks removed
- **6 tablespoons olive oil**
- **1 large tomato,**
  seeded and chopped
- **1 tablespoon plain flour**
- **1 teaspoon paprika**
- **1 sprig fresh parsley**
- **salt**

Serves 4

Put the chickpeas in a bowl, pour in warm water to cover and add the bicarbonate of soda and a pinch of salt. Leave to soak for at least 12 hours, then drain and rinse well. Meanwhile, put the salt cod in a bowl, add cold water to cover and leave to soak for at least 12 hours, changing the water three or four times. (Each time you change the water rinse out the bowl as salt tends to deposit on the base.) Put the chickpeas into a large saucepan and pour in hot, but not boiling, water to cover. Reserve a garlic clove and add the remainder of the bulb to the pan with the bay leaf and one of the onions. Cook over a medium heat for 2 ¼–2 ½ hours. Drain the salt cod, add to the pan and cook for a further 30 minutes. Add the spinach and cook for 8 minutes more. Finely chop the remaining onion. Heat the oil in a frying pan. Add the chopped onion and cook over a low heat, stirring occasionally, for 10 minutes, until lightly golden. Add the tomato and cook, stirring and breaking it up with the side of the spoon, for a further 10 minutes. Stir in the flour and cook, stirring constantly, for 2–3 minutes. Stir in the paprika and remove the pan from the heat. Allow the mixture to cool slightly, then transfer to a food processor, process to a purée and stir into the chickpeas. Season to taste with salt. Pound the parsley with the reserved garlic clove in a mortar, stir in 1 tablespoon of the cooking liquid from the chickpeas, then stir into the pan. Cook for 15–20 minutes and serve in a soup tureen.

Note: Some people like to add little Dumplings (see recipe 150) to this dish. Roll the dumplings in breadcrumbs and fry in olive oil until golden brown all over. Add to the stew after adding the tomato and onion mixture.

Chickpea stew with rice and potatoes

POTAJE CON ARROZ Y PATATAS

- **400 g/14 oz dried chickpeas**
- **pinch of bicarbonate of soda**
- **2 tablespoons olive oil**
- **1 onion**
- **2 cloves**
- **500 g/1 lb 2 oz potatoes, diced**
- **250 g/9 oz long-grain rice**
- **1 clove garlic**
- **pinch of saffron threads**
- **1 sprig fresh parsley**
- **salt**

Serves 4

Put the chickpeas in a bowl, pour in warm water to cover and add the bicarbonate of soda and a pinch of salt. Leave to soak for at least 12 hours, then drain and rinse well. Preheat the oven to 200°C/400°F/ Gas Mark 6. Put the chickpeas in a saucepan, pour in hot, but not boiling, water to cover and add the oil and a pinch of salt. Cook over a medium heat for about 2 ½ hours, until the chickpeas are softening. (The time depends on the type and age of the chickpeas and the softness of the water.) Meanwhile, stud the onion with the cloves and roast in the oven until golden on the outside. Remove from the oven and add to the chickpeas along with the potato, and cook for a further 15 minutes. Add the rice and cook for a further 20 minutes. Pound the garlic, saffron, parsley and a pinch of salt in a mortar, stir in 2 tablespoons of the cooking liquid from the chickpeas, then add to the pan. Season to taste with salt and serve in a soup tureen.

217

Haricot bean stew

JUDÍAS BLANCAS GUISADAS

- 675 g / 1 ½ lb dried haricot beans,
  soaked for 3 hours or overnight
  in cold water and drained
- ½ garlic bulb, roasted
  (see Note below)
- 1 bay leaf
- 2 small onions
- 1 chorizo or Asturian black
  pudding
- 4 tablespoons olive oil
- 1 tablespoon plain flour
- 1 teaspoon paprika
- salt

Serves 6

Put the beans into a saucepan and pour in water to cover. Cover and bring to the boil, then remove the pan from the heat and drain. Return the beans to the pan, pour in fresh cold water to cover, add the roasted garlic, bay leaf, one of the whole onions and the chorizo or black pudding and cook for about 30 minutes over a medium heat. Add 250 ml / 8 fl oz cold water, bring back to the boil and simmer for a further 30 minutes. Do this twice more at 30-minute intervals, then simmer for a further 30 minutes (making a total cooking time of about 2 ½ hours). Chop the remaining onion. Heat the oil in a frying pan. Add the chopped onion and cook over a medium heat, stirring occasionally, for about 10 minutes, until lightly browned. Stir in the flour and cook, stirring constantly, for about 10 minutes, until lightly browned. Stir in the paprika and 3–4 tablespoons of the cooking liquid from the beans. Remove the pan from the heat and allow to cool slightly, then transfer the mixture to a food processor, process to a purée and stir into the beans. Season to taste with salt. Remove the chorizo or black pudding, cut into slices and return to the pan. Remove and discard the bay leaf. Ladle into a soup tureen and serve immediately.

Notes: If the beans are less than a year old, they do not need to be soaked before cooking. To roast the garlic bulb, spear it with a fork and hold it in a gas flame, turning frequently. Alternatively, place on a sheet of foil, douse with olive oil and roast under a preheated grill, turning frequently.

Haricot bean salad

JUDÍAS BLANCAS EN ENSALADA

- **675 g/1 ½ lb dried haricot beans, soaked overnight in cold water and drained**
- **1 small onion, halved, plus 1 tablespoon finely chopped onion**
- **1 bay leaf**
- **3 tablespoons white-wine vinegar**
- **9 tablespoons sunflower oil**
- **1 teaspoon chopped fresh parsley**
- **salt**

Serves 6

Put the beans into a saucepan and pour in water to cover. Cover and bring to the boil, then remove the pan from the heat and drain. Return the beans to the pan, pour in fresh cold water to cover, add the onion halves and bay leaf and cook over a medium heat for about 30 minutes. Add 250 ml/8 fl oz cold water, bring back to the boil and simmer for a further 30 minutes. Do this twice more at 30-minute intervals, then simmer for a further 30 minutes (making a total cooking time of about 2 ½ hours) until the beans are tender but not falling apart (the cooking time depends on the age of the beans). Remove the pan from the heat and drain. Remove and discard the bay leaf and onion halves and leave the beans to cool. Put the beans into a salad bowl. Whisk the vinegar with a pinch of salt in another bowl, then whisk in the oil. Pour the dressing over the beans, add the parsley and chopped onion and toss lightly to mix. Garnish with tomato slices, if you like, and serve.

Haricot beans with egg topping

JUDÍAS BLANCAS CON COSTRA

- **600 g/1 lb 5 oz dried haricot beans, soaked overnight in cold water and drained**
- **1 bay leaf**
- **1 onion, halved, plus 2 tablespoons finely chopped onion**
- **4 tablespoons olive oil**
- **1 kg/2 ¼ lb tomatoes, chopped**
- **1 teaspoon sugar**
- **250 g/9 oz canned peas, drained**
- **3 eggs, lightly beaten**
- **salt**

Serves 6

Put the beans into a saucepan and pour in water to cover. Cover and bring to the boil, then remove the pan from the heat and drain. Return the beans to the pan, pour in fresh cold water to cover, add the bay leaf and onion halves and cook over a medium heat for about 30 minutes. Add 250 ml/8 fl oz cold water, bring back to the boil and simmer for a further 30 minutes. Do this twice more at 30-minute intervals, then simmer for a further 30 minutes until the beans are tender (making a total cooking time of about 2 ½ hours). Meanwhile, heat the oil in a frying pan. Add the chopped onion and cook over a low heat, stirring occasionally, for about 10 minutes, until lightly golden. Add the tomato and cook, stirring and breaking it up with the side of the spoon, for 15 minutes. Remove the pan from the heat and allow to cool slightly, then transfer the mixture to a food processor and process to a purée. Return the purée to the frying pan, stir in the sugar and season to taste with salt. Preheat the oven to 200°C/400°F/Gas Mark 6. Drain the beans well and stir them into the tomato sauce with half the peas. Taste and adjust the seasoning, then pour the mixture into an ovenproof dish. Sprinkle the remaining peas on top, then pour the eggs over them. Bake for about 10 minutes, until the eggs have set. Serve immediately straight from the dish.

220

Haricot beans with black pudding
JUDÍAS BLANCAS GUISADA CON MORCILLAS

- 500 g/1 lb 2 oz dried haricot
  beans, soaked overnight in cold
  water and drained
- 1 small onion, plus 1 large onion,
  finely chopped
- 6 tablespoons olive oil
- 1 bay leaf
- 2 cloves garlic, finely chopped
- 1 black pudding,
  skinned and chopped
- 175 ml/6 fl oz white wine
- 1 tablespoon white-wine vinegar
- 1 sprig fresh parsley
- salt and pepper

Serves 4

Put the beans into a saucepan and pour in water to cover. Bring to the boil, then remove the pan from the heat and drain, reserving the cooking water. Return the beans to the pan, pour in fresh cold water to cover, add the small onion, 1 tablespoon of the oil and the bay leaf and bring back to the boil. Lower the heat and simmer for about 1 ½ hours, then drain. Heat the remaining oil in another saucepan. Add the chopped onion and garlic and cook over a low heat, stirring occasionally, for 8–10 minutes, until lightly browned. Add the black pudding and cook for 2–3 minutes. Add the beans, wine, vinegar and parsley and pour in enough of the reserved cooking liquid to cover. Cover the pan and simmer gently for about 30 minutes, until the beans are tender. (The time depends on the age of the beans and the softness of the water.) Season to taste with salt and pepper, mix well and simmer for about 5 minutes more. Remove and discard the parsley. Serve immediately.

221

Haricot bean garnish
JUDÍAS BLANCAS DE ADORNO

- 300 g/11 oz dried haricot beans,
  soaked for 3 hours in cold water
  and drained
- 1 bay leaf
- 1 small onion, halved
- 80 g/3 oz butter
- 1 teaspoon chopped
  fresh parsley
- salt

Serves 6

Put the beans into a saucepan and pour in water to cover. Cover and bring to the boil, then remove the pan from the heat and drain. Return the beans to the pan, pour in fresh cold water to cover, add the bay leaf and onion halves and cook over a medium heat for about 30 minutes. Add 250 ml/8 fl oz cold water, bring back to the boil and simmer for a further 30 minutes. Do this twice more at 30-minute intervals, then simmer for a further 30 minutes (making a total cooking time of about 2 ½ hours). Drain the beans in a large colander. Melt the butter in a frying pan and add the beans. Season to taste with salt and sprinkle with the parsley. Do not let the beans brown or they will become hard. These beans go well with roast leg of lamb.

White beans with sausages and bacon

JUDÍAS BLANCAS CON SALCHICHAS Y BACON

- 500 g/1 lb 2 oz large dried white beans, such as butter beans, soaked for 2 hours in cold water and drained
- 1 ham hock, about 250 g/9 oz
- 2 bacon rashers, about 5 mm/¼ inch thick
- bouquet garni (1 sprig fresh parsley, 1 bay leaf and 1 clove garlic tied together in muslin)
- 3 tablespoons olive oil
- 6 fresh sausages
- 6 frankfurter sausages
- 40 g/1 ½ oz butter
- 1 teaspoon chopped fresh parsley
- salt

Serves 6

Put the beans into a saucepan and pour in water to cover. Bring to the boil over a low heat, then remove the pan from the heat and drain. Return the beans to a clean pan and pour in fresh cold water to cover, then bring to the boil over a low heat and cook for 15 minutes. Add 250 ml/8 fl oz cold water, bring back to the boil and simmer for a further 15 minutes. Add another 250 ml/8 fl oz cold water, bring back to the boil and cook for 15 minutes more. Add the ham hock, bacon and bouquet garni and cook for a further 1 ½ hours, until the beans are almost tender. (If necessary, add more cold water during the cooking to prevent the beans drying out.) Meanwhile, heat the oil in a frying pan, add the fresh sausages and cook over a medium heat, turning occasionally, until browned all over and cooked through. (Prick the sausages first if they have artificial casings.) Season the beans to taste with salt, add the frankfurters and cook for 10 minutes. Remove and discard the bouquet garni. Melt the butter in another saucepan and add the parsley. Using a slotted spoon, transfer the beans to the butter and parsley mixture and stir well. Cut the ham into six pieces and the bacon rashers into three pieces each. Divide the beans among six warmed plates. Add a piece of ham, two pieces of bacon, a frankfurter and a fried sausage to each and serve immediately.

Note: The cooking liquid from the beans is delicious. To make a soup, mix 2 tablespoons potato flour with 4 tablespoons water and add to the cooking liquid with 25 g/1 oz butter, fresh parsley and 1 egg yolk.

223

Bean stew

FABADA

- 500 g/1 lb 2 oz dried Asturian beans or butter beans, soaked for 3 hours or overnight in cold water and drained
- 1 large onion, cut into 4 pieces
- 2 cloves garlic
- 150 ml/¼ pint olive oil
- ½ pig's ear
- 1 pig's tail or pig's trotter
- 1 teaspoon paprika
- 1 Serrano ham hock, about 100 g/3 ½ oz
- 2 chorizos
- 100 g/3 ½ oz streaky bacon
- 2 Asturian black puddings
- pinch of saffron threads
- salt

Serves 6

Put the beans into a saucepan and pour in cold water to cover. Bring to the boil over a low heat, then remove the pan from the heat and drain. Return the beans to a clean pan, pour in fresh cold water to cover and add the onion, garlic, oil, pig's ear, pig's tail or trotter and the paprika. Mix well and, if necessary, add more cold water to cover the contents of the pan. Bring to the boil over a low heat and cook for 30 minutes. Add the ham hock and chorizos and cook for a further 30 minutes. Add the bacon and cook for 30–60 minutes more, until the beans are almost tender. Add the black puddings and cook for a final 30 minutes. Remove the ham hock, cut it into bite-sized pieces, and return the pieces to the pan. Crush the saffron in a mortar and stir in 2 tablespoons of the cooking liquid from the beans, then stir into the stew. Season to taste with salt and serve.

Notes: It is not usual to serve the tail or the ear, although some people like them and leave them in the stew. If serving the ear, cut it into fine strips first. This bean stew is much better made the previous day and reheated. It is also usual to remove a ladleful of beans, make a purée with them and then use the purée to thicken the stew.

Beans with clams

FABES CON ALMEJAS

- 500 g/1 lb 2 oz dried Asturian
  beans or butter beans, soaked
  overnight in cold water and
  drained
- 3 tablespoons olive oil
- 1 clove garlic
- 1 bay leaf
- 1 small onion
- 3–4 sprigs fresh parsley,
  tied together with kitchen twine
  or thread
- pinch of saffron threads
- 3 tablespoons breadcrumbs
- 400 g/14 oz carpetshell,
  Venus or warty Venus clams
- dash of white-wine vinegar
- salt

Serves 4

Put the beans into a saucepan and pour in cold water to cover. Bring to the boil over a low heat. Meanwhile, put the oil, garlic, bay leaf, whole onion and parsley in another large saucepan and pour in a little cold water. When the beans come to the boil, remove the pan from the heat and drain. Tip the beans into the pan with the parsley and add cold water to cover generously. Cover and cook over a low heat for 1 ½ hours, adding more cold water if necessary. Crush the saffron in a mortar and stir in 2 tablespoons of the cooking liquid from the beans, then stir into the pan. Sprinkle the breadcrumbs over the mixture in the pan, cover and simmer gently over a very low heat for a further 30 minutes, until the beans are tender. (The total cooking time depends on the type and age of the beans and the softness of the water.) Meanwhile, wash the clams in cold water with a little salt and the vinegar. Discard any with broken shells or any that do not shut immediately when sharply tapped. Put them into a frying pan or saucepan, add 175 ml/6 fl oz water, cover and cook over a high heat, shaking the pan occasionally, for 3–5 minutes, until the shells have opened. Remove the clams with a slotted spoon, reserving the cooking liquid. Discard any that remain shut. Remove the clams from their shells or, if you prefer, discard the empty half shells, and leave the clams on the half shell. Put the clams in a bowl and strain the reserved cooking liquid over them through a muslin-lined sieve. Set aside. About 15 minutes before you're ready to serve, add the clams and their cooking liquid to the beans. Serve in a warm deep dish.

225 Pinto or kidney beans with red wine

JUDÍAS PINTAS O ENCARNADAS CON VINO TINTO

- 500 g/1 lb 2 oz dried pinto or
  kidney beans, soaked overnight
  in cold water and drained
- 150 g/5 oz streaky bacon
  in a single piece
- 1 veal knuckle
- 2 cloves
- 5 tablespoons olive oil
- 1 onion, finely chopped
- 2 cloves garlic, finely chopped
- 1 heaped tablespoon plain flour
- 300 ml/½ pint red wine
- salt

Serves 4

Put the beans into a saucepan and pour in water to cover. Bring to the boil, then remove the pan from the heat and drain. Return the beans to the pan, pour in fresh cold water to cover and add the bacon, veal knuckle and cloves. Bring to the boil, then lower the heat and simmer for 1 ½ hours until the beans are beginning to soften. (The time depends on the type and age of the beans and the softness of the water.) Meanwhile, heat the oil in a frying pan. Add the onion and garlic and cook over a low heat, stirring occasionally, for 10 minutes, until beginning to brown, Stir in the flour and cook, stirring constantly, for 2–3 minutes, then gradually stir in the wine a little at a time. Stir the mixture into the beans and simmer for a further 30 minutes. Season to taste with salt. Remove the bacon, cut into pieces and return to the pan. Remove and discard the veal knuckle and cloves. Serve the beans in a warm deep dish.

Note: To reduce the cooking time, once the beans have come to the boil the first time, drain and transfer them to a pressure cooker with the bacon, veal knuckle and cloves. Bring to high pressure and cook for 30 minutes, then remove the lid (once the pressure has reduced) and proceed as described above.

Pinto beans with rice

JUDÍAS PINTAS CON ARROZ

- 400 g/14 oz dried pinto beans, soaked overnight in cold water and drained
- 1 onion, cut into quarters
- 1 bay leaf
- 2 cloves garlic
- 400 g/14 oz long-grain rice
- 4 tablespoons olive oil
- 1 tablespoon plain flour
- ½ teaspoon paprika
- 40 g/1 ½ oz butter
- salt

Serves 4

Put the beans into a saucepan and pour in enough water to cover. Cover and bring to the boil, then remove the pan from the heat and drain. Return the beans to the pan, pour in fresh cold water to cover generously and add half the onion, the bay leaf and one of the garlic cloves, then cook over a medium heat for about 30 minutes. Add 250 ml/8 fl oz cold water, bring back to the boil and simmer for a further 30 minutes. Do this twice more at 30-minute intervals, then simmer for a further 30–90 minutes (making a total cooking time of 2 ½–3 ½ hours). Meanwhile, cook the rice in boiling water and rinse under cold running water as described in recipe 173. Drain well and set aside. Chop the remaining onion and lightly crush the remaining garlic clove. Heat the oil in a frying pan. Add the chopped onion and garlic and cook over a low heat, stirring occasionally, for about 8 minutes, until beginning to brown. Stir in the flour and cook, stirring constantly, for about 10 minutes, until lightly browned. Stir in the paprika, followed immediately by 3–4 tablespoons of the cooking liquid from the beans. Stir the contents of the frying pan into the beans and season to taste with salt. Melt the butter in another saucepan. Add the rice, season with salt and heat through, stirring with a wooden spoon. Spoon the rice into a ring mould and turn out on a deep, round serving dish. Spoon the bean mixture into the centre of the rice and serve immediately.

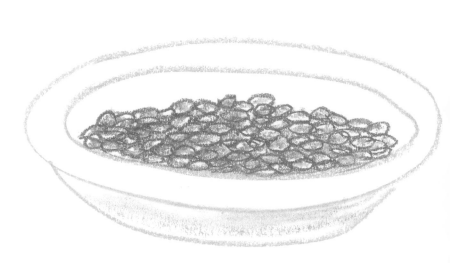

Lentils

Unlike other pulses, it is not necessary to soak lentils. Instead they can be pre-cooked for 15 minutes. In fact, this is better than soaking, which can start fermentation, so making them more indigestible.

227

Lentil stew
LENTEJAS GUISADAS

- 1 onion
- 600 g/1 lb 5 oz lentils
- 1 bay leaf
- 2 cloves garlic, unpeeled
- 275 ml/9 fl oz olive oil
- 2 slices bread
- 1 ripe tomato,
  peeled, seeded and chopped
- ½ teaspoon paprika
- 1 sprig fresh parsley
- salt

Serves 6

Halve the onion and cut one half into pieces. Finely chop the other half. Put the lentils into a saucepan with the bay leaf, the pieces of onion and one of the garlic cloves and pour in water to cover generously. Cover and bring to the boil, then lower the heat and simmer for 1–2 hours, until the lentils are tender. (The cooking time depends on the type of lentil.) Heat the oil in a frying pan. Add the slices of bread and cook, turning occasionally, until crisp and evenly golden. Drain on kitchen paper and set aside. Drain off most of the oil, leaving just enough to cover the base of the frying pan, and reheat. Add the chopped onion and cook over a low heat, stirring occasionally, for about 8 minutes, until beginning to brown. Add the tomato and cook, stirring occasionally, for 10 minutes. Remove the pan from the heat, stir in the paprika and add the mixture to the lentils. Peel the remaining garlic clove, then pound in a mortar with a pinch of salt and the parsley and fried bread. Mix in 2–3 tablespoons of the cooking liquid from the lentils, then stir into the pan containing the lentils. Season to taste with salt and cook for a further 10 minutes. Remove and discard the bay leaf and garlic clove and serve immediately in a soup tureen.

228

Lentils with bacon and sausages
LENTEJAS CON TOCINO Y SALCHICHAS

- 1 small onion
- 2 cloves
- 600 g/1 lb 5 oz Puy lentils
- 1 bay leaf
- 1 carrot, cut into 4 pieces
- 2 cloves garlic, unpeeled
- 250 g/9 oz bacon in a single piece
- 12 small sausages
- 275 ml/9 fl oz olive oil
- salt

Serves 6

Stud the onion with the cloves. Put the lentils into a saucepan, add the onion, bay leaf, pieces of carrot, garlic cloves and bacon and pour in water to cover generously. Cover and bring to the boil, then lower the heat and simmer for 1–1 ½ hours, until the lentils are tender. Drain the lentils, reserving the cooking liquid. Remove the onion, bay leaf, garlic, carrot and bacon. Cut the bacon into small cubes and set aside. Prick the sausages if they have artificial casings. Heat the oil in a frying pan. Add the sausages and cook, turning frequently, for about 5 minutes, until lightly browned and cooked through. Remove from the pan and keep warm. Drain off about half the oil from the frying pan and reheat. Add the cubes of bacon and cook, stirring, for about 3 minutes, then add the lentils. Stir well and season to taste with salt. Put the lentils into a warm serving dish, place the sausages on top and serve immediately.

Note: Some people prefer a little more liquid in the finished dish. If so, reserve and add some cooking liquid from the lentils to achieve the desired consistency. It's worth reserving the stock anyway in case there are lentils left over. You can purée them in a food processor and make a thick soup, garnishing it with croûtons or a little white rice.

229

Lentil salad
LENTEJAS EN ENSALADA

- 1 small onion
- 2 cloves
- 600 g/1 lb 5 oz Puy lentils
- 1 bay leaf
- 1 carrot, cut into 4 pieces
- 2 cloves garlic, unpeeled
- 12 small sausages
- olive oil
- white-wine vinegar
- salt

Serves 4-6

Proceed as described in recipe 228, but do not use the bacon or sausages. When the lentils are cooked, drain them and remove the bay leaf, onion, garlic and carrot. Put the lentils into a glass or china salad bowl and dress with olive oil, vinegar and a pinch of salt, mixing well. Serve warm or cold.

Note: The lentils can also be mixed with mayonnaise and garnished with drained, canned anchovy fillets and sliced tomatoes.

Potatoes

Origin and season
The potato originated in Peru and was introduced to Europe by the Spanish conquistadores. Pedro Cieza was the first to mention them in 1533. From Spain they travelled to the Netherlands and so to other parts of Europe. They are available all year round, although they have two seasons. New potatoes are in season from late autumn to early summer and maincrop potatoes are in season from mid summer to spring. There are hundreds of varieties: some are better for frying, while others, with softer flesh, are better for mashing and soups.

Selection

Potatoes should have no blemishes and should not show any signs of germination. It is especially important that they do not have green patches as this shows they contain a toxic substance. New potatoes should have a thin skin and be nice and firm.

Nutrition

Depending on how they are cooked, potatoes have 90 calories per 100 g / 3 ½ oz. They are easily digestible as they contain potassium, sugar and starch. Potatoes are rich in vitamin C, although some of this is lost when they are cooked, and contain minerals. They are often recommended for those suffering from ulcers.

How to cook

Potatoes can be prepared many different ways to create economical and tasty dishes full of variety. A basic way to cook them (and the starting point for many recipes) is to wash and dry them without peeling; put the potatoes into a pan with enough cold water to cover generously, a dash of milk and a pinch of salt; bring to the boil, then lower the heat to medium and cook for about 30 minutes. The cooking time depends on the variety of potato. If the potatoes have to be peeled and cut into pieces before cooking, either because the recipe calls for it or to save time, the procedure is the same as above.

Tricks

- Do not leave mashed potato standing for long, as it loses 90–100 per cent of its vitamins
- Be careful not to overcook potatoes to be used in salads
- To make potatoes easier to peel, put them into boiling water for 1–2 minutes first
- To prevent potatoes turning black after they have been peeled leave them in a bowl of water
- Potatoes can be used to remove excess salt from a stew. Simply add a raw potato and leave it to cook for a few minutes in the stew before discarding it
- To keep potatoes looking white, add a little vinegar to the cooking water.

230

Mashed potato
PURÉ DE PATATAS

- **1.2 kg/2 ½ lb potatoes**
- **50 g/2 oz butter,**
  cut into 2–3 pieces
- **250 ml/8 fl oz hot milk**
- **salt**

Serves 6

Cut any large potatoes into pieces. Put the potatoes into a large saucepan and add cold water and about a teaspoon of salt. Make sure the water covers them completely. Bring to the boil, then lower the heat and cook for 20–30 minutes, until tender. Drain well. Put the butter in another saucepan over a low heat. Add the potatoes and mash well. When the butter has been fully incorporated, stir with a wooden spoon and gradually stir in the hot milk. Season to taste with salt. Keep the mashed potato warm over a low heat and serve as soon as possible.

Note: The quantity of milk may be varied according to personal taste.

231

Mashed potato balls
ROLAS DE PURÉ DE PATATAS

- **1.2 kg/2 ½ lb potatoes**
- **4 eggs**
- **120 g/4 oz breadcrumbs**
- **sunflower oil, for deep-frying**
- **salt**

Serves 6

Cut any large potatoes into pieces. Put the potatoes into a large saucepan and add cold water and add a teaspoon of salt. Make sure the water covers them completely. Bring to the boil, then lower the heat and cook for 20–30 minutes, until tender. Drain well and mash immediately. Beat two of the eggs in a bowl and stir them into the mash. Season to taste with salt. Shape the mixture into small balls between the palms of your hands. Beat the remaining eggs in a shallow dish and spread out the breadcrumbs in another shallow dish. Roll the potato balls first in the beaten egg and then in the breadcrumbs. Heat the oil in a deep-fryer or deep saucepan to 180–190°C/350–375°F or until a cube of day-old bread browns in 30 seconds. Add the potato balls and cook until golden brown and crisp on the outside. Drain well and serve immediately.

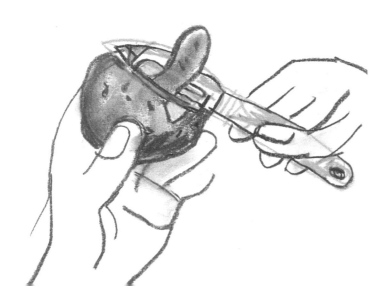

232

Mashed potato with chorizo, bacon and paprika

PURÉ DE PATATAS CON CHORIZO, TOCINO Y PIMENTÓN (REVOLCONAS)

- 1.5 kg/3 ¼ lb potatoes
- 1 clove garlic, unpeeled
- 3 bay leaves
- 175 ml/6 fl oz olive oil
- 1 chorizo,
  about 120 g/4 oz, diced
- 120 g/4 oz bacon, diced
- 1 teaspoon paprika
- salt
- triangles of fried bread
  (see recipe 130)

Serves 6

Cut any large potatoes into pieces. Put the potatoes into a large saucepan with plenty of cold water, a teaspoon of salt, the garlic, bay leaves and 1 tablespoon of the oil. Bring to the boil, then lower the heat and cook for about 20–30 minutes, until tender. Meanwhile, heat the remaining oil in a frying pan. Add the chorizo and bacon and cook, stirring occasionally, for about 5 minutes, until lightly browned. Remove from the pan with a slotted spoon and set aside. Remove the pan from the heat and stir in the paprika, then return the chorizo and the bacon to the pan and keep warm over a low heat. Drain the potato and remove and discard the garlic and bay leaves. Tip into a warm large dish, add the contents of the frying pan, including the oil, and stir well. Serve immediately, garnished with triangles of fried bread.

233

Potato croquettes with salt cod

CROQUETAS DE PURÉ DE PATATAS CON BACALAO

- 250 g/9 oz salt cod fillet
- 1.5 kg/3 ¼ lb red-skinned
  potatoes, unpeeled
- 2 eggs, separated
- sunflower oil
- 1 clove garlic (optional)
- salt
- 2 deep-fried parsley sprigs
  (see recipe 918) or Classic
  Tomato Sauce (see recipe 73)

Serves 6

If the salt cod is not too dry, you can use it straightaway. Otherwise, put in a bowl, add water to cover and leave to soak for several hours, changing the water three or four times (each time you change the water, rinse out the bowl as the salt tends to deposit on the bottom). Drain, then put the cod and the potatoes into a saucepan. Add cold water to cover and bring to the boil. Lower the heat and cook for 20–30 minutes, until the potatoes are tender. Remove the fish and drain. Drain, peel and mash the potatoes before they cool. Remove any skin and bones from the cod and flake the flesh or process in a food processor. Mix the fish with the potato and beat in the egg yolks. If using the garlic, heat 1 tablespoon of the oil in a small frying pan. Add the garlic and cook for a few minutes, until beginning to colour. Remove the garlic from the pan and crush with a pinch of salt in a mortar, then add to the mash. Whisk the egg whites with a pinch of salt in a clean, dry bowl until they form soft peaks. Fold into the potato mixture. Shape the mixture into croquettes with dampened hands. Keep your hands damp to prevent the mash from sticking. Heat the remaining oil in a deep-fryer or deep saucepan to 180–190°C/350–375°F or until a cube of day-old bread browns in 30 seconds. Add the croquettes, in batches of six or eight, and cook until golden brown. Drain well and serve immediately with fried parsley sprigs or with tomato sauce offered separately in a sauce boat.

234

Potatoes baked in béchamel sauce
PATATAS ASADAS AL HORNO CON BECHAMEL

- 1.2 kg/2 ½ lb potatoes, unpeeled
- 1 clove garlic
- 40 g/1 ½ oz butter
- 1 ½ tablespoons olive oil
- 1 ½ tablespoons plain flour
- 1 litre/1 ¾ pints milk
- ½ teaspoon meat extract
- 80 g/3 oz gruyere cheese, grated
- salt

Serves 6

Put the potatoes into a large saucepan of cold water and add 1 tea-spoon salt. Make sure the water covers them completely. Bring to the boil, lower the heat and cook for about 20–30 minutes, until tender but not falling apart. Drain, peel and slice thinly. Rub the garlic clove around the inside of an ovenproof dish and lay half the potato slices in the dish. Preheat the oven to 200°C/400°F/Gas Mark 6. To make a béchamel sauce, melt the butter with the oil in a saucepan. Stir in the flour and cook, stirring constantly, for 2 minutes. Gradually stir in the milk and season lightly with salt (bearing in mind that the cheese and the meat extract will both be salty). Cook, stirring constantly, for about 4 minutes, until thickened, then stir in the meat extract. Pour half the sauce over the potatoes in the dish and top with half the gru-yere. Add the remaining potato slices, pour in the rest of the sauce and sprinkle with the remaining gruyere. Bake for about 15 minutes, until the topping is golden brown. Serve immediately straight from the dish.

235

Potato fritters with grated cheese or nutmeg
BUÑUELOS DE PURÉ DE PATATAS EMPANADOS, CON QUESO RALLADO O NUEZ MOSCADA

- 1.5 kg/3 ¼ lb potatoes, unpeeled
- 20 g/¾ oz butter
- 4 tablespoons warm milk
- 100 g/3 ½ oz gruyere cheese, grated, or a pinch of freshly grated nutmeg
- 4 eggs
- 1 egg white
- 80–120 g/3–4 oz breadcrumbs
- sunflower oil, for deep-frying
- salt
- 1 quantity Classic Tomato Sauce (see recipe 73)

Serves 6

Put the potatoes into a saucepan of cold water and add 1 teaspoon salt. Make sure that the water covers them completely. Bring to the boil, lower the heat and cook for about 20 minutes if they are new potatoes or 30 minutes if not. Drain, peel and mash while still hot. Stir in the butter, warm milk and gruyere or nutmeg. Separate three of the eggs and beat the yolks with the remaining egg. Add to the potatoes, mix well with a wooden spoon and season to taste with salt. Stiffly whisk all the egg whites in a clean, dry bowl and fold them into the mash. Shape the mixture into 5 cm/2 inch square fritters. Spread out the breadcrumbs in a shallow dish and gently roll the fritters in them to coat. Heat the oil in a deep-fryer or deep saucepan to 180–190°C/350–375°F or until a cube of day-old bread browns in 30 seconds. Add the fritters, in batches, and cook until golden brown. Drain well and keep warm until all the batches are cooked. Serve immediately, offering the tomato sauce separately.

236 Important potatoes

PATATAS A LA IMPORTANCIA

- **1 kg/2 ¼ lb potatoes,
  cut into 5-mm/¼-inch slices**
- **80–120 g/3–4 oz plain flour**
- **4 eggs**
- **sunflower oil, for deep-frying**
- **1 clove garlic**
- **pinch of saffron threads**
- **1 onion, very finely chopped**
- **1 tablespoon chopped
  fresh parsley**
- **salt**

Serves 6

Season the potato slices with salt. Reserve 1 tablespoon of the flour and spread out the remainder in a shallow dish. Lightly beat the eggs in another shallow dish. Dip the potato slices first in the flour and then in the beaten egg. Heat the oil in a deep-fryer or saucepan to 180–190°C/350–375°F or until a cube of day-old bread browns in 30 seconds. Add the potato slices, four at a time, and cook un-til golden brown. Remove with a slotted spoon and drain on kitchen paper. Transfer to a flameproof casserole, arranging them in loosely packed layers. Pound the garlic with a pinch of salt in a mortar, stir in the saffron, add a little water and pound again. Transfer 3 tablespoons of the oil to a clean saucepan and heat. Add the onion and cook over a low heat, stirring occasionally, for 5 minutes, until softened. Stir in the reserved flour, then add the contents of the mortar, 1 litre/1 ¾ pints water and a pinch of salt. Strain this mixture over the potatoes, sprinkle with the parsley and simmer over a low heat for 30 minutes. Halfway through the cooking time, preheat the oven to 200°C/400°F/ Gas Mark 6. When the cooking time is up, transfer the casserole to the oven and bake for 10 minutes. Serve immediately straight from the casserole.

237 Potatoes with chorizo

PATATAS CON CHORIZO

- **2 tablespoons olive oil**
- **3 cloves garlic, lightly crushed**
- **2 teaspoons paprika**
- **1 small onion**
- **1 bay leaf**
- **6 black peppercorns**
- **6 pieces of cooking chorizo
  (see Note)**
- **1.5 kg/3 ¼ lb potatoes**
- **salt**

Serves 6

Heat the oil in a frying pan. Add the garlic and cook, stirring occasion-ally, for a few minutes, until beginning to brown. Remove the pan from the heat and stir in the paprika, then pour the contents of the pan into a flameproof casserole. Pour in 1.5 litres/2 ½ pints water, add the onion, bay leaf, peppercorns and chorizo and bring to the boil. Lower the heat, cover and simmer for 1 hour. Insert a knife a little way into each potato and twist slightly as you pull it out to split the potato. Add the potatoes to the casserole. If there is not enough liquid just to cover the potatoes, add a little water. Season to taste with salt, re-cover the casserole and simmer for 45 minutes. Remove the casserole from the heat and leave to stand for 5 minutes before serving.

Note: For this recipe it's best to use the long thin cooking chorizo; the type used for stews rather than the kind intended for slicing and eating raw. The pieces of chorizo (one per serving) should each be about 4 cm/1 ½ inches long.

238

Potato gratin
PURÉ DE PATATAS AL GRATÉN

- 1 kg/2 ¼ lb potatoes,
  cut into large pieces
- 100 g/3 ½ oz butter,
  plus extra for greasing
- 250 ml/8 fl oz hot milk
- 100 g/3 ½ oz cheese, such as
  Cheddar or gruyere, grated
- 2 eggs, separated
- 2 egg whites
- salt

Serves 6

Put the potato into a saucepan, pour in water to cover and add 1 teaspoon salt. Bring to the boil, lower the heat and cook for 20–30 minutes, until tender. Preheat the oven to 200°C/400°F/Gas Mark 4. Grease a gratin dish with butter. Drain and mash the potatoes, while they are still hot, then stir in the butter, hot milk, 80 g/3 oz of the cheese and the egg yolks. Stiffly whisk all the egg whites in a clean, dry bowl and fold into the mixture. Spoon the mixture into the prepared dish, sprinkle with the remaining cheese and use a tablespoon to make a pattern on the top. Bake for about 30 minutes, until the top is golden. Serve immediately straight from the dish.

239

Tuna, mayonnaise and potato roll
BRAZO DE GITANO DE PURÉ DE PATATAS, ATÚN Y MAYONESA

- 1.5 kg/3 ½ lb potatoes
- 50 g/2 oz butter
- 175 ml/6 fl oz hot milk
- 250 g/9 oz canned tuna, drained
- 3 firm tomatoes
- 50 g/2 oz black olives
- salt
- lettuce leaves

  Mayonnaise:
- 2 eggs
- juice of ½ lemon
- 450 ml/¾ pint sunflower oil
- salt

Serves 6

Make the mayonnaise as described in recipe 106, cover and leave to stand in a cool place or in the refrigerator. Boil and mash the potatoes with the butter and milk as described in recipe 230. Flake the tuna and mix it with 3–4 tablespoons of the mayonnaise. Peel, seed and dice one of the tomatoes. Slice the remainder. Soak a clean tea towel in hot water and wring it out well. Spread it out on a work surface and put the mashed potato on it. Use a large spoon to spread out the potato until it is about 1.5 cm/½ inch thick. Spoon the tuna and mayonnaise mixture in a strip along the middle, together with the diced tomato. Using the tea towel to help, roll up the mashed potato like a Swiss roll. Spread some of the mayonnaise on top of the roll and garnish with the tomato slices, olives and lettuce leaves. Chill in the refrigerator for at least 1 hour and serve, with the remaining mayonnaise offered separately.

Note: You can make this roll with cooked minced meat or cooked peeled prawns instead of canned tuna.

240 Fish and potato roll with tomato sauce

BRAZO DE GITANO DE PURÉ DE PATATAS, PESCADO Y SALSA DE TOMATE

- 1.2 kg/2 ½ lb potatoes
- 50 g/2 oz butter
- 275 ml/9 fl oz hot milk
- 500 g/1 lb 2 oz firm white fish fillets
- 2 tablespoons white wine
- ½ small onion
- 1 bay leaf
- pinch of freshly grated nutmeg
- salt
- black or green olives (optional)
- 1 quantity Classic Tomato Sauce (see recipe 73)

Serves 6

Boil and mash the potatoes with the butter and hot milk as described in recipe 230. Meanwhile, put the fish in a saucepan, pour in cold water to cover and add the wine, onion, bay leaf and a pinch of salt. Cover and bring to the boil, then remove the pan from the heat and leave to stand, still covered, for 5 minutes. Lift out the fish with a fish slice and remove and discard any skin and bones. Flake the fish and mix with 3 tablespoons of the tomato sauce and the nutmeg. Preheat the oven to 180°C/350°F/Gas Mark 4. Soak a tea towel in hot water and wring it out well. Spread it out on a work surface and put the mashed potato on it. Make the potato and fish roll as described in recipe 239, working as quickly as possible to prevent the ingredients getting too cold. Place the roll in an ovenproof dish, pour the tomato sauce over it and bake for about 5 minutes, until heated through. Serve immediately, garnished with olives, if you like. If there is any tomato sauce left over, serve it in a sauce boat.

241 Mashed potato with eggs

PURÉ DE PATATAS CON HUEVOS

- 1 kg/2 ¼ lb potatoes
- 65 g/2 ½ oz butter
- 250 ml/8 fl oz hot milk
- 100 g/3 ½ oz cheese, such as Cheddar or gruyere, grated
- 6 eggs
- salt

Serves 6

Boil and mash the potatoes with 50 g/2 oz of the butter and the hot milk as described in recipe 230. Stir in 80 g/3 oz of the cheese and season with salt if necessary. Preheat the oven to 200°C/400°F/Gas Mark 6. Spoon the mash into an ovenproof dish and make six hollows with the back of a spoon. Crack an egg into each one, sprinkle with a little salt and add a small knob of the remaining butter. Sprinkle the remaining cheese over the top and bake for 5–10 minutes, until the egg whites are set. Serve immediately, straight from the dish.

242

- 1 kg/2 ¼ lb potatoes,
  preferably yellow-fleshed
- sunflower oil, for deep-frying
- salt

Serves 6

Chips
PATATAS FRITAS

Cut the potatoes into 2-cm/¾-inch wide strips. Rinse well and leave to soak in cold water for 30 minutes to remove the starch, then pat dry. Put them in a tea towel, add a little salt, gather up the edges of the tea towel and shake to ensure the salt is evenly distributed. Heat the oil in a deep-fryer or deep saucepan to 150–160 °C/300–325°F or until a cube of day-old bread browns in 45 seconds. Add the potato slices, in batches, and cook until they are beginning to colour, then remove from the oil and drain well. When all the potatoes have been cooked at this temperature, heat the oil to 180–190°C/350–375°F or until a cube of day-old bread browns in 30 seconds. Add the chips, in batches, and cook until they are golden brown. Remove from the oil, drain and keep warm until all the batches are cooked. Sprinkle with salt and serve immediately.

Note: Crisps, straw potatoes and other deep-fried potatoes are prepared in the same way as chips, but without soaking them in water for so long. After soaking, pat dry and fry only once until they are golden brown in oil heated to 180–190°C/350–375°F.

243

- 250 g/9 oz salt cod fillet
- 1.5 kg/3 ¼ lb potatoes
- sunflower oil, for deep-frying
- 5 eggs, beaten
- salt

Serves 4

Straw potatoes with scrambled eggs and salt cod
REVUELTO DE PATATAS PAJA, HUEVOS Y BACALAO

Put the salt cod in a bowl, add water to cover and leave to soak for 8 hours, changing the water at least three times. (Each time you change the water rinse out the bowl as the salt tends to deposit on the bottom.) Drain the fish, put into a saucepan and pour in water to cover. Bring to the boil, then remove the pan from the heat. Leave to stand until the water is only just warm. Lift out the fish with a fish slice, remove and discard any skin and bones and flake the flesh. Cut the potatoes into thin julienne strips. This is most easily done with a mandoline. Heat the oil in a deep-fryer or deep saucepan to 180–190°C/350–375°F or until a cube of day-old bread browns in 30 seconds. Add the potato strips, in batches, and cook for about 2 minutes, until golden brown. Remove from the oil and drain. Transfer 1–2 tablespoons of the oil to a large frying pan and reheat. Add the eggs and cook over a low heat, stirring with a fork, until they are beginning to set. Add the potatoes and cod, mix, season with salt and cook until the eggs are set but not dry. Serve immediately.

244

Diced potatoes with scrambled eggs and peas
REVUELTO DE PATATAS EN CUADRADITOS, HUEVOS Y GUISANTES

- **1.5 kg/3 ¼ lb potatoes,**
  cut into 1-cm/½-inch cubes
- **sunflower oil, for deep-frying**
- **6 eggs, beaten**
- **250 g/9 oz canned peas, drained**
- **salt**

Serves 6

Season the potato lightly with salt. Heat the oil in a deep-fryer or deep saucepan to 180–190°C/350–375°F or until a cube of day-old bread browns in 30 seconds. Add the potato, in batches, and cook for 3–5 minutes, until golden brown. Remove from the oil and drain. Transfer 1–2 tablespoons of the oil to a large frying pan set over a low heat and add the potato cubes. Season the eggs with salt, pour into the pan on top of the potatoes and add the peas. Increase the heat to high and cook, stirring constantly, for about 5 minutes, until the eggs are set but not dry. Transfer to a warm serving dish and serve immediately.

Note: This dish can be made with asparagus tips instead of peas.

245

Potatoes baked with salt cod and cream
PATATAS CON BACALAO Y NATA AL HORNO

- **500 g/1 lb 2 oz thick salt**
  cod fillet
- **1 kg/2 ¼ lb large potatoes,**
  unpeeled
- **200 g/7 oz onions, sliced**
- **350 ml/12 fl oz double cream**
- **margarine, for greasing**
- **salt**

Serves 4

Put the salt cod in a bowl, add water to cover and leave to soak for 8 hours, changing the water three or four times. (Each time you change the water rinse out the bowl as the salt tends to deposit on the bottom.) Put the potatoes into a large saucepan of cold water and add 1 teaspoon salt. Make sure the water covers them completely. Bring to the boil, lower the heat and cook for 20–30 minutes, until tender but not falling apart. Drain well and leave to cool. Drain the fish, put into a saucepan, and pour in water to cover. Bring to the boil, then remove the pan from the heat. Leave to stand until the water is only just warm. Lift out the fish with a fish slice, remove and discard any skin and bones and flake the flesh. Preheat the oven to 180°C/350°F/ Gas Mark 4. Grease an ovenproof dish with margarine. Peel and slice the potatoes. Place a third of the potato slices in the prepared dish and cover with half the salt cod, lightly seasoning each layer with salt. Make another layer with half the remaining potato slices. Add the onion in one layer, then add a layer of the remaining salt cod and top with the remaining potato slices, lightly seasoning each layer with salt. Use very thin slices for the top layer if possible. Pour the cream over the top and bake for about 45 minutes, then put the dish under a preheated grill for a few minutes, until the top is golden brown. Serve immediately, straight from the dish.

Potatoes with milk cap mushrooms

PATATAS CON NÍSCALOS

- **500 g/1 lb 2 oz milk cap mushrooms or other wild mushrooms, cut into medium-sized pieces**
- **4 tablespoons olive oil**
- **1 large onion, finely chopped**
- **1.5 kg/3 ¼ lb potatoes, diced**
- **1 tablespoon plain flour**
- **1 teaspoon paprika**
- **1 bay leaf**
- **175 ml/6 fl oz white wine**
- **salt and pepper**

Serves 4

Put the milk cap mushrooms in a saucepan, without added oil, and cook over a low heat until they have released all their juices. Remove the mushrooms and discard the juices. (You can omit this step if you are using other wild mushrooms.) Heat the oil in a saucepan. Add the onion and cook over a low heat, stirring occasionally, for 5 minutes, until softened and translucent. Add the potato and mushrooms and cook, stirring constantly, for 2–3 minutes. Stir in the flour and cook, stirring constantly, for 2– 3 minutes, then add the paprika and bay leaf. Gradually stir in the wine and 750 ml/1 ¼ pints water. Season with salt and pepper to taste and bring to the boil. Lower the heat and simmer for about 45 minutes, until the potato is tender. Remove the bay leaf. Serve immediately in a soup tureen or deep dish.

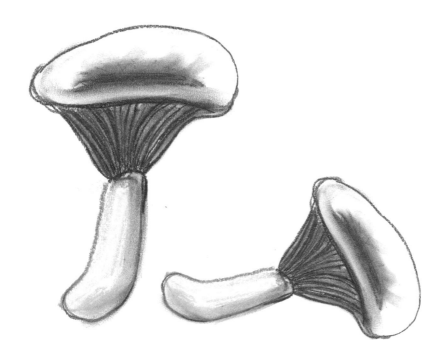

Potatoes with clams

PATATAS GUISADAS CON CHIRLAS

- **250 g/9 oz live warty Venus clams**
- **6 tablespoons olive oil**
- **1 onion, finely chopped**
- **2 ripe tomatoes, peeled, seeded and chopped**
- **1.5 kg/3 ¼ lb potatoes, cut into pieces**
- **1 tablespoon plain flour**
- **1 clove garlic**
- **1 sprig fresh parsley**
- **pinch of saffron threads**
- **salt**

Serves 4-6

Wash the clams in salted water, changing the water twice. Discard any with broken shells or any that do not shut immediately when sharply tapped. Put them in a saucepan, pour in 50 ml/2 fl oz water and add a pinch of salt. Cover and cook over a high heat for 3–5 minutes, until the shells have opened. Remove the pan from the heat and lift out the clams with a slotted spoon. Discard any clams that remain shut. Strain the cooking liquid into a bowl through a muslin-lined sieve and reserve. Remove the clams from their shells and add them to the bowl. Heat the oil in a small frying pan. Add the onion and cook, stirring occasionally, for 3 minutes, then add the tomato and cook, stirring occasionally, for a further 8 minutes. Transfer the onion and tomato mixture to a larger saucepan and set over a low heat. Add the potato and stir in the flour. Pound the garlic in a mortar with a pinch of salt, and the parsley and saffron. Stir in 2–3 table-spoons of the reserved cooking liquid from the clams, then pour into the pan with the potato. Add the clams and their cooking liquid and pour in enough water to generously cover the potatoes. Bring to the boil, then lower the heat and cook for about 20–30 minutes, until the potato is tender. Serve immediately in a soup tureen.

248

Potatoes with green peppers

PATATAS GUISADAS CON PIMIENTOS VERDES

- **6 tablespoons olive oil**
- **1 onion, finely chopped**
- **2–3 green peppers, seeded and diced**
- **2 ripe tomatoes, peeled, seeded and chopped**
- **1.5 kg/3 ¼ lb potatoes, cut into pieces**
- **1 tablespoon plain flour**
- **1 clove garlic**
- **1 sprig fresh parsley**
- **pinch of saffron threads**
- **salt**

Serves 4-6

Heat the oil in a small frying pan. Add the onion and cook, stirring occasionally, for 3 minutes, then add the pepper and tomato and cook, stirring occasionally, for a further 8 minutes. Transfer the mixture to a larger saucepan and set over a low heat. Add the potato and stir in the flour. Pound the garlic in a mortar with a pinch of salt, and the parsley and saffron. Stir in 2–3 tablespoons water, then pour into the pan with the potato. Pour in enough water to generously cover the potatoes. Bring to the boil, then lower the heat and cook for about 20–30 minutes, until the potato is tender. Serve immediately in a soup tureen.

249

Widow's potatoes
PATATAS GUISADAS VIUDAS

- 6 tablespoons olive oil
- 1 large onion, finely chopped
- 1.5 kg/3 ¼ lb red-skinned
  potatoes, cut into medium-sized
  pieces
- 1 teaspoon paprika
- 1 chicken stock cube
- pinch of saffron threads
- 1 tablespoon chopped
  fresh parsley
- salt
Serves 6

Heat the oil in a saucepan. Add the onion and cook over a medium heat, stirring occasionally, for 4–6 minutes, until beginning to brown. Add the potato and cook, stirring frequently, for 5 minutes, then stir in the paprika. Cook, stirring constantly, for a further 2 minutes, then pour in water to cover – about 1 litre/1 ¾ pints – crumble in the stock cube and season lightly with salt. Crush the saffron in a mortar and stir in 2–3 tablespoons water, then pour into the pan with the potato and mix well. Cook over a medium heat for about 20–30 minutes, until the potato is tender. Sprinkle with the parsley, stir and serve immediately in a soup tureen.

250

Gratin potatoes with onions and cream

PATATAS GRATINADAS CON CEBOLLA Y NATA

- 1.2 kg/2 ½ lb potatoes, unpeeled
- 3 tablespoons olive oil
- 3 large onions, sliced
- butter, for greasing
- 80 g/3 oz cheese, such as
  Cheddar or gruyere, grated
- 250 ml/8 fl oz single cream
- salt

Serves 6

Put the potatoes into a large saucepan of cold water and add 1 teaspoon salt. Make sure the water covers them completely. Bring to the boil, lower the heat and cook for 20–30 minutes, until tender. Drain, peel and slice thinly. Heat the oil in a saucepan. Add the onion and cook over a low heat, stirring occasionally, for about 10 minutes, until beginning to brown. Remove from the heat and set aside. Preheat the oven to 180°C/350°F/Gas Mark 4. Grease a deep ovenproof dish with butter and lay half the potato slices in it. Cover with half the onion, sprinkle with half the cheese and season lightly with salt. Add the remaining potatoes and top with the remaining onion. Season lightly with salt and pour the cream over the top of the layers, shaking the dish gently to ensure the cream flows down between the potato slices. Sprinkle the remaining cheese on top. Bake for about 20 minutes, then put the dish under a preheated grill for a few minutes, until the top is golden brown. Serve immediately, straight from the dish.

251

Potatoes with tomato sauce and béchamel

PATATAS CON SALSA DE TOMATE Y BECHAMEL

- sunflower oil, for deep-frying
- 1.5 kg/3 ¼ lb potatoes, sliced
- 250 ml/8 fl oz Classic Tomato
  Sauce (see recipe 73)
- 25 g/1 oz butter or margarine
- 2 tablespoons olive oil
- 1 heaped tablespoon plain flour
- 450 ml/¾ pint milk
- 20 g/¾ oz butter
- salt

Serves 6

Heat the sunflower oil in a deep-fryer or deep saucepan to 180–190°C/350–375°F or until a cube of day-old bread browns in 30 seconds. Add the potato, in batches, and cook until golden brown. Remove with a slotted spoon and drain on kitchen paper. Place half the potato slices in a deep, ovenproof dish and pour in half the tomato sauce to cover and sprinkly lightly with salt. Add the remaining potato slices and cover them with the rest of the tomato sauce. Preheat the oven to 200°C/400°F/Gas Mark 6. Make the béchamel sauce: Melt the butter or margarine with the oil in a saucepan. Stir in the flour and cook, stirring constantly, for 2–3 minutes, then remove the pan from the heat. Gradually stir in the milk, a little at a time. Return the pan to the heat and cook, stirring constantly, for 8–10 minutes. Pour the sauce into the dish with the potatoes. Dot the butter on top and bake for about 15 minutes. Serve immediately, straight from the dish.

252

Fried potato stew

PATATAS REHOGADAS Y GUISADAS

- sunflower oil, for deep-frying
- 1.5 kg/3 ¼ lb potatoes, thinly sliced
- 2 cloves garlic
- 1 sprig fresh parsley
- ½ teaspoon paprika
- 1 chicken stock cube
- 175 ml/6 fl oz white wine
- salt

Serves 6

Heat the oil in a deep-fryer or deep saucepan to 180–190°C/350–375°F or until a cube of day-old bread browns in 30 seconds. Add the potato, in batches, and cook until golden brown. Remove with a slotted spoon and drain on kitchen paper. Put the potato slices into a saucepan. Crush the garlic with a pinch of salt, the parsley and paprika in a mortar. Stir in 2 tablespoons water, add the mixture to the potatoes and mix well with a wooden spoon. Add 1.2 litres/2 pints water, the stock cube and wine and season to taste with salt. Bring to the boil, then lower the heat and cook for 10–15 minutes. Serve immediately, in a warm deep serving dish.

253

Coated potato bake

PATATAS REBOZADAS Y GUISADAS

- 150 g/5 oz plain flour
- 4 eggs
- 1.5 kg/3 ¼ lb potatoes, cut into 5-mm/¼-inch thick slices
- sunflower oil, for deep-frying
- 1 clove garlic
- pinch of saffron threads
- 1 small onion, finely chopped
- 1 tablespoon chopped fresh parsley
- salt

Serves 4–6

Set aside 1 tablespoon of the flour and spread out the remainder in a shallow dish. Beat the eggs in another shallow dish. Season the potato slices with salt and dip them first in the flour and then in the beaten egg. Heat the oil in a deep-fryer or deep saucepan to 180–190°C/350–375°F or until a cube of day-old bread browns in 30 seconds. Add the slices of potato, four at a time, and cook until golden brown. Remove with a slotted spoon and drain on kitchen paper. When all the slices are cooked, put them into a flameproof casserole, arranging them in loosely packed layers. Crush the garlic in a mortar with a little salt and the saffron, then stir in 2 tablespoons water. Transfer 3 tablespoons of the oil to a saucepan. Add the onion and cook over a low heat, stirring occasionally, for 8–10 minutes, until golden brown. Stir in the reserved flour and cook, stirring constantly, for 2–3 minutes, then add the contents of the mortar and 1 litre/1 ¾ pints water. Season to taste with salt. Tip the mixture through a large colander over the potatoes. Sprinkle the parsley over the top and simmer gently for 30 minutes. Preheat the oven to 180°C/350°F/Gas Mark 4. Transfer the casserole to the oven and bake for 10 minutes. Serve immediately, straight from the casserole.

254

Potatoes with milk and eggs

PATATAS CON LECHE Y HUEVOS

- sunflower oil, for deep-frying
- 1.2 kg/2 ½ lb potatoes, sliced
- 3 eggs
- 100 g/3 ½ oz gruyere cheese, grated
- 750 ml/1 ¼ pints milk
- salt

Serves 6

Heat the oil in a deep-fryer or deep saucepan to 150–160°C/300–325°F or until a cube of day-old bread browns in 45 seconds. Season the potato slices with salt and cook, in batches, until just beginning to colour. Remove with a slotted spoon and drain on kitchen paper. Put the potato slices into a deep ovenproof dish. Preheat the oven to 180°C/350°F/Gas Mark 4. Beat the eggs with a pinch of salt in a bowl. Stir in 80 g/3 oz of the gruyere, then gradually whisk in the milk, a little at a time. Pour the mixture over the potatoes and mix gently with a fork. Sprinkle the remaining gruyere over the top. Bake for 20 minutes, stirring occasionally with a fork. If the potatoes seem to be drying out, add a little more milk. Remove the dish from the oven and brown the top under a preheated grill for 10 minutes. Serve the potatoes immediately.

255

Potatoes with tomato, onion and aromatic herbs

PATATAS CON TOMATES, CEBOLLAS Y HIERBAS AROMÁTICAS, AL HORNO

- 1.5 kg/3 ¼ lb potatoes, unpeeled
- 175 ml/6 fl oz olive oil
- 1 large onion,
  sliced and pushed out into rings
- 4 large, ripe tomatoes, sliced
- ½ teaspoon chopped fresh aromatic herbs (parsley, thyme or oregano) or 2 sprigs fresh thyme
- 80 g/3 oz gruyere cheese, grated
- salt

Serves 6

Put the unpeeled potatoes into a large saucepan and add about a teaspoon of salt. Make sure that the water covers them completely. Bring to the boil, then lower the heat and cook for about 20–30 minutes, until tender but not falling apart. Drain well, peel and cut into 1-cm/½-inch thick slices. Preheat the oven to 180°C/350°F/Gas Mark 4. Pour a thin layer of oil into an ovenproof dish. Put half the potato slices into the dish and top with half the onion rings. Next, make a layer with half the tomato slices, then season lightly with salt and add half the aromatic herbs or one of the thyme sprigs. Sprinkle with half the gruyere. Repeat the layers of potato, onion, tomato and herbs. Pour the remaining oil over the dish and sprinkle with the rest of the gruyere. Bake for about 45 minutes, until the tomato slices have softened and browned. Serve the potatoes immediately, straight from the dish.

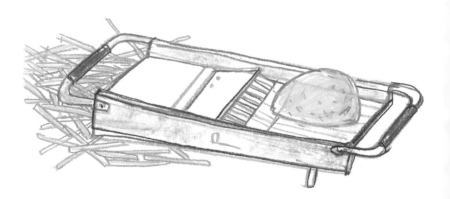

Potatoes baked in tomato sauce

PATATAS AL HORNO CON SALSA DE TOMATE

- 1 quantity Classic Tomato Sauce
  (see recipe 73)
- 500 ml/18 fl oz sunflower oil
- 1.5 kg/3 ¼ lb potatoes,
  thinly sliced
- 150 g/5 oz streaky bacon, diced
- 50 g/2 oz cheese, such as
  Cheddar or gruyere, grated
- 25 g/1 oz butter
- salt

Serves 6

Process the tomato sauce to a purée in a food processor and set aside. Heat the oil in a frying pan. Add the potato slices, in batches, and cook until light golden brown. Remove with a slotted spoon and drain on kitchen paper. Add the bacon to the pan and cook until lightly browned, then drain well and set aside. Preheat the oven to 160°C/ 325°F/Gas Mark 3. Layer the potato slices, bacon and tomato sauce in a deep ovenproof dish, seasoning each layer with salt. Sprinkle the cheese on top and dot with the butter. Bake for about 1 hour, until golden and bubbling. Serve immediately, straight from the dish.

257

Potatoes served with a spicy sauce

PATATAS BRAVAS

- 12 small potatoes, unpeeled
- 2 tablespoons olive oil
- 1 tablespoon white-wine vinegar
- pinch of hot paprika
- 1 clove garlic, finely chopped
- 1 teaspoon chilli powder or
  Worcestershire sauce
- salt

Serves 4

Bring a large saucepan of salted water to the boil. Add the potatoes and cook for 20–25 minutes, until tender but not falling apart. Drain and leave to cool, then peel and slice or dice. Transfer to a plate or tray. Mix together the oil, vinegar, paprika, garlic and the chilli powder or Worcestershire sauce in a bowl. Pour the mixture over the potatoes and serve them as an appetizer.

258

Potatoes stuffed with ham

PATATAS RELLENAS DE JAMÓN

- 6 large potatoes, about 200 g/
  7 oz each, unpeeled
- 80 g/3 oz butter
- 150 g/5 oz Serrano ham,
  finely chopped
- salt

Serves 6

Preheat the oven to 180°C/350°F/Gas Mark 4. Wash and dry the potatoes. Bake for 1–1 ½ hours, until soft. Remove the potatoes from the oven and cut in half widthways. Do not switch off the oven. Using a teaspoon, scoop out the flesh into a bowl without piercing the skins. Lightly season each skin with salt and divide half the butter among them. Mash the potato flesh with a fork, lightly season with salt and mix in the ham. Fill the skins with the mixture and place in a single, fairly tight-fitting layer in an ovenproof dish. Dot the remaining butter over them and bake for a further 10 minutes. Serve immediately.

259

Potatoes with peppers

PATATAS CON PIMIENTOS

- 1 large red pepper
- 6 large potatoes,
  about 200 g/7 oz each, unpeeled
- 450 ml/¾ pint sunflower oil
- 4 large green peppers, seeded
  and cut into large squares
- 2 hard-boiled eggs,
  coarsely chopped
- salt

Serves 6

Preheat the oven to 180°C/350°F/Gas Mark 4. Put the red pepper on a baking sheet and roast, turning occasionally, for 10–20 minutes, until the skin is blistered and charred. Remove from the oven, place in a bowl and cover with a tea towel or kitchen paper. When the pepper is cool enough to handle, peel off the skin, remove the stalk and seeds and cut the flesh into strips. Season with salt and set aside. Put the potatoes into a large saucepan of cold water and add 1 teaspoon salt. Make sure the water covers them completely. Bring to the boil, then lower the heat and cook for 20–30 minutes, until tender but not falling apart. Drain well. Meanwhile, heat the oil in a deep frying pan. Add the green pepper and some salt, cover and cook over a medium heat for 15–20 minutes, until tender. Remove with a slotted spoon and drain. Preheat the oven to 200°C/400°F/Gas Mark 6. Transfer 3 tablespoons of the oil from the frying pan to an ovenproof dish. Peel the potatoes, cut a segment out of the top and a slice off the base of each one so they will stand up. Put them in a single layer in the dish. Season lightly with salt and spoon a little of the oil from the frying pan on to each one. Place a little hard-boiled egg and a few strips of red pepper in the cavity in the top of each potato. Put the green peppers around the edge of the dish and spoon a little more of the oil from the frying pan over the potatoes. Bake for about 10 minutes, until heated through, then serve.

260

Twice cooked potatoes

PATATAS COCIDAS Y REHOGADAS

- 750 g/1 lb 10 oz red-skinned
  or new potatoes, unpeeled
- 1 tablespoon milk
- 50 g/2 oz lard
- 4 tablespoons sunflower oil
- 1 tablespoon chopped
  fresh parsley
- salt

Serves 4

Put the potatoes into a large saucepan of cold water and add the milk and 1 teaspoon salt. Make sure the liquid covers them completely. Bring to the boil, then lower the heat to medium and cook for 20–30 minutes, until tender but not falling apart. Drain well, then peel and cut into pieces. Melt the lard with the oil in a frying pan over a high heat. Add the potato and cook, shaking the pan frequently, until all the pieces of potato are golden brown. Remove with a slotted spoon, season to taste with salt, sprinkle with the parsley and serve immediately.

Note: These potatoes can be served with all kinds of dishes.

Potatoes with chorizo and bacon

PATATAS CON CHORIZO Y BACON

- 40 g/1 ½ oz lard
- 5 tablespoons sunflower oil
- 50 g/2 oz chorizo,
  peeled and thinly sliced
- 100 g/3 ½ oz thickly sliced
  bacon rashers, cut into
  1–cm/½-inch wide strips
- 1.5 kg/3 ¼ lb small potatoes,
  preferably new potatoes
- 1 tablespoon chopped
  fresh parsley
- 1 clove garlic, finely chopped
- salt

Serves 4

Melt the lard with the oil in a saucepan or large frying pan. (It needs to be big enough to hold the potatoes in a single layer.) Add the chorizo and bacon and cook over a medium heat, stirring constantly, for a few minutes, then add the potatoes. Season with salt and cook over a low heat, shaking the pan occasionally, for 45–60 minutes, until the potatoes are evenly browned. Just before serving, sprinkle with the parsley and garlic and stir for a few minutes more. Transfer to a warm serving dish and serve immediately.

Note: Some types of chorizo become hard with prolonged cooking. To prevent this, cook the slices with the bacon, then remove and set aside. About 10 minutes before serving, return the slices of chorizo to the pan.

Potatoes with sausages

PATATAS CON SALCHICHAS ·

- 12 small or new potatoes,
  about 50 g/2 oz each
- 12 small sausages
- 4 tablespoons olive oil
- 1 tablespoon chopped
  fresh parsley
- 2 cloves garlic, finely chopped
- salt

Makes 12

Preheat the oven to 200°C/400°F/Gas Mark 6. Using an apple corer or a small sharp knife, make a hole through the centre of each potato. Place a sausage in each one. Reserve the cut-out pieces of potato. Put the oil into a roasting tin and add the sausage-filled potatoes. Put the reserved potato pieces in the tin, lightly season with salt and sprinkle with half the parsley and half the garlic. Roast for 15 minutes, then turn the potatoes over, season with salt, sprinkle with the remaining parsley and remaining garlic and baste with the oil. Return the tin to the oven and roast, turning and basting three or four more times, for about 30 minutes. Serve immediately in a warm serving dish.

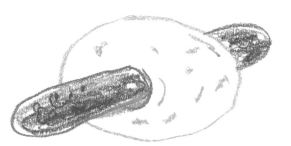

263

Roasted potatoes with Roquefort

PATATAS ASADAS CON ROQUEFORT

- **9 large potatoes, about 100 g/3 ½ oz each, unpeeled**
- **25 g/1 oz butter**
- **50 g/2 oz Roquefort cheese**
- **1 egg, beaten**
- **pinch of freshly grated nutmeg**
- **450 ml/¾ pint hot milk**
- **salt**

Serves 4

Preheat the oven to 180°C/350°F/Gas Mark 4. Wash and dry the potatoes, then bake for about 1 hour, until tender. Remove from the oven, cut in half lengthways and scoop out the flesh into a bowl using a teaspoon, without piercing the skins. Put the flesh in a food processor and process briefly. Transfer to a bowl, beat in the butter, Roquefort, egg and nutmeg and season with salt. Finally, stir in just enough of the hot milk to make a thick mash. Fill the potato skins with the mixture and cook under a preheated grill for about 15 minutes, until golden brown. Serve immediately.

Note: If you like, separate the egg, then add the yolk to the mash with the other ingredients. Whisk the egg white in a clean, dry bowl until it forms soft peaks and then fold it in.

264

American baked potatoes

PATATAS ASADAS A LA AMERICANA

- **4 large potatoes, unpeeled**
- **1 clove garlic**
- **2 tablespoons olive oil**

Serves 4

Preheat the oven to 160°C/325°F/Gas Mark 3. Wash and dry the potatoes. Rub the outside of each potato with garlic, then rub with oil. Do this with your fingers as if giving the potatoes a massage. Lightly prick the skins with a fork three or four times in different places. Wrap each potato in foil and bake for 10 minutes. Increase the oven temperature to 220°C/425°F/Gas Mark 7 and bake for a further 50 minutes. Serve the potatoes immediately, with their foil opened just at the point where the two ends of foil meet.

Note: This recipe requires top-quality potatoes. Allow 1 large potato per serving and serve as an accompaniment to grilled steak or chops. You can cut open each potato with a knife and insert a knob of butter just before serving.

265

Potato cake to accompany cold meats and meat dishes

TORTA DE PATATAS PARA ACOMPAÑAR FIAMBRES Y CARNES

- **750 g/1 lb 10 oz potatoes, unpeeled**
- **3–4 tablespoons olive oil**
- **50 g/2 oz butter or lard**
- **onion and bacon (optional – see Note), finely chopped**
- **salt**

Serves 4

Put the potatoes into a saucepan of cold water and add 1 teaspoon salt. Make sure the water covers them completely. Bring to the boil, then lower the heat to medium and cook for 20–30 minutes, until tender but not falling apart. Drain well and leave to cool. (You can prepare the potatoes to this stage the day before they are required.) Peel the potatoes and push them through a ricer or cut them into thin julienne strips with a mandoline. Heat the oil in a frying pan. Add the potato, shape it into a cake without flattening it too much, and cook for about 10 minutes, until the underside is lightly browned. Turn the cake over by inverting it on to the pan lid or a plate and then sliding it back into the pan. Cook for about 10 minutes, until the second side is lightly browned. Invert the cake on to the pan lid or plate again and drain the oil from the pan. Melt half the butter or lard in the pan, add the potato cake and cook for about 5 minutes, then turn it and cook for a further 5 minutes, until browned and crusty. Transfer to a warm serving dish and cut into triangles. This potato cake can be served with all kinds of dishes.

Note: If you want to add the onion, cook it in the frying pan over a low heat, stirring occasionally, for 5 minutes before adding the potato. If you want to add the bacon, cook it in the frying pan for a few minutes before then adding the potato. Both onion and bacon provide additional flavour.

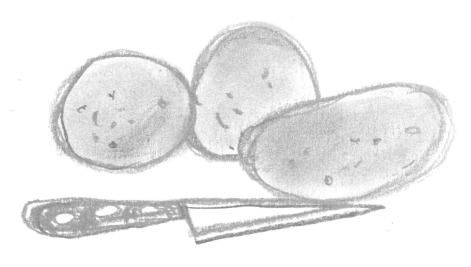

266

Potato salad with tuna and hard-boiled egg

PATATAS EN ENSALADILLA CON ATÚN Y HUEVO DURO

- 1.2 kg/2 ½ lb potatoes, unpeeled
- 2 tablespoons milk
- 225 g/8 oz canned tuna in oil, drained and broken into chunks
- 3 hard-boiled eggs, sliced
- 3 tablespoons white-wine vinegar
- 6 tablespoons sunflower oil
- 1 spring onion, finely chopped
- 1 teaspoon chopped fresh parsley
- salt

Serves 6

Put the potatoes into a large saucepan of cold water and add the milk and a generous pinch of salt. Make sure that the liquid covers them completely. Bring to the boil, then lower the heat to medium and cook for 20–30 minutes, until tender but not falling apart. Drain well, peel and cut into slices. Put the slices into a bowl, alternating with the tuna and hard-boiled eggs. Whisk the vinegar with a little salt using a fork, then pour over the potatoes. Pour the oil over the salad and add the spring onion and parsley. Mix lightly to avoid breaking up the potatoes or eggs and leave until almost cold before serving.

267

Potato and tuna salad

ENSALADA DE PATATAS CON ATÚN

- 225 g/8 oz canned tuna in oil, drained
- juice of 1 lemon
- 4 large potatoes
- 2 tablespoons white-wine vinegar
- 4 tablespoons olive oil
- 4–6 lettuce leaves
- 12 olives
- 2 hard-boiled eggs, cut into quarters
- salt

Serves 4

Coarsely flake the tuna into a bowl and pour the lemon juice over it. Cook the potatoes as described on page 196. Drain, peel and slice, then put the slices in another bowl. Whisk the vinegar with a pinch of salt, then whisk in the oil with a fork. Pour half the vinaigrette over the potatoes. Make a bed of lettuce leaves in a salad bowl. Mix the tuna with the remaining potato and spoon into the salad bowl. Add the olives, pour the remaining vinaigrette over the salad and garnish with the hard-boiled eggs.

Potatoes with mayonnaise, tomatoes and anchovies

PATATAS CON MAYONESA, TOMATES Y ANCHOAS

- **1 quantity Classic Mayonnaise (see recipe 105)**
- **1 kg/2 ¼ lb potatoes, unpeeled**
- **2 tablespoons capers, rinsed, drained and chopped**
- **2 tablespoons milk**
- **1 cucumber, peeled and thinly sliced**
- **3 firm tomatoes, sliced**
- **1 canned red pepper, drained and sliced**
- **1 hard-boiled egg, sliced**
- **50 g/2 oz canned anchovies in oil, drained**
- **100 g/3 ½ oz stoned olives**
- **salt**

Serves 6

Divide the mayonnaise equally between two bowls and stir the capers into one, then set both bowls aside in a cool place. Put the potatoes into a large saucepan of cold water and add the milk and 1 teaspoon salt. Make sure that the liquid covers them completely. Bring to the boil, then lower the heat to medium and cook for about 20–30 minutes, until tender but not falling apart. Drain well and leave to cool slightly, then peel and slice. Meanwhile, spread out the cucumber slices on a plate, sprinkle with a little salt and leave to stand until they have released some of their water. Drain and pat dry with kitchen paper. Mix together the caper mayonnaise, potatoes and cucumber in a bowl, then spoon the mixture on to a serving dish, mounding it up into a dome. Cover with the remaining mayonnaise and garnish with the tomatoes, red pepper, hard-boiled egg, anchovies and olives. Chill in the refrigerator for at least 1 hour before serving.

Pasta

How to cook

Pasta is one of the most versatile ingredients in any mediterranean cook's kitchen. However, it needs careful cooking to prevent its becoming too soggy or remaining too hard. The cooking time depends on the brand of pasta and personal taste. Italians prefer their pasta al dente – only just tender rather than well done, for example.

Macaroni: Allow 50–65 g/2–2 ½ oz dried pasta per person. Bring a large saucepan of salted water to the boil, add the macaroni and cook uncovered. When the water comes back to the boil, lower the heat slightly but make sure the water is still boiling and cook for 10–12 minutes. Drain the macaroni in a large colander and refresh under cold running water. The pasta is now ready to use.

Tagliatelle and spaghetti: These are cooked in the same way as macaroni but are not refreshed under running water. It is important, therefore, to calculate exactly when you are going to serve the pasta so that it is not left standing in hot water for longer than necessary as this will make it slimy. Serve tagliatelle and spaghetti on warm plates.

Cannelloni: Pasta tubes that do not need precooking are now widely available. Just leave them to soak in cold water for 1 hour to allow the pasta to soften or follow the instructions on the packet. If using cannelloni that requires precooking, treat it in the same way as macaroni but do not refresh under running water. When it is tender, remove it from the water very carefully to avoid breaking it and drain on a clean tea towel until required.

Note: Some people add a teaspoon of sunflower or olive oil to the cooking water to prevent the pasta sticking.

269

Pasta dough

PASTA DE LOS ESPAGUETIS

- 500 g/1 lb 2 oz plain flour,
  plus extra for dusting
- 3 eggs
- salt

Serves 6

Put half the flour into a bowl and make a well in the centre. Add the eggs, water and a pinch of salt. Bring the mixture together with your hands and knead the dough well, adding the rest of the flour a little at a time. Shape it into a ball, then throw it on to a work surface quite hard and from quite high, eight or ten times. Roll out the dough on a lightly floured surface and leave to dry for about 30 minutes. Roll it again, without pressing down, and cut into strips 5 mm/¼ inch wide, or wider if preferred. Dangle the pasta over the edge of your work surface to stretch the strips, then cook in the same way as dried pasta but for a much shorter time. The pasta keeps for up to a week as long as it has dried completely before it is stored.

270

Macaroni with chorizo and tomato

MACARRONES CON CHORIZO Y TOMATE

- 350 g/12 oz macaroni
- 3 tablespoons olive oil
- 1 onion, chopped
- 1 kg/2 ¼ lb ripe tomatoes,
  seeded and chopped
- 1 teaspoon sugar
- 100 g/3 ½ oz gruyere or
  Parmesan cheese, grated
- 100 g/3 ½ oz chorizo,
  skinned and chopped
- 25 g/1 oz butter
- salt

Serves 6

Cook the macaroni as described on page 221, refresh under cold running water, drain and set aside. Make a tomato sauce with the oil, onion, tomatoes and sugar as described in recipe 73. Preheat the oven to 180°C/350°F/Gas Mark 4. Reserve 2–3 tablespoons of the tomato sauce and mix the remainder with the macaroni. Stir in half the cheese and pour the mixture into a deep ovenproof dish. Sprinkle the chorizo over the pasta and push the pieces down into the dish to prevent them drying out during cooking. Pour the reserved tomato sauce over the top and sprinkle with the remaining cheese. Dot the top with the butter and bake for 15–30 minutes, until golden brown and bubbling. Serve immediately.

American macaroni

MACARRONES A LA AMERICANA

- **350 g/12 oz macaroni**
- **350 g/12 oz pints canned mushroom soup**
- **450 ml/¾ pint milk**
- **1 teaspoon curry powder**
- **50 g/2 oz gruyere or Parmesan cheese, grated**
- **25 g/1 oz butter**
- **salt**

Serves 4

Preheat the oven to 180°C/350°F/Gas Mark 4. Cook the macaroni as described on page 221, refresh under cold running water, drain and set aside. Pour the soup and milk into a saucepan and heat gently. Add the macaroni and sprinkle in the curry powder. Mix well and pour into a deep ovenproof dish. Sprinkle with the cheese and dot with the butter. Bake for about 15–30 minutes, until golden brown and bubbling. Serve immediately.

272

Macaroni with mayonnaise and tuna
MACARRONES Y CODITOS CON MAYONESA Y ATÚN

- 300 g/11 oz elbow macaroni
- 1 quantity Thick Mayonnaise
  (see recipe 106)
- 100 g/3 ½ oz canned tuna
  in oil or brine, drained
- 500 g/1 lb 2 oz firm tomatoes,
  sliced
- 6 stuffed olives
- 1 hard-boiled egg, finely chopped
- salt

Serves 4

Cook the macaroni as described on page 221. Refresh under cold running water, then drain. Mix together the cold macaroni, half the mayonnaise and the tuna in a bowl and arrange the mixture in the centre of a serving dish. Garnish the edge of the dish with the tomato slices topped with a little of the remaining mayonnaise and the olives. Sprinkle the hard-boiled egg over the pasta. Chill in the refrigerator for 30 minutes before serving.

273

Macaroni with mayonnaise and gruyere
MACARRONES Y CODITOS CON MAYONESA Y QUESO

- 300 g/11 oz macaroni
- 1 quantity Thick Mayonnaise
  (see recipe 106)
- 25 g/1 oz butter
- 80 g/3 oz gruyere cheese, grated

Serves 4

Cook the macaroni as described on page 221. Refresh under cold running water, then drain. Preheat the grill. Put the macaroni, butter and gruyere into a saucepan and heat gently, stirring constantly. Remove the pan from the heat and add about one-third of the mayonnaise, mix well and pour the mixture into a flameproof dish. Pour the remaining mayonnaise over the top and cook under the grill until the mayonnaise has set. Serve immediately straight from the dish.

Note: Sometimes it is necessary to tilt the dish and spoon off any oil that the mayonnaise has released during cooking.

Macaroni with spinach

MACARRONES CON ESPINACAS

- **1.5 kg/3 ¼ lb spinach, coarse stalks removed**
- **300 g/11 oz macaroni**
- **80 g/3 oz butter**
- **1 tablespoon sunflower oil**
- **1 tablespoon plain flour**
- **250 ml/8 fl oz milk**
- **65 g/2 ½ oz gruyere or Parmesan cheese, grated**
- **salt**

Serves 4

Add the spinach to a large pan of salted boiling water. Bring back to the boil, lower the heat and cook for about 10 minutes. Drain well, pressing down with the back of a spoon to squeeze out all the water. Coarsely chop the leaves. Cook the macaroni as described on page 221. Refresh under cold running water, then drain and set aside. Meanwhile, make a béchamel sauce. Melt 25 g/1 oz of the butter with the oil in a saucepan. Stir in the flour and cook, stirring constantly, for 2–3 minutes, but do not allow the flour to brown. Gradually stir in the milk, a little at a time, and season with salt. Cook over a low heat, stirring constantly, for 5 minutes. Preheat the oven to 180°C/350°F/Gas Mark 4. Melt 40 g/1 ½ oz of the remaining butter in another saucepan, add the spinach and toss well to coat. Spoon the spinach into a deep ovenproof dish, spreading it out evenly. Mix the macaroni with half the cheese, then pour the mixture over the spinach. Pour the béchamel sauce on top, sprinkle with the remaining cheese and dot with the rest of the butter. Bake for about 15–30 minutes, until golden brown and bubbling. Serve immediately.

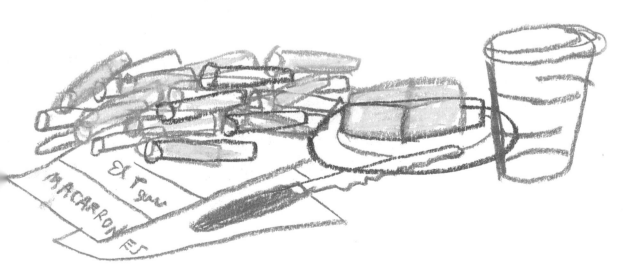

Macaroni with curried mussels

MACARRONES CON MEJILLONES AL CURRY

- 1 kg/2 ¼ lb mussels
- 5 tablespoons white wine
- 1 stick celery, chopped (optional)
- 350 g/12 oz macaroni
- 25 g/1 oz butter
- 2 tablespoons sunflower oil
- 1 large shallot or 1 small onion, very finely chopped
- 1 teaspoon of curry powder
- 1½ tablespoons plain flour
- 500 ml/18 fl oz milk
- 100 g/3 ½ oz cheese, such as Cheddar or gruyere, grated
- 1 teaspoon finely chopped fresh parsley
- salt

Serves 4

Scrape the mussel shells with the blade of a knife and remove the 'beards', then scrub under cold running water. Discard any mussels with broken shells or any that do not shut immediately when sharply tapped. Put them into a large saucepan with the wine, celery, if using, and a pinch of salt. Cover and cook over a medium heat, shaking the pan occasionally, for 4–5 minutes, until the shells have opened. Remove the mussels with a slotted spoon and reserve the cooking liquid. Discard any mussels that remain closed. Remove the mussels from their shells and if they are very big, cut them into two or three pieces with kitchen scissors. Strain the reserved cooking liquid into a bowl through a muslin-lined sieve. Cook the macaroni as described on page 221. Meanwhile, make the sauce. Melt half the butter with the oil in a frying pan. Add the shallot or onion and cook over a low heat, stirring occasionally, for about 5 minutes, until softened but not brown. Stir in the curry powder and flour and cook, stirring constantly, for 2 minutes, then gradually stir in the milk and the reserved cooking liquid. Cook, stirring constantly, for 5–10 minutes, until thickened. Preheat the grill. Drain the macaroni and put it into a flameproof dish. Add the mussels and stir in half the cheese and the parsley. Pour the sauce over the top, sprinkle with the remaining cheese and dot with the rest of the butter. Cook under the grill for 10–15 minutes, until golden brown and bubbling. Serve immediately.

276 Macaroni with canned tuna

MACARRONES CON ATÚN DE LATA

- **350 g/12 oz macaroni**
- **4 tablespoons sunflower oil**
- **1 onion, finely chopped**
- **1 clove garlic, finely chopped**
- **400 g/14 oz ripe tomatoes, peeled, seeded and chopped**
- **5 tablespoons white wine**
- **½ teaspoon sugar**
- **pinch of aromatic herbs**
- **25 g/1 oz butter**
- **50 g/2 oz gruyere cheese, grated**
- **150 g/5 oz canned tuna, drained and flaked**
- **salt**

Serves 4–5

Cook the macaroni as described on page 221. Refresh under cold running water, drain and set aside. Heat the oil in a saucepan. Add the onion and garlic and cook over a low heat, stirring occasionally, for about 5 minutes, until softened and translucent. Add the tomato and cook, stirring and breaking it up with the side of the spoon, for a few minutes, then add the wine, sugar, herbs and a pinch of salt. Cook, stirring occasionally, for 15 minutes, then add the macaroni, butter, gruyere and tuna. Mix well and serve hot.

277 Macaroni with bacon and peas

CODITOS CON BACON Y GUISANTES

- **300 g/11 oz elbow macaroni**
- **2 tablespoons sunflower oil**
- **1 large onion, finely chopped**
- **1 kg/2 ¼ lb ripe tomatoes, seeded and coarsely chopped**
- **1 teaspoon sugar**
- **250 g/9 oz canned peas, drained**
- **80 g/3 oz gruyere cheese, grated**
- **12 thin smoked bacon rashers**
- **salt**

Serves 4–5

Cook the macaroni as described on page 221. Refresh under cold running water, drain and set aside. Heat the oil in a frying pan. Add the onion and cook over a low heat, stirring occasionally, for about 8 minutes, until beginning to brown. Add the tomato and cook, stirring occasionally and breaking it up with the side of the spoon, for about 10 minutes. Allow to cool slightly, then transfer to a food processor and process to a purée. Add the sugar and season to taste with salt. Preheat the oven to 180°C/350°F/Gas Mark 4. Mix together the macaroni, tomato sauce, peas and 65 g/2 ½ oz of the gruyere in an ovenproof dish. Sprinkle the remaining gruyere on top and bake for a few minutes, until the cheese has melted. Meanwhile, roll up the bacon slices and secure with wooden cocktail sticks. Cook in a heavy-based or non-stick frying pan, turning frequently, for 5–10 minutes, until lightly browned and cooked through. Remove and discard the cocktail sticks, place the bacon rolls on top of the pasta and serve immediately.

278

Tagliatelle with prawns and pistachio nuts
CINTAS CON GAMBAS Y PISTACHOS

- 200 g/7 oz raw, unpeeled prawns
- 2 courgettes
- 5 tablespoons olive oil
- 2 shallots, finely chopped
- 50 g/2 oz shelled pistachio nuts
- pinch of dried oregano
- 400 g/14 oz fresh tagliatelle
- 1 tablespoon chopped fresh basil
- salt and pepper

Serves 4

Peel the prawns, reserving the heads and shells. Put the heads and shells into a saucepan, pour in 2 litres/3 ½ pints water and bring to the boil. Lower the heat and simmer for 15 minutes. Meanwhile, slice the courgettes lengthways into thin strips with a vegetable peeler. Season with salt and pepper. Heat half the oil in a frying pan. Add the shallots and cook over a low heat, stirring occasionally, for 5 minutes, until softened and translucent. Add the courgettes and cook, stirring occasionally, for 5 minutes. Add the prawn tails, pistachios and oregano and cook, stirring occasionally, for 3–5 minutes, until the prawns are opaque. Strain the prawn shell stock into a clean saucepan, add a pinch of salt and bring to the boil. Add the tagliatelle and cook for 3–4 minutes, until tender, but still firm to the bite. Drain, add to the frying pan and toss with the sauce. Add the remaining oil and the basil and toss lightly again. Serve immediately.

279

Pasta with peppers and ham
PASTA CON PIMIENTOS Y JAMÓN

- 2 large red peppers
- 200 g/7 oz Serrano ham,
  thinly sliced
- 3 tablespoons olive oil
- 3 red onions, sliced
- 2 tablespoons capers,
  rinsed and drained
- 4 tablespoons chopped
  fresh basil
- 400 g/14 oz tagliatelle
- salt and pepper

Serves 4

Preheat the oven to 200°C/400°F/Gas Mark 6 or preheat the grill. Put the peppers on a baking sheet and place in the oven or under the grill and cook, turning frequently, for about 25 minutes, until charred and blistered. Transfer to a chopping board, cover with a tea towel and leave to cool, then peel off the skins. Halve lengthways, remove and discard the seeds and cut the flesh into thick strips. Cut the ham into strips. Heat the oil in a frying pan. Add the onion and cook over a low heat, stirring occasionally, for about 5 minutes, until softened and translucent. Remove the pan from the heat, stir in the pepper strips, ham, capers and basil, season with salt and pepper and turn into a bowl. Bring a large saucepan of salted water to the boil. Add the tagliatelle, bring back to the boil and cook for 8–10 minutes, until tender but still firm to the bite. Drain well and toss with the mixture in the bowl. Serve warm or cold.

Note: for a contrast of textures, cook the ham in a frying pan until crisp before adding to the recipe.

Seafood noodles
FIDEOS CON MARISCOS (FIDEUÁ)

- **300 g/11 oz raw,**
  unpeeled prawns
- **400 g/14 oz monkfish**
- **175 ml/6 fl oz olive oil**
- **6 small langoustines or**
  Dublin Bay prawns
- **4 tomatoes,**
  peeled, seeded and diced
- **2 cloves garlic, crushed**
- **1 teaspoon paprika**
- **pinch of saffron powder**
- **500 g/1 lb 2 oz very fine noodles**
- **salt**

Serves 6

Peel the prawns, reserving the heads and shells. Set the prawns aside. Cut along either side of the monkfish bone, set the fillets aside and reserve the bone. Pour 1.75 litres/3 pints water into a saucepan, add a pinch of salt, the prawn heads and shells and the monkfish bone and bring to the boil. Lower the heat and simmer for 20 minutes. Meanwhile, cut the monkfish fillets into 2-cm/¾-inch cubes. Remove the pan from the heat, leave to cool slightly then strain the stock into a bowl and set aside. Heat the oil in a paella pan or flameproof earthenware dish. Add the langoustines or Dublin Bay prawns and cook for a few minutes, then add the prawn tails and monkfish. Cook for a few minutes more, then transfer to a plate and set aside. Add the tomato and garlic to the paella pan and cook, stirring occasionally, for 5 minutes. Stir in the paprika and saffron and cook, stirring occasionally, for 8–10 minutes. Preheat the oven to 180°C/350°F/Gas Mark 4. Add the noodles to the paella pan, stir with a wooden spoon and pour in 1.5 litres/2 ½ pints of the reserved stock. Cook over a high heat for 12 minutes, add the seafood, placing it carefully around the dish, and cook for a further 3 minutes. Transfer to the oven and bake for about 5 minutes, until the top is lightly coloured. Serve immediately straight from the dish.

Note: You can also substitute mussels for the langoustines. They are less expensive but are also very tasty. If you are substituting mussels for langoustines, use their strained cooking liquid instead of the fish stock, and shell them before adding them to the dish.

281

Noodles with crayfish

TALLARINES CON CANGREJOS

- 24 live crayfish
- 1 ½ teaspoons sea salt
- 250 g/9 oz fresh noodles
- 250 ml/8 fl oz single cream
- 3 tablespoons chopped
  fresh parsley
- pepper

  Stock:
- 2 carrots
- 1 onion
- 6 black peppercorns
- 1 bay leaf
- 1 sprig fresh parsley
- 1 sprig fresh thyme
- 1 tablespoon olive oil
- salt

Serves 4

Put all the stock ingredients into a saucepan, pour in 2 litres/3 ½ pints water and bring to the boil over a high heat. Meanwhile, wash the crayfish in plenty of cold water. Pull out the bitter gut, by twisting the central lamina at the end of the tail and then pulling it so that the gut comes out in one piece. When the stock is boiling vigorously, add the crayfish, bring back to the boil and cook for 4–6 minutes, depending on their size. Remove from the pan and shell. (Most of the edible meat is in the tail, but you can also crack the claws with a nutcracker and extract the meat.) Flake the flesh. Pour 3 litres/5 ¼ pints water into a large saucepan and bring to the boil. Add the salt and noodles, stir with a fork to prevent the noodles sticking, bring back to the boil and cook for a few minutes, until tender but still firm to the bite. Drain well. Meanwhile, gently heat the cream in another large saucepan, but do not allow it to boil. Stir in the crayfish meat and cook, stirring constantly, for 1 minute, to heat through. Add the noodles and toss over a low heat. Serve immediately, seasoned with pepper and sprinkled with the parsley.

282

Noodles with walnuts and truffles

TALLARINES CON NUECES Y TRUFA

- 1 truffle, about 40 g/1 ½ oz
- 1 egg yolk, lightly beaten
- 150 g/5 oz mascarpone cheese
- 400 g/14 oz fresh noodles
- 12 walnuts,
  shelled, peeled and chopped
- 25–40 g/1–1 ½ oz Parmesan
  cheese, grated
- salt and pepper

Serves 4

Clean the truffle with a small brush and a damp cloth. Stir the egg yolk into the mascarpone with a wooden spoon. Season with salt and pepper. Bring a large saucepan of salted water to the boil. Add the noodles, bring back to the boil and cook for a few minutes, until tender but still firm to the bite. Drain the noodles and toss with the mascarpone mixture. Sprinkle with the walnuts and Parmesan to taste and grate a little truffle to taste over the top. Alternatively, sprinkle the noodles with very thinly sliced truffle.

Note: For a delicious variation, crush the walnuts until they are reduced to a paste, then season them with salt and pepper and add a pinch of freshly grated nutmeg and a pinch of ground cinnamon. Stir in a little oil and mix the paste in with the drained noodles before continuing as above.

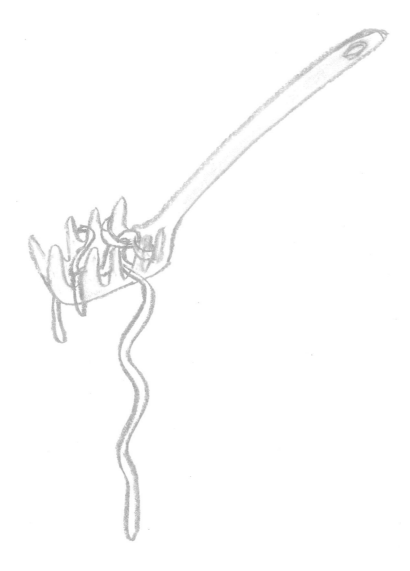

283

Spaghetti alla carbonara

ESPAGUETIS A LA ITALIANA CON BACON Y HUEVOS

- **350 g/12 oz spaghetti**
- **120 ml/4 fl oz olive oil**
- **150 g/5 oz bacon,**
  cut into 1-cm/½-inch strips
- **80 g/3 oz butter**
- **4 eggs, beaten**
- **small pinch of aromatic herbs**
- **80 g/3 oz Parmesan cheese,**
  grated
- **salt**

Serves 4

Cook the spaghetti as described on page 221. Meanwhile, heat the oil in a frying pan. Add the bacon and cook, stirring occasionally, for about 5 minutes, until tender and cooked through. Remove from the pan and drain on kitchen paper. Drain the spaghetti in a large colander and cover with a clean tea towel to prevent it from getting cold. Melt the butter in another large saucepan. Remove the pan from the heat, then add the bacon and eggs, immediately followed by the spaghetti, aromatic herbs and Parmesan. Stir well, then transfer to a warm serving dish and serve immediately.

284

Spaghetti with peas and clams

ESPAGUETIS CON GUISANTES Y ALMEJAS

- **350 g/12 oz spaghetti**
- **500 g/1 lb 2 oz clams**
- **5 tablespoons white wine**
- **1 shallot, finely chopped**
- **50 g/2 oz butter**
- **100 g/3 ½ oz canned peas, drained**
- **80 g/3 oz Parmesan cheese, grated**
- **salt**

Serves 4

Cook the spaghetti as described on page 221. Meanwhile, wash the clams in salted water. Discard any with broken shells or any that do not shut immediately when sharply tapped. Put them into a saucepan, pour in the wine and add the shallot. Cover and cook over a high heat, shaking the pan occasionally, for 3–5 minutes, until the shells have opened. Remove the pan from the heat. Remove the clams with a slotted spoon and reserve the cooking liquid. Discard any that remain closed. Remove the clams from their shells and set aside. Strain the cooking liquid into a bowl through a muslin-lined sieve. Drain the spaghetti. Melt the butter in another large saucepan. Add the spaghetti, clams, peas, reserved cooking liquid and Parmesan. Mix well and heat through briefly, then transfer to warm serving dish. Serve immediately.

285

Spaghetti with clams and porcini
ESPAGUETIS CON ALMEJAS Y SETAS

- 1 ½ small onions
- 1 hake or other white fish head,
  gills removed
- 3 cloves garlic
- 1 sprig fresh parsley
- 25 g/1 oz dried or fresh porcini
- 250 g/9 oz clams
- 4 tablespoons olive oil
- 250 g/9 oz raw prawns, peeled
- 400 g/14 oz canned chopped
  tomatoes
- pinch of saffron threads
- 300 g/11 oz spaghetti
- salt

Serves 4

Cut the half onion into wedges and finely chop the whole onion. Put the fish head into a saucepan with the onion wedges, one of the garlic cloves, and the parsley. Pour in water to cover and bring to the boil, then lower the heat and simmer for about 30 minutes. Meanwhile, if using dried porcini put them into a small bowl and pour in warm water to cover. Set aside to soak. Finely chop the remaining garlic. Scrub the clams under cold running water. Discard any with damaged shells or any that do not shut immediately when sharply tapped. Heat the oil in a saucepan. Add the chopped garlic and the chopped onion and cook over a low heat, stirring occasionally, for 8 minutes, until beginning to brown. Add the prawns, clams and 50 ml/2 fl oz water, cover and cook for 10 minutes. Discard any clams that remain closed. Meanwhile, drain the dried porcini, if using. Chop the porcini (dried or fresh). Add the porcini and the tomato to the pan and cook for a further 5 minutes. Strain the fish stock into a clean pan, add the saffron and a pinch of salt and bring to the boil. Add the spaghetti, bring back to the boil and cook for 10–12 minutes, until tender but still firm to the bite. Drain and add to the sauce. Toss to coat and serve immediately.

286

Spaghetti with peas and porcini
ESPAGUETIS CON GUISANTES Y SETAS

- 350 g/12 oz spaghetti
- 120 g/4 oz butter
- 50 g/2 oz dried or fresh porcini
- 100 g/3 ½ oz canned peas,
  drained
- 70 g/3 oz Parmesan cheese,
  grated
- salt

Serves 4

If you are using dried mushrooms, soak them as described in recipe 285, drain and slice. Cook the spaghetti as described on page 221. Melt the butter in a frying pan, add the mushrooms and cook until softened. Drain the spaghetti well and add it and the peas to the frying pan and toss. Sprinkle with the cheese and serve immediately. This is a dish with a very distinctive taste but it is also delicious.

287

Spaghetti with courgettes
ESPAGUETIS CON CALABACINES

- 500 g/1 lb 2 oz courgettes,
  cut into thick sticks
- 350 g/12 oz spaghetti
- 3 tablespoons olive oil
- 1 onion, finely chopped
- juice of ½ lemon
- 275 ml/9 fl oz double cream
- 80 g/3 oz cheese, such as
  Cheddar or gruyere, grated
- salt

Serves 4

Cook the courgettes in plenty of salted boiling water for 2 minutes, then drain and refresh under cold running water. Set aside in a clean tea towel to dry. Cook the spaghetti as described on page 221. Meanwhile, heat the oil in a frying pan. Add the courgettes and onion and cook over a low heat, stirring occasionally, for 8–10 minutes. Stir in the lemon juice. Drain the spaghetti well and add it to the pan. Stir in the cream, season to taste with salt and serve immediately, offering the cheese separately.

288

Spaghetti Bolognese
ESPAGUETIS CON SALSA BOLOÑESA

- 300 g/11 oz spaghetti
- salt

  Bolognese sauce:
- 2 tablespoons olive oil
- 50 g/2 oz bacon, finely chopped
- 150 g/5 oz minced steak
- 1 large onion, finely chopped
- 1 carrot, finely chopped
- 1–2 sticks celery, finely chopped
- pinch of ground cloves
- 6 tablespoons passata
- 2 tablespoons white wine
- 275 ml/9 fl oz single cream
- 80 g/3 oz Parmesan cheese,
  grated
- salt

Serves 6

First, make the Bolognese sauce. Heat the oil in a saucepan. Add the bacon and cook over a low heat, stirring occasionally, for 4 minutes. Add the minced steak, onion, carrot, celery and cloves, season with salt and cook, stirring frequently, for 10 minutes. Stir in the passata and wine, cover and simmer for 10 minutes. Meanwhile, cook the spaghetti as described on page 221. Drain well and stir into the sauce along with the cream and Parmesan. Serve immediately.

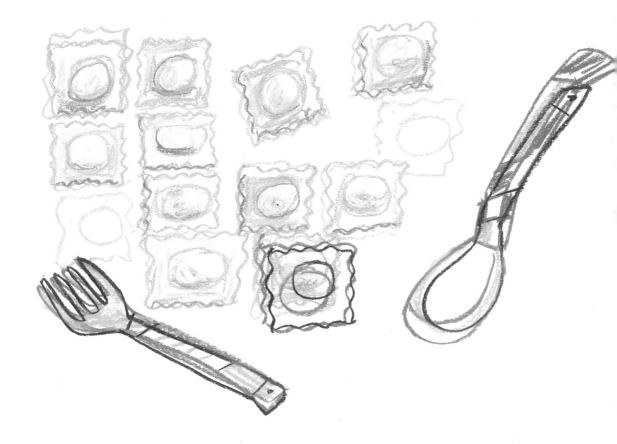

289

Ravioli

RAVIOLIS

Make the pasta dough as described in recipe 269, shape into a ball and leave to rest for 2 hours. Cut it in half and roll out into two very thin squares. Place small heaps of prepared filling (see the following recipes) on one of the squares, spacing them 2.5 cm/1 inch apart. Brush the spaces in between the mounds of filling with water and brush the second dough square with water. Place the second square, damp side down, on top of the first square. Use a fluted pasta wheel to cut between the ravioli, pressing down hard to make sure the edges stick together. Bring a large saucepan of salted water to the boil. Add the ravioli, in batches, and bring back to the boil, then lower the heat and cook for about 20 minutes, until tender. Drain and refresh under cold running water to prevent the ravioli sticking. The ravioli are now ready to be mixed with a sauce and baked. Cook them as soon as they are ready to prevent them drying out.

Note: Ready-made ravioli are widely available, in which case you need only cook them, make the sauce and then bake them – an easier and quicker process.

290

Fillings for ravioli (first version)

RELLENOS PARA RAVIOLIS

- **500 g/1 lb 2 oz spinach,
  coarse stalks removed**
- **50 g/2 oz bread, crusts removed**
- **5 tablespoons hot milk**
- **3 tablespoons olive oil**
- **1 tablespoon finely chopped
  onion**
- **150 g/5 oz sausage meat**
- **1 tablespoon sherry**
- **1 egg, lightly beaten**
- **salt**

Makes about 35

Cook the spinach in salted boiling water for about 10 minutes. Drain it well, pressing down with the back of a spoon to squeeze out all the water. Finely chop the leaves. Put the bread in a bowl, add the hot milk and leave to soak. Heat the oil in a frying pan. Add the onion and cook over a low heat, stirring occasionally, for about 10 minutes, until lightly browned. Stir in the sausage meat. Remove the pan from the heat and put the meat and onion mixture into a bowl. Gently squeeze out the bread and add it to the bowl along with the sherry, egg and a pinch of salt. Mix well with a wooden spoon, then add the spinach. Leave the mixture to cool completely before using it to fill the ravioli.

291

Fillings for ravioli (second version)

RELLENOS PARA RAVIOLIS

- **500 g/1 lb 2 oz spinach,
  coarse stalks removed**
- **3 tablespoons olive oil**
- **2 leeks, halved lengthways, cut
  into 2.5-cm/1-inch lengths, and
  rinsed well**
- **150 g/5 oz lean beef, diced**
- **100 g/3 ½ oz breadcrumbs**
- **50 g/2 oz gruyere or Parmesan
  cheese, grated**
- **1 egg, lightly beaten**
- **1 tablespoon sherry**
- **salt**

Makes about 35

Cook the spinach in salted boiling water for about 10 minutes. Drain it well, pressing down with the back of a spoon to squeeze out all the water. Finely chop the leaves. Heat the oil in a frying pan. Add the leek and cook over a low heat, stirring occasionally, for 10 minutes. Add the beef, cover and cook over a low heat, stirring occasionally, for 15–20 minutes. Mince the meat mixture and spinach with a mincer or in a food processor. Put the resulting mixture into a bowl with the breadcrumbs, cheese, egg, sherry and a pinch of salt. Stir well until the mixture comes together. Leave the mixture to cool completely before using it to fill the ravioli.

292

Tomato sauce for ravioli
SALSA DE TOMATE PARA RAVIOLIS

- 3 tablespoons sunflower oil
- 50 g/2 oz onion, chopped
- 1.5 kg/3 ¼ lb ripe tomatoes, seeded and diced
- 1 teaspoon sugar
- 100 g/3 ½ oz Parmesan or gruyere cheese, grated
- 25 g/1 oz butter
- salt

Serves 4

Heat the oil in a frying pan. Add the onion and cook over a low heat, stirring occasionally, for about 5 minutes, until softened. Add the tomato and cook, breaking it up with the edge of a skimmer or slotted spoon, for 10 minutes. Allow to cool slightly, then transfer to a food processor and process to a purée. Add the sugar and a pinch of salt. Preheat the oven to 200°C/400°F/Gas Mark 6. Spoon a little of the sauce into an ovenproof dish and sprinkle with half the cheese. Place the ravioli on top and pour the remaining tomato sauce over them. Sprinkle with the remaining cheese and dot with the butter. Bake for 20–30 minutes, until golden brown.

293

Béchamel sauce for ravioli
SALSAS BECHAMEL PARA RAVIOLIS

- 50 g/2 oz butter
- 2 tablespoons olive oil
- 1 tablespoon plain flour
- 500 ml/18 fl oz milk
- 2 teaspoons tomato purée
- 50 g/2 oz gruyere cheese, grated
- salt

Serves 4

Melt half the butter with the oil in a saucepan. Stir in the flour and cook, stirring constantly, for 2 minutes. Gradually stir in the milk, a little at a time. Season with salt and cook, stirring constantly, for 6 minutes. Stir in the tomato purée. Preheat the oven to 200°C/400°F/Gas Mark 6. Place the ravioli in an ovenproof dish and pour the béchamel sauce over them. Sprinkle with the cheese and dot with the remaining butter. Bake for about 20–30 minutes, until the cheese has melted.

Porcini ravioli in leek sauce
RAVIOLI DE SETAS CON SALSA DE PUERROS

- 300 g/11 oz plain flour,
  plus extra for dusting
- 1 teaspoon salt
- 3 eggs, lightly beaten
- 2 chicken stock cubes

Filling:
- 25 g/1 oz butter
- 1 shallot, chopped
- 1 clove garlic, crushed
- 500 g/1 lb 2 oz porcini,
  finely chopped
- juice of 1 lemon
- salt and pepper

Sauce:
- 25 g/1 oz butter
- 500 g/1 lb 2 oz leeks,
  halved lengthways, chopped,
  and rinsed well
- 4 tablespoons chicken stock
  (home-made or made with a
  stock cube)
- 100 ml/3 ½ fl oz single cream
- salt and pepper

Serves 4–6

Sift the flour and salt on to a work surface and make a well in the centre. Break the eggs into the well and gradually incorporate the dry ingredients to make a smooth dough. If the dough is too sticky, add a little more flour. Cover and leave to rest while preparing the filling. Melt the butter in a large frying pan. Add the shallot and garlic and cook over a low heat, stirring occasionally, for 5 minutes, until softened. Add the porcini and lemon juice and season to taste with salt and pepper. Cover and simmer gently for 10 minutes, until the liquid has evaporated, then remove from the heat and leave to cool. Roll out the dough on a lightly floured surface. Fill and cut out ravioli as described in recipe 289. To make the sauce, melt the butter in a frying pan. Add the leek and cook over a low heat, stirring occasionally, for 5 minutes, until softened. Add the stock and simmer for a further 10 minutes, until tender. Allow to cool slightly, then transfer to a food processor, add the cream and process until smooth. Strain into a clean pan and reheat gently. Season to taste with salt and pepper and, if necessary, add a little more stock. Bring a large saucepan of water to the boil and crumble in the stock cubes. Add the ravioli, in batches, and bring back to the boil and cook for 4 minutes, until tender but still firm to the bite. Drain and serve immediately with the sauce.

Note: Test the edge of one of the ravioli before draining. As it is thicker there it takes longer to cook. The ravioli may also be served with a mustard and cream sauce.

Duck and foie ravioli with sauce

RAVIOLIS DE PATO Y FOIE CON SALSA

- 400 g/14 oz plain flour,
  plus extra for dusting
- 3 large eggs
- 1 teaspoon olive oil
- salt

  Filling:
- 300 g/11 oz cooked duck fillet
- 100 g/3 ½ oz boar's head,
  in a single piece
- 100 g/3 ½ oz cooked duck
  foie gras, chopped
- 4 tablespoons chopped
  fresh parsley
- pinch of freshly grated nutmeg
- 1 ¼ teaspoons finely chopped
  onion
- 1 teaspoon finely chopped
  gherkin
- 1 teaspoon capers,
  rinsed and drained
- 50 ml/2 fl oz balsamic vinegar
- 50 ml/2 fl oz walnut oil
- 1 teaspoon strong mustard
- salt and pepper

Serves 4

Sift the flour and a pinch of salt on to a work surface and make a well in the centre. Break the eggs into the well and add 2 tablespoons water and the oil. Gradually incorporate the dry ingredients to make a smooth dough. Cover and leave to rest for 2 hours. Heat the duck fillet in the microwave. Cut off the meat and chop. Heat the boar's head in the microwave, drain off the fat into a bowl and reserve. Chop the meat. Mix together the duck and boar's head meat, foie gras, parsley, nutmeg, onion, gherkin and capers in a bowl and stir in the reserved fat. Season with pepper. Roll out the dough on a lightly floured surface. Fill and cut out ravioli as described in recipe 289. Bring a large saucepan of salted water to the boil. Add the ravioli, in batches, and bring back to the boil and cook for 5 minutes, until tender but still firm to the bite. Meanwhile, whisk together the balsamic vinegar, walnut oil and mustard in a bowl. Drain the ravioli, put in a warm serving dish and pour the dressing over them. Serve this dish immediately.

Note: This filling is also delicious in cannelloni. Serve the cannelloni on a bed of chopped mushrooms and finely chopped onion lightly cooked in a little butter. It will make them more succulent.

296

Gnocchi

ÑOQUIS

- **1.5 litres/2 ½ pints milk**
- **300 g/11 oz semolina**
- **100 g/3 ½ oz butter**
- **50 g/2 oz Parmesan or gruyere cheese, grated**
- **4 egg yolks**
- **salt**

Béchamel sauce:
- **25 g/1 oz butter**
- **1 tablespoon olive oil**
- **1 tablespoon plain flour**
- **300 ml/½ pint milk**
- **130 ml/4 ½ fl oz white wine**
- **pinch of freshly grated nutmeg (optional)**
- **salt**

Serves 6

Bring the milk just to the boil in a saucepan. Sprinkle in the semolina and cook, stirring constantly, for 5 minutes. Stir in the butter and cheese. Remove the pan from the heat and stir in the egg yolks, one at a time. Season to taste with salt and leave to cool. Shape the cooled mixture into little balls about the size of walnuts and place them in a flameproof dish. Preheat the grill. To make the béchamel sauce, melt the butter with the oil in a saucepan. Stir in the flour and cook, stirring constantly, for 2 minutes. Gradually stir in the milk and then the wine, season with salt and add the nutmeg, if using. Cook over a low heat, stirring constantly, for 10 minutes. Pour the sauce over the gnocchi and grill lightly before serving.

Cannelloni

CANELONES DE CARNE

- 12 cannelloni tubes or
  12 sheets of egg pasta,
  15 x 7.5 cm/6 x 3 inches
- 80 g/3 ½ oz gruyere cheese,
  grated
- 25 g/1 oz butter
- ¾ quantity Classic Tomato
  Sauce (see recipe 73)

Filling:
- 2 tablespoons olive oil
- 1 small onion, finely chopped
- 150 g/5 oz minced beef
- 1 cooked chicken breast, minced
- 1 cooked lamb's brain
- 25 g/1 oz foie gras

Béchamel sauce:
- 25 g/1 oz butter
- 2 tablespoons sunflower oil
- 2 tablespoons plain flour
- 750 ml/1 ¼ pints milk or
  half milk half stock
- salt

Makes 12 cannelloni

The filling for cannelloni can be made in several ways, some more expensive than others. The base is always meat – minced beef, veal or even better, pork. This can be mixed with various other ingredients such as fried chicken livers, minced cooked chicken breast, a cooked lamb's brain, foie gras, Serrano, York or other dry-cured ham and sausage meat. The idea is to mix the meat with one or more ingredients that add flavour but do not overpower it. Another delicious alternative is to cook a small finely chopped onion with a little chopped tomato to make a paste. If using the cannelloni tubes, prepare according to the instructions on the packet. The type that does not require precooking is the easiest to use. To make the dish a little simpler, you could use good-quality bottled tomato sauce, if you like, instead of making the sauce, but it should be quite thick. To make the filling, heat the oil in a small frying pan. Add the onion and cook over a low heat, stirring occasionally, for about 5 minutes, until softened and translucent. Stir in 2 tablespoons of the tomato sauce and remove from the heat. Mix the onion with all the other filling ingredients in a bowl. Drain the cannelloni tubes, if necessary. Fill the tubes using a teaspoon or divide the filling among the pasta sheets and roll them up. Put them into an ovenproof dish. Preheat the oven to 200°C/400°F/Gas Mark 6.

Make a thin béchamel sauce as described in recipe 77 and stir in the remaining tomato sauce. (You can omit the tomato sauce, if you like.) Strain the sauce over the cannelloni through a coarse sieve. (This is not necessary if the tomato sauce has been omitted.) Sprinkle the gruyere over the top and dot with the butter. Bake for about 20 minutes, until the topping is golden brown. Remove the dish from the oven and leave to stand for about 5 minutes before serving.

Fried cannelloni

CANELONES FRITOS

- 200 g/7 oz plain flour
- 1 egg
- 1 bottle of beer (330 ml/12 fl oz),
  at room temperature
- 1 litre/1 ¾ pints olive oil
- 12 filled cannelloni
  (see recipe 297)
- salt
- 1 quantity Classic Tomato Sauce
  (see recipe 73)

Serves 4

Sift the flour into a bowl and sprinkle in a pinch of salt. Add the egg and mix lightly, then gradually stir in the beer, a little at a time, until the batter has the consistency of a thick béchamel. Heat the oil in a frying pan. Dip the filled cannelloni, one at a time, into the beer batter to coat, then place into the hot oil, seam sides down. Cook until golden brown, then remove with a skimmer or slotted spoon. Drain well and keep warm while cooking the remaining cannelloni. Serve the fried cannelloni plain or with tomato sauce offered separately.

299 Tuna, hard-boiled egg and mushroom cannelloni

CANELONES DE ATÚN, HUEVOS DUROS Y CHAMPIÑONES

- 12 cannelloni tubes or
  12 sheets of egg pasta,
  15 x 7.5 cm/6 x 3 inches
- 100 g/3 ½ oz chestnut
  mushrooms, chopped
- 20 g/¾ oz butter
- juice of ½ lemon
- 3 tablespoons olive oil
- 200 g/7 oz finely chopped onion
- 1 quantity Classic Tomato Sauce
  (see recipe 73)
- 250 g/9 oz canned tuna in oil or
  brine, drained and flaked
- 2 hard-boiled eggs, chopped
- 50 g/2 oz gruyere cheese, grated
- salt

Béchamel sauce:
- 25g/1 oz butter
- 2 tablespoons sunflower oil
- 2 tablespoons plain flour
- 500 ml/18 fl oz milk or half milk
  half stock

Serves 6

If using the cannelloni tubes, prepare them according to the instructions on the packet instructions. Put the mushrooms into a saucepan with the butter and the lemon juice. Cover and cook over a low heat for about 10 minutes. Heat the oil in a frying pan. Add the onion and cook over a low heat, stirring occasionally, for about 5 minutes, until softened but not browned. Remove the pan from the heat and stir in 2 tablespoons of the tomato sauce, the tuna, mushrooms and hard-boiled eggs. Season to taste with salt. Drain the cannelloni tubes, if necessary. Fill the tubes using a teaspoon or divide the filling among the pasta sheets and roll them up. Put them into an ovenproof dish. Preheat the oven to 200°C/400°F/Gas Mark 6. Make the béchamel sauce as described in recipe 77 and stir in 3–4 tablespoons of the tomato sauce to turn it pink. Pour the béchamel sauce over the cannelloni, sprinkle with the gruyere and dot with the butter. Bake for about 20 minutes, until the topping is golden brown. Remove the dish from the oven and leave to stand for 5 minutes before serving.

Note: You can use fresh or leftover cooked fish instead of tuna. If using fresh fish, poach it first.

300

Cannelloni with leftover ragout

CANELONES CON UN RESTO DE RAGOÛT

- 12 cannelloni tubes or
  12 sheets of egg pasta,
  15 x 7.5 cm/6 x 3 inches
- 250 g/9 oz leftover ragout
- 1 quantity Classic Béchamel
  Sauce (see recipe 77)
- 100 g/3 ½ oz gruyere cheese,
  grated
- 25 g/1 oz butter

Serves 6

Cannelloni made with leftover ragout (or meat stew) are delicious and original. Mince the meat, carrots and onion and use this to fill the cannelloni. Put the leftover ragout into an ovenproof dish and place the filled cannelloni on top. Spoon some of the meat sauce over them. Pour the béchamel sauce over the cannelloni. Sprinkle with grated cheese, dot with butter and bake until golden brown. Serve straight from the dish.

301

Spinach cannelloni with hard-boiled egg

CANELONES DE ESPINACAS Y HUEVOS DUROS

- 12 cannelloni tubes or
  12 sheets of egg pasta,
  15 x 7.5 cm/6 x 3 inches
- 1.5 kg/3 ¼ lb spinach,
  coarse stalks removed
- 80 g/3 oz butter
- 3 hard-boiled eggs, chopped
- 100 g/3 ½ oz gruyere, grated
- salt

Béchamel sauce:
- 25 g/1 oz butter
- 2 tablespoons sunflower oil
- 2 tablespoons plain flour
- 500 ml/18 fl oz milk or
  half milk half stock

Serves 6

If using the cannelloni tubes, prepare them according to the instructions on the packet. Cook the spinach in salted boiling water for about 10 minutes. Drain well, pressing down with the back of a spoon to squeeze out all the water, then finely chop the leaves. Melt 50 g/2 oz of the butter in a frying pan and stir in the spinach. Remove the pan from the heat and add the hard-boiled eggs and half the gruyere. Drain the cannelloni tubes, if necessary. Fill the tubes using a teaspoon or divide the filling among the pasta sheets and roll them up. Put them into an ovenproof dish. Preheat the oven to 200°C/400°F/Gas Mark 6. Make the béchamel sauce as described in recipe 77 and pour it over the cannelloni. Sprinkle with the remaining cheese and dot with the remaining butter. Bake for 15–30 minutes, until the topping is golden brown. Remove the dish from the oven and leave to stand for about 5 minutes before serving.

Salmon lasagne with ratatouille

LASAÑA DE SALMÓN CON PISTO

- 350–400 g/12–14 oz lasagne
- 750 g/1 lb 10 oz thin salmon
  fillets
- 350 ml/12 fl oz thick fish stock
  (home-made or made with a
  stock cube) or white wine

Ratatouille:
- 7 tablespoons olive oil
- 2 large onions, chopped
- 2 kg/4 ½ lb courgettes,
  peeled, halved, seeded and diced
- 1 kg/2 ¼ lb ripe tomatoes,
  peeled and chopped
- 1 teaspoon sugar
- 2 green peppers, diced
- salt

Serves 6

Make the ratatouille. Heat 3 tablespoons of the oil in a saucepan. Add the onion and cook, stirring occasionally, for 5 minutes, until soft and translucent. Add the courgette and cook, stirring occasionally, for a further 10 minutes, until lightly browned. Meanwhile, heat 2 tablespoons of the remaining oil in a frying pan. Add the tomato and cook, stirring occasionally and breaking it up with the side of the spoon for 10 minutes. Allow to cool slightly, then transfer to a food processor and process to a purée. Stir in the sugar, season with salt and stir into the courgette. Simmer gently for 20 minutes. Meanwhile, heat the remaining oil in another frying pan. Add the pepper, cover the pan and cook over a low heat, stirring occasionally, for 20 minutes. Add to the courgette and tomato mixture and stir well. Cook the sheets of lasagne according to the instructions on the packet. Put the salmon into a fish kettle or large shallow pan. Add the stock and bring to the boil. Lower the heat and poach for about 10 minutes, until cooked through. Lift out carefully. Make a layer of fish in a deep ovenproof dish, then add a layer of ratatouille, then one of lasagne. Continue with all remaining ingredients. Serve immediately.

Lasagne

LASAÑA

- olive oil, for brushing
- 350–400 g/12–14 oz lasagne
- 80 g/3 oz Parmesan cheese, grated
- 30 g/1 oz butter

Béchamel sauce:
- 50 g/2 oz butter
- 50 g/2 oz plain flour
- 500 ml/18 fl oz milk
- pinch of freshly grated nutmeg
- salt and pepper

Filling:
- 2 tablespoons olive oil
- 50 g/2 oz sausage meat
- 50 g/2 oz ham, chopped
- ½ onion, chopped
- ½ carrot, chopped
- ½ stick celery, chopped
- 1 clove garlic, chopped
- 150 g/5 oz minced beef
- 5 tablespoons red wine
- 300 g/11 oz ripe tomatoes, peeled and chopped
- 1 bay leaf
- pinch of ground cloves
- salt and pepper

Serves 4

Make the filling. Heat the oil in a frying pan. Add the sausage meat and cook over a low heat, stirring frequently, for a few minutes, until lightly browned. Add the ham, onion, carrot, celery and garlic and cook, stirring occasionally, for 5 minutes. Add the minced beef and cook, breaking it up with a wooden spoon, for 5–8 minutes, until browned. Increase the heat to medium, pour in the wine and cook until it has almost evaporated, then add the tomato, bay leaf and cloves and season with salt and pepper. Lower the heat, cover and simmer for 40 minutes. Remove and discard the bay leaf. Make the béchamel sauce as described in recipe 77. Season to taste with salt and pepper and stir in the nutmeg. Preheat the oven to 200°C/400°F/Gas Mark 6. Brush the base of an ovenproof dish with oil. Prepare the lasagne according to the instructions on the packet. Spoon some of the filling into the prepared dish to cover the base and top with a layer of béchamel sauce. Cover with a layer of lasagne sheets and sprinkle with some of the Parmesan. Continue making layers in this way until all the ingredients are used up, ending with a layer of béchamel sauce sprinkled with Parmesan. Dot with the butter and bake for 40 minutes. Remove from the oven and leave to stand for 5 minutes before serving.

Note: The pasta for the lasagne can be made using 400 g/14 oz plain flour, 4 eggs and salt (see recipe 269). Roll out and cut into rectangles. Cook in salted boiling water for a few minutes, then refresh in cold water and spread out on a tea towel to dry.

VEGETABLES AND MUSHROOMS

Vegetables

Sorrel

Origin and season

Sorrel comes from Africa. For a long time it was not very popular because it was considered too sour. Nowadays, cooks use it to give an original touch to their dishes. It can be found in markets from early spring to early autumn.

Selection

Choose the variety with thin arrow-shaped leaves, sometimes known as herb patience or sorrel dock. The leaves should look fresh and have no blemishes.

Nutrition

Sorrel contains about 25 calories per 100 g/3 ½ oz and lots of vitamin C, but the leaves also contain oxalic acid which should not be consumed by people with nephritic colic, asthma, arthritis or with liver complaints.

Tricks

• If sorrel is to be puréed, mix it with lettuce to reduce the acidity
• Sorrel goes very well with chicken
• An infusion of sorrel is wonderful for removing rust stains.

304

French-style sorrel
ACEDER AS A LA FRANCESA

- **2 kg/4½ lb sorrel, stalks removed**
- **50 g/2 oz butter**
- **1 tablespoon plain flour**
- **500 ml/18 fl oz milk**
- **2 egg yolks**
- **salt**

Serves 6

Pour 3–4 litres/5¼–7 pints water into a saucepan and add 1 tablespoon salt. Add the sorrel, bring to the boil over a high heat and cook for 10 minutes. Drain well and chop finely. Melt the butter in a saucepan. Stir in the flour and cook, stirring constantly, for 2 minutes. Gradually stir in the milk, a little at a time, and cook, stirring constantly, for 4 minutes. Lightly season with salt, then add the sorrel and stir well. Cover and simmer over a low heat, stirring occasionally, for 10 minutes. Lightly beat the egg yolks in a bowl, stir in a little of the sorrel mixture to prevent them curdling and stir into the pan. Season to taste with salt and serve as an accompaniment to eggs or meat.

305

Fried sorrel
ACEDERAS REHOGADAS

- **2 kg/4½ lb sorrel, stalks removed**
- **6 tablespoons olive oil**
- **2 cloves garlic, lightly crushed**
- **1½ tablespoons white-wine vinegar**
- **salt**

Serves 6

Pour 3–4 litres/5¼–7 pints water into a saucepan and add 1 tablespoon salt. Add the sorrel, bring to the boil over a high heat and cook for 10 minutes. Drain well and chop. Heat the oil in a saucepan. Add the garlic and cook for a few minutes, until lightly browned. Remove and discard the garlic, add the sorrel to the pan and cook, stirring frequently, until wilted. Remove the pan from the heat and pour the vinegar over the leaves. Reheat gently and serve.

306

Marinated Swiss chard

ACELGAS EN ESCABECHE

- **1.5 kg/3¼ lb Swiss chard, finely chopped**
- **sunflower oil, for deep-frying**
- **4 cloves garlic**
- **3 bay leaves**
- **3 tablespoons white-wine vinegar**
- **salt**

Dough:
- **5 tablespoons plain flour**
- **salt**

Serves 6

Put the Swiss chard into a saucepan, pour in water to cover and add a pinch of salt. Bring to the boil, then lower the heat and simmer for about 20 minutes, until tender. Drain well and, if necessary, chop more finely with a mezzaluna. Make the dough. Sift the flour with a pinch of salt into a bowl and stir in 250–275 ml/8–9 fl oz water to make a dough. Mix the dough with the Swiss chard. Heat the oil in a deep-fryer or saucepan to 180–190°C/350–375°F or until a cube of day-old bread browns in 30 seconds. Using a tablespoon, take small heaps of the Swiss chard mixture, add them to the pan, in batches of four, and cook for 3–4 minutes, until golden. Remove with a slotted spoon and drain on kitchen paper, then transfer to a deep serving dish and keep warm. Prepare the marinade. Transfer 6 tablespoons of the oil to a small frying pan and heat. Add the garlic and cook for a few minutes until lightly browned. Add the bay leaves and cook for a few minutes more. Remove the pan from the heat and add 350 ml/ 12 fl oz water, taking care that the oil does not splatter, and the vinegar. Return the pan to the heat, bring to the boil and simmer for 3–4 minutes. Remove and discard the garlic and bay leaves and pour the marinade over the Swiss chard. Leave the dish to stand for 5 minutes before serving to allow the Swiss chard to absorb the flavour of the marinade.

Note: This dish may also be served cold. Leave the Swiss chard to cool and prepare the marinade in advance to allow it to cool.

307

Fried Swiss chard with croûtons, meat juices and vinegar

ACELGAS REHOGADAS, CON CUSCURROS DE PAN, JUGO DE CARNE Y VINAGRE

- 1.5 kg/3¼ lb Swiss chard
- 250 ml/8 fl oz olive oil
- 50 g/2 oz white bread, crusts removed, cut into small cubes
- 250 ml/8 fl oz leftover meat cooking juices or beef stock (home-made or made with a stock cube)
- 1 tablespoon white-wine vinegar
- salt

Serves 4–6

Finely chop the Swiss chard, put it into a saucepan, pour in water to cover and add a pinch of salt. Bring to the boil, then lower the heat and simmer for about 20 minutes, until tender. Drain well. Heat the oil in a saucepan. Add the cubes of bread and cook, stirring frequently, until golden brown all over. Remove from the pan and set aside. Put the Swiss chard into a large frying pan, pour the meat sauce over the top and cook, stirring with a wooden spoon, for 5 minutes. Stir in the croûtons and vinegar, heat the Swiss chard through for a few minutes more and serve.

308

Swiss chard with tomatoes

ACELGAS CON TOMATE

- 1.75 kg/4 lb Swiss chard, finely chopped
- 3 tablespoons sunflower oil
- 1 onion, chopped
- 1 kg/2¼ lb very ripe tomatoes, seeded and chopped
- 1 teaspoon sugar
- pinch of aromatic herbs
- salt

Serves 6

Put the Swiss chard into a saucepan, pour in water to cover and add a pinch of salt. Bring to the boil, then lower the heat and simmer for about 20 minutes, until tender. Drain well. Heat the oil in a frying pan. Add the onion and cook over a low heat, stirring occasionally, for about 5 minutes, until softened and translucent. Add the tomato and cook, stirring occasionally and breaking it up with the side of the spoon, for 20 minutes. Stir in the sugar, a pinch of salt and the Swiss chard. Add the herbs and cook for 3 minutes. Serve immediately.

309

Deep-fried Swiss chard ribs

PENCAS DE ACELGAS REBOZADAS

- 1.5 kg/3¼ lb Swiss chard
- sunflower oil, for deep-frying
- 80 g/3 oz plain flour
- 2 eggs, lightly beaten
- salt

Serves 4–6

Cut out the ribs of the Swiss chard and cut them into 2.5-cm/1-inch long pieces. Put them into a saucepan, pour in water to cover and add a pinch of salt. Bring to the boil, then lower the heat and simmer for about 35 minutes, until tender. Drain well. Heat the oil in a deep-fryer or saucepan until a cube of day-old bread browns in 30 seconds. Roll each piece of Swiss chard rib in the flour, then dip into the eggs. Carefully add to the hot oil and cook until golden brown. Drain and serve immediately.

310   Baked Swiss chard ribs with Spanish sauce

PENCAS DE ACELGAS AL HORNO CON SALSA ESPAÑOLA

- 2.5 kg/5½ lb Swiss chard
- 6 tablespoons olive oil
- 1 large onion, chopped
- 250 g/9 oz carrots, sliced
- 1 kg/2¼ lb very ripe tomatoes, peeled, seeded and coarsely chopped
- 175 ml/6 fl oz white wine
- 1 bay leaf
- 1 sprig fresh thyme
- 1 sprig fresh parsley
- 1 teaspoon sugar
- 1 clove garlic, finely chopped
- 50 g/2 oz gruyere cheese, grated
- salt

Serves 6

Cut out the ribs of the Swiss chard and cut them into 2.5 cm/1 inch long pieces. Put them into a saucepan, pour in water to cover and add a pinch of salt. Bring to the boil, then lower the heat and simmer for 20 minutes. Drain well. Heat the oil in a large frying pan. Add the onion and cook over a low heat, stirring occasionally, for about 5 minutes, until softened and translucent. Add the carrot and cook, stirring frequently, for a further 10 minutes. Add the tomato and cook, stirring occasionally, for 8 minutes, then add the wine, bay leaf, thyme, parsley, sugar and garlic. Season with salt and pour in 500 ml/18 fl oz water. Cook over a medium heat for 1 hour. Remove and discard the bay leaf, thyme and parsley. Preheat the oven to 200°C/400°F/Gas Mark 6. Allow the tomato mixture to cool a little, then transfer to a food processor and process to a purée. Put half the Swiss chard ribs into an ovenproof dish and spoon a little of the sauce over them. Add the remaining ribs and pour the remaining sauce over them. Sprinkle with the gruyere and bake for about 15 minutes, until the cheese has melted. Serve immediately straight from the dish.

311   Baked Swiss chard ribs with garlic and parsley

PENCAS DE ACELGAS AL HORNO CON AJO Y PEREJIL

- 2.5 kg/5½ lb Swiss chard
- 2 teaspoons chopped fresh parsley
- 3 cloves garlic, finely chopped
- 4 tablespoons sunflower oil
- 3 tablespoons breadcrumbs
- 25 g/1 oz butter
- salt

Serves 6

Cut out the ribs of the Swiss chard and cut them into 4-cm/1½-inch long pieces. Put them into a saucepan, pour in water to cover and add a pinch of salt. Bring to the boil, then lower the heat and simmer for about 35 minutes, until tender. Drain well. Preheat the oven to 200°C/400°F/Gas Mark 6. Lay the Swiss chard ribs in an ovenproof dish and top with the parsley, garlic and oil. Sprinkle with the breadcrumbs and dot with the butter. Bake for 10–15 minutes until lightly browned on top. Serve immediately.

312

Artichokes in vinaigrette
ALCACHOFAS EN VINAGRETA

• 1 lemon, halved
• 12 globe artichokes
• 3 tablespoons white-wine
  vinegar
• 9 tablespoons sunflower oil
• 1 tablespoon chopped
  fresh parsley
• salt

Serves 6

Squeeze the juice from one lemon half and add the juice to a large bowl of water. Break off the artichoke stalks and remove the coarse outer leaves. Cut off the tips of the remaining leaves. Cut the artichokes in half lengthways, and remove and discard the chokes. Rub the artichokes with the remaining lemon half and place in the acidulated water. Bring a large saucepan of salted water to the boil. Add the artichokes and bring back to the boil, then lower the heat, cover and simmer for about 25 minutes, until tender. (Test by gently pulling a leaf; it should come away easily.) Drain well, turning the artichokes upside down and pressing down gently. Place the artichokes in a dish, cut side up. Whisk the vinegar with a pinch of salt in a bowl, then whisk in the oil. Pour the vinaigrette over the artichokes, sprinkle with the parsley and serve.

313

Artichokes in sauce
ALCACHOFAS EN SALSA

• 1 lemon, halved
• 1.5–2 kg/3¼–4½ lb small
  young globe artichokes
• 2 heaped tablespoons
  breadcrumbs
• 2 tablespoons olive oil
• 1 teaspoon chopped
  fresh parsley
• 2 cloves garlic, finely chopped
• salt

Serves 6

Squeeze the juice from one lemon half and add the juice to a large bowl of water. Cut off and reserve one slice from the other half. Remove the coarse outer leaves from the artichokes and cut off the tips of the remaining leaves. Cut the artichokes into halves or quarters lengthways, and remove and discard the chokes. Rub the artichokes with the remaining lemon half and place in the acidulated water. When all the artichokes have been prepared, drain them and put into a saucepan, which should be deep and not too wide. Add the reserved lemon slice, breadcrumbs, oil, parsley and garlic. Pour in just enough water to cover, add a pinch of salt and mix well. Bring to the boil over a high heat, then lower the heat to medium, cover and cook for about 45 minutes, until tender. (Test by gently pulling a leaf; it should come away easily.) Serve immediately.

Note: This dish can be made in advance and reheated.

314

Fried artichokes in sauce

ALCACHOFAS REBOZADAS Y EN SALSA

- 1 lemon, halved
- 12 globe artichokes
- 1 tablespoon plain flour,
  plus extra for dusting
- 500 ml/18 fl oz sunflower oil
- 3 tablespoons olive oil
- 2 onions, finely chopped
- 100 g/3 ½ oz Serrano ham,
  finely chopped
- salt

Serves 6

Squeeze the juice from one lemon half and add the juice to a large bowl of water. Break off the artichoke stalks and remove the coarse outer leaves. Cut off the tips of the remaining leaves. Open out the centres of the artichokes and remove the chokes. Rub the artichokes with the remaining lemon half and place in the acidulated water. Bring a large saucepan of salted water to the boil. Add the artichokes and bring back to the boil, then lower the heat, cover and simmer for about 35 minutes, until tender. (Test by gently pulling a leaf; it should come away easily.) Drain well, turning the artichokes upside down and pressing gently. Reserve 750 ml/1 ¼ pints of the cooking liquid. Cut the artichokes in half lengthways. Dust with the flour and shake off any excess. Heat the sunflower oil in a frying pan. Add the artichokes and cook until golden brown. Remove with a slotted spoon, drain well and put into a flameproof casserole. Heat the olive oil in another frying pan. Add the onion and cook over a low heat, stirring occasionally, for about 8 minutes, until lightly browned. Stir in the flour and cook, stirring constantly, for 2 minutes, then gradually stir in the reserved cooking liquid. Cook, stirring constantly, for 5 minutes, then add the ham. Season to taste with salt and pour the sauce over the artichokes. Bring to the boil, lower the heat and simmer for 10–15 minutes. Serve immediately straight from the dish.

315

Baked artichokes

ALCACHOFAS AL HORNO

- 1 lemon, halved
- 12 globe artichokes
- 25 g/1 oz lard (optional)
- 4 tablespoons white wine
- sunflower oil, for drizzling
- 2 teaspoons finely chopped
  fresh parsley
- 25 g/1 oz breadcrumbs
- salt

Serves 6

Squeeze the juice from one lemon half and add the juice to a large bowl of water. Break off the artichoke stalks and remove the coarse outer leaves. Cut off the tips of the remaining leaves. Cut the artichokes in half lengthways and remove and discard the chokes. Rub the artichokes with the remaining lemon half and place in the acidulated water. Bring a large saucepan of salted water to the boil. Add the artichokes and bring back to the boil, then lower the heat, cover and cook for 30–60 minutes, until tender. (Test by gently pulling a leaf; it should come away easily.) Preheat the oven to 180°C/350°F/ Gas Mark 4. Cut the lard, if using, into three pieces and put it into an ovenproof dish with the white wine. Remove the artichokes from the pan and place cut side up in the dish without draining them. Drizzle a little oil over each artichoke and sprinkle with the parsley and breadcrumbs. Bake for 15 minutes and serve straight from the dish.

316 Artichokes stuffed with Serrano ham

ALCACHOFAS RELLENAS DE JAMÓN SERRANO

- 1 lemon, halved
- 12 globe artichokes
- 150 g/5 oz Serrano ham, finely chopped
- 2½ tablespoons breadcrumbs
- 1 tablespoon white wine
- 1 tablespoon chopped fresh parsley
- 1 clove garlic (optional), finely chopped
- 1 chicken stock cube
- 2 tablespoons sunflower oil
- salt

Serves 6

Squeeze the juice from one lemon half and add the juice to a large bowl of water. Break off the artichoke stalks and remove the coarse outer leaves. Cut off the tips of the remaining leaves. Open out the centres of the artichokes and remove the chokes. Rub the artichokes with the remaining lemon half and place in the acidulated water. Mix together the ham, 1½ tablespoons of the breadcrumbs, the wine, parsley and garlic, if using, in a bowl. Drain the artichokes and fill with the ham mixture. Put the artichokes filling uppermost into a saucepan just large enough to hold them in a single layer. Pour in water to cover. Crumble the stock cube and dissolve it in a little water, then add it to the pan. Sprinkle the remaining breadcrumbs and the oil over the artichokes. Bring to the boil, lower the heat, cover and simmer for 30 minutes. Season with salt if necessary (bearing in mind that the ham and stock cube are both salty). Re-cover the pan and cook for a further 30 minutes, until the liquid has reduced to a sauce and the artichokes are tender. Serve the artichokes in a dish with a little sauce in the base.

317 Artichoke and ham gratin

ALCACHOFAS AL HORNO CON JAMÓN Y BECHAMEL

- 1 lemon, halved
- 12 globe artichokes
- strip of thinly pared lemon rind
- 150 g/5 oz ham, diced
- 25 g/1 oz butter
- 2 tablespoons sunflower oil
- 2 tablespoons plain flour
- 500 ml/18 fl oz milk
- 65 g/2½ oz gruyere cheese, grated
- salt

Serves 6

Squeeze the juice from one lemon half and add the juice to a large bowl of water. Break off the artichoke stalks and remove the coarse outer leaves. Cut off the tips of the remaining leaves. Open out the centres of the artichokes and remove the chokes. Rub the artichokes with the remaining lemon half and place in the acidulated water. Bring a large saucepan of salted water to the boil. Add the lemon rind and artichokes and bring back to the boil, then lower the heat, cover and simmer for 30–60 minutes, until tender. (Test by gently pulling a leaf; it should come away easily.) Drain well, turning the artichokes upside down and pressing gently. Put the artichokes, cut side uppermost, into a flameproof dish. Fill them with the ham. Preheat the grill. Melt the butter with the oil in a saucepan. Stir in the flour and cook, stirring constantly, for 2 minutes. Gradually stir in the milk, a little at a time. Cook, stirring constantly, for 6 minutes. Season with salt and pour the sauce over the artichokes, covering them completely. Sprinkle with the gruyere and cook under the grill for about 10 minutes, until the topping is golden brown. Serve immediately straight from the dish.

318

Artichoke hearts with foie gras and béchamel sauce

FONDOS DE ALCACHOFAS CON FOIE-GRAS Y BECHAMEL

- 1 lemon, halved
- 12 large globe artichokes
- 200 g/7 oz canned foie gras
- 25 g/1 oz butter
- 2 tablespoons sunflower oil
- 2 heaped tablespoons plain flour
- 750 ml/1¼ pints milk
- 65 g/2½ oz gruyere cheese, grated
- salt

Serves 6

Squeeze the juice from one lemon half and add the juice to a large bowl of water. Break off the artichoke stalks and remove the coarse outer leaves. Cut off the remaining leaves at the base. Rub the artichoke hearts with the remaining lemon half and place in the acidulated water. Bring a large saucepan of salted water to the boil. Add the artichoke hearts and cook for 20 minutes. (They should not be fully cooked as they will finish cooking under the grill.) Lift the artichoke hearts out of the water with a slotted spoon and turn them upside down to drain. Remove the chokes with a teaspoon and discard. Fill each artichoke heart with foie gras and put them, filling uppermost, in a single layer in a flameproof dish. Preheat the grill. Melt the butter with the oil in a saucepan. Stir in the flour and cook, stirring constantly, for 2 minutes, then gradually stir in the milk, a little at a time. Season with salt and cook, stirring constantly, for 10 minutes. Pour the béchamel sauce over the artichoke hearts and sprinkle with the gruyere. Cook under the grill until golden and bubbling. Serve immediately straight from the dish.

319

Fried artichokes

ALCACHOFAS REHOGADAS

- 1 lemon, halved
- 1.5–2 kg/3¼–4½ lb small young globe artichokes
- 25 g/1 oz lard (optional)
- 2–4 tablespoons sunflower oil
- 150 g/5 oz Serrano ham, diced
- 1 tablespoon chopped fresh parsley
- salt

Serves 6

Squeeze the juice from one lemon half and add the juice to a large bowl of water. Break off the artichoke stalks and remove the coarse outer leaves. Cut off the tips of the remaining leaves. Cut the artichokes in half lengthways and remove and discard the chokes. Rub the artichokes with the remaining lemon half and place in the acidulated water. Bring a large saucepan of salted water to the boil. Add the artichokes and bring back to the boil, then lower the heat, cover and simmer for about 25 minutes, until tender. (Test by gently pulling a leaf; it should come away easily.) Drain well, turning the artichokes upside down and pressing gently. Melt the lard, if using, with 2 tablespoons of the oil in a saucepan. If you're not using lard, add 2 tablespoons more oil and heat. Add the ham and artichokes and cook gently, stirring occasionally, for 8 minutes. Sprinkle with the parsley and serve immediately.

320

Deep-fried artichokes

ALCACHOFAS REBOZADAS

- 1 lemon, halved
- 12 small globe artichokes
- 50 g/2 oz plain flour
- 2–3 eggs
- sunflower oil, for deep-frying
- salt

Serves 6

Squeeze the juice from one lemon half and add the juice to a large bowl of water. Break off the artichoke stalks and remove the coarse outer leaves. Cut off the tips of the remaining leaves. Cut the artichokes in half lengthways, or into quarters if they are large, and remove and discard the chokes. Rub the artichokes with the remaining lemon half, then place in the acidulated water. Bring a large saucepan of salted water to the boil. Add the artichokes and bring back to the boil, then lower the heat, cover and simmer for about 25 minutes, until tender. (Test by gently pulling a leaf; it should come away easily.) Drain well, turning the artichokes upside down and pressing gently. Spread out the flour in a shallow dish. Lightly beat the eggs in another shallow dish. Roll the artichokes in the flour, shaking off any excess, and then dip into the beaten eggs. Heat the oil in a deep-fryer or saucepan to 180–190°C/350–375°F or until a cube of day-old bread browns in 30 seconds. Add the artichokes and cook until golden brown. Drain well and serve immediately, either on their own or as an accompaniment to meat.

321

Celery hearts with béchamel sauce

APIO CON BECHAMEL

- 6 small or 3 large heads celery
- 40 g/1½ oz butter
- 2 tablespoons sunflower oil
- 3 tablespoons plain flour
- 750 ml/1¼ pints milk
- 65 g/2½ oz gruyere or
  Parmesan cheese, grated
- salt

Serves 6

Cut large heads of celery in half. Cut the celery into pieces about 15 cm/6 inches long. Remove the outside sticks, leaving just the hearts. Rinse thoroughly. Bring a large saucepan of salted water to the boil. Add the celery hearts, cover and cook for 10 minutes. Remove with a skimmer or slotted spoon and leave to drain. Preheat the oven to 180°C/350°F/Gas Mark 4. Melt the butter with the oil in a saucepan. Stir in the flour and cook, stirring constantly, for 2 minutes, then gradually stir in the milk, a little at a time. Cook, stirring constantly, for 3–4 minutes and season with salt. Put the celery hearts into an ovenproof dish and pour in the béchamel sauce to cover. Sprinkle with the cheese and bake for about 15 minutes, until the topping is golden brown. Serve immediately straight from the dish.

Braised celery hearts

APIO EN SU JUGO

- **6 small or 3 large heads celery**
- **3 thin streaky bacon rashers, diced**
- **1 tablespoon olive oil**
- **1 small onion, sliced**
- **2 carrots, sliced**
- **1 tablespoon plain flour**
- **175 ml/6 fl oz white wine**
- **1 tablespoon tomato purée or 2 tablespoons thick tomato sauce**
- **¼ teaspoon meat extract**
- **salt**

Serves 6

Cut large heads of celery in half. Cut the celery into pieces about 15 cm/6 inches long. Remove the outside sticks, leaving just the hearts. Rinse thoroughly. Bring a large saucepan of salted water to the boil. Add the celery hearts, cover and cook for 10 minutes. Remove with a skimmer or slotted spoon and leave to drain. Put the bacon into another large saucepan and cook over a low heat for a few minutes, until the fat runs. Add the oil and heat, then add the onion and carrot and cook, stirring occasionally, for 5 minutes. Stir in the flour and cook, stirring constantly, for a further 5 minutes. Add the celery hearts and pour in the wine and 275 ml/9 fl oz water. Cover and simmer for about 1 hour, until the celery hearts are tender. Remove the celery hearts with a skimmer or slotted spoon and keep warm. Transfer the sauce to a food processor and process to a purée. Add the tomato purée or tomato sauce and the meat extract and process briefly again to mix. If the sauce is too thick, add a little water. Return the sauce to a clean pan and bring to the boil, then pour over the celery hearts and serve immediately.

323

Celery hearts with butter and grated cheese
APIO CON MANTEQUILLA Y QUESO RALLADO

- **6 small or 3 large heads celery**
- **150 g/5 oz butter**
- **100 g/3½ oz gruyere cheese, grated**
- **salt**

Serves 6

Cut large heads of celery in half. Cut the celery into pieces about 15 cm/6 inches long. Remove the outside sticks, leaving just the hearts. Rinse thoroughly. Bring a large saucepan of salted water to the boil. Add the celery hearts, cover and cook for 1 hour, until tender. Re-move with a skimmer or slotted spoon and leave to drain. Preheat the oven to 180°C/350°F/Gas Mark 4. Put the celery hearts into an ovenproof dish, dot with the cheese and sprinkle with the gruyere. Bake for about 15 minutes, until golden brown. Serve immediately straight from the dish.

324

Preparing raw celery for salads
PREPARACIÓN DEL APIO CRUDO PARA MEZCLAR CON ENSALADA

- **1 quantity escarole or lettuce salad**
- **6 tender, very white sticks celery**

Serves 3

Celery has a wonderful flavour that goes well with escarole and lettuce. Prepare your favourite salad. Rinse the celery well, then cut into pieces 2.5 cm/1 inch long. Cut each piece lengthways into three without cutting all the way down. Add the little celery 'flowers' to the salad before serving.

325

Aubergines with garlic
BERENJENAS AL AJO

- **6 aubergines**
- **175 ml/6 fl oz olive oil**
- **2 tablespoons chopped fresh parsley**
- **3 cloves garlic, finely chopped**
- **40 g/1½ oz breadcrumbs**
- **salt**

Serves 6

Cut the aubergines in half lengthways, sprinkle with a little salt and put into a colander, cut sides down, for about 1 hour to draw out some of their juices. Rinse well and pat dry. Heat three-quarters of the oil in a large frying pan. Add the aubergines in a single layer, cut sides down. Cook over a medium heat for 30 minutes, until soft. Preheat the oven to 200°C/400°F/Gas Mark 6. Put the aubergines, cut sides up, side by side in an ovenproof dish. Mix together the parsley and garlic and sprinkle over the aubergines. Sprinkle with the breadcrumbs and drizzle with the remaining oil. Bake for about 10 minutes, until golden brown. Serve immediately straight from the dish.

326

Aubergines au gratin with sauce
BERENJENAS EN SALSA AL GRATÉN

- **7 large aubergines**
- **sunflower oil, for deep-frying**
- **2 chicken stock cubes**
- **1 litre/1¾ pints hot water**
- **25 g/1 oz butter**
- **2 tablespoons plain flour**
- **50 g/2 oz gruyere cheese, grated**
- **salt**

Serves 6

Peel the aubergines and cut into 5-mm/¼-inch thick slices. Put them into a deep dish or a bowl, sprinkling each layer with salt. Leave to stand for about 1 hour to draw out some of their juices. Rinse well and pat dry. Heat the oil in a deep-fryer or saucepan to 180–190°C/350–375°F or until a cube of day-old bread browns in 30 seconds. Add the aubergines, in batches, and cook until golden brown. Remove with a slotted spoon and drain well. Preheat the grill. Dissolve the stock cubes in the hot water. Melt the butter with 1 table-spoon oil in a saucepan. Stir in the flour and cook, stirring constantly, for 2 minutes. Gradually stir in the stock, a little at a time. Cook, stirring constantly, for 8 minutes. Put half the aubergine slices into a deep flameproof dish and pour in half the sauce. Add the remaining slices and pour in the remaining sauce. Sprinkle with the gruyere and cook under a hot grill for about 10 minutes, until golden. Serve immediately straight from the dish.

Aubergines stuffed with mushrooms and béchamel sauce

BERENJENAS RELLENAS CON CHAMPIÑON Y BECHAMEL

- **6 aubergines**
- **200 g/7 oz mushrooms, chopped**
- **25 g/1 oz butter**
- **juice of 1 lemon**
- **5 tablespoons olive oil**
- **1 onion, finely chopped**
- **1 heaped tablespoon plain flour**
- **250 ml/8 fl oz milk**
- **1 egg yolk**
- **80 g/3 oz gruyere cheese, grated**
- **salt**

Serves 6

Cut the aubergines in half lengthways. Remove and discard the seeds and scoop out the flesh with a teaspoon without piercing the skins. Dice the flesh and sprinkle with salt. Sprinkle the inside of the aubergine skins with salt. Leave to stand for 1 hour to draw out some of their juices. Rinse well and pat dry. Preheat the oven to 180°C/350°F/Gas Mark 4. Put the mushrooms, 20 g/¾ oz of the butter and a few drops of the lemon juice into a saucepan and cook over a low heat, stirring occasionally, for 6 minutes. Put the aubergine skins cut sides up in a single layer in an ovenproof dish and add a little of the oil to each, then bake for about 25 minutes while you prepare the filling. Melt the remaining butter with the remaining oil in a saucepan. Add the onion and cook over a low heat, stirring occasionally, for 5 minutes, until softened and translucent. Add the diced aubergine flesh and cook, stirring constantly, for 8 minutes, then add the mushrooms. Stir in the flour and cook, stirring constantly, for 2 minutes. Gradually stir in the milk, a little at a time. Cook over a low heat, stirring constantly, for 10 minutes, adding a little more milk if the mixture is too thick. Beat together the remaining lemon juice and the egg yolk in a bowl, then stir in a little of the aubergine-mushroom béchamel sauce to prevent the yolk curdling. Stir the mixture into the pan. Fill the aubergine skins with the mixture, sprinkle with the gruyere, return the dish to the oven and bake until the cheese has melted. Serve immediately straight from the dish.

Note: The mushrooms can be replaced with chopped Serrano ham.

328

Baked aubergines and tomatoes with grated cheese

BERENJENAS Y TOMATES AL HORNO, CON QUESO RALLADO

- **4 large aubergines**
- **sunflower oil, for deep-frying**
- **1 heaped tablespoon plain flour, plus extra for dusting**
- **2–3 large tomatoes, thinly sliced**
- **50 g/2 oz margarine**
- **450 ml/¾ pint milk**
- **40 g/1½ oz gruyere cheese, grated**
- **salt**

Serves 4

Peel and slice the aubergines. Heat the oil in a deep-fryer or saucepan to 180–190°C/350–375°F or until a cube of day-old bread browns in 30 seconds. Dust the aubergine slices with flour and cook them, in batches, in the hot oil. Remove with a slotted spoon and drain well. Put the tomato slices on a plate, sprinkle each layer with a little salt and leave to stand to draw out some of their juices. Preheat the oven 200°C/400°F/Gas Mark 6. Arrange the aubergine and tomato slices in an overlapping pattern in a round ovenproof dish, putting one slice of tomato after every three slices of aubergine until all the tomatoes and aubergines are used up. Make a thin béchamel sauce with half the margarine, the reserved oil, the flour and milk as described in recipe 77. Lightly season the aubergine and tomato slices with salt and pour the béchamel sauce over them. Sprinkle with the gruyere, dot with the remaining margarine and bake for about 15 minutes, until golden. Serve immediately straight from the dish.

329

Aubergines stuffed with rice

BERENJENAS RELLENAS DE ARROZ

- **6 aubergines**
- **6 tablespoons olive oil**
- **6 tablespoons long-grain rice**
- **2 tablespoons breadcrumbs**
- **50 g/2 oz butter**
- **salt**

Tomato sauce:
- **2 tablespoons olive oil**
- **1 small onion, chopped**
- **500 g /1 lb 2 oz very ripe tomatoes, seeded and chopped**
- **1 teaspoon sugar**
- **salt**

Serves 6

Preheat the oven to 180° C/350°F/Gas Mark 4. Make a very concentrated tomato sauce as described in recipe 73. Cut the aubergines in half lengthways, slash the flesh, season lightly with salt and put them into an ovenproof dish. Pour the oil over them and roast for 30 minutes, until the flesh is soft. Meanwhile, bring a large saucepan of unsalted water to the boil. Add the rice, stir with a wooden spoon to prevent the grains from clumping together and cook over a high heat for 12–15 minutes, until tender. (The cooking time depends on the type of rice.) Drain the rice in a large colander and rinse well under cold running water, stirring to ensure that it is well washed. Drain well again and season lightly with salt while it is still in the colander. Remove the aubergines from the oven but do not switch off the oven. Leave to cool slightly, then scoop out the flesh with a teaspoon without piercing the skins. Remove and discard the seeds, then chop the flesh. Mix together the aubergine flesh, rice and tomato sauce in a bowl and divide the mixture among the aubergine skins. Sprinkle with the breadcrumbs and dot with the butter. Return to the oven and cook for about 25 minutes, until golden. Serve immediately straight from the dish.

330

Aubergines stuffed with meat
BERENJENAS RELLENAS DE CARNE

- 6 aubergines
- 1½ tablespoons sunflower oil
- 200 g/7 oz minced meat
  or leftover meat or 150 g/5 oz
  Serrano ham, chopped
- 1 egg, lightly beaten
- 4 tablespoons breadcrumbs
- 2 cloves garlic, chopped
- 1 sprig fresh parsley, chopped
- salt

Serves 6

Preheat the oven to 180°C/350°F/Gas Mark 4. Cut the aubergines in half lengthways and slash the flesh. Lightly season with salt, place in a roasting tin and drizzle with the oil. Roast for 30 minutes, until soft. Remove from the oven but do not switch off the oven. Leave to cool slightly, then scoop out the flesh with a teaspoon without piercing the skins. Remove and discard the seeds. Chop the flesh, mix with the meat, egg, half the breadcrumbs, the garlic and parsley and season with salt. Divide the mixture among the aubergine skins. Sprinkle with the remaining breadcrumbs and drizzle with the remaining oil. Return to the oven and bake for about 35 minutes, then cook under a preheated grill for a further 10 minutes. Serve immediately straight from the dish.

331

Aubergine omelettes
BERENJENAS EN TORTILLA

- 3 aubergines
- 4 tablespoons olive oil
- 1 onion, finely chopped
- 2 tablespoons plain flour
- 500 ml/ 18 fl oz milk
- 150–175 ml/5–6 fl oz
  sunflower oil
- 6 eggs
- 80 g/3 oz gruyere cheese, grated
- 1 quantity Classic Tomato Sauce
  (see recipe 73)
- salt

Serves 4–6

Peel the aubergines and coarsely chop the flesh, then shred it in a food processor or put through a mincer. Heat the olive oil in a large frying pan. Add the onion and aubergine and cook over a low heat, stirring occasionally, for 10 minutes. Stir in the flour and cook, stirring constantly, for 2 minutes. Gradually stir in the milk, a little at a time. Cook, stirring constantly, for 10 minutes, season with salt and remove the pan from the heat. Preheat the grill. Heat a little of the sunflower oil in another frying pan. Beat one of the eggs with a pinch of salt in a bowl. Tip half the egg mixture into the frying pan and cook until just beginning to set. Put a little of the aubergine mixture in the middle of the omelette, flip it over and slide it out of the pan into a flameproof dish. Continue to make more little omelettes in the same way until the eggs and filling have been used up. Pour the tomato sauce over the omelettes, sprinkle with the gruyere and cook under the grill for 5–10 minutes, until golden and bubbling. Serve immediately straight from the dish.

Note: You can cover the omelettes with Classic Béchamel Sauce (see recipe 77), made with milk or a mixture of equal parts milk and stock, instead of tomato sauce.

332

- 2 kg/4½ lb aubergines
- 175 ml/6 fl oz olive oil
- 2 large onions, finely chopped
- 1.5 kg/3¼ lb ripe tomatoes,
  seeded and chopped
- 1 teaspoon sugar
- salt

Serves 6

Aubergines cooked in tomato sauce
BERENJENAS COCIDAS CON SALSA DE TOMATE

Peel and dice the aubergines and put them into a saucepan. Pour in water to cover, add a pinch of salt and cook for 15 minutes. Drain in a large colander. Heat the oil in a large frying pan. Add the onion and cook over a low heat, stirring occasionally, for about 8 minutes, until lightly browned. Add the tomato, increase the heat to medium and cook, stirring occasionally and breaking up the tomato with the side of the spoon, for about 10 minutes. Allow to cool slightly, then transfer to a food processor and process to a purée. Return to the pan, stir in the sugar and add the diced aubergine. Season to taste with salt and cook over a low heat for about 10 minutes. Serve immediately.

333

- 750 g/1 lb 10 oz striped
  aubergines
- 500 ml/18 fl oz sunflower oil
- 1 clove garlic, chopped
- 1 tablespoon chopped
  fresh parsley
- salt

Serves 4

Aubergine garnish
BERENJENAS ESTILO SETAS

Peel the aubergines, if you like, and cut into slices about 2 cm/¾ inch thick. Put the slices into a colander, sprinkling each layer with salt, and leave to stand for about 1 hour to draw out some of their juices. Rinse thoroughly and pat dry. Heat the oil in one very large or two frying pans. Add the aubergine slices, packing them in tightly. Cover and cook over a low heat for about 20 minutes, until soft. Drain off nearly all the oil, leaving just enough to prevent the aubergine sticking. Sprinkle the garlic and parsley over the aubergine and season lightly with salt. Increase the heat to medium and cook for a few minutes, shaking the pan. Serve immediately.

Note: Striped aubergines do not normally have seeds. This recipe is intended to be used as a garnish for a meat dish. To serve as a vegetable dish, allow 2.5 kg/5 ½ lb aubergines for serving six people.

334

Fried aubergine garnish
BERENJENAS FRITAS DE ADORNO

- **750 g / 1 lb 10 oz striped aubergines (they do not usually have seeds)**
- **50 g / 2 oz plain flour**
- **sunflower oil, for deep-frying**
- **salt**

Serves 4

Peel the aubergines and thinly slice lengthways. Put the slices into a colander, sprinkling each layer with salt, and leave to stand for about 1 hour to draw out some of their juices. Rinse thoroughly and pat dry. Spread out the flour in a shallow dish. Dip the slices in the flour to coat, shaking off any excess. Heat the oil in a deep-fryer or saucepan to 180–190°C/350–375°F or until a cube of day-old bread browns in 30 seconds. Add the aubergine slices, in batches, and cook until golden brown and crisp. Drain well and keep warm while you cook the remaining batches. Sprinkle with a little fine salt and serve.

Note: This recipe is a garnish for a meat dish. To serve as a vegetable dish, allow 2.5 kg / 5 ½ lb aubergines for six people.

335

Watercress salad
BERROS EN ENSALADA

- **1 bunch watercress**
- **1 quantity Vinaigrette (see recipe 98)**

Serves 2–4

Remove and discard the long stalks of the watercress. Wash the leaves well and pat or spin dry. Toss lightly with the vinaigrette.

336

Fantasy salad
ENSALADA FANTASÍA

- **1 bunch watercress**
- **1 avocado**
- **100 g / 3 ½ oz potatoes**
- **2 apples**
- **1 quantity Classic Mayonnaise (see recipe 105)**

Serves 2–4

Boil and slice the potatoes. Remove and discard the long stalks of the watercress. Wash the leaves well and pat dry. Place in a salad bowl. Peel and cut the avocado into wedges. Peel, core and dice the apples. Add to the watercress along with the potato and avocado. Toss gently with the mayonnaise.

337

Watercress as garnish
BERROS PARA ADORNO

- **1 bunch watercress**

Serves 2–4

Remove and discard the longest stalks. Wash the watercress, drain and tie into bunches with chives or pieces of kitchen string.

338

Potatoes with borage
PATATAS CON BORRAJAS

- 2 bunches fresh borage
- 1 kg/2¼ lb potatoes,
  cut into walnut-size pieces
- 4 tablespoons olive oil
- 1 onion, finely chopped
- 1 large or 2 small cloves garlic,
  finely chopped
- 1 teaspoon paprika
- salt
  Serves 4

Scrape off the hairs from the borage stalks and cut the stalks into 2.5-cm/1-inch lengths. Put the borage and potato into a saucepan, pour in water to cover, add a pinch of salt and bring to the boil. Lower the heat and cook for about 25 minutes, until the potatoes are tender. Heat the oil in a large frying pan. Add the onion and garlic and cook over a low heat, stirring occasionally, for about 6 minutes, until the onion is softened and translucent. Remove the pan from the heat and sprinkle in the paprika. Drain the potatoes and borage and add to the frying pan. Return the pan to the heat and cook, stirring occasionally, for 5 minutes. Serve immediately.

339

Fried courgette garnish
CALABACINES FRITOS

- 3 tablespoons plain flour
- 275 ml/9 fl oz beer
- 750 g/1 lb 10 oz courgettes
- sunflower oil, for deep-frying
- salt
  Serves 6

Sift the flour into a bowl and gradually stir in the beer, a little at a time, until the batter has the consistency of a thick custard. Lightly season with salt and leave to stand for 30 minutes. Meanwhile, peel and thinly slice the courgettes. Heat the oil in a deep-fryer or saucepan to 180–190°C/350–375°F or until a cube of day-old bread browns in 30 seconds. One at a time, dip the courgette slices into the batter, and add to the hot oil in batches. Cook until golden brown, then remove with a slotted spoon and drain well. Serve immediately.

340

Fried coated courgettes
CALABACINES REBOZADOS Y FRITOS

- 1.5 kg/3¼ lb fairly large
  courgettes, peeled and thinly
  sliced
- 50 g/2 oz plain flour
- 4 eggs
- sunflower oil, for deep-frying
- 1 teaspoon chopped
  fresh parsley
- salt
  Serves 6

Put the courgette slices in a colander, sprinkling each layer with salt, and leave to stand for at least 1 hour to draw out some of their juices. Rinse thoroughly and pat dry. Spread out the flour in a shallow dish. Lightly beat the eggs in another shallow dish. Heat the oil in a deep-fryer or saucepan to 180–190°C/350–375°F or until a cube of day-old bread browns in 30 seconds. Dip the courgette slices first in the flour, shaking off any excess, then the beaten egg. Add to the hot oil, in batches, and cook until golden brown. Remove with a slotted spoon and drain well, then keep warm while cooking the remaining batches. Serve immediately, sprinkled with the parsley.

341

Fried courgettes with bacon

CALABACINES FRITOS Y BACON

- 1.2 kg / 2½ lb courgettes, peeled and cut into 5-mm/¼-inch slices
- 50 g / 2 oz plain flour
- sunflower oil, for deep-frying
- 6 thin bacon rashers
- 1 large onion, finely chopped
- 2 cloves garlic, finely chopped
- salt

Serves 6

Preheat the oven to 160°C/325°F/Gas Mark 3. Season the courgette slices with salt. Spread out the flour in a shallow dish. Heat the oil in a deep-fryer or saucepan to 180–190°C/350–375°F or until a cube of day-old bread browns in 30 seconds. One at a time, dip the courgette slices in the flour, shaking off the excess, add to the hot oil in batches and cook until golden brown. Remove with a slotted spoon and drain well, then arrange in a spiral in a round ovenproof dish. Keep warm in the oven. Add the bacon to the oil and cook until crisp and golden brown. Drain well and keep warm in the oven. Transfer 5 tablespoons of the oil into another frying pan and heat it. Add the onion and garlic and cook over a medium heat, stirring occasionally, for 5–6 minutes, until the onion is beginning to brown. Increase the oven temperature to 230°C/450°F/Gas Mark 8. Pour the onion mixture over the courgette slices and place the bacon on top. Return the dish to the oven for 4 minutes. Serve immediately straight from the dish.

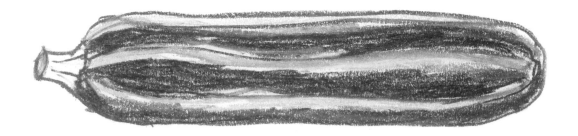

342

Courgettes stuffed with prawns

CALABACINES RELLENOS DE GAMBAS

- **4 courgettes**
- **10 g/¼ oz butter,**
  plus extra for greasing
- **2 shallots, chopped**
- **275 ml/9 fl oz white wine**
- **1 kg/2¼ lb raw prawns, peeled**
- **4 sprigs fresh tarragon**
- **300 ml/½ pint single cream**
- **2 tablespoons mustard**
- **salt and pepper**

Serves 4

Working on one courgette at a time, peel off narrow strips of skin lengthways, leaving wider strips intact in between to create a striped effect. Cut into three pieces and scoop out each courgette and discard some of the flesh. Steam for 10 minutes. Preheat the oven to 180°C/350°F/Gas Mark 4. Grease an ovenproof dish with butter. Melt the remaining butter in a frying pan. Add the shallots and cook over a low heat, stirring occasionally, for 5 minutes. Pour in the wine and cook for a further 5 minutes. Add the prawns and three of the tarragon sprigs, season with salt and pepper and cook for a few minutes until the prawns are opaque. Remove them from the pan and keep warm. Stir the cream and mustard into the pan and simmer for 10 minutes. Meanwhile, chop the remaining tarragon. Put the pieces of courgette into the prepared baking dish and bake for 10 minutes. Add the prawns to the cream sauce and remove the pan from the heat. Remove the tarragon sprigs and stir in the chopped tarragon. Fill the courgettes with the prawns and pour the sauce over them.

343

Courgettes stuffed with mussels

CALABACINES RELLENOS DE MEJILLONES

- **1 kg/2¼ lb mussels**
- **275 ml/9 fl oz white wine**
- **4 courgettes**
- **10 g/¼ oz butter,**
  plus extra for greasing
- **2 shallots, chopped**
- **4 sprigs fresh tarragon**
- **300 ml/½ pint single cream**
- **2 tablespoons mustard**
- **salt and pepper**

Serves 4

Discard any mussels with broken shells or any that do not shut immediately when sharply tapped. Cook the mussels in a saucepan in the wine over a high heat for 3–5 minutes, until they open. Discard any that remain closed, remove the mussels from their shells and strain the cooking liquid through a fine muslin-covered sieve into a bowl. Working on one courgette at a time, peel off narrow strips of skin lengthways, leaving wider strips intact in between to create a striped effect. Cut into three pieces and scoop out each courgette and discard some of the flesh. Steam for 10 minutes. Preheat the oven to 180°C/350°F/Gas Mark 4. Grease an ovenproof dish with butter. Melt the remaining butter in a frying pan. Add the shallots and cook over a low heat, stirring occasionally, for 5 minutes. Add the cooking liquid from the mussels, and 3 of the tarragon sprigs, season with salt and pepper and cook for a few minutes. Stir in the cream and mustard and simmer for 10 minutes. Meanwhile, chop the remaining tarragon. Put the pieces of courgette into the prepared baking dish and bake for 10 minutes. Remove the tarragon sprigs and stir in the chopped tarragon and the mussels. Fill the courgettes with the prawns and pour the sauce over them.

344

- 1.5–2 kg/3¼–4½ lb courgettes, peeled and cut into 5-mm/ ¼-inch thick slices
- 275 ml/9 fl oz sunflower oil
- 100 g/3½ oz dried instant mashed potato
- 20 g/¾ oz butter
- 275 ml/9 fl oz milk
- 1 egg, separated
- 1 egg white
- 25 g/1 oz gruyere cheese, grated
- salt

Serves 4

Courgettes with mashed potato

CALABACINES CON PURÉ DE PATATAS

Put the courgette slices into a colander, sprinkling each layer with salt, and leave to stand for at least 1 hour to draw out some of their juices. Rinse thoroughly and pat dry. Heat the oil in a frying pan. Add the courgettes, in batches, and cook until light golden brown. Remove with a slotted spoon and set aside. Preheat the oven to 200°C/400°F/Gas Mark 6. Make the mashed potato in a saucepan according to the instructions on the packet, using the instant mashed potato, 275 ml/9 fl oz water, the butter, milk and a pinch of salt. It should be quite thick. Remove the pan from the heat and beat in the egg yolk. Whisk the egg whites in a clean, dry bowl until they form firm peaks, then fold into the potato. Put half the courgette slices into an ovenproof dish in an even layer and cover with the mashed potato. Top with the remaining courgettes, sprinkle with the gruyere and bake for 5 minutes, until golden brown. Serve immediately.

345

- 2 kg/4½ lb courgettes
- 5–7 tablespoons olive oil
- 250 g/9 oz onions, chopped
- 1 kg/2¼ lb ripe tomatoes, peeled and chopped
- 1 teaspoon sugar
- 2 green peppers, seeded and diced (optional)
- salt

Serves 6

Courgette ratatouille

PISTO DE CALABACÍN

Peel and dice the courgettes, removing the seeds. Heat 3 tablespoons of the oil in a saucepan. Add the onion and cook over a low heat, stirring occasionally, for about 5 minutes, until softened and translucent. Add the courgette and cook, stirring occasionally, for a further 5 minutes, until lightly browned. Heat 2 tablespoons of the remaining oil in a frying pan. Add the tomato and cook over a low heat, stirring occasionally and breaking it up with the side of the spoon, for 10 minutes. Allow to cool slightly, then transfer to a food processor and process to a purée. Season with salt, add the sugar and process briefly again, then pour the mixture over the courgette and stir well. Cook over a low heat for a further 25 minutes, adding a little water if the mixture is becoming too thick. If using the green peppers, heat 2 tablespoons oil in a small frying pan. Add the peppers, cover and cook over a low heat, stirring occasionally, for about 25 minutes. Stir them into the courgettes just before serving. Serve in a warm deep dish.

Note: This dish can be made in advance and reheated. You can also process the ratatouille in a food processor once it is cooked, then just before serving, add 3 beaten eggs. Serve garnished with triangles of fried bread (see recipe 130).

Courgette ratatouille with potatoes

PISTO DE CALABACÍN CON PATATAS

- **5 tablespoons olive oil**
- **250 g/9 oz onions,
  finely chopped**
- **1 kg/2¼ lb very ripe tomatoes,
  peeled, seeded and chopped**
- **2 green peppers,
  seeded and diced**
- **sunflower oil, for deep-frying**
- **200 g/7 oz potatoes,
  thinly sliced**
- **1 kg/2¼ lb courgettes**
- **1 teaspoon sugar**
- **1 egg, lightly beaten**
- **salt**

Serves 6

Heat 3 tablespoons of the olive oil in a frying pan. Add the onion and cook over a low heat, stirring occasionally, for about 5 minutes, until softened and translucent. Add the tomato, increase the heat to medium and cook, stirring occasionally and breaking up the tomato with the side of the spoon, for a further 15 minutes. Heat the remaining olive oil in a small frying pan. Add the pepper, cover and cook over a low heat, stirring occasionally, for 25 minutes. Heat the sunflower oil in a deep-fryer or saucepan to 180–190°C/350–375°F or until a cube of day-old bread browns in 30 seconds. Add the potato slices and cook for 5–10 minutes, until golden brown. Remove with a slotted spoon and drain well. Peel the courgettes, cut them in half lengthways and remove the seeds, then slice thinly. Put into a saucepan, pour in just enough water to cover and bring to the boil. Lower the heat and simmer for about 5 minutes, then drain well. Stir the sugar into the onion and tomato mixture. Using a slotted spoon, transfer the pepper to the onion and tomato mixture, then add the potato and courgette. Season to taste with salt and cook, stirring constantly, for 5 minutes. Just before serving, stir the egg into the warm ratatouille.

Note: This dish can be made in advance and reheated, but do not add the egg until just before serving.

347

Courgette ratatouille with rice

PISTO DE CALABACÍN CON ARROZ

- 4 tablespoons long-grain rice
- 4 tablespoons olive oil
- 1 large onion, chopped
- 1 clove garlic, finely chopped
- 14 ripe tomatoes,
  peeled, seeded and chopped
- 1.5 kg/3¼ lb courgettes, diced
- salt

Serves 6

Bring a large saucepan of water to the boil. Add the rice, bring back to the boil, then lower the heat and cook for about 15 minutes, until tender. Drain well in a large colander, rinse under cold running water and drain well again. Heat the oil in a frying pan. Add the onion and garlic and cook over a low heat, stirring occasionally, for 2 minutes. Add the tomato and cook, stirring occasionally, for a further 5 minutes, then add the courgette. Season with salt, cover and simmer, stirring frequently, for 35 minutes. Stir in the rice, heat through gently and serve immediately.

Note: This dish can be made in advance and reheated, but do not stir in the rice until just before serving.

348

Ratatouille

PISTO ESTILO FRANCÉS

- 150 ml/¼ pint olive oil
- 300 g/11 oz onions,
  finely chopped
- 3 aubergines, peeled and cut
  into 2-cm/¾-inch cubes
- 2 green peppers,
  seeded and diced
- 4 courgettes, peeled and diced
- 500 g/1 lb 2 oz very ripe
  tomatoes, peeled, seeded
  and chopped
- 2 cloves garlic
- salt

Serves 6

Heat the oil in a large, deep frying pan. Add the onion and cook over a low heat, stirring occasionally, for 10 minutes. Add the aubergine and cook, stirring occasionally, for a further 10 minutes. Add the green pepper and cook, stirring occasionally, for 10 minutes more. Stir in the courgette and tomato, add the garlic and season with salt. Cover and simmer over a low heat for 1 hour. If the ratatouille is very runny, remove the lid for the last 10 minutes to allow some of the liquid to evaporate. Remove and discard the garlic before serving. Serve immediately.

Note: This dish can be prepared in advance and reheated.

349

Courgette ratatouille with tuna

PISTO DE CALABACÍN CON ATÚN

- **120 ml/4 fl oz olive oil**
- **1.5 kg/3¼ lb courgettes,**
  peeled and coarsely chopped
- **1 green pepper,**
  seeded and diced
- **2 large onions, chopped**
- **750 g/1 lb 10 oz tomatoes,**
  peeled, seeded and chopped
- **200 g/7 oz canned tuna,**
  drained and flaked
- **salt**

Serves 6

Heat 4 tablespoons of the oil in a large frying pan. Add the courgette and cook, stirring frequently, for 2–3 minutes, then add 3 table-spoons water and simmer for about 15 minutes, until soft. Heat 3 tablespoons of the remaining oil in another frying pan. Add the green pepper and cook over a medium heat, stirring occasionally, for about 15 minutes, until soft. Remove from the pan and set aside. Add the onion to the pan and cook over a low heat, stirring occasionally, for about 10 minutes, until beginning to brown. Add the tomato and cook, stirring occasionally and breaking it up with the side of the spoon, for 15–20 minutes, until it forms a thick sauce. Transfer the mixture to the pan of courgette, stir in the green pepper and cook, stirring oc-casionally, for 10 minutes. Stir in the tuna, heat through and serve.

Note: This dish can be made in advance and reheated, but do not add the tuna until just before serving.

350

Courgettes with tomato sauce au gratin

CALABACINES CON SALSA DE TOMATE AL GRATÉN

- **2 kg/4½ lb large courgettes,**
  peeled and sliced lengthways
- **20 g/¾ oz butter,**
  plus extra for greasing
- **150 g/5 oz gruyere cheese,**
  grated
- **1 quantity Classic Tomato Sauce**
  (see recipe 73)
- **salt**

Serves 6

Bring a large saucepan of salted water to the boil. Add the courgette slices and cook for 5 minutes. Drain well and set aside in a colander to drain completely. Preheat the oven to 180°C/350°F/Gas Mark 4. Grease an ovenproof dish with butter. Layer the courgette slices in the prepared dish, sprinkling a little of the gruyere between each layer. Pour in the tomato sauce, sprinkle with the remaining cheese and dot with the butter. Bake for 15–20 minutes, until golden brown. Serve immediately straight from the dish.

351

- 2 kg/4½ lb courgettes, peeled
  and cut into 5-mm/¼-inch slices
- 25g/1oz butter
- 2 tablespoons sunflower oil
- 2 heaped tablespoons plain flour
- 500ml/18floz milk
- 80g/3oz gruyere cheese, grated
- salt

Serves 6

Courgettes with béchamel sauce
CALABACINES CON BECHAMEL

Put the courgette slices into a saucepan, pour in water to cover and add a pinch of salt. Bring to the boil, then remove the pan from the heat and drain well. Place the slices in an ovenproof dish. Preheat the oven to 200°C/400°F/Gas Mark 6. To make a béchamel sauce, melt the butter with the oil in another saucepan. Stir in the flour and cook, stirring constantly, for 2 minutes. Gradually stir in the milk, a little at a time. Lightly season with salt and cook, stirring constantly, for 10 minutes. Pour the sauce over the courgette slices, sprinkle with the gruyere and bake for 10–15 minutes, until golden brown. Serve immediately straight from the dish.

352

- 2 kg/4½ lb courgettes,
  peeled and cut into 5-mm/
  ¼-inch thick slices
- 100g/3½oz gruyere cheese,
  grated
- pinch of freshly grated nutmeg
  (optional)
- 3–4 tablespoons breadcrumbs
- 50g/2oz butter
- salt

Serves 6

Baked courgettes with cheese
CALABACINES GRATINADOS CON QUESO

Preheat the oven to 200°C/400°F/Gas Mark 6. Bring a large saucepan of salted water to the boil. Add the courgette slices and cook for 5 minutes, until tender. Drain well. Place a layer of slices in a deep ovenproof dish, sprinkling a little gruyere and nutmeg, if using, over the top. Continue in this way until all the courgette slices are used. Sprinkle the remaining cheese on top, then sprinkle with the breadcrumbs and dot with the butter. Bake for 15–20 minutes, until golden brown. Serve immediately straight from the dish.

353

Courgettes stuffed with York ham and tomatoes
CALABACINES RELLENOS CON JAMÓN DE YORK Y TOMATES

- 6 courgettes, halved lengthways
- 300 g/11 oz York or other
  dry-cured ham, chopped
- 3 tomatoes,
  peeled, seeded and chopped
- 1 teaspoon chopped
  fresh tarragon
- 2–3 tablespoons olive oil
- 3 tablespoons breadcrumbs
- salt

Serves 6

Bring a large saucepan of salted water to the boil. Add the courgettes, bring back to the boil and cook for 10 minutes. Remove the courgettes and leave to drain on a tea towel. When cool enough to handle, scoop out the flesh with a teaspoon without piercing the skins. Chop the flesh. Preheat the oven to 200°C/400°F/Gas Mark 6. Mix together the ham, tomato, courgette flesh and tarragon in a bowl and season to taste with salt. Spoon the mixture into the courgette skins. Put just enough of the oil into an ovenproof dish to cover the base, then place the filled courgettes in the dish side by side, filling uppermost. Sprinkle with the breadcrumbs, drizzle with the remaining oil and bake for about 15 minutes, until lightly browned. Serve immediately straight from the dish.

354

Piperade
PIPERADA

- 120 ml/4 fl oz olive oil
- 1 kg/2¼ lb onions,
  cut into 1-cm/½-inch wedges
- 250 g/9 oz green peppers,
  seeded and cut into thin strips
- 1 kg/2¼ lb very ripe tomatoes,
  peeled, seeded and chopped
- 1–2 cloves garlic (optional),
  finely chopped
- salt

Serves 4–6

Heat the oil in large, deep frying pan. Add the onion and cook over a low heat, stirring occasionally, for 10 minutes. Add the pepper and cook for a further 5 minutes. Add the tomato, season with salt and simmer over a low heat, stirring occasionally, for 1½ hours. If using the garlic, heat 2 tablespoons olive oil in a small frying pan. Add the garlic and cook over a low heat, stirring frequently, for a few minutes, until lightly browned. Remove from the heat and add to the vegetables just before the end of the cooking time.

Note: Piperade is a stew-like dish that originated in the Basque region of France.

Pumpkin

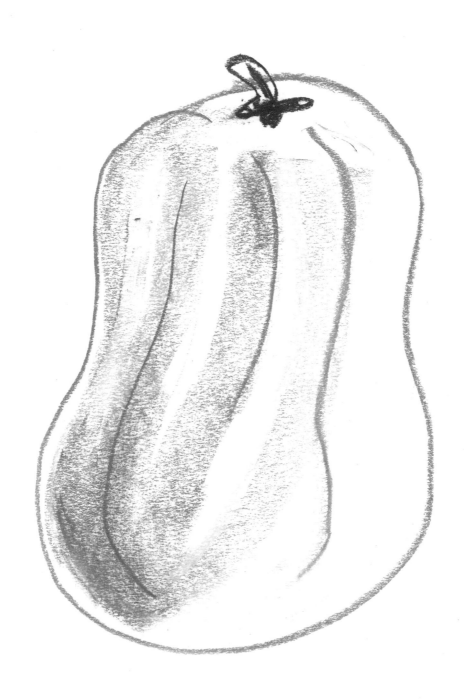

Origin and season

The exact origin of calabaza (or West Indian pumpkin) is not known, but it is a favourite throughout the Caribbean and Central and South America. It is at its best in the autumn. If you can't find this winter squash, use regular pumpkin. The custom of carving pumpkin lanterns at Halloween is popular in many countries, most notably the United States, where pumpkin soup and pumpkin pie also feature as part of the traditional Thanksgiving meal.

Selection

As pumpkins can grow extremely large, they are often sold in pieces. Their skin might be green or orange, but their flesh should have a good orange colour with no signs of mould.

Nutrition

Pumpkins contain a lot of water and so are easy to digest. They contain about 20 calories per 100 g / 3 ½ oz.

Trick

• To extract the maximum flavour, cut the flesh into cubes and cook them in a little water with a few slices of potato and a finely chopped onion. Purée by processing in a food processor, and season well with pepper. Serve the soup in a hollowed-out pumpkin 'shell'.

355

Fried pumpkin

CALABAZA REHOGADA

- 4 leeks, cut into 2.5-cm/
  1-inch lengths, and rinsed well
- 1.5 kg / 3 ¼ lb pumpkin,
  peeled, seeded and cubed
- 250 ml / 8 fl oz olive oil
- 3–4 slices of bread,
  crusts removed, cubed
- 3 cloves garlic, lightly crushed
- salt

Serves 4

Bring a saucepan of salted water to the boil. Add the leek and cook over a medium heat for 20 minutes. Add the pumpkin and cook for about 25 minutes, until the pumpkin is tender. (Test by piercing with a fork.) Drain off the water, cover the pan and set aside. Heat the oil in a large frying pan. Add the bread and cook, stirring frequently, until evenly browned. Remove with a slotted spoon and drain on kitchen paper. Pour off most of the oil, leaving just enough to cover the base of the pan, and return the pan to the heat. Add the garlic and cook for a few minutes until well browned, then remove and discard. Add the pumpkin, leeks and croûtons to the pan and cook over a low heat for 5 minutes. Serve immediately.

Pumpkin purée gratin
PURÉ DE CALABAZA GRATINADO

- 120 ml/4 fl oz olive oil
- 1.5 kg/3¼ lb pumpkin,
  peeled, seeded and cubed
- 25 g/1 oz butter
- 2 heaped tablespoons plain flour
- 500 ml/18 fl oz milk
- pinch of freshly grated nutmeg
- 3 eggs, lightly beaten
- 100 g/3½ oz gruyere cheese,
  grated
- salt

Serves 4–6

Heat 6 tablespoons of the oil in a saucepan. Add the pumpkin and cook over a low heat, stirring occasionally, for 10–15 minutes, until tender. (Test by piercing with a fork.) Transfer to a food processor and process to a purée, then scrape into a bowl. Preheat the oven to 180°C/350°F/Gas Mark 4. Melt the butter with the remaining oil in another saucepan. Stir in the flour and cook, stirring constantly, for 2 minutes. Gradually stir in the milk, a little at a time. Add the nutmeg, season with salt and cook, stirring constantly, for 10 minutes. Stir the sauce into the pumpkin purée, then beat in the eggs. Pour the mixture into an ovenproof dish, sprinkle with the gruyere and bake until golden. Serve immediately straight from the dish.

Cardoons

Origin and season
This tall plant, resembling celery in appearance, comes from the Mediterranean islands of Sicily, the Balearics and Sardinia. It is from the same family as the globe artichoke. It is popular in southern Europe and North Africa. It is at its best in the early winter.

Selection
Choose light-coloured cardoons and allow quite a lot per serving – about 400 g/14 oz – as only the inner ribs and heart are edible.

Nutrition
Cardoons consist of about 90 per cent water and contain about 40 calories per 100 g/3½ oz. The plant is said to have calming properties and is therefore used in some herbal teas.

How to cook

Trim the base. Remove and discard the hard outer stalks. Pull off the inedible strings. Remove the inner stalks, one at a time, rub with ½ lemon and cut into pieces about 4 cm/1½ inches long. Cut the heart into quarters. Put the pieces of cardoon into a large bowl of water mixed with lemon juice. Put 1 tablespoon plain flour into a bowl and mix to a paste with water. Tip this into a saucepan, pour in plenty of water (enough to cover the cardoon once it has been added to the pan) and add a pinch of salt. Partially cover the pan and bring to the boil. Add the cardoon and cook over a medium heat for 1–1½ hours, until tender. Drain well, then cook as preferred.

357

Cardoon with paprika sauce

CARDO CON SALSA DE PIMENTÓN

- 1 cardoon
- 1 lemon
- 2½ tablespoons plain flour
- 3 tablespoons olive oil
- 1 onion, finely chopped
- 1 teaspoon paprika
- salt

Serves 4

Prepare and precook the cardoon, using the lemon and 1 tablespoon of the flour, as described on page 285. Drain well, reserving the cooking liquid. Heat the oil in a frying pan. Add the onion and cook over a low heat, stirring occasionally, for 8–10 minutes, until golden brown. Stir in the remaining flour and cook, stirring constantly, for 2 minutes. Stir in the paprika, then gradually stir in 450 ml/¾ pint of the reserved cooking liquid. Bring to the boil, stirring constantly. Pour the mixture into a large saucepan. If you prefer to remove the onion, strain through a coarse sieve. Add the cardoon and simmer over a low heat for 10 minutes. Serve immediately.

358

Cardoon in milk sauce with saffron and cinnamon

CARDO EN SALSA DE LECHE CON AZAFRÁN Y CANELA

- 1 cardoon
- ½ lemon,
  peeled and coarsely chopped
- 175 ml/6 fl oz olive oil
- 2 cloves garlic
- 2 tablespoons plain flour
- 500 ml/18 fl oz milk
- ½ teaspoon ground cinnamon
- pinch of saffron threads
- 2 slices of fried bread (see
  recipe 130), broken into pieces
- 2 tablespoons chopped
  fresh parsley
- salt and pepper

Serves 4

Prepare the cardoon as described on page 285, but do not precook. Put the pieces of cardoon into a pressure cooker, pour in water to cover and add the lemon and a pinch of salt. Bring to high pressure and cook for 35 minutes (longer for a large cardoon, shorter for a small one). Remove from the heat and leave covered until the pressure has reduced, then remove the cardoon with a slotted spoon, reserving the cooking liquid. Heat the oil in a saucepan. Add one of the garlic cloves and cook for a few minutes, until browned. Stir in the flour and cook, stirring constantly, for 2 minutes. Remove and discard the garlic. Add the cardoon to the pan, stir in the milk and add 250 ml/8 fl oz of the reserved cooking liquid. Sprinkle in the cinnamon and season to taste with salt and pepper. Cover and simmer over a low heat for 30 minutes. Cut the remaining garlic into four pieces and pound in a mortar with the saffron and fried bread. Stir the mixture into the pan, re-cover and simmer gently for a further 10 minutes. Serve immediately, garnished with the parsley.

359

Cardoon gratin

- 1 cardoon
- 1 lemon
- 1 tablespoon plain flour
- 2 tablespoons sunflower oil
- 100 g/3½ oz gruyere cheese, grated
- 50 g/2 oz butter
- salt

Serves 4

Prepare and precook the cardoon, using the lemon and flour, as described on page 285. Drain well. Preheat the grill. Pour the oil into a flameproof dish, add the cardoon, sprinkle with the gruyere and dot with the butter. Cook under the grill for about 5 minutes, until golden brown. Serve immediately straight from the dish.

360

Cardoons with red pepper and anchovies

CARDOS CON PIMIENTOS Y ANCHOAS

- 1 kg/2¼ lb cardoons
- 1 lemon
- 2 tablespoons plain flour
- 2 tablespoons olive oil
- 3 cloves garlic
- 3 canned anchovy fillets, drained
- 3 tablespoons chopped fresh parsley
- 1 red pepper, seeded and sliced
- 1 bouquet garni (1 sprig fresh parsley and 1 bay leaf tied together in muslin)
- salt and pepper

Serves 4

Prepare and precook the cardoons, using the lemon and 1 tablespoon of the flour, as described on page 285. Drain well, reserving the cooking liquid. Heat the oil in a saucepan. Stir in the remaining flour and cook, stirring constantly, for 2 minutes. Add the red pepper and bouquet garni. Gradually stir in 350 ml/12 fl oz of the reserved cooking liquid, a little at a time. Season to taste with salt and pepper and cook over a low heat, stirring constantly, for 5 minutes. Pound the garlic with the anchovies in a mortar, then stir into the sauce, together with the parsley. Mix well and serve the cardoons with the sauce poured over them.

361

Cardoon in garlic and vinegar sauce
CARDO EN SALSA CON AJO Y VINAGRE

- 1 cardoon
- 1 lemon
- 2 tablespoons plain flour
- 5 tablespoons olive oil
- 1 onion, finely chopped
- 1 clove garlic
- 1 sprig fresh parsley
- 1 slice of fried bread
- pinch of ground cumin or pepper
- 1 tablespoon white-wine vinegar
- salt

Serves 4

Prepare and precook the cardoon, using the lemon and 1 tablespoon of the flour, as described on page 281. Drain well, reserving the cooking liquid. Heat the oil in a saucepan. Add the onion and cook over a low heat, stirring occasionally, for about 10 minutes, until lightly browned. Put the garlic, parsley, fried bread, cumin or pepper and a pinch of salt into a mortar and pound with a pestle, then pour the mixture into the pan. Stir in the remaining flour and cook, stirring constantly, for 2 minutes. Stir in the vinegar and some of the reserved cooking liquid. Add the cardoon and pour in enough of the remaining reserved cooking liquid to just cover. Season to taste with salt and simmer for 10 minutes. Serve immediately.

362

Cardoon in vinaigrette
CARDO EN VINAGRETA

- 1 cardoon
- 1 lemon
- 1 tablespoon plain flour
- 3 tablespoons-wine vinegar
- 9 tablespoons sunflower oil
- 1 sprig fresh parsley
- 1 hardboiled egg (optional)
- salt

Serves 4

Prepare and precook the cardoon, using the lemon and flour, as described on page 281. Drain well and put into a deep dish or bowl. Make a vinaigrette with the vinegar, oil and salt as described in recipe 98, and pour it over the cardoon. Finely chop the parsley and chop the hardboiled egg, if using, and sprinkle over the cardoon. Serve immediately.

Note: This dish is usually served hot but it is also very good cold.

363

Baby cardoons
CARDILLOS

- 500 g/1 lb 2 oz baby cardoons
- 2 tablespoons sunflower oil
- 2 tablespoons olive oil
- 1 tablespoon white-wine vinegar
- 1 tablespoon breadcrumbs
- 4 sprigs chopped fresh parsley
- 1 clove garlic, finely chopped
- salt

Serves 4

Clean off any earth and pull off the strings, leaving the baby cardoons attached. Cook them in salted boiling water for about 20 minutes, until tender. Drain well. Heat the sunflower oil in a frying pan and cook the cardoons over a medium heat until lightly browned. Remove from the pan with a slotted spoon and drain. Make a vinaigrette with the oil, vinegar and salt as described in recipe 98. Add the breadcrumbs, parsley and garlic. Serve the baby cardoons with the vinaigrette. These vegetables are usually served with stew.

Onions

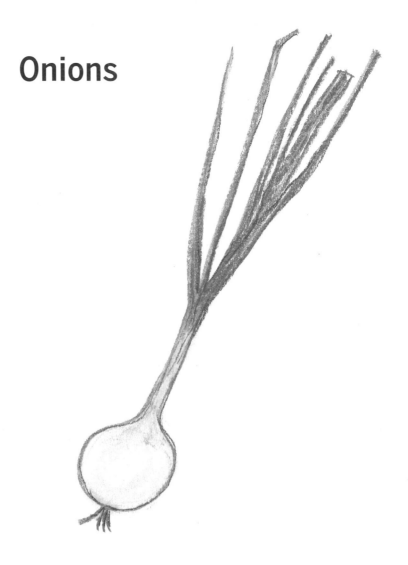

Origin and season

Believed to be one of the oldest vegetables, onions come from Persia (modern Iran). They were popular with the ancient Greeks and the Romans. They are widely grown in Europe, Asia and America and opinion is unanimous on their medicinal, nutritional, gastronomic and even meteorological virtues. Although there are many members of the onion family there are two main types of true onion: the spring onion with a small white bulb and green top, and the winter onion with a dry, brownish skin, also known as a yellow onion. There are many other varieties such as Spanish, red, white and Vidalia onions.

Selection

Winter onions should be firm with no signs of germination. The green part of spring onions should give off a pungent smell. If you buy them in bunches, make sure the ones on the inside of the bunch are not soft or going rotten.

Nutrition

Onions contain 40 calories per 100 g/3 ½ oz. Eaten raw, they are an excellent diuretic and have antiseptic properties. They are rich in vitamin C. A glass of onion juice each morning is an excellent protection against infections, as well as being a good tonic.

Tricks

• If eating raw onions results in bad breath, chew a few coffee beans
• If you use only part of an onion for a recipe, it is not advisable to keep the remainder as it may be harmful to health
• To avoid crying when peeling onions, wear sunglasses or put the onions into the freezer for 15 minutes first
• To reduce pungency, marinate onions in lemon juice for 2 hours
• It is not advisable to use winter onions once they have germinated, although the green sprouts can be used for salads and omelettes.

364

Battered onion garnish

CEBOLLAS REBOZADAS Y FRITAS PARA ADORNO

• 150 g/5 oz plain flour
• 1 egg, separated
• sunflower oil, for deep-frying
• 1 bottle of beer (330 ml/11 fl oz)
• 2 large onions,
  sliced and pushed out into rings
• salt

First version

Sift the flour with a pinch of salt into a bowl. Add the egg yolk and 1 tablespoon of the oil and mix well. Gradually stir in the beer, a little at a time, until the batter has the consistency of thick custard. Whisk the egg white with a pinch of salt in a clean, dry bowl until soft peaks form, then gently fold it into the batter. Heat the remaining oil in a deep-fryer or saucepan to 180–190°C/350–375°F or until a cube of day-old bread browns in 30 seconds. Dip the onion rings, one at a time, into the batter, add to the hot oil and cook, in batches, until golden brown. Do not cook too many at once. Remove the onion rings from the pan and drain well. Serve hot, as a garnish with roasted or grilled meat.

• 3–4 tablespoons plain flour
• 275 ml/9 fl oz soda water
• 1 tablespoon chopped
  fresh parsley
• 2 large onions,
  sliced and pushed out into rings
• sunflower oil, for deep-frying
• salt

Second version

Sift the flour with a pinch of salt into a bowl and gradually stir in the soda water, a little at a time, until the batter has the consistency of thick custard. Sprinkle in the parsley. Dip the onion rings in the batter and cook in the hot oil as described in the previous recipe.

365

Onion purée
CEBOLLAS EN PURE

- **4 tablespoons olive oil**
- **2 kg/4½ lb onions, cut into 1.5-cm/½-inch thick slices**
- **2 tablespoons plain flour**
- **1 teaspoon sugar**
- **5 tablespoons white wine**
- **salt**

Serves 4

Heat the oil in a large, heavy-based saucepan, preferably a cocotte. Add the onion and cook over a very low heat, stirring occasionally, for 30–45 minutes, until very soft. Sprinkle in the flour and sugar and stir in the wine. Season with salt, mix well, cover and cook on a very low heat for about 2 hours.

Note: This dish can be made in advance and reheated. In fact, it is even better that way.

366

Onions stuffed with meat
CEBOLLAS RELLENAS DE CARNE

- **12 onions, 80–100 g/ 3–3½ oz each**
- **1 thick slice of bread, crusts removed**
- **175 ml/6 fl oz hot milk**
- **250 g/9 oz mixed minced pork and beef**
- **1 teaspoon chopped fresh parsley**
- **½ clove garlic, finely chopped**
- **1 tablespoon white wine**
- **2 eggs, lightly beaten**
- **250 ml/8 fl oz sunflower oil**
- **80 g/3 oz plain flour**
- **2 tablespoons olive oil**
- **1 beef stock cube**
- **salt**

Serves 6

Peel the onions and, using a thin sharp knife, make a circular cut around the top and cut a slice off the base of each so that it stands up. Bring a large saucepan of salted water to the boil, add the onions and cook for 15 minutes. Remove the onions with a slotted spoon and reserve the cooking liquid. Meanwhile, tear the bread into pieces and place in a bowl. Pour in the hot milk and leave to soak. Put the minced meat into a bowl and add the soaked bread, drained if necessary, the parsley, garlic, wine, three-quarters of the beaten eggs and a pinch of salt. Mix well. Cut into the onions where the circular cut was made in the tops and scoop out the centres. Fill the cavities with the meat mixture. Heat the sunflower oil in a deep frying pan. Brush the surface of the filling in each onion with the remaining beaten egg and then dust the whole onion with some of the flour. Add the onions to the pan, in batches, and cook until evenly browned. Preheat the oven to 180°C/350°F/Gas Mark 4. Heat the olive oil in a flameproof casserole. Arrange the onions in the casserole, side by side and filling uppermost, in a single layer. Dissolve the stock cube in a bowl with the reserved cooking liquid and pour enough into the casserole to come halfway up the onions. Transfer to the oven and bake, basting occasionally, for about 30 minutes, until tender and browned. (Test by piercing with a skewer or the point of sharp knife.) Serve immediately straight from the casserole.

Shallots

Shallots are small, elongated members of the onion family with a less acerbic flavour than onions. They have brown or red skins and often consist of two or more 'cloves'. Grelots are small, flat French onions that are not always easy to obtain.

How to cook
Peel the shallots and place them in a single layer in a saucepan. Pour in water to cover generously and add a knob of butter (allow 20 g / ¾ oz butter for every 250 g / 9 oz shallots or grelots), a pinch of salt and a few drops of lemon juice. Cover and cook over a medium heat for about 30 minutes, until tender. (Test by piercing with a skewer or the point of a sharp knife.)

How to glaze
Preheat the oven to 180°C/350°F/Gas Mark 4. Peel the shallots or grelots and place them in a single layer in an ovenproof dish. Pour in warm or cold water to cover and add a knob of butter, a pinch of salt and 1 teaspoon sugar. Cut a disc of brown wrapping paper that will just fit in the dish and position it so that it almost touches the shallots or grelots. Bake until all the liquid has evaporated and the shallots or grelots are shiny and tender. (Test by piercing with a skewer or the point of a sharp knife.) Use to garnish any dish.

367

- 12–18 shallots
- 65g/2½oz butter
- dash of lemon juice
- 2 tablespoons olive oil
- 2 tablespoons plain flour
- 500ml/18fl oz milk
- 1½ teaspoons tomato purée
- 50g/2oz gruyere cheese, grated
- salt

Serves 4

Shallots with béchamel sauce

CEBOLLITAS FRANCESAS CON BECHAMEL

Prepare and cook the shallots, using 40g/1½oz of the butter and the lemon juice, as described on page 294. Drain well. Melt the remaining butter with the oil in a saucepan. Stir in the flour and cook, stirring constantly, for 2 minutes. Gradually stir in the milk, a little at a time, then cook, stirring constantly, for 8 minutes. Remove the pan from the heat and stir in the tomato purée. Season to taste with salt. Preheat the oven to 180°C/350°F/Gas Mark 4. Place the shallots in a single layer in an ovenproof dish and pour the béchamel sauce over them. Sprinkle with the gruyere and bake for 10–15 minutes, until the cheese has melted. Serve immediately straight from the dish.

368

- 4 celeriac
- 1 quantity Classic Mayonnaise
  (see recipe 105)
- 2 tablespoons mustard
- salt and pepper

Serves 4

Celeriac

APIO-RÁBANO

Peel the celeriac, cut in half and put into a saucepan. Pour in water to cover, add a pinch of salt and bring to the boil. Lower the heat and cook for 30 minutes. Drain and leave to cool, then cut into strips like straw potatoes. Mix with the mayonnaise and add the mustard, and pepper to taste. Leave to stand for at least 30 minutes before serving to allow the flavours to mingle. Some people like their celeriac raw, grated and lightly blanched before it is mixed with the mayonnaise.

Note: instead of boiling the celeriac, some people prefer to grate and lightly blanch it, before mixing it with the mayonnaise.

Brussels sprouts

Origin and season

As their name suggests, Brussels sprouts were cultivated in Flanders, now Belgium, in the fifteenth century, although the Belgians claim that they were introduced into their country by the Romans. They are in season from mid autumn to early spring

Selection

They should be completely closed with no yellowing leaves. Try to select sprouts that are more or less the same size so that they need the same cooking time.

Nutrition

They contain vitamin C and are rich in minerals.

How to cook

Brussels sprouts should be very green with tightly wrapped leaves and as uniform in size as possible. Remove any limp or coarse leaves and trim the stems. Wash thoroughly in plenty of water with some vinegar or lemon juice added to remove any bugs. Bring a saucepan of salted water to the boil, add a handful of sprouts and cover the pan. Continue adding them handful by handful and re-covering the pan to prevent the temperature of the water dropping below boiling point. When all the sprouts have been added, remove the lid so that they stay green. Some people like to add a pinch of bicarbonate of soda to keep the sprouts bright green, but this is not recommended, as it makes them soft and they already need to be watched carefully while cooking to make sure they do not begin to disintegrate. The cooking time depends on size and freshness but it will be 20–25 minutes. Drain the sprouts well and refresh under cold running water, taking care they do not start to fall apart. They are then ready to be used.

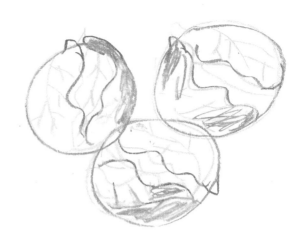

369

- 1.2–1.5 kg / 2½–3¼ lb
  Brussels sprouts
- 100 g / 3½ oz butter or
  175 ml / 6 fl oz olive oil
- 2 cloves garlic (optional),
  lightly crushed
- 2 tablespoons white-wine
  vinegar or 1 teaspoon
  Dijon mustard
- salt and pepper

Serves 4–6

Fried Brussels sprouts

COLES DE BRUSELAS REHOGADAS

Prepare and cook the sprouts as described on page 296, then drain and refresh under cold running water. If using the butter, melt half in a large frying pan. Add the sprouts and cook over a medium–low heat, occasionally stirring gently, for about 5 minutes, until lightly browned. Meanwhile, melt the remaining butter in a small saucepan. Season the sprouts to taste with salt and pour the melted butter over them just before serving. If using the oil instead of butter, heat the oil with the garlic cloves in a frying pan for a few minutes, until the garlic has browned. Remove and discard the garlic and add the sprouts to the pan. Cook for about 5 minutes until lightly browned. Season with pepper and pour the vinegar over them. Alternatively, do not season with pepper and stir in the mustard.

370

- 1.2–1.5 kg / 2½–3¼ lb
  Brussels sprouts
- 25 g / 1 oz butter
- 2 tablespoons olive oil
- 2 tablespoons plain flour
- 500 ml / 18 fl oz milk
- 1 teaspoon chopped
  fresh parsley
- salt

Serves 4–6

Brussels sprouts with béchamel sauce

COLES DE BRUSELAS CON BECHAMEL

Prepare and cook the sprouts as described on page 296, then drain and refresh under cold running water. Melt the butter with the oil in a frying pan. Stir in the flour and cook, stirring constantly, for 2 minutes. Gradually stir in the milk, a little at a time. Season with salt and cook, stirring constantly, for about 8 minutes. Carefully add the sprouts, stirring just enough to make sure that they are coated with sauce. Transfer to a vegetable dish, sprinkle with the parsley and serve immediately.

Note: The béchamel sauce can be made with half milk and half stock.

Brussels sprouts au gratin
COLES DE BRUSELAS GRATINADAS

Prepare and cook the Brussels sprouts as described on page 296. Preheat the oven to 180°C/350°F/Gas Mark 4. Transfer the sprouts and béchamel sauce to an ovenproof dish and sprinkle with 80 g / 3 oz grated gruyere cheese. Bake for 10–15 minutes, until the cheese has melted. Serve immediately straight from the dish.

Cauliflower

Origin and season
The cauliflower is known to have been cultivated in Europe since the Middle Ages but there is dispute over its country of origin. It is available almost all year round, although it is at its best from mid winter to late spring. It is most abundant from early autumn to the middle of winter.

Selection
Always buy cauliflower with its leaves still attached, even if they have been trimmed. Although the leaves are not eaten, they are a good indication of freshness. The head should be crisp, very white and tightly packed.Remember when buying cauliflower that you will lose half the weight during its preparation.

Nutrition
Cauliflower is very rich in vitamin C, possibly richer than orange juice as long as it is eaten raw. The slightly unpleasant smell produced when it is cooking is because of the magnesium and potassium it contains, but there are tricks to avoid this, such as placing a slice of bread soaked in a little milk on top of the cauliflower or adding 2 bay leaves to the pan during cooking.

How to cook

Separate the florets, or if the cauliflower is to be cooked whole, cut out as much of the stalk as possible. If cooking florets, peel the stalks a little so that they become tender when cooked. Rinse the florets in cold water mixed with the juice of ½ lemon. Bring a large saucepan of salted water to the boil. Add the florets and a little milk and cook, uncovered, for about 20 minutes, until tender. Drain well, taking care not to break up the florets, then refresh under cold running water. Tip on to a clean tea towel to drain. Cook a whole cauliflower in the same way, taking care when draining not to damage the florets.

372

Coated cauliflower
COLIFLOR REBOZADA

- 1 small cauliflower,
  about 1kg/2¼lb,
  separated into small florets
- juice of ½ lemon
- a little milk, for cooking
- sunflower oil, for deep-frying
- 50g/2oz plain flour
- 2 eggs, lightly beaten
- salt

Serves 6

Prepare and cook the cauliflower as described on page 299, then re-fresh under cold running water and drain on a clean tea towel. Heat the oil in a deep-fryer or saucepan to 180–190°C/350–375°F or until a cube of day-old bread browns in 30 seconds. Dip each floret in the flour, shaking off any excess, and then in the beaten egg. Add to the hot oil and cook for a few minutes, until golden brown. Do not add too many at a time. Remove with a slotted spoon, drain well and serve immediately. This is delicious served as an accompaniment to meat.

373

Cauliflower fritters
BUÑUELOS DE COLIFLOR

- 1 cauliflower, about 1.5kg/
  3¼lb, separated into florets
- juice of ½ lemon
- a little milk, for cooking
- sunflower oil, for deep-frying
- lemon slices and sprigs
  fresh parsley
- salt

Batter:
- 250g/9oz plain flour
- 3 tablespoons white wine
- 3 tablespoons sunflower oil
- 200ml/7floz milk
- 1 teaspoon easy-blend dried
  yeast
- salt

Serves 6

Prepare and cook the cauliflower as described on page 299, then re-fresh under cold running water and drain on a clean tea towel. Make the batter. Sift the flour with a pinch of salt into a bowl and make a well in the centre. Pour the wine and oil into the well and stir in the flour. Gradually stir in the milk, a little at a time. When the batter is smooth, cover and leave to stand for 30 minutes. When you are ready to cook, stir in the yeast. Heat the oil in a deep-fryer or saucepan to 180–190°C/350–375°F or until a cube of day-old bread browns in 30 seconds. One at a time, dip the florets into the batter, add to the hot oil and cook for about 5 minutes, until golden brown. Do not add too many at a time. Remove with a slotted spoon, drain well and keep warm. When all the florets have been fried, pile them into the middle of a round dish and garnish with the lemon slices and parsley. Serve the fritters immediately.

Note: This can be served with Classic Tomato Sauce (see recipe 73).

374 Cauliflower in caper and paprika sauce

COLIFLOR CON SALSA DE ALCAPARRAS Y PIMENTÓN

- 1 cauliflower, about 1.5 kg/
  3¼ lb, separated into florets
- juice of ½ lemon
- 500 ml/18 fl oz milk, plus a little
  for cooking the cauliflower
- 80 g/3 oz butter
- 3 tablespoons olive oil
- 1 onion, chopped
- 1 clove garlic
- 1 bay leaf
- 2 tablespoons plain flour
- 500 ml/18 fl oz chicken stock
  (home-made or made
  with a stock cube)
- ½ teaspoon paprika
- 2 tablespoons white-wine
  vinegar
- 3 tablespoons capers,
  rinsed and drained
- 3 tablespoons breadcrumbs
- salt

Serves 6

Prepare and cook the cauliflower as described on page 299, then refresh under cold running water and drain on a clean tea towel. Melt 25 g/1 oz of the butter with the oil in a saucepan. Add the onion and cook over a low heat, stirring occasionally, for about 5 minutes until softened. Add the garlic and bay leaf and cook for a few minutes more, then remove the pan from the heat. Stir the flour into the stock. Stir the paprika into the onion, immediately add the flour and stock mixture and stir in the milk. Pour in the vinegar, return the pan to the heat and cook gently, stirring constantly, for 5–6 minutes. Season to taste with salt. Preheat the oven to 180°C/350°F/Gas Mark 4. Pour a little of the sauce into an ovenproof dish and sprinkle half the capers over the base of the dish. Add the florets, pour the remaining sauce over them and sprinkle with the remaining capers. Sprinkle the breadcrumbs over the dish and dot with the remaining butter. Bake for 10–15 minutes, until lightly browned. Remove and discard the bay leaf and garlic. Serve immediately straight from the dish.

375 Cold cauliflower with mayonnaise

COLIFLOR FRÍA CON MAYONESA

- 1 cauliflower, about 1.5 kg/
  3¼ lb, separated into florets
- juice of ½ lemon
- a little milk, for cooking
- 1 quantity Thick Mayonnaise
  (see recipe 106)
- 2 hard-boiled eggs
- salt

Serves 6

Prepare and cook the cauliflower as described on page 299, then refresh under cold running water and drain on a clean tea towel. Put the florets into a round dish and pour the mayonnaise over them to cover completely. Chop one of the hard-boiled eggs and sprinkle it over the florets. Slice the other egg and arrange it around the edge of the dish. Serve cold.

376

Cauliflower pie
BUDÍN DE COLIFLOR

- 1 cauliflower, about 675 g/
  1½ lb, separated into florets
- juice of ½ lemon
- 500 ml/18 fl oz milk, plus a little
  for cooking the cauliflower
- 40 g/1½ oz butter or margarine,
  plus extra for greasing
- 2 tablespoons sunflower oil
- 3 heaped tablespoons plain flour
- pinch of freshly grated nutmeg
- 4 eggs
- 100 g/3½ oz gruyere cheese,
  grated
- 1 quantity Classic Tomato Sauce
  (see recipe 73)
- salt

Serves 6

Prepare and cook the cauliflower as described on page 299, then refresh under cold running water and drain on a clean tea towel. Transfer to a bowl and mash with a fork. Preheat the oven to 160°C/325°F/Gas Mark 3. Grease a 19-cm/7½-inch flan tin with butter or margarine. Melt the remaining butter or margarine with the oil in a saucepan. Stir in the flour and cook, stirring constantly, for 2 minutes. Gradually stir in the milk, a little at a time. Add the nutmeg, season with salt and cook, stirring constantly, for 8 minutes. Remove the pan from the heat. Beat two of the eggs, then beat them into the béchamel sauce. Repeat with the remaining eggs. Stir in the gruyere and when thoroughly incorporated, add the florets. Pour the mixture into the prepared tin and place the tin in a roasting tin. Pour in boiling water to come about halfway up the sides and bake for about 1 hour, until set. To serve, run a round-bladed knife around the edge of the flan tin and turn the pie out on to a round serving dish. Pour the warmed tomato sauce over it and serve immediately.

377

Cauliflower with béchamel sauce
COLIFLOR CON BECHAMEL

- 1 cauliflower, about 1.5 kg/
  3¼ lb, separated into florets
- juice of ½ lemon
- 500 ml/18 fl oz milk, plus a little
  for cooking the cauliflower
- 25 g/1 oz butter
- 2 tablespoons sunflower oil
- 2 tablespoons plain flour
- 80 g/3 oz gruyere cheese, grated
- salt

Serves 6

Prepare and cook the cauliflower as described on page 299, then refresh under cold running water and drain on a clean tea towel. Put the florets into an ovenproof dish. Preheat the oven to 180°C/350°F/Gas Mark 4. Melt the butter with the oil in a saucepan. Stir in the flour and cook, stirring constantly, for 2 minutes. Gradually stir in the milk, a little at a time. Season with salt and cook, stirring constantly, for 10 minutes, then pour the sauce over the florets. Sprinkle with the gruyere and bake for 10–15 minutes, until golden brown. Serve immediately straight from the dish.

Note: For a tasty variation, when the cheese begins to melt, push 65 g/2½ oz peeled almonds or pine nuts into the cauliflower so that half of each nut protrudes. Return the dish to the oven and bake for a few more minutes, taking care that the nuts do not brown too much.

378

Baked cauliflower with butter, lemon, parsley and hard-boiled egg

COLIFLOR AL HORNO CON MANTEQUILLA, LIMÓN, PEREJIL Y HUEVO DURO

- 1 cauliflower,
  about 1.5 kg/3¼ lb
- juice of 2 lemons
- a little milk, for cooking
- 150 g/5 oz butter
- 1 tablespoon chopped
  fresh parsley
- 1 hard-boiled egg, finely chopped
- salt

Serves 6

Preheat the oven to 180°C/350°F/Gas Mark 4. Prepare and cook the cauliflower, without separating it into florets, as described on page 299, and using the juice of half of one of the lemons, then refresh under cold running water and drain on a clean tea towel. Put the cauliflower into a deep ovenproof dish. Dot the butter all over the cauliflower and pour the remaining lemon juice over it. Bake, basting occasionally, for 15–20 minutes, until lightly browned. Remove the dish from the oven, sprinkle with the parsley and hard-boiled egg and serve immediately.

Note: You could sprinkle grated cheese over the cauliflower, but in this case, pour the juice of only 1 lemon into the dish. (You will require the juice of 1 ½ lemons in total because the cauliflower should be washed in acidulated water as described on page 299.) Use slightly less butter and omit the parsley and egg.

379

Cauliflower in toasted butter and breadcrumb sauce

COLIFLOR COCIDA CON SALSA DE MANTEQUILLA TOSTADA Y PAN RALLADO

- 1 cauliflower, about 1.5 kg/3¼ lb,
  separated into large florets
- juice of 1 lemon
- a little milk, for cooking
- 200 g/7 oz butter
- 3 tablespoons breadcrumbs
- salt

Serves 6

Prepare and cook the cauliflower as described on page 299, using the juice of half of the lemon, then drain and keep warm. Melt the butter in a saucepan and cook over a low heat until browned, then remove the pan from the heat and add the remaining lemon juice. Return the pan to the heat and stir in the breadcrumbs, but do not allow the sauce to brown any further. Pour the sauce over the florets and serve.

380

Chicory gratin

ENDIVIAS AL GRATÉN

- 12 heads chicory, trimmed
- 100 g/3½ oz butter
- 65 g/2½ oz gruyere cheese, grated
- salt

Serves 6

Put the chicory heads into a saucepan, pour in enough water to cover and add a pinch of salt. Bring to the boil and, at the same time, bring another saucepan with the same amount of salted water to the boil. When the water in both pans is boiling, use a slotted spoon to transfer the chicory to the second pan. This helps prevent it becoming bitter. Bring back to the boil and cook for about 20 minutes, until tender. Meanwhile, preheat the oven to 180°C/350°F/Gas Mark 4. Drain the chicory well and put into an ovenproof dish. Dot with the butter, sprinkle with the gruyere and bake for 10–15 minutes, until the cheese has melted and browned. Serve immediately straight from the dish.

381

Chicory in béchamel sauce

ENDIVIAS CON BECHAMEL

- 12 heads chicory, trimmed
- 25 g/1 oz butter
- 2 tablespoons sunflower oil
- 2 tablespoons plain flour
- 500 ml/18 fl oz milk
- 100 g/3½ oz gruyere cheese, grated
- salt

Serves 6

Cook the chicory heads in salted boiling water, using two saucepans as described in recipe 380. Drain well and put into an ovenproof dish. Preheat the oven to 180°C/350°F/Gas Mark 4. Melt the butter with the oil in a saucepan. Add the flour and cook, stirring constantly, for 2 minutes. Gradually stir in the milk, a little at a time, and bring to the boil, stirring constantly. Season with salt and simmer over a medium heat, stirring constantly, for 8–10 minutes. Pour over the chicory. Sprinkle with the gruyere and bake for 10–15 minutes, until golden brown. Serve immediately straight from the dish.

382

Chicory with York ham and béchamel sauce

ENDIVIAS CON JAMÓN DE YORK Y BECHAMEL

- **12 heads chicory, trimmed**
- **12 thin slices York ham or other dry-cured ham**
- **25 g/1 oz butter**
- **2 tablespoons sunflower oil**
- **2 tablespoons plain flour**
- **500 ml/18 fl oz milk**
- **100 g/3½ oz gruyere cheese, grated**
- **salt**

Serves 6

Follow the method for recipe 381, but before putting the chicory heads into a flameproof dish wrap each in one of the slices of ham. Pour in the béchamel sauce, sprinkle with the gruyere and cook under a preheated grill until golden brown.

383

Braised chicory
ENDIVIAS AL JUGO

- 12 heads chicory, trimmed
- 25 g/1 oz butter
- 2 tablespoons sunflower oil
- 1 tablespoon plain flour
- 275 ml/9 fl oz veal or beef stock
  (home-made or made
  with a stock cube)
- 1 veal knuckle
- pinch of freshly grated nutmeg
- salt

Serves 6

Cook the chicory heads in salted boiling water, using two saucepans as described in recipe 380, but for only 15 minutes in the second pan. Drain well. Melt the butter with the oil in a saucepan. Stir in the flour and cook, stirring constantly, for 2 minutes. Gradually stir in the stock, a little at a time. Add the veal knuckle and chicory and sprinkle with the nutmeg. Cook for 10–12 minutes, then remove the veal knuckle and transfer the chicory and sauce to a warm serving dish.

Note: This dish can be made in advance. Cook the chicory for just 5 minutes in the sauce and then cook for a further 5 minutes when reheating it.

384

Chicory salad
ENDIVIAS EN ENSALADA

- 6 heads chicory
- 1 quantity Vinaigrette
  (see recipe 98)

Serves 4–6

Trim the chicory heads, separate the leaves and cut them in half lengthways. Wash them well under cold running water, but do not leave to soak as this makes them bitter. Pat dry, put into a bowl and dress with the vinaigrette. Serve the salad quite soon after adding the dressing or it will become soggy.

385

Grapefruit salad with apples and chicory
ENESALADA DE POMELO CO MANZANA Y ENDIVIAS

- 1 pink grapefruit
- 1 eating apple
- juice of ½ lemon
- 2 chicory heads,
  cut into thin strips
- 100 g/3 ½ oz Roquefort cheese,
  crumbled
- 2 tablespoons olive oil
- juice of 1 lemon
- 2 tablespoons natural yogurt
- fresh mint leaves
- salt and pepper

Serves 4

Peel the grapefruit with a sharp knife, removing all traces of pith. Cut out the segments from the membranes and cut them into pieces. Peel, core and dice the apple and toss with half the lemon juice. Put the grapefruit, apple and chicory into a salad bowl and mix well. Prepare the sauce by mashing the cheese with the oil in a bowl, then stir in the lemon juice and season to taste with salt and pepper. Gradually stir in the yogurt, a little at a time. Add the sauce to the salad and chill well before serving, garnished with the mint leaves.

Note: If the flavour of the Roquefort is too strong, it can be replaced with soft, unripened cheese, such as ricotta. The grapefruit can be replaced with orange, in which case cut the apple into thick slices and leave the skin on to give the salad more colour.

386

Escarole salad
ENSALADA DE ESCAROLA

- **300 g/11 oz escarole leaves**
- **1 quantity Vinaigrette (see recipe 98)**
- **1 clove garlic (optional)**

Serves 4

Separate the escarole leaves, discarding all but the pale inner leaves, and wash, then pat dry. If the leaves are long, cut them into two or three pieces. Put into a bowl and dress with the vinaigrette. Serve the salad quite soon after adding the dressing or it will become soggy. If you like, you can rub the inside of the salad bowl with a peeled garlic clove before adding the leaves.

Note: Peeled, diced tomato may be mixed into the salad. Chopped celery may also be added.

Asparagus

Origin and season
Asparagus was known to the ancient Egyptians, regarded as an aphrodisiac by the Greeks and cultivated by the Romans. Since then, however, although wild asparagus grows in central and southern Europe and in North Africa there is little mention of it being eaten until the seventeenth and eighteenth centuries. It is widely cultivated under glass at the end of winter and the beginning of spring. Green asparagus can be thin, medium or fat, while white asparagus is usually fat. Wild asparagus is hard to find and then is available only in small quantities. It tends to be bitter.

Selection
The spears should be straight and even in colour. If you snap off the end, a little moisture should appear. The yellower the spears are, the older they are and the more likely they are too woody. Choose asparagus spears of a uniform length so that they will cook in the same amount of time. When sold in bunches, they will have been selected with this in mind. It is not a good idea to buy spears that are too long. The best time for asparagus is middle to late spring.

Nutrition

Asparagus does not have a high nutritional value, as it consists of 92 per cent water and has only 15 calories per 100 g / 3 ½ oz. It contains vitamins and is a good source of the minerals potassium, iron and calcium. It also contains a substance that can irritate the renal system, so it should be avoided by people with kidney problems. It is good for cleansing the system. Asparagus is a good convalescent food and may be helpful for those suffering from anaemia, rheumatism, some types of eczema, palpitations and diabetes.

How to prepare and cook

Allow 1.5–2 kg / 3 ¼ – 4 ½ lb to serve four. Try to buy asparagus spears that are the same thickness. Peel them from the tip to the base, if necessary, then cut them all to the same length (about 25 cm/10 inches). Make sure you cut off the woody ends. As they are cut put them into cold water. Bring a large saucepan of salted water to the boil. Add the asparagus, submerging it completely and with all the tips pointing in the same direction so that they will not break when lifted out. Cover the pan, bring back to the boil and cook for about 10 minutes for medium asparagus or 20 minutes for fat asparagus. In both cases, check that the spears are cooked by piercing one with the point of a sharp knife. You can also buy a special asparagus pan which is tall enough to allow the spears to stand up, so that the stems cook in water while the tips are gently steamed.

Tricks

- If you're not ready to serve the asparagus immediately, leave it in its cooking water for up to 1 hour. If you need to keep it longer, drain it well, put a doubled napkin in a dish, put the asparagus on the napkin and cover the dish with foil
- Asparagus may be served hot or cold
- Asparagus can be served with various sauces: melted butter with chopped fresh parsley; all kinds of mayonnaise
(see recipes 105–111); vinaigrette with chopped hard-boiled egg, etc. (see recipes 98–101).

387

Ham with asparagus

JAMÓN CON ESPÁRRAGOS

- **2 kg/4½ lb green asparagus, trimmed**
- **6 slices ham**
- **20 g/¾ oz butter**
- **1 tablespoon sunflower oil**
- **1 tablespoon plain flour**
- **450 ml/¾ pint milk**
- **50 g/2 oz gruyere cheese, grated**
- **salt**

Serves 6

Bring a large saucepan of salted water to the boil. Add the asparagus, cover and cook for 10–20 minutes, until tender but not falling apart. Carefully lift out the spears and drain on a folded tea towel. Divide the spears into six portions and wrap each portion in a slice of ham, leaving the tips sticking out. Put into an ovenproof dish in a single layer. Preheat the oven to 180°C/350°F/Gas Mark 4. Melt the butter with the oil in a saucepan. Stir in the flour and cook, stirring constantly, for 2 minutes. Gradually stir in the milk, a little at a time. Season with salt and cook, stirring constantly, for 4 minutes. Remove the pan from the heat and pour the sauce over the rolls of ham, but do not cover the asparagus tips. Sprinkle with the gruyere and bake for 10–15 minutes, until golden brown. Serve immediately straight from the dish.

388

Asparagus with peas

PUNTAS DE ESPÁRRAGOS CON GUISANTES

- 1.5 kg / 3¼ lb peas, shelled
- 3 tablespoons sunflower oil
- 1 spring onion, chopped
- 1 teaspoon sugar
- 100 g / 3½ oz Serrano ham, finely chopped
- 2 kg / 4½ lb fine asparagus, trimmed
- 1 hard-boiled egg, sliced or chopped
- salt

Serves 6

Heat the oil in a saucepan. Add the spring onions and cook over a low heat, stirring occasionally, for 3–4 minutes, but do not allow them to brown. Add the peas and cook, stirring constantly, for a few minutes. Pour in 275 ml / 9 fl oz water, stir in the sugar, cover the pan and simmer for 15 minutes. Add the ham and cook for a further 20 minutes, until the peas are tender. Season to taste with salt. Meanwhile, cut the asparagus into 2.5-cm/1-inch lengths. Bring a large saucepan of salted water to the boil. Add the asparagus, cover and cook for about 10 minutes, until tender but not falling apart. Drain well and combine with the peas and ham in a warm deep serving dish. Garnish with the hard-boiled egg and serve immediately.

389

Scrambled eggs with asparagus and potatoes

PUNTAS DE ESPÁRRAGOS REVUELTAS CON PATATAS Y HUEVOS

- 2 kg / 4½ lb short asparagus, and trimmed
- sunflower oil, for deep-frying
- 1 kg / 2¼ lb potatoes, diced
- 6 eggs, lightly beaten
- salt

Serves 6

Cut the asparagus into 2.5-cm/1-inch lengths. Bring a large saucepan of salted water to the boil, add the asparagus, cover and cook for 10–20 minutes, until tender but not falling apart. Drain well. Heat the oil in a deep frying pan to 180–190°C/350–375°F or until a cube of day-old bread browns in 30 seconds. Add the potato and cook for 5–8 minutes, until evenly browned. Remove with a slotted spoon, drain well, lightly season with salt and set aside. Drain off almost all the oil from the pan, leaving just a thin layer on the base, and reheat. Add the asparagus. Season the eggs with salt and then pour into the frying pan. Cook, stirring frequently with a fork, for a few minutes, until the eggs are creamy. Remove the pan from the heat and leave the eggs to set a little more, then add the potato. Stir well, turn the mixture out on to a warm serving dish and serve immediately.

390

Green asparagus with sauce
ESPÁRRAGOS VERDES EN SALSA

- 4 tablespoons olive oil
- 2 slices of bread, crusts removed
- 1 clove garlic
- 1 sprig fresh parsley
- 2 kg / 4½ lb green asparagus, trimmed
- 1 tablespoon white-wine vinegar
- ½ teaspoon paprika
- 2 eggs, lightly beaten
- salt

Serves 4

Heat the oil in a frying pan. Add the bread, garlic and parsley and cook, turning the bread occasionally, for a few minutes until golden brown on both sides. Transfer the bread, garlic and parsley to a mortar and pound with a pestle. Cut the asparagus into 2.5-cm/1-inch lengths. Add to the pan with the vinegar and cook for 5 minutes. Stir in the paprika, pour in just enough water to cover the asparagus, add the contents of the mortar and season with salt. Simmer for about 20 minutes, until the asparagus is tender. Just before serving, stir in the eggs. Serve immediately.

391

Fried green asparagus with garlic, vinegar and paprika
ESPÁRRAGOS VERDES REHOGADOS CON AJO, VINAGRE Y PIMENTÓN

- 2 kg / 4½ lb green asparagus, trimmed
- 6 tablespoons olive oil
- 3 slices of bread, crusts removed
- 2 cloves garlic
- ½ teaspoon paprika
- 450 ml / ¾ pint hot water
- 3 tablespoons white-wine vinegar
- 1 teaspoon chopped fresh parsley
- salt

Serves 6

Cut the asparagus into 4-cm/1½-inch lengths. Heat the oil in a frying pan. Add the bread and cook, turning occasionally, for a few minutes, until golden brown on both sides. Remove from the pan and set aside. Add the garlic to the pan and cook, stirring frequently, for a few minutes, until golden brown. Transfer to a mortar, add the fried bread and pound with a pestle. Pour the oil from the frying pan into a saucepan and heat. Add the asparagus and cook for 2–3 minutes. Remove the pan from the heat and stir in the paprika, then pour in the hot water. Return the pan to a medium heat, cover and cook, shaking the pan occasionally, for 1 hour. Add the vinegar and a little of the asparagus cooking liquid to the mixture in the mortar and stir well, then stir into the pan containing the asparagus. Season with a little salt and cook for a further 5 minutes. Sprinkle with the parsley and serve immediately.

392

Wild asparagus omelette

ESPÁRRAGOS TRIGUEROS PARA TORTILLA

• **1 bunch wild asparagus, trimmed**
• **4 eggs, lightly beaten**
• **3 tablespoons olive oil**
• **salt**

Serves 2

Cut the asparagus into 2.5-cm/1-inch lengths. Put into a saucepan, add water to cover and bring to the boil. At the same time, bring another saucepan of lightly salted water to the boil. When the asparagus has been boiling for 3 minutes, transfer it to the second pan, using a slotted spoon. Cook for a further 10 minutes, until tender. Drain well. Lightly beat the eggs with a pinch of salt in a bowl, then add the asparagus. Heat the oil in a frying pan. Pour in the egg and asparagus mixture and cook until the underside has set and is golden brown. Turn the omelette by inverting it on to the lid of the pan or a plate and then carefully sliding it back into the pan, and cook until the second side is golden brown. Serve immediately.

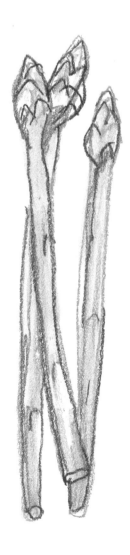

Spinach

Origin and season

Of Persian origin, spinach was introduced to Europe by the Arabs at the end of the Middle Ages. For a long time, it was considered to be a plant that invigorated the body owing to its high iron content. Spinach has two seasons: late winter to late spring and mid to late autumn.

Selection

The leaves should have a uniform green colour, which may be dark or light depending on the variety. Choose the larger leaves for cooking and the smaller, more tender leaves for salads.

Nutrition

Spinach is a vegetable with a relatively low nutritional value and contains about 18 calories per 100 g / 3 ½ oz. It contains vitamins A, B and C, as well as iron, calcium, phosphorus and cobalt. It is not as rich in iron as was once thought. It is not recommended for people with rheumatism, arthritis or nephritic colic. However, it is good for children who suffer from anaemia.

How to prepare and cook

Most recipes require spinach to be precooked. Remove and discard the coarse stalks and wash the spinach in several changes of water. Drain slightly, then put into a saucepan with just the water clinging to its leaves. Add a pinch of salt and cook, stirring occasionally, for 8–10 minutes. Drain well, pressing out as much liquid as you possibly can with the back of a spoon. Allow 2.5–3 kg/5 ½–6 ½ lb spinach for 6 servings.

393

Spinach with béchamel sauce

ESPINACAS CON BECHAMEL

- 3 kg/6 ½ lb spinach,
  coarse stalks removed
- 25 g/1 oz butter
- 2 tablespoons sunflower oil
- 1 tablespoon plain flour
- 275 ml/9 fl oz milk
- 3 slices of bread,
  cut into triangles and fried
  (see recipe 130)
- 2 hard-boiled eggs, sliced
- salt

Serves 6

Cook the spinach as described above. Drain well and chop finely. Melt the butter with the oil in a frying pan. Stir in the flour and cook, stirring constantly, for 2 minutes. Gradually stir in the milk, a little at a time. Cook, stirring constantly, for 8 minutes. Lightly season with salt and add the spinach, in three or four batches, stirring well to prevent it sticking to the pan. Transfer to a warm serving dish and garnish with the triangles of fried bread around the edge and the slices of hard-boiled egg on top. Serve immediately.

Note: Add slightly less milk if you prefer thicker creamed spinach; or slightly more if you prefer it thinner.

394

Scrambled eggs with spinach and prawns

REVUELTO DE ESPINACAS, GAMBAS Y HUEVOS

- 1 kg/2 ¼ lb spinach,
  coarse stalks removed
- pinch of bicarbonate of soda
- 50 g/2 oz butter or
  5 tablespoons sunflower oil
- 300 g/11 oz raw prawns, peeled
- 8 eggs, lightly beaten
- salt

Serves 6

Cook the spinach as described above, adding the bicarbonate of soda to preserve the green colour. Drain well and chop finely. Heat the butter or oil in a frying pan. Add the prawns and cook over a medium heat, stirring occasionally, for 2 minutes. Stir in the spinach and cook, stirring constantly, for 3 minutes. Season the beaten eggs with salt, pour into the pan and cook, stirring frequently, for a few minutes, until the eggs begin to set. Turn the mixture out on to a warm serving dish and serve immediately, garnished with triangles of fried bread (see recipe 130), if you like.

395

Spinach, cream and asparagus vol-au-vent

VOL-AU-VENT DE ESPINACAS CON NATA Y PUNTAS DE ESPÁRRAGOS

- 2 kg/4½ lb spinach,
  coarse stalks removed
- 40 g/1½ oz butter
- 175 ml/6 fl oz single cream
- 1 vol-au-vent case, 15–20 cm/
  6–8 inches in diameter, cooked
- 400 g/14 oz canned
  asparagus tips, drained
- salt

Serves 6

Preheat the oven to 160°C/325°F/Gas Mark 3. Cook the spinach as described on page 315. Drain and chop finely. Melt the butter in a frying pan. Stir in the spinach and add the cream. Mix well. Place the vol-au-vent case on a baking sheet. Remove the pan from the heat and spoon the spinach mixture into the vol-au-vent case. Insert the asparagus spears into the spinach mixture in a circle. Put the pastry lid on the vol-au-vent case and heat through in the oven for 15–20 minutes, until warm. Serve immediately.

396

Spinach and potato stew

ESPINACAS Y PATATAS GUISADAS

- 1.5 kg/3¼ lb spinach,
  coarse stalks removed
- 4 tablespoons olive oil
- 2 cloves garlic
- 1 onion, chopped
- pinch of saffron threads
- 2 slices of fried bread
  (see recipe 130)
- 5 waxy potatoes,
  cut into small pieces
- salt

Serves 6

Cook the spinach as described on page 315 for just 5 minutes. Drain well, reserving a little of the cooking liquid, and chop. Heat the oil in a flameproof earthenware pot or a saucepan. Add the garlic and cook, stirring occasionally, for a few minutes, until lightly browned, then remove from the pan and reserve. Add the onion and cook over a low heat, stirring occasionally, for about 5 minutes, until softened and translucent. Add the spinach and pour in water to cover. Put the saffron, reserved garlic and the fried bread in a mortar and pound with a pestle. Stir in the reserved cooking liquid and pour into the pan. Add the potatoes, season to taste with salt, cover and cook over a medium heat for about 30 minutes, until the potatoes are tender but not falling apart. Serve straight from the pot or transfer to a warm deep serving dish. Ladle into soup plates and eat with spoons.

397

Spinach garnish

ESPINACAS DE ADORNO

- 1.5 kg/3¼ lb spinach,
  coarse stalks removed
- 50 g/2 oz butter

Serves 6

Prepare and cook the spinach as described on page 315. Drain well and chop. Melt the butter in a frying pan, add the spinach and cook, stirring occasionally, for 3–5 minutes. Serve with meat or fish.

Note: You can put this into an ovenproof dish with fish or as a base for macaroni (see page 221). Cover with béchamel sauce (see recipe 77) sprinkle with grated cheese and bake in the oven.

Peas

Origin and season

Peas have been known since ancient times and were already growing wild several thousand years BC. The ancient Egyptians, Greeks and Romans grew them, although the cultivated variety originated in China. Their season is from late spring to early summer.

How do you choose them?

Peas must be very fresh, otherwise they will be starchy and hard. The pods should not show any discoloration. Bear in mind that peas can be bought frozen and canned and that both are good-quality products. You should check the amount of sugar that has been added during processing; in the case of canned peas this should not be more than 5 per cent.

Nutrition

Fresh peas have about 80 calories per 100 g / 3 ½ oz, and they contain starch and sucrose (so they may not be suitable for diabetics) and cellulose.

Tricks

- Do not wash peas when preparing them. To enhance their flavour, add fresh mint leaves to the cooking water
- Peas can be frozen after shelling and freeze quite well. To cook, put them straight into boiling water
- Do not cover the pan when cooking, and add a little bicarbonate of soda to preserve a good green colour
- Do not forget to add a little sugar when cooking peas, as this makes them more tender
- Rinse drained canned peas with warm water to remove the metallic taste and pour lemon juice over them.

398

Simple peas

GUISANTES SENCILLOS

- 3 tablespoons sunflower oil
- 2 spring onions, chopped
- 2.5–3 kg/5½–6½ lb peas, shelled
- 1 teaspoon sugar
- 100 g/3½ oz Serrano ham, finely chopped
- salt

Serves 6

Heat the oil in a saucepan. Add the spring onions and cook over a low heat, stirring occasionally, for 3–4 minutes, but do not allow them to brown. Add the peas and cook, stirring constantly, for a few minutes. Pour in 275 ml/9 fl oz water, stir in the sugar, cover the pan and simmer for 15 minutes. Add the ham and cook for a further 20 minutes, until the peas are tender. Season to taste with salt and serve immediately.

399

Peas and carrots

GUISANTES Y ZANAHORIAS

- 1.5 kg/3¼ lb peas, shelled and pods reserved
- 300 ml/½ pint sunflower oil
- 1 spring onion, finely chopped
- 750 g/1 lb 10 oz young carrots, diced
- 25 g/1 oz butter
- 6 thin rashers bacon
- salt

Serves 6

Tie a couple of handfuls of the reserved pea pods together with kitchen string or tie them in a piece of muslin. Heat 3 tablespoons of the oil in a saucepan. Add the spring onion and cook over a low heat, stirring occasionally, for about 3 minutes, but do not allow it to brown. Add the carrot and pour in 500 ml/18 fl oz water. Simmer for 15 minutes, then add the peas and tied pods, season with salt and cook for a further 20 minutes, until the vegetables are tender. Just before serving, remove and discard the pea pods and use the lid of the pan to drain off nearly all the water. Stir in the butter until it melts. Meanwhile, heat the remaining oil in a frying pan. Add the bacon and cook for 2–4 minutes on each side, until lightly browned. Serve the vegetables in a warm vegetable dish, garnished with the bacon.

Broad beans

Origin and season

Broad beans originated in Persia (modern Iran). In the past they symbolised the migration of souls and did not have a good reputation: Some people believed they caused infertility, while others considered them to be a powerful aphrodisiac – the reason why eating broad beans was forbidden in convents in the Middle Ages. Both fresh and dried beans are available. The best time for fresh beans is from late spring to early summer, when they are small and tender.

Selection

Broad beans should not show any discoloration and they should be firm and flawless.

Nutrition

Fresh broad beans have 36 calories per 100 g/3 ½ oz and some vitamins and minerals. Dried beans have more calories – 250 per 100 g/3 ½ oz. They are also high in fibre, which may have a laxative effect and can cause wind. Consuming them in large quantities outside a well-balanced diet can result in anaemia.

Tricks

• Very young beans can be cooked in their skins, but older dried beans should be soaked and peeled
• To eat broad beans in the pod, trim the ends and pull them to remove any stringy parts, there might be, just as with string beans.

400 Broad beans with eggs

HABAS CON HUEVOS

- 2 kg/4½ lb baby broad beans
- pinch of bicarbonate of soda
- 6 tablespoons olive oil
- 1 onion, very finely chopped
- 100 g/3½ oz Serrano ham, finely chopped
- 3 eggs, lightly beaten
- salt

Serves 6

Baby broad beans can be eaten in their pods. Trim the ends and pull off any strings from the sides. Cut the pods into little squares around the beans. Wash and drain thoroughly. Bring a large saucepan of salted water to the boil. Add the beans and the bicarbonate of soda. Cook, uncovered, for 1 hour. Meanwhile, heat the oil in a frying pan. Add the onion and cook over a low heat, stirring occasionally, for about 5 minutes, until softened and translucent. Add the ham and cook, stirring frequently, for a further 3 minutes. Drain the beans and add them to the pan. Lightly season the eggs with salt and pour them into the pan. Cook, stirring constantly, until the eggs start to set around the beans. Serve immediately.

401 Sautéed broad beans with ham

HABAS SALTEADAS CON JAMÓN

- 2 kg/4½ lb baby broad beans
- 6 tablespoons olive oil
- 2 cloves garlic, chopped
- 2 sprigs chopped fresh parsley
- 100 g/3½ oz Serrano ham, finely chopped
- salt

Serves 6

Baby broad beans can be eaten in their pods. Trim the ends and pull off any strings from the sides. Cut the pods into little squares around the beans. Wash and drain thoroughly. Heat the oil in a saucepan. Add the beans, sprinkle in the garlic and parsley and season with salt. Cook, uncovered, over a low heat, shaking the pan occasionally, for 15 minutes. Add the ham and 5 tablespoons water and cook for a further 30–45 minutes, until the beans are tender. Serve immediately.

402 Broad beans with black pudding

HABAS CON MORCILLA

- 750 g/1 lb 10 oz shelled broad beans
- 1 tablespoon olive oil
- 1 small onion, chopped
- 300 g/11 oz onion-flavoured black pudding, skinned and cut into small pieces
- salt

Serves 6

If using frozen broad beans, cook them according to the instructions on the packet. If using fresh broad beans, pop the broad beans out of their skins by squeezing them between your thumb and index finger. Bring a large saucepan of salted water to the boil. Add the beans and cook, uncovered, for about 1 hour, until tender. Meanwhile, heat the oil in a frying pan. Add the onion and cook over a low heat, stirring occasionally, for about 7 minutes, but do not brown. Drain the beans, add to the onion and cook over a very low heat for 6 minutes. Meanwhile, heat another frying pan. Add the black pudding and cook, stirring occasionally, for 5–8 minutes. Add it to the beans and cook, stirring occasionally, for a further 10 minutes. Serve immediately.

403

Broad beans with milk and egg yolks

HABAS CON LECHE Y YEMAS

- 4 kg/8 ¾ lb broad beans, shelled
- small pinch of bicarbonate of soda
- 25 g/1 oz butter
- 2 tablespoons olive oil
- 1 teaspoon chopped fresh parsley
- 1 heaped tablespoon plain flour
- 450 ml/¾ pint milk
- 2 egg yolks, lightly beaten
- salt

Serves 6

Pop the broad beans out of their skins by squeezing them between your thumb and index finger. Bring a large saucepan of salted water to the boil. Add the bicarbonate of soda and the beans and cook, uncovered, for 20 minutes. Melt the butter with the oil in a saucepan. Using a slotted spoon, transfer the beans to the pan of melted butter. Sprinkle with the parsley and flour and cook, stirring constantly, for 2 minutes. Gradually stir in the milk, a little at a time. Simmer over a low heat for a further 10 minutes, until the beans are tender. Stir a little of the sauce from the beans into the egg yolks to prevent them curdling, then stir into the beans. Serve immediately.

404

Broad beans in sauce

HABAS EN SALSA

- 2 kg/4 ½ lb baby broad beans
- pinch of bicarbonate of soda
- 6 tablespoons olive oil
- 1 onion, chopped
- 2 tablespoons plain flour
- 100 g/3 ½ oz Serrano ham, chopped
- 175 ml/6 fl oz white wine
- salt

Serves 4

Baby broad beans can be eaten in their pods. Trim the ends and pull off any strings from the sides. Cut the pods into little squares around the beans. Wash and drain thoroughly. Bring a large saucepan of salted water to the boil. Add the bicarbonate of soda and the beans. Cook, uncovered, for 35 minutes, until tender. Just before the beans are ready, prepare the sauce. Heat the oil in a frying pan. Add the onion and cook over a low heat, stirring occasionally, for about 6 minutes, until softened but not browned. Stir in the flour and cook, stirring constantly, for a further 5 minutes. Add the ham and cook for a few minutes, then pour in the wine. Drain the beans, reserving the cooking liquid. Pour the sauce into a saucepan and add the beans. Stir well and add just enough of the reserved cooking liquid to cover. Cook, uncovered, over a low heat for 10 minutes. Serve immediately.

405

Stewed broad beans
HABAS GUISADAS

- 4 kg/8¾ lb broad beans, shelled
- very small pinch of bicarbonate of soda
- 4 tablespoons olive oil
- 2 slices of bread, crusts removed
- 1 clove garlic
- 1 small onion, chopped
- 1 teaspoon paprika
- 1 small lettuce, shredded
- 1 tablespoon white-wine vinegar
- salt

Serves 6

Pop the broad beans out of their skins by squeezing them between your thumb and index finger. Bring a large saucepan of salted water to the boil. Add the beans and the bicarbonate of soda and cook, uncovered, for 15 minutes. Drain well. Heat the oil in a frying pan. Add the bread and garlic and cook, turning occasionally, for a few minutes until evenly browned. Remove the bread and garlic from the pan and pound in a mortar. Add the onion to the frying pan and cook over a low heat, stirring occasionally, for about 6 minutes, until softened but not browned. Remove the pan from the heat and stir in the paprika, then immediately add the lettuce and beans and stir well. Stir the vinegar into the mixture in the mortar, then add to the frying pan. Season to taste with salt and, if necessary, add 3–4 tablespoons water. Simmer gently for about 15 minutes, until the beans are tender, adding a little hot water if the mixture seems too thick. Serve immediately.

406

Fried broad bean garnish
HABAS FRITAS DE ADORNO

- 1 kg/2 ¼ lb baby broad beans
- pinch of bicarbonate of soda
- 50 g/2 oz plain flour
- sunflower oil, for deep-frying

Serves 4–6

Baby broad beans can be eaten in their pods. Trim the ends and pull off any strings from the sides. Cut the pods into little squares around the beans. Wash and drain thoroughly. Bring a large saucepan of salted water to the boil. Add the beans and the bicarbonate of soda. Cook, uncovered, for 1 hour. Drain well. Heat the oil in a deep-fryer or saucepan to 180–190°C/350–375°F or until a cube of day-old bread browns in 30 seconds. Coat the beans in the flour and cook them, in batches, for 6 minutes, until lightly browned. Serve as a garnish with meat dishes and roasts.

Fennel

Origin and season

Fennel comes from southern Europe. The ancient Egyptians and Greeks used it as medicine but it was the Italians who first used it as a foodstuff in the Middle Ages. There are two types: wild fennel is used mostly for producing alcohol, while the cultivated variety has a mild flavour and may be eaten raw or cooked. The season is from late autumn to late spring.

Selection

The bulb should feel heavy in the hand and look smooth with no imperfections or discoloration. The best bulbs are small with tightly packed leaves.

Nutrition

Fennel has few calories – 25 per 100 g / 3 ½ oz. It contains calcium, iron and small quantities of vitamins A and C. It also contains an aromatic oil. Eating fennel is said by some to help lactation.

Tricks

- A few fennel leaves can be added to a filling or stuffing to create a very special flavour. They can also be combined with herbs such as tarragon to give more aroma to chicken, whether cooked in the oven or in a pan
- Fennel has a special affinity with fish
- Allow half a fennel bulb per serving. A whole bulb will take about 15 minutes to cook.

Green beans

Origin and season

It is believed that green beans were brought to Europe from South America by Christopher Columbus. It is said that Charles Darwin used to play the trombone to his green beans to encourage them to grow. They are available all year round although the best time to eat them is late spring to autumn, when they are at their most succulent.

Selection

Very fresh green beans are shiny. It is best to choose small beans. To check for freshness, snap the end off one of them; it should break off cleanly, without any stringy part, and look juicy.

Nutrition

Beans contain high levels of vitamin C, potassium, calcium and iron and have only 35 calories per 100 g/3 ½ oz. According to some research, they have an invigorating effect on the heart. Tender green beans are recommended for everyone and are ideal for people on a weight-loss programme as part of a balanced diet.

How to cook

If the beans are large, cut them into smaller pieces. Bring a large saucepan of salted water to the boil. Add the beans, bring back to the boil, and cook, uncovered, for 10–12 minutes, until tender, then refresh in cold water. Drain immediately and pat dry. Alternatively, steam the beans for 12 minutes.

Tricks

- You can add a little bicarbonate of soda to the cooking water to preserve the good green color of beans
- Remember that frozen beans will never be so small as fresh beans, as the smaller varieties do not freeze well.

407

- 1 kg/2¼ lb green beans, trimmed
- 100 g/3½ oz butter
- 1 heaped tablespoon chopped fresh parsley
- juice of 1 lemon
- salt

Serves 4–6

Green beans sautéed in butter, parsley and lemon

JUDÍAS VERDES SALTEADAS CON MANTEQUILLA, PEREJIL Y LIMÓN

Prepare, cook and refresh the beans as described on page 325. Melt the butter in a saucepan or frying pan and add the beans just before it is completely melted. Cook gently for several minutes and just before serving sprinkle with the parsley and add the lemon juice. Serve immediately.

408

- 1.5 kg/3¼ lb green beans, trimmed
- 5 tablespoons sunflower oil
- 2 cloves garlic, lightly crushed
- salt

Serves 6

Green beans fried in oil with garlic

JUDÍAS VERDES REHOGADAS SÓLO CON ACEITE Y AJOS

Prepare, cook and refresh the beans as described on page 325. Heat the oil in a frying pan. Add the garlic and cook for a few minutes, until lightly browned. Remove and discard the garlic. Add the beans to the pan and cook briefly, taking care that they neither disintegrate nor burn. Serve immediately.

409

- 1.5 kg/3¼ lb green beans, trimmed
- 3 tablespoons sunflower oil
- 1 onion, thinly sliced
- 150 g/5 oz bacon or Serrano ham, chopped
- 1 tablespoon chopped fresh parsley
- salt

Serves 6

Green beans fried with bacon

JUDÍAS VERDES REHOGADAS CON TOCINO

Prepare, cook and refresh the beans as described on page 325. Heat the oil in a frying pan. Add the onion and cook over a low heat, stirring occasionally, for about 5 minutes, until softened. Add the bacon or ham and cook, stirring frequently, for a further 5 minutes. Add the beans and cook for 5–10 minutes, until heated through. Season to taste with salt and sprinkle with the parsley. Serve immediately.

410

Green bean salad with foie gras

ENSALADA DE JUDIAS VERDES CON FOIE-GRAS

- 500 g/1 lb 2 oz green beans, trimmed
- 100 g/3½ oz mushrooms
- juice of ½ lemon
- 2 cooked or canned artichoke hearts, drained and thickly sliced
- 200 g/7 oz cooked or canned foie gras, diced
- 1 truffle, cut into julienne strips
- 3 tablespoons olive oil
- salt and pepper

Serves 4

Prepare and cook the beans as described on page 325, but cook them for only 10 minutes, until tender but still crunchy. Refresh in cold water, drain immediately and pat dry. Separate the mushroom stalks from the caps (keep the stalks for soup) and thickly slice the caps. Sprinkle with the lemon juice. Put the artichoke hearts on to plates and add the beans and slices of mushroom. Place the foie gras and truffle on top, drizzle with the olive oil, season with salt and pepper and serve.

411

Green beans with tomato sauce

JUDÍAS VERDES CON SALSA DE TOMATE

- 1.5 kg/3¼ lb green beans, trimmed
- 1 tablespoon chopped fresh parsley
- salt

Tomato sauce:
- 3 tablespoons sunflower oil
- 1 onion, finely chopped
- 750 g/1 lb 10 oz very ripe tomatoes, peeled, seeded and chopped
- 1 teaspoon sugar

Serves 6

Make the tomato sauce as described in recipe 73, and process to a purée in a food processor. Prepare and cook the beans as described on page 325, but cook them for only 10 minutes. Drain well and return to the pan; do not refresh under cold running water. Add the tomato sauce and cook over a low heat, uncovered, for about 10 minutes, until the beans are tender. Sprinkle with the parsley and serve.

412

Green beans with vinegar and egg yolk sauce

JUDÍAS VERDES CON SALSA DE VINAGRE Y YEMAS

- 1.5 kg/3¼ lb green beans, trimmed
- 6 tablespoons olive oil
- 1 heaped tablespoon plain flour
- 2 egg yolks
- 1 tablespoon white-wine vinegar
- salt

Serves 6

If the beans are long and wide, cut them in half lengthways and widthways. Heat the oil in a saucepan. Add the beans and cook, stirring occasionally, for about 5 minutes. Stir in the flour and cook, stirring constantly, for 2 minutes. Stir in cold water to cover. Season with salt and cook, uncovered, over a low heat for 15–20 minutes, until tender. Lightly beat the egg yolks with the vinegar in a bowl, then gradually whisk in a few spoonfuls of the sauce from the beans. Remove the pan from the heat and stir the egg mixture into the beans to heat through. Serve immediately.

413

Green beans in vinaigrette

JUDÍAS VERDES CON VINAGRETA

- 1.5 kg/3¼ lb green beans, trimmed
- 2 tablespoons white-wine vinegar
- 6 tablespoons sunflower oil
- 1 tablespoon chopped shallot (optional)
- 1 teaspoon chopped fresh parsley
- 2 large firm tomatoes, sliced
- salt

Serves 6

Prepare, cook and refresh the beans as described on page 325. Make a vinaigrette with the vinegar, oil and salt as described in recipe 98. Put the beans in a serving dish and sprinkle with the shallot, if using, and the parsley. Pour the vinaigrette over the beans and toss to coat thoroughly. Lightly season the tomato slices with salt and use them to garnish the beans.

414 📷 Coated green beans

JUDÍAS VERDES REBOZADAS

- 600 g/1 lb 5 oz young flat
  green beans
- 500 ml/18 fl oz sunflower oil
- 50 g/2 oz plain flour
- 1–2 eggs
- 2 slices of fried bread
  (see recipe 130)
- 1 large clove garlic
- 3–4 sprigs fresh parsley
- 3 tablespoons white-wine
  vinegar
- salt

Serves 4

The beans should be so young that they do not have any strings. Cook them in salted boiling water for 8–12 minutes, until tender. Alternatively, steam them in a pressure cooker for 6 minutes. Drain well and pat dry. Heat the oil in a deep-fryer or deep saucepan to 180–190°C/350–375°F or until a cube of day-old bread browns in 30 seconds. Beat the eggs in a shallow dish and spread out the flour in another shallow dish. One at a time, dip the beans first in the flour and then in the egg. Add them to the oil, in batches, and cook until golden. Drain well and put into a deep serving dish. Pound the fried bread, garlic and parsley in a mortar and stir in the vinegar and 275 ml/9 fl oz of the oil used to fry the beans. Mix well, pour over the beans and leave to stand for 15 minutes before serving.

415 Green beans with mayonnaise

JUDÍAS VERDES CON MAYONESA

- 1.5 kg/3¼ lb green beans,
  trimmed
- 1–2 tomatoes, sliced
- salt

Mayonnaise:
- 2 eggs
- juice of 1 small lemon
- 500 ml/18 fl oz sunflower oil
- salt and pepper

Serves 6

Make the mayonnaise as described in recipe 105, using a food processor. Prepare, cook and refresh the beans as described on page 325. Put into a serving dish while still warm or leave to cool completely. Cover them with the mayonnaise and garnish with the tomato slices.

Lettuce

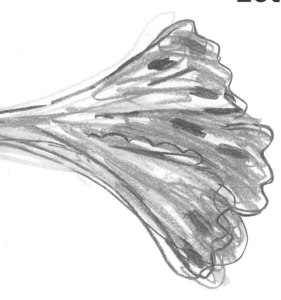

Origin and season

The precise origins of lettuce are not known but the ancient Greeks are known to have liked it and attributed therapeutic qualities to it, such as combating insomnia and easing coughs. Lettuce contains a milky-looking substance in its fibres which has a soporific effect (the origin of the word lettuce is lactua meaning milk). In the Middle Ages, priests were recommended to eat lettuce in order to diminish their interest in the opposite sex. Although it is available all year round, the best time for lettuce is spring.

Selection

The stalk should be white and surrounded by firm leaves without any marks. There may be traces of pesticide on the outer leaves so it is advisable to remove them and wash the lettuce in water mixed with lemon juice or vinegar.

Nutrition

Lettuce has only 20 calories per 100 g / 3 ½ oz. When fresh it provides vitamins A C and E, and calcium, iron, potassium and magnesium.

Tricks

- To keep lettuce as fresh as possible in the refrigerator, wrap it in a tea towel or put it in a plastic bag
- Toss lettuce in a dressing only just before serving to prevent it becoming limp.

416

Lettuces in jus
LECHUGAS AL JUGO

- 2 lettuce hearts, washed
  and trimmed if necessary
- 6 tablespoons olive oil
- 1 tablespoon plain flour
- 175 ml / 6 fl oz white wine
- 1 tablespoon meat extract
- salt

Serves 4

Tie each lettuce heart into shape with fine kitchen string to prevent them opening during cooking. Heat the oil in a saucepan. Add the lettuces in a single layer and cook, turning occasionally, for 3 minutes. Sprinkle the flour over them and add the wine, 350 ml / 12 fl oz water and a pinch of salt (remember that the meat extract will be salty). Cover and cook over a low heat for 15 minutes. Put the lettuces on a warm serving dish and remove and discard the string. Stir the meat extract into the pan, pour the cooking juices over the lettuces and serve immediately.

417

Braised lettuces
LECHUGAS GUISADAS

- 4 tablespoons olive oil
- 1 large onion,
  cut into thin wedges
- 6 lettuce hearts, washed
  and trimmed if necessary
- 3 tomatoes, peeled, seeded
  and cut into quarters
- 175 ml / 6 fl oz white wine
- ½ teaspoon meat extract
- salt

Serves 6

Heat the oil in a large saucepan. Spread out the onion wedges over the base of the pan and top with the lettuce hearts in a single layer. Place the tomato quarters among the lettuces. Lightly season with salt (remember that the meat extract will be salty). Add the wine, cover and cook over a low heat for 5 minutes. Gradually add 475 ml / 16 fl oz water, a little at a time, and cook for 15 minutes, until tender. (Check by piercing the stalks with a skewer or the point of a sharp knife.) Transfer the lettuce hearts to a long dish. Stir the meat extract into the pan, pour the sauce over the lettuces and serve.

Note: This dish can be made in advance and reheated. Do not add the meat extract until just before serving.

Stuffed lettuces

LECHUGAS RELLENOS

- **4 small lettuces**
- **40 g/1½ oz butter**
- **1 onion, very finely chopped**
- **250 g/9 oz leftover roasted meat, chopped**
- **65 g/2½ oz ham, chopped**
- **1 egg, lightly beaten**
- **2 tablespoons breadcrumbs**
- **50 g/2 oz thinly sliced bacon**
- **275 ml/9 fl oz chicken stock (home-made or made with a stock cube)**
- **salt and pepper**

Serves 4

Remove and discard the outer lettuce leaves and cut out as much of the stalk as possible while keeping the lettuces whole. Bring a large saucepan of salted water to the boil. Add the lettuces, bring back to the boil and cook for 2 minutes. Remove from the pan and drain well. Melt 25 g/1 oz of the butter in a frying pan. Add the onion and cook over a low heat, stirring occasionally, for 5 minutes, until softened. Transfer to a bowl, add the meat, ham, egg and breadcrumbs and mix well. Season with salt and pepper and then use the mixture to fill the lettuce heads. Tie the lettuces in shape with fine kitchen string to prevent them opening during cooking. Line an ovenproof dish with the bacon, add the lettuces and dot with the remaining butter. Pour in the stock and bake for 30 minutes. Serve immediately.

Red cabbage

Trick

- To preserve the colour of red cabbage, add a tablespoon of vinegar to the cooking water.

419

Red cabbage with apple and red wine

LOMBARDA CON MANZANAS Y VINO TINTO

- 5 tablespoons olive oil
- 1.5 kg/3¼ lb red cabbage, shredded
- 250 g/9 oz onions, thinly sliced
- generous pinch of aromatic herbs
- 2 cloves garlic, finely chopped
- 2 eating apples, peeled, cored and thinly sliced
- 2 tablespoons red-wine vinegar
- 500 ml/18 fl oz red wine
- 5 tablespoons boiling water
- salt

Serves 6

Preheat the oven to 160°C/325°F/Gas Mark 3. Heat the oil in a flame-proof casserole. Add the cabbage and cook, stirring constantly, until it is well coated with the oil, then cover and cook over a medium heat for 10 minutes. Transfer about two-thirds of the cabbage to a plate, leaving a third as a layer in the base of the pan. Put half the onion on top of the layer of cabbage, season with salt, add half the aromatic herbs and sprinkle with half the garlic. Top with half the apples. Make another layer of cabbage, then herbs, then garlic, then apple, finishing with the remaining cabbage. Pour the vinegar, wine and boiling water into the casserole, cover, transfer to the oven and cook for about 2 hours, until the cabbage is tender. Serve immediately straight from the casserole.

420

Red cabbage with apple

LOMBARDA CON MANZANA

- 100 g/3½ oz onions, finely chopped
- 25 g/1 oz butter
- 1 red cabbage, about 750 g/1 lb 10 oz, shredded
- 175 ml/6 fl oz red wine
- 1 teaspoon vinegar
- 500 g/1 lb 2 oz eating apples, peeled, cored and sliced
- salt and pepper

Serves 4

Put the onions into a large microwave-proof dish, add the butter, cover and microwave on high power for 2 minutes. Add the cabbage, wine and vinegar, cover and microwave for 3 minutes. Add the apples and mix well, season with salt and pepper, cover and cook for 3 minutes. Taste and adjust the seasoning, if necessary, re-cover the dish and microwave for a further 2 minutes. Check how tender the cabbage is and, if necessary, microwave for a further 2 minutes, then check again. Add a little hot water if necessary.

421

Red cabbage with red wine and onion

LOMBARDA CON VINO TINTO Y CEBOLLA

- **5 tablespoons olive oil**
- **1 red cabbage, about 1.5 kg/ 3¼ lb, shredded**
- **250 g/9 oz onions, thinly sliced**
- **2 tablespoons red-wine vinegar**
- **500 ml/18 fl oz red wine**
- **1 tablespoon plain flour**
- **salt and pepper**

Serves 6

Heat the oil in a heavy-based flameproof casserole or cocotte. Add the cabbage and cook over a low heat, stirring constantly, until it is well coated with the oil. Cover the casserole, increase the heat to medium and cook for 10 minutes. Transfer two-thirds of the cabbage to a plate, leaving only a third as a layer in the base of the casserole. Make a layer of onion on top of the cabbage and cover with another layer of cabbage. Continue making layers in this way until the onions and cabbage are used up. Pour in the vinegar and wine, sprinkle in the flour and season with salt and pepper. Cover and cook over a low heat for about 2 hours, until the cabbage is tender and there is no liquid left in the base of the casserole. Serve immediately.

Note: this dish can be made in advance and reheated. It can also be cooked in a preheated oven at 160°C/325°F/Gas Mark 3 for 2 hours. It is delicious as an accompaniment to roasted meat and game.

422

Red cabbage salad
ENSALADA DE LOMBARDA

- **2 red cabbages,**
  about 500 g/1 lb 2 oz each
- **salt**

  Vinaigrette:
- **2 tablespoons red wine vinegar**
- **6 tablespoons olive oil**
- **salt and pepper**

Serves 6

Remove and discard the tough outer leaves of the cabbages. Separate the leaves and cut out the stalks. Shred the leaves, wash in plenty of cold water and drain well. Bring a large saucepan of salted water to the boil. Add the cabbage, pushing it down with a spoon so that it is covered by the water. Cook for 5 minutes, then drain well in a large colander and leave to stand until just warm. Meanwhile, make the vinaigrette. Whisk together the vinegar and oil and season to taste with salt and pepper. Put the cabbage into a serving dish and dress with the vinaigrette. Serve warm or cold.

Turnips

Origin and season
The precise origin of turnips is not known but it is believed that prehistoric man ate them. The ancient Greeks liked them very much and used them medicinally as well as for food. They were eaten in large quantities in the Middle Ages, but nowadays they are less popular. Turnip is a winter vegetable, although it also grows in spring and autumn. It may be round or long.

Selection
Whether round or long, a turnip should feel heavy in the hand and be firm to the touch. Soft turnips will be fibrous. When a turnip is cut, a drop of liquid should appear. If it has a noticeable smell, the turnip will be hot. Do not buy turnips with any blemishes.

Nutrition

Turnips contain a lot of water and have about 28 calories per 100 g/ 3 ½ oz. They contain vitamins A and B, and calcium and potassium. Taken as a syrup, they are recommended to combat coughs. They are quite hard to digest. According to the sixteenth-century scholar Sir Thomas Elyot, 'They increase the seduction of man and increase his carnal appetite.'

Tricks

- Never peel turnips in advance, as they will oxidize and may cause intestinal problems
- Very young and tender turnips do not need to be peeled – simply scraping them with the tip of a knife is enough
- The leaves can be added to a stock to give it a delightful flavour.

How to prepare and cook

Most recipes require turnips to be washed and peeled. Cut them in half lengthways or into medium slices, even when they are small. Bring a large saucepan of salted water to the boil, add the turnips, making sure they are covered, and cook for 10 minutes. Drain well before using.

423

Turnips with béchamel sauce and egg yolks

NABOS CON BECHAMEL Y YEMAS

- 2 kg/4½ lb young turnips, sliced
- 25 g/1 oz butter
- 2 tablespoons sunflower oil
- 2 tablespoons plain flour
- 450 ml/¾ pint milk
- pinch of freshly grated nutmeg
- 2 egg yolks
- salt

Serves 6

Prepare and cook the turnips as described on page 336. Melt the butter with the oil in a saucepan. Stir in the flour and cook, stirring constantly, for 2 minutes. Gradually stir in the milk, a little at a time. Cook, stirring constantly, for 5 minutes. Season with salt. Add the turnip and nutmeg, mix well and cook, stirring occasionally, for about 25 minutes, until the turnips are tender. (Test by piercing one with a skewer or the point of a sharp knife.) Lightly beat the egg yolks in a bowl and stir in a little of the sauce to prevent them curdling, then stir into the pan. Serve immediately.

424

Turnip gratin

NABOS CON BECHAMEL Y QUESO RALLADO, GRATINADOS

- 2 kg/4½ lb turnips, sliced
- 40 g/1½ oz butter
- 2 tablespoons sunflower oil
- 3 tablespoons plain flour
- 750 ml/1¼ pints milk
- ½ teaspoon meat extract
- 80 g/3 oz gruyere cheese, grated
- salt

Serves 6

Prepare and cook the turnips as described on page 336. Preheat the oven to 200°C/400°F/Gas Mark 6. Melt the butter with the oil in a saucepan. Stir in the flour and cook, stirring constantly, for 2 minutes. Gradually stir in the milk, a little at a time. Cook, stirring constantly, for 5 minutes. Stir in the meat extract and season to taste with salt. Put the turnip slices into an ovenproof dish, pour the sauce over them and sprinkle with the gruyere. Bake for 10–15 minutes, until golden brown. Serve immediately.

425

Turnips with carrots

NABOS CON ZANAHORIAS

- 750 g/1 lb 10 oz carrots, peeled
- 750 g/1 lb 10 oz turnips, peeled
- 6 tablespoons olive oil
- 1 large onion, finely chopped
- 1 tablespoon plain flour
- 1 teaspoon sugar
- salt

Serves 6

Cut the carrots and the turnips lengthways into halves or quarters, depending on their thickness. Heat the oil in a saucepan. Add the onion and cook over a low heat, stirring occasionally, for about 6 minutes, until softened and translucent. Add the carrots and turnips. Stir in the flour, then add the sugar and a pinch of salt. Mix well and add just enough water to cover. Cook over a medium heat for about 30 minutes, until the vegetable are tender. Transfer the vegetables and sauce to a warm dish and serve immediately.

426

- 1kg/2¼lb small turnips
- 150ml/¼ pint cider
- 50g/2oz lard
- 275ml/9floz hot chicken stock
  (home-made or made
  with a stock cube)
- 1 bouquet garni
  (1 sprig fresh parsley, 1 bay leaf
  and 1 clove garlic tied in muslin)
- chopped fresh parsley (optional)
- salt and pepper
  Serves 6

Turnips in cider
NABOS A LA SIDRA

Bring a large saucepan of salted water to the boil. Add the turnips and cook for 5 minutes. Drain well. Heat the cider in another saucepan and cook until it has reduced by half, then remove the pan from the heat. Melt the lard in a heavy-based saucepan or cocotte. Add the turnips and cook over a low heat, stirring occasionally, for about 5 minutes, until lightly browned. Pour in the cider and stock, add the bouquet garni and season to taste with salt and pepper. Cover and simmer over a very low heat for 30 minutes. Remove and discard the bouquet garni. Serve immediately, garnished with chopped parsley if you like.

427

- 1kg/2¼lb turnips, sliced
- 65g/2½oz butter
- 1 teaspoon sugar
- salt
  Serves 6

Glazed turnips
NABOS GLASEADOS

Put the turnip into a saucepan, pour in just enough water to cover and add the butter, sugar and a pinch of salt. Cook over a medium-low heat for 20 minutes, until the water has evaporated. Serve immediately as an accompaniment to meat.

Cucumber

Origin and season

Cucumbers have grown wild in the foothills of the Himalayas for 6,000 years and, although nobody really knows how, they appeared in ancient Egypt, where they were a favourite vegetable of the pharaohs. The celebrated Roman gourmet Apicius invented a recipe based on cucumber with honey, oil and eggs. The best cucumbers are available from early summer to early autumn, as this is usually the period of least rain and the cucumbers have lots of flavour and are not bitter. However, the season is from mid spring to mid autumn.

Selection

Choose firm cucumbers without any blemishes. The skin should be shiny and smooth. Except in the case of the English cucumbers, which are ridged. Try to find cucumbers that are not too fat as they will have fewer seeds.

Nutrition

Cucumbers contain about 15 calories per 100 g / 3 ½ oz. A light food, they are a source of minerals and vitamins but are difficult to digest. The skin contains a bitter laxative substance that could cause irritation to the intestinal wall, so it is advisable to peel cucumbers before eating them.

Tricks

- Peel cucumbers from head to tail in order to avoid the bitterness that can sometimes be given off
- To draw out some of their water, slice cucumbers, then sprinkle with salt and leave to stand. Alternatively, put the slices in a tea towel and twist it, pressing hard, so that the water is released and the cucumber is ready to be seasoned
- Cucumber makes a good face mask for oily skin to help close the pores. Process the flesh in a food processor or blender with a pot of natural yogurt. Leave the mask on for about 10 minutes and rinse off with water.

428

Cucumbers for salads

PEPINOS PARA ENSALADA

- 4 cucumbers
- 1 quantity Vinaigrette
  (see recipe 98)
- 1 tablespoon chopped fresh
  parsley (optional)

Serves 4–6

Choose cucumbers that are very green and firm. Peel and thinly slice, then sprinkle with salt and leave to stand for at least 2 hours. Rinse well and pat dry, then put the slices on a plate and sprinkle with the vinaigrette and chopped parsley, if using. Chill in the refrigerator until ready to serve. The slices can be served alone or mixed with tomatoes and peppers.

429

Cucumber boats with salad

BARCAS DE PEPINOS CON ENSALADILLA

- 6 cucumbers
- 1 small onion, chopped
- 2 cloves garlic, chopped
- 250 g/9 oz raw unpeeled prawns
- 3 firm tomatoes, diced
- 1 small green pepper or 1 small
  canned or bottled red pepper,
  drained and diced
- 2 hard-boiled eggs

  Mayonnaise:
- 1 egg
- juice of 1 lemon
- 250 ml/8 fl oz sunflower oil
- salt

Serves 6

Halve the cucumbers lengthways. Sprinkle with salt and leave to stand, cut side down, for 30 minutes. Meanwhile, make the mayonnaise as described in recipe 105. Using the tip of a knife, scrape out the seeds and remove the centres from the cucumbers so that they resemble little boats. Chop the scooped-out flesh and reserve. Sprinkle the onion and garlic into the cucumbers, put them in a dish, cover with foil and chill in the refrigerator for 1 hour. Meanwhile, put the prawns into a saucepan, pour in water to cover and add a pinch of salt. Bring to the boil, then drain and peel. Mix together the tomato, pepper, reserved cucumber flesh, prawns and mayonnaise in a bowl and divide among the cucumber boats. Chop the hardboiled egg and sprinkle over the boats. Cover with foil again and chill in the refrigerator for another hour before serving.

Stuffed cucumbers

PEPINOS RELLENOS

- **90 g / 3 ¼ oz butter,**
  plus extra for greasing
- **1 kg / 2 ¼ lb cucumbers,**
  cut into 4-cm / 1 ½-inch lengths
- **100 g / 3 ½ oz mushrooms**
- **juice of ½ lemon**
- **150 g / 5 oz ham,**
  coarsely chopped
- **1 tablespoon chopped**
  fresh parsley
- **2 tablespoons day-old**
  breadcrumbs
- **salt and pepper**

Tomato sauce:
- **3 tablespoons sunflower oil**
- **1 small onion, chopped**
- **1 kg / 2 ¼ lb very ripe tomatoes,**
  peeled, seeded and chopped
- **1 bouquet garni (1 sprig fresh**
  parsley, 1 clove garlic and 1 bay
  leaf tied in muslin)
- **3 tablespoons dry white wine**
- **1 teaspoon sugar**
- **salt**

Serves 6

Preheat the oven to 180°C/350°F/Gas Mark 4. Grease an ovenproof dish with butter. Scoop out the cucumber seeds with a teaspoon and put the pieces of cucumber into the prepared dish. Remove and discard the mushroom stalks, cut the caps into large pieces, place in a bowl and sprinkle with lemon juice. Stir in the ham. Melt 25 g/1 oz of the butter in a saucepan. Add the mushroom mixture and cook over a low heat, stirring occasionally, for 5 minutes. Season with salt and pepper and stir in the parsley and breadcrumbs. Remove the pan from the heat. Season the pieces of cucumber with salt and pepper and fill them with the mushroom mixture. Dot with the remaining butter, cover the dish with foil and bake for 40 minutes, until the cucumbers are tender but still crunchy. Meanwhile, make the tomato sauce. Heat the oil in a frying pan. Add the onion and cook over a low heat, stirring occasionally, for about 7 minutes, until beginning to brown. Add the tomato, bouquet garni and wine and cook, stirring occasionally and breaking up the tomato with the side of the spoon, for 15 minutes. Remove and discard the bouquet garni, allow the sauce to cool a little, then process the sauce in a food processor. Stir in the sugar and season to taste with salt. Serve the stuffed cucumbers with the hot tomato sauce offered separately.

Peppers

Origin and season
Peppers come from the Americas and were brought to Europe by Christopher Columbus. They are available all year round.

Selection
The skin should be smooth and shiny, without any blemishes and with a distinct colour. Allow about 250 g / 9 oz per person.

Nutrition
Peppers contain about 30 calories per 100 g / 3 ½ oz. They are a rich source of vitamin C. They are difficult to digest when eaten raw but present no problems when cooked. In small quantities they stimulate the appetite. The skin irritates the intestine and is hard to digest, so it is advisable to peel peppers before eating them (see below).

Tricks
- To peel peppers easily, put them into an oven preheated to 180°C/350°F/Gas Mark 4 or under a preheated grill for about 10 minutes, turning them once. Alternatively, spear them on a long-handled fork and hold them directly in a flame. When they have been roasted, wrap them in a tea towel or sheet of newspaper, put them into a plastic bag and tie the top, or place in a bowl and cover with crumpled kitchen paper. Leave to cool, then peel off the skins
- Peppers freeze perfectly, but their smell can contaminate other food, so freeze them in a closed container or a sealed freezer bag.

431

Red peppers with hard-boiled eggs

PIMIENTOS ROJOS CON HUEVOS DUROS

- **1 kg / 2¼ lb red peppers**
- **1 quantity vinaigrette (see recipe 98)**
- **2 hard-boiled eggs, sliced**

Serves 6

Roast and peel red peppers as described on page 342, then remove and discard the seeds and cut the flesh into strips. Put into a dish, add the vinaigrette and leave to marinate for 30 minutes. Drain slightly and serve with the slices of hard-boiled egg.

432

Fried green pepper garnish

PIMIENTOS VERDES FRITOS, PARA ADORNAR LA CARNE

- **1 kg / 2¼ lb green peppers**
- **350 ml / 12 fl oz olive oil**
- **salt**

Serves 6

Cut out the stalks and remove the seeds from the peppers. If they are large, cut them into strips or rings. If they are small, cut them in half lengthways or even leave them whole. Season the insides of the peppers with salt. Heat the oil with 2 tablespoons water in a deep frying pan. Add the peppers, season with salt, cover and cook over a low heat for about 10 minutes, until tender. Drain off the oil and serve as a garnish for a meat dish.

Green peppers stuffed with meat

PIMIENTOS VERDES RELLENOS DE CARNE

- 12 green peppers
- 500 ml/18 fl oz sunflower oil

Filling:
- 300 g/11 oz minced meat
  (half pork and half beef)
- 100 g/3 ½ oz Serrano ham,
  minced
- 1 slice of bread, crusts removed
  and soaked in hot milk
- 1 clove garlic, finely chopped
- 1 teaspoon chopped
  fresh parsley
- 1 egg, lightly beaten
- 1 tablespoon white wine
- salt

Sauce:
- 1 large onion, chopped
- 1 large ripe tomato,
  seeded and quartered
- 2 carrots, sliced
- 1 tablespoon plain flour
- 175 ml/6 fl oz white wine
- salt

Serves 6

Cut out the stalks and remove the seeds from the peppers. Make the filling. If you are mincing the meat yourself, mince the ham at the same time. Otherwise, thoroughly mix the meat and ham together in a bowl. Gently squeeze out the bread, if necessary, and add it to the bowl with the garlic, parsley, egg and wine. Season with salt and mix well.Fill the peppers with the meat mixture, using a teaspoon, and secure with wooden cocktail sticks. Heat the oil with 2 tablespoons water in a deep frying pan. Add the peppers, three at a time, and cook over a low heat for 10 minutes. Using a slotted spoon, transfer the cooked peppers to a clean saucepan, arranging them in a single layer. Drain all but about 5 tablespoons of the oil from the frying pan and reheat. Add the onion and cook over a low heat, stirring occasionally, for about 10 minutes, until browned. Add the tomato and carrot and cook, stirring occasionally, for a further 5 minutes. Stir in the flour and cook, stirring constantly, for 2 minutes, then stir in the wine and 1 litre/1 ¾ pints water. Simmer for 15 minutes. Allow to cool a little, then transfer to a food processor, process until smooth and pour into the saucepan of peppers. Season with salt and cook over a low heat, stirring occasionally, for 15 minutes. If the sauce is too thick, add a little hot water. Serve in a warm deep dish.

Note: This dish can be made in advance and is quite delicious when it is reheated.

434 Peppers stuffed with meat and rice

PIMIENTOS RELLENOS DE CARNE PICADA Y ARROZ CRUDO

- **6 round green peppers**
- **6 tablespoons long-grain rice**
- **375 g/13 oz minced meat**
- **½ clove garlic, finely chopped**
- **1 tablespoon finely chopped fresh parsley**
- **175 ml/6 fl oz sunflower oil**
- **25 g/1 oz plain flour**
- **1 egg, lightly beaten**
- **salt**

  Sauce:
- **1 onion, chopped**
- **1 tablespoon plain flour**
- **pinch of saffron threads**
- **1 beef stock cube**
- **salt**

  Serves 6

Cut out the stalks and remove the seeds from the peppers. Season the insides of the peppers with salt. Put 1 tablespoon of the rice into each one. Mix together the meat, garlic and parsley in a bowl and season with salt. Using a teaspoon, divide the mixture among the peppers. Heat the oil in a deep frying pan. Coat the opening of the peppers first with the flour and then with the beaten egg. Add the peppers to the frying pan, cut sides down, and cook until the egg has set. Lay the peppers on their sides and cook, turning occasionally, for 5 minutes. You may need to do this in two batches to allow sufficient room. Transfer the cooked peppers to a clean saucepan. Make the sauce. Drain all but about 4 tablespoons of the oil from the frying pan and reheat. Add the onion and cook over a low heat, stirring occasionally, for about 7 minutes, until beginning to brown. Stir in the flour and cook, stirring constantly, for 2 minutes. Lightly season with salt, add the saffron and pour in 500 ml/18 fl oz water. Cook, stirring constantly, for 3 minutes, then strain into the pan of peppers. Crumble the stock cube into a little water, then add it to the pan. Pour in water to half cover the peppers, cover and cook over a low heat for about 30 minutes, until tender. Serve the peppers immediately with their sauce or leave to cool, and reheat just before serving.

435 Peppers stuffed with quail

PIMIENTOS RELLENOS DE CODORNICES

- **5 tablespoons olive oil**
- **6–12 oven-ready quail**
- **6 rashers of bacon**
- **6–12 large peppers**
- **50 g/2 oz butter**
- **salt**

  Sauce:
- **1 onion, finely chopped**
- **20 grapes, peeled and seeded**
- **5 tablespoons red wine**
- **5 tablespoons white wine**
- **a little meat sauce**
- **1 bay leaf**

  Serves 6

Preheat the oven to 200°C/400°F/Gas Mark 6. Heat the oil in a frying pan. Add the quail and cook over a low heat, turning occasionally, for a few minutes, but do not allow them to brown. Remove the quail from the pan and reserve the oil. Lightly season the quail with salt and put a rasher of bacon into the cavity of each one. Cut out the stalks and remove the seeds from the peppers. Put each quail into a pepper and add a little of the butter. Put into an ovenproof dish and bake for about 1 hour. Meanwhile, make the sauce. Reheat the oil in the frying pan. Add the onion and cook over a low heat, stirring occasionally, for 5 minutes, until softened. Add the grapes, red and white wine, meat sauce and bay leaf, season to taste with salt and cook for 10 minutes. Remove and discard the bay leaf. Serve the quail in the peppers and offer the sauce separately.

Leek

Origin and season

The origin of leeks is unknown, although it is certain that they have been grown for a very long time. The ancient Egyptians liked them, so much so that the pharaoh used to give his soldier bunches of leeks instead of gold. The Greeks used them to combat infertility and the Roman emperor Nero ate great quantities of them to clear his voice. They are available nearly all year round, but their best season is from mid autumn to mid spring.

Selection

Leeks should be straight, white and not too fat, with shiny green leaves. Allow about 150 g/5 oz per serving.

Nutrition

Leeks contain about 40 calories per 100 g/3 ½ oz. They provide the minerals potassium and magnesium and contain a lot of water, so they have diuretic and laxative properties. Although they contain sugars, these are easily assimilated by the body. They are wonderful for the skin and hair. Leek skin should be eaten, as this is where nearly all the nutritional value is concentrated. The green part is where most of the vitamins are.

Tricks

- Always remove the roots and dark green outer leavese and wash leeks under cold running water to remove any earth that may be trapped between the leaves
- Give leeks an original touch by preparing them with honey or brown sugar. Cook them in butter and when they are beginning to brown, add a spoonful of honey and cook until golden and glazed. Finally, add a dash of vinegar for sharpness. Serve the leeks with this sauce poured over them.

436

Leeks with vinaigrette or mayonnaise
PUERROS CON VINAGRETA O CON MAYONESA

- 2–3 leeks per serving,
  trimmed and rinsed well
- salt

Serves 6

Bring a saucepan of salted water to the boil. Add the leeks and cook for about 15 minutes, until tender. Drain and serve warm. They may be served with a vinaigrette (see recipe 98), capers and canned anchovy fillets or with Classic Mayonnaise (see recipe 105).

437

Leeks au gratin
PUERROS GRATINADOS

- 12–18 leeks,
  trimmed and rinsed well
- 3 tablespoons olive oil
- 2 thick rashers of smoked bacon,
  cut into strips
- 80 g/3 oz gruyere cheese, grated
- 25 g/1 oz butter
- salt

Serves 6

Bring a saucepan of salted water to the boil. Add the leeks and cook for about 15 minutes, until tender. Preheat the oven to 200°C/400°F/ Gas Mark 6. Drain the leeks well and put them into an ovenproof dish. Heat the oil in a frying pan. Add the bacon and cook over a medium heat, stirring occasionally, for about 5 minutes, until lightly browned. Remove from the pan, drain and add to the dish. Sprinkle with the gruyere and dot with the butter. Bake for 10–15 minutes, until golden brown. Serve immediately straight from the dish.

438

Leeks with béchamel sauce
PUERROS CON BECHAMEL

- 12 large leeks,
  trimmed and rinsed well
- 25 g/1 oz butter
- 2 tablespoons sunflower oil
- 1 heaped tablespoon plain flour
- 500 ml/18 fl oz milk
- 1 tablespoon tomato purée
- 80 g/3 oz gruyere cheese, grated
- 2 tablespoons chopped
  fresh parsley
- salt

Serves 6

Bring a saucepan of salted water to the boil. Add the leeks and cook for about 15 minutes, until tender. Drain well. Preheat the oven to 200°C/400°F/Gas Mark 6. Melt the butter with the oil in a saucepan. Stir in the flour and cook, stirring constantly, for 2 minutes. Gradually stir in the milk, a little at a time. Cook, stirring constantly, for 10 minutes, then lightly season with salt and stir in the tomato purée. Put the leeks into an ovenproof dish and pour the béchamel sauce over them. Sprinkle with the gruyere and bake for 10–15 minutes, until golden brown. Sprinkle the parsley on top in two lines and serve immediately.

439

Curried leeks
PUERROS AL CURRY

- 12 large leeks,
  trimmed and rinsed well
- 25 g/1 oz butter
- 2 tablespoons sunflower oil
- 1 heaped tablespoon plain flour
- 500 ml/18 fl oz milk
- ½ teaspoon curry powder
- 80 g/3 oz gruyere cheese, grated
- 2 tablespoons chopped
  fresh parsley
- salt

Serves 6

Bring a saucepan of salted water to the boil. Add the leeks and cook for about 15 minutes, until tender. Drain well. Preheat the oven to 200°C/400°F/Gas Mark 6. Melt the butter with the oil in a saucepan. Stir in the flour and cook, stirring constantly, for 2 minutes. Gradually stir in the milk, a little at a time. Cook, stirring constantly, for 10 minutes, then lightly season with salt and stir in the curry powder. Put the leeks into an ovenproof dish and pour the béchamel sauce over them. Sprinkle with the gruyere and bake for 10–15 minutes, until golden brown. Sprinkle the parsley on top in two lines and serve immediately.

440

Leek tart with rice
TARTA DE PUERROS CON ARROZ

- 3 tablespoons olive oil,
  plus extra for brushing
- 4 leeks, trimmed,
  sliced and rinsed well
- 2 large onions, finely chopped
- 1 bay leaf
- ½ teaspoon dried thyme
- 150 ml/¼ pint white wine
- 3 eggs
- 300 ml/½ pint milk
- 50 g/2 oz gruyere cheese, grated
- 225 g/8 oz cooked rice

Sauce:
- 1 large red pepper, roasted
  and peeled (see page 342)
- ½ chicken stock cube
- 150 ml/¼ pint warm water
- 4 tablespoons single cream
- salt and pepper

Serves 6

Preheat the oven to 180°C/350°F/Gas Mark 4 and preheat the grill. Brush an ovenproof dish with oil. Heat the oil in a saucepan. Add the leek, onion, bay leaf and thyme and cook over a low heat, stirring occasionally, for 5 minutes, until softened and translucent. Pour in the wine, cover and simmer for 12 minutes. Beat the eggs in a bowl, then stir in the milk and gruyere. Mix the leek and onion with the cooked rice in another bowl and add the egg mixture. Spoon into the prepared dish and bake for 30 minutes. Meanwhile, make the sauce. Remove and discard the seeds from the pepper and coarsely chop the flesh. Dissolve the stock cube in the warm water. Put the pepper and stock into a food processor and process to a purée, then pour into a saucepan and bring to the boil. Simmer for 2 minutes. Stir in the cream and heat through but do not allow to boil. Season to taste with salt and pepper. Turn the leek tart out on to a plate and serve immediately, offering the sauce separately.

Radish

Origin and season

Radishes are a very old vegetable, although it is difficult to determine their exact origin. The ancient Greeks ate radishes to prevent gall stones and stop haemorrhaging. Radishes can be found all year round. Early spring ones are the hottest. The best time for radishes is from the late spring to early autumn.

Selection

Radishes should be smooth and not too fat with very shiny green leaves. They lose their crispness and the leaves wilt within 48 hours of harvesting. Be careful when buying bunches without leaves, as this could indicate that the radishes are already deteriorating; be sure the radishes are firm to the touch.

Nutrition

Radishes contain about 20 calories per 100 g / 3 ½ oz. Though difficult to digest, they are rich in iron and vitamins B and C and often form part of a balanced weight-loss diet.

Tricks

- If the pinker radishes are very fresh, they do not need to be peeled, but they should be washed in plenty of water and thoroughly dried
- Do not discard the leaves; add them to a soup for extra flavour
- The best way to keep radishes is with the stalks and leaves in water, but do not submerge the radish.

441

Orange and radish salad
ENSALADA DE NARANJAS Y RABANOS

- 2 bunches radishes, trimmed
- 1 tablespoon icing sugar
- 6 tablespoons lemon juice
- 6 oranges
- 50 g/2 oz shelled walnuts, sliced
- salt and pepper

Serves 4

Coarsely grate the radishes into a bowl. Add the sugar, a pinch of salt, a pinch of pepper and the lemon juice. Cut the rinds off the oranges with a sharp knife, removing all traces of the bitter pith. Thinly slice the flesh. Mix the oranges and radishes together and garnish with the walnuts. Chill in the refrigerator before serving.

442

Radish salad
ENSALADA CON RABANOS

- 150 g/5 oz mixed salad leaves
- ½ bunch radishes,
  trimmed and sliced
- salt and pepper

Dressing:
- 150 ml/¼ pint natural yogurt
- 1 tablespoon lemon juice
- 1 tablespoon chopped
  fresh chives

Serves 4

Put the salad leaves and radishes into a salad bowl. Mix together all the dressing ingredients and pour over the salad. Season to taste with salt and pepper and toss lightly. Chill in the refrigerator for 1 hour before serving.

Notes: Wash the salad leaves but do not allow them to soak for too long as they will lose their vitamins. Give the salad a personal touch by adding fresh herbs, such as parsley, chives, mint or basil. Diced apple is a very tasty addition. A little mustard or a pinch of herbs can be added to the yogurt dressing.

Beetroot

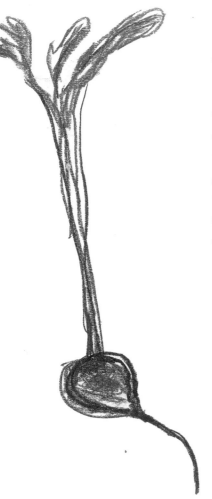

Origin and season

Beetroots come from North Africa. The ancient Greeks valued them for their therapeutic properties, principally to combat stomach problems. As well as the root itself, the tender tops can also be eaten as a green vegetable. Beetroots are available all year round.

Selection

Although there are various types of beetroot, the most common is the red one. It can be bought raw, but does take a long time to cook. Ready-cooked beetroots are also available. A good rule when buying cooked beetroots is that the tastiest ones are those that look least attractive. A dull, wrinkled appearance means they have been cooked in the oven, while shiny smooth beetroots have been cooked in water or steamed and will have less flavour.

Nutrition

Beetroots contain about 42 calories per 100 g / 3 ½ oz and are rich in sugar and potassium. They can be difficult to digest so should be eaten in moderation.

How to cook

Wash beetroots whole with the skin and leaves intact. Do not cut these off as the beetroots will lose their lovely red colour. Put the beetroots into a saucepan with plenty of cold water and a pinch of salt. Bring to the boil and cook over a medium heat for about 1 ½ hours, until tender. Check by piercing with a skewer or the point of a sharp knife. Remove from the pan and leave to cool. Peel, then slice or dice and dress with oil, vinegar and salt.

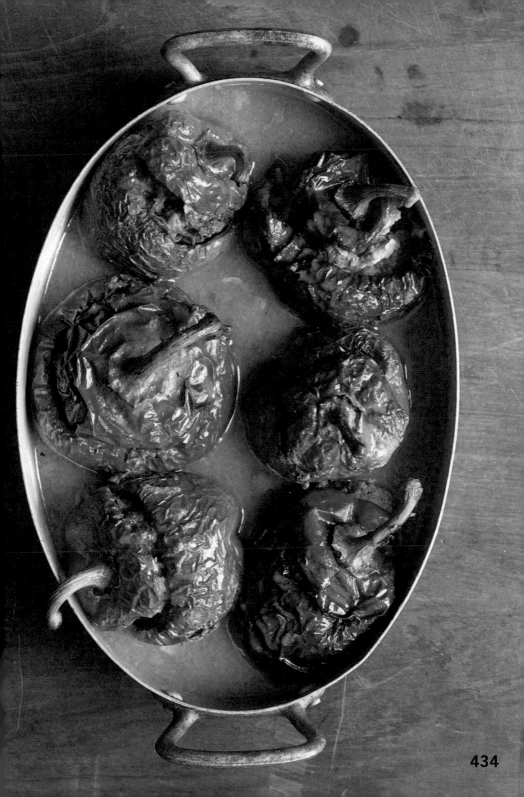

443

Stuffed beetroots

REMOLACHAS RELLENAS

- 4 cooked beetroots
- 2 hard-boiled eggs, halved
- 100 g/3½ oz long-grain rice, cooked
- 1 apple, peeled, cored and diced
- ½ small onion, finely chopped
- 1 tablespoon chopped fresh parley
- 1 tablespoon red-wine vinegar
- 3 tablespoons olive oil
- salt and pepper

Serves 4

Peel the beetroots and cut a slice like a little hat off the top of each one. Hollow out the centres, taking care not to break the 'shells'. Dice the scooped-out flesh and set aside. Scoop the yolks out of the hard-boiled eggs and set aside. Finely chop the whites. Mix together the diced beetroot, egg whites, rice, apple, onion and parsley in a bowl. Whisk together the vinegar and oil in another bowl, stir in the egg yolks and season with salt and pepper, then pour over the beetroot and rice mixture. Season to taste with salt and pepper and use to fill the beetroot shells. Store in the refrigerator until ready to serve.

Cabbage

Origin and season

Cabbage is one of the oldest European vegetables and has grown naturally for 6,000 years in places such as the Balearic Islands and Sardinia. The ancient Romans used it as a remedy for melancholy. It is a winter vegetable with a season from the end of autumn until the middle of spring. There are two main types, one from Milan and the one called Savoy.

Selection

A cabbage should feel heavy in the hand and the leaves should be well established. When calculating quantities remember that cabbage reduces by about half during cooking.

Nutrition

Cabbage is one of the richest vegetable sources of vitamins and minerals. It contains as much vitamin C as lemon juice and is rich in calcium, magnesium and sulphur. It has only 25 calories per 100 g / 3 ½ oz when eaten raw and 15 calories per 100 g / 3 ½ oz when cooked. The leaves are thought by some to be helpful for those with bronchitis and rheumatism. Unfortunately, cabbage fibres contain a substance that ferments in the intestine and can produce wind.

Tricks

- Cooking cabbage in two stages will prevent it causing wind
- To avoid the unpleasant smell of cooking cabbage, put a piece of bread in the water. If this still doesn't help, be patient; studies are currently being carried out to produce a variety that does not have this characteristic odour
- Remove the cabbage from leftover cabbage soup, otherwise it will turn the soup sour
- To retain the vitamins and minerals in cabbage do not leave it soaking for too long and try to eat it raw in salads.

444

Cabbage with mayonnaise

REPOLLO CON MAYONESA

- 2 kg / 4 ½ lb cabbage
- 4 boiled new potatoes, cut into 2–4 pieces, or tomato slices
- salt

Mayonnaise:
- 2 eggs
- juice of 1 lemon or 4 tablespoons white-wine vinegar
- 750 ml / 1 ¼ pints sunflower oil
- salt

Serves 6

Remove and discard the tough outer leaves of the cabbage. Cut into quarters and remove the stalk, then slice the leaves into 2-cm/¾-inch strips. Wash well. Bring a large saucepan of salted water to the boil. Add the cabbage, pushing it down into the water with a spoon. Bring back to the boil, cover and simmer for about 30 minutes, until tender. Meanwhile, make the mayonnaise as described in recipe 105. Drain the cabbage well. If it is to be served hot, put it into a warm round or oval dish and garnish with the potato. Cover with the mayonnaise and serve straight away. If the cabbage is to be served cold or just warm, garnish it with slices of tomato, then cover with the mayonnaise.

Note: An alternative is to heat some oil in a frying pan. Add 1–2 garlic cloves and cook for a few minutes, until lightly browned. Remove and discard the garlic, add the cabbage to the pan and cook, stirring frequently, for a few minutes. Remove the cabbage from the pan, drain well and place in an ovenproof dish. Spoon the mayonnaise over the cabbage and bake in a preheated oven, 200°C/400°F/Gas Mark 6, for about 10 minutes, until browned.

445

Cabbage in jus
REPOLLO AL JUGO

- 2 kg/4½ lb Savoy cabbage
- 65 g/2½ oz lard
- 150 g/5 oz streaky bacon,
  thinly sliced
- 1 onion, thinly sliced and pushed
  out into rings
- 2 carrots, thinly sliced
- 500 ml/18 fl oz chicken stock
  (home-made or made
  with a stock cube)
- 2 bay leaves
- salt

Serves 6

Prepare and cook the cabbage as described in recipe 444. Drain well. Melt the lard in a saucepan. Add the bacon and cook over a medium heat, stirring occasionally, for about 5 minutes, until browned. Remove from the pan and set aside. Add the onion to the pan and cook over a low heat, stirring occasionally, for about 5 minutes, until softened and translucent. Add the cabbage, carrot and half the bacon and mix well. Pour the stock over the mixture and add the remaining bacon and the bay leaves. Cover and simmer over a low heat, stirring occasionally, for 1½ hours. Serve immediately.

446

Cabbage pie with tomato sauce
BUDÍN DE REPOLLO CON SALSA DE TOMATE

- 1 quantity Classic Tomato Sauce
  (see recipe 73)
- 1.5 kg/3¼ lb Savoy cabbage
- 40 g/1½ oz butter,
  plus extra for greasing
- 100 g/3½ oz Serrano ham,
  finely chopped
- 3 eggs
- 3 tablespoons milk
- salt

Serves 6

Process the tomato sauce in a food processor and set aside. Prepare and cook the cabbage as described in recipe 444. Drain well. Preheat the oven to 160°C/325°F/Gas Mark 3. Grease an ovenproof dish with butter.Melt the butter in a frying pan. Add the cabbage and ham and cook over a medium heat, stirring frequently, for 5 minutes. Remove the pan from the heat. Beat the eggs with the milk in a bowl, then stir into the cabbage mixture. Spoon the mixture into the prepared dish, then place the dish in a roasting tin and pour in boiling water to come about halfway up the sides. Transfer to the oven and bake for about 1 hour, until set. Turn off the oven, open the door and leave the pie to stand for 8 minutes. Meanwhile, reheat the tomato sauce. Turn out the pie on to a warm serving dish and pour the tomato sauce over it. Serve immediately.

447

Cabbage pie
PASTEL DE REPOLLO

- 1.5 kg/2¼ lb cabbage
- 2 tablespoons olive oil, plus extra for brushing
- 750 g/1 lb 10 oz sausage meat
- 3 eggs, lightly beaten
- 2 tablespoons of milk
- 100 g/3½ oz Serrano ham, chopped
- 350 g/12 oz thinly sliced bacon

Serves 6

Prepare and cook the cabbage as described in recipe 444. Drain well. Preheat the oven to 160°C/325°F/Gas Mark 3. Brush an ovenproof dish with oil. Mix together the sausage meat and eggs in a bowl, then add the milk. Heat the oil in a frying pan. Add the cabbage and ham and cook over a medium heat, stirring occasionally, for about 5 minutes, until lightly browned. Remove the pan from the heat. Line the prepared dish with the some of the bacon. Add a layer of the sausage meat mixture, then a layer of cabbage and ham. Continue making layers in this way until all the ingredients are used up, ending with a layer of bacon. Put the dish into a roasting tin and pour in boiling water to come about halfway up the sides. Bake for 1½ hours, until set. Remove the dish from the oven, cover with foil, put a weight on top and leave to cool. Refrigerate until ready to serve. This dish is best eaten the following day.

448

Fried cabbage garnish
HOJAS DE REPOLLO FRITAS (PARA ADORNO DE LA CARNE)

- 1 cabbage, about 1 kg/2¼ lb
- sunflower oil, for deep-frying
- 50 g/2 oz plain flour
- salt

Serves 6

Cut the stalk and carefully separate the cabbage leaves without breaking them. Bring a large saucepan of salted water to the boil. Add the cabbage leaves, gently pushing them down into the water with a spoon. Bring back to the boil, cover and simmer for about 30 minutes, until tender. Carefully remove the leaves from the pan, drain and place on a clean tea towel to dry. Heat the oil in a deep-fryer or deep saucepan to 180–190°C/350–375°F or until a cube of day-old bread browns in 30 seconds. Meanwhile, fold in the two outside edges of each cabbage leaf and roll the leaf up so that it is about the size of a large croquette with straight ends. Coat in the flour and add to the hot oil, in batches of four. Cook for a few minutes, until golden brown. Drain well and use to garnish meat. These rolls go very well with stews, casseroles and meat cooked in a sauce.

449

• 1 cabbage, about 1 kg/2¼ lb
• 150 g/5 oz cooked meat or
  York ham, finely chopped
• 25 g/1 oz butter
• 2 tablespoons sunflower oil
• 2 tablespoons plain flour
• 500 ml/18 fl oz milk
• 80 g/3 oz gruyere cheese, grated
• salt

Serves 6

Cabbage leaves stuffed with York ham in béchamel sauce
HOJAS DE REPOLLO RELLENAS DE JAMÓN DE YORK CON BECHAMEL

Prepare and cook the cabbage leaves as described in recipe 448. Carefully remove the leaves from the saucepan, drain and place on a clean tea towel to dry. Divide the meat or ham among the leaves and roll up like cannelloni. Put them into an ovenproof dish in a single layer. Preheat the oven to 200°C/400°F/Gas Mark 6. Melt the butter with the oil in a saucepan. Stir in the flour and cook, stirring constantly, for 2 minutes. Gradually stir in the milk, a little at a time. Cook, stirring constantly, for 10 minutes. Season with salt and pour the sauce over the cabbage rolls. Sprinkle with the gruyere and bake for 10–15 minutes, until golden brown. Serve immediately straight from the dish.

Note: The béchamel sauce can also be made by using half milk and half stock.

450

• 5 tablespoons olive oil
• 1 onion, chopped
• 100 g/3½ oz streaky bacon,
  diced
• 1.5–2 kg/3¼–4½ lb
  mangetouts (snow peas),
  trimmed
• 2 tablespoons plain flour
• 1 litre/1¾ pints chicken stock
  (home-made or made
  with a stock cube)
• 2 egg yolks
• salt

Serves 6

Mangetouts
TIRABEQUES

Heat the oil in a saucepan. Add the onion and cook over a low heat, stirring occasionally, for about 5 minutes, until softened and translucent. Add the bacon and cook, stirring occasionally, for a further 5 minutes. Add the mangetouts, increase the heat to high, cover and cook, shaking the pan occasionally, for 10 minutes. Season with salt and stir in the flour. Cook, stirring constantly, for 2 minutes, then stir in the stock. Bring to the boil, lower the heat, cover and simmer for 30 minutes. Lightly beat the egg yolks in a bowl and stir in a little of the cooking liquid from the mangetouts to prevent them curdling, then stir into the pan. Serve immediately.

Note: If there is too much liquid in the saucepan containing the mangetouts, remove some before adding the egg yolks.

Tomatoes

Origin and season

Tomatoes, which are actually a fruit rather than a vegetable, come from Peru and Mexico and were brought to Europe by the conquistadores of the sixteenth century. In some countries, such as pre-revolutionary France, they were considered to be inedible as they are part of the nightshade family. Nowadays, tomatoes are among the most commonly eaten fruits. They are available all year round but the best time for them is early autumn when they have had all the sun they need.

Selection

Tomatoes are best bought fully ripe. They should be firm to the touch and the skin should be smooth and without blemishes. Green tomatoes are indigestible; allow them to ripen by wrapping them in newspaper and leaving them to ripen in a dark place.

Nutrition

Tomatoes have about 20 calories per 100 g / 3 ½ oz. They stimulate the appetite and are rich in vitamins A, B and C. They also contain iron and magnesium. Their high level of acidity can cause stomach problems for some people.

Tricks

- There are two ways to peel tomatoes. Put them in a heatproof bowl and pour in boiling water to cover. Leave for 3 seconds, then drain, peel off the skins and refresh in cold water. Alternatively, run the blunt edge of a knife blade over the tomato, pressing quite hard, then peel off the skin with the sharp edge
- To store leftover tomato purée, cover it with a layer of oil
- To reduce the acidity of a tomato sauce, add a pinch of sugar
- When making a tomato sauce, give it a different touch by adding a few fresh basil leaves at the last minute
- Raw tomatoes do not freeze well but tomato sauce can be frozen successfully
- The best way to keep tomatoes is to stand them on their bases without touching each other.

451

Tomatoes stuffed with meat

TOMATES RELLENOS DE CARNE

- **12 tomatoes**
- **300 g/11 oz minced meat (half beef and half pork)**
- **1 egg, lightly beaten**
- **1 clove garlic, finely chopped**
- **1 teaspoon chopped fresh parsley**
- **2 heaped tablespoons breadcrumbs**
- **2 tablespoons olive oil**
- **salt**

Serves 4–6

Cut out the stalks and cores of the tomatoes with the point of a knife and scoop out the seeds and flesh with a teaspoon. Sprinkle a little salt in the cavities and leave the tomatoes to drain, upside down, for about 1 hour. Preheat the oven to 180°C/350°F/Gas Mark 4. Mix together the minced meat, egg, garlic, parsley and breadcrumbs in a bowl and season with salt. Using a teaspoon, fill the tomatoes with the mixture, leaving some of it protruding. Pour the oil over the base of an ovenproof dish and place the tomatoes in the dish in a single layer. Bake for about 1 hour until cooked through and tender. Serve immediately straight from the dish.

452

Tomatoes stuffed with béchamel sauce and grated cheese

TOMATES RELLENOS DE BECHAMEL Y QUESO RALLADO

- **12 ripe tomatoes**
- **5 tablespoons olive oil**
- **25 g/1 oz butter**
- **2 tablespoons sunflower oil**
- **2 tablespoons plain flour**
- **500 ml/18 fl oz milk**
- **100 g/3½ oz gruyere cheese, grated**
- **2 eggs, separated**
- **salt**

Serves 4–6

Cut out the stalks and cores of the tomatoes with the point of a knife and scoop out the seeds and flesh with a teaspoon. Sprinkle a little salt in the cavities and leave the tomatoes to drain, upside down, for about 1 hour. Preheat the oven to 180°C/350°F/Gas Mark 4. Put the tomatoes into an ovenproof dish and divide the olive oil among the cavities. Bake for about 20 minutes. Meanwhile, make the béchamel sauce. Melt the butter with the sunflower oil in a saucepan. Stir in the flour and cook, stirring constantly, for 2 minutes. Gradually stir in the milk, a little at a time. Cook, stirring constantly, for 10 minutes. Lightly season with salt, remove the pan from the heat and stir in half the gruyere and the egg yolks. (Take care that the sauce is not too hot or the egg yolks will curdle.) Whisk the egg whites in a clean, dry bowl until they form soft peaks, add a little salt and fold into the sauce. Fill the tomatoes with the sauce, sprinkle with the remaining cheese, return to the oven and bake for 10–15 minutes, until golden brown. Serve immediately straight from the dish.

453

Baked tomatoes with parsley and garlic

TOMATES AL HORNO CON PEREJIL Y AJO PICADO

- **6 large ripe tomatoes, halved widthways**
- **1 tablespoon chopped fresh parsley**
- **1½ teaspoons chopped garlic**
- **6 tablespoons breadcrumbs**
- **6 tablespoons olive oil**
- **salt**

Serves 6

Scoop out the seeds from the tomatoes with a teaspoon and sprinkle the insides of the 'shells' with salt. Leave the tomato halves to drain, upside down, for 1 hour. Preheat the oven to 180°C/350°F/Gas Mark 4. Put the tomatoes into an ovenproof dish, cut sides up and in a single layer. Divide the parsley and garlic among them and sprinkle with the breadcrumbs. Drizzle the oil over the tomatoes and bake for about 1 hour, until the flesh is well roasted and soft. Serve immediately straight from the dish.

Note: Smaller tomatoes that have been prepared in this way make a good accompaniment to meat dishes.

454

Tomatoes filled with Russian salad

TOMATES RELLENOS DE ENSALADILLA RUSA

- **6 large tomatoes**
- **300 g/11 oz Russian Salad (see recipe 21)**
- **lettuce leaves**

Serves 4–6

Cut out the stalks and cores of the tomatoes with the point of a knife and scoop out the seeds and some of the flesh with a teaspoon. Sprinkle a little salt in the cavities and leave the tomatoes to drain, upside down, for about 1 hour. Fill the tomatoes with the Russian Salad and chill in the refrigerator for at least 1 hour. Just before serving, garnish with the lettuce.

Notes: This dish can be served as an appetizer in summer. In Spain you can buy ready-made Russian salad. Alternatively, to save time buy cans of ready prepared vegetables that can be mixed with Mayonnaise (see recipe 105).

455

Tomatoes filled with sardines, green peppers and olives

TOMATES RELLENOS DE SARDINAS EN ACEITE, PIMIENTOS VERDES Y ACEITUNAS

- **12 tomatoes**
- **3 tablespoons olive oil**
- **2 green peppers,**
  seeded and diced
- **9 large canned sardines in oil,**
  drained
- **100 g/3½ oz pimiento-stuffed**
  olives, halved
- **lettuce leaves**
- **salt**

  Vinaigrette:
- **1 tablespoon white-wine vinegar**
- **3 tablespoons sunflower oil**
- **½ teaspoon mustard**
- **1 teaspoon chopped**
  fresh parsley
- **salt**

Serves 6

Cut out the stalks and cores of the tomatoes with the point of a knife and scoop out the seeds and some of the flesh with a teaspoon. Sprinkle a little salt in the cavities and leave the tomatoes to drain, upside down, for about 1 hour. Heat the oil in a frying pan. Add the green pepper, cover and cook over a low heat, shaking the pan occasionally, for 10 minutes. Just before the end of the cooking time, lightly season with salt. Meanwhile, make the vinaigrette as described in recipe 98. Remove the skin and bones from the sardines and flake the flesh into a bowl with a fork. Add the pepper and vinaigrette, mix well and divide the mixture among the tomatoes. Chill in the refrigerator for 2 hours, then top with the olives and garnish with the lettuce leaves and serve.

456

Fried tomato slices

RODAJAS DE TOMATE EMPANADAS Y FRITAS

- **6 large ripe, fleshy tomatoes**
- **6 tablespoons breadcrumbs**
- **1 egg, lightly beaten**
- **vegetable oil, for frying**
- **salt**

Serves 4

Thickly slice some fleshy tomatoes, sprinkle with salt on both sides and leave to drain for 30 minutes. Pat dry and dip in breadcrumbs, then in beaten egg and finally in breadcrumbs again. Fry on both sides in plenty of hot oil. Serve immediately. These slices make an attractive garnish for meat and some fish dishes.

457 Tomato sorbet

TOMATE EN SORBETE

- 1.5 kg/3¼ lb very ripe tomatoes,
  peeled, seeded
  and chopped
- 1 small onion, chopped
- 1 sprig fresh mint
- 1 sprig fresh basil
- 1 sprig fresh marjoram
- 1 tablespoon tomato purée
- juice of 2 lemons
- 2 tablespoons brown sugar
- slices of lemon

Serves 4–6

Put the tomato, onion, mint, basil and marjoram into a saucepan and cook over a low heat, stirring occasionally, for 30 minutes. Remove and discard the herbs, allow to cool slightly, then process in a food processor and pour into a freezer-proof container. Stir in the tomato purée, lemon juice and sugar and leave to cool. Stand the container on a tray of ice in the freezer for at least 4 hours. Just before serving, take the sorbet out of the freezer, beat gently to break the ice and serve in glasses, garnished with slices of lemon. Serve the sorbet at the beginning of a meal.

458 Preserved tomatoes

TOMATITOS EN CONSERVA

- 1 kg/2¼ lb small tomatoes
  (the greener the better)
- 1 tablespoon black peppercorns
- 2 onion, chopped
- 1 tablespoon sugar
- 750 ml/1¼ pints strong vinegar
- 1 sprig fresh tarragon
- 1 sprig fresh fennel
- 1 tablespoon wholegrain
  mustard
- salt

Serves 6

Put the tomatoes into a large saucepan of boiling water for 1 minute, then drain. Put them into a sterilized glass pickling jar, add the peppercorns, onion, sugar and a pinch of salt. Bring the vinegar to the boil in a small saucepan and simmer for 10 minutes. When the tomatoes have cooled, pour the vinegar over them. Close the lid and leave to marinate for 24 hours. Add the tarragon, fennel and mustard, seal the jar so that it is airtight and leave for 2 months before using.

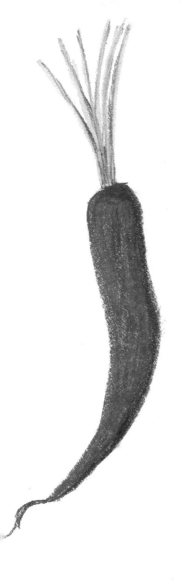

Carrots

Origin and season

Carrots have been grown for more than 5,000 years. Until the Renaissance they were considered a medicinal rather than a culinary plant, and up to the middle of the nineteenth century they were beige in colour; their now familiar orange colour is the result of cross-breeding. The best time for carrots is spring and early summer, when they are smaller in size and have almost no skin. At this time of year they are very tender and can be eaten raw. Thicker carrots appear in winter and are ideal for stews.

Selection

In spring the best carrots are small and shiny with fresh green feathery tops. The larger winter carrots should not have any cracks as they will have a hard, yellow part in the middle that has to be removed before the carrots can be eaten. In general, the more orange the carrot, the sweeter and more tender it will be. It is better to buy carrots loose, rather than in plastic bags; if they are not well ventilated, dampness forms and causes mould. If the carrots are served as an accompaniment allow 150 g / 5 oz per serving.

Nutrition

Many virtues have been attributed to carrots, including giving the skin a good colour, improving the eyesight and helping to maintain good humour. They contain 26 calories per 100 g / 3 ½ oz and are a rich source of vitamins A, B, C and E. They also contain carotene, pro-vitamin A that the body converts into retinol, and the minerals potassium, iron, calcium and zinc.

Tricks

- To retain vitamins and minerals, scrape carrots with a knife rather than peeling them
- Cook carrots in salted boiling water with a pinch of sugar for 10–15 minutes
- If they are to be steamed, dice them first
- Wetting your hand before peeling carrots will prevent any trace of colour being left on your skin.

459

Carrots in sauce
ZANAHORIAS EN SALSA

- 6 tablespoons olive oil
- 1 onion, finely chopped
- 1.5 kg/3¼ lb carrots, cut into 5-mm/¼-inch thick slices
- 1 tablespoon plain flour
- 175 ml/6 fl oz white wine
- 1 teaspoon chopped fresh parsley
- salt

Serves 6

Heat the oil in a saucepan. Add the onion and cook over a medium heat, stirring occasionally, for 6 minutes, until softened and translucent. Add the carrot and cook, stirring occasionally, for a further 5 minutes. Stir in the flour and cook, stirring constantly, for 5 minutes, then add the wine, season with salt and pour in water to cover. Cook over a medium heat, stirring occasionally, for 30–60 minutes, depending on the variety and freshness of the carrots. Serve in a warm deep dish, garnished with the parsley.

460

Carrot salad appetizer
ZANAHORIAS EN ENSALADA PARA ENTREMESES

- 750 g/1 lb 10 oz carrots
- 1 quantity Vinaigrette (see recipe 98)

Serves 6

Scrape the carrots with a knife, then wash and dry them. Cut into small thin sticks with a mandoline, like straw potatoes. Dress the carrot with the vinaigrette and serve as an appetizer with tomatoes, lettuce and beetroot.

Notes: Carrots are delicious and extremely healthy when mixed with escarole in salads. Use only the freshest and most tender available.

461

Glazed carrots
ZANAHORIAS GLASEADAS

- **500 g/1 lb 2 oz tender carrots**
- **50 g/2 oz butter**
- **1 heaped teaspoon sugar**
- **salt**

Serves 4

If the carrots are small, leave them whole, otherwise halve them lengthways. Put into a saucepan, pour in 500 ml/18 fl oz water and add the butter, sugar and a generous pinch of salt. Cut a disc of brown wrapping paper slightly larger than the diameter of the pan and position it in the pan so that it nearly touches the carrots. Cook over a high heat until all the water has evaporated. Serve immediately as a garnish to meat dishes.

Mixed vegetable dishes

462

Vegetable stew
MENESTRA DE VERDURAS VERDES

- 750 g/1 lb 10 oz small young globe artichokes
- 1 lemon, halved
- 4 tablespoons olive oil
- 3 shallots, chopped
- 150 g/5 oz Serrano ham, chopped
- 1 tablespoon plain flour
- 1 small lettuce, shredded
- 500 g/1 lb 2 oz green beans, trimmed
- 1 kg/2¼ lb peas, shelled
- 2 tablespoons white wine
- salt

Serves 6

Remove and discard the tough outer leaves of the artichokes and cut off the tops of the remaining leaves. Cut the artichokes lengthways into halves or quarters, depending on their size, and remove the chokes with a teaspoon. Rub the artichokes all over with the lemon halves to prevent them turning black. Heat the oil in a saucepan. Add the shallots and cook over a low heat, stirring occasionally, for about 8 minutes, until beginning to brown. Add the ham and cook for 3 minutes, then stir in the flour and add the lettuce, artichokes, beans and peas. Cook, stirring occasionally, for a further 5 minutes, then pour in the wine and season with salt. Stir well and add enough water to just cover the vegetables. Cover the pan and simmer, stirring occasionally, for about 45 minutes. Add a little more water during cooking, if necessary. Serve immediately, garnished with slices of hard-boiled egg, if you like.

Note: You can add broad beans to the stew.

463

Classic vegetable soup
MENESTRA DE VERDURAS CORRIENTE

- 4 tablespoons olive oil
- 1 small onion, finely chopped
- 100 g/3½ oz Serrano ham, diced
- 6 lettuce leaves, shredded
- 1 tablespoon plain flour
- 500 g/1 lb 2 oz carrots, diced
- 750 g/1 lb 10 oz small young globe artichokes
- 1 lemon, halved
- 2 turnips, diced
- 500 g/1 lb 2 oz green beans, trimmed and cut into short lengths
- 1 kg/2¼ lb peas, shelled
- salt

Serves 6

Heat the oil in a saucepan. Add the onion and cook over a low heat, stirring occasionally, for about 5 minutes, until softened and translucent. Add the ham and lettuce and cook for a few minutes, then stir in the flour. Add the carrot and pour in enough water to cover. Simmer gently for 10–15 minutes. Meanwhile, remove and discard the tough outer leaves of the artichokes and cut off the tops of the remaining leaves. Cut the artichokes lengthways into halves or quarters, depending on their size, and remove the chokes with a teaspoon. Rub the artichokes all over with the lemon halves to prevent them turning black. Add the artichokes, turnip, beans, peas and a pinch of salt to the pan. (If you're unsure about how tender the artichokes are, cook them separately and add them to the soup later.) Simmer over a low heat, stirring occasionally, for 30–45 minutes, until the vegetable are tender but not falling apart. If the soup is too liquid, remove some of the stock before serving. Garnish with slices of hard-boiled egg, if you like.

Note: This is a very flexible recipe; you can use different vegetables, depending on the time of year.

464

Vegetable pie
BUDÍN DE VERDURAS

- 1.5 kg/3¼ lb spinach
  or 1 kg/2¼ lb Swiss chard
- 300 g/11 oz carrots, thinly sliced
- 750 g/1 lb 10 oz peas, shelled
- 50 g/2 oz butter,
  plus extra for greasing
- 2 eggs
- 3 tablespoons milk
- salt

  Sauce:
- 20 g/¾ oz butter
- 2 tablespoons olive oil
- 1½ tablespoons plain flour
- 500 ml/18 fl oz milk
- 1 tablespoon tomato purée
- salt

  Serves 6

Cook the vegetables in separate pans. If using the spinach, remove the coarse stalks, put the leaves into a saucepan with just the water clinging to them after washing and cook for 8–10 minutes. Drain well, pressing out as much liquid as possible with the back of a spoon, then chop. If using the the Swiss chard, chop it and put it into a saucepan. Pour in water to cover and add a pinch of salt. Bring to the boil, lower the heat and simmer for about 20 minutes, until tender. Drain well. Cook the carrot in a saucepan of salted boiling water for 10–15 minutes, until tender. Drain well, reserve a few slices and chop the remainder. Cook the peas in a saucepan of salted boiling water for 20–30 minutes, until tender. Drain well. Preheat the oven to 180°C/350°F/Gas Mark 4. Grease a cake tin with butter. Cut out a piece of greaseproof paper to fit the base of the tin and grease with butter, then place in the tin. Arrange the reserved carrot slices and some peas in a decorative pattern on the paper. Melt the butter in a large frying pan. Add the spinach or Swiss chard, carrot and peas and cook, stirring occasionally, for 5 minutes. Lightly beat the eggs with the milk in a bowl and pour into the pan. Transfer the vegetable mixture to the prepared tin and press down gently to remove any air bubbles. Put the tin into a roasting tin and pour in boiling water to come about halfway up the sides. Bake for about 1 hour, until set. Meanwhile, make the sauce. Melt the butter with the oil in a saucepan. Stir in the flour and cook, stirring constantly, for 2 minutes. Gradually stir in the milk, a little at a time. Season with salt and cook, stirring constantly, for 10–15 minutes, until thickened. Stir in the tomato purée. When the pie is cooked, turn off the oven and open the door. Leave the pie to stand for 5–8 minutes. Run a round-bladed knife around the edge of the pie, then turn out on to a warm serving dish. Carefully remove the paper and pour the sauce over the pie. Serve immediately.

Note: The vegetables can be varied according to the season.

465

Vegetable flan
FLAN DE VERDURAS

- 750 g/1 lb 10 oz shelled or frozen peas
- 500 g/1 lb 2 oz green beans, trimmed and cut into 2-cm/ ¾-inch lengths
- 500 g/1 lb 2 oz carrots, sliced
- 300 g/11 oz turnips, diced
- margarine, for greasing
- 4–5 eggs
- 175 ml/6 fl oz milk
- salt
- 1 quantity Béchamel Sauce with Tomato (see recipe 78) or Classic Béchamel Sauce (see recipe 77) with ½ teaspoon curry powder

Serves 6

Cook the vegetables in separate saucepans. Cook the peas in salted boiling water for 20–30 minutes, until tender or according to the instructions on the packet. Drain well. Cook the green beans in salted boiling water for 12–15 minutes, until tender, then drain well. Cook the carrot in salted boiling water for 10–15 minutes, until tender, then drain well. Cook the turnip in salted boiling water for 10 minutes, then drain well. This can be done in advance or even the night before. Preheat the oven to 180°C/350°F/Gas Mark 4. Line the base of a flan dish with foil and generously grease the whole dish, including the foil, with margarine. Put the carrots in the base of the dish, put the green beans on top, then the turnips and, finally, the peas. Lightly beat the eggs with the milk in a bowl. Lightly season with salt and carefully pour over the vegetables. Gently move the vegetables slightly to make sure that the egg mixture penetrates. Put the dish into a roasting tin and pour in hot water to come about halfway up the sides. Bake for 1 hour, until set. Remove from the oven and leave to stand for about 5 minutes. Run a round-bladed knife around the edge of the flan, then turn out on to a warm serving dish. Pour the sauce over the flan or serve separately in a sauce boat.

466

Aubergine, courgette, tomato and pepper medley
REVUELTO DE BERENJENAS, CALABACINES, TOMATES Y PIMIENTOS

- 6 tablespoons olive oil
- 1 onion, chopped
- 750 g/1 lb 10 oz ripe tomatoes, peeled, seeded and chopped
- 3 large courgettes, peeled and cut into large pieces
- 3 large aubergines, peeled and cut into large pieces
- 1 green pepper, seeded and cut into thin strips
- 1 tablespoon plain flour
- 1–3 tablespoons leftover meat sauce or 1 chicken stock cube
- salt

Serves 6

Heat the oil in a saucepan. Add the onion and cook over a low heat, stirring occasionally, for 10 minutes, until lightly browned. Add the tomato and cook, stirring occasionally, for a further 8 minutes. Add the courgettes, aubergines and green pepper, season with salt and cook, stirring occasionally, for 10 minutes. Stir in the flour and add the meat sauce or the stock cube dissolved in a little water. Mix well and cook over a medium heat, stirring occasionally, for 30–40 minutes, until all the vegetables are tender. Serve in a warm deep dish.

Note: This dish can be made earlier and reheated before serving.

Stuffed mixed vegetables

RELLENO DE VERDURAS VARIADAS

- **2 courgettes, halved**
- **4 tomatoes**
- **4 potatoes**
- **4 small onions**
- **4 small red or green peppers**
- **50–80 g/2–3 oz plain flour**
- **500 ml/18 fl oz sunflower oil**

Stuffing:
- **1 thick slice bread,**
  crusts removed
- **3–4 tablespoons warm milk**
- **1 clove garlic**
- **1 sprig fresh parsley**
- **250 g/9 oz minced meat**
  (half beef and half pork)
- **2 eggs, lightly beaten**
- **1 tablespoon white wine**
- **salt**

Sauce:
- **6 tablespoons sunflower oil**
- **1 large onion, chopped**
- **1 heaped tablespoon plain flour**
- **2 carrots, thinly sliced**
- **175 ml/6 fl oz white wine**
- **salt**

Serves 6–8

Prepare the stuffing. Put the bread into a bowl and add the milk, then leave to soak for 10 minutes. Pound the garlic with a pinch of salt and the parsley in a mortar. Mix together the meat, bread, squeezed out if necessary, eggs, wine and garlic mixture in a bowl. Bring the mixture together as if making meatballs. Using a sharp knife or an apple corer, make a cavity about the size of a walnut in the centre of the courgette halves, tomatoes, potatoes and onions. Fill the cavities with a little of the stuffing. Cut out the stalk from the peppers and remove the seeds, then fill with the stuffing. Dust all the stuffed vegetables with the flour. Heat the oil in a deep frying pan. Add the stuffed vegetables, one at a time, and cook until browned all over. Remove with a slotted spoon and, with the exception of the tomatoes, place in a single layer in another large saucepan. Set the tomatoes aside on a plate. Make the sauce. Heat the oil in a frying pan. Add the onion and cook over a low heat, stirring occasionally, for about 10 minutes, until lightly browned. Stir in the flour and cook, stirring constantly, for 3–5 minutes, until lightly browned. Add the carrots, pour in the wine and 1.5 litres/2 ½ pints water and simmer for 15 minutes. Allow to cool slightly, then process in a food processor, season with salt and pour into the pan of stuffed vegetables. Cook over a low heat for 45 minutes, then add the tomatoes and cook for a further 15 minutes. Remove from the heat and leave to stand for 5 minutes before serving.

Note: This dish can be made earlier and reheated before serving.

468   Ratatouille with squid in julienne strips

PISTO CON JULIANA DE CALAMARES

- 150 ml/¼ pint olive oil
- 2 large onions, finely chopped
- 3 aubergines, peeled and diced
- 2 green peppers,
  seeded and cut into pieces
- 4 courgettes, diced
- 500 g/1 lb 2 oz ripe tomatoes,
  peeled, seeded and chopped
- 2 cloves garlic, finely chopped
- 4 prepared squid, cleaned and
  cut into thin strips
  (see page 468)
- salt

Serves 4

Reserve 2 tablespoons of the oil and heat the remainder in a large frying pan. Add the onion and cook over a low heat, stirring occasionally, for 5 minutes, until softened and translucent. Add the aubergine and cook, stirring occasionally, for 10 minutes. Add the pepper and cook, stirring occasionally, for a further 10 minutes. Add the courgette, tomato and garlic and season with salt. Cover and simmer gently for 1 hour. Heat the reserved oil in another frying pan. Add the strips of squid and cook over a high heat, stirring constantly, for 2–3 minutes, until lightly coloured. Remove from the heat. If the ratatouille has too much liquid, drain some off, then put the strips of squid on top and serve.

Notes: the strips of squid can be coated in flour before being fried. Instead of adding chopped garlic to the ratatouille, crush the cloves and mix with 4 tablespoons olive oil, then pour this over the served dish. In this case, use only 4 tablespoons oil to cook the vegetables.

469   Manchegan ratatouille

PISTO MANCHEGO

- 150 ml/¼ pint olive oil
- 200 g/7 oz chorizo, diced
- 200 g/7 oz ham, diced
- 1 kg/2¼ lb onions, chopped
- 1 kg/2¼ lb green peppers,
  seeded and diced
- 1 kg/2¼ lb courgettes, diced
- 1 kg/2¼ lb ripe tomatoes,
  peeled and chopped
- croûtons
- salt

Serves 10

Heat the oil in a saucepan. Add the chorizo and ham and cook over a low heat, stirring occasionally, for 5 minutes. Remove with a slotted spoon and set aside. Add the onion and green pepper to the pan and cook, stirring occasionally, for 10 minutes. Add the courgette and tomato, mix well, cover and simmer gently for 30 minutes. Season to taste with salt, add the chorizo and ham and heat through for a few minutes. Serve immediately with the croûtons.

Note: This recipe comes from the Spanish region of La Mancha.

Mushrooms and truffles

Cultivated mushrooms

Origin and season
Mushrooms have been cultivated since the time of Napoleon. They are available all year round but the best season for them is autumn.

Selection
There should be no cracks or holes in the caps, which should feel firm to the touch. Avoid mushrooms with blemishes on the caps. The cap and stalk should be firmly attached; if they separate too easily, it is a sign of poor quality.

Nutrition
Mushrooms have very few calories – 35 per 100 g / 3 ½ oz. They are rich in vitamin C and phosphorus.

Tricks
• If mushrooms are cleaned with fresh water and lemon juice and wrapped in a tea towel, they will remain in good condition in the refrigerator for several days. Do not let them come into contact with metal as it will turn them black.

Wild mushrooms

Origin and season

The term 'wild mushrooms' includes all the types of mushrooms that grow naturally in the wild, even though some varieties are now cultivated. Some, such as milk cap mushrooms, appear in autumn, while others, such as morels, in spring. Porcinis, also known by their French name cep, are especially highly prized autumn mushrooms, but are available dried throughout the year.

Selection

The fresher wild mushrooms are, the better. However, do not pick them unless you are absolutely certain you can identify them properly. Some poisonous mushrooms look very similar to edible ones. If in any doubt, it is better to buy them at a greengrocer's.

Nutrition

In general, mushrooms have few calories: 25–50 per 100 g / 3 ½ oz. They are rich in proteins.

Tricks

- Always wash wild mushrooms very carefully as they may contain small bugs and a lot of earth. It is best to wash them in water with a dash of vinegar
- Although canned wild mushrooms are available all year round, they do not have half the flavour of fresh ones
- Dried mushrooms are available all year, and are a good choice if fresh are not available. They must be reconstituted in liquid. They tend to be strongly flavoured so only small quantities are needed.

How to prepare mushrooms for a sauce

Choose the freshest white mushrooms. If they are large, separate the stalks from the caps. Trim the stalks and cut them widthways into two or three pieces. Wash the caps and brush with a fine brush to remove any traces of earth, then cut into two or four pieces and put into cool water with a few drops of lemon juice. Wash well and drain immediately. Put a knob of butter (about 20 g / ¾ oz butter to 250 g / 9 oz mushrooms), a pinch of salt and the juice of ½ lemon into a saucepan. Cover and cook over a medium heat, shaking the pan occasionally, for about 6 minutes. The mushrooms are then ready to be made into a sauce. They can also be cut into thin slices for use in sauces to accompany meat, and for omelettes.

470

Garlic mushrooms
CHAMPIÑONES AL AJILLO

- **9 tablespoons sunflower oil**
- **1.5 kg / 3¼ lb**
  button mushrooms
- **3 cloves garlic, chopped**
- **2 tablespoons chopped**
  fresh parsley
- **salt**

Serves 6

Preheat the oven to 180°C/350°F/Gas Mark 4. Divide the oil and mushrooms among six flameproof earthenware ramekins or other individual cooking dishes. (If you don't have individual dishes, just cook the ingredients all together in a frying pan and divide between six serving dishes or ramekins when you are done.) Add some salt and garlic to each and cook for 5 minutes. Increase the temperature to 220°C/425°F/Gas Mark 7 and cook, shaking the dishes occasionally, for a further 5 minutes. Sprinkle the parsley over the mushrooms and serve immediately.

471

Mushrooms in béchamel sauce
CHAMPIÑONES CON BECHAMEL

- 1.2 kg/2¼ lb mushrooms
- 50 g/2 oz butter
- juice of ½ lemon
- 2 tablespoons sunflower oil
- 3 tablespoons plain flour
- 750 ml/1¼ pints milk
- 2 egg yolks, lightly beaten
- 2 tablespoons chopped
  fresh parsley
- 6 triangles of fried bread
  (see recipe 130), optional
- salt and pepper

Serves 6

If the mushrooms are small, leave them whole, otherwise cut the caps and stalks into large pieces. Put them into a pan with half the butter and the lemon juice. Cook, shaking the pan occasionally, for 6 minutes, then remove from the heat and set aside. Melt the remaining butter with the oil in another saucepan. Stir in the flour and cook, stirring constantly, for 2 minutes. Gradually stir in the milk, a little at a time. Cook, stirring constantly, for 10–12 minutes. Stir a little of the sauce into the egg yolks to prevent them curdling, then stir into the pan of sauce. Season to taste with salt and pepper and remove the pan from the heat. Drain the mushrooms and stir them into the béchamel sauce. Serve in warm individual dishes, sprinkled with the parsley and garnished with the triangles of fried bread if you like.

Note: This mixture can be used to fill small individual vols-au-vent or a large vol-au-vent.

472

Mushroom appetizer
CHAMPIÑONES PARA ENTREMESES

- 5 tablespoons olive oil
- 1 onion, chopped
- 2 small carrots, diced
- 2 cloves garlic
- 275 ml/9 fl oz white wine
- 2 sprigs fresh parsley
- 1 bay leaf
- 750 g/1 lb 10 oz
  button mushrooms
- 2 ripe tomatoes,
  peeled, seeded and chopped
- 1 tablespoon chopped
  fresh parsley
- salt and pepper

Serves 4

Heat 3 tablespoons of the oil in a saucepan. Add the onion, carrot and garlic and cook over a low heat, stirring occasionally, for 5 minutes. Pour in the wine, add the parsley sprigs and bay leaf, season with salt and pepper and cook for a further 5 minutes. Add the mushrooms and tomato and cook for 5 minutes. Remove and discard the parsley sprigs, bay leaf and garlic. Tip the mixture into a warm serving dish, drizzle with the remaining oil and sprinkle with the chopped parsley. Mix well and chill in the refrigerator before serving.

473

Stuffed mushrooms
CHAMPIÑONES RELLENOS DE UN PICADITO CON CHALOTA

- **4 large flat cap mushrooms**
- **2 shallots, chopped**
- **2 tablespoons olive oil**
- **juice of ½ lemon**
- **salt**

Serves 4

Use large flat cap mushrooms for stuffing. Separate the caps and stalks, and chop the stalks. Heat the oil in a small frying pan. Add the stalks and shallots and cook over a low heat, stirring occasionally, for about 5 minutes. Season with salt, stir in a few drops of the lemon juice and cook for a further for 5–8 minutes. Divide the filling among the mushroom caps and then bake as in recipe 470.

474

Mushroom brochettes
BROCHETAS DE CHAMPIÑONES

- **500 g/1 lb 2 oz button mushrooms**
- **250 g/9 oz bacon in 2 thick slices**
- **7 tablespoons olive oil**
- **½ teaspoon fresh rosemary leaves**
- **salt and pepper**

Serves 4

Preheat the grill. Separate the mushroom caps and stalks (the stalks can be kept for soup). Cut the bacon into strips about 1.5 cm/⅝ inch wide. Put the oil into a bowl, add the rosemary and season with salt and pepper. Mix well. Thread the mushroom caps on to skewers, alternating with pieces of bacon. Brush the brochettes with the oil mixture. Cook under the grill, turning and brushing with more oil occasionally, for about 15 minutes, until cooked through and tender. Serve immediately.

Note: The brochettes can also be cooked on a medium-hot barbecue.

475
Mushrooms with rosemary
CHAMPIÑONES AL ROMERO

- **500 g / 1 lb 2 oz large mushrooms**
- **juice of ½ lemon**
- **50 g / 2 oz butter**
- **100 g / 3 ½ oz Serrano ham,**
  very finely chopped (optional)
- **2 sprigs fresh rosemary,**
  leaves removed and chopped
- **salt and pepper**

Serves 4

Separate the mushroom stalks and caps. Sprinkle the caps with the lemon juice and chop the stalks. Melt 10 g / ¼ oz of the butter in a frying pan or saucepan. Add the stalks and cook, stirring occasionally, for 6–7 minutes. If using the ham, add it to the pan after about 3 minutes and cook with the stalks. Season with salt and pepper, remove the mixture from the pan and set aside. Put the mushroom caps into the frying pan, gill sides up. Season with salt and pepper, cover and cook over a low heat for 1 minute. Drain off and reserve the liquid released by the mushrooms, return the pan to the heat and cook for a further 10 minutes, until tender. (Check by piercing a mushroom with the point of a knife – it should penetrate but the mushroom should feel firm.) Fill the caps with the chopped mixture. Mix the rosemary with the remaining butter, put it in a saucepan with the reserved cooking juices and cook over a low heat, stirring vigorously with a wooden spoon or whisk. Pour the rosemary sauce over the mushrooms and serve immediately.

476
Raw mushroom salad
ENSALADA DE CHAMPIÑONES CRUDOS

- **750 g / 1 lb 10 oz mushrooms**
- **6 tablespoons sunflower oil**
- **juice of 1 lemon**
- **1 tablespoon chopped**
  fresh parsley
- **salt and pepper**

Serves 4–6

Separate the mushroom caps and stalks. Slice the stalks and caps and put into a bowl. Pour in the oil and lemon juice, season with salt and pepper and mix well. Sprinkle with the parsley and chill in the refrigerator for 2 hours before serving.

477

Milk cap mushrooms

NÍSCALOS

- **500 g/1 lb 2 oz milk cap mushrooms**
- **1½ tablespoons olive oil**
- **1 tablespoon chopped fresh parsley**
- **1 clove garlic, very finely chopped**
- **salt**

Serves 4

Separate the mushroom stalks and caps. Discard the stalks. Wash the caps under cold running water, rubbing each side carefully with your fingers to remove any earth or sand. Cut them into large pieces and put them into a frying pan with no added oil. Cover and cook over a medium heat, shaking the pan occasionally, for 10 minutes. Drain off the liquid from the mushrooms. Season with salt, drizzle with the oil and sprinkle with the parsley and garlic. Mix well and cook over a low heat, stirring occasionally, for 3 minutes. Serve immediately.

Note: Milk cap mushrooms are usually used to garnish a meat dish, but if they are served as a first course allow 250 g/9 oz per serving. If milk cap mushrooms are not available, this recipe will work well with other wild mushroom varieties.

478

Wild mushrooms in sauce

SETAS EN SALSA

- **3 tablespoons olive oil**
- **2 shallots, finely chopped**
- **100 g/3½ oz Serrano ham, finely chopped**
- **1 kg/2¼ lb wild mushrooms, such as porcinis, cut into large pieces**
- **6 tablespoons sherry**
- **3 tablespoons single cream**
- **salt and pepper**

Serves 4

Heat the oil in a large frying pan. Add the shallots and cook over a low heat, stirring occasionally, for about 8 minutes, until beginning to brown. Add the ham and cook, stirring frequently, for 2–3 minutes, then add the mushrooms. Cook, stirring occasionally, for about 8 minutes, until lightly browned. Add the sherry and cook for a further 8 minutes. Season to taste with salt and pepper. Pour the cream over the mushrooms and heat through, stirring constantly, but do not allow the cream to boil. Serve immediately.

479

Stuffed porcini
SETAS GRATINADAS

- 24 large porcini mushrooms
- 120 ml/4 fl oz olive oil,
  plus extra for brushing
- 2 shallots, chopped
- 2 tablespoons chopped
  fresh parsley
- 2 tablespoons breadcrumbs
- 5 tablespoons white wine
- 175 ml/6 fl oz stock (home-made
  or made with a stock cube)
- salt

Serves 6

Separate the mushroom caps and stalks. Chop the stalks. Heat 3 tablespoons of the oil in a frying pan. Add the stalks and shallots and cook, stirring occasionally, for 4 minutes, then stir in the parsley. Preheat the oven to 190°C/375°F/Gas Mark 5. Brush an ovenproof dish with oil. Put the mushroom caps in the prepared dish, gill sides up. Season with salt, divide the shallot mixture among the caps and sprinkle with the breadcrumbs. Mix together the wine and stock in a jug and pour over the mushrooms. Bake for 10 minutes and serve straight from the dish.

480

Truffles
CRIADILLAS DE TIERRA

- 500 g/1 lb 10 oz truffles,
  thinly sliced
- 4 tablespoons olive oil
- 1 onion, finely chopped
- 2 tablespoons plain flour
- 175 ml/6 fl oz white wine
- salt

Serves 3

Put the truffles into a saucepan, pour in enough water to cover and bring just to the boil. Lower the heat, cover and simmer for 10 minutes. Meanwhile, make the sauce. Heat the oil in another saucepan. Add the onion and cook over a low heat, stirring occasionally, for 8–10 minutes, until lightly browned. Stir in the flour and cook, stirring constantly, for 3–5 minutes, until lightly coloured. Stir in the wine and 750 ml/1¼ pints water, lightly season with salt and cook for 2–3 minutes more. Drain the truffles and return them to the pan. Strain the sauce over them, cover and cook over a low heat for 30 minutes. Taste and adjust the seasoning, if necessary, and serve.

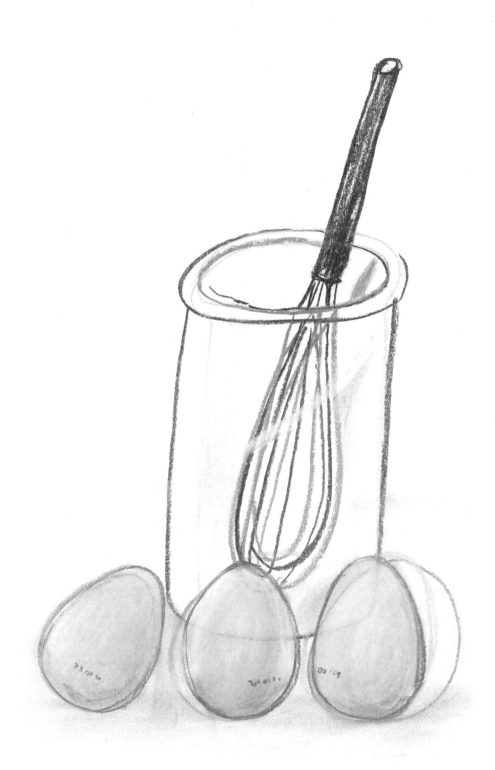

EGGS, FLANS AND SOUFFLES

Eggs

Buying eggs

Eggs may be from free-range or intensively reared hens or may come from birds that have limited access to the outside. If they are labelled organic, the hens will have been reared in a natural and humane way and the producer will have observed regulations concerning the use of any chemicals and antibiotics. Although there are different grades of egg, most of those on sale in supermarkets and other retail outlets are grade A, the lower grades mainly being used commercially. The grade is marked on the container, together with the size of the eggs, such as medium or large, the country of origin and the use-by date. It will also state whether the eggs are free-range and organic. In Spain eggs are sold at different prices according to their category. There are extra, 1st and 2nd class eggs, etc., and on those sold in boxes there should be the date on which they were laid and the date by which they should be used. The most important thing about an egg is that it is fresh.

How to choose eggs

In the past, a customer could look at each egg to see the size of the air sac inside the shell, as the bigger the sac, the older the egg. This is not very practical nowadays and it is easier to rely on the use-by date. The colour of the shell is no guide to the quality of the egg: a brown egg is as nutritious as a white one. The colour simply varies according to the breed of hen. A large egg is not necessarily more nutritious than a smaller one because proportionately it contains less yolk.

Tricks

- A new-laid egg is indigestible – wait at least 24 hours before eating it
- Never wash eggs before storing them, as the shell becomes permeable in water
- When storing eggs in the refrigerator do not put them near strong-smelling foods such as melon, which can give the eggs a flavour as the shell is porous. Store them in the refrigerator in their container or put them in the egg rack, pointed end down
- Remember to wash your hands after handling eggs as the shells may carry harmful bacteria
- Whenever possible, remove the eggs from the refrigerator at least an hour before they are needed. This ensures that whites will whisk stiffly, mayonnaise will come out better and so on
- Fresh eggs may be stored in the refrigerator for up to 2 weeks. An unshelled hard-boiled egg will keep for 4 days. A leftover egg yolk covered in a little cold water will keep for 2 days
- Don't let eggs come into contact with silver containers or cutlery as it turns them black
- When whisking egg whites do not let even a drop of egg yolk fall into them as it will prevent them frothing. Always use a clean, dry bowl, preferably copper or other metal, glass or china. Plastic bowls are less suitable
- Eggs can be frozen as long as they have been beaten first.

Soft-boiled eggs

How to cook

Pour enough water into a saucepan to cover all the eggs (never more than six at a time) and add salt (1 tablespoon for 4–6 eggs). Bring to the boil, plunge in the eggs and cook for exactly 3 minutes.

Variation

Put the eggs into a saucepan, add water to cover and 1 tablespoon salt. Bring to the boil over a high heat, remove the eggs immediately and serve. Soft-boiled eggs may be served in egg cups or even in tea cups and are often accompanied by strips of buttered toast.

481

Soft-boiled eggs with anchovy and smoked trout butter

HUEVOS PASADOS POR AGUA CON MANTEQUILLA DE ANCHOAS Y TRUCHA

- **40 g/1½ oz canned anchovy fillets, drained**
- **25 g/1 oz butter, softened**
- **50 g/2 oz smoked trout**
- **4 slices bread**
- **2 eggs**

Serves 2

Pound the anchovies in a mortar, then mix with half the butter to a smooth paste. Put the trout and remaining butter into a food processor and process to a smooth paste. Toast the bread, then cut into lengthways strips, about 2 cm/¾ inch wide. Spread half the strips with the anchovy butter and half with the smoked trout butter. Soft-boil the eggs as described above and serve in egg cups, accompanied by the strips of buttered toast.

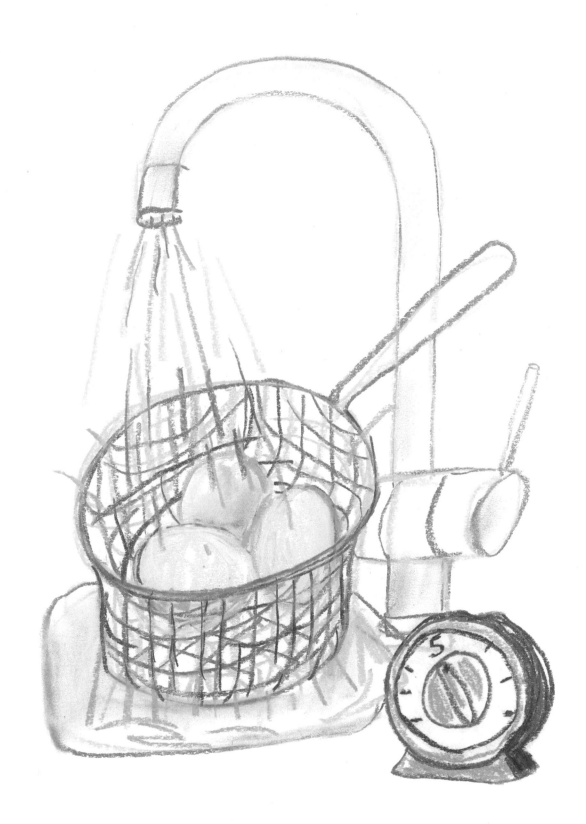

Hard-boiled eggs

How to cook

Pour enough water to cover the eggs into a saucepan, add 1 table-spoon salt and bring to the boil. Add the eggs carefully and stir gently with a wooden spoon so that when they set the yolks will be in the middle. Cook medium eggs for 12 minutes. (Add 1 minute for bigger eggs and subtract 1 minute for smaller eggs.) Drain off the hot water, fill the pan with cold water and leave the eggs in the water until required.

482

Hard-boiled egg croquettes
CROQUETAS DE HUEVOS DUROS

- **8 eggs**
- **2 tablespoons olive oil,**
  plus extra for brushing
- **25 g/1 oz butter**
- **4 tablespoons plain flour**
- **750 ml/1¼ pints milk**
- **80–120 g/3–4 oz fine**
  breadcrumbs
- **sunflower oil, for deep-frying**
- **4 deep-fried parsley sprigs**
  (see recipe 918)
- **salt**

Serves 6

Hard-boil six of the eggs as described on page 392. Shell and halve lengthways, then cut each half into three pieces. Brush a baking sheet with olive oil. Melt the butter with the olive oil in a saucepan. Stir in the flour and cook, stirring constantly, for 2 minutes. Gradually stir in the milk, a little at a time. Season with salt and cook, stirring constantly, for 10 minutes. Remove the pan from the heat. Using two spoons, add the pieces of egg, one at a time, and coat in the béchamel sauce, then place on the prepared baking sheet. Leave to cool for 1 hour. Beat the remaining eggs in a shallow dish and spread out the breadcrumbs in another shallow dish. Dip the egg pieces first in the beaten egg and then in the breadcrumbs to coat. Heat the sunflower oil in a deep-fryer or saucepan to 180–190°C/350–375°F or until a cube of day-old bread browns in 30 seconds. Add the egg pieces, in batches if necessary, and cook until golden brown. Remove and drain on kitchen paper. Serve the croquettes garnished with the parsley.

483

Eggs mimosa
HUEVOS DUROS MIMOSA

- **9 eggs**
- **1 quantity Classic Mayonnaise**
  (see recipe 105)
- **40 g/1½ oz canned anchovy**
  fillets, drained and chopped
- **fresh parsley or**
  watercress sprigs
- **salt**

Serves 6

Hard-boil the eggs as described on page 392. Shell and halve lengthways, then scoop out the yolks with a teaspoon, without piercing the whites, and set the whites aside. Mix together 250 ml/8 fl oz of the mayonnaise, five of the egg yolks and the anchovies in a bowl. Cut a thin slice off the base of each egg white half so that it stands straight. Using a teaspoon, fill the egg white halves with the mayonnaise mixture. Place on a serving dish, cover with the remaining mayonnaise and sift the remaining egg yolks over them. (Use a nylon rather than a metal sieve.) Garnish with the parsley or watercress and chill in the refrigerator for 1–2 hours before serving.

484

Hard-boiled egg fritters
BUÑUELOS DE HUEVOS DUROS

- 11 eggs
- 25 g/1 oz butter
- sunflower oil, for deep-frying
- 3 tablespoons plain flour
- 750 ml/1¼ pints milk
- 120 g/4 oz breadcrumbs
- 1 quantity Classic Tomato Sauce (see recipe 73)
- salt

Serves 6

Hard-boil nine of the eggs as described on page 392. Shell and halve widthways, then scoop out the yolks with a teaspoon, without piercing the whites. Melt the butter with 2 tablespoons of oil in a saucepan. Stir in the flour and cook, stirring constantly, for 2 minutes. Gradually stir in the milk, a little at a time. Season with salt and cook, stirring constantly, for 8–10 minutes. Add the cooked egg yolks and stir until they are fully incorporated into the sauce. Using a teaspoon, fill the egg white halves with this mixture, allowing the outside of the egg halves to be coated too. Leave to stand for at least 30 minutes. Beat the remaining eggs in a shallow dish and spread out the breadcrumbs in another shallow dish. Dip the egg halves first in the beaten egg and then in the breadcrumbs. Heat the oil in a deep-fryer or saucepan to 180–190°C/350–375°F or until a cube of day-old bread browns in 30 seconds. Add the egg halves, in batches if necessary, and cook until golden brown. Remove with a slotted spoon and drain on kitchen paper. Serve immediately, offering the tomato sauce separately.

485

Hard-boiled eggs with prawns
HUEVOS DUROS CON GAMBAS

- 350 g/12 oz raw unpeeled prawns
- 9 eggs
- 3 tablespoons sunflower oil
- 1 onion, chopped
- 3 tablespoons plain flour
- 5 tablespoons white wine
- salt

Serves 6

Bring a large saucepan of salted water to the boil. Add the prawns and cook for 2–3 minutes. Drain well, reserving 450 ml/¾ pint of the cooking liquid. Remove the heads and peel the prawns, then cut the tails into two or three pieces. Hard-boil the eggs as described on page 392. Shell and halve lengthways, then scoop out the yolks with a teaspoon, without piercing the whites. Preheat the oven to 180°C/350°F/Gas Mark 4. Heat the oil in a frying pan. Add the onion and cook over a low heat, stirring occasionally, for about 8 minutes, until beginning to brown. Stir in the flour and cook, stirring constantly, for 2 minutes. Gradually stir in the wine, a little at a time, then stir in the reserved cooking liquid. Cook, stirring constantly, for 5 minutes. Strain into a bowl, season to taste with salt and keep warm. Mix together three-quarters of the egg yolks, the prawns and 2–3 tablespoons of the sauce in another bowl. Cut a thin slice off the base of each egg white half so it stands straight. Using a teaspoon, fill the egg whites with the prawn mixture. Put them into an ovenproof dish, pour the remaining sauce over them and bake for about 5 minutes. Sift the remaining egg yolks over the dish and serve immediately. (Use a nylon rather than a metal sieve.)

486

Hard-boiled eggs with salad
HUEVOS DUROS CON ENSALADILLA

- 9 eggs
- 1 bunch watercress

Vegetable salad:
- 500 g/1 lb 2 oz peas, shelled
- 250 g/9 oz carrots, diced
- 2 potatoes, unpeeled
- 1 quantity Classic Mayonnaise (see recipe 105)
- salt

Serves 6

First cook the vegetables. Bring a saucepan of salted water to the boil. Add the peas and cook for 20–30 minutes, until tender. Put the carrot in another pan, pour in water to cover and add a pinch of salt. Bring to the boil and cook for 20–30 minutes, until tender. Put the potatoes into a third pan, pour in water to cover and add a pinch of salt. Bring to the boil and cook for 20–30 minutes, until tender but not falling apart. Drain all the vegetables well and leave to cool. Peel and dice the potatoes. Meanwhile, hard-boil the eggs as described on page 392. Shell and halve lengthways, then scoop out the yolks with a teaspoon, without piercing the whites. Cut a thin slice off the base of each egg white half so that it stands straight. Mix the mayonnaise with the vegetables. Using a teaspoon, fill the egg white halves with this mixture. Sift the egg yolks over the top. (Use a nylon rather than metal sieve.) Chill in the refrigerator for 1 hour. Serve garnished with the watercress.

Note: The potatoes can be replaced with 500 g/1 lb 2 oz Russian Salad (see recipe 21).

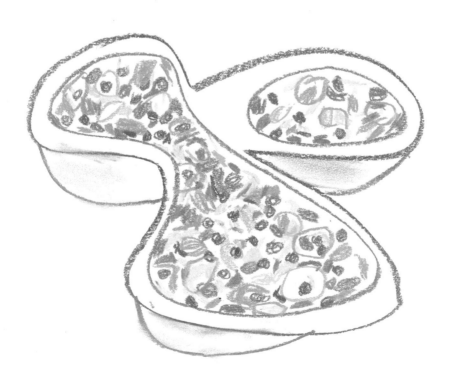

487 Hard-boiled eggs au gratin

HUEVOS DUROS GRATINADOS

- 9 eggs
- 65 g/2 ½ oz butter,
  plus extra for greasing
- 250 g/9 oz mushrooms,
  thinly sliced
- juice of ½ lemon
- 4 tablespoons sunflower oil
- 2 onions, finely chopped
- 2 tablespoons plain flour
- 500 ml/18 fl oz milk
- pinch of freshly grated nutmeg
- 3 tablespoons breadcrumbs
- salt

Serves 6

Hard-boil the eggs as described on page 392. Shell and halve lengthways, then scoop out the yolks with a teaspoon, without piercing the whites. Cut a thin slice off the base of each egg white half so it stands straight. Preheat the oven to 200°C/400°F/Gas Mark 6. Grease an ovenproof dish with butter. Put the mushrooms, the lemon juice and 20 g/¾ oz of the butter into a saucepan, cover and cook over a low heat for 6 minutes. Heat half the oil in a frying pan. Add the onion and cook over a low heat, stirring occasionally, for about 8 minutes, until beginning to brown. Melt 25 g/1 oz of the remaining butter with the remaining oil in a saucepan. Stir in the flour and cook, stirring constantly, for 2 minutes. Gradually stir in the milk, a little at a time. Season with salt and cook, stirring constantly, for 8–10 minutes. Mix together 2 tablespoons of the sauce, the egg yolks, onion, mushrooms and nutmeg in a bowl. Using a teaspoon, fill the egg white halves with this mixture, place in an ovenproof dish and pour the remaining sauce over them. Sprinkle with the breadcrumbs, dot with the remaining butter and bake for 10–15 minutes, until golden brown. Serve immediately straight from the dish.

488 Hard-boiled eggs with hunter's sauce

HUEVOS DUROS CON SALSA CAZADORA

- ½ clove garlic
- 9 eggs
- 4 tablespoons olive oil
- 200 g/7 oz onions, thinly sliced
- 1 kg/2 ¼ lb ripe tomatoes,
  peeled, seeded and chopped
- 250 g/9 oz mushrooms, chopped
- 1 sprig fresh thyme
- 5 tablespoons white wine
- 1 teaspoon sugar
- salt and pepper

Serves 6

Crush the garlic with a pinch of salt in a mortar and stir in 5 tablespoons water. Hard-boil the eggs as described on page 392. Shell and halve lengthways, then cut a thin slice off the base of each egg half so it stands straight and put on a serving dish. Heat the oil in a frying pan. Add the onion and cook over a low heat, stirring occasionally, for about 5 minutes, until softened and translucent. Add the tomato and cook, stirring occasionally and breaking it up with the side of the spoon, for 5 minutes. Add the mushrooms, garlic mixture, thyme and wine, season with pepper and cook for 10 minutes. Stir in the sugar and stir until it dissolves. Pour the sauce over the eggs and serve immediately.

489

Eggs in port jelly
HUEVOS EN GELATINA AL OPORTO

- **8 leaves gelatine**
- **1 litre/1¾ pints chicken stock (home-made or made with a stock cube)**
- **8 eggs**
- **2 tablespoons port**
- **4 slices of ham, chopped**
- **100 g/3½ oz cooked green beans**
- **500 g/1 lb 2 oz Russian Salad (see recipe 21)**

Serves 4

Soak the gelatine in a small bowl of cold water for 10 minutes. Meanwhile, pour the stock into a saucepan and bring to the boil. Squeeze out the gelatine and stir it into the stock. Remove the pan from the heat and leave to cool, stirring occasionally. Meanwhile, hard-boil the eggs as described on page 392, then leave to stand in cold water until required. Stir the port into the cooled stock. Spoon a little of the stock into the base of 4 individual oval moulds to make a layer about 1 cm/½ inch deep. Chill in the refrigerator for 15 minutes, until set. Shell the eggs. Cut the beans into thin strips and arrange decoratively on the base of the moulds once the stock has set. Cover with the ham, put the eggs on top and surround with some of the Russian Salad. Pour in the remaining stock to fill the moulds and chill in the refrigerator until set. To serve, dip the base of the moulds in warm water and turn out on to individual plates. If using hard-boiled eggs, the dish can be kept in the refrigerator for up to 2 days.

Note: This dish is delicious with coddled eggs (see page 398) instead of hard-boiled eggs.

Coddled eggs

How to cook

Bring a saucepan of water with 2 tablespoons salt to the boil. Pass the eggs under cold running water, put them into a wire basket and plunge into the boiling water. When the water comes back to the boil, cook for exactly 5 minutes and remove the pan from the heat. Run cold water into the pan until it is completely cold. This must happen quickly to prevent any further cooking. Leave the eggs in cold water until needed. Shell the eggs very carefully and gently. The eggs can be reheated in warm water for a maximum of 2–3 minutes.

490 Coddled eggs with wine sauce

HUEVOS MOLLETS CON SALSA DE VINO

- 6 eggs
- 3 tablespoons olive oil
- 2 onions, chopped
- 2 tablespoons plain flour
- 500 g/1 lb 2 oz very ripe
  tomatoes, seeded and chopped
- 150 ml/¼ pint dry white wine
- ¼ teaspoon meat extract
- 100 g/3½ oz Serrano ham,
  chopped
- salt and pepper

Serves 6

Coddle the eggs as described on page 398 and leave to stand in cold water. Heat the oil in a frying pan. Add the onion and cook over a low heat, stirring occasionally, for about 8 minutes, until lightly browned. Stir in the flour, add the tomato and cook, stirring frequently, for 5 minutes. Pour in the wine and 275 ml/9 fl oz water and season with salt and pepper. Increase the heat to medium and cook for a further 10 minutes. Carefully shell the eggs and put them into a warm deep serving dish. Stir the meat extract into the frying pan and strain the sauce over the eggs. Sprinkle with the ham, and serve immediately with triangles of fried bread (see recipe 130).

491 Little spinach tarts with coddled eggs

TARTALETAS DE ESPINACAS Y HUEVOS MOLLETS

- 6 eggs
- pinch of bicarbonate of soda
  (optional)
- 1 kg/2¼ lb spinach,
  coarse stalks removed
- 3 tablespoons olive oil
- 750 g/1 lb 10 oz tomatoes,
  seeded and coarsely chopped
- ½ teaspoon sugar
- 6 cooked tartlet cases
  (see recipe 2)
- 20 g/¾ oz butter
- 1 tablespoon plain flour
- 250 ml/8 fl oz milk
- salt

Serves 6

Coddle the eggs as described on page 398 and leave to stand in cold water. Bring a saucepan of salted water to the boil, add a pinch of bicarbonate of soda, then add the spinach, pushing it down into the water with a spoon. Bring back to the boil and cook for 5 minutes, then drain well, pressing down with the back of a spoon to squeeze out as much liquid as possible. Chop very finely. Preheat the oven to 180°C/350°F/Gas Mark 4. Heat 2 tablespoons of the oil in a frying pan. Add the tomato and cook over a medium-low heat, stirring occasionally and breaking it up with the side of the spoon, for 20 minutes. Transfer to a food processor and process to a thick purée. Scrape into a bowl, season with salt and stir in the sugar. Keep warm. Place the tartlet cases on a baking sheet and warm through in the oven. Melt the butter with the remaining oil in a saucepan. Stir in the flour and cook, stirring constantly, for 2 minutes. Gradually stir in the milk, a little at a time. Season with salt and cook, stirring constantly, for 10 minutes. Stir in the spinach and cook for a few minutes more, until heated through. Divide the spinach mixture among the tartlets and keep warm. Carefully shell the eggs and put one on top of each tartlet. Pour a spoonful of hot tomato sauce over each of the eggs and serve immediately.

Poached eggs

How to cook

The most important thing when poaching eggs is to make sure they are fresh. Pour some water into a saucepan or deep frying pan, add 1 tablespoon lemon juice or a good dash of vinegar for each 1 litre/1 ¾ pints water and bring to the boil. Crack each egg into a tea cup and tip it into the water from just above the water level, to prevent the yolk breaking and the white spreading. (Poach up to three eggs at a time.) When the water comes back to the boil, turn the heat down to low and cook for 3 minutes in very hot but not boiling water. Remove with a slotted spoon, put into a cake tin and leave to cool. When the eggs are needed, gradually pour in hot, but not boiling water, a little at a time, to warm them. Do not leave them for more than 3 minutes in this water. Remove very carefully. If they are still dripping water, drain well on a tea towel.

492

Poached eggs with asparagus

HUEVOS ESCALFADOS CON ESPÁRRAGOS

- **18 fresh or canned asparagus spears**
- **50 g/2 oz butter**
- **8 eggs**
- **475 ml/16 fl oz milk**
- **6 slices of bread**
- **2 tablespoons sunflower oil**
- **2 tablespoons plain flour**
- **pinch of freshly grated nutmeg**
- **2 tablespoons white-wine vinegar**
- **salt**

Serves 6

If using fresh asparagus, trim and cook in a saucepan of salted boiling water for 20 minutes, until tender. If using canned asparagus, drain and heat gently. Melt half the butter in a frying pan. Lightly beat two of the eggs in a shallow dish and pour the milk into another shallow dish. Dip the slices of bread first in the milk and then in the beaten eggs. Reserve the remaining milk. Add the bread to the frying pan, in batches, and cook until golden brown on both sides. Remove with a fish slice and keep warm. Melt the remaining butter with the oil in a frying pan. Stir in the flour and cook, stirring constantly, for 2 minutes. Gradually stir in the reserved milk, a little at a time. Cook, stirring constantly, for 6–8 minutes, until thickened. Season with salt, stir in the nutmeg and keep warm. Poach the remaining eggs, three at a time, with the vinegar, as described on page 400. Transfer the bread to a warm serving dish and put an egg on each slice. Cover with the sauce and place the asparagus on top. Serve immediately.

Note: you can use chopped truffles or ham instead of asparagus.

493

Poached eggs with mushrooms

HUEVOS ESCALFADOS CON CHAMPIÑONES

- **300 g/11 oz mushrooms**
- **65 g/2½ oz butter**
- **juice of ½ lemon**
- **6 slices of bread**
- **8 eggs**
- **475 ml/16 fl oz milk**
- **2 tablespoons white wine vinegar**
- **1 tablespoon sunflower oil**
- **2 tablespoons plain flour**
- **salt**

Serves 6

Separate six of the mushroom caps from the stalks and keep the caps whole. Thinly slice the remainder. Put all the mushrooms into a saucepan with 20 g/¾ oz of the butter and the lemon juice. Cover and cook over a low heat for 6 minutes, then remove from the heat and keep warm. Soak and fry the bread, using two of the eggs, the milk and 20 g/¾ oz of the remaining butter, as described in recipe 492. Meanwhile, poach the remaining eggs, three at a time, with the vinegar as described on page 400. Melt the remaining butter with the oil in a saucepan. Stir in the flour and cook, stirring constantly, for 2 minutes. Gradually stir in the reserved milk, a little at a time. Season with salt and cook, stirring constantly, for 6–8 minutes, until thickened. Transfer the slices of bread to a warm serving dish and divide the sliced mushrooms among them. Top each with an egg and cover with a tablespoonful of sauce. Finally, put a whole mushroom cap on top of each egg to garnish. Serve immediately.

Poached eggs in jelly

HUEVOS ESCALFADOS EN GELATINA

- 500 g/1 lb 2 oz gelatine (ready-made or powdered)
- 1 tablespoon sherry (optional)
- 100 g/3½ oz canned peas, drained
- 1 thick slice ham, about 100 g/3½ oz, cut into 6 squares
- 6 eggs
- 2 tablespoons white-wine vinegar
- lettuce leaves

Serves 6

Make the gelatine according to the instructions on the packet and, when cool, stir in the sherry. If using ready-made gelatine, melt it in a heatproof bowl set over a pan of barely simmering water. Pour 3 tablespoons of gelatine into each of six individual moulds or ramekins to cover the base. Chill in the refrigerator for about 15 minutes, until nearly set. Arrange a 'necklace' of peas on the gelatine and put a square of ham in the middle. Poach the eggs, three at a time, with the vinegar, as described on page 400, then drain and leave to cool. Carefully put 1 into each mould or ramekin and pour in the remaining gelatine to cover (it should not be too hot or it will set the eggs). Chill in the refrigerator until set. Make a bed of lettuce on individual plates, turn out the moulds and serve. This dish can be made the night before it is needed.

Eggs en cocotte

How to cook

These eggs are somewhere between poached and shirred eggs. To cook them successfully you will need individual ovenproof cocottes or ramekins. Preheat the oven to 200°C/400°F/Gas Mark 6. Put a small knob of butter, about the size of a hazelnut, into each dish and melt it in the oven or over a pan of barely simmering water for about 1 minute. Alternatively, grease the dishes with the butter. Break an egg into each dish, making sure that the yolk remains whole. Season with salt and put the dishes into a roasting tin. Pour in boiling water to come about halfway up the sides and bake for 4–5 minutes, until the whites have set but the yolks are still runny. Serve the eggs straight from the dishes or remove them carefully, making sure that the yolks do not break. They can also be served cold.

495

- 1 ox kidney, about 400 g/14 oz, trimmed, cored and diced
- 3 tablespoons olive oil
- 1½ tablespoons plain flour
- 175 ml/6 fl oz sherry
- 6 eggs
- salt

Serves 6

Eggs en cocotte with kidneys in sherry

HUEVOS EN CAZUELITAS CON RIÑONES AL JEREZ

Put the pieces of kidney into a frying pan, cover and cook over a medium heat, gently shaking the pan, for 2 minutes. Drain off and discard the cooking juices and transfer the pieces of kidney to a plate. Preheat the oven to 200°C/400°F/Gas Mark 6. Heat the oil in a saucepan. Stir in the flour and cook, stirring constantly, for 10 minutes. Gradually stir in the sherry and 450 ml/¾ pint water, a little at a time. Season with salt and cook, stirring constantly, for 5 minutes. Add the pieces of kidney and cook for a further 3 minutes. Divide the pieces of kidney among six cocottes or ramekins, adding about 1 tablespoon of the sauce to each one. Break an egg into each dish, season with salt and cook as described on page 403. Top each egg with a little of the remaining sauce and serve immediately.

496

- 6 cheese portions
- 20 g/¾ oz butter
- 6 eggs
- 100 g/3½ oz York or other dry-cured ham, chopped
- 6 small pieces of truffle
- salt

Serves 6

Eggs en cocotte with cheese and ham

HUEVOS EN CAZUELITAS CON QUESO EN PORCIONES Y JAMÓN

Preheat the oven to 200°C/400°F/Gas Mark 6. Put a cheese portion and a knob of the butter, about the size of a hazelnut, into each of six cocottes or ramekins. Put the dishes into a roasting tin, pour in boiling water to come about halfway up the sides and bake for about 15 minutes, until the cheese is very soft or almost melted. Break an egg into each dish, lightly season with salt and cook as described on page 403. Sprinkle the ham around the edge of each dish and top each yolk with a piece of truffle. Serve immediately.

497

Eggs en cocotte with mushrooms

HUEVOS EN CAZUELITAS CON CHAMPIÑONES

- **250 g/9 oz mushrooms, thinly sliced**
- **40 g/1½ oz butter**
- **juice of ½ lemon**
- **6 eggs**
- **salt**

Serves 6

Preheat the oven to 200°C/400°F/Gas Mark 6. Put the mushrooms, half the butter and the lemon juice into a saucepan, season with salt, cover and cook over a low heat for 6 minutes. Meanwhile, divide the remaining butter among six cocottes or ramekins. Break an egg into each, season lightly with salt and cook as described on page 403. Remove from the oven and top the eggs with the mushrooms. Serve immediately.

498

Eggs en cocotte with ham, cream and grated cheese

HUEVOS EN CAZUELITAS CON JAMÓN, NATA Y QUESO RALLADO

- **12 tablespoons single cream**
- **100 g/3½ oz York or other dry-cured ham, chopped**
- **6 eggs**
- **50 g/2 oz gruyere cheese, grated**
- **salt**

Serves 6

Preheat the oven to 200°C/400°F/Gas Mark 6. Put 2 tablespoons of the cream into each of six cocottes or ramekins and divide the ham among them. Break an egg into each one, season lightly with salt and sprinkle with the gruyere. Cook as described on page 403. Serve immediately.

499

Eggs en cocotte with tomato sauce and bacon

HUEVOS EN CAZUELITAS CON SALSA DE TOMATE Y BACON

- **5 tablespoons olive oil**
- **750 g/1 lb 10 oz very ripe tomatoes, peeled, seeded and chopped**
- **1 teaspoon sugar**
- **6 thin rashers bacon, halved lengthways**
- **6 eggs**
- **salt**

Serves 6

Preheat the oven to 200°C/400°F/Gas Mark 6. Make a tomato sauce with 3 tablespoons of the oil, the tomatoes and sugar, as described in recipe 73. Meanwhile, heat the remaining oil in a frying pan. Add the bacon and cook, stirring occasionally, for about 5 minutes, until lightly browned. Remove from the pan and drain. Roll up and secure with wooden cocktail sticks. Keep warm. Put 1 heaped tablespoon of the tomato sauce into each of six cocottes or ramekins. Break an egg into each one, season lightly with salt and cook as described on page 403. Remove the cocktail sticks from the bacon rolls and top each egg with two rolls. Serve immediately.

Shirred eggs

How to cook

You will need individual ovenproof egg dishes to cook these eggs successfully. Put about 10 g/¼ oz butter into each dish and melt in a preheated oven, at 160°C/325°F/Gas Mark 3, for 1–2 minutes. Remove from the oven and break an egg into each dish. Season the egg whites lightly with salt and cook for 3–4 minutes until the whites have set but the yolks are still runny. Serve immediately.

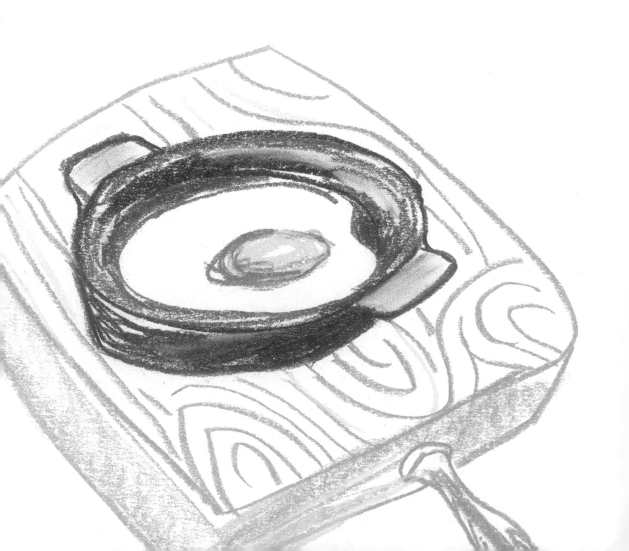

500 Shirred eggs with chicken livers

HUEVOS AL PLATO CON HIGADITOS DE POLLO

- 3 tablespoons olive oil
- 1 small onion, finely chopped
- 6 small chicken livers,
  trimmed and cut into 4 pieces
- 1 tablespoon potato flour
- 2 tablespoons sherry
- 50 g/2 oz butter
- 6 eggs
- 1 tablespoon chopped
  fresh parsley
- salt

Serves 6

Preheat the oven to 160°C/325 °F/Gas Mark 3. Heat the oil in a small frying pan. Add the onion and cook over a low heat, stirring occasionally, for 5 minutes, until softened and translucent. Add the chicken livers and cook, stirring frequently, for 3 minutes. Remove from the pan with a slotted spoon and set aside. Stir the potato flour into the frying pan and cook, stirring constantly, for 2 minutes. Gradually stir in the sherry, a little at a time, then stir in 275 ml/9 fl oz water. Cook, stirring constantly, for 2–3 minutes, then return the livers and onion to the pan and season with salt. Remove from the heat and keep warm. Divide the butter among six egg dishes and melt in the oven. Break an egg into each dish and cook as described on page 406. Gently reheat the sauce and spoon it over the egg whites. Sprinkle with the parsley and serve immediately.

501 Shirred eggs with green asparagus

HUEVOS AL PLATO CON ESPÁRRAGOS VERDES

- 1 bunch of green asparagus,
  trimmed
- 80 g/3 oz butter
- 6 eggs
- salt

Serves 6

Bring a large saucepan of salted water to the boil. Add the asparagus and cook over a medium heat for about 20 minutes, until tender. Meanwhile, preheat the oven to 160°C/325°F/Gas Mark 3. Drain the asparagus well. Melt half the butter in a frying pan. Add the asparagus and cook over a low heat for 5–10 minutes. Meanwhile, divide the remaining butter among six egg dishes. Melt in the oven, then break an egg into each dish and cook as described on page 406. Remove the asparagus from the pan and divide among six warm plates. Add the eggs and serve immediately.

502

Shirred eggs with mashed potato

HUEVOS AL PLATO CON PURÉ DE PATATAS

- 1 kg/2¼ lb potatoes
- 80 g/3 oz butter
- 250 ml/8 fl oz warm milk
- 100 g/3½ oz gruyere cheese, grated
- 6 eggs
- salt

Serves 6

Boil and mash the potatoes with 50 g/2 oz of the butter and the milk as described in recipe 230. Stir in all but 15 g/½ oz of the gruyere. Preheat the oven to 160°C/325°F/Gas Mark 3. Melt 10 g/¼ oz of the remaining butter in an ovenproof dish, then add the mashed potato. Using the back of a spoon, make six hollows in the mash, sprinkle with the remaining cheese and bake for 5 minutes. Remove the dish from the oven and break an egg into each hollow. Lightly season the whites with salt and top the yolks with the remaining butter. Return to the oven and cook as described on page 406. Serve immediately straight from the dish.

503

Shirred eggs, soufflé style, with grated cheese and ham

HUEVOS AL PLATO, ESTILO SOUFFLÉ, CON QUESO RALLADO Y JAMÓN

- 20 g/¾ oz butter
- 6 eggs, separated
- 3 egg whites
- 80 g/3 oz Parmesan cheese, grated
- 1 slice ham, chopped
- salt

Serves 6

Preheat the oven to 160°C/325°F/Gas Mark 3. These eggs are best served in one large dish. Put the butter into an ovenproof dish and melt in the oven. Meanwhile, stiffly whisk all the egg whites in a clean, dry bowl, then fold in all but 3 tablespoons of the Parmesan. Spoon the egg whites into the dish with the butter and smooth the surface, then, using the back of a spoon, make six hollows. Tip the egg yolks into the hollows, sprinkle the remaining cheese over the egg whites and lightly season the yolks with salt. Bake for about 10 minutes, until the cheese is lightly browned. Sprinkle the ham over the yolks and serve immediately.

Fried eggs

How to cook

To fry eggs well it is best to cook them one at a time. If you need to cook them more quickly, use two small frying pans simultaneously. Always use the freshest possible eggs and check that they are not cracked. Break the egg into a cup. Heat plenty of oil in a small frying pan. Slide the egg into the pan and use a fish slice or slotted spoon to baste the white with oil. When the white has set and the egg is loose in the pan, remove with a fish slice and serve. Season the eggs after they have been removed from the pan, otherwise the oil will spatter.

504

Fried eggs with straw potatoes and bacon

HUEVOS FRITOS CON PATATAS PAJA Y BACON

- 1 kg/2¼ lb potatoes,
  cut into julienne strips
- sunflower oil, for deep-frying
- 6 rashers smoked bacon
- 6 eggs
- salt

Serves 6

Deep-fry the potato strips in the oil in a deep frying pan as described in recipe 243. Drain well, season with salt, place in the centre of a round serving dish and keep warm. Drain off half the oil and re-heat the pan. Add the bacon and cook for 4–5 minutes, until lightly browned. Remove from the pan, drain well and place around the edge of the serving dish like the rays of the sun. Fry the eggs as described on page 411. Put the eggs between the rashers of bacon and serve immediately.

505

Eggs in buns

HUEVOS EN BOLLOS

- 6 muffins or individual brioches
- 6 egg yolks
- 4 egg whites
- 1 teaspoon plain flour, sifted
- sunflower oil, for deep-frying
- salt

Tomato sauce:
- 1½ tablespoons sunflower oil
- 750 g/1 lb 10 oz ripe tomatoes,
  peeled, seeded and chopped
- 1 teaspoon sugar
- salt

Serves 6

Make a thick tomato sauce as described in recipe 73. Cut a thin layer off the top of each muffin or brioche and scoop out a hollow in the centre of each. Put a little tomato sauce in the hollows and add an egg yolk to each. Lightly season with salt and put some more tomato sauce around the yolks. Stiffly whisk the egg whites with a pinch of salt in a clean, dry bowl and gently fold in the flour. Divide the egg whites among the muffins or brioches, spooning some on top of each egg yolk and making an attractive pyramid shape using the tines of a fork. Heat the oil in a deep-fryer or deep frying pan to 180–190°C/350–375°F or until a cube of day-old bread browns in 30 seconds. Put a muffin or brioche on to a slotted spoon and lower it into the oil without taking it off the spoon. Use a tablespoon to baste the egg white quickly with oil so that it cooks without the yolk setting. Remove from the oil, transfer to a serving dish and keep warm while cooking the remaining muffins or brioches in the same way. Serve immediately or keep the cooked muffins or brioches in a preheated oven, now turned off to prevent the yolks setting.

Notes: Some people like to stick pine nuts into the egg white. It is attractive but is optional.

506

Fried eggs with rice
HUEVOS FRITOS CON ARROZ

- 350 g/12 oz long-grain rice
- 50 g/2 oz butter
- sunflower oil, for deep-frying
- 6 rashers smoked bacon
  or 3 bananas, peeled
  and halved lengthways
- 1 quantity Classic Tomato Sauce
  (see recipe 73)
- 6 eggs

Serves 6

Boil and drain the rice, then cook in the butter as described in recipe 173. Heat the oil in a frying pan. Add the bacon or bananas and cook for about 5 minutes, until lightly browned. Remove from the pan, drain and keep warm. Heat the tomato sauce. Fry the eggs as described on page 411. Make a ring of rice on a warm round serving dish. Spoon the tomato sauce into the middle and put the bacon or bananas on top of the rice. Place the fried eggs around the rice and serve immediately.

507

Fried eggs in breadcrumbs
HUEVOS FRITOS ENCAPOTADOS

- 750 ml/1¼ pints sunflower oil,
  plus extra for brushing
- 8 eggs
- 20 g/¾ oz butter
- 2 tablespoons olive oil
- 3 tablespoons plain flour
- 750 ml/1¼ pints milk
- 50 g/2 oz breadcrumbs
- deep-fried parsley sprigs
  (see recipe 918)
- 1 quantity Classic Tomato Sauce
  (see recipe 73)
- salt

Serves 6

Brush a marble slab or baking sheet with oil. Heat half the sunflower oil in a frying pan. Fry six of the eggs as described on page 411. Transfer to the marble slab or baking sheet and trim the edges to give them a neat round shape. Melt the butter with the olive oil in a saucepan. Stir in the flour and cook, stirring constantly, for 2 minutes. Gradually stir in the milk, a little at a time. Cook, stirring constantly, for about 8 minutes, until thickened. Season with salt, remove the pan from the heat and leave to cool slightly, stirring occasionally. Spoon enough sauce over each fried egg to cover it completely. Refrigerate until the eggs are completely cold. Beat the remaining eggs in a shallow dish and spread out the breadcrumbs in another shallow dish. Dip the coated eggs first in the beaten eggs and then in the breadcrumbs. Add the remaining sunflower oil to the frying pan and heat to 180–190°C/350–375°F or until a cube of day-old bread browns in 30 seconds. Add the coated eggs to the hot oil and cook, in batches, until golden brown. Serve immediately, garnished with the fried parsley, and offer the tomato sauce separately.

Scrambled eggs

How to cook

Allow 2 eggs per serving. Break the eggs into a saucepan and beat for 30 seconds with a fork. Immediately add a pinch of salt, 2 tablespoons milk for every 4 eggs and 20 g/¾ oz butter (also for every 4 eggs). Put the pan in a roasting tin half filled with very hot water set over a low heat. Whisk constantly, especially around the sides of the pan where the eggs will set first. When the mixture is thick and creamy, remove the pan from the heat as the eggs will continue to cook off the heat. Stir in a dash of single cream and serve immediately.

508

Scrambled eggs with rice and prawns

HUEVOS REVUELTOS CON ARROZ Y GAMBAS

- **pinch of saffron threads**
- **400 g/14 oz long-grain rice**
- **250 g/9 oz raw prawns, peeled**
- **130 g/4½ oz butter**
- **12 eggs**
- **6 tablespoons milk**
- **4 tablespoons single cream**
- **salt**

Serves 6

Bring 3 litres/5¼ pints unsalted water to the boil in a saucepan. Crush the saffron in a mortar with a little water and add to the pan. Add the rice and cook over a high heat for about 15 minutes, until tender. Drain well, refresh under cold running water, drain again and set aside. Put the prawns, 20 g/¾ oz of the butter and a pinch of salt into a small saucepan. Cover and cook for about 5 minutes. Melt 50 g/2 oz of the remaining butter in a frying pan. Add the rice, season with salt and heat through. Meanwhile, beat the eggs with a fork in another saucepan. Add the prawns, milk, remaining butter and a pinch of salt. Put the pan into a roasting tin half filled with very hot water and cook as described above. Stir in the cream. If you like, spoon the rice into a ring mould and turn out on to a warm serving plate. Put the scrambled eggs and prawns into the middle and serve immediately. Alternatively, serve the scrambled eggs and prawns with the rice on the side.

Note: You can add 100 g/3½ oz cooked or canned peas to the rice while it is frying.

509

Scrambled eggs on toast with truffles
HUEVOS REVUELTOS EN TOSTADAS CON TRUFAS

- 50 g/2 oz truffles
- 500 ml/18 fl oz sunflower oil
- 6 slices of bread
- 6 tablespoons milk
- 13 eggs
- 100 g/3½ oz butter
- 4 tablespoons single cream
- salt

Serves 6

Drain the truffles, reserving the liquid from the cans. Cut six thin slices of truffle for the garnish and set aside. Finely chop the remainder. Heat the oil in a frying pan. Put the slices of bread in a shallow dish, add the milk and leave to soak. Lightly beat one of the eggs in another shallow dish. Add the slices of bread, then transfer to the frying pan, in batches, and cook until golden brown on both sides. Remove from the pan, drain and keep warm. Lightly beat the remaining eggs with the soaking milk, the butter and the reserved truffle liquid in a saucepan. Put the pan into a roasting tin half filled with very hot water and cook as described on page 415. Stir in the cream and chopped truffles. Divide the scrambled eggs among the slices of fried bread, garnish each portion with a truffle slice and serve immediately.

510

Scrambled eggs on toast with sausages
HUEVOS REVUELTOS EN TOSTADAS CON SALCHICHAS

- 13 eggs
- 500 ml/18 fl oz sunflower oil
- 6 slices of bread
- 6 tablespoons milk
- 6 frankfurter sausages
- 40 g/1½ oz butter
- 4 tablespoons single cream
- 6 tablespoons Classic Tomato Sauce (see recipe 73)
- salt

Serves 6

Heat the oil in a frying pan and lightly beat one egg in a shallow dish. Soak the slices of bread in the milk and then in the beaten egg and fry, as described in recipe 509. Remove from the pan, drain and keep warm. Bring a saucepan of water just to boiling point, add the frankfurters, then lower the heat and warm through. Lightly beat the remaining eggs with the butter and the soaking milk in a saucepan. Put the pan into a roasting tin half filled with very hot water and cook as described on page 415. Stir in the cream and divide the scrambled eggs among the slices of fried bread. Halve the frankfurters and put a half on either side of each slice of fried bread. Spoon the warmed tomato sauce on the other two sides. Serve immediately.

511

Artichoke hearts with scrambled eggs

FONDOS DE ALCACHOFAS CON HUEVOS REVUELTOS

- 4–6 large globe artichokes
- ½ lemon
- 8 eggs
- 4–5 tablespoons milk
  or single cream
- 40 g/1½ oz butter
- 1 truffle, cut into 6 slices
- salt

Serves 4–6

Break off the stems from the artichokes and cut off and discard the tough outer leaves. Trim the remaining leaves to about halfway and remove and discard the chokes. Trim the bases of the artichokes so they will not tip over when filled. Rub all over with the lemon half to prevent discoloration. Bring a saucepan of salted water to the boil, add the artichokes and cook for about 30 minutes, until tender. Remove from the pan and drain upside down, covered with a tea towel to keep warm. Lightly beat the eggs with half the milk or cream and 25 g/1 oz of the butter in a saucepan. Put the pan into a roasting tin half filled with very hot water and cook as described on page 415. Stir in the remaining milk or cream and butter. Place the artichokes in a warm serving dish, fill with the scrambled eggs and top each with a slice of truffle. Serve immediately.

512

Scrambled eggs with potatoes and peas or asparagus

HUEVOS REVUELTOS CON PATATAS Y GUISANTES O ESPÁRRAGOS

- 500 g/1 lb 2 oz shelled peas
- pinch of bicarbonate of soda
- 750 ml/1¼ pints sunflower oil
- 1.5 kg/3¼ lb potatoes, diced
- 8 eggs
- salt

Serves 4

Bring a saucepan of salted water to the boil. Add the peas and bicarbonate of soda and cook for about 30 minutes, until tender. Drain well. Meanwhile, heat the oil in a frying pan to 180–190°C/350–375°F or until a cube of day-old bread browns in 30 seconds. Add the potato and cook for about 15 minutes, until golden brown. Remove from the pan with a slotted spoon, drain and keep warm. Drain off most of the oil from the pan, leaving just enough to prevent the eggs from sticking, and heat. Meanwhile, lightly beat the eggs with a pinch of salt in a bowl. Add to the pan and cook, whisking constantly, until creamy. Stir in the peas and potato and serve immediately.

Note: You can use drained canned peas instead of fresh or replace the peas with fresh or canned green or white asparagus. Instead of stirring the potato into the eggs, you could arrange it around the edge of a serving dish with the eggs in the centre.

513

Portuguese scrambled eggs with straw potatoes and salt cod

HUEVOS REVUELTOS CON PATATAS PAJA Y BACALAO (A LA PORTUGUESA)

- 250 g/9 oz salt cod fillet
  (not soaked)
- 1.2 kg/2½ lb potatoes,
  cut into fine julienne strips
- sunflower oil, for deep-frying
- 1 large onion, finely chopped
- 8 eggs
  Serves 4

To serve the cod raw, Portuguese-style, remove and discard any skin and bones, then flake the flesh finely. If you prefer to cook it, put it into a saucepan, pour in water to cover and bring to the boil. Lift out the fish with a fish slice, remove and discard any skin and bones and flake the flesh. Cook the potato strips in the hot oil as described in recipe 243. Drain well and set aside. Transfer about 6 tablespoons of the oil to a large frying pan and heat. Add the onion and cook over a low heat, stirring occasionally, for about 10 minutes, until golden brown. Increase the heat to high, add the straw potatoes and fish, break the eggs into the pan and cook, stirring constantly, until the eggs begin to set. Serve immediately.

514

Scrambled eggs with tomato

HUEVOS REVUELTOS CON TOMATES

- 9 eggs
- salt
- 3 tablespoons milk
- 30 g/1 oz butter

Tomato sauce:
- 2 tablespoons sunflower oil
- 2 onions, finely chopped
- 1 kg/2¼ lb ripe tomatoes,
  peeled, seeded and chopped
- ½ teaspoon sugar
- salt
  Serves 6

Make a thick tomato sauce as described in recipe 73 and keep warm. Beat the eggs with a pinch of salt in a saucepan for 30 seconds, then add the milk and butter. Put the pan into a roasting tin half filled with very hot water and cook as described on page 415. Stir in the tomato sauce and serve immediately, with several triangles of fried bread (see recipe 130).

515

Scrambled eggs with grated cheese
HUEVOS REVUELTOS CON QUESO RALLADO

- **12 eggs**
- **5 tablespoons milk**
- **40 g/1½ oz butter**
- **100 g/3½ oz gruyere
  or Parmesan cheese, grated**
- **salt**

Serves 6

Beat the eggs in a saucepan for 30 seconds, add the milk, half the butter and the gruyere. Put the pan into a roasting tin half filled with very hot water and cook as described on page 415. Remove the pan from the heat and stir in the remaining butter. Season to taste with salt and serve immediately, with buttered toast or triangles of fried bread (see recipe 130).

Omelettes

How to cook

Allow 1½–2 eggs per serving, but it is advisable not to use more than 6 eggs at a time, as the fatter the omelette, the more difficult it is to produce a good one. Over a high heat, heat enough sunflower oil to cover the base of a frying pan. Meanwhile, beat the eggs vigorously with a pinch of salt in a bowl for 1 minute. Tip the eggs into the pan and pull them from the edge of the pan to the centre with a fork or spatula. Cook until the underside is set and lightly browned. Fold the omelette using a spatula.

Tricks

- To make a Spanish omelette succulent, add 1 teaspoon baking powder to the eggs and, if it is a potato omelette, add 150 ml/¼ pint milk to the eggs. Add a dash of milk to the beaten eggs when preparing a folded omelette
- To flip an omelette professionally, tilt the pan, holding the handle in your left hand so that the omelette slides towards the edge. Holding a spatula in your right hand, roll the omelette under from the edge opposite the handle. Then gently hit the handle of the pan with your right hand and the omelette will slide in the pan and roll over on itself. Adjust the shape slightly with a fork, slide the omelette on to a plate and serve immediately. If this does not work out the first time, do not despair. Even great chefs take time to learn the trick.

516

French omelette

TORTILLA A LA FRANCESA

- **2 tablespoons sunflower oil**
- **4 eggs**
- **½ tablespoon chopped fresh parsley**
- **salt**

Serves 2

Heat the oil in a frying pan. Beat the eggs vigorously with a pinch of salt for 1 minutes. Add the parsley and cook as described above. Serve immediately.

517

Soufflé omelette with parsley or cheese

TORTILLA SOUFFLÉ CON PEREJIL O QUESO

- 3 eggs
- 3 tablespoons sunflower oil
- ½ teaspoon chopped fresh
  parsley or 2 tablespoons
  grated gruyere cheese
- salt

Serves 2

Separate two of the eggs. Whisk the whites in a clean, dry bowl until they form soft peaks. Heat the oil in a frying pan. Beat the remaining egg and the egg yolks with a pinch of salt in a bowl. Fold in the egg whites and parsley, if using, and cook as described on page 422. Alternatively, beat the egg and egg yolks with the cheese, fold in the egg whites and cook as described on page 422. Serve immediately.

518

Omelette with grated cheese, ham and croûtons

TORTILLA CON QUESO RALLADO, JAMÓN Y CUSCURROS DE PAN FRITO

- 250 ml/8 fl oz sunflower oil
- 2 slices of bread,
  crusts removed, cubed
- 6 eggs
- 50 g/2 oz gruyere cheese, grated
- 5 tablespoons milk
- 150 g/5 oz Serrano ham,
  chopped
- salt

Serves 6

Heat the oil in a frying pan. Add the bread cubes and cook, stirring occasionally, for a few minutes, until golden brown. Remove from the pan and drain well. Beat the eggs vigorously in a bowl for 1 minute. Add the gruyere, milk and ham and season lightly with salt. (Bear in mind that the cheese and ham are salty.) Transfer enough oil to another frying pan just to cover the base and heat. Add the egg mixture and cook as described on page 422, until beginning to set. Sprinkle with the croûtons and cook until the omelette sets around the edges but is still liquid in the middle – about 6 minutes. Fold it in half, transfer to a warm dish and serve immediately.

519

Ham omelette

TORTILLA DE JAMÓN

- 3 tablespoons sunflower oil
- 25 g/1 oz Serrano ham, diced
- 4 eggs
- salt

Serves 2

If the ham is very salty, leave to soak in warm milk for 10 minutes, then drain and pat dry. Heat 1 tablespoon of the oil in a frying pan. Add the ham and cook, stirring occasionally, for a few minutes, until lightly browned. Remove with a slotted spoon. Add the remaining oil to the pan and heat. Meanwhile, beat the eggs vigorously in a bowl for 1 minute. Add the ham and season lightly with salt. Tip into the pan and cook as described on page 422. Serve immediately.

520

Omelette with mushrooms, asparagus, spinach, truffles or prawns

TORTILLA DE CHAMPIÑONES O ESPÁRRAGOS, O ESPINACAS, O TRUFAS, O GAMBAS

- 100 g/3½ oz mushrooms, thinly sliced or 100 g/3½ oz asparagus tips, trimmed or 50 g/2 oz leftover cooked spinach or 2 truffles, thinly sliced or 100 g/ 3½ oz raw prawns, peeled
- 15–25 g/½–1 oz butter
- dash of lemon juice (optional)
- 1 tablespoon Madeira wine (optional)
- 3 tablespoons sunflower oil
- 3 eggs
- salt

Serves 2

If using the mushrooms, cook them with 15 g/½ oz butter and the lemon juice as described in recipe 470. If using the asparagus, bring a saucepan of salted water to the boil. Add the asparagus and cook for about 10 minutes, until tender. Drain well and gently pat dry. Melt 20 g/¾ oz butter in a frying pan. Add the asparagus and cook over a low heat for a few minutes. If using leftover cooked spinach, melt 25 g/1 oz butter in a frying pan. Add the spinach and cook, stirring occasionally, for a few minutes. If using truffles, put them into a frying pan, add 20 g/¾ oz butter and the Madeira and heat gently. If using prawns, melt 25 g/1 oz butter in a frying pan. Add the prawns and a pinch of salt and cook over a medium-high heat, stirring frequently, for 3–5 minutes, until opaque. Remove from the pan. Heat the oil in a frying pan. Meanwhile, beat the eggs vigorously with a pinch of salt in a bowl for 1 minute. If using mushrooms, asparagus, spinach or truffles, tip the eggs into the pan and cook as described on page 422. Using a slotted spoon put the chosen filling in the middle, fold over the omelette and serve. If using prawns, put them into the pan before adding the eggs. Serve immediately.

521

Omelette with tuna in brine

TORTILLA DE ATÚN ESCABECHADO

- **5 tablespoons sunflower oil**
- **1 small onion, chopped**
- **50 g/2 oz tuna in brine**
- **4 eggs**
- **salt**

Serves 2

Heat 2 tablespoons of the oil in a frying pan. Add the onion and cook over a low heat, stirring occasionally, for about 5 minutes, until softened but not browned. Add the tuna and cook for a few minutes, breaking up the fish with a fork or slotted spoon. Heat the remaining oil in another frying pan. Meanwhile, beat the eggs vigorously with a pinch of salt in a bowl for 1 minute. Tip into the frying pan and cook as described on page 422. When the eggs begin to set, put the tuna mixture in the middle, fold over the omelette and serve immediately.

Note: This dish can be served with Classic Tomato Sauce (see recipe 73) poured around the omelette.

522

Little omelettes filled with aubergine

TORTILLITAS RELLENAS DE BERENJENAS

- **500 g/1 lb 2 oz aubergines, peeled**
- **5 tablespoons sunflower oil**
- **250 g/9 oz onions, finely chopped**
- **1 heaped tablespoon plain flour**
- **300 ml/½ pint milk**
- **8 eggs**
- **50 g/2 oz gruyere cheese, grated**
- **salt**

  Tomato sauce:
- **3 tablespoons sunflower oil**
- **100 g/3½ oz onion, chopped**
- **1.5 kg/3¼ lb tomatoes, peeled, seeded and chopped**
- **1 teaspoon sugar**
- **salt**

Serves 4

Make the tomato sauce as described in recipe 73. Put the aubergines through a mincer or process in a food processor. Heat 3 tablespoons of the oil in a frying pan. Add the onion and aubergine and cook over a low heat, stirring occasionally, for 8–10 minutes, until lightly browned. Stir in the flour and cook, stirring constantly, for 2 minutes. Gradually stir in the milk, a little at a time. Season with salt and cook, stirring constantly, for about 10 minutes, until thickened. Preheat the oven to 200°C/400°F/Gas Mark 6. Using the remaining oil and the eggs, make little one-egg omelettes in a small frying pan as described on page 422. As each one sets, put a spoonful of the aubergine mixture in the middle, fold over and slide on to an ovenproof dish. When all the omelettes have been cooked, pour the tomato sauce over them, sprinkle with the gruyere and bake for about 8 minutes, until golden brown. Serve immediately straight from the dish, allowing two omelettes per serving.

Spanish potato omelette

TORTILLA DE PATATAS A LA ESPAÑOLA

- **500 ml/18 fl oz sunflower oil**
- **1 kg/2 ¼ lb potatoes, halved lengthways and thinly sliced**
- **8 eggs**
- **2 tablespoons olive oil**
- **salt**

Serves 6

Heat the sunflower oil in a frying pan. Add the potato slices and cook, stirring occasionally, until softened and lightly browned. Season with salt, remove from the pan and drain well. Beat the eggs vigorously with a pinch of salt in a large bowl for 1 minute. Add the potato slices and stir with a fork. Heat the olive oil in a large frying pan. Tip in the egg mixture and cook, gently shaking the pan occasionally, until the underside is set and lightly browned. Invert the omelette on to the pan lid or a plate, then gently slide it back into the pan, cooked side up. Cook, gently shaking the pan occasionally, until the underside is set and golden brown. Serve immediately.

Note: The omelette can be made with Chips (see recipe 242) and accompanied by Classic Mayonnaise (see recipe 105), either poured over it or offered separately.

524

Spanish potato omelette with sauce

TORTILLA DE PATATAS GUISADA

- 500 ml/18 fl oz sunflower oil
- 1.3 kg/3 lb potatoes, halved lengthways and thinly sliced
- 8 eggs
- 2 tablespoons olive oil
- salt

  Sauce:
- 4 tablespoons olive oil
- 1 onion, finely chopped
- 1½ tablespoons plain flour
- pinch of saffron threads
- 1 tablespoon chopped fresh parsley
- 100 g/3½ oz Serrano ham, chopped
- 100 g/3½ oz canned peas, drained
- salt

  Serves 6

Make a thick Spanish Potato Omelette with the sunflower oil, potatoes, eggs, olive oil and salt (see recipe 523). Keep it warm in the frying pan. To make the sauce, heat the olive oil in another frying pan. Add the onion and cook over a low heat, stirring occasionally, for about 7 minutes, until beginning to brown. Stir in the flour and cook, stirring constantly, for 2 minutes. Gradually stir in 750 ml/1¼ pints water, a little at a time. Crush the saffron and parsley in a mortar and stir in a little of the sauce, then stir into the frying pan. Simmer for 5 minutes, then strain into a saucepan. Add the ham and simmer for a further 5 minutes, then add the peas and season lightly with salt (bearing in mind that the ham is salty). Pour the sauce over the omelette and cook over a low heat for 2 minutes. Slide the omelette on to a warm serving dish with the sauce-covered side up. Cut into squares and serve. Alternatively, slide the omelette on to a serving dish before adding the sauce. Cut the omelette into squares and pour the sauce over them. This way, the omelette will be drier in the middle.

525

Green pepper omelette

TORTILLA DE PIMIENTOS VERDES

- 3 tablespoons olive oil
- 1 green pepper, seeded and cut into strips
- 4 eggs
- 1 quantity Classic Tomato Sauce (see recipe 73)
- salt

  Serves 2

Heat the oil in a frying pan. Add the green pepper, season with salt, cover and cook over a low heat for 15 minutes. Drain off the oil. Beat the eggs vigorously with a pinch of salt in a bowl for 1 minute. Add to the pepper and mix well, then cook as described in recipe 523. Serve immediately, covered in tomato sauce if you like.

526

Three-layer omelette with tomato sauce

TRES PISOS DE TORTILLAS CON SALSA DE TOMATE

- **500 ml/18 fl oz sunflower oil**
- **4 large potatoes, halved lengthways and thinly sliced**
- **12 eggs**
- **150 g/5 oz canned tuna, drained and flaked**
- **500 g/1 lb 2 oz canned peas, drained**
- **100 g/3½ oz Serrano ham, finely chopped**
- **1 quantity Classic Tomato Sauce (see recipe 73)**
- **salt**

Serves 6

Make a Spanish potato omelette with half the sunflower oil, the potatoes, four of the eggs and salt as described in recipe 523. Transfer to a serving dish and keep warm. Beat four of the remaining eggs vigorously with a pinch of salt in a bowl for 1 minute and add the tuna. If necessary, add more oil to the frying pan and reheat. Tip in the egg mixture and cook as described in recipe 523. Put the tuna omelette on top of the potato omelette and keep warm. Beat the remaining eggs vigorously with a pinch of salt in a bowl for 1 minute and add the peas and ham. If necessary, add more oil to the pan and reheat. Tip in the egg mixture and cook as described in recipe 523. Put the ham and pea omelette on top of the tuna omelette. Pour the warmed tomato sauce over the stack of omelettes and serve immediately.

Note: The base of this dish should always be a potato omelette but you can vary the other two layers according to taste. For example, instead of tuna, use prawns and substitute asparagus for the peas or substitute chorizo for the ham.

Savoury custards and soufflés

527

- **25 g/1 oz butter,**
  plus extra for greasing
- **2 tablespoons sunflower oil**
- **4 tablespoons plain flour**
- **500 ml/18 fl oz milk**
- **5 eggs, separated**
- **250 g/9 oz cooked peeled**
  prawns or 150 g/5 oz finely
  chopped Serrano ham (optional)
- **3 egg whites**
- **1 quantity Classic Tomato Sauce**
  (see recipe 73)
- **pinch of freshly grated nutmeg**
  or ground pepper
- **salt**

Serves

Egg custard with tomato sauce
FLAN DE HUEVOS CON SALSA DE TOMATE

Make the tomato sauce as described in recipe 73. Preheat the oven to 180°C/350°F/Gas Mark 4. Generously grease an 18-cm/7-inch flan tin with butter. Melt the butter with the oil in a frying pan. Stir in the flour and cook, stirring constantly, for 2–3 minutes, but do not allow the flour to brown. Gradually stir in the milk, a little at a time. Season with salt and the nutmeg or pepper and cook, stirring constantly, for about 10 minutes, until thickened. Remove the pan from the heat and leave to cool. Stir in the egg yolks one at a time. Stir in the prawns or ham, if using. Stiffly whisk all the egg whites with a pinch of salt in a clean, dry bowl until stiff. Gently fold them into the sauce in three or four batches, then pour the mixture into the prepared tin. Put the tin in a roasting tin and pour in boiling water to come about halfway up the sides. Bake for about 1 hour, until set. Just before serving, reheat the tomato sauce. Remove the tin from the oven, run a round-bladed knife around the edge and turn the custard out on to a warm serving dish. Pour the hot tomato sauce over it and serve immediately.

Note: The custard may also be served with a Classic Béchamel Sauce (see recipe 77) mixed with 2–3 tablespoons tomato sauce or 1 tablespoon tomato purée. Alternatively, make a béchamel sauce with half milk and half stock.

Savoury custard

FLAN SALADO

- **butter, for greasing**
- **8 eggs**
- **100 g/3 ½ oz Serrano ham, finely chopped**
- **5 tablespoons sherry**
- **pinch of freshly grated nutmeg**
- **750 ml/1 ¼ pints warm milk**
- **salt**

Béchamel sauce:
- **20 g/¾ oz butter**
- **2 tablespoons sunflower oil**
- **1 tablespoon plain flour**
- **275 ml/9 fl oz milk**
- **1 tablespoon tomato purée or 2 tablespoons Classic Tomato Sauce (see recipe 73)**
- **salt**

Serves 6

Preheat the oven to 160°C/325°F/Gas Mark 3. Grease a ring mould with butter. Beat the eggs in a bowl, add the ham, sherry and nutmeg and season with salt (bearing in mind that the ham is salty). Mix well, then gradually stir in the milk, a little at a time. Pour the mixture into the prepared mould and bake (not in a water bath) for 30–40 minutes, until set. Meanwhile, make the béchamel sauce as described in recipe 77 and stir in the tomato purée or tomato sauce. Keep the sauce warm. Remove the custard from the oven and turn out on to a serving dish. Fill the centre with the béchamel sauce and serve immediately.

529

· 20 g/¾ oz butter,
  plus extra for greasing
· 8 eggs
· 100 g/3½ oz Serrano ham,
  finely chopped
· 5 tablespoons sherry
· pinch of freshly grated nutmeg
· 750 ml/1¼ pints warm milk
· 1 quantity Classic Béchamel
  Sauce (see recipe 77)
· 200 g/7 oz mushrooms
· juice of ½ lemon
· salt

Serves 6

Savoury custard with mushrooms

FLAN SALADO CON CHAMPIÑONES

Preheat the oven to 160°C/325°F/Gas Mark 3. Grease a ring mould with butter. Beat the eggs in a bowl, add the ham, sherry and nutmeg and season with salt (bearing in mind that the ham is salty). Mix well, then gradually stir in the milk, a little at a time. Pour the mixture into the prepared mould and bake (not in a water bath) for 30–40 minutes, until set. Meanwhile, make the béchamel sauce as described in recipe 77. Keep the sauce warm. Cut the mushrooms into large pieces and put into a saucepan with the butter. lemon juice and a pinch of salt. Cook over a medium heat for 6 minutes. Remove the custard from the oven and turn out on to a serving dish. Fill the centre with the béchamel sauce and place the mushrooms around the custard. Serve immediately.

530

· 80 g/3 oz butter,
  plus extra for greasing
· 4 tablespoons plain flour
· 4 teaspoons potato flour
· 500 ml/18 fl oz milk
· 100 g/3½ oz gruyere cheese,
  grated
· 5 eggs, separated
· 3–4 egg whites
· salt

Serves 6–8

Cheese soufflé

SOUFFLÉ DE QUESO

Preheat the oven to 180°C/350°F/Gas Mark 4. Generously grease a 22 cm soufflé dish with butter. Melt the butter in a frying pan. Stir in the flour and potato flour and cook, stirring constantly, for 2 minutes. Gradually stir in the milk, a little at a time. Bring to the boil, stirring constantly, then lower the heat and simmer, still stirring, for 5 minutes. Remove the pan from the heat and stir in the gruyere. Leave to cool slightly. Stir in the egg yolks, one at a time, then season to taste with salt. Whisk half the egg whites in a clean, dry bowl until stiff. Gently fold into the mixture. Repeat with the remaining egg whites. Pour the mixture into the prepared dish and bake for 20 minutes. Increase the oven temperature to 220°C/425°F/Gas Mark 7 and bake for a further 10–15 minutes, until risen and golden brown. Serve immediately. A soufflé cannot wait even a few minutes as it will collapse.

Note: The basic method for soufflés is always the same, only the flavouring ingredients change. For a prawn soufflé, put 250 g/9 oz peeled raw prawns into a saucepan with 25 g/1 oz butter and a pinch of salt. Cover and cook over a medium heat for 6–8 minutes, then stir the mixture into the sauce. Continue as above.

531

Custards with tomato sauce
FLANECILLOS CON SALSA DE TOMATE

- **butter, for greasing**
- **7 eggs**
- **120 ml/4 fl oz milk**
- **pinch of freshly grated nutmeg**
- **salt**

  Tomato sauce:
- **3 tablespoons sunflower oil**
- **750 g/1 lb 10 oz ripe tomatoes,**
  peeled, seeded and chopped
- **1 teaspoon sugar**
- **salt**

Serves 4

Make the tomato sauce as described in recipe 73. Preheat the oven to 160°C/325°F/Gas Mark 3. Grease four individual flan tins with butter. Beat the eggs in a bowl, add the milk and nutmeg, season with salt and mix well. Pour the egg mixture into the prepared tins. Put the flan tins into a roasting tin, pour in boiling water to come halfway up the sides and bake for about 15 minutes, until set. Put the tomato sauce in a warm serving dish and turn the custards out on top of the sauce. Serve immediately.

Note: This dish can also be made with Béchamel Sauce with Tomato (see recipe 78) instead of tomato sauce.

532

- 1.2 kg/2½ lb potatoes,
  cut into pieces
- 50 g/2 oz butter, cut into small
  pieces, plus extra for greasing
- 250 ml/8 fl oz hot milk
- 4 eggs, separated
- pinch of freshly grated nutmeg
- 3 egg whites
- salt

Serves 4–6

Potato soufflé
SOUFFLÉ DE PATATAS

Put the potato into a saucepan, pour in water to cover and add a pinch of salt. Bring to the boil and cook for 20–30 minutes, until tender but not falling apart. Meanwhile, preheat the oven to 200°C/400°F/Gas Mark 6. Grease a 22 cm soufflé dish with butter. Drain the potato well and push through a sieve or press through a ricer into a bowl. Immediately add the butter, then gradually stir in the milk, a little at a time. Stir the egg yolks into the mash and add the nutmeg. Whisk half the egg whites with a pinch of salt in a clean, dry bowl until stiff. Gently fold into the mixture. Repeat with the remaining egg whites. Tip the mixture into the prepared dish and bake for 45 minutes, until golden brown. Serve immediately.

533

- 40 g/1½ oz butter,
  plus extra for greasing
- 2 tablespoons sunflower oil
- 1½ tablespoons plain flour
- 750 ml/1¼ pints milk
- 4 eggs, separated
- 225 g/8 oz cooked long-grain
  rice
- 100 g/3½ oz gruyere cheese,
  grated
- 2 egg whites
- salt

Serves 4–6

Rice soufflé
SOUFFLÉ DE ARROZ BLANCO

Preheat the oven to 180°C/350°F/Gas Mark 4. Grease a 22 cm soufflé dish with butter. Melt 25 g/1 oz of the butter with the oil in a saucepan. Stir in the flour and cook, stirring constantly, for 2 minutes. Gradually stir in the milk, a little at a time. Season with salt and cook, stirring constantly, for 8 minutes, until thickened. Remove the pan from the heat and leave to cool slightly. Stir in the egg yolks, one at a time, then add half the rice and all but 15 g/½ oz of the gruyere. Dot with the remaining butter. Whisk the egg whites with a pinch of salt in a clean, dry bowl until stiff. Fold in the remaining rice, then fold the rice and egg whites into the rice and egg yolk mixture. Tip into the prepared dish, sprinkle with the remaining cheese and bake for 20 minutes. Increase the oven temperature to 220°C/425°F/Gas Mark 7 and bake for a further 15 minutes, until risen and golden brown. Serve immediately.

FISH AND SEAFOOD

Fish

Before preparing fish for any recipe, rinse all fish under cold running water and immediately pat dry.

534

Fish poached in quick white wine stock

CALDO CORTO CON VINO BLANCO

• 1 kg / 2 ¼ lb fish, such as sole,
  hake or whiting

Quick white wine stock:
• 1 bay leaf
• 1 thick slice of onion
• 1 large carrot, sliced
• 175 ml / 6 fl oz white wine
• juice of ½ lemon
• salt

Serves 4–6

Put all the stock ingredients into a large saucepan, pour in 2 litres / 3 ½ pints water and bring to the boil. Lower the heat and simmer for about 10 minutes, then remove the pan from the heat and leave to cool. When ready to poach the fish, remove the rack from a fish kettle and pour in the stock. Put the fish on the rack and replace the rack so that it is positioned over the vegetables. If the stock does not cover the fish, add some water. Set the kettle over a medium heat, cover and bring just to the boil. If you are cooking flat fish, such as sole, turn off the heat immediately and leave the fish in the stock for 5–6 minutes. If you are cooking round fish, such as hake, lower the heat and simmer gently for a few minutes, until the flesh flakes easily. Lift up the rack and place it diagonally across the top of the fish kettle so that the fish drains well without getting cold. Wring out a clean tea towel in very hot water and place it over the fish to keep it warm until you are ready to serve.

Notes: To cook fish in a red wine or red-wine vinegar stock, prepare the stock and cook as described above, substituting red wine or red-wine vinegar for the white wine. This stock can be used to give colour and flavour to fish such as trout and pike. If you do not have a fish kettle, you can cook the fish in the stock in a frying pan. Lift it out with a slotted spoon and drain in a colander set over the frying pan.

535

Fish poached in quick stock with milk

CALDO CORTO CON LECHE

- 1 kg/2¼ lb fish, such as sole,
  hake or whiting

Quick stock with milk:
- 250 ml/8 fl oz milk
- ½ lemon, peeled and sliced
- 1 bay leaf
- salt

Serves 4

Bring the milk just to the boil in a saucepan, then remove from the heat and leave to cool. Remove the rack from a fish kettle, pour in the milk, add the lemon, bay leaf and a pinch of salt and pour in 1.5 litres/2½ pints water. Put the fish on the rack and replace the rack. There should always be plenty of stock to cover the fish. Increase the quantities as necessary. Poach the fish until the flesh flakes easily. This stock is mainly used for fish such as turbot and skate.

Note: If you do not have a fish kettle, you can cook the fish in the stock in a frying pan. Lift it out with a slotted spoon and drain in a colander set over the frying pan.

Fish cooked in salt crust

PESCADO A LA SAL

- **1 whole fish, such as sole, sea bream, grouper or sea bass, about 1.5 kg/3¼ lb, gutted but not skinned**
- **3–4 kg/6½–8¾ lb coarse sea salt**

Serves 4–6

Do not clean the fish. (Cleaning the fish allows the salt to enter through the cut flesh and spoils the flavour.) Scale the fish with the back of a knife, then rinse and pat dry. Preheat the oven to 200°C/400°F/Gas Mark 6. Make a thick layer of salt in the base of a deep earthenware dish large enough to hold the fish. Place the fish on top and cover it completely with more salt, then sprinkle a little water over the top to form a crust. Bake for about 40 minutes, depending on the size of the fish. Remove the dish the oven, cover the crust with a tea towel or some thick paper and break it with a hammer or a pestle. Carefully transfer the fish to a serving dish without breaking, and serve. Mayonnaise and its variations or hollandaise sauce make excellent accompaniments.

Note: This dish is easy to prepare but it is essential to use a thick, meaty, chunky fish.

537

Gulas in garlic
GULAS AL AJILLO

- **2 tablespoons olive oil**
- **1 clove garlic, sliced**
- **1 chilli, sliced**
- **120 g / 4 oz gulas**

Serves 2–4

Heat the oil in a flameproof dish. Add the garlic and cook, stirring frequently, for a few minutes, until browned. Add the chilli and then the gulas, stirring them with a wooden fork. Serve piping hot.

Note: Usually made from ling, a member of the cod family, gulas are white 'sausages' with a dark line down the back made from squid ink. They are healthy and nutritious, with no cholesterol, are low in calories and have a high protein content. You may find them in Spanish speciality shops but they are not widely available outside Spain. If you can't find gulas, you can try other seafood sausages, but follow the cooking time and temperature specified by your fishmonger or on the packet.

Eel

Baby eels, also known as glass-eels, are white or transparent and 6–9 cm/2 ½–3 ½ inches long. They are highly valued in Spain and parts of France and fetch very high prices during their short season.

How to prepare

For perfect results, buy live eels. Take great care as they escape easily! To kill an eel, hold it firmly by the tail with a cloth and hit it hard on the head with something heavy. To remove the skin, cut around the head with a small sharp knife. Using a cloth, grasp the skin and pull it firmly towards the tail. It should come off in one piece. It is sometimes easier to do this if you hang the eel from a meat hook or other firm support. You can also buy fish pliers that make keeping hold of the skin easier. Cut off the head and the tail. Slit open the belly and remove the intestines. Wash the eel thoroughly in cold water and cut into pieces.

538

- **12 tablespoons olive oil**
- **12 cloves garlic**
- **600 g/1 lb 5 oz baby eels**
- **2 chillies, sliced**

Serves 6

Baby eels in individual dishes
ANGULAS EN CAZUELITAS

Put 2 tablespoons of the oil and two of the garlic cloves into each of six individual gratin dishes and set over a high heat until the garlic browns. Remove and leave the oil to cool, then divide the eels among them and add 2 slices of chilli to each. Return the dishes to a high heat and cook, stirring frequently with a wooden fork, until the mixture comes to the boil. Remove from the heat, place each one on a plate and cover with another plate. Serve immediately with wooden forks.

539

- **6 herring,**
  scaled, cleaned and boned
- **sunflower oil, for brushing**
- **salt**

Mustard sauce:
- **80 g/3 oz butter**
- **1 tablespoon plain flour**
- **250 ml/8 fl oz hot water**
- **2 egg yolks**
- **1–2 teaspoons mustard**
- **salt**

Serves 6

Grilled herring served with mustard sauce
ARENQUES ASADOS, SERVIDOS CON SALSA DE MOSTAZA

Preheat the grill. Lightly season the herring inside and out with salt. Brush oil all over the insides of the fish, then slash the outsides twice with a sharp knife and brush with oil. Gently reshape the fish and place on the grill rack. Cook, turning once, for 15–20 minutes, until the flesh flakes easily. Meanwhile, make the mustard sauce. Melt the butter in a saucepan. Add the flour and cook, stirring constantly, for 2 minutes. Gradually stir in the water, a little at a time. Cook, stirring constantly for 10 minutes, until thickened. Remove the pan from the heat and stir in the egg yolks one at a time, then the mustard and season to taste with a little salt. When the herring are ready, transfer them to a warm dish and serve immediately, offering the mustard sauce separately.

540

- **120 g/4 oz canned anchovy**
  fillets in oil
- **50 g/2 oz butter**
- **8 sprigs fresh parsley**
- **6 herring,**
  scaled, cleaned and boned
- **3 tablespoons olive oil**
- **1 teaspoon mustard**
- **salt**

Serves 6

Grilled herring with anchovies
ARENQUES ASADOS CON ANCHOAS

Preheat the grill. Cut six fillets in half lengthways and set aside. Drain the remainder and pound to a paste with the butter and two parsley sprigs in a mortar. Divide the paste among the herring cavities, close the fish and secure with wooden cocktail sticks. Place the fish on a grill rack. Mix together the oil and mustard and brush half over the one side of each herring, then grill for about 10 minutes. Carefully turn the fish, brush with the remaining oil and mustard mixture and grill for a further 5–10 minutes, until the flesh flakes easily. Transfer to a warm serving dish and garnish with the reserved anchovies in the shape of crosses and the remaining parsley sprigs. Serve immediately.

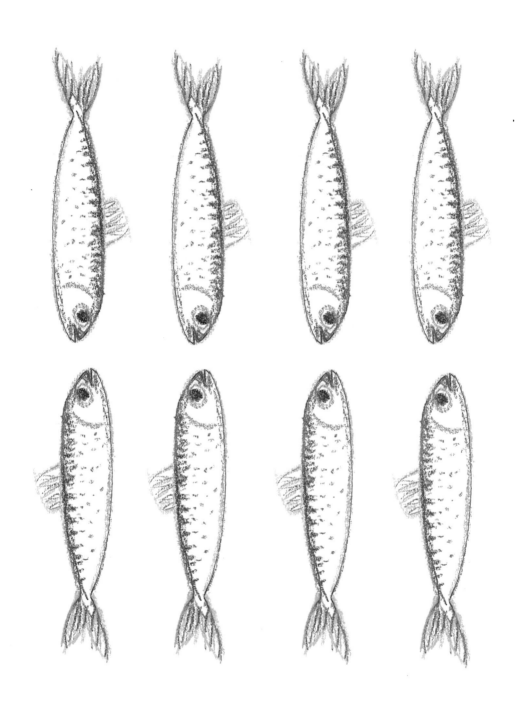

Tuna

As tuna is closely related to bonito (see recipes 557–565), the same recipes can be used for both fish.

Tuna au gratin

GRATINADO DE ATÚN DE LATA

- **1 kg/2¼ lb mussels**
- **5 tablespoons white wine**
- **50 g/2 oz butter**
- **2 tablespoons sunflower oil**
- **3 tablespoons plain flour**
- **500 ml/18 fl oz milk**
- **500 g/1 lb 2 oz canned tuna,**
  drained and flaked
- **1 tablespoon chopped**
  fresh parsley
- **2 spring onions or large shallots,**
  very finely chopped
- **juice of 1 lemon**
- **2 eggs, separated (optional)**
- **3 tablespoons breadcrumbs**
- **salt**

Serves 6

Scrape the mussel shells with the blade of a knife and remove the 'beards', then scrub under cold running water. Discard any mussels with broken shells or any that do not shut immediately when sharply tapped. Put them into a saucepan with the wine, 5 tablespoons water and a pinch of salt. Cover and cook over a high heat, shaking the pan occasionally, for 4–5 minutes, until the shells have opened. Remove the mussels with a slotted spoon and reserve the cooking liquid. Discard any mussels that remain closed. Strain the cooking liquid through a muslin-lined strainer into a bowl. Remove the mussels from their shells, cut in half with kitchen scissors if they are large, and put into the bowl of cooking liquid. Preheat the oven to 200°C/400°F/Gas Mark 6. Heat half the butter with the oil in a saucepan. Stir in the flour and cook, stirring constantly, for 2 minutes. Gradually stir in the milk, a little at a time. Cook, stirring constantly, for about 10 minutes until thickened. Add the tuna, parsley and spring onions or shallots. Using a slotted spoon, add the mussels and stir in 175 ml/6 fl oz of the reserved cooking liquid. Season to taste with salt and add the lemon juice. Whisk the egg whites, if using, in a clean, dry bowl until stiff. Beat the egg yolks, if using, in another bowl, stir in a little of the sauce to prevent them curdling and add to the pan. Remove the pan from the heat and fold in the egg whites. Divide the mixture among individual gratin dishes, sprinkle with the breadcrumbs and dot with the remaining butter. Bake for 5–10 minutes, until golden brown. Serve immediately straight from the dishes.

Salt cod

How to de-salt

Choose pieces of salt cod that are very white with dark skin and not too thick. Soak them in a bowl of cold water for 12 hours, changing the water four times. Each time the water is changed, remove the cod and thoroughly rinse the bowl before adding fresh water and replacing the fish, as salt tends to deposit on the bottom. If time is short, flake the salt cod and soak in warm water for 3 hours, changing the water three times, as described above. However, this method is only recommended for such dishes as croquettes and purées.

542

Salt cod with garlic

BACALAO AL AJO ARRIERO

- 500 g / 1 lb 2 oz salt cod fillet
- 100 g / 3½ oz canned red peppers, drained, or 2 dried red peppers, soaked in water
- 275 ml / 9 fl oz sunflower oil
- 1 large onion, finely chopped
- 3–4 cloves garlic, finely chopped
- 2 tablespoons olive oil

Serves 6

The night before you are going to cook the cod, remove and reserve the skin and flake the flesh. Soak the cod as described above. The next day, drain the cod and pat dry. Cut the skin into fine strips with kitchen scissors. Seed the peppers, if necessary, and cut into strips. Heat the sunflower oil in a flameproof casserole. Add the onion and garlic and cook over a very low heat, stirring occasionally, for about 10 minutes, until very soft and translucent. If using dried peppers, add them to the casserole and cook for a few minutes more. If using canned peppers, heat the olive oil in a small frying pan, add the peppers and cook over a low heat, stirring occasionally, for 5 minutes. Add the cod and strips of skin to the casserole and cook, shaking the casserole occasionally to release the gelatine, for 10 minutes. Add the canned peppers, if using. Mix well and simmer over a low heat for about 1 hour, until cooked through.

Note: As a variation, prepare the dish as described above, but omit the peppers. Just at the end of the cooking time, beat 2–3 eggs in a bowl, then stir them into the casserole and cook, stirring constantly, for a few minutes, until the eggs are scrambled with the salt cod. Serve immediately.

543

Salt cod bites

FRITOS DE BACALAO

- 1 kg/2¼ lb potatoes, unpeeled
- 500 g/1 lb 2 oz salt cod fillet
- 1 clove garlic, chopped
- 1 tablespoon chopped
  fresh parsley
- 3 eggs, separated
- sunflower oil, for deep-frying
- salt

Serves 6

Put the potatoes and cod (not desalted) into a saucepan, pour in water to cover and bring to the boil. Lower the heat and simmer for about 30 minutes, until the potatoes are tender. Lift the cod out of the pan and set aside to cool slightly. Drain the potatoes and when they are cool enough to handle, peel and mash them in a bowl. Remove and discard any skin and bones from the cod and flake the flesh, then mix into the mashed potatoes. Stir in the garlic and parsley and add the egg yolks one at a time. Whisk the egg whites with a pinch of salt in a clean, dry bowl until stiff, then gently fold into the mixture. Heat the oil in a deep-fryer or deep saucepan to 180–190°C/350–375°F or until a cube of day-old bread browns in 30 seconds. Use two spoons to shape the fish and potato mixture into little balls, then add them to the hot oil and cook, in batches, until golden brown. Remove with a slotted spoon, drain well and keep warm while you cook the remaining balls. Serve immediately.

544

Salt cod fritters with tomato sauce

BUÑUELOS DE BACALAO CON SALSA DE TOMATE

- **500 g/1 lb 2 oz salt cod fillet, soaked overnight as described on page 448**
- **sunflower oil, for deep-frying**
- **1 quantity Classic Tomato Sauce (see recipe 73)**

Batter:
- **250 g/9 oz plain flour**
- **½ teaspoon easy-blend dried yeast**
- **1 egg, separated**
- **1 tablespoon sunflower oil**
- **1 tablespoon rum or brandy**
- **1 egg white**
- **salt**

Serves 6

Put the cod into a saucepan, pour in water to cover and bring just to the boil. Remove the pan from the heat, cover and leave to stand for 10 minutes. Lift out the fish, remove any skin and bones and flake the flesh into large pieces. To make the batter, mix together the flour, yeast and a pinch of salt in a bowl. Make a well in the centre and add the egg yolk, oil and rum or brandy. Mix well and add just enough water to give the consistency of a thin purée. Cover and leave to stand for 2 hours. Just before frying the fritters, whisk both the egg whites with a pinch of salt in a clean, dry bowl until stiff, then gently fold them into the batter. Heat the oil in a deep-fryer or deep saucepan to 180–190°C/350–375°F or until a cube of day-old bread browns in 30 seconds. Dip the pieces of cod into the batter, three at a time, add to the hot oil and cook until golden brown. Remove with a slotted spoon, drain well and keep warm while you cook the remaining fritters. Reheat the tomato sauce. Serve the fritters immediately, offering the tomato sauce separately.

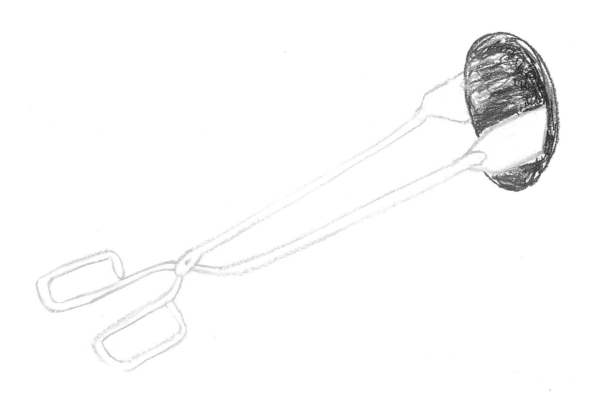

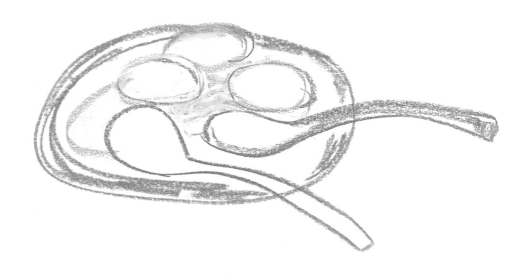

545

Potato and salt cod bouillabaisse
BOUILLABAISSE DE PATATAS Y BACALAO

- **5 tablespoons olive oil**
- **2 onions, finely chopped**
- **3 cloves garlic, lightly crushed**
- **2 tomatoes,**
  peeled, seeded and chopped
- **pinch of dried mixed herbs or**
  1 bouquet garni
  (1 sprig fresh thyme, 1 bay leaf
  and 1 sprig fresh parsley tied
  together in muslin)
- **1 kg/2 ¼ lb red-skinned**
  potatoes, cut into 1.5-cm/
  ½-inch thick slices
- **pinch of saffron threads**
- **400 g/14 oz salt cod fillet,**
  soaked overnight as described
  on page 448
- **fried bread (see recipe 130)**
- **salt**

Serves 6

Heat the oil in a large, heavy pot. Add the onions and cook over a low heat, stirring occasionally, for about 5 minutes, until soft and translucent. Add the garlic and cook, stirring frequently, for a few minutes, then add the tomatoes and cook, stirring occasionally, for 5 minutes. Pour in 2 litres / 3 ½ pints water, add the herbs or bouquet garni and potatoes and bring to the boil. Crush the saffron in a mortar and stir in 2 – 3 tablespoons of the cooking liquid, then add to the pot. Simmer for about 20 minutes. Meanwhile, drain the cod, remove any skin and bones and coarsely flake the flesh. Add to the pot and cook for a further 10 minutes, until the potatoes are tender. Season to taste with salt. Serve immediately, with slices of fried bread if you like.

Note: Bouillabaisse is a traditional Provençal fish soup which is more like a stew in its consistency. This Spanish version uses the salt cod fillet so prized in Spain.

546

Salt cod with spinach and béchamel sauce

BACALAO CON ESPINACAS Y BECHAMEL

- 500g/1lb 2oz salt cod fillet,
  soaked overnight as described
  on page 448
- 3kg/6½lb spinach,
  coarse stalks removed
- 20g/¾oz butter,
  plus extra for greasing
- 5 tablespoons olive oil
- 1 onion, finely chopped
- 50g/2oz gruyere cheese, grated
- salt

Béchamel sauce:
- 25g/1oz butter
- 2 tablespoons sunflower oil
- 1½ tablespoons plain flour
- 500ml/18fl oz milk
- salt

Serves 6

Drain the cod and put into a saucepan. Pour in water to cover and bring just to the boil. Remove the pan from the heat, cover and leave to stand for 10 minutes. Lift out the fish, remove any skin and bones and finely flake the flesh. Cover and set aside. Bring a large saucepan of salted water to the boil. Add the spinach, push it down into the water with a spoon and cook for about 10 minutes. Drain well, refresh under cold running water and drain again, pressing out as much liquid as possible with the back of a spoon, then chop. Preheat the oven to 200°C/400°F/Gas Mark 6. Grease an ovenproof dish with butter. Make the béchamel sauce as described in recipe 77. Heat the olive oil in a frying pan. Add the onion and cook over a low heat, stirring occasionally, for about 5 minutes, until softened and translucent. Add the spinach and cook, stirring frequently, for a few minutes more. Spoon the spinach mixture into the prepared dish, spreading it evenly over the base. Add the cod and pour in the béchamel sauce. Sprinkle with the gruyere, dot with the butter and bake for 10–15 minutes, until golden brown. Serve immediately straight from the dish.

547

Salt cod in green sauce
BACALAO EN SALSA VERDE

- 1 kg/2¼ lb salt cod, cut into
  pieces, soaked overnight as
  described on page 448
- sunflower oil, for deep-frying
- 2 tablespoons plain flour,
  plus extra for dusting
- 6 tablespoons olive oil
- 1 large onion, finely chopped
- 1 clove garlic
- 2–3 sprigs fresh parsley
- 250 ml/8 fl oz white wine
- 1 bay leaf
- 1 tablespoon chopped
  fresh parsley
- salt

Serves 6–8

Drain the cod and put into a saucepan. Pour in water to cover and bring just to the boil. Remove the pan from the heat, cover and leave to stand for 10 minutes. Lift out the pieces of fish and pat dry. Reserve the cooking liquid. Heat the sunflower oil in a deep-fryer or saucepan to 180–190°C/350–375°F or until a cube of day-old bread browns in 30 seconds. Dust each piece of fish in flour, add to the hot oil and cook, in batches, until golden brown. Remove with a slotted spoon and drain. Heat the olive oil in a frying pan. Add the onion and cook over a low heat, stirring occasionally, for 7–8 minutes, until beginning to brown. Meanwhile, crush the garlic with a pinch of salt and the parsley sprigs in a mortar and stir in 3–4 tablespoons of the reserved cooking liquid. Stir the flour into the frying pan and cook, stirring constantly, for 2 minutes. Stir in the garlic mixture, wine and 500 ml/18 fl oz of the reserved cooking liquid. Add the bay leaf and cook for 5–8 minutes. Place the cod in a flameproof dish and strain the sauce over it. Cook over a low heat, gently shaking the dish occasionally, for 10 minutes. Sprinkle with the chopped parsley and serve immediately straight from the dish.

548

Salt cod with peppers and tomato sauce

BACALAO CON PIMIENTOS Y SALSA DE TOMATE

- 750 g–1 kg/1 lb 10 oz–2¼ lb salt cod fillet, cut into 12 pieces, soaked overnight as described on page 448
- 500 g/1 lb 2 oz canned red peppers, drained, seeded and cut into 2-cm/¾-inch wide strips
- sunflower oil, for deep-frying
- 80 g/3 oz plain flour
- 1 quantity Classic Tomato Sauce (see recipe 73)

Serves 6

Drain the cod. Wrap each piece in a red pepper strip and secure with a wooden cocktail stick. Heat the oil in a deep-fryer or saucepan to 180–190°C/350–375°F or until a cube of day-old bread browns in 30 seconds. Coat each piece of wrapped cod in some of the flour, add to the hot oil, four at a time, and cook until golden brown. Remove with a slotted spoon, drain and put into a flameproof dish. Pour the tomato sauce over the pieces of cod and cook over a low heat, shaking the dish occasionally, for about 10 minutes, until the sauce has thickened. Serve immediately, straight from the dish.

Note: You can substitute fresh roasted peppers for canned ones.

549

Salt cod with potatoes and mayonnaise

BACALAO CON PATATAS Y MAYONESA

- 500 g/1 lb 2 oz salt cod fillet, soaked overnight as described on page 448
- 500 ml/18 fl oz milk
- 500 g/1 lb 2 oz potatoes, unpeeled
- sunflower oil, for deep-frying
- 80 g/3 oz plain flour
- 1 quantity Classic Mayonnaise (see recipe 105)

Serves 6

Put the cod into a dish, pour in the milk and leave to soak for 1 hour. Drain, remove the skin and any bones and flake the flesh into large pieces. Put the potatoes into a saucepan, pour in water to cover and add a pinch of salt. Bring to the boil and cook for about 30 minutes, until tender. Meanwhile, heat the oil in a deep-fryer or saucepan to 180–190°C/350–375°F or until a cube of day-old bread browns in 30 seconds. Lightly dust the pieces of cod with some of the flour, add to the hot oil, in batches, and cook until golden brown. Remove with a slotted spoon, drain well and keep warm while you cook the remaining batches. Drain the potatoes, then peel and cut them into large pieces. Put them around the edge of a warm serving dish and put the cod in the middle. Serve immediately with the mayonnaise either poured over the dish or served separately in a sauce boat.

550

Salt cod and mashed potato baked with mayonnaise

BACALAO CON PURÉ DE PATATAS Y MAYONESA, AL HORNO

- 750 g/1 lb 10 oz salt cod, soaked overnight as described on page 448

Mashed potato:
- 1 kg/2¼ lb potatoes, unpeeled
- 40 g/1½ oz butter
- 450 ml/¾ pint hot milk
- salt

Mayonnaise:
- 2 eggs
- 750 ml/1¼ pints sunflower oil
- juice of 1 lemon
- salt

Serves 6

Make the mayonnaise in a food processor as described in recipe 105. Put the potatoes into a saucepan, pour in water to cover and add a pinch of salt. Bring to the boil and cook for about 30 minutes, until tender. Drain well, then peel and mash. Stir in the butter, then gradually stir in the milk, a little at a time. The mash should be quite thick, so you may not need all the milk. Preheat the oven to 160°C/325°F/ Gas Mark 3. Drain the cod and put into a saucepan. Pour in water to cover and bring just to the boil. Remove the pan from the heat, cover and leave to stand for 10 minutes. Lift out the fish, remove any skin and bones and flake the flesh into large pieces. Spoon the mashed potato around the edge of an ovenproof dish and put the cod in the middle. Cover with the mayonnaise. Roll a small piece of foil around your finger to make a funnel and insert it into the mashed potato one side of the dish. Bake for about 15 minutes, until the top is golden brown. Tip the dish a little so that excess liquid drains out of the foil funnel. You can also remove the liquid with a spoon. Serve immediately, straight from the dish.

551

Salt cod with straw potatoes and scrambled eggs

BACALAO CON PATATAS PAJA Y HUEVOS REVUELTOS

- 350 g/12 oz salt cod fillet
- sunflower oil, for deep-frying
- 500 g/1 lb 2 oz potatoes, cut into thin julienne strips
- 3 onions, thinly sliced and pushed out into rings
- 4 eggs
- salt

Serves 6

Flake the cod and rinse well under cold running water. Set aside. Heat the oil in a frying pan to 180–190°C/350–375°F or until a cube of day-old bread browns in 30 seconds. Add the potatoes, in batches, and cook for a few minutes, until golden brown. Remove with a slotted spoon, drain and set aside. Drain off all but about 4–5 tablespoons of the oil from the pan and reheat. Add the onion and cook over a low heat, stirring occasionally, for about 8 minutes, until lightly browned. Add the cod and cook for about 5 minutes, until lightly browned. Break the eggs straight into the pan and quickly mix with a fork, as if making scrambled eggs. When they begin to set but are still creamy, add the straw potatoes. Lightly season with salt, stir rapidly and then tip the mixture into a warm serving dish. Serve immediately.

Brandade
BRANDADA (PURÉ DE BACALAO)

- 300 g/11 oz salt cod fillet, soaked overnight as described on page 448
- 175 ml/6 fl oz double cream
- triangles of fried bread (see recipe 130)

Béchamel sauce:
- 5 tablespoons olive oil
- 4 tablespoons plain flour
- 250 ml/8 fl oz milk
- salt

Serves 4

Drain the cod, remove any skin and bones and flake the flesh. Put it into a saucepan, pour in water to cover and bring just to the boil. Remove the pan from the heat, cover and leave to stand for 10 minutes. Drain the cod and process to a purée in a food processor. Make the béchamel sauce as described in recipe 77, using the olive oil instead of a mixture of butter and oil. Stir the cod into the béchamel sauce, then stir in the cream and heat through gently. Serve the purée immediately, garnished with fried bread triangles.

Note: Brandade or brandada is a salt cod purée that is much loved throughout Spain.

Sea bream

Sea bream are firm-fleshed fish and have a shape that makes them good for steaming or cooking on a barbecue. If sea bream is unavailable, use the same weight of another firm-fleshed fish such as hake, whiting or sea bass.

553

Sea bream baked with lemon juice, parsley and butter

BESUGO AL HORNO CON ZUMO DE LIMÓN, PEREJIL Y MANTEQUILLA

- **4 tablespoons sunflower oil**
- **1 sea bream or snapper, about 1.5 kg/3¼ lb, trimmed, scaled and cleaned**
- **1 sprig fresh parsley**
- **2 lemon slices**
- **juice of 1 lemon**
- **80 g/3 oz butter**
- **salt**

Serves 6

Preheat the oven to 190°C/375°F/Gas Mark 5. Pour the oil into an ovenproof dish. Season the fish inside and outside with salt. Using a sharp knife, slash the fish diagonally once on either side, place the parsley in the cavity and insert the lemon slices into the slashes. Put the fish into the dish, pour in the lemon juice, dot with the butter and bake for 20–25 minutes. Serve immediately, straight from the dish.

554 Sea bream baked with garlic, parsley and vinegar

BESUGO AL HORNO CON AJO, PEREJIL Y VINAGRE

- 250 ml/8 fl oz olive oil
- 1 large potato, sliced
- 1 sea bream or snapper,
  about 1.5 kg/3¼ lb,
  trimmed, scaled and cleaned
- 2–3 large sprigs fresh fennel
- 3 tablespoons white-wine
  vinegar
- 3 cloves garlic, finely chopped
- 1 tablespoon chopped
  fresh parsley
- salt

Serves 6

Preheat the oven to 180°C/350°F/Gas Mark 4. Heat the oil in a small frying pan. Add the potato slices and cook, turning occasionally, for about 10 minutes, until softened but not browned. Remove with a fish slice, lightly season with salt and put into a large ovenproof dish. Reserve the oil. Season the fish inside and out with salt and reshape. Put one of the fennel sprigs in the cavity and put the fish in the dish. Insert one of the remaining fennel sprigs underneath it and place the other on top. Pour 2 tablespoons of the reserved oil over the fish and bake for about 10 minutes. Remove the dish from the oven and increase the oven temperature to 220°C/425°F/Gas Mark 7. Remove and discard the fennel. Carefully pour half the vinegar inside the cavity, then sprinkle in half the garlic and half the parsley. Close the fish, pour the remaining vinegar over it and sprinkle with the remaining garlic and parsley. Return to the oven for about 8 minutes, until the flesh flakes easily, and serve immediately straight from the dish.

555 Sea bream baked with white wine and breadcrumbs

BESUGO AL HORNO CON VINO BLANCO Y PAN RALLADO

- 4 tablespoons olive oil
- ½ small onion, thinly sliced
- 1 sea bream or snapper,
  about 1.5 kg/3¼ lb,
  trimmed, scaled and cleaned
- 175 ml/6 fl oz white wine
- juice of 1 lemon
- 4 tablespoons breadcrumbs
- 50 g/2 oz butter
- salt

Serves 6

Preheat the oven to 190°C/375°F/Gas Mark 5. Heat the oil in a flameproof casserole. Add the onion and cook over a low heat, stirring occasionally, for about 5 minutes, until softened and translucent. Remove the casserole from the heat and scoop the onion into the centre. Season the fish inside and out with salt and slash twice with a sharp knife. Place on top of the onion. Mix the wine with 5 tablespoons water in a bowl and pour it over the fish. Add the lemon juice, sprinkle with the breadcrumbs and dot with the butter, making sure that there is a large piece in each slash. Bake the fish, basting occasionally, for about 20 minutes, until the flesh flakes easily. Serve immediately straight from the dish.

556

Grilled sea bream with mayonnaise sauce

BESUGO A LA PARRILLA CON SALSA MAYONESA

• 1 sea bream or snapper,
  about 1.5 kg/3 ¼ lb,
  trimmed, scaled and cleaned
• 2 thin rashers bacon, halved
• olive oil, for brushing
• 2 sprigs fresh fennel or thyme
• salt

  Mayonnaise sauce:
• 1 egg
• 250 ml/8 fl oz sunflower oil
• juice of ½ lemon
• 1 tablespoon capers,
  rinsed, drained and chopped
• 2 canned anchovy fillets,
  drained and chopped
• 1 teaspoon chopped
  fresh parsley
• salt

Serves 6

Preheat the grill. To make the sauce, first make a mayonnaise with the egg, oil, lemon juice and salt in a food processor as described in recipe 107. Transfer to a bowl and stir in the capers, anchovies and parsley. Cover and leave in a cool place or in the refrigerator. Slash the fish twice on each side with a sharp knife. Season with salt and put a piece of bacon into each of the slashes. Brush the fish all over with oil and brush the grill rack with oil. Put the fennel or thyme sprigs into the cavity of the fish and grill, turning the fish and brushing it with more oil occasionally, for 15 minutes, until the flesh flakes easily. Serve immediately with the mayonnaise sauce offered separately.

Bonito

As bonito is closely related to tuna, the same recipes can be used for both fish (see recipe 541).

557

Bonito with onion and tomato
BONITO CON CEBOLLA Y TOMATE

- **6 tablespoons olive oil**
- **2 large onions, chopped**
- **1 teaspoon plain flour**
- **750 g/1 lb 10 oz ripe tomatoes, peeled, seeded and chopped**
- **175 ml/6 fl oz white wine**
- **pinch of dried mixed herbs or 2 bay leaves or 1 sprig fresh thyme**
- **1.2 kg/2 ½ lb thick bonito fillets**
- **salt**

Serves 6

Heat the oil in a large frying pan. Add the onion and cook over a low heat, stirring occasionally, for about 5 minutes, until softened and translucent. Stir in the flour and cook, stirring constantly, for 2 minutes. Add the tomato and cook, stirring occasionally and breaking it up with the side of the spoon, for 5 minutes. Pour in the wine, add the herbs, season with salt and cook for about 15 minutes. Add the bonito, cover and cook over a low heat for a further 10 minutes. Serve immediately.

558

- 120 ml / 4 fl oz olive oil
- 3 large onions, finely chopped
- 2 bonito fillets,
  about 1.2 kg / 2 ½ lb total weight
- 175 ml / 6 fl oz white wine
- 1 bay leaf
- salt

Serves 6

Bonito with onion and white wine
BONITO CON CEBOLLA Y VINO BLANCO

Heat the oil in a frying pan. Add the onion and cook over a low heat, stirring occasionally, for 5 minutes, until softened and translucent. Place the bonito fillets on top, season with salt and pour in the wine. Add the bay leaf, cover and cook over a low heat, shaking the pan occasionally, for 15 minutes. If necessary, add a little water during cooking. Transfer the fish to a warm serving dish, top with the onion and serve.

559

- 1.5-kg / 3 ¼-lb bonito tail
- 6 rashers smoked bacon
- 5 tablespoons olive oil
- 1 onion, chopped
- 2 carrots, thinly sliced
- 250 ml / 8 fl oz white wine
- 1 sprig fresh thyme
- cooked potatoes (optional)
- salt

Serves 6

Bonito cooked with bacon
BONITO ASADO CON BACON

Ask your fishmonger to fillet the fish or do it yourself: remove and discard the skin from the bonito. Cut out the backbone and remove any other bones, then put the two fillets back together. Lightly season with salt and cover the fish with the bacon. Tie together in several places with kitchen string, rather like a rolled roast. Heat the oil in a large saucepan. Add the onion and carrot and cook over a low heat, stirring occasionally, for 5 minutes. Add the fish and cook, turning once, for a few minutes, until lightly browned on both sides. Pour in the wine, add the thyme, cover and cook, stirring occasionally, for 25 minutes. Lift out the fish and remove the string and bacon. Remove and discard the thyme and stir in a little water if the sauce seems too thick. Heat well, then pass the sauce through a food mill into a bowl. Cut the fish into slices like meat and serve it with the sauce on top. Garnish with a few cooked potatoes if you like.

Note: If there is any fish left over, flake it and mix with a thin béchamel sauce (see recipe 77). Put into an ovenproof dish, sprinkle with grated cheese and dot with butter. Bake in a preheated oven, 200°C/400°F/ Gas Mark 6, for 10–15 minutes, until golden and serve immediately straight from the dish.

Roasted bonito with green mayonnaise

BONITO ASADO CON MAYONESA VERDE

- 1.2 kg/2 ½ lb bonito
- 5 tablespoons olive oil
- 3 tablespoons white wine
- 3 sprigs fresh parsley
- salt

  Green mayonnaise:
- 2 eggs
- juice of ½ lemon
- 450 ml/¾ pint sunflower oil
- 1 teaspoon chopped
  fresh parsley
- 2 tablespoons capers, rinsed,
  drained and coarsely chopped
  capers
- 2 small gherkins,
  coarsely chopped
- salt

Serves 6

Preheat the oven to 200°C/400°F/Gas Mark 6. Make the green mayonnaise as described in recipe 107, and set aside in a cool place or in the refrigerator. Season the bonito with salt and brush both sides with the oil. Put the fish into a roasting tin and pour the wine over it. Roast, basting occasionally and turning once, for 20 minutes, until golden brown. Transfer to a warm serving dish, garnish with the parsley and serve with the green mayonnaise.

561

Fried bonito with green mayonnaise

BONITO EMPANADO CON MAYONESA VERDE

- **2 eggs**
- **120 g / 4 oz breadcrumbs**
- **sunflower oil, for deep-frying**
- **1.2 kg / 2 ½ lb thin bonito fillets**
- **salt**
- **sprigs fresh parsley**

Green mayonnaise:
- **4 eggs**
- **juice of 1 lemon**
- **900 ml / 1 ½ pints sunflower oil**
- **2 teaspoons chopped**
  fresh parsley
- **4 tablespoon capers, rinsed,**
  drained and coarsely chopped
- **4 small gherkins,**
  coarsely chopped
- **salt**

Serves 6

Make the green mayonnaise as described in recipe 107 and set aside in a cool place or in the refrigerator. Beat the eggs in a shallow dish and spread out the breadcrumbs in another shallow dish. Heat the oil in a deep-fryer or saucepan to 180–190°C/350–375°F or until a cube of day-old bread browns in 30 seconds. Lightly season the fish with salt and coat first in the beaten egg and then in the bread-crumbs, gently pressing them into place. Add the fish to the pan, in batches, and cook until golden brown. Remove from the pan, drain and keep warm while you cook the remaining batches. Garnish with the parsley and serve immediately, offering the green mayonnaise on the side.

Bonito marmitako

MARMITAKO DE BONITO

- **4 tablespoons olive oil**
- **400 g/14 oz bonito fillet,**
  cut into 2-cm/¾-inch cubes
- **1 large onion, finely chopped**
- **2 tomatoes,**
  peeled, seeded and chopped
- **1 kg/2¼ lb potatoes,**
  thickly sliced
- **2 cloves garlic**
- **2 sprigs fresh parsley**
- **1 bay leaf**
- **½ chilli,**
  seeded and finely chopped
- **1 fish or vegetable stock cube**
- **100 g/3½ oz canned peas,**
  drained
- **100 g/3½ oz canned red**
  peppers, drained, seeded
  and diced
- **salt**

Serves 6–8

Heat the oil in a flameproof casserole. Add the bonito and cook, stirring frequently, for 2–3 minutes, until lightly browned. Remove from the casserole with a slotted spoon and set aside. Add the onion to the casserole and cook over a low heat, stirring occasionally, for about 8 minutes, until lightly browned. Add the tomato and cook, stirring occasionally, for a further 5 minutes, then add the potato slices and pour in water to cover. Season with salt and bring to the boil, then lower the heat. Pound the garlic with the parsley and a pinch of salt in a mortar and stir in 2 tablespoons of the cooking liquid, then add to the casserole along with the bay leaf and chilli. Mix well and cook over a low heat for 30 minutes. Crumble in the stock cube, add the peas, red peppers and bonito and cook for 10 minutes. Remove and discard the bay leaf and serve the marmitako straight from the casserole.

Note: Marmitako is a Basque word meaning 'from the pot'.

563

Cold bonito loaf
PASTEL DE BONITO FRÍO

- 1 kg/2¼ lb bonito fillets,
  chopped
- 6 tablespoons breadcrumbs
- 1 egg, lightly beaten
- 175 ml/6 fl oz sherry
- 1 thick slice Serrano ham,
  cut lengthways into 5-mm/
  ¼-inch wide strips
- 1 thick rasher bacon,
  cut lengthways into 5-mm/
  ¼-inch wide strips
- lettuce and tomato
- salt and pepper

Quick stock:
- 2 bay leaves
- ½ small onion, halved
- 5 tablespoons white wine
- salt

Serves 6–8

Put the bonito into a bowl, sprinkle with the breadcrumbs, add the egg and sherry and season with salt and pepper. Using your hands, mix together well, then spread out the mixture into a rectangle on a clean tea towel. Top with alternating strips of ham and bacon. Using the tea towel to help, roll up the mixture, then wrap the tea towel around it and tie at both ends. Put the roll into a saucepan. Pour in water to cover, add all the quick stock ingredients and season with salt. Bring to the boil, then lower the heat, cover and cook for 45 minutes. Drain off the stock and transfer the roll, still wrapped in the tea towel, to a flat dish. Place a weight, such as a chopping board, on top and leave to stand in the refrigerator for at least 2 hours. Remove the tea towel and cut the loaf into slices. Serve garnished with lettuce and tomato.

564

Cold bonito pie
BUDÍN DE BONITO FRÍO

- 750 g/1 lb 10 oz potatoes,
  unpeeled
- 3 tablespoons olive oil,
  plus extra for brushing
- 1 onion, finely chopped
- 200 g/7 oz canned skipjack
  tuna (bonito) in oil, drained
- 1 tablespoon tomato purée
- tomato slices and lettuce or
  prawns (optional)
- 1 quantity Classic Mayonnaise
  (see recipe 105)
- salt

Serves 6

Put the potatoes into a saucepan, pour in water to cover and add a pinch of salt. Bring to the boil, then lower the heat and simmer for about 30 minutes, until tender. Meanwhile, heat the oil in a frying pan. Add the onion and cook over a low heat, stirring occasionally, for 5 minutes, until softened and translucent. Mash the tuna in a bowl and mix with the tomato purée. Drain the potatoes, then peel and mash them. Stir in the tuna mixture and onion, together with the oil from the pan, and mix well. Brush a loaf tin with oil and spoon in the mixture, pressing it down with the back of the spoon to eliminate any air pockets. Chill in the refrigerator for at least 4 hours. Run a round-bladed knife around the edge of the tin and turn the pie out on to a serving dish. Garnish with slices of tomato and lettuce or prawns, if you like, and serve, offering the mayonnaise separately.

565

Bonito in aspic with mayonnaise
ASPIC DE BONITO CON MAYONESA

- 1 sachet fish aspic jelly powder
- 150 g/5 oz canned peas, drained
- 100 g/3½ oz canned red
  peppers, drained
- 300 g/11 oz canned skipjack
  tuna (bonito) in oil, drained
  and flaked
- 2 hard-boiled eggs, chopped
- 1 onion, finely chopped
- tomato slices and lettuce leaves

  Mayonnaise:
- 1 egg
- 250 ml/8 fl oz sunflower oil
- juice of ½ lemon
- ½ teaspoon mustard
- salt
  Serves 6–8

Make the mayonnaise in a food processor as described in recipe 106 and set aside in a cool place or the refrigerator. Dissolve the aspic powder according to the instructions on the packet but use only half the quantity of water. Pour a thin layer of jelly into a tart tin. Place some of the peas in a ring around the edge of the tin. Cut two strips of red pepper and place them in an x in the middle of the tin. Chill in the refrigerator until set. Put the remaining jelly in a cool place but not the refrigerator. Dice the remaining red peppers. Mix together the tuna, hard-boiled eggs, onion, the remaining peas and the diced peppers in a bowl. Stir in the mayonnaise and the cooled jelly. Mix well, then tip into the tart tin and chill in the refrigerator for at least 2 hours. To serve, run a round-bladed knife around the edge of the tin and turn the aspic out on to a round serving dish. Garnish with slices of tomato and a few lettuce leaves.

566

Mackerel with garlic sauce and lemon juice
CABALLA CON SALSA DE AJO Y ZUMO DE LIMÓN

- 6 mackerel, about 400 g/14 oz
  each, cleaned and boned
- 250 ml/8 fl oz olive oil
- 80 g/3 oz plain flour
- 4 cloves garlic, lightly crushed
- 2 bay leaves
- ½ lemon, sliced
- juice of 1½ lemons
- salt
  Serves 6

Season the mackerel inside and out with salt. Heat the oil in a frying pan. Coat the mackerel, two at a time, in the flour, shaking off the excess, add to the pan and cook for about 5 minutes on each side until golden brown. Remove from the pan and place in a single layer in an ovenproof dish. Preheat the oven to 180°C/350°F/Gas Mark 4. Drain off all but 5–6 tablespoons of the oil from the pan and reheat. Add the garlic and cook, stirring frequently, for a few minutes, until beginning to brown, then add the bay leaves and cook for a few minutes more. Add the lemon slices and heat well, then remove the pan from the heat and stir in the lemon juice and 175 ml/6 fl oz water. Strain the sauce over the mackerel and warm through in the oven for about 5 minutes. Serve hot.

567

Mackerel fillets with mustard sauce

FILETES DE CABALLA CON SALSA DE MOSTAZA

- **12 mackerel fillets**
- **65 g / 2 ½ oz butter**
- **1 tablespoon sunflower oil**
- **1 tablespoon plain flour**
- **500 ml / 18 fl oz milk**
- **3 tablespoons Bordeaux or Dijon mustard**
- **juice of ½ lemon**
- **1 tablespoon chopped fresh parsley**
- **salt**

Serves 6

Preheat the oven to 180°C/350°F/Gas Mark 4. Put the mackerel fillets in a single layer in a large ovenproof dish. Make the mustard sauce. Melt 20 g / ¾ oz of the butter with the oil in a saucepan. Stir in the flour and cook, stirring constantly, for 2 minutes. Gradually stir in the milk, a little at a time. Cook, stirring constantly, for about 10 minutes, until thickened. Remove the pan from the heat, stir in the mustard and lemon juice and season to taste with salt. Pour the sauce over the mackerel fillets, sprinkle with the parsley and dot with the remaining butter. Bake for 10–15 minutes, then serve straight from the dish.

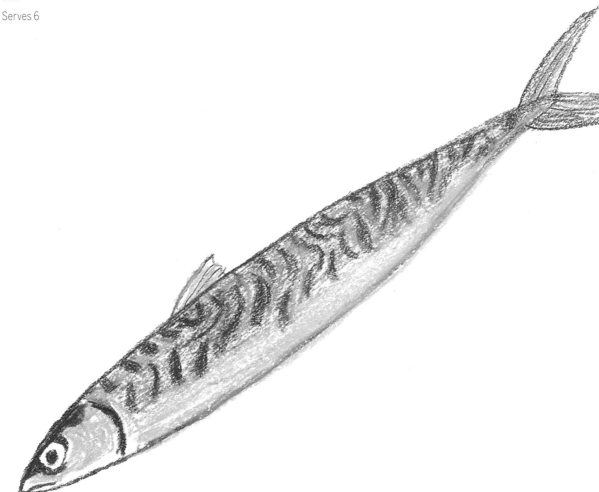

Squid

How to clean

Pull the head away from the body – the intestines will come away at the same time. Cut away the ink sac, if required, from among the intestines and put it in a bowl of water. Cut off the tentacles from the head, if using, and squeeze out the beak. Discard the head and beak. Remove and discard the transparent quill from the body sac and remove any remaining membrane. Rinse well under cold running water and peel off the skin. Pat dry.

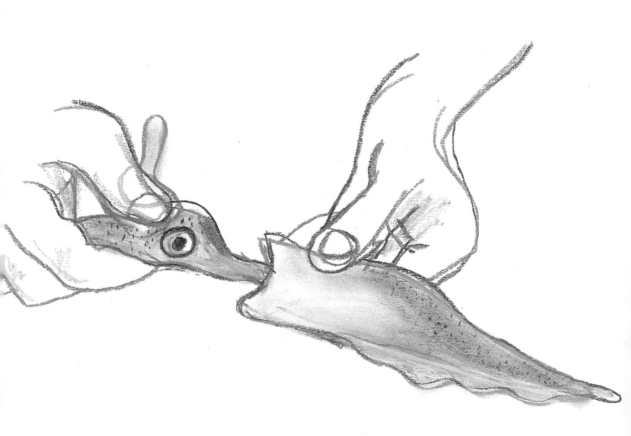

568

Calamari
CALAMARES FRITOS ENVUELTOS

- 4 tablespoons plain flour,
  plus extra for dusting
- 250 ml/8 fl oz soda water
- sunflower oil, for deep-frying
- 1.2 kg/2½ lb squid, cleaned and
  cut into 1-cm/½-inch wide rings
- 1 lemon, cut into wedges
- salt
Serves 6

Sift the flour with a pinch of salt into a bowl. Gradually stir in the soda water, a little at a time, to make a thick batter. Heat the oil in a deep-fryer or deep saucepan to 180–190°C/350–375°F or until a cube of day-old bread browns in 30 seconds. Dust the squid rings with flour, shaking off the excess, then dip them into the batter to coat. Add them to the hot oil, in batches, and cook until golden brown. Remove with a slotted spoon, drain well and keep warm while you cook the remaining batches. Serve with the lemon wedges.

Note: A pinch of saffron powder added to the batter of these squid rings gives it a nicer colour.

569

Simple fried squid
CALAMARES FRITOS SENCILLOS

- 1.2 kg/2½ lb squid, cleaned and
  cut into 1-cm/½-inch wide rings
- 80 g/3 oz plain flour
- sunflower oil, for deep-frying
- lemon wedges
- salt
Serves 6

Lightly season the squid rings with salt and coat them in the flour shaking off the excess. Heat the oil in a deep-fryer or saucepan to 180–190°C/350–375°F or until a cube of day-old bread browns in 30 seconds. Add the squid rings, in batches, and cook until golden brown. Remove with a slotted spoon, drain well and keep warm while you cook the remaining batches. Serve the squid garnished with the lemon wedges.

Note: This dish can be made with breadcrumbs added to the flour.

Squid in its ink with rice (first version)

CALAMARES EN SU TINTA CON ARROZ BLANCO

- 1 kg/2¼ lb small squid,
  cleaned with their ink sacs
  reserved
- 175 ml/6 fl oz red wine
- 5 tablespoons olive oil
- 1 onion, chopped
- 1 tomato,
  peeled, seeded and chopped
- 1 tablespoon plain flour
- 250 ml/8 fl oz sunflower oil
- 1 slice of bread, crusts removed
- 1 sprig fresh parsley
- 1 clove garlic
- 1 sachet squid ink
- 400 g/14 oz long-grain rice
- 40 g/1½ oz butter
- salt

Serves 6

Put the ink sacs into a bowl with half the red wine. Leave the squid body sacs whole if they are very small or cut into pieces if larger. Heat the olive oil in a frying pan. Add the onion and cook over a low heat, stirring occasionally for about 10 minutes, until lightly browned. Add the tomato and cook, stirring occasionally, for a further 5 minutes. Stir in the flour and cook, stirring constantly, for 2 minutes. Gradually stir in 500 ml/18 fl oz water, a little at a time. Heat the sunflower oil in another frying pan. Add the bread, parsley and garlic and cook, stirring and turning the bread, for a few minutes, until golden brown. Transfer the fried bread, parsley and garlic to a mortar and pound together, then add to the onion and tomato mixture. Stir in the remaining red wine. Use the back of a spoon to mash the ink sacs into the wine, stir in the sachet of ink and pour the mixture into the frying pan. Add the squid before the sauce comes to the boil and simmer over a low heat for 1½–2 hours. Cook and refresh the rice as described in the first part of recipe 173, frying it in the butter afterwards. Spoon it into a ring mould and turn out on to a warm serving dish. Season the squid to taste with salt and spoon it and its sauce into the middle of the rice. Serve immediately. Alternatively, serve the rice on the side.

Note: To prepare this recipe using small squid or cuttlefish, allow 4–6 squid/cuttlefish per serving, depending on size. Clean the squid, chop the tentacles and use them to stuff the body sacs, then prepare and cook as in the recipe above.

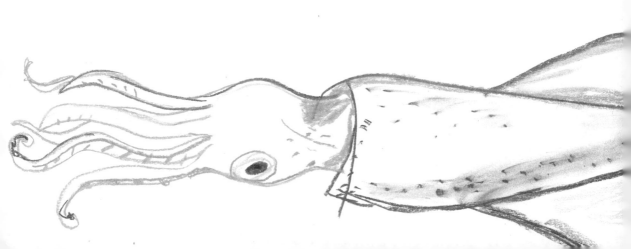

571

Squid in its ink with rice (second version)

CALAMARES EN SU TINTA CON ARROZ BLANCO

- 1 kg/2¼ lb small squid,
  cleaned with their ink sacs
  reserved in water
- 175 ml/6 fl oz olive oil
- 1 kg/2¼ lb onions,
  finely chopped
- 1 clove garlic, finely chopped
- 2 sprigs fresh parsley
- 1 sachet squid ink
- 2 tablespoons Classic Tomato
  Sauce (see recipe 73)
- 5 tablespoons white wine
- 1 tablespoon breadcrumbs
  (optional)
- salt

Serves 6

Leave the squid body sacs whole if they are very small or cut into pieces if larger. Put the oil, onion and garlic into a flameproof casserole and heat gently. Cook over a very low heat, stirring occasionally, for about 10 minutes, until softened but not coloured. Add the squid and cook, stirring occasionally, for 15 minutes. Meanwhile, crush the ink sacs with the parsley and stir in the sachet of ink. Pour the mixture into the pan, and add the tomato sauce and wine. Simmer gently for about 10 minutes. If the sauce seems too thin, stir in the breadcrumbs to thicken. Season to taste with salt and serve. Leave the squid body sacs whole if they are very small or cut into pieces if larger.

Note: To prepare this recipe using small squid or cuttlefish, allow 4–6 squid/cuttlefish per serving, depending on size. Clean the squid, chop the tentacles and use them to stuff the body sacs, then prepare and cook as in the recipe above.

572

Stuffed squid

CALAMARES RELLENOS

- 6–8 squid, about
  65 g/2½ oz each, cleaned
- 300 g/11 oz lean pork, minced
- 2 hard-boiled eggs, chopped
- 250 ml/8 fl oz olive oil
- 1 tablespoon plain flour,
  plus extra for dusting
- 1 onion, finely chopped
- 5 tablespoons white wine
- 1 sprig fresh parsley
- very small pinch of saffron
  powder
- salt

Serves 6

Finely chop the squid tentacles and leave the body sacs whole. Mix together the chopped squid, pork and hard-boiled eggs in a bowl. Divide the mixture among the body sacs, but do not overfill them or they will burst during cooking. Secure with trussing thread or wooden cocktail sticks. Heat 150 ml/¼ pint of the oil in a frying pan. Dust the squid with flour and add them to the pan, two at a time, and cook, turning occasionally, for a few minutes, until lightly browned. Remove from the pan and set aside. Heat the remaining oil in a saucepan. Add the onion and cook over a low heat, stirring occasionally, for about 8 minutes, until beginning to brown. Stir in the flour and cook, stirring constantly, for 5 minutes, until lightly coloured. Gradually stir in the wine and 1 litre/1¾ pints water and add the parsley and saffron. Add the squid to the pan, cover and cook over a low heat for 1 hour. Season to taste with salt. Remove and discard the trussing thread or cocktail sticks and serve the squid in a warm deep dish with the sauce.

Pomfret

Pomfrets are thin-bodied fish that provide very good eating. They come from the same family as butterfish, so if you could also use butterfish in the following recipes, but you will need 4–6 per person. If using butterfish, clean, remove the head and tails and rub off the scales. Reduce the cooking time accordingly, if using smaller fish.

573

Baked pomfret fillets
FILETES DE CASTAÑOLA AL HORNO

- 1 small pomfret, 750 g–1 kg/
  1 lb 10 oz–2 ¼ lb, cleaned,
  filleted and skinned
- 175 ml/6 fl oz sunflower oil
- 5 tablespoons white wine
- 1 large onion, finely chopped
- 1 tablespoon chopped
  fresh parsley
- salt

Serves 6–8

Preheat the oven to 180°C/350°F/Gas Mark 4. Put the pomfret fillets into an ovenproof dish in a single layer, season with salt and pour the oil and wine over them. Mix together the onion and parsley and sprinkle a little over each fillet. Bake for about 20 minutes, until the flesh flakes easily, and serve immediately straight from the dish.

574

Pomfret fillets with onions and tomatoes
FILETES DE CASTAÑOLA CON CEBOLLA Y TOMATE

- **6 tablespoons olive oil**
- **2 onions, very finely chopped**
- **1 clove garlic**
- **3 large ripe tomatoes,**
  peeled, seeded and chopped
- **½ teaspoon sugar**
- **1 pomfret, 750 g–1 kg/**
  1 lb 10 oz–2¼ lb, cleaned,
  filleted and skinned
- **175 ml/6 fl oz white wine**
- **1 sprig fresh thyme or**
  2 bay leaves
- **salt**

Serves 4

Heat the oil in a large frying pan. Add the onion and cook over a low heat, stirring occasionally, for 5–6 minutes, until softened and translucent. Add the garlic, tomato and sugar and cook, stirring occasionally and breaking up the tomato with the side of the spoon, for 10 minutes. Add the pomfret fillets, wine and thyme sprigs or bay leaves and season with salt. Cover and simmer gently, adding a little water if necessary, for about 20 minutes, until the fish flakes easily. Remove and discard the thyme or bay leaves and garlic and serve immediately.

Note: This dish can be made in advance and reheated before serving.

575

Dentex in sauce
DENTÓN EN SALSA

- **750 ml/1¼ pints sunflower oil**
- **6 x 150-g/5-oz slices dentex,**
  sea bream or snapper
- **1 tablespoon plain flour,**
  plus extra for dusting
- **1 onion, chopped**
- **2 cloves garlic**
- **pinch of saffron threads**
- **500 ml/18 fl oz fish stock**
  (home-made or made
  using a stock cube)
- **1 tablespoon chopped**
  fresh parsley
- **100 g/3½ oz canned peas,**
  drained
- **1 bay leaf**
- **salt**

Serves 6

Reserve 3 tablespoons of the oil and heat the remainder in a frying pan. Season the fish with salt on both sides and dust with flour. Add the fish to the pan and cook for 4–5 minutes, until golden brown. Transfer the fish to a flameproof casserole. Heat the reserved oil in a frying pan. Add the onion and garlic and cook over a low heat, stirring occasionally, for about 10 minutes, until lightly browned. Remove the pan from the heat. Pound the onion and garlic with the saffron and a pinch of salt in a mortar, stir in 2 tablespoons of the stock and pass the mixture through a vegetable mill into a bowl. Return the pan to the heat and stir in the flour. Cook, stirring constantly, for 2 minutes. Gradually stir in the remaining fish stock, a little at a time, and strain in the mixture from the mortar. Cook, stirring constantly, for 2 minutes, season to taste with salt and pour the sauce over the fish. Sprinkle with the parsley, add the peas and bay leaf and cook over a medium heat, gently shaking the casserole occasionally, for 10 minutes. Remove and discard the bay leaf and serve immediately, straight from the casserole.

Note: See also recipes for sea bream (553–556) for alternative ways to prepare dentex.

Sole

How to prepare

To prevent the fillets shrinking, once they have been removed from the fish hold them by one end and gently bang both sides on to a work surface. Although not a flat fish, John Dory is often prepared in the same way as sole. It has a similar flavour and texture, but is not quite such a fine quality fish.

576

Sole fillets with spinach, béchamel sauce and langoustines

FILETES DE LENGUADO CON ESPINACAS, BECHAMEL Y LANGOSTINOS

- 3–4 sole, about 300 g/11 oz each, cleaned, filleted and skinned, trimmings reserved
- 500 g/1 lb 2 oz unpeeled langoustines or Dublin Bay prawns
- 2 kg/4½ lb spinach, coarse stalks removed
- 50 g/2 oz butter, plus extra for greasing
- 50 g/2 oz gruyere or Parmesan cheese, grated
- salt

Quick stock:
- 1 bay leaf
- 1 thick slice of onion
- 1 large carrot, sliced
- 175 ml/6 fl oz white wine
- juice of ½ lemon
- salt

Béchamel sauce:
- 25 g/1 oz butter
- 3 tablespoons sunflower oil
- 1 tablespoon plain flour
- 120 ml/4 fl oz milk
- small pinch of curry powder (optional)
- salt

Serves 6

Make the quick stock in advance as described in recipe 534. Remove the rack from a fish kettle, put the fish trimmings on the base and pour in the stock. Fold the sole fillets in half and put them on the rack with the langoustines. Replace the rack and bring the stock just to the boil. Remove the fish kettle from the heat and lift the rack to rest diagonally across the top so that the fish and shellfish drain. Strain and reserve 120 ml/4 fl oz of the stock. Meanwhile, put the spinach into a large saucepan with just the water clinging to its leaves after washing. Add a pinch of salt and cook for 8–10 minutes, until tender. Drain well, pressing out as much liquid as possible with the back of a spoon. Chop coarsely. Melt the butter in a saucepan. Add the spinach and cook, stirring frequently, for 5 minutes. Grease an ovenproof dish with butter and spoon the spinach over the base. Place the fish fillets on top. Peel the langoustines and put them in the dish. Preheat the oven to 200°C/400°F/Gas Mark 6. Make the béchamel sauce. Melt the butter with the oil in a saucepan. Stir in the flour and cook, stirring constantly, for 2 minutes. Gradually stir in the milk and reserved stock. Cook, stirring constantly, for about 10 minutes, until thickened. Season to taste with salt and stir in the curry powder, if using. Pour the sauce over the fish, sprinkle with the gruyere and bake for 15–20 minutes, until golden brown. Serve immediately, straight from the dish.

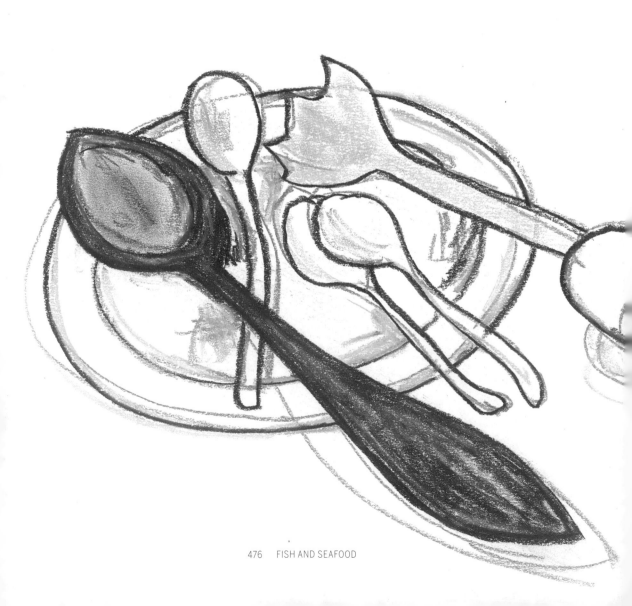

577

Sole fillets in whisky
FILETES DE LENGUADO AL WHISKY

- **3 sole, about 350 g/12 oz each, cleaned, filleted and skinned, trimmings reserved**
- **50 g/2 oz butter, plus extra for greasing**
- **150 g/5 oz mushrooms, sliced**
- **juice of ½ lemon**
- **2 tablespoons sunflower oil**
- **1 tablespoon plain flour**
- **3 tablespoons whisky**
- **2 egg yolks**
- **200 ml/7 fl oz double cream**
- **pinch of curry powder**
- **25 g/1 oz gruyere cheese, grated**
- **salt**

Quick stock:
- **1 bay leaf**
- **1 thick slice onion**
- **1 large carrot, sliced**
- **175 ml/6 fl oz white wine**
- **juice of ½ lemon**
- **salt**

Serves 6

Make the quick stock as described in recipe 534. Remove the rack from a fish kettle, pour in half the stock and set aside to cool. Put the fish trimmings in a saucepan, add the remaining stock and bring to the boil. Lower the heat and simmer for 35 minutes, then remove the pan from the heat and strain into a bowl. Put the sole fillets on the rack of the fish kettle and replace the rack. Bring the stock to the boil, then remove the kettle from the heat. Lift the rack to rest diagonally across the top of the fish kettle so that the fish can drain. Grease an ovenproof dish with butter, put the sole fillets in it and cover with a tea towel wrung out in hot water, or with foil, to keep them warm. Put the mushrooms, 20 g/¾ oz of the butter, the lemon juice and a pinch of salt into a saucepan. Cook over a low heat for 6 minutes, then set aside. Preheat the oven to 200°C/400°F/Gas Mark 6. Melt the remaining butter with the oil in a saucepan. Stir in the flour and cook, stirring constantly, for 2 minutes. Gradually stir in 450 ml/¾ pint of the strained concentrated stock, a little at a time. Cook, stirring constantly, for 5 minutes, add the whisky and cook, still stirring for a further 3–4 minutes, until thickened. Add the mushrooms and their cooking juices. Remove the pan from the heat. Mix the egg yolks with the cream in a bowl and stir into the sauce, then add the curry powder and season to taste with salt. Pour the sauce over the fish, sprinkle with the gruyere and bake for about 15 minutes, until golden brown. Serve immediately.

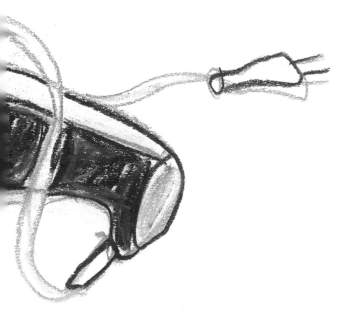

578

Sole fillets with béchamel sauce au gratin

FILETES DE LENGUADO CON BECHAMEL GRATINADA

- 250 g/9 oz raw unpeeled prawns
- 3 large sole, 350–400 g/
  12–14 oz each, cleaned, filleted
  and skinned, trimmings reserved
- 25 g/1 oz butter
- 2 tablespoons sunflower oil
- 1 heaped tablespoon plain flour
- 275 ml/9 fl oz milk
- pinch of curry powder (optional)
- 2 egg yolks
- 65 g/2½ oz gruyere cheese,
  grated
- salt

Serves 6

Peel the prawns, reserving the heads and shells. Set the prawn tails aside. Put the heads and shells with the trimmings from the sole in a saucepan, pour in water to cover and add a pinch of salt. Bring to the boil, then lower the heat and simmer for 5 minutes. Strain the stock into a bowl, pressing down on the contents of the sieve to extract all the liquid. Lightly season the sole fillets with salt, fold them in half and put into an ovenproof dish in a single layer. Preheat the oven to 180°C/350°F/Gas Mark 4. Melt the butter with the oil in a saucepan. Stir in the flour and cook, stirring constantly, for 2 minutes. Gradually stir in the milk, a little at a time, then stir in 275 ml/9 fl oz of the prawn and fish stock. Cook, stirring constantly, for about 10 minutes, until thickened. Add the prawns and cook, stirring constantly, for a further 5 minutes. Season to taste with salt and stir in the curry powder, if using. Lightly beat the egg yolks in a bowl and stir in a little of the béchamel sauce to prevent them curdling, then stir them into the sauce. Pour the sauce over the fish fillets, sprinkle with the gruyere and bake for 10 minutes. Meanwhile, preheat the grill. Remove the dish from the oven and put under the grill for a further 10 minutes, until golden brown. Serve immediately, straight from the dish.

579

Sole fillets baked with white wine and chopped onions

FILETES DE LENGUADO AL HORNO, CON VINO BLANCO
Y PICADITO DE CEBOLLAS

- 2 large sole, 350–400 g/
  12–14 oz each, cleaned, filleted
  and skinned, trimmings reserved
- 175 ml/6 fl oz sunflower oil
- 175 ml/6 fl oz white wine
- 1 small onion, finely chopped
- 1 tablespoon finely chopped
  fresh parsley
- ½ teaspoon dried mixed herbs
- salt

Serves 4

Put the fish trimmings into a saucepan, pour in just enough water to cover and add a pinch of salt. Bring to the boil, then lower the heat and cook for 30 minutes. Strain the stock into a bowl. Preheat the oven to 180°C/350°F/Gas Mark 4. Pour 50 ml/2 fl oz of the oil into an ovenproof dish. Lightly season the sole fillets with salt and put them in the dish in a single layer. Pour the wine over them, then pour in the remaining oil. Mix together the onion, parsley and dried herbs in a bowl and sprinkle over the fish. Pour in 175 ml/6 fl oz of the fish stock and gently shake the dish to make sure it penetrates. Bake for 15–20 minutes, until the fish flakes easily. Serve immediately, straight from the dish.

Note: Grouper fillets can be used in place of sole in this dish but the cooking time should be increased slightly.

580

Baked sole fillets with tomato sauce, mushrooms, mussels and grated cheese

FILETES DE LENGUADO AL HORNO CON SALSA DE TOMATE, CHAMPIÑONES, MEJILLONES Y QUESO RALLADO

- **1 quantity Classic Tomato Sauce (see recipe 73)**
- **500 g/1 lb 2 oz mussels**
- **175 ml/6 fl oz white wine**
- **1 bay leaf**
- **200 g/7 oz mushrooms, sliced**
- **20 g/¾ oz butter**
- **juice of ½ lemon**
- **3 large sole, 350–400 g/ 12–14 oz each, cleaned, filleted and skinned**
- **50 g/2 oz gruyere or Parmesan cheese, grated**
- **salt**

Serves 6

Strain the tomato sauce and set aside. Preheat the oven to 200°C/ 400°F/Gas Mark 6. Scrape the mussel shells with the blade of a knife and remove the 'beards', then scrub under cold running water. Discard any mussels with broken shells or any that do not shut immediately when sharply tapped. Put the mussels into a saucepan and add 50 ml/2 fl oz of the wine, 120 ml/4 fl oz water, the bay leaf and a pinch of salt. Cover and cook over a medium heat, shaking the pan occasionally, for 4–5 minutes, until the shells have opened. Remove the mussels from the pan with a slotted spoon and discard any that remain shut. Strain the cooking liquid through a muslin-lined sieve into a bowl. Remove the mussels from their shells and put them into the bowl. Put the mushrooms, butter, lemon juice and a pinch of salt into a saucepan. Cover and cook over a low heat for 8 minutes. Stir the mushrooms into the tomato sauce and add the remaining wine. Spoon a little sauce on to the base of an ovenproof dish and add the sole fillets in a single layer. Drain the mussels and put them on top of the fish in an even layer. Pour the remaining tomato sauce mixture over them and sprinkle with the gruyere or Parmesan. Bake until golden brown. Serve immediately, straight from the dish.

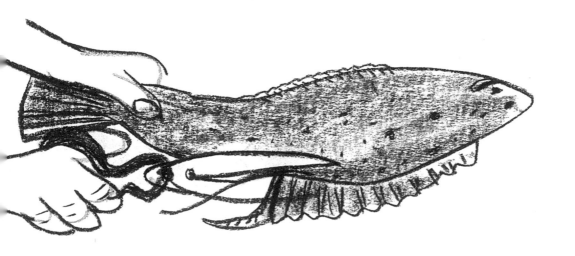

581

Sole fillets in tartlets with mushroom and béchamel sauce

CAZOLETAS DE FILETES DE LENGUADO CON CHAMPIÑONES Y BECHAMEL

- 2 large sole, 400–500 g/
  14 oz–1 lb 2 oz each, cleaned,
  filleted and skinned,
  trimmings reserved
- 120 g/4 oz mushrooms, sliced
- 20 g/¾ oz butter
- juice of ½ lemon
- 8 cooked tartlet cases
  (see recipe 1) or cooked
  individual vol-au-vent cases
- 1 black truffle, sliced (optional)
- salt

Quick stock:
- 1 bay leaf
- 1 thick slice of onion
- 1 large carrot, sliced
- 175 ml/6 fl oz white wine
- juice of ½ lemon
- salt

Béchamel sauce:
- 25 g/1 oz butter
- 2 tablespoons sunflower oil
- 1 heaped tablespoon plain flour
- 250 ml/8 fl oz milk
- 2 egg yolks
- salt

Serves 8

Make the quick stock as described in recipe 534. Remove the rack from a fish kettle and pour in the cold stock. Loosely roll up the sole fillets and secure with wooden cocktail sticks. Place them on the rack and return it to the fish kettle. Bring to the boil, then lift out the fish and transfer to a plate. Cover with a tea towel wrung out in hot water or foil and keep warm. Add the fish trimmings to the stock and cook for 20 minutes. Strain and set aside. Put the mushrooms, butter, lemon juice and a pinch of salt into a saucepan. Cover and cook over a medium heat for 6 minutes. Remove from the heat and set aside. Preheat the oven to 180°C/350°F/Gas Mark 4. Make the béchamel sauce. Melt the butter with the oil in a saucepan. Stir in the flour and cook, stirring constantly, for 2 minutes. Gradually stir in the milk, a little at a time, then stir in 150 ml/¼ pint of the strained concentrated stock. Cook, stirring constantly, for about 10 minutes, until thickened. Lightly beat the egg yolks in a bowl and gradually stir in some of the béchamel sauce to prevent them curdling, then add them to the pan. Drain the mushrooms and add to the sauce, then remove the pan from the heat. Season to taste with salt. Heat the tartlet cases or vol-au-vent cases in the oven for about 5 minutes or according to the instructions on the packet. Remove and discard the cocktail sticks from the rolled fish fillets and place a roll in each tartlet case or vol-au-vent. Pour in some of the béchamel sauce and place a slice of truffle on top of each, if you like. Serve immediately.

Note: This dish can be served with or without the tartlet cases. If you are not using the tartlet cases, simply place the rolls of fish in an ovenproof dish, allowing at least two fillets per serving.

582

Sole fillets stuffed with ham in sauce
ROLLITOS DE FILETES DE LENGUADO RELLENOS CON JAMÓN EN SALSA

- 6 sole, 200 g/7 oz each,
  cleaned, filleted and skinned
- 200 g/7 oz Serrano ham,
  chopped
- 2 hard-boiled eggs, chopped

Quick stock:
- 1 bay leaf
- 1 thick slice of onion
- 1 large carrot, sliced
- 3 tablespoons white wine
- juice of ½ lemon
- salt

Béchamel sauce:
- 25 g/1 oz butter
- 2 tablespoons sunflower oil
- 1 tablespoon plain flour
- 250 ml/8 fl oz milk
- 1 tablespoon chopped
  fresh parsley
- salt

Serves 6

Make the quick stock as described in recipe 534, and leave to cool. Remove the rack from a fish kettle and pour in the cold stock. Loosely roll up the sole fillets and secure with wooden cocktail sticks. Place them on the rack and return it to the fish kettle. Bring to the boil over a medium heat. Turn off the heat and lift the rack to rest diagonally across the fish kettle. Cover the sole fillets with a clean tea towel wrung out in hot water to keep them warm. Make the béchamel sauce. Melt the butter with the oil in a saucepan. Stir in the flour and cook, stirring constantly, for 2 minutes. Gradually stir in the milk, a little at a time. Cook, stirring constantly, for 5 minutes, then stir in 250 ml/8 fl oz of the quick stock and cook, stirring constantly, for a further 5 minutes. Season to taste with salt, remove the pan from the heat and stir in the parsley. Remove and discard the cocktail sticks from the fish rolls and put the rolls on a warm dish. Fill the centres with the ham. Pour the béchamel sauce over the rolls and sprinkle with the hard-boiled eggs (this should be mostly yolk with just a little white). Serve immediately.

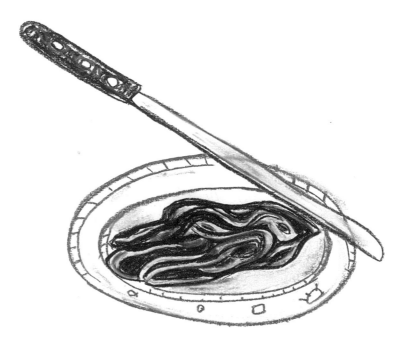

583

Sole fillets with rice
FILETES DE LENGUADO CON ARROZ

- 120 g/4 oz mushrooms, finely chopped
- 100 g/3½ oz butter
- a few drops of lemon juice
- 120 g/4 oz Serrano or York ham, chopped
- 500 g/1 lb 2 oz long-grain rice
- pinch of saffron threads
- 3 large sole, 350–400 g/ 12–14 oz each, cleaned, filleted and skinned
- 2 tablespoons sunflower oil
- 1 heaped tablespoon plain flour
- 250 ml/8 fl oz milk
- salt

Quick stock:
- 1 bay leaf
- 1 thick slice onion
- 1 carrot, sliced
- 3 tablespoons white wine
- juice of ½ lemon
- salt

Serves 6

Make the quick stock as described in recipe 534, and leave to cool. Put the mushrooms, 15 g/½ oz of the butter, the lemon juice and a pinch of salt into a saucepan. Cover and cook over a medium heat for 6 minutes. Add the ham, mix well and set aside. Cook the rice and sauté in 50 g/2 oz of the remaining butter as described in the first part of recipe 173, but do not add any peas. Put the rice into a tart tin, pressing down lightly, then turn out on to the centre of a warm round serving dish and keep warm. Remove the rack from a fish kettle and pour in the cold stock. Fold the sole fillets, put them on the rack and return it to the fish kettle. Bring to the boil over a medium heat. Turn off the heat and lift the rack to rest diagonally across the fish kettle. Cover the sole fillets with a clean tea towel wrung out in hot water, to keep them warm. Melt the remaining butter with the oil in a saucepan. Stir in the flour and cook, stirring constantly, for 2 minutes. Gradually stir in the milk, a little at a time. Cook, stirring constantly, for 5 minutes, then add about 150 ml/¼ pint of the quick stock and cook, stirring constantly, for a further 5 minutes. Season to taste with salt. Arrange the sole fillets around the edge of the rice on the serving dish. Use a spoon to fill the fillets with the mushroom mixture, then pour the béchamel sauce over them and serve immediately.

584

Sole fritters
FILETES DE LENGUADO EN BUÑUELOS

- sunflower oil, for deep-frying
- 3 sole, 350–400 g/12–14 oz, cleaned, filleted and skinned
- 1 quantity Fritter Batter (see recipes 58–60)
- 2 sprigs fresh parsley
- 1 quantity Classic Tomato Sauce (see recipe 73)
- salt

Serves 6

Heat the oil in a deep-fryer or saucepan to 180–190°C/350–375°F or until a cube of day-old bread browns in 30 seconds. Lightly season the sole fillets with salt and dip them into the batter. Add them to the hot oil, in batches, and cook until golden brown. Remove with a slotted spoon, drain and keep warm while you cook the remaining batches. Serve immediately, garnished with the parsley, and offer the tomato sauce, if using, separately.

585

Breaded sole fillets with rice and tomato sauce

FILETES DE LENGUADO EMPANADOS CON ARROZ BLANCO Y SALSA
DE TOMATE

- **2 eggs**
- **80 g/3 oz breadcrumbs**
- **sunflower oil, for deep-frying**
- **4 sole, about 200 g/7 oz each,**
  cleaned, filleted and skinned
- **1 quantity Classic Tomato Sauce**
  (see recipe 73)

Rice:
- **500 g/1 lb 2 oz long-grain rice**
- **50 g/2 oz butter**
- **salt**

Serves 4–6

Cook the rice and refresh under cold running water as described in the first part of recipe 173. Beat the eggs in a shallow dish and spread out the breadcrumbs in another shallow dish. Heat the oil in a deep-fryer or saucepan to 180–190°C/350–375°F or until a cube of day-old bread browns in 30 seconds. Dip the sole fillets first in the beaten egg and then in the breadcrumbs, pressing them on well with your hands. Add to the hot oil, in batches, and cook until golden brown. Remove with a fish slice, drain and keep warm while you cook the remaining batches. Heat the tomato sauce. Finish cooking the rice by sautéing in the butter as described in recipe 173, then put it into a tart tin, pressing down lightly. Turn out on to the centre of a warm serving dish and place the breaded fish fillets around the edge. Pour 2 tablespoons of the tomato sauce over the rice and serve immediately, offering the rest of the tomato sauce separately.

586

Fried sole fillets with brandy and tomato mayonnaise

FILETES DE LENGUADO REBOZADOS Y FRITOS, SERVIDOS CON MAYONESA
DE COÑAC Y TOMATE

- **2 eggs**
- **80 g/3 oz plain flour**
- **sunflower oil, for deep-frying**
- **4 large sole, 300–400 g/**
  11–14 oz each, cleaned,
  filleted and skinned
- **salt**
- **2 quantities Mayonnaise with**
  Brandy and Tomato (see recipe
  108, but using ½ the mustard)

Serves 4–6

Beat the eggs in a shallow dish and spread out the flour in another shallow dish. Heat the oil in a deep-fryer or saucepan to 180–190°C/350–375°F or until a cube of day-old bread browns in 30 seconds. Lightly season the sole fillets with salt and coat them first in the flour, shaking off any excess, and then in the beaten eggs. Add to the hot oil, in batches, and cook until golden brown. Remove with a fish slice, drain and keep warm while you cook the remaining batches. Serve immediately, offering the mayonnaise separately.

587

Sole with butter

LENGUADOS MOLINERA CON MANTEQUILLA

- sunflower oil, for deep-frying
- 6 sole, 150–200 g/5–7 oz each, cleaned, filleted and skinned
- 50 g/2 oz plain flour
- 2 tablespoons chopped fresh parsley
- lemon wedges
- 150 g/5 oz butter
- juice of 1 lemon, strained
- salt

Serves 6

Heat the oil in a deep-fryer or saucepan to 180–190°C/350–375°F or until a cube of day-old bread browns in 30 seconds. Lightly season both sides of the sole with salt and coat them in the flour, shaking off any excess. Add them to the hot oil, two at a time, and cook until golden brown. Remove with a fish slice and keep warm while you cook the remaining fish. Transfer the cooked fish to a warm serving dish, sprinkle with the parsley and garnish with the lemon wedges. Melt the butter in a pan but do not allow it to brown. Remove the froth that rises to the surface with a spoon. Stir in the lemon juice and pour the hot butter over the fish. Serve immediately.

588

Baked sole with white wine

LENGUADO GRANDE ENTERO CON VINO BLANCO, AL HORNO

- 3 tablespoons sunflower oil
- 1 extra-large sole, about 1.5 kg/3¼ lb, or 2 large sole, about 600 g/1 lb 5 oz each, cleaned and skinned
- juice of 1 lemon
- 175 ml/6 fl oz white wine
- ¼ teaspoon paprika (optional)
- 2 tablespoon breadcrumbs
- 1 tablespoon chopped fresh parsley
- 50 g/2 oz butter
- salt

Serves 6

Preheat the oven to 180°C/350°F/Gas Mark 4. Pour the oil into a large ovenproof dish. Lightly season both sides of the sole with salt and place in the dish. Pour the lemon juice over the top, then the wine and gently rub the paprika, if using, over the fish with your fingertips. Sprinkle with the breadcrumbs and parsley and dot with the butter. Cover the dish with foil and bake for 15 minutes. Remove the foil and bake the fish for a further 5 minutes. Serve immediately, straight from the dish.

Note: Grouper can be used in place of sole in this dish but the cooking time should be increased slightly.

589

Baked stuffed sea bass
LUBINA RELLENA AL HORNO

- 1 sea bass or grouper, about
  1.5 kg/3¼ lb, scaled, trimmed,
  cleaned and boned
- 5 tablespoons sunflower oil
- juice of 1 lemon
- 50 g/2 oz butter
- 1 small onion
- salt

  Stuffing:
- 1 thick slice of bread,
  crusts removed
- 175 ml/6 fl oz hot milk
- 120 g/4 oz mushrooms,
  finely chopped
- 10 g/¼ oz butter
- a few drops of lemon juice
- 2 tablespoons olive oil
- 1 small onion, finely chopped
- 1 teaspoon chopped
  fresh parsley
- 1 egg, lightly beaten
- salt
  Serves 6

Season the fish inside and out with salt. Prepare the stuffing. Put the bread into a bowl, add the milk and leave to soak. Meanwhile, put the mushrooms, butter, lemon juice and a pinch of salt into a saucepan. Cover and cook over a medium heat for about 6 minutes. Heat the olive oil in a frying pan. Add the onion and cook over a low heat, stirring occasionally, for about 8 minutes, until beginning to brown. Remove the pan from the heat. Preheat the oven to 180°C/350°F/ Gas Mark 4. Gently squeeze out the bread, if necessary, and put it into a bowl with the onion, mushrooms, parsley, egg and a pinch of salt. Mix well and then use to fill the cavity of the fish. Sew up the opening with fine trussing thread, leaving a length hanging to help to pull out the stitches when the fish is ready to be served. Alternatively, secure the cavity with wooden cocktail sticks. Pour the sunflower oil into an ovenproof dish and add the fish. Slash the uppermost side twice without cutting into the flesh. Pour the lemon juice over the fish, sprinkle with salt and place knobs of butter under the fish. Bake, basting occasionally, for about 20 minutes, until the flesh flakes easily. Remove and discard the trussing thread or cocktail sticks and serve immediately.

590

Fried sea bass
LUBINAS DE RACIÓN FRITAS

- 6 sea bass or grouper,
  300–400 g/11–14 oz each,
  scaled, trimmed and cleaned
- sunflower oil, for deep-frying
- 50 g/2 oz plain flour
- 25 g/1 oz butter
- juice of 1 lemon
- 1 tablespoon chopped
  fresh parsley
- salt
  Serves 6

Slash the fish twice on both sides with a sharp knife. Season inside and out with salt. Heat the oil in a deep-fryer or saucepan to 180–190°C/350–375°F or until a cube of day-old bread browns in 30 seconds. Coat the fish in the flour, skaing off the excess, add them, two at a time, to the hot oil and cook until golden brown. Transfer to a serving dish and keep warm while you cook the remaining fish. Drain off the oil from the frying pan, add the butter and melt over a low heat. Remove the pan from the heat and stir in the lemon juice and parsley. Return the pan to the heat and warm through, stirring constantly. Pour the lemon butter over the fish and serve immediately.

Hake

Whiting can be used in place of hake in recipes 591, 592, 603, 604, 605. If you can't find fillets of hake, ask your fishmonger to fillet the fish for you.

591

Cooked hake, served with mayonnaise, vinaigrette or hollandaise sauce

MERLUZA COCIDA, SERVIDA CON SALSA MAYONESA, VINAGRETA U HOLANDESA

- 1.5–2 kg/3 ¼–4 ½ lb hake fillet, in a single piece
- sprigs fresh parsley
- lemon slices

To serve:
- 1 quantity Classic Mayonnaise (see recipe 105) or Vinaigrette (see recipes 98–101) or Hollandaise Sauce (see recipe 84)

Quick stock:
- 1 large carrot, sliced
- 1 large onion, cut into 4 slices
- juice of ½ lemon
- 1 bay leaf
- 175 ml/6 fl oz white wine
- salt

Serves 6

Remove the rack from a fish kettle. Pour in 2.5 litres/4 ¼ pints water and add all the stock ingredients. Bring to the boil, then lower the heat and simmer for 15 minutes. Remove the fish kettle from the heat and leave the stock to cool completely. Put the hake on the rack and replace the rack in the fish kettle so that the vegetables are underneath. Bring to the boil over a medium heat, then lower the heat and simmer very gently for 15–17 minutes, until the flesh flakes easily. Lift the rack to rest diagonally on top of the fish kettle and cover the hake with a clean tea towel wrung out in hot water, to keep it warm. Leave to drain for 5–10 minutes. Place a folded napkin in the base of a serving dish, put the hake on to it and garnish with parsley sprigs and lemon slices. Serve with your chosen sauce.

592

- 1 hake tail, about 1.5 kg/3¼ lb, boned
- 50 g/2 oz butter
- 150 g/5 oz gruyere cheese, grated
- 3 tablespoons sunflower oil
- 4 ripe tomatoes, peeled and halved
- salt

Serves 6

Hake baked with tomatoes and cheese

COLA DE MERLUZA AL HORNO, CON TOMATES Y QUESO RALLADO

Preheat the oven to 180°C/350°F/Gas Mark 4. Lightly season the hake inside and out with salt. Put half the butter and half the gruyere in the cavity and close the cavity to reshape the tail. Put the oil into an ovenproof dish. Reserve two tomato halves and put the remainder into the centre of the dish. Lightly season with salt. Place the hake on top of the tomatoes. Slash the fish twice and rub the tail with the remaining butter. Place a tomato half on each slash and sprinkle with the remaining cheese. Bake for about 20 minutes, until the fish is browned and the flesh flakes easily. Serve the hake immediately straight from the dish.

593

- 5 tablespoons olive oil
- 6 hake steaks
- 1 large onion
- 3 large ripe tomatoes, peeled, halved and seeded
- 100 g/3½ oz gruyere cheese, grated
- salt

Serves 6

Hake steaks with tomato, onion and grated cheese

RODAJAS DE MERLUZA CON TOMATE, CEBOLLA Y QUESO RALLADO

Preheat the oven to 160°C/325°F/Gas Mark 3. Put 4 tablespoons of the oil into an ovenproof dish and add the hake steaks in a single layer. Lightly season with salt and drizzle ½ teaspoon of the remaining oil over each steak. Cut the onion into six thin slices, discarding the thick end pieces, and place a slice on each steak. Put a tomato half on top. Sprinkle each steak with the gruyere and bake for about 25 minutes, until the fish flakes easily. Serve immediately straight from the dish.

594

Breaded hake fillets with green mayonnaise

FILETES DE MERLUZA EMPANADOS, SERVIDOS CON SALSA MAYONESA VERDE

- 6 hake fillets, 1.2 kg/2½ lb, total weight
- 250 ml/8 fl oz milk
- 2 eggs
- 80 g/3 oz breadcrumbs
- sunflower oil, for deep-frying
- 6 canned rolled anchovies, drained
- salt

Green mayonnaise:
- 2 eggs
- juice of 1 lemon
- 500 ml/18 fl oz sunflower oil
- 1 sprig fresh parsley
- 3 tablespoons capers, rinsed, drained and coarsely chopped
- 2 gherkins, coarsely chopped
- salt

Serves 6

Make the green mayonnaise as described in recipe 107. It should be quite thick. Put the hake fillets in a shallow dish, pour in the milk and leave to soak, turning occasionally, for 30 minutes. Meanwhile, beat the eggs in a shallow dish and spread out the breadcrumbs in another shallow dish. Drain the fish fillets, season with salt and dip them first in the beaten egg and then in the breadcrumbs. Heat the oil in a deep-fryer or saucepan to 180–190°C/350–375°F or until a cube of day-old bread browns in 30 seconds. Add the hake fillets, in batches, and cook until golden brown. Remove with a fish slice, drain well, transfer them to a serving dish and keep warm while you cook the remaining batches. Place a rolled anchovy on each fillet to garnish and serve immediately, offering the green mayonnaise separately.

Note: If using frozen hake fillets, leave to thaw completely before soaking in the milk.

595

Fried hake

FILETES DE MERLUZA REBOZADOS Y FRITOS

- 2 eggs
- 80 g/3 oz plain flour
- sunflower oil, for deep-frying
- 6 hake or whiting fillets 1.2 kg/2½ lb total weight
- 1 lemon, cut lengthways into 6 slices
- salt

Serves 6

Beat the eggs in a shallow dish and spread out the flour in another shallow dish. Heat the oil in a deep-fryer or deep saucepan to 180–190°C/350–375°F or until a cube of day-old bread browns in 30 seconds. Season the hake fillets with salt, then coat first in the flour, shaking off any excess, and then in the beaten egg. Add to the hot oil, in batches, and cook until golden brown. Remove with a fish slice, drain well, transfer to a serving dish and keep warm while you cook the remaining batches. Garnish with the lemon slices and serve immediately.

Note: To make the hake fillets more succulent, put them into a shallow dish, pour in milk to cover and leave to soak for 10 minutes. Turn the fish over, leave for a further 10 minutes and then drain and pat dry. Proceed as described above.

596

Fillets of hake wrapped in York ham

FILETES DE MERLUZA ENVUELTOS EN JAMÓN DE YORK

- 12 hake fillets, 750g–1kg/
  1lb 10 oz–2¼lb total weight
- 250 ml/8 fl oz milk
- 6 thin slices of York or
  other dry-cured ham, halved
- 2 eggs
- 50g/2oz plain flour
- sunflower oil, for deep-frying
- 1 lemon, cut into wedges
- salt

Serves 6

Put the hake fillets into a deep dish, pour the milk over them and leave to soak for 30 minutes, turning them twice. Drain and pat dry. Season with salt, wrap each fillet in half a slice of the ham and secure with a wooden cocktail stick. Beat the eggs in a shallow dish and spread out the flour in another shallow dish. Heat the oil in a deep-fryer or saucepan to 180–190°C/350–375°F or until a cube of day-old bread browns in 30 seconds. Dip the wrapped fillets first in the flour and then in the beaten egg. Add to the hot oil, in batches, and cook until golden brown. Remove with a fish slice, drain well and keep warm while you cook the remaining batches. Serve immediately, garnished with the lemon wedges.

597

Hake in garlic sauce

MERLUZA EN ALLADA

- 2 large potatoes, thickly sliced
- 3 tablespoons olive oil
- 1 onion, chopped
- 8 cloves garlic, sliced
- 1 heaped teaspoon paprika
- 4 hake or other white fish steaks
- salt

Serves 4

Put the potato slices into a flameproof casserole, pour in water to cover and add a pinch of salt. Bring to the boil, lower the heat and cook for 20 minutes. Meanwhile, heat the oil in a frying pan. Add the onion and cook over a low heat, stirring occasionally, for about 5 minutes, until softened and translucent. Add the garlic and cook, stirring occasionally for a further 5 minutes. Remove the pan from the heat and stir in the paprika. Season the hake steaks lightly with salt and add to the potato slices at the end of the cooking time. Bring back to the boil and cook for a further 5 minutes. Drain off nearly all the water from the casserole, add the onion mixture and cook for a further 5 minutes. You can either serve the dish immediately or heat it through in a preheated oven at 180°C/350°F/Gas Mark 4 for a few more minutes.

598

Baked hake tail with béchamel sauce and mushrooms

COLA DE MERLUZA AL HORNO CON BECHAMEL Y CHAMPIÑONES

- 1 hake tail,
  1.2–1.5 kg / 2¼–3¼ lb
- 50 g / 2 oz butter
- 2 tablespoons sunflower oil
- 1 heaped tablespoon plain flour
- 500 ml / 18 fl oz milk
- 80 g / 3 oz gruyere cheese, grated
- 120 g / 4 oz mushrooms,
  stalks removed
- a few drops of lemon juice
- salt

Serves 6

Preheat the oven to 180°C/350°F/Gas Mark 4. Lightly season the hake with salt and put it into a deep ovenproof dish. Melt half the butter with the oil in a saucepan. Stir in the flour and cook, stirring constantly, for 2 minutes. Gradually stir in the milk, a little at a time. Season with salt and cook, stirring constantly, for about 10 minutes, until thickened. Pour the sauce over the fish, sprinkle with the gruyere and bake for about 25 minutes, until golden brown. Put the mushroom caps, remaining butter, the lemon juice and a pinch of salt into a saucepan and cook for about 6 minutes, until tender. Remove from the heat and set aside. At the end of the cooking time, remove the dish from the oven and place the mushroom caps in a line along the fish, then return the dish to the oven and cook for 5 minutes more. Serve immediately, straight from the dish.

599

Hake fried in flour

RODAJAS DE MERLUZA FRITA SÓLO CON HARINA

- **6 thick hake steaks**
- **sunflower oil, for deep-frying**
- **50 g/2 oz plain flour**
- **1 lemon, cut into 6 thick slices**
- **salt**

Serves 6

Season the hake steaks on both sides with salt. Heat the oil in a deep-fryer or saucepan to 180–190°C/350–375°F or until a cube of day-old bread browns in 30 seconds. Coat the fish steaks with the flour, shaking off any excess, add to the oil, in batches of two, and cook until golden brown. Remove with a fish slice, drain and keep warm while you cook the remaining batches. Garnish each steak with a slice of lemon and serve immediately.

600

• 6 thick hake steaks
• sunflower oil, for deep-frying
• 50 g/2 oz plain flour
• 2 eggs, beaten
• 1 lemon, cut into wedges
• salt

Serves 6

Fried hake steaks

RODAJAS DE MERLUZA FRITAS REBOZADAS

Season the hake steaks on both sides with salt. Heat the oil in a deep-fryer or saucepan to 180–190°C/350–375°F or until a cube of day-old bread browns in 30 seconds. Coat the fish steaks first in the flour, shaking off any excess, and then in the beaten egg. Add the steaks to the hot oil, in batches of two, and cook until golden brown. Remove with a fish slice, drain and keep warm while you cook the remaining batches. Serve immediately garnished with the lemon wedges.

601

• 6 frozen hake steaks
• 250 ml/8 fl oz milk
• 50 g/2 oz plain flour
• 2 eggs, beaten
• sunflower oil, for deep-frying
• 1 lemon, cut into wedges
• salt

Serves 6

Fried frozen hake

RODAJAS DE MERLUZA CONGELADA FRITAS

Put the hake steaks into a bowl of cold water with 3 tablespoons salt and leave to thaw. Drain well, put the steaks into a deep dish and pour in the milk to cover. Leave to soak, turning several times, for 30 minutes. Drain well, then coat the steaks first in the flour, shaking off any excess, and then in the beaten egg. Cook the steaks in hot oil as described in recipe 600. Serve immediately, garnished with the lemon wedges.

602

• sunflower oil, for deep-frying
• 3 slices of bread, about 2 cm/
  ¾ inch thick, crusts removed,
  cut into small squares
• 6 thick hake steaks
• 50 g/2 oz plain flour
• 1 tablespoon chopped
  fresh parsley
• 40 g/1½ oz butter
• 3 tablespoons capers,
  rinsed and drained
• salt

Serves 6

Hake steaks garnished with croûtons and capers

RODAJAS DE MERLUZA FRITAS ADORNADAS CON CURRUSQUITOS DE PAN FRITO Y ALCAPARRAS

Heat the oil in a frying pan. Add the bread squares and cook for a few minutes, until lightly golden. Remove with a slotted spoon, drain and set aside. Reserve the oil in the frying pan. Season the hake steaks on both sides with salt and coat them in the flour, shaking off any excess. Sprinkle some of the parsley over each steak and press down gently to make sure it adheres to the fish. Reheat the oil to 180–190°C/350–375°F or until a cube of day-old bread browns in 30 seconds. Add the steaks to the hot oil, in batches of two, and cook until golden brown all over. Remove with a fish slice, drain and keep warm while you cook the remaining steaks. Drain off most of the oil from the frying pan, leaving just enough to cover the base. Melt the butter in the pan and skim off the froth with a spoon. Add the capers and croûtons and stir for 1–2 minutes. Pour the sauce over the steaks and serve immediately.

603

Hake cooked with clams
RODAJAS DE MERLUZA GUISADA CON CHIRLAS

- sunflower oil, for deep-frying
- 6 thick hake steaks
- 50 g/2 oz plain flour
- 250 g/9 oz Venus clams
- 4 tablespoons olive oil
- 1 small onion, chopped
- 1 clove garlic, chopped
- 5 tablespoons white wine
- ½ teaspoon meat extract
- 1 tablespoon chopped
  fresh parsley
- salt

Serves 6

Heat the sunflower oil in a deep-fryer or saucepan to 180–190°C/350–375°F or until a cube of day-old bread browns in 30 seconds. Season the hake steaks on both sides with salt and coat in the flour, shaking off the excess. Reserve the remaining flour. Add the steaks to the hot oil, in batches, and cook until golden brown. Remove with a fish slice, drain and keep warm in a flameproof dish, while you cook the remaining batches. Wash the clams under cold running water and discard any with broken shells or any that do not shut immediately when sharply tapped. Put them into a saucepan and pour in water to cover. Cover and cook over a high heat, shaking the pan occasionally, for 3–5 minutes, until the shells have opened. Remove the pan from the heat and lift out the clams with a slotted spoon. Discard any that remain shut. Strain the cooking liquid through a muslin-lined sieve into a bowl. Remove the clams from their shells, put into another bowl and add a little of the reserved cooking liquid. Heat the olive oil in a frying pan. Add the onion and garlic and cook over a low heat, stirring occasionally, for 5 minutes, until softened and translucent. Stir in the reserved flour and cook, stirring constantly, for about 4 minutes, until lightly coloured. Gradually stir in the wine, a little at a time, and the reserved cooking liquid. Cook, stirring constantly, for 10 minutes, then remove the pan from the heat and stir in the meat extract. Pass the sauce through a food mill and then pour it over the hake steaks. Scatter the clams and sprinkle the parsley on top. If there does not seem to be enough sauce, add a little warm water. Season to taste with salt and cook over a medium heat, gently shaking the dish occasionally, for about 10 minutes, until the sauce has thickened. Serve immediately, straight from the dish.

Hake steaks in green sauce

RODAJAS DE MERLUZA EN SALSA VERDE

- **4 tablespoons olive oil**
- **1 onion, chopped**
- **1 clove garlic**
- **2–3 sprigs fresh parsley**
- **1 tablespoon plain flour**
- **6 thick hake or whiting steaks,**
  about 200 g/7 oz each
- **1 tablespoon very finely**
  chopped fresh parsley
- **120 g/4 oz canned peas,**
  drained (optional)
- **1–2 hard-boiled eggs,**
  chopped (optional)
- **salt and pepper**

Serves 6

Heat the oil in a frying pan. Add the onion and cook over a low heat, stirring occasionally, for 5 minutes, until softened and translucent Meanwhile, crush the garlic with the parsley sprigs and a pinch of salt in a mortar. Stir the flour into the frying pan and cook, stirring constantly, for 2 minutes. Gradually stir in 450 ml/¾ pint water, a little at a time. Cook, stirring constantly, for 5 minutes. Stir 2 tablespoons of the sauce into the garlic mixture, mix well and then stir into the frying pan. Pass the sauce through a food mill or push through a coarse sieve into a flameproof dish. Lightly season the hake steaks with salt and add to the dish. The sauce should just cover them, but if not, add a little more water. Lightly season with pepper, sprinkle with the chopped parsley and add the peas, if using. Cook over a medium heat, gently shaking the dish occasionally, for about 15 minutes. Taste and adjust the seasoning, occasionally, if necessary. Sprinkle with the hard-boiled eggs, if using, and serve immediately straight from the dish.

Note: This dish can be made using 1.5 kg/3 ¼ lb grouper steaks in place of the hake but the cooking time will need to be increased.

605

Basque hake
RODAJAS DE MERLUZA A LA VASCA

- 1 bunch thin asparagus, trimmed
- 500 g/1 lb 2 oz peas, shelled
- 4 tablespoons olive oil
- 1 onion, chopped
- 1 clove garlic, chopped
- 1 tablespoon plain flour
- 1 sprig fresh parsley
- 6 thick hake steaks,
  about 200 g/7 oz each
- 1 tablespoon chopped
  fresh parsley
- 1 hard-boiled egg, chopped
- salt

Serves 6

Bring a large saucepan of salted water to the boil. Add the asparagus, submerging it completely, cover, bring back to the boil and cook for about 10 minutes, until tender. Drain well and set aside. Bring another saucepan of salted water to the boil, add the peas and cook for 20–30 minutes, until tender. Drain well and set aside. Heat the oil in a frying pan. Add the onion and garlic and cook over a low heat, stirring occasionally, for 5–7 minutes, until the onion is softened and translucent. Stir in the flour and cook, stirring constantly, for 2 minutes. Gradually stir in 250 ml/8 fl oz water and add the parsley sprig. Cook, stirring constantly, for 8 minutes. Remove from the heat and pass through a food mill or push through a sieve into a bowl. Lightly season the hake steaks with salt, put them into a flameproof dish and pour the sauce over them, adding about 450 ml/¾ pint water, if necessary (the fish should be covered). Cook over a medium heat, gently shaking the dish occasionally, for 12 minutes. Sprinkle the parsley over the steaks, add the peas, asparagus and hard-boiled egg and heat gently for about 5 minutes to warm through. Season to taste with salt and serve immediately, straight from the dish.

Notes: You can substitute drained canned asparagus and/or peas for the fresh vegetables. Grouper can be used in place of hake in this dish.

Baked hake with wine and cream sauce

RODAJAS DE MERLUZA AL HORNO CON SALSA DE VINO Y NATA

- **5 tablespoons olive oil**
- **6 thick hake steaks**
- **3–4 tablespoons breadcrumbs**
- **25 g/1 oz butter**
- **1 shallot, very finely chopped**
- **175 ml/6 fl oz white wine**
- **250 ml/8 fl oz single cream**
- **salt**

Serves 6

Preheat the oven to 180°C/350°F/Gas Mark 4. Pour 3 tablespoons of the oil into an ovenproof dish. Season the hake steaks on both sides with salt, put them into the dish, sprinkle with the breadcrumbs and dot with the butter. Bake for about 15 minutes. Meanwhile, heat the remaining oil in a frying pan. Add the shallot and cook over a low heat, stirring occasionally for about 5 minutes, until softened and translucent. Add the wine and cook for a further 8 minutes. Remove the pan from the heat and gradually stir in the cream. Pour the sauce over the fish and return the dish to the oven but turn off the heat. Leave for about 5 minutes to warm through, then serve immediately straight from the dish.

607

- 3 tablespoons sunflower oil
- 6 thick hake steaks
- 120 ml/4 fl oz white wine
- juice of 1½ lemons
- 4 sprigs fresh parsley
- 2 tablespoons breadcrumbs
- 40 g/1½ oz butter
- 100 g/3½ oz mushrooms, sliced
- 250 ml/8 fl oz single cream
- salt

Serves 6

Baked hake with cream and mushroom sauce

RODAJAS DE MERLUZA AL HORNO CON SALSA DE NATA Y CHAMPIÑONES

Preheat the oven to 180°C/350°F/Gas Mark 4. Pour the oil into an ovenproof dish. Season the hake steaks on both sides with salt and put them into the dish in a single layer. Pour in the white wine and 5 tablespoons of the lemon juice and place the parsley sprigs between the steaks. Sprinkle 1 teaspoon of the breadcrumbs over each steak and dot with 25 g/1 oz of the butter. Bake for about 10 minutes, until golden brown. Meanwhile, put the mushrooms, the remaining butter and the remaining lemon juice into a saucepan. Cover and cook over a medium heat for 6 minutes. Stir in the cream and warm the sauce through but do not allow to boil. Remove the parsley sprigs from the dish and discard. Lower the oven temperature to 110°C/225°F/Gas Mark ¼. Pour the mushroom sauce over the hake steaks, return the dish to the oven and cook for a further 5 minutes. Serve immediately, straight from the dish.

Note: Grouper can be used in place of hake in this dish.

608

- 6 fresh or frozen hake steaks
- 250 ml/8 fl oz sunflower oil
- 2 potatoes, thinly sliced
- 2 cloves garlic, finely chopped
- 1 tablespoon chopped fresh parsley
- juice of 1 lemon
- salt

Serves 6

Quick hake

MERLUZA RÁPIDA

If using frozen hake, put the steaks into a bowl of cold water with 3 tablespoons salt and leave for about 1 hour, until thawed. Drain, rinse under cold running water and pat dry. Preheat the oven to 180°C/350°F/Gas Mark 4. Heat the oil in a frying pan. Add the potato slices and cook over a low heat for 5–8 minutes, until softened but not browned. Remove with a slotted spoon and put into an ovenproof dish. Put the hake steaks on top. Drain off nearly all the oil from the frying pan, leaving just enough to coat the base. Add the garlic and cook over a low heat, stirring frequently, for a few minutes, until beginning to brown. Remove the pan from the heat, stir in the parsley and pour the mixture over the fish. Bake for about 15 minutes, until the steaks are opaque and the flesh flakes easily. Remove the dish from the oven, season with salt and sprinkle with the lemon juice.

Notes: This dish can be cooked on the hob rather than in the oven, but it will be drier. The secret of this dish's flavour is that neither the salt nor the lemon juice are added until just before serving.

609

Frozen hake with onion
RODAJAS DE MERLUZA CONGELADA CON CEBOLLA

- **5 tablespoons sunflower oil**
- **2 large onions, chopped**
- **6 thick frozen hake steaks, thawed (see recipe 608)**
- **juice of 1 lemon**
- **salt**

Serves 6

Pour the oil into a saucepan and add about two-thirds of the onion. Season the hake steaks on both sides with salt, put them on top of the onion and pour in the lemon juice. Sprinkle the remaining onion on top of the fish. Cover and cook over a low heat for 15 minutes. Carefully transfer the steaks to a warm serving dish with a fish slice and serve immediately.

610

Hake with almond, garlic and white wine sauce
COLA DE MERLUZA AL HORNO CON SALSA DE ALMENDRAS, AJOS
Y VINO BLANCO

- 500 ml/18 fl oz sunflower oil
- 2 potatoes, thinly sliced
- 1.2–1.5 kg/2½–3¼ lb hake, cleaned and filleted
- 50 g/2 oz plain flour
- salt

Sauce:
- 3 slices of bread, 1 cm/ ½ inch thick, crusts removed
- 2 tablespoons olive oil
- 1 small onion, chopped
- 3 cloves garlic
- 2 sprigs fresh parsley
- 8 almonds
- 275 ml/9 fl oz white wine
- salt

Serves 4

Heat the sunflower oil in a frying pan. Add the slices of bread for the sauce and cook, turning occasionally, until golden brown on both sides. Remove from the pan and set aside. Add the potato slices to the pan and cook for 5–10 minutes, until softened and just beginning to colour. Transfer to an ovenproof dish with a slotted spoon. Lightly season the hake fillets with salt and coat with the flour, shaking off the excess. Add the hake fillets to the pan, one at a time, and cook until golden brown. Remove with a fish slice and place on top of the potatoes. Preheat the oven to 180°C/350°F/Gas Mark 4. To make the sauce, heat the oil in a frying pan. Add the onion and cook over a low heat, stirring occasionally, for about 8 minutes, until beginning to brown. Pound the fried bread with the garlic, parsley and almonds in a mortar, then add to the pan. Pour in the wine and 5 tablespoons water, lightly season with salt and cook for 5 minutes. Pass the mixture through a food mill and pour it over the hake fillets. Bake for 10 minutes, then serve immediately straight from the dish

611

Fried hake cheeks
COCOCHAS REBOZADAS FRITAS

- 600 g/1 lb 5 oz hake cheeks
- sunflower oil, for deep-frying
- 50 g/2 oz plain flour
- 2 eggs, beaten

Serves 6

Ask your fish supplier to skin and bone the hake cheeks. Heat the sunflower oil in a deep-fryer or saucepan to 180–190°C/350–375°F or until a cube of day-old bread browns in 30 seconds. One at a time, lightly coat the hake cheeks first in the flour, and then in the beaten egg. Add to the hot oil, in batches of two, and cook until golden brown. Remove with a slotted spoon, drain on kitchen paper and keep warm while you cook the remaining batches. Serve immediately.

Note: This dish can be made with cod cheeks.

Fried whiting biting their tails

PESCADILLAS FRITAS QUE SE MUERDEN LA COLA

- **6 whiting, 350–400 g/12–14 oz each, scaled, trimmed and cleaned, with heads and tails**
- **sunflower oil, for deep-frying**
- **40 g/1½ oz plain flour**
- **1 lemon, cut into wedges**
- **salt**

Serves 6

Season the whiting inside and out with salt. Place the tails in the mouths and press down gently so that the teeth get a good grip. Heat the oil in a deep-fryer or saucepan to 180–190°C/350–375°F or until a cube of day-old bread browns in 30 seconds. Coat the whiting in the flour, shaking off any excess, add to the hot oil, in batches of two, and cook until golden brown. Remove with a fish slice, drain and keep warm while you cook the remaining batches. Serve immediately, garnished with the lemon wedges.

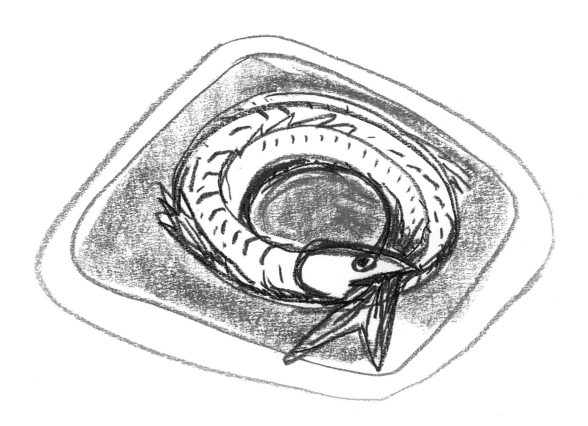

613 Fried coated whiting

PESCADILLAS ABIERTAS, REBOZADAS Y FRITAS

- 6 whiting, 350–400 g/
  12–14 oz each, scaled,
  trimmed, cleaned and boned
- 2 eggs
- 40 g/1½ oz plain flour
- sunflower oil, for deep-frying
- salt
- 1½ lemons, cut into wedges

Serves 6

Season the whiting with salt. Beat the eggs in a shallow dish and spread out the flour in another shallow dish. Heat the oil in a deep-fryer or saucepan to 180–190°C/350–375°F or until a cube of day-old bread browns in 30 seconds. Dip the fish first in the flour, shaking off any excess, and then in the beaten egg. Add to the hot oil, in batches, and cook until golden brown. Remove with a fish slice, drain and keep warm while you cook the remaining batches. Serve immediately, garnished with the lemon wedges.

614 Whiting baked with wine and currants

PESCADILLAS AL HORNO CON VINO Y PASAS

- 3 tablespoons olive oil
- 6 whiting, 350–400 g/
  12–14 oz each, scaled,
  trimmed, cleaned and boned
- 1 tablespoon breadcrumbs
- 50 g/2 oz butter
- 175 ml/6 fl oz muscatel wine
- juice of 1½ lemons
- 80 g/3 oz currants
- 2 egg yolks
- salt

Serves 6

Preheat the oven to 180°C/350°F/Gas Mark 4. Pour the oil into an ovenproof dish. Season the whiting with salt, fold them in half, skin side outside, and put into the dish. Sprinkle with breadcrumbs and dot with 20 g/¾ oz of the butter. Pour in half the wine and half the lemon juice and bake for 15 minutes. Meanwhile put the currants and the remaining wine into a small saucepan and heat gently until warmed through. Remove the pan from the heat and set aside. Melt the re-maining butter in a frying pan. Stir in the remaining lemon juice and the wine and currants and cook for a few minutes, stirring constantly. Lightly beat the egg yolks in a bowl and gradually stir in a little of the sauce to prevent the yolks curdling, then stir into the frying pan. Pour the sauce over the whiting, shaking the dish so it penetrates. Return the dish to the oven, switch off the heat and leave for about 5 minutes. Serve straight from the dish.

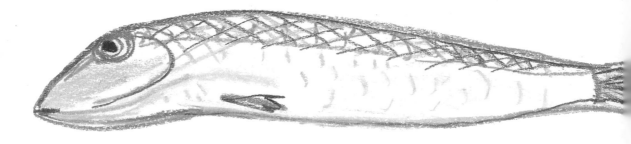

615

Baked whiting
PESCADILLA AL HORNO

- 4 tablespoons sunflower oil
- 1.5-kg/3¼-lb whiting fillet
- 1 tablespoon chopped
  fresh parsley
- 1½ tablespoons breadcrumbs
- 50g/2oz butter
- juice of 1 lemon
- salt

Serves 6

Preheat the oven to 180°C/350°F/Gas Mark 4. Pour the oil into an ovenproof dish and add the whiting, skin side down. Season with salt, sprinkle with the parsley and breadcrumbs and dot with the butter and drizzle with the lemon juice. Bake for about 15 minutes. Serve immediately, straight from the dish.

616

Swordfish with onions and white wine
PEZ ESPADA CON CEBOLLA Y VINO BLANCO

- 450ml/¾ pint sunflower oil
- 1kg/2¼lb thin swordfish steaks
- 50g/2oz plain flour
- 2 large onions,
  cut into long thin strips
- 175ml/6floz white wine
- salt

Serves 6

Heat the oil in a frying pan. Lightly season the swordfish steaks on both sides with salt and coat in the flour, shaking off the excess. Add to the pan, in batches, and cook over a medium heat until golden brown. Remove from the pan and set aside. Transfer 3 tablespoons of the oil from the frying pan to a saucepan and reheat. Add the onion and cook over a low heat, stirring occasionally, for about 5 minutes. Pour in the wine and 175ml/6floz water and simmer, stirring occasionally, for 10 minutes. Add the steaks and simmer for a further 10 minutes, until the flesh flakes easily. Serve immediately.

617

Swordfish with toasted sauce
PEZ ESPADA CON SALSA TOSTADA

- 1½ tablespoons plain flour
- 250ml/8floz sunflower oil
- 4 swordfish steaks
- 2 small onions, thinly sliced and
  pushed out into rings
- 175ml/6floz fish stock (home-
  made or made with a stock cube)
- 2 tablespoons sherry (optional)
- 1 tablespoon capers, rinsed and
  drained
- salt and pepper

Serves 4

Heat the flour in a non-stick frying pan, stirring constantly, until browned, then set aside. Heat the oil in a large frying pan. Add the swordfish steaks and cook for about 5 minutes on each side. Remove from the pan and set aside. Pour off nearly all the oil from the frying pan, leaving just enough to cover the base. Add the onion and cook over a low heat, stirring occasionally, for about 5 minutes, until translucent. Stir in the flour, then gradually stir in the stock, a little at a time, followed by the sherry, if using. Season to taste and cook, stirring constantly, for a few minutes more, until thickened a little. Add the steaks and simmer very gently for 5 minutes. Stir in the capers and warm through. Serve immediately.

618

Swordfish with prawn and clam sauce

FILETES DE PEZ ESPADA CON SALSA DE GAMBAS Y ALMEJAS

- 250 g/ 9 oz carpetshell
  or Venus clams
- 250 g/9 oz raw unpeeled prawns
- 1 kg/2¼ lb thin swordfish steaks
- 40 g/1½ oz plain flour
- 500 ml/18 fl oz sunflower oil
- 1 large onion, chopped
- 3 tablespoons sherry
- pinch of saffron threads
  or powder
- 1 clove garlic
- salt

Serves 6

Scrub the clams under cold running water and discard any with damaged shells or any that do not shut when sharply tapped. Put them into a saucepan, pour in 175 ml/6 fl oz water, cover and cook over a high heat, shaking the pan occasionally, for 3–5 minutes, until the shells have opened. Remove the clams with a slotted spoon and discard any that remain shut. Strain the cooking liquid through a muslin-lined sieve into a bowl. Remove the clams from their shells and put them in the bowl. Peel the prawns and set them aside. Put the heads and shells in a saucepan, pour in water to cover and add a pinch of salt. Bring to the boil, then lower the heat and simmer for 10 minutes. Strain the stock into a bowl and set aside. Lightly season the sword fish steaks with salt. Reserve 1 tablespoon of the flour and spread out the remainder in a shallow dish. Heat the oil in a frying pan. Lightly coat the fish steaks in the flour, shaking off any excess, add to the hot oil and cook for about 5 minutes on each side, until golden brown. Remove from the pan with a fish slice, drain and put into a flame-proof dish. Measure the prawn stock and add enough of the reserved cooking liquid from the clams to make it up to 450 ml/¾ pint. Transfer about 4 tablespoons of the oil from the frying pan to a saucepan and reheat. Add the onion and cook over a low heat, stirring occasionally, for about 8 minutes, until beginning to brown. Stir in the reserved flour and cook, stirring constantly, for 2 minutes. Gradually stir in the sherry, a little at a time, then the prawn and clam stock. Crush the saffron with the garlic in a mortar, stir in 2 tablespoons water and add to the sauce. Strain the sauce over the swordfish steaks and add the prawns and clams. Season to taste with salt and cook over a medium heat, shaking the dish occasionally, for about 8 minutes, until the sauce has thickened. Add a little more water if necessary. Serve immediately, straight from the dish.

619

Monkfish with milk
RAPE CON LECHE

- 25 g/1 oz butter
- 3 tablespoons sunflower oil
- 1 large onion, finely chopped
- 1½ tablespoons plain flour
- 750 ml/1¼ pints milk
- ½ tablespoon tomato purée
- 6 monkfish (Aus: stargazer) fillets, about 1.5 kg/3¼ lb total weight
- salt

Serves 6

Ask your fish supplier for the monkfish backbone. Melt the butter with the oil in a frying pan. Add the onion and cook over a very low heat, stirring occasionally, for about 10 minutes, until softened but not browned. Stir in the flour and cook, stirring constantly, for 2 minutes. Gradually stir in the milk, a little at a time, then stir in the tomato purée, add the monkfish bone, if available, and lightly season with salt. Lightly season the monkfish fillets with salt and add them to the sauce. Simmer gently for about 8 minutes, until the flesh flakes easily. Remove and discard the bone and serve immediately.

620

American-style monkfish with tomatoes, Cognac and white wine

RAPE A LA AMERICANA CON TOMATE, COÑAC Y VINO BLANCO

- 120 ml/4 fl oz olive oil
- 6 monkfish (Aus: stargazer) fillets, about 1.5 kg/ 3¼ lb total weight
- 40 g/1½ oz plain flour
- 5 tablespoons Cognac or other brandy
- 1 shallot, very finely chopped
- 1 large clove garlic, lightly crushed
- pinch of dried mixed herbs
- 275 ml/9 fl oz dry white wine
- 6 very ripe tomatoes, seeded and chopped
- juice of 1 lemon
- 1 tablespoon finely chopped fresh parsley
- salt and pepper

Serves 6

Heat 6 tablespoons of the oil in a frying pan. Season the monkfish fillets with salt and coat lightly in the flour, shaking off any excess. Add to the pan and cook for about 5 minutes, until the flesh has become opaque. Drain off and discard the liquid released by the fish, add the remaining oil and cook for a further 5 minutes, until the fillets are light golden brown. Meanwhile, warm the Cognac or brandy in a small saucepan, ignite and leave until the flames have died down. Set aside. Sprinkle the shallot over the fillets, add the garlic, sprinkle in the dried herbs and pour in the brandy. Add the wine and tomato, lightly season with salt and pepper, cover and cook over a medium-high heat for 10 minutes. Lift out the fillets with a fish slice and put them into a warm deep serving dish. Pass the sauce through a food mill, stir in the lemon juice and pour it over the monkfish. Sprinkle with the parsley and serve immediately.

621

Monkfish in sauce with tomatoes and peas

RAPE EN SALSA CON TOMATES Y GUISANTES

- 250 ml/8 fl oz sunflower oil
- 40 g/1½ oz plain flour
- 6 monkfish (Aus: stargazer) fillets, about 1.5 kg/3¼ lb total weight
- 1 large onion, finely chopped
- 2 tomatoes, peeled, seeded and chopped
- 2 cloves garlic
- pinch of saffron threads
- 100 g/3½ oz canned peas, drained
- 1 tablespoon chopped fresh parsley

Serves 6

Heat the oil in a frying pan. Reserve 1 tablespoon of the flour and spread out the remainder in a dish. Lightly coat the monkfish fillets in the flour, shaking off any excess, add to the pan and cook for about 5 minutes. Remove from the pan with a fish slice and set aside. Transfer 4 tablespoons of the oil from the frying pan to a saucepan and reheat. Add the onion and cook over a low heat, stirring occasionally, for about 8 minutes, until browned. Add the tomato and cook, stirring frequently, for 10 minutes. Stir in the reserved flour and cook, stirring constantly, for 2 minutes. Gradually stir in 450 ml/¾ pint water, a little at a time. Crush the garlic with the saffron and a pinch of salt in a mortar. Stir in 2 tablespoons of the sauce, then add to the pan. Season to taste with salt and simmer for 10 minutes. Add the fillets. If there is not enough liquid to cover them, add some more water. Cook for a further 10 minutes, then add the peas and heat through gently. Transfer to a warm serving dish, sprinkle with the parsley and serve.

Monkfish and potato soup

BOUILLABAISSE DE RAPE Y PATATAS

- 1 kg/2¼ lb monkfish
  (Aus: stargazer) fillet,
  cut into chunks
- pinch of saffron threads
- 2 cloves garlic
- 5 tablespoons white wine
- 6 tablespoons olive oil
- juice of ½ lemon
- 1 onion, very finely chopped
- 500 g/1 lb 2 oz potatoes,
  cut into fairly thick slices
- 450 ml/¾ pint fish stock (home-
  made or made with a stock cube)
- 1 tablespoon chopped
  fresh parsley
- salt

Serves 6

Put the monkfish chunks into a non-metallic bowl. Crush the saffron with one of the garlic cloves and a pinch of salt in a mortar. Stir in the wine, then pour the mixture over the fish and add 2 tablespoons of the oil, the lemon juice and 5 tablespoons water. Mix well and leave to marinate in the refrigerator, stirring occasionally, for 3–4 hours. Heat the remaining oil in a saucepan. Add the onion and the remaining garlic clove and cook over a low heat, stirring occasionally, for about 10 minutes, until lightly browned. Add the potato slices and cook, stirring frequently, for 5 minutes. Pour in the fish stock. If there is not enough liquid to cover the ingredients, add a little water. Season with salt and cook over a high heat for 20 minutes. Add the monkfish chunks, together with their marinade, stir well and cook for a further 10 minutes. Taste and adjust the seasoning if necessary. Serve immediately, sprinkled with the parsley.

623

Monkfish and vegetable stew
ESTOFADO DE RAPE CON VERDURAS

- 800 g/1¾ lb monkfish
  (Aus: stargazer) fillets
- 40 g/1½ oz plain flour
- 4 tablespoons olive oil
- 200 g/7 oz diced mixed
  vegetables, fresh, frozen and
  thawed or canned and drained
- 100 ml/3½ fl oz white wine
- 200 ml/7 fl oz fish stock (home-
  made or made with a stock cube)
- 150 ml/¼ pint single cream
- 2 tablespoons Classic Tomato
  Sauce (see recipe 73)
- 1 sprig fresh parsley, chopped
- salt and pepper

Serves 4

Cut the monkfish fillets into medallions, coat them in the flour and shake off any excess. Heat half the oil in a frying pan, add the fish and cook for 7 minutes, until the flesh flakes easily. Remove with a fish slice and keep warm. Heat the remaining oil in another frying pan. Add the mixed vegetables and cook over a medium-low heat, stirring occasionally, until tender. Remove the pan from the heat, drain off the oil and keep warm. Drain off most of the oil from the first frying pan, add the wine and cook over a medium heat until reduced by half. Lower the heat, add the stock and cream and cook until thickened, then stir in the tomato sauce and heat through. Spoon the sauce over individual warm serving plates, add the fish and vegetables and garnish with the parsley.

624

- 1.5 kg/3¼ lb skate wings
- 150 g/5 oz butter
- 2 tablespoons pickled capers, drained, plus 2 tablespoons vinegar from the jar
- salt

Stock:
- 5 tablespoons white-wine vinegar
- 1 onion, cut into wedges
- 2 bay leaves
- 10 black peppercorns

Serves 6

Skate in black butter and caper sauce

RAYA COCIDA CON SALSA DE MANTEQUILLA NEGRA Y ALCAPARRAS

Put the skate into a saucepan with all the stock ingredients, season with salt and pour in water to cover. Bring to the boil, lower the heat and simmer gently for 15 minutes. Lift out the skate wings with a fish slice and remove and discard the skin, if this has not already been done. Drain the fish well and transfer to a warm serving dish. Melt the butter in a frying pan. As soon as it begins to turn brown and smell nutty, remove the pan from the heat and carefully add the capers and vinegar. Return the pan to the heat and warm through, then pour the sauce over the fish and serve immediately.

Skate in gelatine with green mayonnaise
RAYA EN GELATINA CON MAYONESA DE ALCAPARRAS

- 1 kg/2¼ lb skate wings
- 2 tablespoons powdered gelatine
- 2 tablespoons sherry
- lettuce leaves and 2 sliced tomatoes
- 1 quantity Green Mayonnaise (see recipe 107)
- salt

Stock:
- 5 tablespoons white-wine vinegar
- 1 onion, cut into wedges
- 2 bay leaves
- 10 black peppercorns

Serves 6

Cook the skate with the stock ingredients and add enough water to cover, as described in recipe 624. Drain well and flake the fish. Pour 500 ml/18 fl oz water into a heatproof bowl and sprinkle the gelatine over the surface. Leave to sponge for 5 minutes, then set the bowl over a pan of barely simmering water and heat until the gelatine has dissolved and the mixture is clear. Remove from the heat and stir in the sherry. Put a little gelatine into a 5-cm/2-inch deep round mould to cover the base, and chill in the refrigerator for 15 minutes, until set. Put the fish into the mould, pour in the remaining gelatine and chill for about 3 hours, until set. Run a round-bladed knife around the edge of the mould and invert on to a serving dish. Garnish with the lettuce leaves and slices of tomato and serve with the mayonnaise.

Note: This dish can be made with any fish that has quite firm flesh, such as sea bream, hake and sea bass.

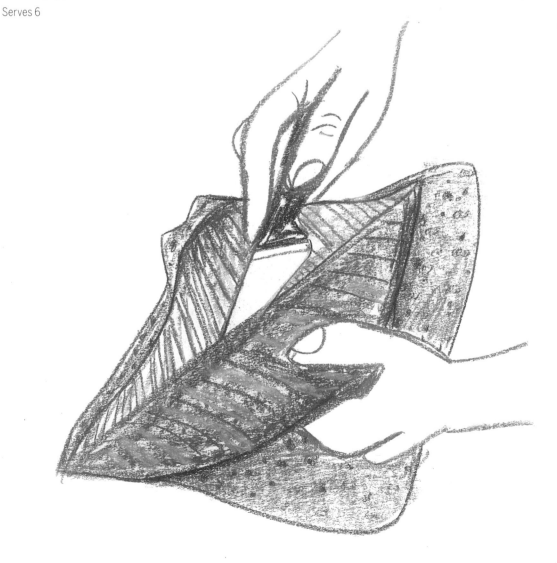

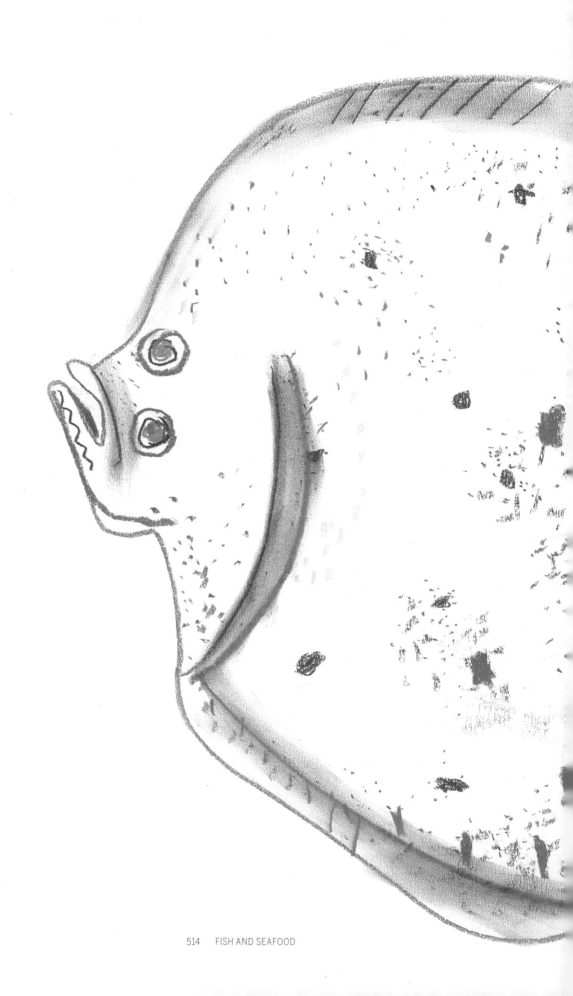

Turbot

A large European flatfish that is highly prized for its fine flavour, turbot is sold whole, and as fillets, steaks and tronçons (slices). It can be difficult to obtain outside Europe, in which case substitute the best-quality local flatfish available, such as halibut.

How to prepare

When buying a whole turbot, ask the fishmonger to prepare the fish for you (removing the head, tail and frill and cleaning it). Rinse the fish thoroughly, sprinkle with salt and put it on a slightly inclined rack in a diamond-shaped fish kettle to drain for about 2 hours. Rinse the fish again and rinse the fish kettle and rack. Put the turbot on the rack, dark side down. Using a sharp knife, make two deep incisions, one on each side of the backbone. If you don't have a diamond-shaped fish kettle, cut the fish into large pieces and place into an oblong fish kettle or a frying pan. If you use a frying pan, lift the portions out with a fish slice and drain in a colander set over the pan.

626

Poached turbot

RODABALLO COCIDO

• **200 g/7 oz turbot per serving, trimmed and cleaned**

Quick stock with milk:
• **250 ml/8 fl oz milk**
• **½ lemon, peeled and sliced**
• **1 bay leaf**
• **salt**

Makes enough for 1 serving

Make the stock as described in recipe 534 and allow to cool. Remove the rack from a diamond-shaped fish kettle and pour in the stock. Place the turbot on the rack and replace it. Bring the stock just to the boil, then lower the heat and poach the fish very gently for 15–20 minutes. Do not take the fish out of the stock in advance of serving it, unlike other fish. It can be left in its concentrated stock for up to 30 minutes, but should not cook any further before being served. If it is to be served cold, leave the fish to cool in the stock. Put it on to a doubled-over napkin to drain. Remove the skin before serving.

Note: To serve turbot hot, it may be accompanied by Hollandaise Sauce (see recipe 84), Mousseline Sauce (see recipe 87), or Black Butter and Caper Sauce (see recipe 96). To serve it cold, it can be accompanied by all varieties of mayonnaise (see recipes 105–109).

627

Turbot with mussels
RODABALLO AL HORNO CON MEJILLONES

- 1 turbot, 1.2–1.5 kg/2½–3¼ lb, trimmed and cleaned
- 1 kg/2¼ lb mussels
- 175 ml/6 fl oz white wine
- 25 g/1 oz butter
- 2 tablespoons sunflower oil
- 1 heaped tablespoon plain flour
- 250 ml/8 fl oz fish stock (home-made or made with a stock cube)
- 2 egg yolks
- 1 tablespoon chopped fresh parsley
- salt

Quick stock with milk:
- 250 ml/8 fl oz milk
- ½ lemon, peeled and sliced
- 1 bay leaf
- salt and black peppercorns

Serves 6

Remove the rack from a diamond-shaped fish kettle. Prepare the stock as described in recipe 534, in the kettle. Put the turbot on the rack and return it to the fish kettle. Bring the stock just to the boil, then lower the heat and poach the fish very gently for 20 minutes. Meanwhile, scrape the mussel shells with the blade of a knife and remove the 'beards', then scrub under cold running water. Discard any mussels with broken shells or any that do not shut immediately when sharply tapped. Put them into a saucepan, pour in the wine, cover and cook over a high heat, shaking the pan occasionally, for 4–5 minutes, until they have opened. Remove the mussels with a slotted spoon and discard any that remain shut. Strain the cooking liquid through a muslin-lined sieve into a bowl. Remove the mussels from their shells and set aside. Melt the butter with the oil in a saucepan. Stir in the flour and cook, stirring constantly, for 2 minutes. Gradually stir in the reserved cooking liquid, a little at a time, followed by the stock. Cook, stirring constantly, for about 10 minutes, until thickened. Season to taste with salt. Remove the turbot from the fish kettle and carefully remove the skin and bones. Cut the flesh into large pieces and put into a warm serving dish. Lightly beat the egg yolks in a bowl and stir in a little of the sauce to prevent them curdling, then add to the sauce, together with the mussels. Mix well and pour the sauce over the turbot. Sprinkle with the parsley and serve.

628

Cooked salmon

SALMÓN COCIDO

- 200 g / 7 oz salmon per serving

Special quick stock:
- 1 bay leaf
- 1 thick slice of onion
- 1 large carrot, sliced
- 175 ml / 6 fl oz white wine
- juice of ½ lemon
- salt

Serves 4–6

Make the stock as described in recipe 534. Allow to cool, then remove the rack from a fish kettle, and pour in the stock. Place the salmon in the rack and return it to the kettle. Bring the stock just to the boil, then lower the heat so that the salmon cooks very gently. Allow about 20 minutes per 1 kg / 2 ¼ lb fish. Salmon may be served hot or cold, with various sauces.

Notes: For this dish you can use fillets, steaks, a whole tail or even the whole fish if there are a lot of guests and a big enough fish kettle is available. To serve cooked salmon hot, it may be accompanied by Hollandaise Sauce (see recipe 84) or Mousseline Sauce (see recipe 87). To serve it cold, it can be accompanied by all varieties of mayonnaise (see recipes 105–109). It is usual to put a doubled-over napkin into the serving dish to absorb any water from the cooked fish. Garnish with cooked potatoes and sprigs of fresh parsley. You can also cook the salmon in quick white wine stock (see recipe 534).

629

Grilled salmon

SALMÓN ASADO

- 250 ml/8 fl oz sunflower oil
- 3 large salmon steaks or
  6 small salmon steaks
- salt

Serves 6

Pour the oil into a large dish and add the salmon steaks in a single layer, turning to coat. Leave to marinate in the refrigerator, turning occasionally, for 1 hour. Preheat the grill. Remove the steaks from the marinade and drain slightly, then season with salt on both sides. Brush the grill rack with oil (from marinating the salmon) and discard any remaining marinade. Cook the steaks under the grill for about 4 minutes on each side. They are fully cooked when the central bones can be removed easily with a fork. Serve in a warm dish, offering a sauce separately.

Note: Serve mayonnaise with this dish (see recipes 105–109).

630

Oven-roasted salmon with butter

RODAJAS DE SALMÓN AL HORNO CON MANTEQUILLA

- 250 ml/8 fl oz sunflower oil
- 3 large salmon steaks or
  6 small salmon steaks
- 100 g/3½ oz butter
- 1 tablespoon chopped
  fresh parsley
- 1 lemon, cut into wedges
- salt

Serves 6

Put the oil into a large dish and add the salmon steaks in a single layer, turning to coat. Leave to marinate in the refrigerator, turning occasionally, for 1 hour. Preheat the oven to 180°C/350°F/Gas Mark 4. Remove the steaks from the marinade and drain slightly, then season with salt on both sides. Discard the marinade. Put the steaks into an ovenproof dish in a single layer, dot with the butter and roast, basting occasionally, for about 20 minutes, until golden brown. Take the salmon out of the oven, sprinkle with the parsley and garnish with the lemon wedges on the side of the dish. To do this, separate the rind from the flesh to just over halfway up each wedge, then hook the wedges over the edge of the dish. Serve immediately.

631

Salmon medallions cooked in egg and breadcrumbs

MEDALLONES DE SALMÓN EMPANADOS

- 500 g/1 lb 2 oz mushrooms
- 40 g/1½ oz butter
- juice of ½ lemon
- 2 eggs
- 40 g/1½ oz plain flour
- 80 g/3 oz breadcrumbs
- 1 litre/1¾ pints sunflower oil
- 1 kg/2¼ lb salmon fillets, skinned
- 500 ml/18 fl oz single cream
- salt

Serves 6

Put the mushrooms, butter, lemon juice and a pinch of salt into a saucepan and cook over a medium heat, shaking the pan occasionally, for 6 minutes. Remove from the heat and keep warm. Beat the eggs in a shallow dish, spread out the flour in another shallow dish and spread out the breadcrumbs in a third. Heat the oil in a deep-fryer or saucepan to 180–190°C/350–375°F or until a cube of day-old bread browns in 30 seconds. Season the salmon fillets with salt and coat first in the flour, then in the beaten egg and finally in the breadcrumbs. Add the fish to the hot oil, in batches, and cook until golden brown. Remove with a fish slice, drain and keep warm in a serving dish while you cook the remaining batches. Return the pan of mushrooms to a low heat, gradually stir in the cream and heat through gently but do not allow to boil. Pour the mushroom sauce over the salmon and serve immediately.

Note: You can substitute a thin béchamel sauce for the cream. Make it with 1 tablespoon plain flour, 20 g/1½ oz butter, 2 tablespoons sunflower oil and 500 ml/18 fl oz milk, as described in recipe 77.

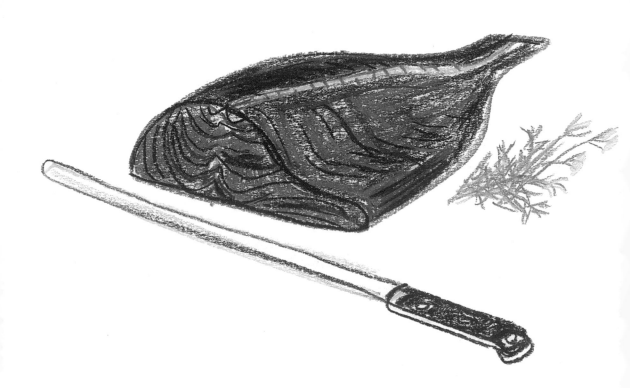

Fisherwoman's salmon, baked with prawns and mussels

SALMÓN A LA PESCADORA,(AL HORNO CON GAMBAS Y MEJILLONES)

- 2 large salmon fillets, 500g/ 1lb 2oz each
- 40g/1½ oz plain flour
- 6 tablespoons olive oil
- 1 small onion, finely chopped
- 275ml/9 fl oz white wine
- juice of 1 lemon
- 250g/9oz large raw prawns, peeled
- 65g/2½ oz butter
- 500g/1lb 2oz mussels
- 2 egg yolks
- 1 tablespoon milk
- 1 tablespoon chopped fresh parsley
- salt

Serves 6

Preheat the oven to 180°C/350°F/Gas Mark 4. Season the salmon fillets with salt on both sides and coat with the flour, shaking off any excess. Pour the oil into a large ovenproof dish and add the onion, salmon fillets, wine and lemon juice. Sprinkle in the prawns and dot the fillets with half the butter. Cover the dish with foil and bake for about 15 minutes. Meanwhile, scrape the mussel shells with the blade of a knife and remove the 'beards', then scrub under cold running water. Discard any mussels with broken shells or any that do not shut immediately when sharply tapped. Put them into a saucepan, pour in 250 ml/8 fl oz water and add a pinch of salt. Cook over a high heat, shaking the pan occasionally, for 3–5 minutes, until the shells have opened. Remove the mussels with a slotted spoon and discard any that remain closed. Strain the cooking liquid through a muslin-lined sieve into a bowl. Remove the mussels from their shells and add them to the bowl. Using a fish slice, carefully transfer the salmon fillets to a warm serving dish. Place the prawns around them and cover the dish with foil. Keep warm. Strain the salmon cooking liquid into a saucepan. Lightly beat the egg yolks with the milk in a bowl. Place the pan of salmon cooking liquid over a low heat, add the mussels with their cooking liquid and warm through, stirring occasionally. Stir a little of this mixture into the egg yolks to prevent them curdling, then stir into the pan. Stir in the parsley, pour the sauce over the salmon and serve immediately.

Note: For a slightly thicker sauce, mix 2 teaspoons potato flour with the milk, then add it to the salmon cooking liquid and cook, stirring constantly, for 2–3 minutes. Then add this to the egg yolks.

633

Salmon fillets marinated in watermelon juice

SALMON FILLETS MARINATED IN WATERMELON JUICE
LOMOS DE SALMON MARINADOS CON ZUMO DE SANDIA

- 4 tablespoons soy sauce
- 4 tablespoons sake
- 4 tablespoons watermelon juice
- pinch of freshly grated ginger
- 500 g/1 lb 2 oz salmon fillets, skinned
- 2 tablespoons sunflower oil
- 3 tablespoons sesame seeds
- ¼ watermelon, peeled, seeded and cubed

Serves 4

Mix together the soy sauce, sake, watermelon juice and ginger in a large non-metal dish, add the salmon fillets, turning to coat, and leave to marinate for at least 2 hours in the refrigerator. Preheat the oven to 180° C/350°F/Gas Mark 4. Pour the oil into an ovenproof dish. Drain the salmon fillets, discarding the marinade, and add the fillets to the dish in a single layer and sprinkle with the sesame seeds. Bake for about 7 minutes, until the flesh flakes easily. Transfer to a warm serving dish, garnish with the watermelon and serve.

Note: If cooking the salmon on a barbecue, brush both sides with oil. To make watermelon juice, process chunks of watermelon and strain.

634

Salmon with orange vinaigrette

SALMON CON VINAGRETA DE NARANJA

- 250 ml/8 fl oz olive oil
- 4 salmon fillets
- salt

Vinaigrette:
- 10 strips of shallot
- ½ orange
- 2 tablespoons balsamic vinegar
- 2 tablespoons olive oil

Serves 4

Pour the oil into a large non-metal dish and add the salmon fillets, turning to coat. Leave to marinate, turning occasionally, for about 20 minutes. Preheat the grill. Brush the grill rack with a little of the oil from the marinade and discard the remaining marinade. Season the salmon fillets on both sides and cook under the grill for about 4 minutes on each side, until the flesh flakes easily. Meanwhile, prepare the vinaigrette. Cut the shallots into pieces. Squeeze the juice from the orange and cut three strips of rind, avoiding the bitter pith. Chop the rind finely. Mix together the orange juice, balsamic vinegar, oil and a pinch of salt in a bowl. Stir in the shallots and orange zest. Serve the salmon in a warm serving dish and offer the vinaigrette separately.

635

Baked red mullet

SALMONETES AL HORNO

- 6 red mullet or snapper, 200 g/ 7 oz each, scaled and cleaned
- 6 lemon slices, halved
- 4 tablespoons olive oil
- juice of 1 lemon
- 80 g/3 oz butter
- salt

Serves 6

Preheat the oven to 180°C/350°F/Gas Mark 4. Season the cavities of the fish with salt. Slash the fish on either side of the backbones with a sharp knife and insert a half slice of lemon into each cut. Pour the oil into an ovenproof dish and add the fish in a single layer. Lightly season with salt, pour the lemon juice over and dot with the butter. Bake for about 15 minutes, until the flesh flakes easily, and serve immediately straight from the dish.

Red mullet cooked in parcels

SALMONETES AL HORNO ENVUELTOS EN PAPEL (PAPILLOTES)

- **6 red mullet or snapper,**
  about 200 g/7 oz each,
  scaled and cleaned
- **6 tablespoons olive oil**
- **½ teaspoon dried mixed herbs**
  or 6 sprigs fresh thyme or fennel
- **1 large onion,**
  very finely chopped
- **salt**

Serves 6

Preheat the oven to 180°C/350°F/Gas Mark 4. Cut out six squares of foil or baking paper with sides 5 cm/2 inches longer than the fish, then cut into heart shapes. Season the fish inside and out with salt. Brush the sheets with some of the oil, brush both sides of each fish with oil and place each one on a foil or baking paper sheet. Sprinkle the dried herbs over the fish or put a fresh herb sprig into each cavity. Divide the onion among them and wrap the foil or baking paper around them. Put the parcels on to a baking sheet and bake for about 15 minutes. Serve the fish in a dish with the parcels half open.

Note: This dish has the advantage that the fish can wait quite some time before being served without drying out. Also, the smell of fish is not so strong. If you use baking paper, it might require a shorter cooking time than foil.

637

- 6 red mullet or snapper,
  about 200 g/7 oz each,
  scaled and cleaned
- 4 tablespoons olive oil
- 1 small onion,
  very finely chopped
- juice of ½ lemon
- 175 ml/6 fl oz rancio-style wine
  such as muscatel
- 2 tablespoons breadcrumbs
- 50 g/2 oz butter
- salt

Serves 6

Red mullet baked with breadcrumbs and rancio wine

SALMONETES AL HORNO CON PAN RALLADO Y VINO RANCIO

Preheat the oven to 180°C/350°F/Gas Mark 4. Season the fish with salt inside and out and slash on either side of the backbones with a sharp knife. Pour the oil into an ovenproof dish and sprinkle in the onion. Add the fish in a single layer and pour the lemon juice and wine over them. Sprinkle with the breadcrumbs and dot with the butter. Bake for about 15 minutes, until the fish are browned. Serve immediately, straight from the dish.

Note: A tawny brown, rich uniquely flavoured wine with a full aroma of overly ripe fruit, rancio wines are wood-aged and heated fortified wines, such as Madeira. Vino raucio, or raucio-style, is not rancid, as the name suggests, but is made by aging the wine in barrels left in the hot sun, which gives it a unique, fruity flavour.

638

- 250 ml/8 fl oz olive oil
- juice of 1 lemon
- 6 red mullet or snapper,
  about 200 g/7 oz each,
  scaled and cleaned
- 80 g/3 oz breadcrumbs
- salt
- 1 quantity Green Mayonnaise
  (see recipe 107)

Serves 6

Grilled red mullet with green mayonnaise

SALMONETES EMPANADOS A LA PARRILLA, CON SALSA MAYONESA VERDE

Mix together the oil and lemon juice in a dish. Season the fish with salt inside and out and add to the dish, turning to coat. Leave to marinate in the refrigerator, turning occasionally, for 2 hours. Preheat the grill. Drain the fish and coat them in the breadcrumbs. Brush the grill rack with a little of the marinade and discard the remaining marinade. Put the fish on the rack and cook under the grill for about 10 minutes on each side, until the flesh flakes easily. Serve immediately, offering the mayonnaise separately.

639

- 1.5 kg / 3¼ lb fresh sardines or sprats, scaled, cleaned and boned
- sunflower oil, for deep-frying
- 50 g / 2 oz plain flour
- 2 eggs, lightly beaten
- 1 lemon, cut into wedges
- salt

Serves 6

Sardines coated in egg and fried

SARDINAS REBOZADAS CON HUEVO Y FRITAS

Open out the fish and lightly season with salt on both sides. Heat the oil in a deep-fryer or saucepan to 180–190°C/350–375°F or until a cube of day-old bread browns in 30 seconds. Coat each fish first in the flour, holding it by the tail and shaking to remove any excess, and then in the beaten egg. Add to the hot oil, in batches, and cook until golden brown. Remove with a slotted spoon, drain well and keep warm while you cook the remaining batches. Garnish with the lemon wedges and serve immediately.

640

- 5 tablespoons olive oil
- 1.5 kg / 3¼ lb large fresh sardines or sprats, scaled, cleaned and boned
- 150 ml / ¼ pint white wine
- juice of ½ lemon
- 1 tablespoon chopped fresh parsley
- 3 tablespoons breadcrumbs
- 40 g / 1½ oz butter
- salt

Serves 6

Baked sardines with white wine and breadcrumbs

SARDINAS AL HORNO CON VINO BLANCO Y PAN RALLADO

Preheat the oven to 180°C/350°F/Gas Mark 4. Pour the oil into an ovenproof dish. Lightly season the fish with salt on both sides and put them into the dish in a single layer. Pour in the wine and lemon juice, sprinkle with the parsley and breadcrumbs and dot with the butter. Bake, basting occasionally, for about 15 minutes, until the flesh flakes easily. Serve immediately, straight from the dish.

641 Baked sardines stuffed with spinach

SARDINAS AL HORNO RELLENAS DE ESPINACAS

- 1.5 kg/3¼ lb spinach, coarse stalks removed
- 100 g/3½ oz butter
- 1.5 kg/3¼ lb large fresh sardines or sprats, scaled, cleaned and boned
- 4 tablespoons olive oil
- 2 tablespoons breadcrumbs
- salt

Serves 6

Preheat the oven to 180°C/350°F/Gas Mark 4. Cook the spinach as described on page 315. Drain well, pressing out as much liquid as possible with the back of a spoon, then chop. Melt 80 g/3 oz of the butter in a frying pan, add the spinach and cook, stirring occasionally, for 5 minutes. Season to taste with salt. Remove from the heat and keep warm. Put the fish on a work surface, skin side down. Lightly season with salt and divide the spinach among them, then roll up the fish. Pour the oil into an ovenproof dish, making sure that the base is covered. Put the rolled-up fish into the dish in a single layer, sprinkle with the breadcrumbs and dot with the remaining butter. Bake for 15 minutes, then serve immediately straight from the dish.

642 Sardines in pastry parcels

SARDINAS EN HOJAS DE BRICK

- 12 canned sardines or 18 canned sprats, drained
- 4 sheets of brik pastry or 8 sheets of filo pastry, thawed if frozen
- 50 g/2 oz butter, melted
- 4 small tomatoes, peeled, seeded and chopped
- 6 fresh basil leaves, chopped
- 4 cloves garlic, finely chopped
- 4 fresh chives
- 1 lemon, cut into wedges
- mixed salad leaves dressed with an oil and lemon vinaigrette

Serves 4

Preheat the oven to 200° C/400°F/Gas Mark 6. Remove the backbones from the fish, flake the flesh and set aside. Spread out the pastry sheets on a work surface and brush with some of the melted butter. If using filo, put the sheets together in pairs at an angle to each other. Divide the flaked fish, tomato, basil and garlic among the pastry sheets. Gather up the edges like money pouches and tie each with a chive. Brush a baking sheet with some of the remaining melted butter and place the parcels on it. Brush them all over with melted butter and bake for about 20 minutes, until golden brown. Serve the parcels on a bed of dressed mixed salad leaves, garnished with the lemon wedges.

Notes: Brik is the name of a North African dish made with a very flaky pastry. This pastry (also known as malsouqa, wasqa and ouarka) is extremely difficult to make but is available from specialist stores. Filo pastry is a good alternative or you could even use wonton wrappers, which are available from Chinese supermarkets. When they are in season, use fresh sardines for this dish.

643

- 6 trout, about 150 g / 5 oz each
- 250 ml / 8 fl oz milk
- 50 g / 2 oz plain flour
- sunflower oil, for deep-frying
- salt

Serves 6

Fried trout

TRUCHAS FRITAS

Scale and clean the trout, then wash and pat dry. Season inside and out with salt and leave to stand for about 10 minutes to allow the salt to soak in. Heat the oil in a large frying pan. Dip the fish first in the milk, and then in the flour. Add the fish to the hot oil, in batches of two, and cook for about 10 minutes. Drain and keep warm while you cook the remaining fish. Serve immediately, garnished with lemon wedges if you like.

Note: Choose trout that weigh about 150 g / 5 oz each (smaller ones do not have much flesh and larger ones do not fry well).

644

- 4 trout, cleaned
- 300 g / 11 oz canned red peppers, drained and cut into strips
- 1 chilli,
  seeded and cut into pieces
- 4 thin slices of Serrano ham
- 3 tablespoons olive oil
- 1 clove garlic, finely chopped
- 1 tablespoon white-wine vinegar
  or lemon juice
- salt

Serves 4

Trout with ham and peppers

TRUCHAS CON JAMON Y PIMIENTOS

Preheat the oven to 200°C/400°F/Gas Mark 6. Season the trout with salt and pepper. Divide the red peppers and chilli among the slices of ham. Roll up each slice of ham and put one inside the cavity of each fish. Put the trout into a roasting tin in a single layer. Pour the oil over them and sprinkle with the garlic. Season with salt and bake for about 12 minutes, until the flesh flakes easily. Transfer the trout to a warm serving dish. Add the vinegar or lemon juice to the roasting tin and bring the mixture to the boil, then pour it over the trout and serve immediately.

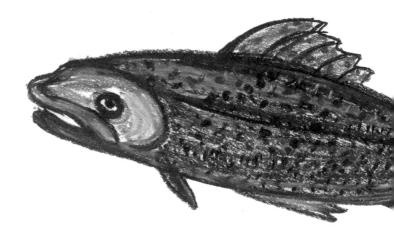

645

Sea trout poached in special quick stock
TRUCHA ASALMONADA EN CALDO CORTO ESPECIAL

- 25 g/1 oz butter
- 2 tablespoons olive oil
- 150 g/5 oz carrots, chopped
- 1 onion, chopped
- 1 rasher of smoked bacon, chopped
- pinch of dried mixed herbs
- 500 ml/18 fl oz white wine
- 1 sea trout, about 500 g/ 1 lb 2 oz, scaled and cleaned
- Hollandaise Sauce (see recipe 84)
- salt and pepper

Serves 3

Melt the butter with the oil in a deep frying pan. Add the carrot, onion and bacon and cook over a low heat, stirring occasionally, for 10 minutes. Lightly season with salt and pepper and add the mixed herbs. Stir in the wine and 500 ml/18 fl oz water, bring to the boil, lower the heat and simmer gently for 30 minutes. Strain the stock into a bowl and leave to cool. Season the trout inside and out with salt and leave to stand for about 10 minutes. Remove the rack from a fish kettle. Pour in the stock, put the trout on the rack and return the rack to the fish kettle. The fish should be completely covered in liquid. Cover the fish kettle and set over a very low heat so that the stock is barely simmering. Cook for about 15 minutes, until the flesh flakes easily. Place a folded napkin in a serving dish, add the trout and serve immediately, offering the hollandaise sauce separately.

Note: This stock is also suitable for salmon, sea bass or grouper.

646

Trout with ham, almonds and garlic
TRUCHAS CON JAMÓN, ALMENDRAS Y AJO

- 6 trout, about 250 g/9 oz each, cleaned
- 500 ml/18 fl oz sunflower oil
- 6 small slices of Serrano ham
- 40 g/1½ oz plain flour
- 100 g/3½ oz cooked ham, finely chopped
- 8 blanched almonds, finely chopped
- 3 cloves garlic, finely chopped
- 2 sprigs fresh parsley, finely chopped
- 3 tablespoons sherry
- juice of 1 lemon
- salt and pepper

Serves 6

Season the trout with salt and pepper. Heat the oil in a frying pan. Add the Serrano ham and cook, turning once, for 1–2 minutes, then remove and drain. Put a slice of Serrano ham into the cavity of each fish. Coat the trout in the flour, shaking off the excess, and then add to the frying pan, in batches, and cook until golden brown all over. Transfer to an ovenproof dish in a single layer. Preheat the oven to 200°C/400°F/Gas Mark 6. Transfer 120 ml/4 fl oz of the oil to a small frying pan and heat. Add the chopped ham, almonds, garlic and parsley and cook for about 5 minutes, until the garlic and almonds are lightly browned. Stir in the sherry and lemon juice, then pour the sauce over the trout. Bake for 10 minutes and serve immediately, straight from the dish.

647 📷 Navarra trout with ham
TRUCHAS CON JAMÓN (A LA NAVARRA)

- 6 trout, about 250 g/9 oz each,
  scaled and cleaned
- 6 thin slices of Serrano ham
- 750 ml/1¼ pints sunflower oil
- 1 onion, finely chopped
  (optional)
- 1 kg/2¼ lb tomatoes,
  peeled, seeded and chopped
- 1 teaspoon sugar
- 1 large red pepper,
  seeded and cut into strips
- 50 g/2 oz plain flour
- salt

Serves 6

Season the trout inside and out with salt and leave to stand for about 10 minutes. Place a slice of ham inside the cavity of each fish and close the cavity with a wooden cocktail stick. Using 3 tablespoons of the oil, the onion, if using the tomato and sugar, make a thick tomato sauce as described in recipe 73. Stir in the red pepper and cook, stirring occasionally, for 10 minutes, then transfer to a serving dish and keep warm. Meanwhile, heat the remaining oil in a frying pan. Coat the trout in the flour, shaking off any excess, add to the hot oil, in batches if necessary, and cook until golden brown. Transfer to the serving dish and serve immediately.

Note: Some people prefer to serve the trout without the tomato sauce. Also, some people prefer to wrap the ham around the trout, holding it in place with a wooden cocktail stick and frying the fish without coating them in flour.

648 Trout au bleu
TRUCHAS AZULADAS

- very fresh trout,
  about 250 g/9 oz, cleaned,
  but not scaled or rinsed
- 250 ml/8 fl oz red-wine vinegar

Quick stock with red wine:
- 450 ml/¾ pint red wine
- 2 carrots, sliced
- 1 onion, cut into wedges
- 1 bay leaf
- 1 sprig fresh parsley
- 2–3 black peppercorns
- 1 tablespoon salt
- 1 quantity Hollandaise Sauce
  (see recipe 84) or
  Special Vinaigrette
  (see recipe 99 or 100)

Serves 6

Make a quick stock with 2.5 litres/4¼ pints water and all the stock ingredients as described in recipe 534. Remove the rack from a fish kettle, pour in the stock and bring to the boil. Meanwhile, put the trout into a deep dish. Bring the vinegar to the boil in a saucepan and pour it over the trout, turning to coat. Transfer the trout to the rack and return the rack to the fish kettle. Cover the kettle and cook the trout over a very low heat for 10 minutes. Place a folded napkin in a serving dish. Lift out the rack, drain the fish and place them on the napkin. Serve immediately with the hollandaise sauce or special vinaigrette.

Note: The name of this dish, which translates as 'bluish trout', refers to a method of cooking fish (especially trout) where a freshly killed fish is immersed in boiling stock, which turns its skin a bluish colour.

649

- **6 trout, about 250 g/9 oz, cleaned but not scaled**
- **175 ml/6 fl oz red-wine vinegar**
- **2 tablespoons gelatine powder**
- **1 quantity Classic Mayonnaise (see recipe 105)**
- **lettuce leaves or watercress, tomato slices or hard–boiled egg slices**

Quick stock:
- **1 bay leaf**
- **1 thick slice of onion**
- **2 carrots, sliced**
- **juice of ½ lemon**
- **4–5 black peppercorns**
- **1 tablespoon salt**
- **275 ml/9 fl oz white wine**

Serves 6

Cold trout in gelatine

TRUCHAS FRÍAS EN GELATINA

First prepare the quick stock, using all the ingredients and 3 litres/5¼ pints water as described in recipe 534. Add the wine just as the stock comes to the boil and simmer for 20 minutes. Remove the rack from a fish kettle, pour in the stock and bring to the boil. Meanwhile, put the trout into a deep dish. Pour the vinegar and 500 ml/18 fl oz water into a small saucepan and bring to the boil. Remove the pan from the heat, leave to cool slightly, then pour the mixture over the trout, turning to coat. Transfer the trout to the rack and return the rack to the fish kettle, plunging the fish into the boiling stock. Immediately remove the kettle from the heat and leave to cool completely. Lift out the rack and drain the trout. Carefully remove the skin from the base of the head until just before the tail, then place the fish in a serving dish. Strain 500 ml/18 fl oz of the stock into a heatproof bowl. Sprinkle the gelatine over the surface and leave to sponge for 5 minutes. Set the bowl over a pan of barely simmering water and leave until the gelatine has dissolved completely and the mixture is clear. Remove the bowl from the heat and leave to cool until beginning to set. Brush some of the gelatine over each trout and repeat three or four times. Chill in the refrigerator for at least 3–4 hours. Allow the remaining gelatine to set, then chop it and place it around the trout. Garnish with lettuce leaves or watercress, tomatoes and hard-boiled eggs. Serve the trout accompanied by the mayonnaise in a sauce boat.

Shellfish

650

Small crabs
CANGREJOS DE MAR PEQUEÑOS

- **36 small crabs,
  such as blue crabs**
- **4 tablespoons olive oil**
- **1 clove garlic**
- **pinch of dried mixed herbs or
  1 bouquet garni (1 sprig fresh
  thyme, 2 bay leaves and 1 sprig
  fresh parsley tied together in
  muslin)**
- **3 black peppercorns**
- **salt**

Makes 36 appetizers

Wash the crabs in salted water, but do not leave them in the water. Remove the legs, if you like. Crush four or five crabs in a mortar. Heat the oil in a frying pan. Add the garlic and cook, stirring occasionally, for a few minutes, until lightly browned. Add the crushed crabs, stir well and add the whole crabs (with or without legs) and the dried herbs or bouquet garni. Pour in water to cover, add the peppercorns and season with salt. Bring to the boil and cook over a high heat for 5 minutes. Remove the pan from the heat, drain the crabs and leave to cool. Serve as an appetizer or add to a paella just before serving.

Note: The crabs are served as appetizers and used to garnish paella when crayfish are not available.

651 **Fisherman's cold spider crab**

CENTOLLO FRÍO A LA PESCADORA

- 175 ml/6 fl oz white-wine vinegar
- 10 black peppercorns
- 3 bay leaves
- 2 spider crabs (mud crabs)
- 300 g/11 oz hake fillet
- 1 tablespoon white wine
- 1 thick slice of onion
- 3 hard-boiled egg yolks
- ¼ teaspoon mustard
- juice of 1 lemon
- 4 tablespoons sunflower oil
- salt

Serves 2

Pour 5 litres/9 pints water into a saucepan, add the vinegar, peppercorns, two of the bay leaves and a pinch of salt and bring to the boil over a high heat. Plunge in the crabs, cover, bring back to the boil and cook over a high heat for 8 minutes. Drain well and leave to cool. Meanwhile, put the hake fillet into a saucepan, pour in water to cover and add the remaining bay leaf, and the wine, onion and a pinch of salt. Bring to the boil, then remove the pan from the heat. Lift out the hake, remove and discard any skin and bones and flake the flesh. Once the crabs are cold, open them carefully without breaking the back shells. Remove and discard the gills. Take out the white meat from the body and the legs and cut it into pieces. Scoop out the brown meat into a bowl and reserve any roe from a hen crab. Wash and dry the back shells and set aside. Pound the brown meat, roe, hard-boiled egg yolks, mustard and lemon juice in a mortar. Gradually whisk in the oil, a little at a time, and season to taste with salt. Mix together the hake, white crab meat and the sauce in a bowl, then divide the mixture between the crab shells. Store in the refrigerator until ready to serve.

Crayfish

Crayfish are freshwater crustaceans that look like small lobsters. European crayfish are 18–20 cm/7–8 inches long, slightly smaller than Australian Murray River or Marron crayfish.

How to clean
Wash in plenty of cold water just before cooking (if this is done in advance, they release all their water). Remove the bitter intestines by twisting the central lamina at the end of the tail and pulling it so that the gut comes out whole. The crayfish are now ready to be cooked.

652

Crayfish
CANGREJOS DE RÍO

• 24 crayfish
• 250 ml/8 fl oz white wine
• 2 carrots, chopped
• 1 onion, chopped
• 6 black peppercorns
• 2 bay leaves
• 1 sprig fresh parsley
• 1 sprig fresh thyme
• 1 tablespoon sunflower oil
• salt

Serves 4

Prepare the crayfish as described above. Put all the remaining ingredients into a saucepan, pour in 2 litres/3 ½ pints water and add a pinch of salt. Bring to the boil over a high heat and plunge in the crayfish so that they are covered by the stock. Bring back to the boil and cook for 4–6 minutes, depending on the size of the crayfish. Drain well and serve warm or cold.

653

Crayfish tails in béchamel sauce with brandy

COLAS DE CANGREJOS CON SALSA BECHAMEL Y COÑAC

- **36–48 cooked crayfish**
- **80 g/3 oz butter**
- **2 tablespoons sunflower oil**
- **2 tablespoons plain flour**
- **500 ml/18 fl oz milk**
- **1 teaspoon tomato purée**
- **2 tablespoons brandy**
- **1 truffle**
- **warm vol-au-vent cases (optional)**
- **salt and pepper**

Serves 6

Pull off and reserve the crayfish heads and peel the tails. Set the tails aside in a saucepan. Put the heads and 50 g/2 oz of the butter into a saucepan and heat gently, stirring constantly. Tip the mixture into a mortar and pound. Strain through a muslin-lined sieve into a bowl, then twist the muslin with your hands to extract all the juices. Set aside. Melt the remaining butter with the oil in a saucepan. Stir in the flour and cook, stirring constantly, for 2 minutes. Gradually stir in the milk, a little at a time. Cook, stirring constantly, for about 10 minutes, until thickened. Season to taste with salt and pepper and stir in the tomato purée. Heat the brandy in a small saucepan for about 30 seconds, ignite it and pour it over the crayfish tails, stirring until the flames die down. Stir into the béchamel sauce along with the truffle and the crayfish juices. Cook, stirring constantly, for 1 minute more. Taste and adjust the seasoning, if necessary, and serve immediately either in the warmed vol-au-vent cases or individual dishes.

654

Bordeaux crayfish
CANGREJOS DE RÍO AL ESTILO BURDEOS

- 3 tablespoons olive oil
- 2 large carrots,
  very finely chopped
- 1 small onion,
  very finely chopped
- 1 shallot, very finely chopped
- 36 large crayfish
- 250 ml/8 fl oz dry white wine
- 3 tablespoons brandy
- 2 very ripe tomatoes,
  seeded and chopped
- pinch of dried mixed herbs or
  1 bouquet garni (1 clove garlic,
  1 sprig fresh parsley, 1 sprig
  fresh thyme and 2 bay leaves
  tied together in muslin)
- pinch of cayenne pepper
- 25 g/1 oz butter
- 1 tablespoon chopped
  fresh parsley
- salt and pepper
Serves 6

Heat the oil in a saucepan. Add the carrot, onion and shallot, cover and cook over a low heat for 5 minutes. Add 250 ml/8 fl oz water, re-cover and cook for a further 10 minutes. Meanwhile, prepare the crayfish as described on page 536. Put them into a frying pan with the wine and a pinch of salt, cover and cook over a high heat until they change colour. Warm the brandy in a small saucepan for a few seconds, ignite it and pour it over the crayfish, stirring until the flames have died down. Remove the pan from the heat and set aside. Add the tomato to the pan of vegetables and cook, stirring occasionally and breaking it up with the side of the spoon, for 5 minutes. Add the crayfish mixture and dried herbs or bouquet garni, season with pepper and cook for about 5 minutes, then remove the crayfish with a slotted spoon and keep warm. Cook the sauce for a further 10 minutes, then pass it through a sieve into a clean saucepan, pressing down hard and adding a little hot water if necessary. Add the cayenne pepper, season to taste with salt and add the butter and crayfish. Sprinkle with the parsley and cook for a few minutes more. Serve immediately.

655

Crayfish omelette
TORTILLA DE COLAS DE CANGREJOS DE RÍO

- 6 crayfish
- 20 g/¾ oz butter
- 2 eggs
- 3 tablespoons sunflower oil
- salt and pepper
Serves 1

Clean and cook the crayfish as described on page 536, then remove the heads and peel the tails. If the tails are large, cut them into two or three pieces. Melt the butter in a saucepan. Add the crayfish, season with salt and pepper and cook, stirring occasionally, for 1–2 minutes. Lightly beat the eggs with a pinch of salt. Heat the oil in a frying pan, pour in the eggs and cook as described on page 422. Drain the crayfish and sprinkle them over the omelette, then fold the omelette and slide it out of the pan. Serve immediately.

Mediterranean prawns

Also known as crevettes, these European prawns are not quite so large or so fine as langoustines (Dublin Bay prawns). They are very good for soups and can be served as a less expensive substitute for langoustines. Medium-size prawns are the best buy. Remove their heads before cooking, as they have a very strong flavour, and cook in the same way as langoustines (see page 552). Readers in Australia and New Zealand can use any of the large Pacific prawns – tiger prawns, king prawns, banana prawns or bay prawns.

656

Crevette and asparagus fan
ABANICO DE CARABINEROS Y ESPARRAGOS

- 24 asparagus spears, trimmed
- 24 raw crevetttes

Sauce:
- 2 tablespoons olive oil
- 1 onion, chopped
- 1 carrot, chopped
- 175 ml/6 fl oz white wine
- 1 litre/1¾ pints double cream
- 1 bouquet garni
  (1 sprig fresh thyme, 2 bay
  leaves and 1 sprig fresh parsley
  tied together in muslin)
- 2 sprigs fresh tarragon
- 3 tablespoons butter (optional)
- salt and pepper

Serves 6

Bring a saucepan of salted water to the boil, add the asparagus with the tips pointing upwards, cover and bring back to the boil. Lower the heat and simmer for about 15 minutes, until the asparagus is tender. Remove the pan from the heat but leave the asparagus in the water. Meanwhile, bring another saucepan of salted water to the boil. Add the crevettes and cook for 3 minutes, then drain well. Remove the heads and peel the crevettes. Pound the heads and shells in a mortar. Heat the oil in a frying pan. Add the crushed heads and shells and cook, stirring frequently, for 3–4 minutes. Add the onion and carrot and cook, stirring occasionally, for a further 3 minutes. Pour in the wine and cook until reduced by half. Stir in the cream, add the bouquet garni and tarragon and cook over a low heat for 30 minutes. Pass the sauce through a food mill into a clean saucepan. If it seems too thin, cook until reduced to the desired consistency. (You could also stir in 40 g/1½ oz butter to thicken it.) Season to taste with salt and pepper, add the crevettes and heat through. Place the asparagus spears and crevettes alternately on a warm serving dish and serve immediately accompanied by the sauce.

Spiny lobsters

Varieties

There is confusion about the names of some crustaceans. The French word cigale refers to slipper or flat lobsters, while the Spanish cigalas is more usually applied to spiny lobsters in spite of the similar-sounding name. To add to the confusion, the spiny lobster is also known as the rock lobster, Florida lobster, thorn lobster, crawfish and langouste. It is often mistakenly called a crayfish, which is a smaller freshwater crustacean, and crayfish are also often called crawfish, especially in the United States. Australian rock lobsters are also often known as crays or crayfish. The Australian equivalents of the European slipper or flat lobsters are the Balmain bug and Moreton Bay bug. In the end, it makes little difference whether you use slipper lobsters or spiny lobsters as they have a similar flavour, neither has claws, all the meat is in the tail and both make good eating.

How to cook

Bring a large saucepan of salted water to the boil. Add the lobsters, making sure that they are fully immersed. When the water comes back to the boil, remove the pan from the heat and leave to cool for 8 minutes. Lift out the lobsters, drain well and serve cold.

Spiny lobster with mayonnaise and spiny lobster with vinaigrette

CIGALAS CON MAYONESA Y CIGALAS CON VINAGRETA

- 2 x 800 g/1 ⅓ lb spiny lobsters
- 1 quantity Classic Mayonnaise (see recipe 105) or Vinaigrette (see recipe 98)
- 1 tablespoon finely chopped fresh parsley (optional)
- 1 tablespoon finely chopped spring onion (optional)
- 1 tablespoon brandy (optional)
- salt and pepper

Serves 4

To serve with mayonnaise, cook the lobsters as described on page 540 and serve cold, offering the mayonnaise separately. To serve with the vinaigrette, make a salpicón the night before it is required. To do this, take the vinaigrette and add the onion, parsley, hard-boiled egg and brandy. Season to taste with salt and pepper. Cook the lobsters as described on page 540 and leave to cool, then remove the meat from the tails and cut into slices about 2 cm/¾ inch thick. Put the slices into a deep dish, pour the salpicón over them and leave in the refrigerator for 3–5 hours. Serve cold.

Note: This dish can be prepared with prawns rather than spiny lobster, leaving the peeled prawns whole. It can also be made with lobster, for which allow 1 lobster, weighing about 600 g/1 lb 5 oz for 2 servings.

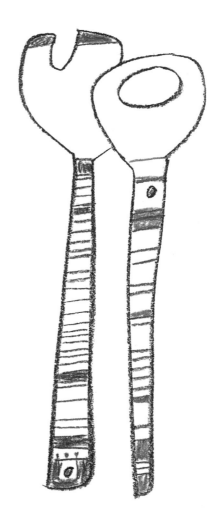

Prawns

How to cook

Bring a large saucepan of salted water to the boil. Add the raw prawns, lower the heat and simmer for 2–4 minutes, depending on their size. Drain well and leave to cool.

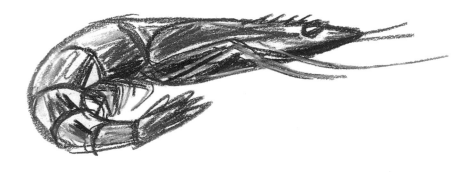

658

Prawn cocktail

CÓCTEL DE GAMBAS

• 1.5 kg/3¼ lb raw unpeeled
  prawns
• 1 large lettuce
• 1 quantity Mayonnaise with
  Tomato and Brandy
  (see recipe 108)
• 1 hard-boiled egg, finely chopped
• salt

Serves 6

Cook the prawns as described above. Drain well and leave to cool. Shred the lettuce and peel the prawns. Make a bed of lettuce in the base of six champagne glasses or sundae dishes and top each with 1 tablespoon of the mayonnaise. Divide the prawns among the glasses or dishes and cover them with the remaining mayonnaise. Sprinkle with the hard-boiled egg and chill in the refrigerator for 1–2 hours before serving.

659

Fish and prawn salad

- 6 tablespoons olive oil
- 12 large prawns, peeled
- 2 strips of chilli
- 150 g/5 oz kingklip fillets
- 150 g/5 oz precooked crab meat
- juice of 2 lemons
- 1 tablespoon chopped fresh mint
- 1 lettuce, shredded
- salt and pepper

Serves 4

Heat half the oil in a frying pan. Add the prawns and chilli and cook over a medium heat, stirring occasionally, for a few minutes, until the prawns are opaque. Remove from the pan, drain well and set aside. Steam the kingklip fillets for 3 minutes. Cut the prawns into pieces and flake the fish and crab meat. Put into a bowl with the remaining oil and the lemon juice and mint, season with salt and pepper and leave to marinate in the refrigerator. To serve, make a bed of lettuce on a round dish and put the fish mixture on top. Pour the marinade over the salad and serve.

Note: Kingklip, also called congrio, is an eel-like fish with pink, orange, brown or black markings. It can be found off the coasts of South America and South Africa. If you can't find it, use another firm-fleshed, mild fish such as monkfish.

Lobster

Spanish cooks distinguish between hen lobsters (langosta) and their male counterparts (bogavante). In fact, chefs and gourmets throughout the world generally agree that female lobsters are usually heavier, are better value and have a better flavour. Cook and prepare bogavante the same way as langosta. It is not advisable to buy one that weighs more than 1 kg/2 ¼ lb as the meat will not be as good.

How to prepare and cook

Allow 500–600 g/1 lb 2 oz–1 lb 5 oz lobster for 2 servings. Tie the lobster. Pour 3–4 litres/5 ¼–7 pints water into a saucepan, add 1 thickly sliced carrot, 1 wedge of onion, 1 bay leaf, 1 sprig fresh thyme, 1 sprig fresh parsley, 5 tablespoons dry white wine, 1 teaspoon salt and 6 black peppercorns. Cook over a high heat for 20 minutes, then plunge in the lobster so that it is completely submerged, cover the pan, lower the heat and cook for 8 minutes per 1 kg/2 ¼ lb. Remove the pan from the heat and leave to cool for about 15 minutes. Then lift the lobster out of the water, untie it and leave it to drain. Remove the head from the tail. Cut open the tail on the underside of the shell with a large pair of scissors. Remove the meat in one piece. Using the point of a knife, remove and discard the black intestinal tract that runs along its length. Break off the claws, then break them into pieces at the joints. Crack the shells and remove the meat. Remove and discard the stomach sac from the head. Remove and reserve the tomalley (liver) and any roe. To kill lobster painlessly, put it into the freezer for 2 hours before plunging it into boiling liquid.

660

Lobster served with mayonnaise

LANGOSTA COCIDA, SERVIDA CON SALSA MAYONESA

- **2 lobsters, about 500 g/**
  1 lb 2 oz each
- **1 quantity Classic Mayonnaise**
  (see recipe 105)
- **lettuce leaves**
- **2 tomatoes, thickly sliced**
- **2 hard-boiled eggs, sliced**

Serves 4

Prepare the lobster as described on page 546 and remove the meat. Cut the tail meat into slices. Put the head and tail shell on an elongated dish. Place the slices of tail meat in the tail shell and put the legs around the edge of the dish with the edible parts of the head and claw meat. Garnish with the lettuce leaves, tomato and hard-boiled egg. Offer the mayonnaise in a sauce boat.

661

Lobster and melon salad

ENSALADA DE LANGOSTA Y MELON

- 400 g/14 oz green beans, trimmed
- 2 lobsters, about 600 g/ 1 lb 5 oz each
- 1 cantaloupe melon, halved and seeded
- juice of 1 lemon
- 120 ml/4 fl oz olive oil
- 200 g/7 oz mixed salad leaves
- 1 sprig fresh dill, chopped
- 6 fresh chives
- salt and ground pink peppercorns

Stock:
- 1 carrot, sliced
- 1 onion, sliced
- 1 leek, sliced and rinsed well
- 1 bouquet garni (1 sprig fresh thyme, 1 bay leaf, 1 sprig fresh parsley tied together in muslin)
- 5 tablespoons dry white wine
- 6 black peppercorns
- 1 teaspoon salt

Serves 4

Cook the beans in salted boiling water for 5–10 minutes, until crisp-tender. Drain, refresh under cold water and drain again. Put into a bowl and set aside. Put all the ingredients for the stock into a saucepan, pour in 2.5 litres/4 ¼ pints water and bring to the boil. Lower the heat and simmer for 30 minutes. Plunge in the lobsters so that they are completely submerged, cover and cook for 8 minutes. Remove the lobsters with a slotted spoon and leave to drain and cool. Using a melon baller, scoop out balls of the melon flesh. Set aside. Separate the heads from the tails of the lobsters and cut open the tails on the underside of the shell with a large pair of scissors. Remove the flesh from the tails, then remove and discard the black intestinal tracts. Cut the flesh from the tails in half. Remove any edible meat from the head, and crack the claws and remove the edible meat. Mix together a pinch of salt, a pinch of pink pepper and the lemon juice in a bowl, then whisk in the oil. Toss the salad leaves with some of the dressing and toss the green beans separately with some of the dressing. Make a bed of the salad leaves on a serving dish and pile a cone of green beans in the centre. Put the halved lobster tails and other meat on top and brush with the remaining dressing. Sprinkle with the dill and chives, arrange the melon balls around the edge and serve.

Note: A few drops of port poured over the melon adds extra flavour.

662

Lobster mousse with leek fondue
ESPUMA DE LANGOSTA EN MOLDE CON FONDUE DE PUERROS

- 1 leaf of gelatine
- 300 ml/½ pint canned
  lobster bisque or other
  creamy lobster soup
- 1 teaspoon Dijon mustard
- 300 ml/½ pint double cream
- 2 tablespoons brandy
- 20 g/¾ oz butter
- 3 leeks,
  cut into strips and rinsed well
- 1 tablespoon flaked almonds,
  toasted
- salt and pepper

Serves 4

Put the gelatine into a small bowl of cold water to soak for 5 minutes. Meanwhile, pour the soup into a bowl and stir in the mustard. Whisk the cream in another bowl until stiff. Heat the brandy in a small saucepan, then remove from the heat. Squeeze out the gelatine and stir it into the brandy until dissolved, then stir into the soup mixture. Fold in the cream and divide the mixture among four individual moulds. Cover and chill in the refrigerator for 6 hours, until set. Melt the butter in a frying pan. Add the leek and cook over a low heat, stirring occasionally, for a few minutes, until crisp-tender. Turn the mousse out of the moulds on to individual plates and surround each one with strips of leek. Sprinkle the almonds over the mousses and serve.

Note: If using plastic moulds, brush them with a little oil to make it easier to turn out the mousses. If the moulds are not plastic, put foil in the base of each one.

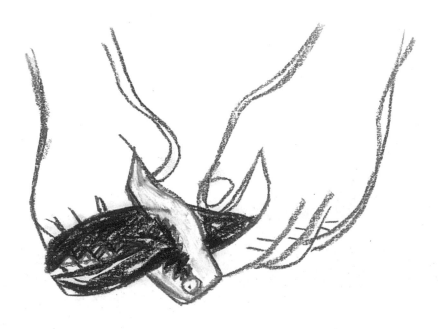

663

Lobster with béchamel sauce

LANGOSTA CON BECHAMEL AL HORNO

- 2 lobsters, about 600 g/
  1 lb 5 oz each
- 130 g/4 ½ oz butter
- 500 ml/18 fl oz hot milk
- 1 heaped tablespoon plain flour
- a pinch of curry powder
- 1 large truffle, thinly sliced
- 2 egg yolks
- juice of ½ lemon
- 50 g/2 oz Parmesan cheese,
  grated
- salt

Quick stock:
- 1 carrot, thickly sliced
- 1 onion wedge
- 1 bouquet garni (1 sprig fresh
  thyme, 1 bay leaf, 1 sprig fresh
  parsley tied together in muslin)
- 5 tablespoons dry white wine
- 6 black peppercorns
- 1 teaspoon salt

Serves 4

Pour 4 litres/7 pints water into a saucepan, add all the stock ingredients and cook the lobsters as described on page 468. When the lobsters have cooled, cut them in half lengthways. Cut off the legs and break off the claws. Loosen the meat in the tail and remove the black intestinal tracts. Remove and reserve the tomalley and any roe from the heads, and remove and discard the stomach sac. Break the claws into pieces at the joints and crack them open. Place the lobster halves, cut sides uppermost, in a large flameproof dish. Put the tomalley, roe, claws and legs into a saucepan with 100 g/3 ½ oz of the butter. Heat gently, stirring and breaking up the lobster pieces as much as possible. When the butter begins to froth, add the milk and bring to the boil. Strain through a muslin-lined sieve into a bowl and reserve. Twist the muslin to extract any remaining liquid. Leave to stand for 15 minutes, then skim off any pink coloured butter that has risen to the surface, and set the butter aside in a bowl. Melt the remaining butter in a saucepan. Stir in the flour and cook, stirring constantly, for 2 minutes. Gradually stir in the strained milk, a little at a time. Cook, stirring constantly, for about 10 minutes, then season to taste with salt and add the curry powder and truffle. Gradually stir in the reserved pink butter. Remove the pan from the heat. Preheat the grill. Lightly beat the egg yolks and lemon juice in a bowl and stir in a few spoonfuls of the béchamel sauce, then stir into the pan. Pour the sauce over the half lobsters, sprinkle with the Parmesan and cook under the grill for 4–5 minutes, until golden brown. Serve immediately.

Langoustines

Langoustines are also known as lobsterettes, Dublin Bay prawns and, in some places, as scampi, especially when deep-fried.

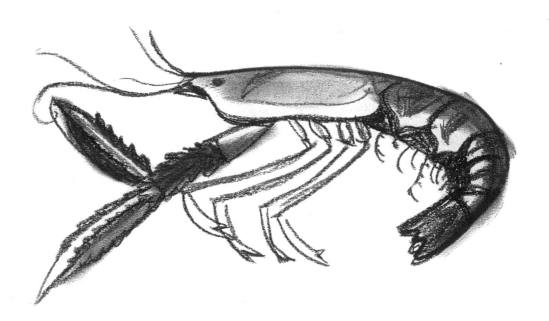

How to cook

Allow about 6 langoustines per serving. Do not cook them too far in advance or they will not be so juicy. If using frozen langoustines, let them thaw fully before using. To cook langoustines, bring a saucepan of salted water to the boil. Add the langoustines so that they are completely submerged and cook for 2 minutes, then remove them from the water with a slotted spoon. However, as langoustines can survive only a short time once they are out of the water, they are usually sold already cooked.

664 Breaded scampi

LANGOSTINOS EMPANADOS Y FRITOS

- 36 langoustines
  (Dublin Bay prawns), peeled
- 2 eggs
- 50 g/2 oz plain flour
- 120 g/4 oz breadcrumbs
- sunflower oil, for deep-frying
- 1 quantity Classic Mayonnaise
  (see recipe 105)
- salt and pepper

Serve 6

Bend the langoustines into nice shapes, season with salt and pepper and leave to stand for about 10 minutes. Meanwhile, beat the eggs in a shallow dish. Spread out the flour in another shallow dish and spread out the breadcrumbs in a third. Heat the oil in a deep-fryer or saucepan to 180–190°C/350–375°F or until a cube of day-old bread browns in 30 seconds. One at a time, coat the langoustines in the flour, then in the beaten egg and, finally, in the breadcrumbs. Thread them on to six metal skewers, submerge in the hot oil and cook for 5–6 minutes, until golden brown. Remove from the oil and drain, then serve immediately, offering the mayonnaise separately.

665 Langoustines with American sauce and rice

LANGOSTINOS CON SALSA AMERICANA Y ARROZ BLANCO

- 36 langoustines
  (Dublin Bay prawns), unpeeled
- 500 g/1 lb 2 oz long-grain rice
- 120 g/4 oz butter
- 175 ml/6 fl oz sunflower oil
- 2 shallots, chopped
- 3 large ripe tomatoes,
  seeded and chopped
- pinch of dried mixed herbs
- pinch of cayenne pepper
- 1 sprig fresh parsley
- 175 ml/6 fl oz dry white wine
- 5 tablespoons brandy
- a few drops of red food colouring
  (optional)
- 4 –5 tablespoons single cream
- salt and pepper

Serves 6

Pull off and reserve the heads of the langoustines and peel the tails. Put the tails in a bowl and cover with cling film. Boil the rice and fry it in half the butter as described in recipe 173. Spoon it into a cake tin. To make the American sauce, melt half the remaining butter with half the oil in a frying pan. Add the langoustine heads, season with salt and pepper and cook over a high heat, stirring frequently, for about 5 minutes. Remove the heads from the pan and set aside. Add the shallots, tomato, dried herbs, cayenne pepper and parsley to the pan and cook, stirring occasionally, for 5 minutes. Reduce the heat to medium, pour in the wine and cook for 10–15 minutes. Melt the remaining butter with the remaining oil in another frying pan. Add the langoustine tails and cook, stirring occasionally, for a few minutes, until golden. Heat the brandy in a small saucepan, ignite it and pour it over the langoustines. When the sauce has finished cooking, add the langoustine heads and strain into a bowl, pressing down hard with the back of a spoon. Pour the sauce over the langoustine tails, adding the food colouring, if using. Cook over a low heat for 6 minutes, then remove the pan from the heat and stir in the cream. Season to taste with salt and pepper. Put the langoustines and their sauce in a warm serving dish, turn out the rice and serve immediately.

Notes: If the sauce is too thin, stir in a paste made from 1 teaspoon potato flour mixed with a little water before adding the cream. This dish can be made using crayfish in place of langoustines

666

Langoustines in sauce
LANGOSTINOS EN SALSA

- 250 g/9 oz langoustines
  (Dublin Bay prawns), unpeeled
- 1 bay leaf
- 1 tablespoon olive oil
- 1 clove garlic, chopped
- 1 onion, chopped
- 1 leek, sliced and rinsed well
- 1 sprig fresh tarragon
- 2 tablespoons fried tomato
- 2 tablespoons brandy
- boiled rice or pasta
- salt

Serves 4

Peel the langoustines, reserving the heads and shells, put the tails in a dish and cover with cling film. Put the heads and shells in a saucepan, pour in 250 ml/8 fl oz water, add the bay leaf and a pinch of salt and bring to the boil. Lower the heat and simmer for 20 minutes. Heat the oil in a frying pan. Add the garlic, onion and leek and cook over a low heat, stirring occasionally, for 5 minutes, until softened. Add the tarragon and tomato and cook for a few minutes more, then add the langoustine tails and cook for about 4 minutes, until opaque. Add the brandy and ignite. Transfer the heads and shells mixture to a food processor, discarding the bay leaf. Process to a purée and strain the sauce over the langoustine tails. Heat through briefly, taste and adjust the seasoning, if necessary, and serve immediately with rice or pasta.

Notes: A little Tabasco sauce or other hot sauce can be added at the last minute for a spicy flavour. This dish can also be made with king prawns.

667

Seafood cocktail
COCTEL DE MARISCOS

- 4 tablespoons Classic
  Mayonnaise (see recipe 105)
- 1 tablespoon tomato purée
- 2 tablespoons lemon juice
- 2 tablespoons double cream
- 6 grapes, peeled and seeded
- 1 stick celery, sliced
- 1 apple,
  peeled, cored and chopped
- 1 red pepper, seeded and diced
- 1 head chicory, cut into strips
- 500 g/1 lb 2 oz cooked peeled
  langoustines (Dublin Bay
  prawns), prawns and spiny
  lobster
- pinch of paprika
- salt and pepper

Serves 4

Mix together the mayonnaise, tomato purée and lemon juice in a bowl and season with pepper. Whisk the cream in another bowl until stiff, and fold it into the mayonnaise mixture. Mix together the grapes, celery, apple, red pepper, chicory and shellfish in another bowl. Add half the sauce and mix well. Stir the paprika into the remaining sauce and pour it over the top.

Note: This dish looks lovely served in glasses or glass sundae dishes on a bed of crushed ice or in glasses that have been rinsed in cold water and put into the freezer.

Mussels

How to clean and cook

These days mussels sometimes come precleaned, but if yours are not (you'll see the thread-like beard hanging from the shell and sandy water around them) you must clean them. Holding each mussel in your hand with the wide part of the shell near your fingers and the pointed end in the palm of your hand, scrape the shells with a knife and pull off the 'beards'. Scrub under cold running water and discard any mussels with broken shells or any that do not shut immediately when sharply tapped. Put the mussels into a saucepan with 250 ml/8 fl oz water (for 2–3 kg/4½–6½ lb mussels) and a pinch of salt. Cover and cook over a high heat, shaking the pan occasionally, for 4–5 minutes, until the shells have opened. Remove the pan from the heat and lift out the mussels with a slotted spoon. Discard any that remain closed. Depending on the dish you are preparing, either remove the mussels from their shells or leave them on the half shell and discard the empty half shells. Strain the cooking liquid through a muslin-lined sieve into a bowl. The mussels are now ready to cook according to the recipe chosen.

668 Mussels in vinaigrette

MEJILLONES EN VINAGRETA

- 1 kg/2¼ lb mussels
- ½ onion finely, chopped
- 200 g/7 oz canned red peppers, drained and chopped
- 200 g/7 oz canned peas
- 1 quantity Vinaigrette (see recipe 98)

Serves 4

Prepare and cook the mussels as describedabove, pouring enough water into the saucepan to cover them completely. Drain and reserve the mussels on the half shell, discarding any that remain closed. Mix together onion, red pepper and peas and spread this mixture over each mussel. Spoon the vinaigrette over the mussels.

Note: These are also ideal served as an appetizer.

669

Fried mussels

MEJILLONES REBOZADOS Y FRITOS

- 1 kg/2 ¼ lb large mussels
- 1 egg
- 80 g/3 oz breadcrumbs
- sunflower oil, for deep-frying
- salt
- 1 quantity Classic Mayonnaise
  (see recipe 105)

Serves 4

Prepare and cook the mussels as described on page 555. Drain, and discard any mussels that remain closed. Remove the mussels from their shells, put them between two clean tea towels and place a weight, such as a heavy chopping board, on top. Beat the egg with a pinch of salt in a shallow dish and spread out the breadcrumbs in another shallow dish. Heat the oil in a deep-fryer or saucepan to 180–190°C/350–375°F or until a cube of day-old bread browns in 30 seconds. Coat each mussel first in the beaten egg and then in the breadcrumbs, add them to the hot oil and cook until golden brown. Remove with a slotted spoon and drain. Stick a wooden cocktail stick into each mussel and serve immediately, offering the mayonnaise separately if you like.

Note: These are also ideal served as an appetizer.

670

Mussels with poulette sauce

MEJILLONES EN SALSA BECHAMEL CLARITA (POULETTE)

- 3 kg/6 ½ lb mussels
- 5 tablespoons white wine
- 25 g/1 oz butter
- 2 tablespoons sunflower oil
- 1 heaped tablespoon plain flour
- 2 egg yolks
- juice of 1 lemon
- 1 tablespoon chopped
  fresh parsley
- salt

Serves 6

Prepare the mussels as described on page 555 and cook in the wine mixed with 275 ml/9 fl oz water. Drain, and reserve the mussels on the half shell, discarding any that remain closed. Strain the cooking liquid through a muslin-lined sieve into a bowl. Melt the butter with the oil in a saucepan. Stir in the flour and cook, stirring constantly, for 2 minutes. Gradually stir in the reserved cooking liquid, a little at a time, adding more water if necessary. Cook, stirring constantly, for 5 minutes. Lightly beat the egg yolks and lemon juice in a bowl and stir in a few spoonfuls of the sauce to prevent the yolks curdling, then stir into the pan. Season to taste with salt, stir in the parsley and add the mussels. Cook for a few minutes to warm through. Serve in a warm deep serving dish.

Note: Poulette sauce is a variety of béchamel sauce that is thickened with egg and usually includes parsley.

671

- 1.5–2 kg/3¼–4½ lb mussels
- 175 ml/6 fl oz white wine
- 1 shallot, finely chopped
- 50 g/2 oz butter
- 2 tablespoons sunflower oil
- 2 tablespoons plain flour
- 500 ml/18 fl oz milk
- ½ teaspoon curry powder
- 1 tablespoon chopped
  fresh parsley
- 2 egg yolks
- juice of ½ lemon
- 3 tablespoons breadcrumbs
- salt

Serves 6

Curried mussels
CONCHAS DE MEJILLONES AL CURRY

Prepare the mussels as described on page 555. Put them into a saucepan, pour in 175 ml/6 fl oz water and the wine and add the shallot and a pinch of salt. Cover and cook over a high heat, shaking the pan occasionally, for 4–5 minutes, until the shells have opened. Remove the pan from the heat and lift out the mussels with a slotted spoon. Discard any that remain closed. Remove the mussels from their shells, cut them in half, put them into a bowl and cover. Return the pan to the heat and cook for a further 10 minutes to concentrate the cooking liquid. Strain through a muslin-lined sieve into a bowl and set aside. Preheat the oven to 200°C/400°F/Gas Mark 6. Melt 40 g/1½ oz of the butter with the oil in a saucepan. Stir in the flour and cook, stirring constantly, for 2 minutes. Gradually stir in the milk, a little at a time, then stir in 250 ml/8 fl oz of the reserved cooking liquid. Cook, stirring constantly, for about 5 minutes, until thickened. Stir in the curry powder and parsley and season to taste with salt. Lightly beat the egg yolks and lemon juice in a bowl and stir in a little of the sauce to prevent the yolks curdling, then stir into the pan. Add the mussels, then divide the mixture among six individual ovenproof dishes or scrubbed scallop shells. Sprinkle with the breadcrumbs, dot with the remaining butter and bake for about 10 minutes, until golden brown. Serve immediately.

672

- 2 kg/4½ lb large mussels
- 175 ml/6 fl oz white wine
- 1 shallot, chopped
- pinch of mixed dried herbs
- salt

Garlic and parsley butter:
- 250 g/9 oz butter, softened
- 2 cloves garlic,
  very finely chopped
- 3 tablespoons chopped
  fresh parsley

Serves 6

Mussels with garlic and parsley butter
MEJILLONES CON MANTEQUILLA, AJO Y PEREJIL, (AL ESTILO CARACOLES)

Preheat the oven to 200°C/400°F/Gas Mark 6. Prepare the mussels as described on page 555. Put them into a saucepan, pour in the wine and 175 ml/6 fl oz water and add the shallot, dried herbs and a pinch of salt. Cover and cook over a high heat, shaking the pan occasionally, for 4–5 minutes, until the shells have opened. Remove the pan from the heat and lift out the mussels with a slotted spoon. Discard any that remain closed. Divide the mussels on the half shells, open side uppermost, among six individual ovenproof plates. Beat the butter with the garlic and parsley until thoroughly combined. Using a round-bladed knife, place a little of the flavoured butter on each mussel, covering it well. Put the dishes into the oven for just 3 minutes, until the garlic and parsley butter has melted. Serve immediately.

673

Mussel, bacon and mushroom brochettes

PINCHOS DE MEJILLONES, BACON Y CHAMPIÑONES

- **3 kg/6½ lb large mussels**
- **250 g/9 oz mushrooms**
- **juice of ½ lemon**
- **9 thin rashers of bacon**
- **sunflower oil, for brushing**
- **salt**

Serves 6

Preheat the oven to 200°C/400°F/Gas Mark 6. Prepare and cook the mussels as described on page 555. Drain, discarding any mussels that remain closed. Remove them from their shells. Separate the mushroom caps from the stalks. Cut the bacon into pieces twice the size of the mussels and fold them in half. Thread six skewers so that there is a mushroom cap at both ends and in the middle with pairs of mussels alternating with the folded pieces of bacon in between. Season the brochettes with salt and brush with the oil. Place the brochettes in a roasting tin or ovenproof dish so that the skewers are resting on the rim. Bake, turning the brochettes occasionally, for 8–10 minutes, until cooked through. Serve immediately.

Queen or king scallops

VIEIRAS O CONCHAS PEREGRINAS

- **9 scallops**
- **150 g/5 oz butter**
- **1 onion, very finely chopped**
- **pinch of dried mixed herbs**
- **pinch of cayenne pepper**
- **275 ml/9 fl oz white wine**
- **200 g/7 oz mushrooms, sliced**
- **juice of ½ lemon**
- **4 tablespoons Classic Tomato
  Sauce (see recipe 73)**
- **4 tablespoons breadcrumbs**
- **salt**

Serves 6

Hold one of the scallops, flat side uppermost, in one hand and slide a thin-bladed knife between the two shells. Keeping the blade flat against the top shell, sever the ligament attaching the scallop to the shell and lift off the top shell. Remove and discard the 'skirt' and the black stomach sac. Slide the knife under the scallop and sever the ligament attaching the scallop to the shell. Pull off and discard the ligament from the scallop. Separate the white muscle and orange coral and reserve. Repeat with the remaining scallops. Thoroughly scrub the rounded half shells and dry with kitchen paper. Melt 40 g/1½ oz of the butter in a saucepan. Add the onion and cook over a low heat, stirring occasionally, for 5 minutes, until softened. Add the white scallop meat, sprinkle with the dried herbs and cayenne pepper, season with salt and pour in the wine. Cook for 5 minutes. Put the mushrooms, 25 g/1 oz of the remaining butter, the lemon juice and a pinch of salt into a saucepan and cook over a low heat for 6 minutes. Remove from the heat and set aside. Remove the scallops from the pan with a slotted spoon and cut them into slices about 1.5 cm/5/8 inch thick. Slice the coral. Generously grease the inside of the reserved shells with some of the remaining butter and divide the scallop meat, mushrooms and coral among them, placing the coral on top in the centre. Stir the tomato sauce into the onion and wine mixture and cook for a few minutes, then pour this sauce over the scallops. Sprinkle with the breadcrumbs, dot with the remaining butter and bake for about 5 minutes, until golden brown. Serve immediately.

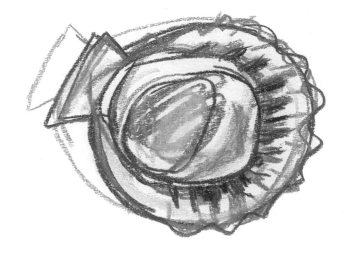

Scallop salad with Parmesan tuiles

ENSALADA DE VIEIRAS CON TEJAS DE PARMESANO

- 16 shelled scallops
  (see recipe 674) without coral
- 6 tablespoons olive oil
- juice of ½ lemon
- 1 tablespoon balsamic vinegar
- 150 g/5 oz watercress
- sea salt and pepper

Tuiles:
- butter, for greasing
- 2 slices of bread,
  left out overnight to harden
- 100 g/3½ oz Parmesan cheese,
  grated

Serves 4

Preheat the oven to 180°C/350°F/Gas Mark 4. Grease a baking sheet with butter. To make the tuiles, put the bread in a food processor and process to make breadcrumbs, then mix with the Parmesan. Spoon small heaps of the mixture on to the prepared baking sheet and flatten gently into rounds with a teaspoon. Bake for 5 minutes, then lift the rounds off the baking sheet with a palette knife and drape them over a rolling pin or bottle to give them the shape of a curved roof tile. Leave to cool. Meanwhile, brush both sides of the scallops with some of the oil. Mix together the remaining oil, the lemon juice, vinegar and a little salt and pepper in a bowl. Make a bed of watercress on four individual plates and sprinkle with the dressing. Heat a non-stick frying pan, add the scallops and cook for 20 seconds on each side until cooked through. Divide them among the plates and pour the cooking juices over them. Serve immediately with the Parmesan tuiles.

Note: You can also sprinkle a little curry powder over the scallops at the last minute to add extra flavour.

Oysters au gratin

OSTRAS GRATINADAS

- **36 oysters**
- **1 clove garlic**
- **2 kg/4½ lb rock salt**
- **grated rind of 2 green lemons**
- **150 g/5 oz butter,**
  chilled and cut into pieces
- **1 sprig fresh parsley**
- **salt and pepper**

Serves 6

If your oysters have not been shucked, wrap one hand in a tea towel and grasp one of the oysters, flat side uppermost. Insert an oyster knife into the hinge – the narrowest point of the shell. Work the knife backwards and forwards or twist to prise open the shells. Slide the blade of the knife along the inside of the top shell and sever the ligament that joins the oyster to the upper shell. Remove the upper shell. Keeping the bottom shell upright to avoid spilling the juices, slide the blade under the oyster and sever the second ligament. Lift out the oyster and strain the juices through a muslin-lined sieve into a saucepan. Repeat with the remaining oysters. Add the garlic to the pan and cook over a medium-low heat until the liquid has reduced by two-thirds. Meanwhile, wash and dry the cup-shaped oyster shells, then stand them on a bed of rock salt on a baking sheet. Return the oysters to their shells and sprinkle with the lemon rind. Preheat the grill. Remove the garlic from the pan and gradually whisk in the butter, one piece at a time. Cook over a medium heat, whisking constantly, until creamy. Season to taste with salt and pepper. Pour a spoonful of this sauce over each oyster and cook under the grill for 2–3 minutes, until beginning to brown. Garnish with the parsley and serve immediately.

Note: You can add 250 ml/8 fl oz dry white wine to the oyster juices before reducing them. If you don't like the flavour of green lemons, substitute a pinch of saffron.

Assorted pies and fish dishes

677

Fine hake pie
BUDÍN FINO DE MERLUZA

- 750 g/1 lb 10 oz hake or
  other white fish fillets
- 225 g/8 oz day-old French bread,
  crusts removed
- 450 ml/¾ pint hot milk
- 25 g/1 oz butter,
  plus extra for greasing
- 4 eggs, separated
- pinch of freshly grated nutmeg
- 2 egg whites
- salt

  Béchamel sauce:
- 25 g/1 oz butter
- 2 tablespoons sunflower oil
- 2 tablespoons plain flour
- 500 ml/18 fl oz milk
- 1 egg yolk

Serves 6

Put the fish into a saucepan, pour in water to cover, add a pinch of salt and bring to the boil. Remove the pan from the heat and leave to cool. Meanwhile, put the bread into a bowl, pour in the milk and leave to soak. Preheat the oven to 180°C/350°F/Gas Mark 4. Grease a 20-cm/8-inch cake tin with butter. Lift the fish out of the pan, reserving the cooking liquid, remove and discard any skin and bones and flake the flesh. Add the soaked bread and any remaining hot milk, breaking it up with a fork, then add half the butter. Stir in the egg yolks, nutmeg and a pinch of salt. Whisk all the egg whites in a clean, dry bowl until stiff, and fold into the fish mixture. Spoon the mixture into the prepared tin. Put the tin in a roasting tin and pour in boiling water to come about halfway up the sides. Bake for about 1 hour, until set. Meanwhile, make the béchamel sauce as described in recipe 77, adding 250 ml/8 fl oz of the reserved cooking liquid. Lightly beat the egg yolk in a bowl, stir in a little of the sauce to prevent it curdling, then stir into the sauce. Run a round-bladed knife around the edge of the cake tin and turn the pie out on to a warm serving dish. Pour the sauce over it and serve immediately.

Note: You can also serve this pie with Classic Tomato Sauce (see recipe 73) or a slightly thicker béchamel with cooked peeled prawns.

678

Hot or cold fish pie with potatoes and tomatoes
BUDÍN DE PESCADO CON PATATAS Y TOMATE, FRÍO O CALIENTE

- 750 g/1 lb 10 oz white fish fillets,
  such as hake or whiting
- 2 potatoes, unpeeled
- 25 g/1 oz butter,
  plus extra for greasing
- 2–3 tablespoons breadcrumbs
- 2 eggs
- 1 egg white
- salt

Tomato sauce:
- 500 g/1 lb 2 oz ripe tomatoes
- 2 tablespoons sunflower oil
- 1 teaspoon sugar
- salt

Quick stock:
- 2 tablespoons white wine
- 2 thick slices of onion
- 1 bay leaf
- salt

Serves 6

Make the quick stock as described in recipe 534 and set aside to cool. Make the tomato sauce as described in recipe 73. After processing it in a food processor, simmer the tomato sauce for a further 25–35 minutes, until thickened, then remove from the heat and set aside. Remove the rack from a fish kettle. Pour in the quick stock, put the fish on the rack and return the rack to the fish kettle. Bring the stock to the boil, then remove the fish kettle from the heat and leave to stand for 10 minutes. Lift out the fish and leave to cool, then remove and discard any skin and bones and flake the flesh carefully. Meanwhile, put the potatoes into a saucepan, pour in water to cover and add a pinch of salt. Bring to the boil and cook for about 30 minutes, until tender. Preheat the oven to 180°C/350°F/Gas Mark 4. Grease a loaf tin with butter, sprinkle with the breadcrumbs and tip out any excess. Drain, peel and mash the potatoes, then put them into a saucepan. Stir in the butter, flaked fish and tomato sauce. Separate one of the eggs and beat the yolk with the whole egg in a bowl, then stir into the mash. Whisk both egg whites in a clean, dry bowl until they form soft peaks, then fold them into the mash. Spoon the mixture into the prepared tin. Put the tin in a roasting tin, pour in boiling water to come about halfway up the sides and bake for 30–45 minutes, until a knife inserted into the pie comes out clean. Run a round-bladed knife around the edge of the tin and turn the pie out on to a serving dish.

Note: The pie may be served hot covered with Classic Tomato Sauce (see recipe 73) or Classic Béchamel Sauce (see recipe 77). It may also be served cold, garnished with slices of tomato and hard-boiled egg or with prawns, and with a sauce boat of mayonnaise.

Glasses of fish and shellfish with vegetable sauce

COPAS DE PESCADO Y MARISCO CON SALSA DE HORTALIZAS (PIPIRRANA)

- **500 g/1 lb 2 oz raw unpeeled prawns**
- **3 bay leaves**
- **250 g/9 oz monkfish (Aus: stargazer) fillet**
- **500 g/1 lb 2 oz white fish fillet, such as hake or whiting**
- **1 quantity Vegetable Sauce (see recipe 113)**
- **salt**

Serves 6

Bring a large saucepan of salted water to the boil. Add the prawns and one of the bay leaves, lower the heat and simmer for 2–4 minutes, depending on the size of the prawns. Drain well, leave to cool, then peel the prawns. Put the monkfish and white fish in separate saucepans. Add 1 bay leaf and a pinch of salt to each and pour in water to cover. Bring to the boil, then remove the pans from the heat and leave to stand for 10 minutes. Lift out the fish and remove and discard any skin and bones. Cut the flesh into bite-size pieces. Divide the prawns and fish among individual glasses or glass sundae dishes and leave to stand in a cool place or the refrigerator. About 10 minutes before serving, stir the vegetable sauce well and divide it among the glasses.

Note: You can vary the fish and shellfish according to taste.

680

Fish balls

ALBÓNDIGAS DE PESCADO

- 130 g/4½ oz day-old bread,
  crusts removed
- 250 ml/8 fl oz hot milk
- 500 g/1 lb 2 oz hake fillet
- 1 egg
- 1 clove garlic, finely chopped
- 1 teaspoon chopped
  fresh parsley
- sunflower oil, for deep-frying
- 50 g/2 oz plain flour
- triangles of fried bread
  (see recipe 130) or boiled rice
- salt

  Sauce:
- 1 onion, chopped
- 1 tablespoon plain flour
- 1 bay leaf
- pinch of saffron threads
- salt

Serves 6

Put the bread into a bowl, pour in the milk and leave to soak. Put the hake into a saucepan, pour in water to cover, add a pinch of salt and bring to the boil. Immediately remove the pan from the heat. Drain the fish well, reserving the cooking liquid, then remove any skin and bones and flake the flesh with a fork. Strain the cooking liquid and leave to cool. Put the fish into a bowl and add the soaked bread, egg, garlic, parsley and a pinch of salt. Mix well, then form the mixture into small balls like meatballs. Heat the oil in a deep-fryer or saucepan to 180–190°C/350–375°F or until a cube of day-old bread browns in 30 seconds. Coat the fish balls in the flour, add to the hot oil, in batches of five at a time, and cook until golden brown. Remove with a slotted spoon and drain. Make the sauce. Transfer 6 tablespoons of the oil to a frying pan and reheat. Add the onion and cook over a low heat, stirring occasionally, for about 10 minutes, until golden brown. Stir in the flour and cook, stirring constantly, for about 5 minutes, until lightly browned. Gradually stir in 500 ml/18 fl oz of the reserved cooking liquid and add the bay leaf. Crush the saffron in a mortar and stir in 2 tablespoons of the sauce, then add to the pan and cook for a further 10 minutes. Strain the sauce, add the fish balls and serve immediately with triangles of fried bread or boiled rice in moulds.

Note: The fish balls can be served with Classic Tomato Sauce (see recipe 73) instead of the sauce in this recipe.

681

Provençal fish stew
BOUILLABAISSE

- 2 onions, coarsley chopped
- 3 cloves garlic, lightly crushed
- 2 tomatoes, peeled, seeded and coarsley chopped
- 1 bay leaf
- 1 sprig fresh parsley
- 1 sprig fresh fennel
- thinly pared rind of 1 orange
- 500 g/1 lb 2 oz monkfish (Aus: stargazer) fillet, sliced
- 500 g/1 lb 2 oz small crabs
- 1 sea bream, about 500 g/ 1 lb 2 oz, trimmed, scaled and cleaned
- 120 ml/4 fl oz olive oil
- pinch of saffron threads
- 500 g/1 lb 2 oz hake steaks
- 2 red mullet or snapper, scaled and cleaned
- 1 sea bass, about 500 g/ 1 lb 2 oz, trimmed, scaled and cleaned
- 1 sprig fresh thyme
- 1 day-old French bread loaf, about 500 g/1 lb 2 oz, cut into 1.5-cm/⅝-inch thick slices
- salt and pepper

Serves 8

Put the onion, garlic, tomato, bay leaf, parsley, fennel and orange rind into a saucepan and put the monkfish, crabs and sea bream on top. Add the oil, pour in boiling water to cover the fish and season with salt and pepper. Crush the saffron in a mortar, stir in 1 tablespoon water and add to the pan. Bring to the boil over a high heat and cook for 5 minutes. Add the remaining fish and more water if necessary. Bring back to the boil and cook for 8 minutes. Remove the pan from the heat and transfer the fish to a warm serving dish. Put the slices of bread in a soup tureen and strain the cooking liquid over them. Serve immediately with the fish.

Note: For a similar recipe using salt cod, see recipe 545.

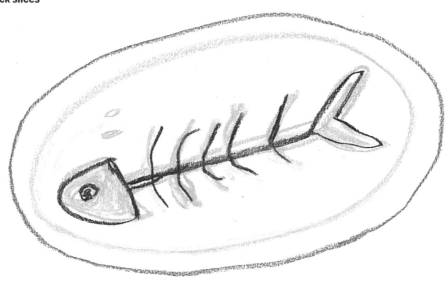

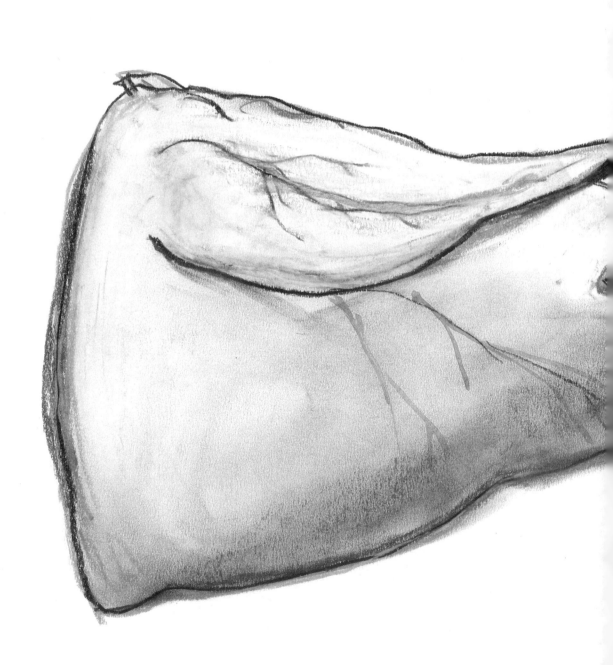

MEAT

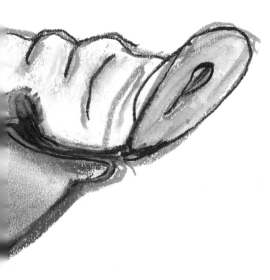

Meat has been an important part of the human diet since prehistoric times – ever since the invention of weapons to hunt animals and tools to turn them into food.

Frozen meat

Once frozen meat has thawed, it should never be refrozen. This is because freezing does not destroy micro-organisms but leaves them 'sleeping', stopping their reproduction. However, once the meat has thawed, the bacteria 'wake up' again and start to multiply rapidly. If you buy frozen meat, do not leave it in the back of a parked car for any length of time and, ideally, put it into the freezer within an hour of purchase, so that any bacteria do not have a chance to proliferate. Can meat be cooked without defrosting it first? It depends on the kind of meat and the way it is to be cooked. If it is to be cooked for a long time on a low heat in a sauce, there is no problem if it hasn't thawed first; just make sure it is fully cooked, right through. It is especially important for minced meat to be cooked through evenly. This is because most bacteria reside on the outside of the meat (due to contact with other contaminated surfaces) which, in the case of minced meat, is then mixed into the interior. Roasts or large cuts for grilling must be defrosted to avoid the outside cooking while the inside remains raw. The best way to defrost frozen meat is slowly in the refrigerator. Remove all the packaging, put it on a plate and cover with cling film. However, if you're in a hurry, it can be defrosted more quickly in a microwave oven, following the manufacturer's instructions.

Selection

The colour of meat is a guide to its quality and flavour. Beef, for example, should be a dull, dark red rather than a shiny coral. This shows that it has been aged long enough to become tender. Similarly, the fat should be firm and waxy and either cream or white in colour, depending on the type of meat. It is important to choose the appropriate cut of meat for the method of cooking. The flank, for example, is ideal for pot-roasting or making meatballs, but is not so good for frying, as it releases a lot of juice and will dry out. The rump is much better for this purpose, as it is succulent but does not release too much juice when cooked. Other good cuts for braising and pot roasts are topside and silverside. Wonderful escalopes, perfect for grilling and frying, can be obtained from the top of the leg, while brisket, breast and ribs are perfect for stews and casseroles. Other less commonly used parts, such as the tail and snout, have a delicious texture because of their gelatine content.

Beef

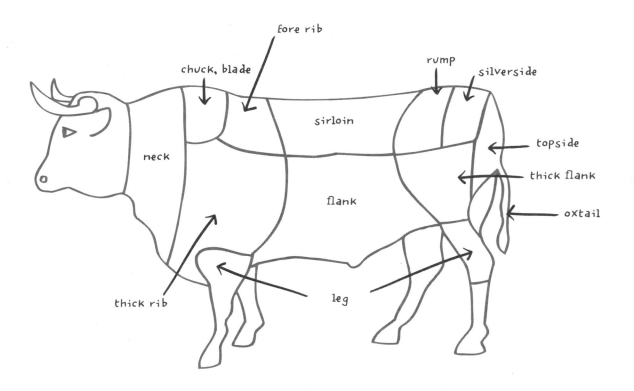

Allow about 130 g/4 ½ oz boneless beef per serving for grilling and frying. Allow about 150 g/5 oz boneless beef per serving for roasting, as it shrinks slightly. Allow 200 g/7 oz boneless beef per serving for stewing, as it is the method that reduces the volume most.

Buying beef	Suitable cuts	Weight per serving	Cooking time
Fried, grilled or griddled	Fillet steak, Hamburgers, Sirloin, Rump	130–150 g/4½–5 oz	2 minutes each side for rare 3–4 minutes each side for medium 4–6 minutes each side for well done
Roasted *	Fillet, Fore rib, Sirloin, Rump, Silverside, Topside	150 g/5 oz (boneless) 250 g/9 oz (on the bone)	15 minutes per 500 g/1 lb 2 oz
Stewed or braised	Topside, Oxtail, Thick rib, Flank, Brisket	185–200 g/6½–7 oz	2–2 ½ hours

*Make sure that the oven is preheated

Tips

Grilled, griddled or fried steak:
Fillet steak, sirloin, entrecôte, porterhouse, T-bone, châteaubriand and rump steak are the best cuts. There are many suitable accompaniments for steak including:

• Chips: traditional, matchstick or straw potatoes
• Mashed potato
• All kinds of vegetables: peas, green beans, fried green peppers,
• onion fritters, fried tomatoes, roasted tomatoes, etc.
• Green salad

Accompaniments are not suggested for each recipe as this is a matter of personal taste.

Stews, casseroles and pot roasts:
Use a good-quality, heavy-based saucepan or flameproof casserole to ensure even cooking.

682

Grilled or griddled steak
FILETES A LA PLANCHA

- **1 fillet steak, about 150 g/15 oz**
- **olive oil, for brushing**
- **1 thin slice lemon**
- **½ teaspoon mustard or
  1 tablespoon butter mixed with
  a little finely chopped fresh
  parsley, chilled**
- **salt**

Serves 1

Brush both sides of the steak with the oil and leave to stand in the refrigerator for 30–60 minutes. Preheat the grill or a ridged griddle pan. Grill or griddle the steak for 2–4 minutes on each side, until done to your liking. Season with salt after cooking. Serve garnished with the lemon and mustard or parsley butter.

Note: Fillet steak and tournedos may be served with Béarnaise Sauce (see recipe 84) or Butter and Anchovy Sauce (see recipe 95), offered separately.

683

Fried steak

FILETES FRITOS

• 1 fillet steak, about 150 g/15 oz
• 1 tablespoon olive oil

Serves 1

Season both sides of the steak with salt. Pour just enough of the oil into a frying pan to cover the base and heat. Add the steak and cook over a high heat for 2–6 minutes on each side, until done to your liking. (4 minutes each side will produce medium steak.) Put the steak on a warm serving dish and pour the cooking juices over it.

Note: Seasoning the steak with salt before cooking helps release the juices, which then mix with the oil to make a delicious sauce.

684

Fillet steaks with port and mustard sauce

FILETES DE SOLOMILLO CON SALSA DE OPORTO Y MOSTAZA

• 6 fillet steaks,
  about 150 g/15 oz each
• 4 tablespoons olive oil
• ½ teaspoon mustard
• 5 tablespoons port
• salt

Serves 6

Brush both sides of the steaks with a little of the oil and leave to stand in the refrigerator for 30 minutes. Heat the remaining oil in a frying pan. Season the steaks with salt, add to the pan and cook over a high heat for 2–4 minutes on each side, until done to your liking. Transfer to a serving dish and keep warm. Stir the mustard and port into the frying pan and cook for 2–3 minutes. Pour the sauce over the steaks and serve immediately.

685

Fillet steaks in wine sauce
SOLOMILLO CON SALSA DE VINO

- **2 thick fillet steaks, about 150 g/5 oz each**
- **2 tablespoons sunflower oil**
- **1 tablespoon chopped fresh parsley**
- **4 raspberries**
- **salt and ground pink peppercorns**

Wine sauce:
- **5 tablespoons olive oil**
- **2 large shallots, chopped**
- **500 ml/18 fl oz red wine**
- **1 tablespoon plain flour**
- **40 g/1½ oz butter**

Serves 2

Make the sauce. Heat the oil in a frying pan. Add the shallots and cook over a low heat, stirring occasionally, for 6–8 minutes, until lightly browned. Pour in the wine, add 175 ml/6 fl oz water and simmer gently for about 10 minutes. Mix the flour with the butter in a small bowl, then stir into the frying pan. Heat a ridged griddle pan. Brush both sides of the steaks with the oil, add to the pan and cook over a high heat for 2–4 minutes on each side, until done to your liking. Season with salt and pepper. Transfer the steaks to a warm serving dish. Stir the cooking juices into the sauce, then pour the sauce over the steaks. Garnish with the parsley and raspberries and serve immediately.

Note: To create a decorative effect, rotate the steaks on the griddle pan half way through cooking so that the ridges make a diamond pattern on the meat. Turn and repeat on the other side.

686

Fillet or sirloin steaks with mushrooms, shallots and ham
FILETES DE SOLOMILLO O LOMO, CON UN PICADITO DE CHAMPIÑON, CEBOLLA Y JAMÓN

- **6 fillet or sirloin steaks, about 150 g/5 oz each**
- **5 tablespoons olive oil**
- **200 g/7 oz mushrooms, sliced**
- **20 g/¾ oz butter**
- **juice of ½ lemon**
- **150 g/5 oz shallots, chopped**
- **100 g/3½ oz Serrano ham, chopped**
- **salt**

Serves 6

Brush both sides of the steaks with a little of the oil and leave to stand in the refrigerator for 30 minutes. Put the mushrooms, butter and lemon juice into a saucepan, season with salt and cook over a medium heat for 6 minutes. Remove from the heat and set aside. Heat 3 tablespoons of the oil in a frying pan. Add the shallots and cook over a low heat, stirring occasionally, for about 5 minutes, until softened and translucent. Stir in the ham and cook for 2–3 minutes, then add the mushrooms and their cooking juices. Keep warm over a very low heat. Heat the remaining oil in a frying pan or ridged griddle pan, add the steaks and cook over a high heat for 2–4 minutes on each side, until done to your liking. Season with salt, transfer to a warm serving dish and spoon a little of the mushroom, onion and ham mixture, together with the cooking juices, on top of each steak. Serve immediately.

Note: This dish can also be made using veal in place of beef.

687

Fillet steaks with butter and anchovies
FILETES DE SOLOMILLO CON MANTEQUILLA Y ANCHOAS

- 6 fillet steaks,
  about 150 g/5 oz each
- 3 tablespoons olive oil
- 8 canned anchovy fillets, drained
- 100 g/3½ oz butter
- juice of 1 lemon
- 1 tablespoon chopped
  fresh parsley
- salt

Serves 6

Brush both sides of the steaks with a little of the oil and leave to stand for 30 minutes in the refrigerator. Heat the remaining oil in a griddle pan or frying pan. Add the steaks and cook over a high heat for 2–4 minutes on each side, until done to your liking. Lightly season with salt, transfer to a serving dish and keep warm. Pound the anchovies and 25 g/1 oz of the butter to a paste in a mortar. Stir in the remaining butter and heat gently in the griddle pan or frying pan. When the butter has melted, stir in the lemon juice and parsley. Mix well and pour the sauce over the steaks or serve separately in a sauce boat.

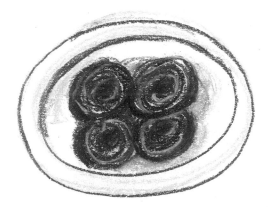

688

Flambéed pepper steaks
FILETES DE SOLOMILLO A LA PIMIENTA Y FLAMEADOS CON COÑAC

- 6 fillet steaks,
  about 150 g/5 oz each
- 3 tablespoons black
  peppercorns, lightly crushed
- 3 tablespoons olive oil
- 6 tablespoons brandy
- salt

Serves 6

Season both sides of each steak with salt. Spread the peppercorns over both sides of each steak, pressing them down firmly. Heat the oil in a heavy-based frying pan. Add the steaks, three at a time, and cook over a high heat for 2–4 minutes on each side, until done to your liking. Return the first batch of steaks to the pan when the second batch has finished cooking. Pour the brandy into a small saucepan and heat gently, then ignite it and carefully spoon it over the steaks while it is still burning. Transfer the steaks to a warm serving dish, pour the sauce over them and serve immediately.

689

Fillet steaks with mushrooms, truffles and cream

FILETES DE SOLOMILLO CON CHAMPIÑON, TRUFA Y NATA

- 100 g/3½ oz mushrooms, chopped
- juice of ½ lemon
- 40 g/1½ oz butter
- 1 canned or bottled truffle, drained and chopped, liquid reserved
- 6 slices of bread
- 6 fillet steaks, 150 g/5 oz each
- sunflower oil, for brushing
- 3 tablespoons brandy
- 4–5 tablespoons single cream
- salt and pepper

Serves 6

Put the mushrooms, lemon juice, half the butter and a pinch of salt into a saucepan. Cook over a medium heat, stirring occasionally, for 6 minutes. Add the truffle and its liquid and mix well. Remove the pan from the heat and keep warm. Toast the bread on both sides and spread with the remaining butter. Keep warm. Heat a heavy-based frying pan. Brush both sides of the steaks with the oil, add to the pan and cook over a high heat for 2–4 minutes. Season with salt, turn the steaks and cook for 2–4 minutes more, until done to your liking. Transfer the steaks to a warm serving dish. Heat the brandy in a small saucepan, ignite it and carefully pour it over the steaks while still burning. When the flames have died down, place a slice of toast under each steak. Stir the cream into the mushroom mixture and heat through gently but do not allow to boil. Season to taste with salt, pour the sauce over the steaks and serve immediately with Mashed Potato (see recipe 230) or Potato Balls (see recipe 231).

690

Steak with olives and white wine

FILETES CON ACEITUNAS Y VINO BLANCO

- 130 g/4½ oz olives, stoned
- 4 tablespoons olive oil
- 6 sirloin or rump steaks, about 130 g/4½ oz each
- 5 tablespoons white wine
- 1 teaspoon tomato purée or Classic Tomato Sauce (see recipe 73)
- ½ teaspoon meat extract
- salt

Serves 6

Put the olives into a saucepan, pour in water to cover, bring to the boil and simmer for 2 minutes. Drain well, pat dry and cut in half. Heat the oil in a frying pan. Season both sides of the steaks with salt, add them to the pan, in three batches, and cook over a high heat for 2–4 minutes on each side, until done to your liking. Remove from the pan and keep warm. Pour off half the cooking juices and return the pan to the heat. Add the olives, stir in the wine, tomato purée or tomato sauce and meat extract and cook for 3–4 minutes. Transfer the steaks to a warm serving dish and pour the sauce over them. Serve immediately.

Note: This dish can also be made using veal in place of beef.

Steak in breadcrumbs

FILETES EMPANADOS

691

- 6 rump steaks, about 130 g/
  4½ oz each
- 1 clove garlic
- 1 sprig fresh parsley
- 2 eggs
- 80 g/3 oz breadcrumbs
- sunflower oil, for deep-frying
- salt

Serves 6

One at a time, place the steaks between two sheets of greaseproof paper and pound thinly and evenly with a meat mallet, the bottom of a small saucepan or the side of a rolling pin. Pound the garlic with the parsley and a pinch of salt to a paste in a mortar. Spread the paste over both sides of each steak. Lightly beat the eggs in a shallow dish and spread out the breadcrumbs in another shallow dish. Dip the steaks first in the beaten egg and then in the breadcrumbs, making sure they are evenly covered. Chill in the refrigerator for 15 minutes. Heat the oil in a deep-fryer or frying pan to 180–190°C/350–375°F or until a cube of day-old bread browns in 30 seconds. Add the steaks, in batches, and cook until golden brown. Remove with a fish slice, drain well and keep warm while you cook the remaining batches. Serve immediately.

Note: You can omit the garlic and parsley if you like. Simply season the steaks with salt before coating them with egg and breadcrumbs.

Beef roulades with ham, olives and hard-boiled eggs

FILETES DE CEBÓN, RELLENOS DE JAMÓN, ACEITUNAS Y HUEVO DURO

- **6 rump or thick flank steaks, about 130 g/4½ oz each**
- **12 olives, stoned and chopped**
- **100 g/3½ oz Serrano ham, chopped**
- **2 hard-boiled eggs, chopped**
- **40 g/1½ oz plain flour**
- **250 ml/8 fl oz sunflower oil**
- **1 small onion, very finely chopped**
- **5 tablespoons white wine**
- **1 clove garlic**
- **1 sprig fresh parsley**
- **salt**

Serves 6

One at a time, place the steaks between two sheets of greaseproof paper and pound thinly and evenly with a meat mallet, the bottom of a small saucepan or the side of a rolling pin. Mix together the olives, ham and hard-boiled eggs. Reserve 2 tablespoons of the mixture and divide the remainder among the steaks. Roll up the steaks and secure with a wooden cocktail stick or tie with fine kitchen string. Reserve 1 tablespoon of the flour and spread out the remainder in a shallow dish. Heat the oil in a frying pan. Lightly coat the steaks in flour, shaking off any excess, add to the pan, in two batches, and cook over a medium heat, turning frequently for 4–5 minutes until golden brown all over. Remove with a slotted spoon, drain and keep warm. Transfer 6 tablespoons of the oil from the frying pan into a saucepan and reheat. Add the onion and cook over a low heat, stirring occasionally, for about 10 minutes, until golden brown. Stir in the reserved flour and cook, stirring constantly, for 2 minutes. Gradually stir in the wine and 1 litre/1¾ pints water. Add the steaks to the pan. Pound the garlic with the parsley and a pinch of salt in a mortar, stir in 2–3 tablespoons of the sauce and stir into the saucepan. Cook over a medium-low heat for about 25 minutes, until the roulades are tender. Just before serving, lift out the roulades and remove and discard the cocktail sticks on string, then place on a warm serving dish. Stir the reserved stuffing into the sauce and bring to the boil, then pour the sauce over the meat. Serve immediately, with croûtons, boiled rice or Mashed Potato (see recipe 230).

Note: This dish can also be made using veal in place of beef.

693

Beef roulades with York ham and olives
FILETES RELLENOS DE JAMÓN YORK Y ACEITUNAS

- 6 rump or thick flank steaks, about 130 g/4 ½ oz each
- 3 large, thin slices of York ham, halved
- 100 g/3 ½ oz pimiento-stuffed green olives, chopped
- 250 ml/8 fl oz sunflower oil
- 1 onion, chopped
- 1 clove garlic, chopped
- 2 tablespoons plain flour
- 300 ml/½ pint white wine
- 2 beef stock cubes
- pinch of mixed dried herbs
- juice of 1 lemon
- salt and pepper

Serves 6

One at a time, place the steaks between two sheets of greaseproof paper and pound thinly and evenly with a meat mallet, the bottom of a small saucepan or the side of a rolling pin. Lightly season each steak with salt and pepper, top with a half-slice of ham and divide the olives among them, putting them in the centre of each steak. Roll up each steak and secure with a wooden cocktail stick or tie with fine kitchen string. Heat the oil in a saucepan. Add the roulades, two at a time, and cook over a medium heat, turning frequently, for 4–5 minutes, until evenly browned. Remove with a slotted spoon, drain and set aside. Pour off most of the oil from the pan, leaving 2–3 tablespoons, and reheat. Add the onion and garlic and cook over a low heat, stirring occasionally, for about 10 minutes, until golden brown. Stir in the flour and cook, stirring constantly, for 2 minutes. Gradually stir in the wine and 450 ml/¾ pint water, crumble in the stock cubes, add the herbs and bring to the boil. Lower the heat, add the roulades and simmer for 1 hour. Add the lemon juice and simmer for a further 15 minutes, until the roulades are tender. Lift the roulades out of the pan, remove and discard the cocktail sticks or string and put them on a warm serving dish. Pass the sauce through a food mill or process in a food processor and pour it over the meat. Serve with Mashed Potato (see recipe 230) or boiled rice.

Note: This dish can also be made using veal in place of beef.

694

Beef in beer with onions
FILETES DE CEBÓN GUISADOS CON CERVEZA Y CEBOLLA

- 5 tablespoons olive oil
- 6 thick slices of beef, such as topside, thick flank or rump
- 3 large onions, thinly sliced and pushed out into rings
- 500–750 ml/ 18 fl oz–1¼ pints beer
- salt

Serves 6

Heat the oil in a saucepan. Add the beef, in batches, and cook over a medium heat for 1 minute on each side, then remove from the pan and set aside. Put half the onion rings into the pan, place the beef on top and season with salt, then put the remaining onion rings on top of the meat. Cover and cook over a low heat for about 10 minutes, until the onion is softened and translucent. Pour in enough beer to cover the meat. Re-cover the pan and cook over a medium-low heat for 1–1½ hours, until tender. (Move the meat occasionally with a wooden spoon or tongs during the cooking time to prevent it sticking to the pan.) Transfer the meat and sauce to a warm serving dish, top with the onion and serve immediately with boiled rice or Mashed Potato (see recipe 230).

695

Rib of beef with parsley, butter and lemon
LOMO DE VACA CON PEREJIL, MANTEQUILLA Y LIMÓN

- **1–2 thick slices of boned beef fore rib, 800 g–1 kg/1¾–2¼ lb total weight**
- **2 tablespoons olive oil**
- **50 g/2 oz butter**
- **juice of 1 lemon**
- **1 tablespoon chopped fresh parsley**
- **salt and pepper**

Serves 6

Preheat the grill. Brush both sides of the beef with the oil and cook under the grill for 4 minutes, then turn over and cook over a medium heat for a further 8 minutes or until done to your liking. Remove the meat from the grill, season both sides with salt and pepper and place on a serving dish. Cut it into strips about 4 cm/1½ inches wide and keep warm. Drain all the juices released into a saucepan, add the butter and melt over a low heat. Stir in the lemon juice and parsley, pour the sauce over the meat and serve immediately.

Note: You can also make this dish with rump steak.

696

Rib of beef with red wine sauce
LOMO DE VACA CON SALSA DE VINO TINTO

- **4 tablespoons sunflower oil**
- **1–2 thick slices of boned beef fore rib, 800 g–1 kg/1¾–2¼ lb total weight**
- **2 shallots, chopped**
- **300 ml/½ pint red wine**
- **3 tablespoons single cream**
- **salt and pepper**

Serves 6

Heat the oil in a large frying pan. Add the beef and cook over a medium heat for 5 minutes on each side. (Cook for a little longer if you prefer your beef well done.) Season with salt and pepper on both sides, then transfer to a serving dish, cut into strips about 4 cm/1½ inches wide and keep warm. Add the shallots to the pan and cook over a low heat, stirring occasionally, for about 5 minutes, until softened and translucent. Add the wine and cook over a low heat for 8–10 minutes, until reduced. Stir in the cream and heat gently but do not allow to boil. Pour the sauce over the meat and serve immediately, with boiled or sautéed potatoes, or a side salad.

Note: You can substitute 80 g/3 oz butter for the cream. Add one-third to the sauce and beat well until it has been incorporated, then add half the remaining butter and beat well again. When that has been completely incorporated, beat in the rest.

697

Hamburgers
FILETES PICADOS O HAMBURGUESAS

- 750 g/1 lb 10 oz lean meat, minced (see note for combinations)
- 2 small onions, chopped
- 2 eggs, lightly beaten
- olive oil, for drizzling
- salt and pepper

Preheat the grill. Mix the meat with the onion in a bowl, add the eggs and season. Shape into eight evenly sized balls and flatten into patties, before drizzling with oil. Cook under a medium grill for 4 minutes each side, depending on how rare you like your meat.

Note: Generally, hamburgers are tastier if made with a mixture of minced beef and sausage meat or lean minced pork. Good proportions for hamburger mince are about 500 g/1 lb 2 oz minced beef to 250 g/9 oz pork or sausage meat. For meatballs or meat loaf it is usual to combine about 400 g/14 oz minced beef with 150 g/5 oz pork or sausage meat.

698

Hamburgers in a light batter
FILETES PICADOS (HAMBURGUESAS) REBOZADOS

- 6 hamburgers (see recipe 697)
- 2 eggs
- 40 g/1½ oz plain flour
- 250 ml/8 fl oz sunflower oil
- salt

Serves 6

Season the hamburgers on both sides with salt. Beat the eggs in a shallow dish and spread out the flour, shaking off the excess, in another shallow dish. Coat the hamburgers first in the flour and then in the beaten egg. Heat the oil in a frying pan. Add the hamburgers, in batches, and cook over a medium heat for 4–5 minutes on each side, until cooked through. Serve immediately.

Note: These hamburgers are also delicious if simply seasoned with salt and coated in flour before frying.

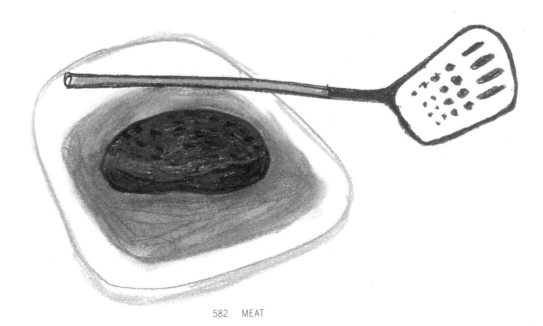

699

Hamburgers in onion sauce

FILETES PICADOS (HAMBURGUESAS) EN SALSA CON CEBOLLA

- **40 g / 1 oz plain flour**
- **250 ml / 8 fl oz sunflower oil**
- **6 hamburgers (see recipe 697)**
- **1 large onion, thinly sliced**
- **175 ml / 6 fl oz white wine**
- **salt**

Serves 6

Reserve 1 teaspoon of the flour and spread out the remainder in a shallow dish. Heat the oil in a frying pan. Season the hamburgers on both sides and coat them in the flour, shaking off the excess. Add to the pan, in batches, and cook over a medium heat for 4–5 minutes on each side until cooked through. Transfer the cooked hamburgers to a large saucepan, arranging them in a single layer. Drain off nearly all the oil from the frying pan, leaving about 3 tablespoons to cover the base, and reheat. Add the onion and cook over a low heat, stirring occasionally, for about 8 minutes, until beginning to brown. Stir in the reserved flour and cook, stirring constantly, for 1 minute. Gradually stir in the wine and 5 tablespoons water, a little at a time. Cook, stirring constantly, for about 5 minutes, until thickened, then pour the sauce into the saucepan with the hamburgers. Bring to the boil, then lower the heat and simmer for 8 minutes. Place the hamburgers on a warm serving dish. Scoop up the onion with a slotted spoon and place it on top. Pour the sauce over the dish and serve immediately with Mashed Potato (see recipe 230) or fried potatoes.

700

Meatballs

ALBÓNDIGAS

- **500 g / 1 lb 2 oz minced beef**
- **1 sprig fresh parsley, chopped**
- **1 clove garlic,**
  very finely chopped
- **1 egg, lightly beaten**
- **4 tablespoons breadcrumbs**
- **3 tablespoons white wine**
- **40 g / 1½ oz plain flour**
- **500 ml / 18 fl oz sunflower oil**
- **salt**

  Sauce:
- **4 tablespoons olive oil**
- **100 g / 3½ oz onions, chopped**
- **2 ripe tomatoes, chopped**
- **small pinch of saffron threads**
- **salt**

Serves 6

Put the beef, parsley, garlic, egg, breadcrumbs, wine and a pinch of salt into a bowl and mix well. Shape the mixture into small balls, rolling them between the palms of your hands. Lightly coat the meatballs in the flour. Heat the oil in a frying pan. Add the meatballs, in batches, and cook over a medium heat, turning frequently, until golden brown all over. Using a slotted spoon, transfer the meatballs to a saucepan, arranging them in a single layer. Heat the oil in another frying pan. Add the onion and cook over a low heat, stirring occasionally, for about 5 minutes. Add the tomato and cook, stirring occasionally and breaking it up with the side of the spoon, for 6–8 minutes. Stir in 500 ml / 18 fl oz water and season. Bring the sauce to the boil, allow to cool slightly, then pass it through a food mill and pour it over the meatballs. Crush the saffron threads in a mortar, then stir in 100 ml / 4 fl oz water and pour into the saucepan. Simmer the meatballs in the sauce for 15–20 minutes, then serve.

Note: You can also make the meatballs with minced veal or a mixture of minced beef and pork. Simmr veal meatballs for 10 minutes only.

701

- 1 small onion or 1 shallot, finely chopped
- 1 clove garlic, finely chopped
- 1 heaped tablespoon finely chopped fresh parsley
- ½–1 teaspoon mustard
- 1 egg yolk
- 400 g/14 oz minced lean steak, such as fillet
- salt and pepper

Serves 2

Steak tartare (first version)

STEAK TÁRTARO

Put the onion or shallot, garlic, parsley, mustard and egg yolk into a bowl, season with salt and quite a lot of pepper and mix well to form a paste. Add the meat and shape into patties.

Note: This dish and the one following are classics. Modern times have given rise to concern over foodborne illnesses caused by uncooked or undercooked meat or eggs. Many people continue to enjoy such dishes, but caution should be applied, especially when serving the very young or very old, or those with compromised immune systems.

702

- 1 small onion or 1 shallot, finely chopped
- 1 clove garlic, finely chopped
- 1 heaped tablespoon finely chopped fresh parsley
- ½–1 teaspoon mustard
- 2 egg yolks
- 200 g/7 oz spinach, coarse stalks removed
- 100 g/3½ oz mushrooms, chopped
- 400 g/14 oz minced lean steak, such as fillet
- salt and pepper

Serves 2

Steak tartare (second version)

STEAK TÁRTARO

To give the steak tartare an original touch, cook the spinach as described on page 315, then chop. Prepare the paste as described in recipe 701, then add the spinach and mushrooms. Add the meat and shape into patties.

Note: This dish and the one following are classics. Modern times have given rise to concern over illnesses caused by uncooked or undercooked meat or eggs. Many people continue to enjoy such dishes, but caution should be applied, especially when serving the very young or very old, or those with compromised immune systems.

703

Pepper steak
STEAK A LA PIMIENTA

- 6 entrecôte or fillet steaks, about 150 g/5 oz each
- 4 tablespoons black or green peppercorns, lightly crushed
- salt

Serves 4–6

Press the peppercorns firmly on to both sides of each steak. Cook the steaks under the grill or in a frying pan over a high heat for 2–4 minutes on each side, until done to your liking. Season both sides of the meat with salt after cooking. It is important to warm the plates on which the meat will be served. There are several recipes in this book for sauces to accompany these steaks, such as Red Wine Sauce (see recipe 88), or Shallot Sauce for Fried Meat (see recipe 93). See Chapter 4 for more ideas.

704

Carpaccio with lemon
CARPACCIO DE CARNE AL LIMÓN

- 8 very thin slices of sirloin steak (see note below)
- 4 tablespoons olive oil
- juice of 1 lemon
- lettuce or watercress
- salt and pepper

Sauce:
- 1 egg
- juice and grated rind of 1 lemon
- 450 ml/¾ pint olive oil
- salt

Serves 4

Put the slices of sirloin in a non-metallic dish. Beat the oil with the lemon juice in a bowl, then pour the mixture over the meat and leave to marinate in the refrigerator for 30 minutes. Meanwhile, make the sauce. Put the egg, lemon juice, a pinch of salt and a dash of the oil in a food processor. Gently combine the ingredients with a spatula or the handle of a spoon, then process for 20 seconds. With the motor running, add the remaining oil through the feeder hole. Pour into a sauce boat, stir in the lemon rind and chill in the refrigerator. Drain the steak, place on individual plates and season with salt and pepper on both sides. Garnish with the lettuce or watercress and serve immediately, offering the sauce separately.

Note: The secrets of a good carpaccio are to use high-quality meat and to slice it extremely thinly. Put a piece of sirloin weighing at least 750 g/1 lb 10 oz into the freezer for 2–3 hours so that it firms up but does not freeze completely. It will then be easier to slice thinly. Foodborne illnesses caused by uncooked or undercooked meat or eggs. Many people continue to enjoy such dishes, but caution should be applied, especially when serving the very young or very old, or those with compromised immune systems.

Minced beef and potato pie

CARNE PICADA CON PURÉ DE PATATAS Y HUEVOS DUROS, AL HORNO

- **50 g/2 oz raisins (optional)**
- **1 kg/2¼ lb potatoes**
- **40 g/1½ oz butter**
- **250 ml/8 fl oz hot milk**
- **6 tablespoons olive oil**
- **1 large onion, finely chopped**
- **500 g/1 lb 2 oz minced beef**
- **2 hard-boiled eggs, cut into wedges or thickly sliced**
- **1 egg, lightly beaten**
- **1½ tablespoons sugar**
- **salt**

Serves 6

Put the raisins, if using, into a bowl and pour in hot water to cover. Leave to soak. Cook and mash the potatoes, using the butter and hot milk as described in recipe 230. Keep warm. Preheat the oven to 200°C/400°F/Gas Mark 6. Meanwhile, heat 4 tablespoons of the oil in a frying pan. Add the onion and cook over a low heat, stirring occasionally, for about 8 minutes, until beginning to brown. Add the minced beef and cook, stirring frequently, for about 4 minutes, until lightly browned. Season with salt. Drain the raisins, if using, and stir them into the pan. Spoon the mixture into an ovenproof dish and put the hard-boiled eggs on top. Mix the mashed potato with the beaten egg and spread over the meat. Drizzle with the remaining oil and sprinkle with the sugar. Bake for 15–20 minutes and serve straight from the dish.

Oven roasts

ASADO AL HORNO

- **1 boneless beef for roasting, 1.5 kg/3 ¼ lb**
- **lard or sunflower oil**
- **meat extract**
- **salt**

Serves 4–6

Preheat the oven to 200°C/400°F/Gas Mark 6. Tie the beef with fine kitchen string so it forms a neat shape. Melt the lard or heat the sunflower oil in a roasting tin over a medium heat. Add the beef and cook, turning frequently, until evenly browned all over. Season with salt and spread with meat extract, then place in the oven and cook until the beef is done to your liking. A boneless piece of beef weighing 1.5 kg/3 ¼ lb cooked for about 30 minutes will be rare and quite red in the middle. Beef is often served rare, but this is a matter of personal taste. (See the table below for approximate cooking times).

Remove the beef from the roasting tin, cover with foil and leave to rest for 10–15 minutes before carving. Add a little boiling water to the roasting tin and bring to the boil, scraping up any bits from the base of the tin, then strain into a sauce boat and serve with the meat.

Boneless beef:
Rare – 10–15 minutes per 500 g/1 lb 2 oz
Medium – 20 minutes per 500 g/1 lb 2 oz
Well done – 25 minutes per 500 g/1 lb 2 oz

Beef on the bone:
Rare – 20 minutes per 500 g/1 lb 2 oz
Medium – 25 minutes per 500 g/1 lb 2 oz
Well done – 30 minutes per 500 g/1 lb 2 oz

707

Fillet of beef in pastry

SOLOMILLO EN HOJALDRE

- 2 tablespoons sunflower oil
- 1 beef fillet, 1 kg/2¼ lb
- 20 g/¾ oz lard or 2 tablespoons olive oil
- ½ onion, finely chopped
- 500 g/1 lb 2 oz mushrooms, sliced
- 1 truffle canned, drained, thinly sliced and cut into slivers
- 400 g/14 oz puff pastry dough, thawed if frozen
- plain flour, for dusting
- 1 egg yolk, lightly beaten
- 200 ml/7 fl oz beef stock
- salt and pepper

Serves 6

Heat the sunflower oil in a roasting tin. Season the beef with salt and pepper, add to the tin and cook over a medium heat, turning frequently, until evenly browned all over. Remove the meat from the roasting tin and put it on to a tea towel to absorb any juice it releases. Preheat the oven to 200° C/400°F/Gas Mark 6. Melt the lard or heat the olive oil in a frying pan. Add the onion and cook over a low heat, stirring occasionally, for 5 minutes, until softened and translucent. Add the mushrooms, increase the heat to high and cook, stirring frequently, for 10 minutes, or until the mushrooms have released their juice and most of it has evaporated. Remove the pan from the heat, stir in the truffle and leave to cool. Roll out the dough on a lightly floured surface to a sheet large enough to enclose the fillet of beef completely. Trim the edges neatly and reserve the trimmings. Spread the mushroom mixture over the beef, then place the meat on the dough. Brush the edges with the egg yolk and wrap the dough around the beef to make a parcel. Roll out the dough trimmings and cut out leaf or star shapes. Brush them with beaten egg yolk and place them on top of the parcel. Cut a slit in the middle of the top and insert a rolled-up cylinder of foil to make a funnel. Brush the remaining egg yolk over the parcel to glaze. Carefully transfer the parcel to a baking sheet and bake for 25 minutes, then turn off the oven, open the oven and cover the parcel with foil. Leave the covered beef en croûte in the warm by the oven for 10 minutes for rare and 18 minutes for medium before cutting the parcel into slices and serving.

Note: For an accompanying sauce, heat some cream in the pan used to cook the onion and mushrooms, adding a few extra slices of mushroom, the juice from the can of truffles and a little pepper. Do not allow the sauce to boil.

708

Roast beef in a pan

ASADOS EN CACEROLA

- **1.5 kg/3 ¼ lb beef**
- **lard or sunflower oil**
- **meat extract**
- **salt**

Serves 4–6

You can 'roast' in a cocotte or flameproof casserole, but this is not the same as a pot roast, which is typically cooked in liquid with vegetables. Melt the lard or heat the oil over a medium heat. Add the beef and cook, turning frequently, until browned all over. Season with salt and spread with meat extract. Lower the heat and cook for 1 ½ hours, uncovered, turning the meat every 10 minutes. When the beef is cooked to your liking, remove it from the cocotte or casserole and make a gravy by adding a little water to the pan juices and cook over low heat until slightly thickened.

Note: Allow about 10 minutes cooking time per 500 g/1 lb 2 oz meat for rare, or longer until cooked to your liking.

709

Beef, carrot, onion and pea stew
RAGOÛT CON ZANAHORIAS, CEBOLLITAS FRANCESAS Y GUISANTES

- 250 ml/8 fl oz olive oil
- 1.5 kg/3¼ lb stewing steak,
  cut into 4-cm/1½-inch cubes
- 1 onion, finely chopped
- 1 tablespoon plain flour
- 250 ml/8 fl oz white wine
- pinch of mixed dried herbs
- 500 g/1 lb 2 oz carrots,
  sliced lengthways
- 2 tablespoons Classic Tomato
  Sauce (see recipe 73)
- 250 g/9 oz shallots
- 20 g/¾ oz butter
- 100 g/3½ oz drained canned,
  frozen or shelled fresh peas
- salt

Serves 6

Heat the oil in a saucepan. Add the beef, in batches, and cook over a medium heat, stirring occasionally, for 5–8 minutes, until evenly browned. Remove with a slotted spoon and set aside. Pour off nearly all the oil from the pan, leaving 2–3 tablespoons, and reheat. Add the onion, lower the heat and cook, stirring occasionally, for 10 minutes, until lightly browned. Stir in the flour and cook, stirring constantly, for 5 minutes. Return the beef to the pan, stir in the wine and add water to cover. Season with salt and sprinkle in the herbs. Bring to the boil, cover and simmer for 1½ hours. Add the carrot, re-cover the pan and simmer for a further 45 minutes. Stir in the tomato sauce, if using. Meanwhile, put the shallots and butter into a small saucepan, add water to cover and simmer gently for about 20 minutes, until tender but not falling apart. About 10–15 minutes before serving, add the shallots and the peas to the stew. Serve hot.

710

Beef cooked in red wine
CARNE ADOBADA Y GUISADA EN VINO TINTO

- 1.5 kg/3¼ lb top rump
  or thick flank, cut into
  4-cm/1½-inch cubes
- 1 large onion, halved
- 1 large carrot, thickly sliced
- 2 bay leaves
- 1 bouquet garni
  (1 sprig fresh parsley, 1 clove
  garlic and 3 sprigs fresh thyme
  tied together in muslin)
- 500 ml/18 fl oz red wine
- 50 ml/2 fl oz red-wine vinegar
- 2 tablespoons olive oil
- 150 g/5 oz streaky bacon,
  cut into thin strips
- 500 ml/18 fl oz hot water
- salt and pepper

Serves 6

Put the beef into a deep, non-metallic dish. Cut one of the onion halves into three wedges and add to the dish along with the carrot, bay leaves and bouquet garni. Season with salt and pour in the wine and vinegar. Cover with cling film and leave to marinate in a cool place, but not the refrigerator, stirring occasionally, for 6–10 hours. Drain the beef, reserving the marinade. Put the oil and bacon into a large saucepan and cook over a medium heat for 3–4 minutes. Meanwhile, chop the remaining onion half, add it to the pan and cook, stirring occasionally, for 8–10 minutes, until lightly browned. Add the beef and cook, stirring frequently, for about 10 minutes, until evenly browned. Pour in the reserved marinade, bring to the boil and cook until the liquid has reduced by half. Lower the heat, add the hot water, cover and simmer for 2–3 hours, until the beef is tender. Remove and discard the bay leaves and bouquet garni and serve the stew in a warm, deep dish garnished with triangles of fried bread (see recipe 130) or accompanied by Mashed Potato (see recipe 230).

Beef bourguignonne

CARNE GUISADA CON VINTO TINTO (BOURGUIGNON, ESTILO FRANCES)

- 3 tablespoons olive oil
- 200 g/7 oz streaky bacon, diced
- 1 onion, chopped
- 1.5 kg/3¼ lb stewing steak,
  cut into 2.5-cm/1-inch cubes
- 2 heaped tablespoons plain flour
- 1 litre/1¾ pints red wine
- pinch of freshly grated nutmeg
- 250 g/9 oz shallots
- 20 g/¾ oz butter
- salt and pepper

Serves 6

Heat the oil in a large saucepan. Add the bacon and onion and cook over a low heat, stirring occasionally, for about 10 minutes, until the onion is lightly browned. Remove with a slotted spoon and set aside. Add the beef to the pan and cook over a medium heat, stirring frequently, for 8 – 10 minutes, until evenly browned. Stir in the flour and cook, stirring constantly, for 2 minutes. Gradually stir in the wine, a little at a time. Add the nutmeg, season with pepper and bring to the boil. Lower the heat, return the bacon and onions to the pan and mix well. If necessary, add a little hot water to ensure the beef is covered. Cover the pan and simmer, stirring occasionally, for about 2 ½ hours, until the beef is tender. Meanwhile, put the shallots in a single layer in a saucepan. Add water to cover, a pinch of salt and the butter. Cook for about 20 minutes, until tender. Taste the stew and adjust the seasoning, if necessary, then add the shallots and cook, stirring occasionally, for 10 minutes. Serve in a warm deep dish, with boiled or fried potatoes around the edge. An alternative accompaniment would be macaroni with a little butter and grated cheese..

Note: If you like, you can stir in 3 tablespoons of Classic Tomato Sauce (see recipe 73) or 1 ½ tablespoons tomato purée after browning the meat and before adding the flour.

712

Pot roast beef with carrots and onions

RABILLO DE CADERA O TAPILLA GUISADA CON ZANAHORIAS Y CEBOLLITAS

- 150 g/5 oz lardons or strips of streaky bacon
- 1 boned thin rib or topside of beef, 1.5 kg/3¼ lb
- 4 tablespoons olive oil
- 4 pieces of ham rind
- 1 small onion, chopped
- 500 g/1 lb 2 oz veal shin
- 3 tablespoons brandy
- 2 carrots, sliced
- ½ teaspoon mixed dried herbs or 1 bouquet garni (1 sprig fresh parsley, 1 clove garlic, 1 bay leaf and 1 sprig fresh thyme tied together in muslin)
- 1 chicken stock cube
- 175 ml/6 fl oz white wine
- 250 g/9 oz baby carrots, halved lengthways
- 250 g/9 oz shallots
- 20 g/¾ oz butter
- salt and pepper

Serves 6

Using a larding needle, thread the lardons or strips of bacon through the beef, then tie it into a neat shape with fine kitchen string. Heat the oil in a large saucepan. Add the ham rind and onion and cook over a low heat, stirring occasionally, for 5 minutes, until the onion is softened and translucent. Add the beef and veal shin and cook, turning occasionally, for about 10 minutes, until evenly browned all over. Meanwhile, heat the brandy in a small saucepan, ignite it and add it to the meat when the flames have died down. Add the sliced carrots and dried herbs or bouquet garni, pour in water to cover and season with salt and pepper. Cover and cook on a medium-low heat for 3 hours. Dissolve the stock cube in 2–3 tablespoons of the cooking liquid in a bowl and add to the pan with the wine and baby carrots. Cook for a further 30 minutes, then taste and adjust the seasoning if necessary. Meanwhile, put the shallots in a single layer in a pan, add the butter and a pinch of salt and pour in water to cover. Simmer for about 20 minutes, until tender. Lift the beef out of the pan and remove and discard the string. Cut into slices and place them on a warm serving dish. Lift out the veal shin, carve the meat off the bone and place on top of the beef. Arrange the baby carrots and shallots around the edge. Remove and discard the bouquet garni, if used, pass the sauce through a food mill or process in a food processor and pour it over the meat.

Note: To serve cold, prepare in the same way as described above but use smaller quantities.

713

- 1 sachet powdered gelatine
- 250 ml/7 fl oz cooking liquid from a stew or meat stock (home-made or made with a stock cube)
- 1 carrot, thinly sliced
- 50 g/2 oz canned or cooked peas
- 150 g/5 oz diced leftover beef
- 100 g/3½ oz Serrano ham, finely diced
- 500 g/1 lb 2 oz veal shin, cooked and finely diced
- 1 tomato, sliced
- 1 beetroot, cooked and sliced
- lettuce leaves

Serves 6

Terrine

PASTEL-TERRINA

Dissolve the gelatine in 500 ml/18 fl oz water, following the instructions on the packet. Mix some of the sauce from the stew or the stock with the gelatine and spoon a layer into the base of a loaf tin. Transfer to the refrigerator and leave to set. Arrange half of the slices of carrot and the peas in a layer on top of the gelatine. Add a layer of the beef, then one of the ham and finally a layer of the veal. Top the terrine with the remaining carrot and peas and pour in the remaining gelatine mixture. Chill in the refrigerator for several hours until the gelatine is set. Turn the terrine out of the tin and serve it cold, garnished with the sliced tomato and beetroot, and the lettuce leaves.

714

- 4 tablespoons olive oil
- 1 large onion, chopped
- 1 kg/2¼ lb ripe tomatoes, seeded and chopped
- 1 teaspoon sugar
- 1 large red pepper
- 1 kg/2¼ lb left-over cooked topside of beef, cut into large pieces
- boiled rice
- salt

Serves 6

Old clothes

ROPA VIEJA

Preheat the oven to 200°C/400°F/Gas Mark 6. Heat the oil in a frying pan. Add the onion and cook over a low heat, stirring occasionally, for about 5 minutes, until softened and translucent. Add the tomato and cook, stirring occasionally and breaking it up with the side of the spoon, for 15 minutes. Pass the mixture through a food mill or process in a food processor. Transfer to a clean pan, stir in the sugar and season with salt. Meanwhile, put the red pepper on a baking sheet and roast for about 30 minutes, until soft. Remove from the oven, cover with a plate or tea towel and leave it to cool, then peel and seed. Cut the flesh into 2-cm/¾-inch strips. Add the red pepper and pieces of meat to the sauce and bring to the boil. Serve immediately with little mounds of the boiled rice (see recipe 173).

Notes: This is one of the many variations on ropa vieja, a dish whose name translates as 'old clothes'. Typically the meat is cooked for so long that it can be shredded – or will fall apart by itself – hence the name. This version, with left-over meat, is a quick alternative.

715

Stewed topside
REDONDO GUISADO

- 4 tablespoons olive oil
- 1 topside of beef, 2–2.5 kg/
  4½–5½ lb
- 2 large onions, chopped
- 2 tablespoons plain flour
- 275 ml/9 fl oz white wine
- 1 bay leaf
- salt
  Serves 8–10

Heat the oil in a large saucepan. Add the beef and cook over a medium heat, turning frequently, for 8–10 minutes, until evenly browned all over. Remove from the pan and set aside. Add the onion to the pan and cook over a low heat, stirring occasionally, for about 10 minutes, until lightly browned. Stir in the flour and cook, stirring constantly, for 2 minutes. Gradually stir in the wine, a little at a time. Cook, stirring constantly, for 5 minutes, then return the beef to the pan. Season with salt, add the bay leaf and pour in water to cover. Cover the pan and simmer gently, turning the beef occasionally, for about 2½ hours, until tender. Lift out the beef and cut into slices about 1.5 cm/⅝ inch thick. Remove and discard the bay leaf and pass the sauce through a food mill or process in a food processor. Serve the meat accompanied by Mashed Potato (see recipe 230) and the sauce in a sauce boat.

Notes: A peeled and halved apple can be added to the dish and passed through the food mill or processed in the food processor with the sauce. If you have time, lard the topside with a few pieces of bacon. It makes it more succulent.

716

Leftover topside (first version)
RESTOS DEL REDONDO

- sunflower oil, for deep-frying,
  plus extra for brushing
- 25 g/1 oz butter
- 2 heaped tablespoons plain flour
- 500 ml/18 fl oz milk
- 6–12 slices of cooked
  topside of beef
- 2 eggs
- 80 g/3 oz breadcrumbs
- salt
  Serves 6

Brush the inside of a ceramic dish with oil. Melt the butter with 3 tablespoons of the oil in a frying pan. Stir in the flour and cook, stirring constantly, for 2 minutes. Gradually stir in the milk, a little at a time. Cook the sauce, stirring constantly, for about 10 minutes, until thickened. Season with salt and remove the pan from the heat. One at a time, dip the slices of beef into the sauce to coat, then put them in the prepared dish. Leave to stand for 1 hour in the refrigerator. Beat the eggs in a shallow dish and spread out the breadcrumbs in another shallow dish. Heat the remaining oil in a deep-fryer or frying pan to 180–190°C/350–375°F, or until a cube of day-old bread browns in 30 seconds. Coat each slice of beef first in the beaten egg and then in the breadcrumbs. Add to the hot oil, in batches if necessary, and cook until golden brown. Remove with a slotted spoon, drain, and keep warm while you cook the remaining batches. Serve immediately.

717

Leftover topside (second version)
RESTOS DEL REDONDO

- 3 tablespoons olive oil
- 2 onions, very finely chopped
- 1 bay leaf
- 1 clove garlic, lightly crushed
- 80 g/3 oz butter
- 2 tablespoons plain flour
- 1 tablespoon white-wine vinegar
- 250 ml/8 fl oz milk
- 250 ml/8 fl oz chicken stock
- 6–12 slices of cooked
  topside of beef
- 2 tablespoons capers
- 2 tablespoons breadcrumbs
- 50 g/2 oz butter
- salt

Serves 6

Preheat the oven to 200°C/400°F/Gas Mark 6. Heat the oil in a frying pan. Add the onion and cook over a low heat, stirring occasionally, for about 5 minutes, until softened and translucent. Add the bay leaf and garlic and cook for a few minutes more. Add 25 g/1 oz of the butter, stir in the flour and cook, stirring constantly, for 2 minutes. Gradually stir in the vinegar, then the milk and, finally, the stock. Cook the sauce, stirring constantly, for about 10 minutes, until thickened. Season with salt and remove the pan from the heat. Remove and discard the bay leaf and garlic and put 3 tablespoons of the sauce into the base of an ovenproof dish. Place the slices of beef on top. Rinse and drain the capers, and stir them into the remaining sauce. Pour the sauce over the beef. Sprinkle with the breadcrumbs and dot with the remaining butter. Bake for about 15 minutes, until the top is golden brown. Serve immediately, straight from the dish.

718

Beef with tomatoes and olives
CARNE GUISADA CON TOMATES Y ACEITUNAS

- 250 ml/8 fl oz sunflower oil
- 1.5 kg/3¼ lb stewing steak,
  such as chuck, flank or brisket,
  cut into chunks
- 2 large onions, finely chopped
- 2 tablespoons plain flour
- 500 g/1 lb 2 oz very ripe
  tomatoes, peeled and chopped
- 150 g/5 oz Serrano ham,
  chopped
- 175 ml/6 fl oz white wine
- pinch of mixed dried herbs or
  1 bouquet garni (1 sprig fresh
  parsley, 1 clove garlic and 1 bay
  leaf tied together in muslin)
- 100 g/3½ oz pimiento-stuffed
  green olives
- salt

Serves 6

Heat the oil in a saucepan. Add the beef, in batches if necessary, and cook, stirring occasionally, for about 10 minutes, until evenly browned. Remove with a slotted spoon and set aside. Drain off most of the oil, leaving about 4 tablespoons to cover the base of the pan, and reheat. Add the onion and cook over a low heat, stirring occasionally, for about 8 minutes, until beginning to brown. Stir in the flour and cook, stirring constantly, for 2 minutes. Add the tomato and cook, stirring occasionally and breaking it up with the side of the spoon, for a further 5 minutes. Return the beef to the pan, add the ham and pour in the wine. Season with salt, add the dried herbs or bouquet garni, mix well and cook for about 5 minutes. Pour in water to cover, cover the pan and simmer over a medium heat for about 2 hours, until tender. Meanwhile, put the olives in a saucepan, add water to cover and bring to the boil, then lower the heat and simmer for 1 minute. Drain well and set aside. Uncover the stew, stir in the olives and cook, uncovered, for a further 10 minutes. Remove and discard the bouquet garni, if used. Serve in a warm deep dish, garnished with triangles of fried bread (see recipe 130).

719

- 150 g/5 oz lardons or strips of streaky bacon
- 250 ml/8 fl oz sunflower oil
- 1 silverside, 1.2 kg/2½ lb
- 2 large onions, chopped
- 8 black peppercorns
- 250 ml/8 fl oz white wine
- 500 g/1 lb 2 oz carrots, cut into chunks
- 1 eating apple, peeled, cored and chopped (optional)
- salt

Serves 6

Pot roasted silverside

CONTRA GUISADA

Using a larding needle, thread the lardons or strips of bacon through the silverside, then tie it into a neat shape with fine kitchen string. Heat the oil in a large saucepan. Add the silverside and cook over a medium heat, turning frequently, for about 10 minutes, until evenly browned all over. Remove from the pan and set aside. Add the onion to the pan and cook over a low heat, stirring occasionally, for 8–10 minutes, until beginning to brown. Return the silverside to the pan, pour in 250 ml/8 fl oz water, add the peppercorns and season with salt. Cover and simmer over a very low heat, stirring occasionally, for 1½ hours. Pour in the wine, add the carrot and the apple, if using, re-cover the pan and cook for a further 45 minutes, until the silverside is tender. Lift out the silverside from the pan, remove and discard the string and carve into fairly thin slices. Transfer to a warm serving dish. Remove all but two of the chunks of carrot from the pan and place on the serving dish. Pass the sauce through a food mill into a saucepan or process in a food processor and transfer to a pan. Heat through gently, adding more water if necessary, then pour over the silverside and serve.

Note: This dish can be served with boiled or mashed potatoes, or with little piles of vegetables placed all around the serving dish.

720

- 25 g/1 oz saltpetre
- 1 topside of beef, 1 kg/2¼ lb
- 350 g/12 oz salt
- 6 black peppercorns
- 1 bay leaf
- 1 sprig fresh thyme
- 2 leeks, thickly sliced and rinsed well
- 2 carrots, thickly sliced
- 2 beef shin bones
- 175 ml/6 fl oz white wine

Serves 6–8

Salt beef

CARNE FIAMBRE

Spread the saltpetre over the beef and leave to stand in a cool place, but not the refrigerator, for a few hours or even overnight. Put the beef into a large saucepan, pour in 4 litres/7 pints water and add the salt, peppercorns, bay leaf and thyme. Leave to soak, stirring the brine occasionally, for 24 hours. Remove the beef, rinse it in cold water and put it into a clean saucepan. Add the leek, carrot and shin bones, pour in the wine and add water to cover. Bring to the boil, then lower the heat to medium and cook for 3 hours. Drain the beef, then put it on a plate and place a weight, such as a chopping board, on top. Leave to cool completely, then slice and serve with Russian Salad (see recipe 21) or green salad.

Note: Saltpetre is a restricted substance in many countries.

Stewed oxtail

RABO DE BUEY GUISADO

- **2 oxtails, cut into pieces**
- **2 large onions**
- **2 cloves**
- **4 black peppercorns**
- **1 bay leaf**
- **250 g/9 oz carrots,**
  halved lengthways
- **350 ml/12 fl oz white wine**
- **salt**

Serves 6

Pour 3 litres/5¼ pints water into a saucepan and add the pieces of oxtail. There should be enough water for the meat to float; if not, add some more. Bring to the boil and skim off the froth that rises to the surface with a slotted spoon. Stud each onion with a clove and add to the pan with the peppercorns, bay leaf, carrots, wine and a pinch of salt. Simmer, uncovered, for 2–3 hours, until the meat is falling off the bones and the cooking liquid has reduced. Lift out the pieces of oxtail, cut off the meat and plac e on a warm serving dish. Remove and discard the bay leaf and peppercorns, then pass the sauce through a food mill or process it in a food processor. Pour the sauce over the meat and serve immediately with the Mashed Potato (see recipe 230) or Chips (see recipe 242).

Note: Oxtails were once made from the tails of oxen, but the term now refers to the tail of any beef cattle. This cut of meat is quite boney and requires long, slow cooking.

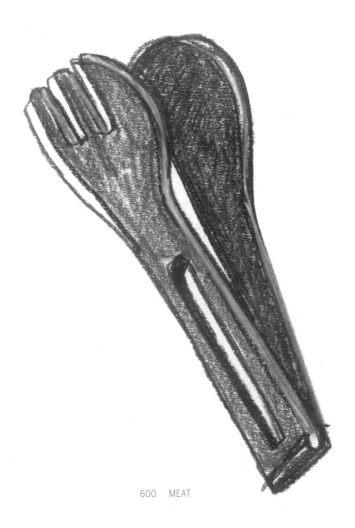

Veal

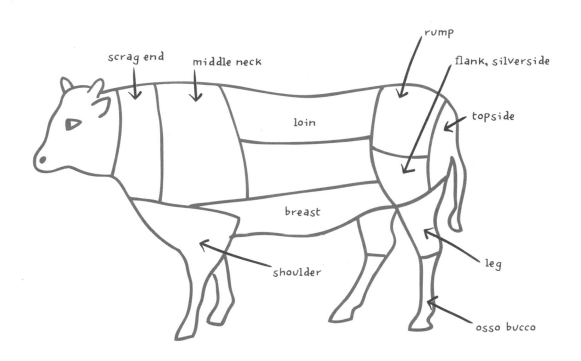

Allow 150 g / 5 oz boneless veal per serving
(130 g / 4 ½ oz for breaded escalopes).
Allow 200–225 g / 7–8 oz veal per serving for roasting,
as it will shrink considerably.
Allow 225–250 g / 8–9 oz stewing veal per serving.

Buying veal	Suitables cuts	Weight per serving	Cooking time
Fried, grilled or griddled	Chops, Leg fillets, Rump, Escalopes, Shoulder	185 g / 6½ oz 150 g / 5 oz (plain escalopes) 130 g / 4½ oz (breaded escalopes)	10 minutes for chops 8–10 minutes for fillets and escalopes, first over a high heat and then over a lower one
Roasted *	Leg, Loin, Rib or shoulder	250 g / 9 oz (boneless)	20 minutes per 500 g / 1 lb 2 oz
Stewed or braised	Breast, Scrag end and middle neck, Flank, Silverside, Osso bucco	200–250 g / 7–9 oz	2 hours for stews 1½–2½ hours for casseroles and pot roasts

*Make sure that the oven is preheated

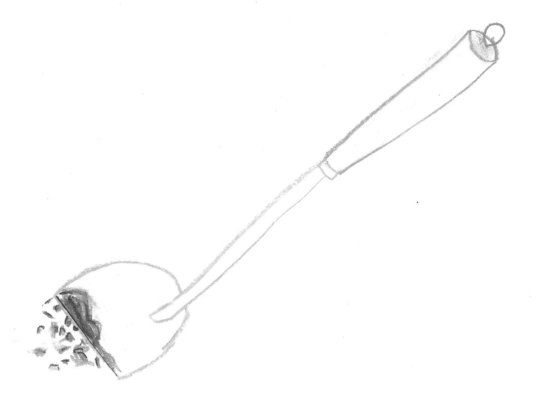

722

- **6 loin or leg fillets of veal,
  about 150 g/5 oz each**
- **50 g/2 oz lard or 3 tablespoons
  sunflower oil**
- **salt**

Serves 6

Fried veal fillets

FILETES FRITOS

Season the fillets with salt on both sides. Melt the lard or heat the oil in a frying pan. Add the veal, in batches, and cook over a high heat for 3 minutes on each side. Turn the meat with tongs to avoid piercing it and so letting out the juices. Lower the heat, cover the pan and cook for a further 2 minutes. Serve immediately with vegetables, Mashed Potato (see recipe 230) or fried potatoes or Chips (see recipe 242).

723

- **6 veal escalopes**
- **4 tablespoons olive oil**
- **50 g/2 oz butter**
- **juice of 1 lemon**
- **1 tablespoon chopped
  fresh parsley**
- **salt**

Serves 6

Fried veal escalopes with lemon and butter

FILETES FRITOS CON LIMÓN Y MANTEQUILLA

Season the escalopes with salt on both sides. Heat the oil in a frying pan. Add the escalopes and cook over a medium heat for 3 – 4 minutes on each side, turning them with tongs. Transfer to a serving dish and keep warm. Pour off most of the oil from the pan, add the butter and when it has melted, stir in the lemon juice. Add the parsley and pour the sauce over the escalopes. Serve immediately.

724

Veal escalopes filled with bacon and gruyere

FILETES DE TERNERA RELLENOS CON BACON Y GRUYÈRE

- 6 veal escalopes
- 6 thin slices of bacon
- 6 thin slices of gruyere cheese
- pinch of mixed dried herbs
- 50 g/2 oz butter
- 2 tablespoons olive oil
- juice of ½ lemon
- 2 tablespoons single cream (optional)
- 1 teaspoon chopped fresh parsley
- salt

Serves 6

Season the escalopes with salt on both sides. Place a slice of bacon in the centre of each escalope and top with a slice of gruyere. Sprinkle with some of the dried herbs, then fold the escalope like a turnover and pinch all around the edge with a cocktail stick. Melt half the butter with the oil in a frying pan. Add the escalopes and cook over a high heat for 2 minutes on each side. Lower the heat and cook for a further 5 minutes on each side. Remove the escalopes from the pan and keep warm. Drain off the oil from the pan, then add the remaining butter and the lemon juice. If necessary, stir in 1–2 tablespoons hot water. Stir well, then remove the pan from the heat and stir in the cream, if using. Sprinkle the escalopes with the parsley and pour the sauce over them. Serve immediately, with straw potatoes (see recipe 243) or Mashed Potato (see recipe 230).

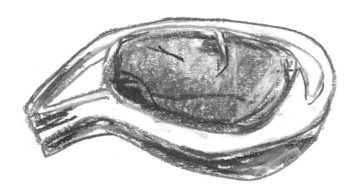

725

Veal escalopes with port, mustard and parsley sauce

FILETES DE TERNERA CON SALSA DE OPORTO, MOSTAZA Y PEREJIL

- 6 veal escalopes
- 5 tablespoons olive oil
- 5 tablespoons port
- 2 teaspoons Dijon mustard
- 1 tablespoon chopped fresh parsley
- salt

Serves 6

Lightly season the escalopes with salt on both sides. Heat the oil in a frying pan. Add the escalopes, in batches, and cook over a medium heat for 3–4 minutes on each side, turning them with tongs. Set aside and keep warm. Pour off most of the oil from the pan, leaving just enough to cover the base. Add the port and mustard and cook, stirring constantly, for 2–3 minutes. Add the parsley, pour the sauce over the escalopes and serve immediately.

Fillet mignon with mushrooms and béchamel sauce

FILETES MIGNON CON CHAMPIÑONES Y BECHAMEL

- 250 g/9 oz chestnut mushrooms
- 50 g/2 oz butter
- juice of ½ lemon
- 250 ml/8 fl oz sunflower oil
- 2 tablespoons plain flour
- 750 ml/1¼ pints milk
- 6 slices of bread, crusts removed and cut into rounds
- 6 slices of veal fillet
- salt

Serves 6

Separate the mushroom caps from the stalks and put the caps into a saucepan with 20 g/¾ oz of the butter, the lemon juice and a pinch of salt. Cook over a low heat for about 6 minutes, then set aside and keep warm. Meanwhile, finely chop the stalks. Melt the remaining butter with 2 tablespoons of the oil in another saucepan. Stir in the flour and cook, stirring constantly, for 2 minutes. Gradually stir in the milk, a little at a time. Add the mushroom stalks and cook, stirring constantly, for about 10 minutes, until the sauce has thickened. Remove from the heat and keep warm. Preheat the grill. Heat the remaining oil in a frying pan. Add the bread and cook, turning occasionally, until golden brown on both sides. Remove with a fish slice, drain and place on a flameproof serving dish. Pour off most of the oil from the pan. Season the veal slices with salt on both sides and add to the pan, in batches, and cook over a medium heat for 3 – 4 minutes on each side. Place a slice of veal on top of each fried bread round, pour the sauce over the top and garnish with the mushroom caps. Put the dish under the grill for about 5 minutes, until lightly browned, then serve.

727

Veal escalopes with chopped mushrooms
ESCALOPINES DE TERNERA REBOZADOS Y CON PICADITO DE CHAMPIÑONES

- 500 g/1 lb 2 oz mushrooms
- 50 g/2 oz butter
- juice of ½ lemon
- sunflower oil, for deep-frying
- 40 g/1½ oz plain flour
- 3 tablespoons brandy
- 2 eggs
- 12 small veal escalopes
- salt and pepper

Serves 6

Separate the mushroom caps from the stalks. Put the caps into a saucepan with 25 g/1 oz of the butter, the lemon juice, 2 tablespoons water and a pinch of salt. Cook over a low heat for about 8 minutes, until tender. Set aside and keep warm. Meanwhile, finely chop the stalks. Melt the remaining butter with 2 tablespoons of the oil in another saucepan. Stir in 1 tablespoon of the flour and cook, stirring constantly, for 5 minutes, until lightly browned. Gradually stir in the brandy and 250 ml/8 fl oz water, a little at a time. Add the mushroom stalks, season and cook, stirring constantly, for about 8 minutes, until thickened. Remove from the heat and keep warm. Spread out the remaining flour in a shallow dish and beat the eggs in another shallow dish. Heat the oil in a deep-fryer or frying pan to 180–190°C/350–375°F or until a cube of day-old bread browns in 30 seconds. Season the escalopes on both sides and coat them first in thc flour, shaking off any excess, then in the beaten egg one at a time. Add them to the hot oil, in batches, and cook until golden brown. Remove with a fish slice, drain and keep warm while you cook the remaining batches. Put the escalopes on a warm serving dish, garnish with the mushroom caps and serve immediately, offering the sauce separately.

728

Veal rolls with bacon and anchovies
ROLLITOS DE TERNERA CON BACON Y ANCHOAS

- 6 slices of veal flank,
  rump or topside
- 12 thin slices of bacon
- 6 canned anchovy fillets, drained
- 4 tablespoons olive oil
- 1 onion, chopped
- 1 tablespoon plain flour
- 175 ml/6 fl oz white wine
- 1 bay leaf
- salt and pepper

Serves 6

Season the veal slices with salt and pepper, place two slices of bacon on each slice of veal and top with an anchovy fillet. Roll up each veal slice and tie with fine kitchen string. Heat the oil in a saucepan. Add the veal rolls and cook, turning frequently, until browned all over. Remove from the pan, drain and set aside. Add the onion to the pan and cook over a low heat, stirring occasionally, for about 8 minutes, until beginning to brown. Stir in the flour and cook, stirring constantly, for 2 minutes. Gradually stir in the wine, a little at a time, then stir in 175 ml/6 fl oz water. Add the bay leaf, return the veal rolls to the pan and add 175 ml/6 fl oz water to cover them. Season and bring to the boil. Lower the heat to medium, cover and cook for 1–1¼ hours. Lift the veal rolls out of the pan, remove and discard the string and place the rolls on a warm serving dish. Discard the bay leaf. Pass the sauce through a food mill or process in a food processor, then pour over the meat. Serve with Mashed Potato (see recipe 230).

729

Veal rolls with bacon and minced beef

ROLLITOS DE TERNERA CON BACON Y CARNE PICADA

- 6 slices of veal flank,
  rump or topside
- 250 g/9 oz minced beef
- 1 thick rasher of bacon,
  cut into 6 strips
- 6 sprigs fresh parsley
- 4 tablespoons olive oil
- 1 onion
- 1 tablespoon plain flour
- 175 ml/6 fl oz white wine
- 1 bay leaf
- salt

Serves 6

Season the veal slices with a little salt on both sides, then divide the minced beef among the slices, placing it on top and pressing it down gently. Put a strip of bacon and a parsley sprig in the middle of each slice. Roll up each slice of veal and tie it with fine kitchen string. From this point, proceed as described in recipe 728.

730

Veal chops with tomatoes and green peppers

CHULETAS DE TERNERA CON REVUELTO DE TOMATES Y PIMIENTOS VERDES

- 500 ml/18 fl oz sunflower oil
- 6 ripe tomatoes, peeled,
  seeded and chopped
- 1 teaspoon sugar
- 4 green peppers,
  seeded and diced
- 6 veal chops
- salt

Serves 6

Heat 2 tablespoons of the oil in a frying pan. Add the tomato and cook over a high heat, stirring occasionally and breaking it up with the side of the spoon, for about 20 minutes, until pulpy. Stir in the sugar, season with salt and set aside. Heat 375 ml/13 fl oz of the remaining oil with 2 tablespoons water in another frying pan. Season the pepper with salt, add to the hot oil, cover and cook over a low heat for 10 minutes. Drain off the oil, add the pepper to the tomato and mix well. Heat the remaining oil in a large frying pan. Season the chops with salt on both sides, add them to the pan, in two batches, and cook over a high heat for 1–2 minutes on each side, then lower the heat and cook for a further 3–4 minutes on each side. Put the chops on a warm serving dish and top each with some of the tomato and pepper mixture. Surround with fried potatoes and serve immediately.

731

Veal chops with almonds and Malaga wine

CHULETAS DE TERNERA CON ALMENDRAS Y VINO DE MÁLAGA

- **5–6 tablespoons olive oil**
- **6 veal chops**
- **100 g/3½ oz flaked almonds**
- **175 ml/6 fl oz Malaga wine**
  or sweet sherry
- **salt**

Serves 6

Heat the oil in a frying pan. Add the chops, in batches, and cook over a high heat for 1–2 minutes on each side, then lower the heat and cook for a further 3–4 minutes on each side. Season with salt, transfer to a serving dish and keep warm. Add the almonds to the pan and cook, stirring frequently, for a few minutes, until golden brown. Stir in the wine or sherry, then spoon the almonds and sauce over the chops. Serve immediately.

Note: This dish can also be made using pork chops in place of veal.

732

Veal chops in parcels

CHULETAS DE TERNERA EN PAPILLOTE

- **25 g/1 oz butter**
- **2 shallots, very finely chopped**
- **120 g/4 oz mushrooms, chopped**
- **1 teaspoon lemon juice**
- **1 tablespoon chopped**
  fresh parsley
- **120 ml/4 fl oz olive oil,**
  plus extra for brushing
- **6 veal chops**
- **3 very thin slices of**
  Serrano ham, halved
- **salt and pepper**

Serves 6

Preheat the oven to 160°C/325°F/Gas Mark 3. Melt the butter in a frying pan. Add the shallots and cook over a low heat, stirring occasionally, for about 5 minutes, until softened. Add the mushrooms and lemon juice, season with salt and cook, stirring occasionally, for 6 minutes or until the mushrooms have released their juice and some of it has been evaporated. Stir in the parsley and cook for 1 minute more. Set aside. Heat the oil in a frying pan. Add the chops, in batches, and cook over a high heat for 1 minute on each side. Remove from the pan and set aside. Brush six sheets of baking paper or foil with oil. Season both sides of each chop with salt and pepper and put a chop on each piece of baking paper or foil. Put one-sixth of the mushroom mixture on top of each chop, and cover it with a half slice of ham. Fold over the baking paper or foil and seal the edges. Put the parcels on a baking sheet and bake, turning the parcels once, for 20 minutes. Serve the parcels half open on a warm serving dish.

733

Veal chops and chicken livers in parcels

CHULETAS DE TERNERA EN PAPILLOTE CON HIGADITOS DE POLLO

- 6 veal chops
- 6 chicken livers, trimmed
- 6 sprigs fresh parsley
- 1 onion, thinly sliced
- 6 tablespoons sunflower oil
- 6 tablespoons white wine
- salt and pepper

Serves 6

Preheat the oven to 180°C/350°F/Gas Mark 4. Season the chops on both sides with salt and pepper and place each one on a sheet of baking paper or foil. Halve the chicken livers without cutting all the way through. Put a liver on each chop and season with salt. Place a parsley sprig on top and divide the onion slices among the chops. Pour 1 tablespoon oil and 1 tablespoon wine over each one. Fold over the baking paper or foil and seal the edges. Place the parcels on a baking sheet and bake for 20 minutes. Serve the parcels half open on a warm serving dish.

Note: Foil provides more insulation than baking paper, so the food inside a baking paper parcel might need to be cooked for less time than food wrapped in foil.

734

Veal chops in sauce

CHULETAS EN SALSA

- 120 ml/4 fl oz olive oil
- 6 veal chops
- 175 ml/6 fl oz dry
  or medium sherry
- ½ teaspoon potato flour
- 25 g/1 oz butter
- ½ teaspoon meat extract
- juice of ½ lemon
- 1 teaspoon chopped
  fresh parsley
- salt

Serves 6

Heat the oil in a frying pan. Add the chops, in batches, and cook over a high heat for 1–2 minutes on each side, then lower the heat and cook for a further 3–4 minutes on each side. Season the chops on both sides with salt, place on a serving dish and keep warm. Drain off nearly all the oil from the pan, then pour in the sherry and 175 ml/6 fl oz water and cook over a high heat, stirring frequently, until reduced by half. Mix the potato flour with a little water and stir into the pan. Add the butter, meat extract and lemon juice and mix well. Pour this sauce over the chops, sprinkle with the parsley and serve with Mashed Potato (see recipe 230) or fried potatoes, Chips (see recipe 242) or vegetables.

735

- 1 leg, loin or rib of veal,
  1.5 kg/3¼ lb
- 100 g/3½ oz lard or 5–6
  tablespoons sunflower oil
- 1 small onion, cut into wedges
  (optional)
- ½ lemon
- salt

Serves 6

Roast veal

ASADO DE TERNERA AL HORNO

Preheat the oven to 160°C/325°F/Gas Mark 3. Tie the veal into a neat shape with fine kitchen string. Rub the veal all over with the lard or brush with the oil and place it in a roasting tin. Roast, turning once or twice, for 30 minutes. Season with salt and pour 5 tablespoons hot water over the meat. Put the onion wedges, if using, around the veal and return the tin to the oven. Increase the oven temperature to 180°C/350°F/Gas Mark 4 and roast for one hour, turning the veal occasionally, adding more water if necessary and basting occasionally with the cooking juices. Turn off the oven, open the door for 2 minutes, close it again and leave the veal to rest in the warm oven for about 5 minutes before carving it. Discard the onion wedges, if used, and serve the cooking juices separately in a sauce boat.

736

- 1 loin or rib of veal,
  1.5 kg/3¼ lb, roasted
  (see recipe 735)
- 2 eggs
- juice of ½ lemon
- 500 ml/18 fl oz sunflower oil
- 2 hard-boiled eggs,
  finely chopped
- salt

Serves 6

Roast veal with mayonnaise and hard-boiled eggs

ASADO DE TERNERA, PRESENTADO CON MAYONESA Y HUEVO DURO

Using the eggs, lemon juice, oil and a pinch of salt, make the mayonnaise in a food processor as described in recipe 105. It should be quite thick. Carve the meat, place in a warm serving dish and cover with the mayonnaise. Sprinkle with the hard-boiled eggs and garnish with vegetables. Serve immediately, offering the cooking juices separately. This dish is splendid and very tasty.

737

Veal pot roast
ASADO DE TERNERA HECHO EN CACEROLA

- 1 silverside, topside or
  leg of veal, 1.5 kg/3¼ lb
- 5–6 tablespoons sunflower oil
  or 100 g/3½ oz lard
- 1 onion, coarsely chopped
- pinch of mixed dried herbs
  or 1 bouquet garni (1 sprig
  fresh parsley, 2 bay leaves
  and 1 clove garlic tied together
  in muslin)
- 2 veal knuckle bones
- salt
  Serves 6

Tie the veal into a neat shape with fine kitchen string. Heat the oil or melt the lard in a large, heavy saucepan. Add the veal and cook over a medium heat, turning frequently, for about 10 minutes, until evenly browned all over. Add the onion, dried herbs or bouquet garni, knuckle bones and a pinch of salt. Pour in 175 ml/6 fl oz water, cover and cook over a medium-low heat, turning the veal every 15 minutes, for 1 hour. Lift out the veal, remove and discard the string and leave to rest for about 5 minutes before carving. Remove the bones and strain the cooking juices into a sauce boat. There is usually plenty, but if not, stir a little hot water into the pan before straining it.

Note: A cast-iron cocotte or casserole is ideal for cooking this dish.

738

Leg of veal with pineapple
BABILLA DE TERNERA CON PIÑA

- 1 leg of veal, about 1.5 kg/3¼ lb
- 8 cloves
- 5 tablespoons rum
- 50 g/2 oz currants
- 2-cm/¾-inch piece of chilli
- 500 g/1 lb 2 oz canned pineapple
  slices in syrup
- 4 tablespoons olive oil
- 1 heaped tablespoon plain flour
- 275 ml/9 fl oz white wine
- 25 g/1 oz margarine or butter
- salt
  Serves 6

Tie the veal into a neat shape with fine kitchen string and stud with the cloves. Put it into a heavy-based saucepan or cocotte and add the rum, currants, chilli and the syrup from the pineapple slices. Chop two slices of the pineapple and add to the pan, then leave the veal to marinate in the refrigerator, turning it occasionally, for at least 1 hour. Reserve the remaining pineapple. Remove the veal from the pan, pour the marinade into a bowl, remove the currants with a slotted spoon and reserve. Heat the oil in the cocotte or saucepan. Add the veal and cook, turning frequently, for about 10 minutes, until evenly browned all over. Sprinkle in the flour, pour in the marinade and wine, season with salt and bring to the boil. Lower the heat and cook, turning the veal occasionally, for about 1½ hours, until tender. Towards the end of the cooking time, melt the margarine or butter in a frying pan. Add the reserved pineapple slices and cook over a high heat for 5 minutes, until golden brown on both sides. Remove with a fish slice, drain and keep warm. Lift the veal out of the pan, remove and discard the string and carve the meat into thin slices. Pass the sauce through a food mill or process in a food processor. Put the veal on a warm serving dish and garnish with the pineapple slices and the reserved currants. Serve immediately, offering the sauce separately.

Note: The dish can be served with yellow rice (see recipe 191).

739

Roast veal with orange
CONTRA DE TERNERA ASADA CON NARANJA

- 1 leg fillet, silverside or topside
  of veal, 1.5 kg/3¼ lb
- 5 tablespoons brandy
- 100 g/3½ oz lard or
  6 tablespoons sunflower oil
- 5 tablespoons hot water
- 2 tablespoons sugar
- 20 g/¾ oz butter
- 1 large orange or 2 small
  oranges, sliced
- juice of 2 oranges
- 1 tablespoon grated orange rind
- Mashed Potato (see recipe 230)
- salt

Serves 6

Preheat the oven to 180°C/350°F/Gas Mark 4. Tie the veal into a neat shape with fine kitchen string and put it into a roasting tin. Heat the brandy in a small saucepan, ignite it and pour it over the veal. When the flames have died down, spread the lard over the veal or pour the oil over it. Roast for about 20 minutes, until beginning to brown, then season with salt, add the hot water and baste the meat. Cook, turning the meat and basting occasionally, for 1 hour, until tender. Meanwhile, pour 250 ml/8 fl oz water into a saucepan, add the sugar and butter and bring to the boil, stirring until the sugar has dissolved. Cook for about 6 minutes, then add the orange slices and bring back to the boil. Remove the pan from the heat and set aside. When the veal is tender, turn off the oven, open the door for 2 minutes and then close it again and leave the meat to rest for about 15 minutes before carving. Carve the veal and place the slices on a warm serving dish. Drain the orange slices. Garnish the meat with little mounds of the mashed potato and the orange slices. Stir the orange juice and grated rind into the cooking juices and heat through, then serve separately in a sauce boat.

740

Osso buco in mushroom sauce
OSSO BUCCO EN SALSA CON CHAMPIÑONES

- 5–6 tablespoons olive oil
- 6 pieces of osso buco
  (sliced hind knuckle)
- 40 g/1½ oz plain flour
- 250 g/9 oz mushrooms,
  thickly sliced
- 3 large, ripe tomatoes, peeled,
  seeded and chopped
- 250 ml/8 fl oz white wine
- 250 ml/8 fl oz veal or chicken
  stock (home-made or made
  with a stock cube)
- salt and pepper

Serves 6

Heat the oil in a large saucepan. Coat the pieces of osso buco in the flour, shaking off the excess, add to the pan and cook over a medium heat, turning occasionally, for 8–10 minutes, until lightly browned. Add the mushrooms and cook, stirring occasionally, for 5 minutes, then add the tomatoes. Pour in the wine and stock, season with salt and pepper, cover and cook over a low heat for about 1 hour, until tender. Serve in a warm deep dish.

741

Osso buco in sauce

OSSO BUCCO EN SALSA

- **450 ml / ¾ pint sunflower oil**
- **6 pieces of osso buco (sliced hind knuckle)**
- **40 g / 1½ oz plain flour**
- **1 onion, finely chopped**
- **1 clove garlic, finely chopped**
- **3 tomatoes, seeded and chopped**
- **½ teaspoon mixed dried herbs or 1 bouquet garni (1 sprig fresh parsley, 1 sprig fresh thyme and 2 bay leaves tied together in muslin)**
- **1 tablespoon grated lemon rind**
- **250 ml / 8 fl oz white wine**
- **250 ml / 8 fl oz veal or chicken stock (home-made or made with a stock cube)**
- **250 g / 9 oz shallots**
- **20 g / ¾ oz butter**
- **a dash of lemon juice**
- **1 tablespoon chopped fresh parsley**
- **salt and pepper**

Serves 6

Reserve 5 tablespoons of the oil and heat the remainder in a frying pan. Coat the pieces of osso buco in the flour, shaking off the excess, add to the pan and cook over a medium heat, turning occasionally, for 8–10 minutes, until golden brown on both sides. Remove from the pan and keep warm. Heat 3 tablespoons of the reserved oil in another frying pan. Add the onion and garlic and cook over a low heat, stirring occasionally, for about 8 minutes, until beginning to brown. Add the tomato and cook, stirring occasionally and breaking it up with the side of the spoon, for about 10 minutes. Add the dried herbs or bouquet garni and stir in the lemon rind. Put the pieces of osso buco into a saucepan. Pour the wine and stock into the tomato and onion mixture, season with salt and pepper and pour the sauce over the meat. Cover and simmer over a low heat for 1 hour, until tender. Meanwhile, put the shallots, butter, lemon juice and a pinch of salt into another saucepan, add water to cover and cook for about 20 minutes, until tender. Drain well. Heat the remaining oil in a third saucepan. Add the shallots and cook, turning frequently, until browned all over. Remove from the pan and set aside. Transfer the pieces of osso buco to a warm serving dish. Remove and discard the bouquet garni, if used, pass the sauce through a food mill or process in a food processor and pour it over the meat. Garnish the dish with the shallots and sprinkle with the parsley. Serve immediately.

Note: Some people prefer not to pass the sauce through a food mill or process in a food processor which results in a sauce which is less smooth and has more texture.

Veal stew with whisky sauce and rice

GUISO DE TERNERA EN SALSA DE WHISKY CON ARROZ BLANCO

- 2 onions
- 1.5 kg/3¼ lb stewing veal, such as breast or flank, cut into cubes
- 4 carrots, halved lengthways
- 1 bay leaf
- 5 tablespoons white wine
- 500 g/1 lb 2 oz long-grain rice
- 80 g/3 oz butter
- 2 tablespoons sunflower oil
- 1 tablespoon plain flour
- 3 tablespoons whisky
- 1 tablespoon chopped fresh parsley
- salt

Serves 6

Finely chop one of the onions and cut the other in half. Put the veal, carrots, onion halves, bay leaf, wine and a pinch of salt into a saucepan, pour in water to cover and bring to the boil. Skim off the froth that rises to the surface, then cover and cook over a medium heat for 1–1½ hours, until the veal is tender. Meanwhile, cook and rinse the rice as described in recipe 173. Remove the veal from the pan with a slotted spoon and set aside. Strain and reserve the cooking liquid. Melt 25 g/1 oz of the butter with the oil in a saucepan. Add the chopped onion and cook over a low heat, stirring occasionally, for about 10 minutes, until lightly browned. Stir in the flour and cook, stirring constantly, for 2 minutes. Stir in the whisky, then gradually stir in 750 ml/1¼ pints of the reserved cooking liquid, a little at a time. Cook, stirring constantly, for about 10 minutes, until thickened. Add the veal and heat through for about 5 minutes. Meanwhile, season the rice with salt and fry in the remaining butter (see recipe 173). Spoon the rice into a ring mould and turn it out on to a warm serving dish. Spoon the meat and sauce into the middle and sprinkle with the parsley. Alternatively, serve the rice in a mound on the side. Serve immediately.

743

Veal stew with lemon juice
GUISO DE TERNERA CON ZUMO DE LIMÓN

- 1.5 kg/3¼ lb stewing veal, such as breast or flank, cut into cubes
- 40 g/1½ oz plain flour
- 6 tablespoons olive oil
- 1 onion, chopped
- juice of 3 lemons
- grated rind of 1 lemon
- 1 veal or chicken stock cube
- 250 g/9 oz shallots
- 15 g/½ oz butter
- 1 teaspoon sugar
- 1 teaspoon Dijon mustard
- ½ teaspoon meat concentrate
- 175 ml/6 fl oz muscatel wine
- salt and pepper

Serves 6

Coat the cubes of veal in the flour, shaking off any excess. Heat the oil in a saucepan. Add the onion and cook over a low heat, stirring occasionally, for about 5 minutes, until softened and translucent. Add the veal and cook over a medium heat, stirring frequently, for 8–10 minutes, until browned all over. Stir in 1 tablespoon of the flour and cook, stirring constantly, for 2 minutes. Gradually stir in 750 ml/1¼ pints water and the lemon juice and add the lemon rind. Crumble in the stock cube and stir well. Cover and cook over a medium heat for about 1½ hours, until the veal is tender. Meanwhile, put the shallots and butter into a saucepan, pour in water to cover and cook for about 20 minutes, until tender. Shortly before serving, heat the sugar in another saucepan until it is the colour of caramel. Stir in the mustard, meat concentrate and wine, then stir into the stew. Season to taste with salt and pepper. Drain the shallots, add to the stew and cook for a further 8 minutes. Serve with triangles of fried bread (see recipe 130) or little mounds of boiled rice.

744

Veal stew with leeks
TERNERA GUISADA CON PUERROS

- 25 g/1 oz butter or margarine
- 2 tablespoons olive oil
- 1 kg/2¼ lb stewing veal, such as breast or flank, cut into cubes
- 800 g/1¾ lb leeks, thinly sliced and rinsed well
- 175 ml/6 fl oz dry white wine
- juice of ½ lemon
- 250 ml/8 fl oz milk
- 50 g/2 oz currants
- 1 bouquet garni (1 sprig fresh parsley, 1 bay leaf and 1 clove garlic tied together in muslin)
- salt

Serves 6

Melt the butter or margarine with the oil in a saucepan. Add the veal and cook over a medium heat, stirring frequently, for about 8 minutes, until golden brown all over. Remove with a slotted spoon and keep warm. Add the leek to the pan and cook over a low heat, stirring occasionally, for 10 minutes, until softened. Return the veal to the pan, pour in the wine, lemon juice and milk and add the currants and bouquet garni. Cover and simmer gently for 40 minutes, until the veal is tender. Remove and discard the bouquet garni and serve immediately with boiled rice or tagliatelle.

745

Veal stew
TERNERA GUISADA

- 600 g/1 lb 5 oz stewing veal, such as breast or flank, cut into cubes
- 2 tablespoons plain flour
- 4 tablespoons olive oil
- 1 onion, chopped
- 120 ml/4 fl oz dry white wine
- 120 ml/4 fl oz veal or chicken stock (home-made or made with a stock cube)
- 1 sprig fresh thyme, chopped
- 1 sprig fresh sage, chopped
- pinch of freshly grated nutmeg
- 2 eggs
- juice of ½ lemon
- 1 tablespoon chopped fresh parsley
- salt and pepper

Serves 4

Coat the veal in the flour, shaking off any excess. Heat the oil in a saucepan. Add the onion and cook over a low heat, stirring occasionally, for about 8 minutes, until beginning to brown. Add the veal, in batches, and cook over a medium heat, stirring frequently, for 5–8 minutes, until evenly browned. Return all the veal to the pan. Pour in the wine and cook over a high heat until reduced, then add the stock. Lower the heat and simmer gently for 45 minutes, adding more stock or water, if necessary, until the veal is tender. Season with salt and pepper halfway through the cooking time and add the thyme, sage and nutmeg. Beat the eggs with the lemon juice and parsley and stir into the pan, then remove from the heat and serve.

Stewed breast of veal

FILETES DE FALDA DE TERNERA GUISADOS

- **5 tablespoons olive oil**
- **1.3 kg/3 lb breast of veal,
  cut into 6 slices**
- **1 onion, finely chopped**
- **3 cloves garlic, lightly crushed**
- **2 ripe tomatoes, peeled,
  seeded and diced**
- **275 ml/9 fl oz white wine**
- **a pinch of mixed dried herbs
  or 1 bouquet garni
  (1 sprig fresh parsley, 1 sprig
  fresh thyme and 2 bay leaves
  tied together in muslin)**
- **250 g/9 oz shallots**
- **40 g/1½ oz butter**
- **juice of ½ lemon**
- **200 g/7 oz mushrooms,
  thickly sliced**
- **50 g/2 oz olives, stoned
  and halved lengthways**
- **salt**

Serves 6

Heat the oil in a heavy-based saucepan or a cocotte. Add the veal, in batches, and cook over a medium heat, stirring frequently for 5–8 minutes until evenly browned on both sides. Remove the veal from the pan and set aside. Add the onion and garlic to the pan and cook over a low heat, stirring occasionally, for about 5 minutes, until softened and translucent. Return the veal to the pan, add the tomato and pour in the wine and 175 ml/6 fl oz water. Season with salt, stir in the dried herbs or bouquet garni and bring to the boil. Lower the heat, cover and simmer for 1 hour, until the veal is tender. Meanwhile, put the shallots, half the butter, half the lemon juice and a pinch of salt into a saucepan and cook for about 20 minutes, until tender. Drain and set aside. Put the mushrooms, the remaining lemon juice, the remaining butter and a pinch of salt into a saucepan. Cover and cook for 6 minutes. When the veal is tender, add the shallots, the mushrooms and their cooking juices and the olives to the stew, mix well and cook over a medium heat for 5 minutes more. Remove and discard the bouquet garni, if used, and serve immediately.

747

Blanquette of veal
BLANQUETA DE TERNERA

- 1.5 kg/3¼ lb breast of veal,
  cut into cubes
- 1 bay leaf
- 1 small onion, halved
- 2 carrots, sliced
- 5 tablespoons white wine
- 500 g/1 lb 2 oz long-grain rice
- 80 g/3 oz butter
- 2 tablespoons sunflower oil
- 1½ tablespoons plain flour
- 250 ml/8 fl oz milk
- 2 egg yolks
- juice of ½ lemon
- 2 teaspoons chopped
  fresh parsley
- salt

Serves 6

Put the veal into a saucepan, pour in water to cover and add the bay leaf, onion, carrot, wine and a pinch of salt. Bring to the boil and skim off the froth that rises to the surface, then lower the heat and simmer for 1–1½ hours, until the veal is tender. Meanwhile, cook and rinse the rice as described in recipe 173. Remove the veal from the pan with a slotted spoon and keep warm. Strain and reserve the cooking liquid. Melt 25 g/1 oz of the butter with the oil in a saucepan. Stir in the flour and cook, stirring constantly, for 2 minutes. Gradually stir in the milk and 500 ml/18 fl oz of the reserved cooking juices. Beat the egg yolks with the lemon juice and stir in a little of the sauce, then pour into the pan. Sprinkle in the parsley and season to taste with salt. Remove the pan from the heat and keep warm. Season the rice with salt and fry in the remaining butter (see recipe 173). Fill half of a long serving dish with the rice and the other half with the veal and sauce. Serve immediately.

748

Classic stuffed breast of veal
ALETA DE TERNERA RELLENA CLÁSICA

- 3 carrots
- 1 boned breast of veal,
  1.5 kg/3¼ lb
- 250 g/9 oz minced veal
- 120-g/4-oz piece of Serrano
  ham, cut into 2-cm/¾-inch
  wide strips
- 1 hard-boiled egg,
  cut into wedges
- 4 tablespoons olive oil
- 1 large onion, chopped
- 1 eating apple, peeled,
  cored and chopped
- 175 ml/6 fl oz dry white wine
- salt

Serves 8–9

Cut two of the carrots into lengthways strips, discarding the centres. Slice the remaining carrot. Open out the breast of veal, spread the minced veal in the centre and place the strips of ham and strips of carrot on top and all along it. Add the hard-boiled egg and season with salt. Roll up the veal and tie securely with fine kitchen string. Heat the oil in a saucepan. Add the veal and cook over a medium heat, turning frequently, for 8–10 minutes, until evenly browned all over. Remove from the pan and set aside. Add the onion to the pan and cook over a low heat, stirring occasionally, for about 10 minutes, until golden brown. Return the veal to the pan, add the apple, sliced carrot and a pinch of salt and pour in the wine. Bring to the boil, pour in enough water almost to cover the veal and bring back to the boil. Lower the heat, cover and simmer for 1¼ hours, until the veal is tender and the sauce has reduced. Lift the veal out of the pan and remove and discard the string. Cut into slices about 1 cm/½ inch thick and place on a warm serving dish. Pass the sauce through a food mill or process in a food processor and transfer to a sauce boat. Serve immediately with little mounds of vegetables or Mashed Potato (see recipe 230).

749

Rolled breast of veal filled with spinach and omelette

ALETA DE TERNERA RELLENA CON ESPINACAS Y TORTILLAS

- 1 kg/2¼ lb spinach, coarse stalks removed
- 1 boned breast of veal, 750 g/1 lb 10 oz
- 200 g/7 oz minced veal
- 100 g/3½ oz Serrano ham, minced
- 2 eggs
- 120 ml/4 fl oz sunflower oil
- 5 tablespoons white wine
- 175 ml/6 fl oz hot water
- salt

Serves 6

Cook the spinach as described on page 315, drain well and chop. Pre-heat the oven to 180°C/350°F/Gas Mark 4. Open out the breast of veal and season lightly with salt. Mix together the minced veal and ham and spread the mixture on top of the breast of veal. Using 1 egg and 1½ tablespoons of the oil each, make two flat omelettes in a small frying pan. Place the omelettes on top of the minced meat, next to each other. Put the spinach on top of the omelettes in a strip, about 6 cm/2½ inches wide. Carefully roll up the veal so that none of the filling moves, then tie it with fine kitchen string. Heat the remaining oil in a roasting tin. Add the veal roll and cook over a medium heat, turning frequently, for 8–10 minutes, until evenly browned all over. Lightly season with salt and roast in the oven for 30 minutes. Pour the wine over the veal, return the tin to the oven and roast for a further 15 minutes. Pour half the hot water over the veal, return it to the oven and roast, basting occasionally, for a further 30 minutes, adding the remaining hot water, if necessary. If serving hot, leave the meat to rest for about 10 minutes before removing the string and carving. This dish is also very tasty served cold.

Stewed shoulder of veal

ESPALDILLA DE TERNERA GUISADA

- 50 g/2 oz lard or 5 tablespoons sunflower oil
- 1 boned and rolled shoulder of veal, 2-kg/4½-lb, bones reserved
- 2 onions, coarsely chopped
- 250 g/9 oz carrots, thickly sliced
- 2 ripe tomatoes, peeled, seeded and chopped
- pinch of mixed dried herbs or 1 bouquet garni (1 sprig fresh parsley, 2 bay leaves and 1 sprig fresh thyme tied together in muslin)
- 250 ml/8 fl oz white wine
- 175 ml/6 fl oz warm water
- 1 tablespoon potato flour
- ¼ teaspoon meat extract
- 1 teaspoon paprika
- salt

Serves 6

Preheat the oven to 180°C/350°F/Gas Mark 4. Melt the lard or heat the oil in a flameproof casserole. Add the veal, veal bones, onion and carrot and cook over a medium heat, turning the meat frequently, for 8–10 minutes, until evenly browned all over. Add the tomato, dried herbs or bouquet garni and a pinch of salt, pour in the wine and the warm water and bring to the boil. Transfer the casserole to the oven and cook, turning the veal and basting occasionally, for 1½ hours, until tender. Remove the veal from the casserole, cut it into slices and keep warm. Set the casserole over a medium-low heat and skim off any fat from the surface of the cooking liquid. Mix the potato flour with a little water and the meat extract in a bowl, then stir into the casserole. Remove and discard the bones and the bouquet garni, if used, and pass the cooking liquid through a food mill or process in a food processor. Stir in the paprika, season to taste with salt and add a little hot water if the sauce is very thick. If it is too thin, cook for a little longer before adding the paprika. Pour the sauce over the veal, and serve immediately with either Mashed Potato (see recipe 230) or fried potatoes.

751

- 1 leg, silverside or topside
  of veal, 1.5 kg/3¼ lb
- 5 tablespoons sunflower oil
  or 80 g/3 oz lard
- 750 g/1 lb 10 oz onions and
  coarsely chopped
- 2 cloves garlic, lightly crushed
- 150 ml/¼ pint sherry
- 2 cloves
- salt and pepper

Serves 6

Veal with onions and sherry

TERNERA CON CEBOLLA Y VINO DE JEREZ

Tie the veal into a neat shape with fine kitchen string. Heat the oil or melt the lard in a heavy-based saucepan or a cocotte. Add the veal and cook over a medium heat, turning frequently, for 8 – 10 minutes, until evenly browned all over. Add the onion, garlic, sherry, cloves and 350 ml/12 fl oz water, season with salt and pepper and bring to the boil. Lower the heat, cover and simmer for about 1¾ hours, until the veal is tender. Lift the veal out of the pan, remove and discard the string and cut the veal into slices. Pass the cooking juices through a food mill or process in a food processor. Serve immediately with boiled potatoes or macaroni tossed in butter and grated cheese.

752

- 1.5 kg/3¼ lb breast,
  leg or middle neck of veal,
  cut into cubes
- 175 ml/6 fl oz white-wine vinegar
- 175 ml/6 fl oz olive oil
- 1 bulb garlic, peeled
- 1 large onion, chopped
- pinch of mixed dried herbs
  or 1 bouquet garni
  (1 bay leaf, 2 sprigs fresh parsley
  and 1 sprig fresh thyme tied
  together in muslin)
- 1 teaspoon paprika
- salt

Serves 6

Braised veal

TERNERA ESTOFADA

Put all the ingredients into a large, heavy-based saucepan and season with the salt. Cover with a tight-fitting lid and cook over a low heat, stirring occasionally, for about 2 hours, until the veal is tender. If necessary, stir in a little hot water to prevent the meat drying out. Remove and discard the garlic and the bouquet garni, if used. Serve in a warm deep dish with triangles of fried bread (see recipe 130).

Veal casserole with porcini
TERNERA A LA CAZUELA CON SETAS

- **100 g/3 ½ oz lard or**
  6 tablespoons sunflower oil
- **1 topside of veal, 1.5 kg/3 ¼ lb**
- **175 ml/6 fl oz Malaga wine**
  or sweet sherry
- **750 g/1 lb 10 oz porcini,**
  cut into large pieces
- **1 teaspoon potato flour**
- **½ teaspoon meat concentrate**
- **salt**

Serves 6

Melt the lard or heat the oil in a heavy-based saucepan or a cocotte. Add the veal and cook over a medium heat, turning frequently, for 8 – 10 minutes, until evenly browned all over. Pour in the wine or sherry and 175 ml/6 fl oz water, season lightly with salt, cover and cook, stirring occasionally, for 30 minutes. Add the porcini to the pan, re-cover and cook for a further 30 minutes, until the veal is tender. Lift out the veal, cut it into slices, place on a serving dish and keep warm. Mix the potato flour and meat concentrate with a little water in a small bowl, then stir into the sauce. Bring to the boil, stirring constantly. Taste and adjust the seasoning, if necessary, then spoon the sauce and mushrooms over the veal. Serve immediately.

Note: This dish can be made with dried porcini. Rehydrate them according to the instructions on the packet.

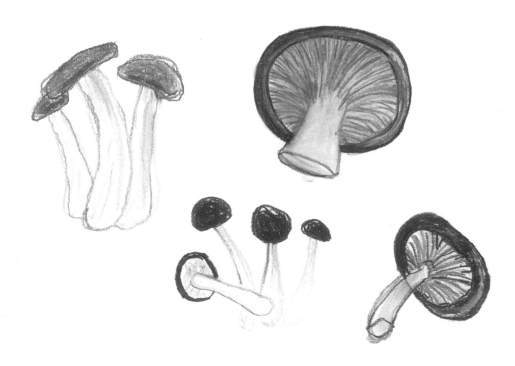

Veal with garlic and tomato

TERNERA AL AJILLO CON TOMATE

- 4 tablespoons olive oil
- 1.5 kg/3¼ lb breast or flank
  of veal, cut into 6-cm/2½-inch
  long strips
- 1 tablespoon breadcrumbs
- 1 bulb garlic, peeled
- 1 veal or chicken stock cube
  dissolved in 275 ml/9 fl oz
  boiling water
- salt

  Tomato sauce:
- 3 tablespoons sunflower oil
- 1 kg/2¼ lb very ripe tomatoes,
  peeled, seeded and chopped
- pinch of mixed dried herbs
  or 1 bouquet garni
  (1 bay leaf and 1 sprig fresh
  thyme tied together in muslin)
- 1 teaspoon sugar
- salt

Serves 6

Make a thick tomato sauce as described in recipe 73. Remove and discard the bouquet garni, if used, before processing in a food processor. Heat the oil in a heavy-based saucepan or a cocotte. Add the veal and cook over a medium heat, stirring occasionally, for about 8–10 minutes, until evenly browned. Sprinkle in the breadcrumbs, add the tomato sauce, garlic cloves and stock, and season lightly with salt. Cover and simmer over a low heat for 1½ hours, until the veal is tender. Remove and discard the garlic and serve immediately accompanied by fried potatoes, boiled rice or triangles of fried bread (see recipe 130).

Pork

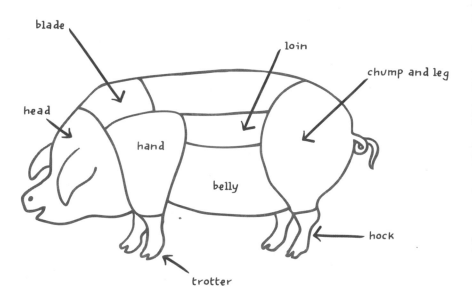

blade

loin

chump and leg

head

hand

belly

hock

trotter

Selection

Pork should be pink or light red, depending on the cut. It shrinks considerably when roasted, fried or stewed, losing almost one-third of its weight. A loin of pork weighing 1.5 kg/3 ¼ lb when raw will be just 1 kg/2 ¼ lb after roasting. Pork is very tasty but the meat from some of the traditional breeds can be quite fatty and indigestible. If you are worried about the fat content, look for specially bred lean pork (but be aware that the meat is often drier, the more lean it is).

Sausages

Method for poaching sausages

Some sausages, especially larger sausages popular in Spain, Italy and France, are often poached rather than fried. Prick the skin in several places with a cocktail stick. Bring a large saucepan of water to the boil, add the sausages and bring back to the boil. Lower the heat so that the water is barely simmering with just a few bubbles around the side of the pan. Poach for 10–12 minutes, depending on the type of sausage, then remove and serve.

Method for frying sausages

Prick the skin in several places with a fork or a cocktail stick. Put them in a frying pan, pour oil over them and set the pan over a low heat. Cook, turning occasionally, until they are cooked through and evenly browned.

Buying pork	Suitable cuts	Weight per serving	Cooking time
Fried, grilled or griddled	Chops, Leg steaks, Fillet	200 g / 7 oz 150 g / 5 oz	6 minutes each side, first over a high heat and then over a low heat
Roasted *	Fillet, Loin, Leg	200–225 g / 7–8 oz (boneless)	30 minutes per 500 g / 1 lb 2 oz
Stewed or braised	Hand and spring, Spare rib, Blade	200 g / 7 oz	1½–1¾ hours

*Make sure that the oven is preheated

755

Roast loin of pork

LOMO DE CERDO ASADO

• **1 boned loin of pork, 1.5 kg / 3¼ lb**

• **2–3 tablespoons lard or sunflower oil (optional)**

• **juice of ½ lemon**

• **salt and pepper**

Serves 6

Tie the pork into a neat shape with fine kitchen string and season with salt and pepper at least 1 hour before cooking. Preheat the oven to 230°C/450°F/Gas Mark 8. Put the pork into a roasting tin. If the meat has plenty of fat, put the tin into the oven without any additional fat. If most of the fat has been trimmed, spread the lard or brush the oil over the pork before putting it into the oven. Roast, turning frequently, for 10–15 minutes, until browned all over. Lower the oven temperature to 180°C/350°F/Gas Mark 4, pour 3–4 tablespoons hot water over the pork and return to the oven. Roast, occasionally basting the meat with the cooking juices, for 1¼ hours, until the juices run clear when the thickest part is pierced with the point of a sharp knife. Remove the pork from the oven and leave to rest for 5 minutes before removing and discarding the string and carving the meat into thin slices. Mix a few drops of the lemon juice into the cooking juices and pour into a sauce boat. Serve the pork with Mashed Potato, fried parsley potatoes, Potato Balls (see recipe 231), watercress, noodles or tagliatelle. Offer the sauce separately.

Notes: Some people like to rub the meat with a peeled garlic clove after it has been seasoned. As roast pork is delicious cold with a salad, remember to roast a larger quantity of meat and keep a piece to serve cold.

Fillet or loin of pork with mustard

CINTA O LOMO DE CERDO ASADO CON MOSTAZA

- **1 fillet or boned loin of pork, 1.5 kg/3¼ lb**
- **2 tablespoons Dijon mustard**
- **175 ml/6 fl oz white wine**
- **hot water**
- **salt**

Serves 6

Tie the pork into a neat shape with fine kitchen string and season with salt 1 hour before cooking. Preheat the oven to 230°C/450°F/Gas Mark 8. Spread the mustard all over the pork, then put the meat into a roasting tin. Put the pork into the oven and roast, turning frequently, for 10–15 minutes, until browned all over. Lower the oven temperature to 180°C/350°F/Gas Mark 4. Pour the wine over the pork and baste well, then return to the oven and roast, basting occasionally, for 1¼ hours, until the juices run clear when the thickest part is pierced with the point of a sharp knife. Turn off the oven, open the door for 2–3 minutes, close it again and leave the pork to rest for about 6 minutes. Take the pork out of the oven, remove and discard the string and carve the pork into thin slices. Place them in a serving dish and keep warm. Put 2–3 tablespoons hot water into the roasting tin and bring to the boil over a medium heat, stirring and scraping up any bits from the base of the pan. Strain into a sauce boat. Serve the pork with Mashed Potato (see recipe 230) or macaroni tossed in butter and grated cheese, offering the sauce separately.

757 Fillet or loin of pork with milk

CINTA O LOMO DE CERDO CON LECHE

• 1 fillet or boned loin of pork,
 1.5 kg/3¼ lb
• 25 g/1 oz lard or 2 tablespoons
 sunflower oil
• 1 litre/1¾ pints warm milk
• 4 cloves garlic, unpeeled
• 4 black peppercorns
• mashed potato or apple sauce
• salt

Serves 6

Tie the pork into a neat shape with fine kitchen string and season with salt 1 hour before cooking. Melt the lard or heat the oil in a heavy-based saucepan or a cocotte. Add the pork and cook over a medium heat, turning frequently, for about 10 minutes, until browned all over. Pour in the milk, add the garlic and the peppercorns and bring to the boil over a medium heat. Lower the heat, cover and simmer gently, turning occasionally, for about 2½ hours, until the pork is tender. Remove the pork from the pan and keep warm. If the remaining cooking liquid is very thin, cook over a high heat until reduced. Remove and discard the string from the pork, carve the meat into thin slices and place on a warm serving dish. Garnish with Mashed Potato (see recipe 230) or apple sauce. Strain the cooking liquid or put it through a food mill or process in a food processor. Beat well and serve separately in a sauce boat.

Pork fillet in a salt crust

CINTA DE CERDO ASADA CON COSTRA DE SAL

- **1.5–2 kg/3¼–4½ lb coarse salt**
- **1 pork fillet, 1.5 kg/3¼ lb**

Serves 6

Preheat the oven to 180°C/350°F/Gas Mark 4. Make a 1-cm/½-inch deep layer of salt in the base of a roasting tin. Put the pork on top and cover with the remaining salt in a thick layer. Press down firmly with wet hands so that the salt forms a crust. Put the roasting tin in the oven and cook for 1¾ hours, until the salt crust begins to crack. Remove the tin from the oven, break the salt crust, lift out the pork and brush off any remaining salt. Carve into slices. Serve hot, with any accompaniment you like, or cold.

759

- 1 boned loin of pork,
  1.5 kg/3¼ lb
- 50 g/2 oz lard or 3 tablespoons
  sunflower oil
- 1 thick slice of bacon,
  about 100 g/3½ oz, diced
- 1 Savoy cabbage, shredded
- salt

Serves 6

Braised loin of pork with cabbage

LOMO DE CERDO BRASEADO CON REPOLLO

Tie the pork into a neat shape with fine kitchen string and season with salt at least 1 hour before cooking. Melt the lard or heat the oil in a heavy-based saucepan or a cocotte. Add the bacon and cook over a medium heat, stirring frequently, for about 5 minutes, until browned. Add the pork and cook, turning frequently, for about 10 minutes, until browned all over. Lower the heat and cover the pan. Bring a large saucepan of salted water to the boil. Add the cabbage, pushing it under the surface with a slotted spoon, and cook for about 15 minutes, until tender. Drain well and add to the pan with the meat, placing it all around the pork. Re-cover the pan and cook, stirring occasionally, for a further 45 minutes. Remove the pan from the heat and leave to stand for 5 minutes, then lift out the pork, remove and discard the string and carve the meat into thin slices. Put them on a warm serving dish and arrange the cabbage all around the edge of the dish. Pour the cooking juices over the pork or serve separately in a sauce boat.

760

- 1 fillet or boned loin of pork,
  1.5 kg/3¼ lb
- 2 tablespoons Dijon mustard
- 25 g/1 oz lard or 2 tablespoons
  sunflower oil
- 200 g/7 oz canned pineapple
  slices in syrup
- 1 teaspoon potato flour
- salt

Serves 6

Roast pork with pineapple

CERDO ASADO CON PIÑA

Tie the pork into a neat shape with fine kitchen string and season with salt 1 hour before cooking. Preheat the oven to 230°C/450°F/ Gas Mark 8. Spread the mustard all over the pork. Melt the lard of heat the oil in a roasting tin over a medium-low heat. Add the meat and cook, turning frequently, for about 10 minutes, until browned all over. Transfer to the oven, lower the temperature to 180°C/350°F/ Gas Mark 4 and roast, turning occasionally and basting with the cooking juices, for about 1¼ hours, until the juices run clear when the thickest part is pierced with the point of a sharp knife. Add a little hot water, if necessary. Remove the pork from the oven. Remove and discard the string and carve the meat into thin slices. Place them on a serving dish and keep warm. Drain the slices of pineapple, reserving the syrup. Coat the pineapple slices with the cooking juices in the roasting tin, then cut them in half. Put some of the half slices on top of the pork and the rest around the edge of the dish. Mix the potato flour with 3 tablespoons water in a bowl, pour into the roasting tin and add the reserved pineapple syrup. Cook over a low heat, stirring frequently, until thickened and hot, then serve in a sauce boat.

761

Fillet or loin of pork with apples

CINTA O LOMO DE CERDO CON MANZANAS

- 1 fillet or boned loin of pork,
  1.5 kg/3¼ lb
- 50 g/2 oz lard or 3 tablespoons
  sunflower oil
- 6 small eating apples,
  peeled and cored
- 3 teaspoons sugar
- 50 g/2 oz butter
- 3 tablespoons sherry
- 1 teaspoon potato flour
- salt

Serves 6

Tie the pork into a neat shape with fine kitchen string and season with salt at least 1 hour before cooking. Preheat the oven to 230°C/450°F/Gas Mark 8. Spread the lard or brush the oil all over the pork, place the meat in a roasting tin and transfer to the oven. Roast, turning frequently, for about 10 minutes, until browned all over. Lower the temperature to 180°C/350°F/Gas Mark 4, pour 1 tablespoon water over the pork, return it to the oven and roast, adding 1–2 tablespoons water occasionally, for a further 45 minutes. Remove the roasting tin from the oven and put the apples around the pork. Divide the sugar and butter among the cavities in the apples, pour the sherry over them and return the tin to the oven. Lower the temperature to 160°C/325°F/Gas Mark 3 and roast for 30 minutes, until the pork juices run clear when the thickest part is pierced with the point of a sharp knife and the apples are soft but not falling apart. Lift out the pork from the roasting tin, remove and discard the string and carve the meat into thin slices. Put them on a warm serving dish and place the apples around the edge. Mix the potato flour with a little cold water, stir into the cooking juices and cook over a low heat, stirring frequently, until thickened, then pour over the pork. Serve immediately.

762

Pork fillet with apples and chestnuts

CINTA DE CERDO CON MANZANAS Y CASTAÑAS

- 1 pork fillet, 1 kg/2¼ lb
- 50 g/2 oz lard or 3 tablespoons sunflower oil
- 5 eating apples, peeled and cored
- 3 teaspoons sugar
- 50 g/2 oz butter
- 3 tablespoons sherry
- 200 g/7 oz canned peeled and cooked chestnuts, drained
- 150 ml/¼ pint milk
- 1 teaspoon potato flour
- salt

Serves 6

Tie the pork into a neat shape with fine kitchen string and season with salt at least 1 hour before cooking. Preheat the oven to 230°C/450°F/Gas Mark 8. Spread the lard or brush the oil all over the pork, place the meat in a roasting tin, and transfer to the oven. Roast, turning frequently, for about 10 minutes, until browned all over. Lower the temperature to 180°C/350°F/Gas Mark 4 and roast, turning occasionally and basting with 3 tablespoons water, for a further 45 minutes. Meanwhile, put the apples into an ovenproof dish. Divide the sugar and butter among the cavities and pour the sherry over them. Thity minutes before the end of the cooking time, arrange the apples alongside the pork and return it to the oven. If necessary, lower the oven temperature to 160°C/325°F/Gas Mark 3. The apples should be soft but not falling apart. Shortly before the end of the cooking time, put the chestnuts in a small saucepan, add the milk and heat through gently, then drain and keep warm. Lift the pork out of the roasting tin, remove and discard the string and slice the meat thinly. Put the slices on a warm serving dish with the apples and chestnuts around the edge. Mix the potato flour with 2–3 tablespoons water in a bowl. Stir into the cooking juices and cook over a low heat, stirring frequently, for a few minutes, until thickened. Pour over the pork and serve immediately.

763

- 1 pork fillet, 1.5 kg/3¼ lb
- 500 ml/18 fl oz white wine
- 3 tablespoons
  white-wine vinegar
- 1 onion, cut into 4 pieces
- 2 carrots, sliced
- 1 clove garlic
- 6 black peppercorns
- pinch of mixed dried herbs
  or 1 bouquet garni
  (1 bay leaf, 1 clove garlic, 1 sprig
  fresh parsley and 1 sprig fresh
  thyme tied together in muslin)
- 50 g/2 oz lard or 3 tablespoons
  sunflower oil
- 1 teaspoon potato flour
- 1 tablespoon tomato purée
- salt

Serves 6

Braised marinated pork
CINTA DE CERDO ADOBADA Y GUISADA

Tie the pork into a neat shape with fine kitchen string and put it into an earthenware, ceramic or glass bowl with the wine, vinegar, onion, carrot, garlic, peppercorns and dried herbs or bouquet garni. Cover and leave to marinate in the refrigerator for 8–10 hours. Preheat the oven to 230°C/450°F/Gas Mark 8. Drain the pork, reserving the marinade and vegetables. Season the meat generously with salt, spread the lard or brush the oil over it and place in a roasting tin. Put the pieces of onion and carrot around it and transfer to the oven. Roast, turning frequently, for about 10 minutes, until the pork and onion pieces begin to brown. Lower the oven temperature to 180°C/350°F/Gas Mark 4, baste the pork with the reserved marinade, return it to the oven and roast, turning the meat and basting occasionally with the cooking juices, for 1¼ hours, until the juices run clear when the thickest part is pierced with the point of a sharp knife. Lift the pork out of the roasting tin, remove and discard the string and carve the meat into thin slices. Put on a serving dish and keep warm. Mix the potato flour with 2–3 tablespoons water in a bowl, then stir into the cooking juices along with the tomato purée. Heat through, stirring, then pass the sauce through a food mill or process in a food processor. Serve the pork with boiled potatoes or macaroni tossed in butter and grated cheese, with the sauce poured over the top.

764

- 1 fillet or boned loin of pork,
  1.5 kg/3¼ lb
- 2 cloves garlic
- 6 black peppercorns
- pinch of paprika
- pinch of dried oregano
- 50 g/2 oz lard or 5 tablespoons
  sunflower oil
- salt

Serves 6

Marinated pork confit
CINTA O LOMO DE CERDO EN ADOBO (PARA CONSERVAR)

Cut the pork into slices and put into a bowl. Pound the garlic with the paprika and a pinch of salt in a mortar. Stir in a few spoonfuls of water, and pour over the pork. Add the oregano and pour in water to cover. Leave to stand in a cool place, but not the refrigerator, for 4–5 days. Drain the slices of pork. Melt the lard or heat the oil in a frying pan, add the pork slices and cook over a medium heat for about 3 minutes on each side. As each slice is cooked, place it in an earthenware pot. Finally, pour in the oil or lard until the meat is completely covered. The meat will keep for a long time like this. To serve, heat the pork slices in the fat covering them.

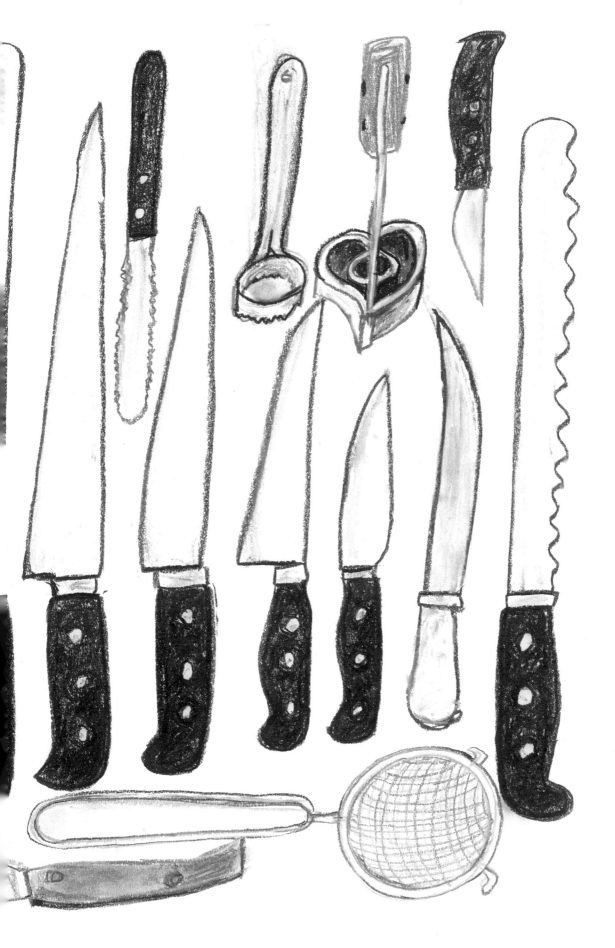

765

Pork medallions with mustard, wine and orange juice

FILETES DE CINTA DE CERDO CON MOSTAZA, SALSA DE VINO Y ZUMO DE NARANJA

- **3 tablespoons Dijon mustard**
- **12 thin pork fillet medallions**
- **200 ml/7 fl oz olive oil**
- **1 onion, chopped**
- **1 tablespoon plain flour**
- **175 ml/6 fl oz white wine**
- **juice of 1 large orange**
- **1 tablespoon very finely chopped fresh parsley**
- **salt**

Serves 6

Spread the mustard over both sides of each medallion and sprinkle with salt. Heat the oil in a heavy-based frying pan. Add the medallions, in batches, and cook over a medium heat for 3–5 minutes on each side, or until done to your liking. Remove with a fish slice and keep warm. Pour off most of the oil from the pan, leaving just enough to cover the base, and reheat. Add the onion and cook over a low heat, stirring occasionally, for 6–8 minutes, until beginning to brown. Stir in the flour and cook, stirring constantly, for 2 minutes. Gradually stir in the wine, orange juice and 450 ml/¾ pint water, a little at a time. Cook, stirring constantly, for 5–10 minutes, until thickened, then pass through a food mill or process in a food processor. Transfer to a clean saucepan. Add the parsley and pork medallions and heat for about 2 minutes. Using a slotted spoon, transfer the pork medallions to a warm serving dish and spoon a little sauce over them. Serve immediately, with Mashed Potato (see recipe 230) offering the remaining sauce separately.

766

Pork medallions with mustard and cream sauce

FILETES DE CERDO CON SALSA DE MOSTAZA Y NATA LÍQUIDA

- **12 thin pork fillet medallions**
- **1 tablespoon lard**
- **4 tablespoons sunflower oil**
- **1 tablespoon Dijon mustard**
- **250 ml/8 fl oz single cream**
- **salt**

Serves 6

Season the pork medallions on both sides with salt about 1 hour before cooking. Melt the lard with the oil, in a frying pan. Add the medallions, in batches, and cook over a medium heat for 3–5 minutes on each side, or until done to your liking. Using a fish slice, transfer the medallions to a serving dish and keep warm. Stir the mustard into the pan, add the cream and cook gently, stirring constantly, but do not allow to boil. Pour the sauce over the pork and serve immediately with fried potatoes, if you like.

767

Pork medallions with béchamel sauce
FILETES DE CINTA DE CERDO CON BECHAMEL

- 12 thin pork fillet medallions
- 1 tablespoon lard
- 4 tablespoons sunflower oil
- 1 tablespoon Dijon mustard
- 1 tablespoon plain flour
- 250 ml/8 fl oz milk
- salt

Serves 6

Season the pork medallions on both sides with salt about 1 hour before cooking. Melt the lard with the oil in a frying pan. Add the medallions, in batches, and cook over a medium heat for 3–5 minutes on each side, or until done to your liking. Using a fish slice, transfer the medallions to a serving dish and keep warm. Stir the mustard into the pan, along with the flour and cook, stirring constantly, for 2 minutes. Gradually stir in the milk, a little at a time. Cook, stirring constantly, for about 6 minutes, until thickened, then pour the sauce over the pork medallions.

768

Pork chops with onion sauce
CHULETAS DE CERDO CON CEBOLLAS EN SALSA

- 6 pork chops
- 250 ml/8 fl oz sunflower oil
- 3 large onions, thinly sliced
- 20 g/¾ oz butter
- 1 tablespoon plain flour
- 200 ml/7 fl oz milk
- salt and pepper

Serves 6

Season the chops with salt and pepper 1 hour before cooking. Reserve 2 tablespoons of the oil and heat the remainder in a frying pan. Add the chops, in batches, and cook over a medium heat for 4–5 minutes on each side. Transfer to a plate and keep warm. Pour off nearly all the oil from the pan, leaving 2–3 tablespoons to cover the base, and reheat. Add the onion and cook over a low heat, stirring occasionally, for about 5 minutes, until softened and translucent. Pour in just enough hot water to cover the onion and simmer for about 15 minutes. Remove the pan from the heat and keep warm. Melt the butter with the reserved oil in another frying pan. Stir in the flour and cook, stirring constantly, for 2 minutes. Gradually stir in the milk, a little at a time. Cook, stirring constantly, for about 5 minutes, until thickened. Stir in the onions with their cooking juices and cook for a further 5 minutes. Put the chops into a warm serving dish, pour the onion sauce over them and serve immediately.

Note: This dish can be garnished with sautéd potatoes.

769 Pork chops with honey, lemon and curry powder

CHULETAS DE CERDO CON MIEL, LIMÓN Y CURRY

- **6 tablespoons olive oil**
- **6 tablespoons clear honey**
- **3 tablespoons lemon juice**
- **1½ teaspoons curry powder**
- **6 pork chops**
- **250 ml/8 fl oz sunflower oil**
- **salt**

Serves 6

Mix together the olive oil, honey, lemon juice, curry powder and a pinch of salt in a non-metallic dish. Add the chops, turning to coat, and set aside to marinate in the refrigerator, turning occasionally, for 30 minutes. Heat the sunflower oil in a frying pan. Drain the chops, reserving the marinade. Add the chops to the pan, in batches, and cook over a medium heat for 4 – 5 minutes on each side. Remove from the pan and keep warm. Pour the reserved marinade into the pan and bring to the boil, then pour over the chops and serve immediately.

Note: This dish may be accompanied by boiled rice or Mashed Potato (see recipe 230). It is also delicious with fried apple slices.

770 Pork chops with prunes

CHULETAS DE CERDO CON CIRUELAS PASAS

- **500 g/1 lb 2 oz prunes, stoned**
- **450 ml/¾ pint red wine**
- **2 cinnamon sticks**
- **2 tablespoons sugar**
- **6 pork chops**
- **50 g/2 oz lard or**
  3 tablespoons olive oil
- **1 kg/2¼ lb small new potatoes**
- **1 tablespoon chopped**
  fresh parsley
- **275 ml/9 fl oz sunflower oil**
- **1 tablespoon potato flour**
  or cornflour
- **salt and pepper**

Serves 6

If using traditional prunes, put them in a bowl, pour in water to cover and leave to soak for at least 6 hours, then drain. If using ready-to-eat prunes, soaking is not necessary. Put the prunes, wine, cinnamon and sugar into a saucepan, pour in water to cover, stir well and cook over a low heat for about 20 minutes, until the prunes are tender. Set aside to cool. Meanwhile, season the chops with salt and pepper 1 hour before cooking. Melt the lard or heat the olive oil in a frying pan. Add the potatoes and cook, occasionally shaking the pan, for 35 – 40 minutes, until tender and golden brown all over. Remove from the heat, season with salt, sprinkle with the parsley and keep warm. Heat the sunflower oil in another frying pan. Add the chops, in batches, and cook over a medium heat for 4 – 5 minutes on each side. Drain the prunes, reserving the cooking liquid. Put the chops on a warm serving dish, and arrange the potatoes on one side of them and the prunes on the other. Gently heat the reserved cooking liquid in a saucepan. Mix the potato flour or cornflour with a little water in a small bowl, stir it into the pan and cook over a low heat, stirring frequently, for a few minutes, until thickened. Pour into a sauce boat and serve.

771

Pork chops with tomato sauce
CHULETAS DE CERDO CON SALSA DE TOMATE

- 6 pork chops
- 120 ml / 4 fl oz olive oil
- 1 onion, chopped
- 6 tomatoes, seeded and chopped
- 1 clove garlic, chopped (optional)
- 120 ml / 4 fl oz white wine
- pinch of mixed dried herbs
  or 1 bouquet garni
  (1 bay leaf and 1 sprig fresh
  thyme, tied together in muslin)
- salt

Serves 6

Season the chops with salt 1 hour before cooking. Heat 2 table-spoons of the oil in a frying pan. Add the onion and cook over a low heat, stirring occasionally, for about 5 minutes, until softened and trans-lucent. Add the tomato, garlic, if using, wine, dried herbs or bouquet garni and a pinch of salt. Mix well, increase the heat to high and cook, stirring occasionally and breaking up the tomato with the side of the spoon, for about 20 minutes. Remove and discard the bouquet garni, if used. Pass the sauce through a food mill or process in a food processor and pour it back into the frying pan. Cook over a low heat, stirring occasionally, until thickened to your liking. Heat the remaining oil in another frying pan. Add the chops, in batches, and cook over a medium heat for 4–5 minutes on each side. Transfer to a warm serving dish, cover each chop with tomato sauce and garnish with Chips (see recipe 242).

772

Pork chops with onion and mustard sauce
CHULETAS DE CERDO CON SALSA DE CEBOLLAS Y MOSTAZA

- 3 tablespoons sunflower oil
- 1 onion, coarsely chopped
- 1 tablespoon plain flour
- 250 ml / 8 fl oz chicken stock
  (home-made or made
  with a stock cube)
- 2 tablespoons white-wine
  vinegar
- 25 g / 1 oz lard or
  2 tablespoons olive oil
- 4 pork chops
- 1 teaspoon Dijon mustard
- salt and pepper

Serves 4

Heat the sunflower oil in a frying pan. Add the onion and cook over a low heat, stirring occasionally, for about 8 minutes, until beginning to brown. Stir in the flour and cook, stirring constantly, for 2 minutes. Gradually stir in the stock, a little at a time. Stir in the vinegar, cover and simmer very gently for 5–6 minutes. Meanwhile, melt the lard or heat the olive oil in another frying pan. Season the chops with salt and pepper, add to the pan and cook over a low heat for about 8 minutes on each side. Transfer the chops to the pan of sauce and simmer over a low heat for 5 minutes. Transfer the chops to a warm serving dish. Stir the mustard into the sauce, then pour it over the chops and serve.

773

Suckling pig
COCHINILLO ASADO

- **1 piglet**
- **generous pinch mixed dried herbs**
- **olive oil, for brushing**
- **250 ml/8 fl oz white wine**
- **salt**

Serves 6

You will require a young piglet about a month and a half old. It should be thoroughly cleaned, wih no hairs or stubble remaining, and halved lengthways. Season generously with salt several hours before roasting. Preheat the oven to 160°C/325°F/Gas Mark 3. Put the dried herbs inside the animal and brush inside and out with the oil. Put the piglet in a large roasting tin and place in the oven. Roast, turning occasionally and basting with the cooking juices, for about 1½ hours. Pour the wine over the skin of the animal and continue to roast, basting frequently, until the wine has all been used up and a meat thermometer inserted into the thickest part of the rump reads 75°C/165°F – 77°C/170°F. Serve the meat carved into large pieces.

Note: The classic method of cooking this dish is to roast a suckling pig in a baker's oven – it tastes much better than when roasted at home, but can be difficult to arrange!

774

Pork hock with sausages, cabbage and potatoes

CODILLOS DE JAMÓN FRESCO CON SALCHICHAS, REPOLLO Y PATATAS

- **1 onion**
- **4 cloves**
- **2 pork hocks**
- **225 g/8 oz streaky bacon in a single piece**
- **2 carrots**
- **1.5 kg/3¼ lb Savoy cabbage, shredded**
- **6 small potatoes**
- **3 tablespoons olive oil**
- **6 frankfurter sausages**
- **salt**

Serves 6

Stud the onion with the cloves. Put the studded onion, pork hocks, bacon and carrots into a flameproof casserole. Pour in 3 litres/5¼ pints water and bring to the boil, then lower the heat and simmer gently for 30 minutes. Bring a large saucepan of salted water to the boil. Add the cabbage pushing it under the surface with a slotted spoon. Cover, bring back to the boil and cook over a high heat for 5 minutes. Remove with a slotted spoon, drain and add to the meat. Simmer gently for a further 20 minutes, then add the potatoes. Cook for a further 30 minutes, until the potatoes are tender but not falling apart. Remove the cabbage with a slotted spoon and set aside. Heat the oil in a frying pan. Prick the frankfurters with a cocktail stick, add to the frying pan and cook over a low heat for a few minutes. Remove from the pan and keep warm. Add the cabbage to the frying pan and cook for a few minutes, then transfer to a warm serving dish. Put the potatoes around the edge. Add the pork hocks and frankfurters to the dish. Cut the bacon into 2 cm/¾-inch strips and sprinkle it over the cabbage. Serve immediately.

Note: Pork hocks are also called shanks, and sometimes knuckles, and come from the hog's lower leg. Use the cooking liquid from this dish to make a delicious soup, with the carrots and any leftover potatoes diced.

775

Sausages in cloaks
SALCHICHAS ENCAPOTADAS

- **12 frankfurter sausages**
- **1 egg, lightly beaten**

Dough:
- **300 g/11 oz plain flour,**
  plus extra for dusting
- **150 g/5 oz butter**
- **½ teaspoon salt**

Makes 12

First make the dough as described in recipe 1, and leave to rest for at least 1 hour. Preheat the oven to 200°C/400°F/Gas Mark 6. Roll out the dough on a lightly floured surface and cut out 12 rectangles measuring about 18 x 16 cm/7 x 6 ¼ inches each. Put a frankfurter on each dough rectangle at an angle. Roll over the dough diagonally, pressing down a little with your fingers to seal. Brush the beaten egg over the sausage rolls, place them on a baking sheet and bake for about 30 minutes, turning them over once the tops have browned and brushing the undersides with the egg. Serve hot.

Note: This dish can made with thawed frozen puff pastry. Bake according to the directions on the packet.

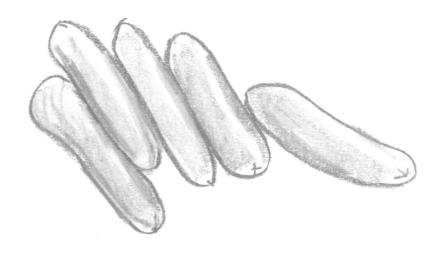

776 Frankfurter sausages with mustard sauce

SALCHICHAS DE FRANKFURT CON SALSA DE MOSTAZA

- **40 g/1½ oz butter**
- **1 tablespoon sunflower oil**
- **1 tablespoon plain flour**
- **250 ml/8 fl oz milk**
- **1 tablespoon Dijon mustard**
- **12 frankfurter sausages**
- **6 slices of bread**
- **3 tablespoons breadcrumbs**
- **salt**

Serves 6

Melt half the butter with the oil in a frying pan. Stir in the flour and cook, stirring constantly, for 2 minutes. Gradually stir in the milk, a little at a time. Cook, stirring constantly, for 5 minutes, then remove the pan from the heat and stir in the mustard. Season to taste with salt and keep warm. Preheat the grill. Bring a saucepan of water to the boil, add the frankfurters and bring back to the boil. Lower the heat so that the water is barely simmering and poach for 6 minutes. Meanwhile, toast the slices of bread on both sides, then place them on a flameproof serving dish. Remove the frankfurters from the water, drain well and halve widthways. Place them on top of the toast. Spoon a little of the sauce over each frankfurter, leaving their ends uncovered. Sprinkle with the breadcrumbs and dot with the remaining butter. Cook under the grill for a few minutes, until the topping is golden brown. Serve immediately.

777

York ham with spinach and Madeira sauce

JAMÓN DE YORK CON ESPINACAS Y SALSA DE VINO MADEIRA

- **6 slices of York or other dry-cured ham**
- **1 quantity Madeira Sauce (see recipe 89)**

Spinach with béchamel sauce:
- **2.5 kg/5½ lb spinach, coarse stalks removed**
- **25 g/1 oz butter**
- **2 tablespoons sunflower oil**
- **1 tablespoon plain flour**
- **275 ml/9 fl oz milk**
- **salt**

Serves 6

First, prepare the spinach with béchamel sauce as described in recipe 393. Put the slices of ham and the Madeira sauce in a saucepan and warm through. To serve, put the creamed spinach on one side, or at each end, of a warm serving dish. Remove the slices of ham from the sauce, using a fork to separate them, fold them in half and place them on the other side of the dish. Reheat the sauce, pour it over the ham and serve.

Note: This dish is best made with small slices of ham that are a little thicker than usual. You can substitute 1 kg/2¼ lb frozen spinach for fresh spinach if you like.

778

York ham with béchamel sauce and mushrooms

JAMÓN DE YORK CON BECHAMEL Y CHAMPIÑONES

- 120 g/4 oz mushrooms, sliced
- 20 g/¾ oz butter
- juice of ½ lemon juice
- 6 thick slices of York or other dry-cured ham
- salt

  Béchamel sauce:
- 25 g/1 oz butter
- 2 tablespoons sunflower oil
- 2 tablespoons plain flour
- 450 ml/¾ pint milk
- 450 ml/¾ pint chicken stock (home-made or made with a stock cube)
- small pinch of curry powder
- salt

Serves 6

Put the mushrooms, butter, lemon juice and a pinch of salt into a saucepan. Cover and cook over a low heat for 6 minutes. Meanwhile, make the béchamel sauce. Melt the butter with the oil in a frying pan. Stir in the flour and cook, stirring constantly, for 2 minutes. Gradually stir in the milk, a little at a time. Cook, stirring constantly, for a further 2 minutes, then gradually stir in the stock, a little at a time. Sprinkle in the curry powder and season to taste with salt. Cook, stirring constantly, for 5 minutes, then add the mushrooms and their cooking juices. Remove the pan from the heat. Pile the slices of ham together and add to the sauce. Leave to stand until they have warmed through. Just before serving, use a fork to separate the slices of ham and place them, one at a time, on a warm serving dish, folding them in half. Reheat the béchamel sauce and pour it over the ham. Serve immediately.

779

Californian ham with pineapple

JAMÓN CALIFORNIANO CON PIÑA

- 1 canned ham, 3 kg/6½ lb
- 300 g/11 oz brown sugar
- 10–14 cloves
- 500 ml/18 fl oz grapefruit juice
- 3–4 canned pineapple slices, drained and halved
- 6 canned or bottled morello cherries in syrup, drained and halved

Serves 10–14

Preheat the oven to 180°C/350°F/Gas Mark 4. Trim the edges of the ham, leaving a piece about the size of a large beef roast. (The trimmings can be used for another recipe). Using a sharp knife, score a diamond pattern in the top. Coat the ham all over with the sugar, pressing it into the meat to prevent it falling off. Insert a clove into each corner of the diamonds. Put the ham into a roasting tin, pour the grapefruit juice over it and bake for 1 hour or according to the instructions on the packet. Arrange the pineapple slices and cherries on top of the ham and return to the oven for about 5 minutes to allow the pineapple to warm through. Cut the ham into slices, place on a warm serving dish and serve with boiled rice or Potato Balls (see recipe 231).

780

Californian ham in beer

JAMÓN CALIFORNIANO EN CERVEZA

- 1 canned ham, 3 kg/6½ lb
- 300 g/11 oz brown sugar
- 10–14 cloves
- 500 ml/18 fl oz beer
- 3–4 canned pineapple slices,
  drained and halved
- 6 canned or bottled morello
  cherries in syrup, drained
  and halved

Serves 10–14

Preheat the oven to 180°C/350°F/Gas Mark 4. Trim the edges of the ham, leaving a piece about the size of a large beef roast. Using a sharp knife, score a diamond pattern in the top. Coat the ham all over with the sugar, pressing it into the meat to prevent it falling off. Insert a clove into each corner of the diamonds. Put the ham into a roasting tin, pour the beer over it and bake for 1 hour or according to the instructions on the packet. Arrange the pineapple slices and cherries on top of the ham and return to the oven for about 5 minutes to allow the pineapple to warm through. Cut the ham into slices, place on a warm serving dish and serve with boiled rice or Potato Balls (see recipe 231).

Ham sandwiches

EMPAREDADOS DE JAMÓN DE YORK

- **3 large slices or 6 small slices of York or other dry-cured ham**
- **12 slices of bread**
- **300 ml/½ pint milk**
- **2 eggs**
- **sunflower oil, for deep-frying**

Makes 6

If using the large slices of ham, cut in half. Using the bread, make six ham sandwiches and soak them briefly in the milk. Put the sandwiches on a work surface, lightly weigh them down with a lid or a plate and leave to stand for 30 minutes. Remove the weight and cut each sandwich diagonally in half. Lightly beat the eggs in a shallow dish. Heat the oil in a deep-fryer or frying pan to 180–190°C/350–375°F or until a cube of day-old bread browns in 30 seconds. One at a time, coat the sandwiches in the beaten egg. Add to the hot oil, in batches, and cook, turning once, until golden brown on both sides. Remove with a fish slice, drain and keep warm while you cook the remaining batches. Serve hot.

782

Ham croquettes
CROQUETAS DE JAMÓN DE YORK

- 2 tablespoons sunflower oil
- 40 g/1½ oz butter
- 4 tablespoons plain flour
- 750 ml/1¼ pints milk
- 2 eggs
- 175 g/6 oz breadcrumbs
- vegetable oil, for deep-frying
- salt
- fresh or deep-fried parsley
  sprigs (see recipe 918), optional

Filling:
- 200 g/7 oz York ham, very finely
  chopped, or 150 g/5 oz Serrano
  ham, finely chopped

Serves 6

Make a béchamel sauce by heating the sunflower oil in a saucepan. Add the butter and when it has melted, stir in the flour with a wooden spoon. Gradually stir in the milk, a little at a time, and cook, stirring constantly, until the béchamel sauce thickens. Season with salt and stir in your chosen filling, then spread the mixture out in a fish kettle or large dish to cool for at least 2 hours. Using two tablespoons, shape scoops of the mixture into croquettes. Finish forming the croquettes with your hands. Beat the eggs in a shallow dish. Spread out the breadcrumbs in another shallow dish. Roll each croquette lightly in the breadcrumbs, then in the beaten egg and finally in the breadcrumbs again, making sure that each one is evenly covered. Heat the vegetable oil in a deep-fryer or deep saucepan to 180–190°C/350–375°F or until a cube of day-old bread browns in 30 seconds. Add the croquettes, in batches of about six at a time, and cook until crisp and golden brown. Using a slotted spoon, transfer them to a large colander set over a baking pan and place in a warm oven until all the croquettes have been cooked. Serve immediately on a dish garnished with sprigs of fresh or deep-fried parsley.

783

Fried fillets of York ham with béchamel sauce
FILETES DE JAMÓN DE YORK CON BECHAMEL Y EMPANADOS

- 3 thick slices of York
  or other dry-cured ham,
  about 120 g/4 oz each
- sunflower oil, for deep frying,
  plus extra for brushing

Béchamel sauce:
- 25 g/1 oz butter
- 2 tablespoons sunflower oil
- 2 heaped tablespoons plain flour
- 500 ml/18 fl oz milk
- salt

Coating:
- 2 eggs
- 80 g/3 oz breadcrumbs

Serves 3

Preheat the oven to 200°C/400°F/Gas Mark 6. Cut the slices of ham into strips about 2 cm/¾ inch wide. Make the béchamel sauce as described in recipe 77. Coat and cook the ham as described in recipe 716. Serve hot, garnished with fried parsley sprigs as described in recipe 918.

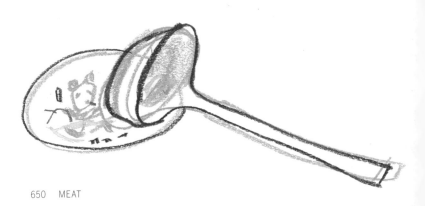

Lamb

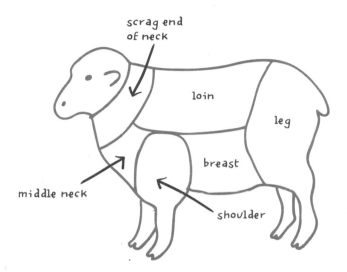

scrag end
of neck

loin

leg

breast

middle neck

shoulder

Spring lamb

This is the name given to lamb that is less than one year old – usually between five and seven months – but has been weaned. It is the most commonly available type of lamb. The meat of spring lamb should be a clear red colour with firm, creamy white fat.
Allow about 200 g/7 oz per serving.

Milk lamb

The meat from milk lamb – an animal 30–40 days old – is a pale rosy pink. Also called milk-fed lamb in some places, it has less nutritional value than spring lamb but is delicious. Although very popular in Spain and other southern European countries, milk lamb is less widely available elsewhere.
Allow about 250 g/9 oz per serving.

Spring lamb

Buying lamb	Suitable cuts	Weight per serving	Cooking time
Fried, grilled or griddled	Best end of neck chops and cutlets, Loin chops	200–225 g/7–8 oz (with bone)	5 minutes on each side (medium)
Roasted *	Leg, Shoulder	200–225 g/7–8 oz (with bone)	20 minutes per 500 g/1 lb 2 oz
Stewed or braised	Shoulder, Scrag and middle neck, Breast	200–225 g/7–8 oz	1¼ hours for stews 1½ hours for casseroles

*Make sure that the oven is preheated

Milk lamb

Buying lamb	Suitable cuts	Weight per serving	Cooking time
Fried, grilled or griddled	Best end of neck chops and cutlets, Loin chops	250 g/9 oz	3 minutes on each side
Roasted *	Half a milk lamb	250 g/9 oz	30 minutes per 500 g/1 lb 2 oz
Stewed or braised	Chops, Shoulder, Scrag and middle neck	250 g/9 oz	1½ hours

*Make sure that the oven is preheated

784

- ½ milk lamb
- 1 clove garlic
- 40 g/1½ oz lard or 3–4
  tablespoons sunflower oil
- 1 teaspoon white-wine vinegar
- salt

Serves 6

Roast milk lamb

CORDERO LECHAL ASADO

Preheat the oven to 180°C/350°F/Gas Mark 4. Rub the lamb with the garlic, spread the lard or oil all over it and sprinkle with salt. Put it into a roasting tin and roast until done to your liking, basting occasionally with the cooking juices, allowing 30 minutes per 500 g/1 lb 2 oz. About 15 minutes before the end of the cooking time, brush the vinegar all over the lamb. Serve hot.

785

- 1 leg of lamb, 1.5–2 kg/
  3¼–4½ lb
- 2 cloves garlic
- 40 g/1½ oz lard or 3–4
  tablespoons sunflower oil
- 1 teaspoon white-wine vinegar
- haricot bean garnish
  (see recipe 221)
- salt

Serves 6–8

Roast leg of spring lamb

PIERNA DE CORDERO PASCUAL ASADA

Rub the lamb all over with the garlic, spread the lard or brush the oil all over it and sprinkle with salt. Leave to stand in the refrigerator for 1 hour. Preheat the oven to 230°C/450°F/Gas Mark 8. Put the lamb into a roasting tin and roast for 15 minutes, then lower the oven temperature to 180°C/350°F/Gas Mark 4. Roast, basting occasionally, until the lamb is cooked to your liking, allowing about 20 minutes per 500 g/1 lb 2 oz. About 15 minutes before the end of the cooking time, brush the vinegar all over the lamb. When the meat is cooked, turn off the oven but leave the lamb to rest in it for about 5 minutes. Remove the leg from the roasting tin and carve, collecting all the juices released. Put a little hot water into the roasting tin, add the juices from the carving and cook over a medium heat, stirring and scraping up any bits from the base of the tin. Garnish the lamb with the haricot bean garnish and serve immediately, offering the sauce separately. The meat can be accompanied by fried or Mashed Potato (see recipe 230), if you like.

Sepulvedana roast lamb

CORDERO ASADO A LA SEPULVEDANA

- 40 g/1½ oz lard or 3–4
  tablespoons sunflower oil
- 1 milk lamb
- salt

  Basting sauce:
- 2 sprigs fresh parsley
- 2 cloves garlic, unpeeled
- 1 bay leaf
- ½ large onion
- 2 tablespoons
  white-wine vinegar
- juice of 1 lemon
- salt, to taste

Serves 6–8

Preheat the oven to 180°C/350°F/Gas Mark 4. Spread the lard or brush the oil all over the lamb, season with salt and put the meat into a roasting tin. Roast for about 15 minutes, until the lamb is beginning to brown. Meanwhile, put all the ingredients for the basting sauce in a saucepan, pour in 275 ml/9 fl oz water and bring to the boil. Lower the heat and simmer for 5 minutes. Remove from the heat and strain into a jug. When the lamb is beginning to brown, pour the basting sauce over it. (You could put some potatoes in the roasting tin around the lamb if you like.) Roast, basting occasionally, until the lamb is cooked to your liking, allowing about 30 minutes per 500 g/1 lb 2 oz. When the lamb is cooked, turn off the oven but leave the lamb to rest in it for about 5 minutes before carving it.

Note: This style of cooking roast lamb is popular in the Sepulvedana region of Spain.

787

Roast lamb with egg and tomato sauce
CORDERO ASADO SERVIDO CON SALSA DE YEMAS Y PURÉ DE TOMATE

- 40g/1½oz lard or 3–4 tablespoons sunflower oil
- 1 leg of lamb, 1.5–2kg/ 3¼–4½lb
- 1 small onion, halved
- 1 bouquet garni (2 sprigs fresh parsley, ½ bay leaf and 1 clove garlic tied together in muslin)
- 175ml/6floz white wine
- 4 tablespoons tomato purée
- 2 egg yolks
- juice of 1 lemon
- 1½ tablespoons chopped fresh parsley
- 25g/1oz butter
- salt and pepper

Serves 6–8

Preheat the oven to 230°C/450°F/Gas Mark 8. Spread the lamb with the lard or brush it with the oil, season with salt and pepper and put the meat into a roasting tin. Put an onion half on either side, add the bouquet garni and roast for 10 minutes. Lower the oven temperature to 180°C/350°F/Gas Mark 4 and roast for a further 15 minutes, then pour the wine over the lamb. Return to the oven and roast, basting occasionally with the cooking juices, for 15 minutes more. Add the tomato purée to the cooking juices and return the lamb to the oven for a further 5–10 minutes, until cooked to your liking. Carve the lamb, place it on a serving dish, cover it with foil and keep warm. Pour the cooking juices into a heatproof bowl and use a tablespoon to skim off the fat from the surface. Set the bowl over a pan of barely simmering water. Beat the egg yolks with the lemon juice and parsley in another bowl. Stir in a little of the cooking juices to prevent the egg yolks curdling, then add to the cooking juices, together with the butter, beating constantly with a whisk. Continue to beat until the sauce is shiny, then remove from the heat and pour into a warm sauce boat. Serve the lamb with the sauce immediately.

788

Stuffed leg of lamb
PIERNA DE CORDERO PASCUAL RELLENA

- 100g/3½oz mushrooms, finely chopped
- 20g/¾oz butter
- juice of ½ lemon
- 6 sausages, skinned
- 5 tablespoons sherry
- pinch of mixed dried herbs
- 1 boned leg of lamb, 1.2–1.5kg/2½–3¼lb
- 40g/1½oz plain flour
- 3 tablespoons olive oil
- salt

Serves 6–8

Preheat the oven to 180°C/350°F/Gas Mark 4. Put the mushrooms, butter, lemon juice and a pinch of salt in a saucepan, cover and cook over a low heat for 6 minutes. Remove the pan from the heat. Mix together the meat from the sausages, half the sherry, the dried herbs and the mushrooms in a bowl, spoon the mixture into the centre of the leg of lamb and sew or tie up the leg with fine kitchen string, forming a neat shape. Season the lamb with salt and lightly coat it in the flour, shaking off any excess. Put the lamb into a roasting tin with the oil and remaining sherry and roast, turning it several times and basting occasionally with the cooking juices, for 1–1¼ hours, until browned all over and cooked to your liking. Lift the lamb out of the roasting tin, remove and discard the string and carve the meat into slices. Make a sauce with the cooking juices as described in recipe 785. Serve the lamb with Chips (see recipe 242) or Mashed Potato (see recipe 230), offering the sauce separately.

789

Roast lamb in a salt and rosemary crust
ASADO DE CORDERO EN COSTRA DE SAL Y ROMERO

- 120 g/4 oz coarse salt
- 1 egg white
- 2 fresh rosemary sprigs
- 250 g/9 oz plain flour
- 1 tablespoon olive oil
- 1 boned rack of lamb,
  bones and fat reserved
- 1 carrot, sliced
- 1 leek , sliced and rinsed well
- 1 clove garlic, lightly crushed
- 50 g/2 oz breadcrumbs
- 1 tablespoon chopped
  fresh parsley
- 2 egg yolks
- salt and pepper

Serves 4

Prepare the salt crust the night before. Mix together the coarse salt and egg white in a bowl, then add the rosemary needles, flour and 5 – 6 tablespoons water. Work the mixture with your fingers until it is even, then leave to stand in the refrigerator overnight (or at least 2 hours). Heat the oil in a saucepan. Add the lamb bones and any scraps of meat and cook over a medium heat, stirring occasionally, for about 10 minutes, until browned. Add the carrot, leek and garlic and cook over a medium heat, stirring occasionally, for about 10 minutes, until browned. Drain off as much fat as possible, and reserve, then pour in just enough water to cover and cook over a medium heat until the liquid has reduced by a third. Strain through a fine sieve into a clean saucepan. Preheat the oven to 220°C/425°F/Gas Mark 7. Mix together the breadcrumbs and parsley. Season the lamb with salt and pepper and sprinkle the breadcrumb and parsley mixture over it, then roll it in its fat. Spread out the salt crust on a clean work surface, wrap the lamb in it, put it in a roasting tin and bake for 20 minutes. Remove from the oven and leave to stand for 25 minutes (the salt crust will keep it warm). Lightly beat the egg yolks with 1 tablespoon water and a pinch of salt in a bowl. Heat the strained liquid and stir 2 tablespoons into the egg yolks, then stir them into the liquid and heat through. Pour into a sauceboat. Break the salt crust and remove the lamb, brushing off all traces of salt. Carve into slices and serve immediately with the sauce.

Note: For a luxurious touch, stir a little single cream and a finely chopped truffle into the sauce.

790

- 1 small head of celery
- 3 carrots
- 1 onion
- 1 teaspoon mixed dried herbs
  or 1 bouquet garni (1 sprig fresh
  parsley, 2 bay leaves,
  1 sprig fresh thyme and 1 clove
  garlic tied together in muslin)
- 4 black peppercorns
- 1 leg of lamb, 1.5–2 kg/
  3¼–4½ lb, boned
- salt

Serves 6–8

English-style leg of lamb

PIERNA DE CORDERO COCIDA A LA INGLESA

Put the celery, carrots, onion, dried herbs or bouquet garni, peppercorns and a pinch of salt into a large saucepan of water, leaving enough room to add the lamb, and bring to the boil. Add the lamb and bring back to the boil, then lower the heat and simmer gently until cooked to your liking, allowing 15 minutes per 500 g/1 lb 2 oz. Lift the lamb out of the pan, drain and carve. Serve hot with mint jelly.

791

- 4 tablespoons olive oil
- 1 leg of lamb, 1.2 kg/2½ lb,
  boned and the bone reserved
- 1 onion
- 3 cloves
- 2 carrots, chopped
- 1 bay leaf
- pinch of mixed dried herbs
- 1 ham hock
- 200 g/7 oz fresh or frozen peas
- 175 ml/6 fl oz white wine
- 8 spinach leaves
- salt and pepper

Serves 4

Leg of lamb with pea sauce

PIERNA DE CORDERO CON SALSA DE GUISANTES

Ask your butcher for the bone when he has removed it from the leg. Heat the oil in a heavy-based saucepan or a cocotte. Add the lamb and cook over a medium heat, turning frequently, for about 10 minutes, until browned all over. Stud the onion with the cloves and add to the pan with the carrot, bay leaf, dried herbs, ham hock and lamb bone. Season with salt and pepper, pour in 500 ml/18 fl oz water and bring to the boil. Add the peas, lower the heat and simmer gently for 45 minutes. Add the wine and simmer for a further 45 minutes. Meanwhile, put the spinach in a saucepan with just the water clinging to its leaves after washing. Add a pinch of salt, cover and cook for 8 minutes. Remove from the heat and drain well, squeezing out as much liquid as possible. Remove the lamb from the pan, wrap in foil and keep warm. Remove and discard the ham hock, lamb bone, carrot, bay leaf and onion (if it has not disintegrated) from the pan. Transfer the cooking liquid to a food processor, add the spinach and process until smooth. Carve the lamb, put it on a warm serving dish and spoon a little of the sauce over it. Serve immediately, offering the remaining sauce separately.

Note: This dish may be accompanied by fried potato balls or steamed potatoes, placed around the edge of the serving dish.

792

Boned shoulder of lamb
PALETILLA DE CORDERO DESHUESADA

- 1 boned shoulder of lamb,
  1–1.2 kg/ 2¼–2½ lb
- 2 cloves garlic
- 40 g/1½ oz lard or 3–4
  tablespoons sunflower oil
- 1 teaspoon white vinegar
- salt

Serves 4–6

Tie the lamb into a neat shape with fine kitchen string. Rub the lamb all over with the garlic, spread the lard or brush the oil all over it and sprinkle with salt. Leave to stand in the refrigerator for 1 hour. Preheat the oven to 230°C/450°F/Gas Mark 8. Put the lamb into a roasting tin and roast for 15 minutes, then lower the oven temperature to 180°C/350°F/Gas Mark 4. Roast, basting occasionally, until the lamb is cooked to your liking, allowing about 20 minutes per 500 g/1 lb 2 oz. About 15 minutes before the end of the cooking time, brush the vinegar all over the lamb. When the meat is cooked, turn off the oven but leave the lamb to rest in it for about 5 minutes. Remove the leg from the roasting tin and carve, collecting all the juices released. Put a little hot water into the roasting tin, add the juices from the carving and cook over a medium heat, stirring and scraping up any bits from the base of the tin. Serve immediately, offering the sauce separately. The meat can be accompanied by fried or Mashed Potato (see recipe 230), if you like.

793

Shoulder of lamb with potato and onion
PALETILLA DE CORDERO CON PATATAS Y CEBOLLA (PANADERA)

- 1 clove garlic
- 1 boned and rolled shoulder of
  lamb, 1.2–1.5 kg/2½–3¼ lb
- 80 g/3 oz lard or 5 tablespoons
  sunflower oil
- 2 large onions, thinly sliced
- 600 g/1 lb 5 oz potatoes,
  preferably new potatoes,
  cut into 1.5-cm/⅝-inch
  thick slices
- 275 ml/9 fl oz chicken stock
  (home-made or made
  with a stock cube)
- salt

Serves 4–6

Preheat the oven to 230°C/450°F/Gas Mark 8. Rub the garlic all over the lamb, then spread some of the lard or oil over it, reserving the remaining lard or oil. Put the lamb into a roasting tin and roast for 10 minutes. Lower the oven temperature to 180°C/350°F/Gas Mark 4 and roast, turning the lamb occasionally, for a further 20 minutes. Meanwhile, melt the remaining lard or heat the remaining oil in a frying pan. Add the onion and cook over a low heat, stirring occasionally, for 6–8 minutes, until beginning to brown. Add the potatoes, increase the heat to medium, season with salt and cook for a further 5–10 minutes. Put the potato slices and onion in the roasting tin around the lamb. Pour the stock over the lamb and return the tin to the oven. Roast, basting three or four times, for a further 20 minutes until the potatoes are tender and the meat is cooked to your liking. Lift the lamb out of the roasting tin, remove and discard the string, carve the meat into slices and put them in the centre of a warm serving dish. Arrange the potatoes and onions around the lamb. Pour the cooking juices into a sauce boat and serve with the roast.

794

Braised shoulder of lamb
PALETILLA DE CORDERO DESHUESADA BRASEADA

- **4 tablespoons olive oil**
- **2 large onions, chopped**
- **1 boned and rolled shoulder of lamb, 1.5–1.8 kg/3¼–4 lb**
- **40 g/1½ oz plain flour**
- **5 tablespoons white wine**
- **450 ml/¾ pint chicken stock (home-made or made with a stock cube)**
- **½ teaspoon mixed dried herbs or 1 bouquet garni (1 sprig fresh parsley, 2 bay leaves, 1 sprig fresh thyme and 1 clove garlic tied together in muslin)**
- **salt**

Serves 6

Heat the oil in a heavy-based saucepan or a cocotte. Add the onion and cook over a low heat, stirring occasionally, for 10 – 12 minutes, until golden brown. Remove with a slotted spoon and set aside. Lightly coat the lamb in the flour, tapping off any excess, add to the saucepan and cook over a medium heat, turning frequently, for 8 – 10 minutes, until evenly browned all over. Return the onion to the pan, pour in the wine and stock and add the dried herbs or bouquet garni and a pinch of salt. Mix well, cover the pan with a tight-fitting lid, increase the heat to medium and bring to the boil. Lower the heat and simmer gently for 45 – 60 minutes, until the lamb is tender. Lift the lamb out of the pan, remove and discard the string, carve the meat into slices and place on a warm serving dish. Remove and discard the bouquet garni, if used, and pass the cooking liquid through a food mill or process in a food processor. Pour the sauce over the meat and serve immediately with fried potatoes or fried whole green peppers.

Note: Some people like to add sliced stoned olives to this dish. Simmer the olives in a little water for 2 minutes, then drain and add to the meat about 5 minutes before the end of the cooking time.

795

Lamb with quinces
CORDERO CON MEMBRILLOS

- juice of 1 lemon
- 12 black peppercorns
- 1 teaspoon Dijon mustard
- 150 ml/¼ pint natural yogurt
- 1 boned leg or shoulder of lamb,
  2 kg/4½ lb
- 6 tablespoons olive oil
- 1 onion, chopped
- 1 carrot, chopped
- 1 leek, chopped and rinsed well
- 1 bulb garlic, unpeeled
- 6 quinces
- 300 ml/½ pint meat stock
  (home-made or made
  with a stock cube)
- 1 bay leaf
- 1 tablespoon sugar
- salt

Serves 4

The night before you are planning to serve, mix together the lemon juice, peppercorns, mustard and yogurt in a bowl. Rub this mixture all over the lamb, put the meat on a plate and leave to marinate overnight in the refrigerator. Remove the lamb from the refrigerator and scrape off the marinade. Heat 4 tablespoons of the oil in a large saucepan. Add the lamb and cook over a medium heat, turning frequently, for 8–10 minutes, until evenly browned all over. Remove from the pan and set aside. Add the onion, carrot, leek, garlic bulb and one of the quinces to the pan and cook over a low heat, stirring occasionally, for 8–10 minutes, until golden brown. Pour in 250 ml/8 fl oz of the stock, add the bay leaf, season with salt and return the lamb to the pan. Cover and simmer gently for 3 hours, until the lamb is tender. Meanwhile, heat the remaining oil in a frying pan. Add the remaining quinces and cook over a low heat, stirring occasionally, for 5 minutes. Add the remaining stock and the sugar and cook, turning the quinces once, for about 10 minutes, until softened. Remove the lamb from the pan, carve into slices and put on a warm serving dish. Place the quinces all around it. Remove and discard the bay leaf from the sauce and pass the sauce through a food mill or process in a food processor. Season with salt if necessary. Serve immediately.

Note: This dish can be made with other fruit, such as pears, peaches, dried peaches or dried apricots.

796

Braised lamb
CORDERO ESTOFADO

- 1.5 kg/3¼ lb stewing lamb,
  such as boneless shoulder,
  breast, middle neck or scrag
  end of neck, cut into pieces
- 175 ml/6 fl oz white-wine vinegar
- 175 ml/6 fl oz olive oil
- 1 bulb garlic, unpeeled
- 1 large onion, halved
- 1 bay leaf
- 1 teaspoon paprika
- salt

Serves 6

Put all the ingredients into a saucepan, mix well and cover the pan. Cook over a low heat, stirring occasionally, for about 2 hours, until the meat is tender. If necessary, add a little hot water during cooking.

797

Lamb stew with peas, artichokes and potatoes

GUISO DE CORDERO CON GUISANTES, ALCACHOFAS Y PATATAS

- **2 shoulders of lamb,**
  each 1.5–1.8 kg/3¼–4 lb,
  cut into pieces
- **1 lemon, halved**
- **1 kg/2¼ lb globe artichokes**
- **5–6 tablespoons olive oil**
- **1 large onion, finely chopped**
- **1 kg/2¼ lb peas, shelled**
- **1 tablespoon plain flour**
- **5 tablespoons white wine**
- **500 ml/18 fl oz sunflower oil**
- **500 g/1 lb 2 oz potatoes, diced**
- **salt**

Serves 6

Ask your butcher to cut the shoulders of lamb into pieces. Squeeze the juice from one of the lemon halves and add it to a large bowl of water. Break off the artichoke stalks and remove the coarse outer leaves. Cut off the tips of the remaining leaves, open them out and remove the chokes. Cut the artichokes lengthways into halves or quarters, depending on their size. Rub them with the remaining lemon half and put them into the acidulated water. Heat the olive oil in a saucepan. Add the onion and cook over a low heat, stirring occasionally, for about 5 minutes, until softened and translucent. Add the lamb and cook over a medium heat, turning frequently, for about 8 minutes, until evenly browned. Drain the artichokes and add them to the pan together with the peas. Stir in the flour and cook, stirring constantly, for 2 minutes. Gradually stir in the wine and add water to cover. Season with salt, cover and cook over a medium-low heat, stirring occasionally, for about 45 minutes. Meanwhile, heat the sunflower oil in a frying pan. Add the potatoes and cook over a low heat for 5–6 minutes without browning. Remove with a slotted spoon, drain well and add to the stew. Mix well, re-cover the pan and cook, stirring occasionally, for a further 20 minutes, until the lamb is tender. Serve in a warm deep dish.

798

Lamb stew with courgettes

RAGÚ DE CORDERO CON CALABACINES

- 2 tablespoons olive oil
- 100 g/3½ oz onion,
  finely chopped
- 150 g/5 oz courgettes, diced
- 1 small aubergine,
  peeled and diced
- 150 g/5 oz green peppers,
  seeded and cut into thin strips
- 150 g/5 oz tomatoes, peeled,
  seeded and diced
- 1 kg/2¼ lb boneless stewing
  lamb, cut into cubes
- 1 sprig fresh thyme
- pinch of paprika
- 6 fresh mint leaves, chopped
- salt and pepper

Serves 4

Heat the oil in a saucepan. Add the onion and cook over a low heat, stirring occasionally, for 5 minutes, until softened and translucent. Add the courgette, aubergine, pepper and tomato and cook, stirring frequently, for 10 minutes. Add the lamb and cook, stirring, for 5 minutes more. Season with salt and pepper, then add the thyme and paprika. Cover the pan and cook over a low heat for 30 minutes, until the lamb is tender. Sprinkle with the mint and serve immediately.

Note: You could add sliced green beans to the stew.

799

Lamb stew with carrots and turnips

GUISO DE CORDERO CON ZANAHORIAS Y NABOS

- **5 tablespoons olive oil**
- **1 onion, chopped**
- **1.5–2 kg/3¼–4½ lb stewing lamb, such as shoulder, breast, middle neck or scrag end of neck, cut into pieces**
- **250 g/9 oz young carrots, thinly sliced**
- **1 clove**
- **1 sprig fresh thyme**
- **1 clove garlic**
- **2 very ripe tomatoes, peeled, seeded and quartered, or 1 tablespoon tomato purée**
- **5 tablespoons white wine**
- **750 g/1 lb 10 oz turnips, diced**
- **400 g/7 oz potatoes, diced**
- **250 ml/8 fl oz chicken stock (home-made or made with a stock cube)**
- **salt**

Serves 6

Heat the oil in a saucepan. Add the onion and cook over a low heat, stirring occasionally, for about 5 minutes, until softened and translucent. Add the lamb and cook over a medium heat, stirring frequently, for about 8 minutes, until evenly browned. Add the carrot, clove, thyme, garlic clove, tomatoes or tomato purée and a pinch of salt and pour in the wine. Cover the pan and cook for 45 minutes. Add the turnip and potato, pour in the stock, re-cover the pan and cook for about 1 hour more, until the lamb is tender. Serve in a warm deep dish, garnished with fried bread (see recipe 130) if you like.

800

Lamb with garlic and tomato
CORDERO AL AJILLO Y TOMATE

- **4 tablespoons olive oil**
- **1.5 kg/3¼ lb stewing lamb,**
  such as boneless shoulder,
  breast, middle neck or scag
  end of neck, cut into pieces
- **1 tablespoon breadcrumbs**
- **1 bulb garlic, peeled**
- **1 veal or chicken stock cube**
  dissolved in 275 ml/9 fl oz
  boiling water
- **salt**

Tomato sauce:
- **3 tablespoons sunflower oil**
- **1 kg/2¼ lb very ripe tomatoes,**
  peeled, seeded and chopped
- **pinch of mixed dried herbs or**
  1 bouquet garni
  (1 bay leaf and 1 sprig fresh
  thyme tied together in muslin)
- **1 teaspoon sugar**
- **salt**

Serves 6

Make a thick tomato sauce as described in recipe 73. Remove and discard the bouquet garni, if used, before processing in a food processor. Heat the oil in a heavy-based saucepan or a cocotte. Add the lamb and cook over a medium heat, stirring occasionally, for about 8–10 minutes, until evenly browned. Sprinkle in the breadcrumbs, add the tomato sauce, garlic cloves and stock and season lightly with salt. Cover and simmer over a low heat for 1½ hours, until the lamb is tender. Remove and discard the garlic and serve immediately accompanied by fried potatoes, boiled rice or triangles of fried bread (see recipe 130).

801

Lamb cutlets with béchamel sauce

CHULETITAS DE CORDERO CON BECHAMEL

- **18 lamb cutlets**
- **sunflower oil, for deep-frying,**
  plus extra for brushing
- **2 eggs**
- **80 g / 3 oz breadcrumbs**
- **salt**

  Béchamel sauce:
- **25 g / 1 oz butter**
- **2 tablespoons sunflower oil**
- **2 tablespoons plain flour**
- **500 ml / 18 fl oz milk**
- **salt**

  Serves 6

Scrape away the meat and connective tissue from the top 5 cm/ 2 inches of the cutlet bones. Season the cutlets with salt. Heat 6 tablespoons of oil in a frying pan. Add the cutlets, in batches, and cook over a medium heat for about 3 minutes on each side, or until cooked to your liking. Remove from the pan and set aside. Reserve the oil in the frying pan. Brush a work surface or chopping board with oil. Make the béchamel sauce. Melt the butter with the oil in another frying pan. Stir in the flour and cook, stirring constantly, for 2 minutes. Gradually stir in the milk, a little at a time. Season with salt and cook, stirring constantly, for about 10 minutes, until thickened. Remove the pan from the heat. Holding the cutlets by the bone, dip them, one at a time, into the béchamel sauce to coat. Put them on to the oiled work surface or chopping board and leave to cool. Beat the eggs in a shallow dish and spread out the breadcrumbs in another shallow dish. Add the remaining oil to the reserved oil in the frying pan or transfer both lots of oil to a deep-fryer and heat until a cube of day-old bread browns in 30 seconds. Coat each lamb cutlet, first in the beaten egg and then in the breadcrumbs. Add to the hot oil, in batches, and cook until golden brown all over. Remove with a fish slice, drain and keep warm while you cook the remaining batches. Serve immediately.

802

Lamb chops with kidneys
CHULETAS DE CORDERO CON RIÑONES

- 65 g/2 ½ oz butter, softened
- 1 tablespoon chopped
  fresh parsley
- 1 tablespoon chopped
  fresh tarragon
- 8 lamb chops
- 6 tablespoons olive oil
- 4 rashers of bacon
- 4 lambs' kidneys, cored
- 16 cherry tomatoes
- salt

Serves 4

Beat the butter with the herbs in a bowl until thoroughly combined. Cover and chill in the refrigerator until required. Season the chops with salt. Heat the oil in a frying pan. Add the chops and cook over a medium heat for about 3 minutes on each side, until evenly browned and cooked to your liking. Remove from the pan and keep warm. Add the bacon and kidneys to the pan and cook for a few minutes on each side, until the bacon is golden brown and the kidneys are just firm. Remove and keep warm. Melt 1 tablespoon of the herb butter in a small saucepan. Add the tomatoes and cook, stirring occasionally, for 3–5 minutes, until softened but not falling apart. Remove the pan from the heat. Divide the chops, bacon, kidneys and tomatoes among four warm individual plates. Top each chop with ½ tablespoon of the remaining herb butter and serve immediately.

POULTRY

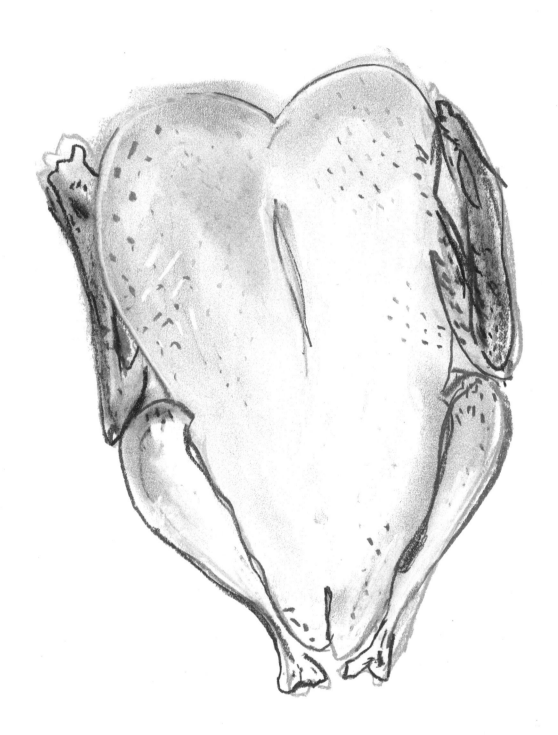

Chicken

History and curious facts

Chicken are domestic birds, members of the Gallinacean family, that originated in Asia more than six thousand years ago. Their heads are adorned with a red crest and they have abundant plumage and strong ankles armed with spurs. These days their size and weight can vary greatly, depending on the breed and place of origin. There are noticeable differences between male and female birds as a result of many years of careful cross-breeding designed to improve either meat or egg production. Today chicken is a very popular foodstuff and a favourite with all consumers, although not long ago it was seen only on the tables of the better-off. This development is the result of research by the agricultural and farming industries into improving the birds' diet and using procedures in their rearing that cut the costs of production and, consequently, the price to the consumer. There are many different breeds of chicken, coming from a variety of geographical locations. The most widespread and intensively reared are the American and Mediterranean breeds, which, in turn, subdivide into different groups with similar sizes and characteristics.

Value for money

The quality of chicken meat is assessed on the age, weight and sex of the bird. Much can be judged from the bird's appearance – the texture of the leg and breast meat and the cleanness and smoothness of the skin. The colour of the skin, however, is not an indicator of quality, some chickens have yellow skin, while others, white. This is the result of variations in feed and processing. .

Intensively reared chickens cost considerably less than organic and free-range birds, and supermarkets, in particular, sell whole chickens and chicken portions at very low prices. In fact, chicken is currently one of the cheapest animal proteins available.

Nutrition

Chicken is a rich source of high-quality protein and provides all the essential amino acids that the human body requires for growth and maintenance. It is relatively low in calories and the white meat, in particular, is low in fat.

Chicken meat (per 100 g/3½ oz)	Calories (kcal)	Protein (grams)	Carbohydrates (grams)	Fats (grams)
Raw chicken	173	20	0.5	10
Roast chicken	192	28	0	10
Braised chicken	233	20	0	17
Fried chicken	305	20	0	25

Chicken is easily digestible. Traditionally, it has been considered suitable for people suffering from a wide variety of digestive disorders and plays in the diet of the elderly. It is a good source of iron, phosphorus and B group vitamins, especially niacin. Younger birds have less fat and are good for roasting and frying, while older birds are better for stewing and braising. The amount of fat varies according to the age, type and quality of the bird. Contrary to popular belief, there is no difference in the nutritional value of white and dark meat, except that the former contains more nicotinic acid, a B group vitamin, than the latter. The white meat contains less connective tissue and fat than the dark meat, making it slightly more digestible. The fat content is higher in the skin than in the rest of the meat, so people with dietary concerns may be advised to eat skinless chicken.

How to prepare

These days, most chickens are sold as oven-ready. However, if this is not the case, here is what you do. To make plucking easier, submerge the chicken in boiling water for 1 minute, holding it by the legs. This process does have the disadvantage that the meat may lose some flavour. After doing this it is advisable to the bird it over a candle or other flame. First, check carefully that no wrapping or identification tag is left on the bird, then begin the process of opening the wings and extending them. Stretch out the bird, holding it by the neck and legs. Pass the whole surface of the chicken over a flame so that all the remaining feathers are scorched, but take care not to burn the skin. The next step is to clean the chicken. Put it on a work surface, breast side up, and then pull hard on the skin of the neck so that it is smooth. Make a small cut near the parson's nose (the protuberance from the rear end of the bird) and under it. Insert two fingers into this hole and pull gently. All the innards should come out together: liver, lungs, heart, etc. Check that nothing remains. To clean the feet, which are delicious when used in stock, submerge them in boiling water for 30 seconds, then use a cloth to pull the skin off as if it were a glove. Another way is to burn the skin and remove it in pieces.

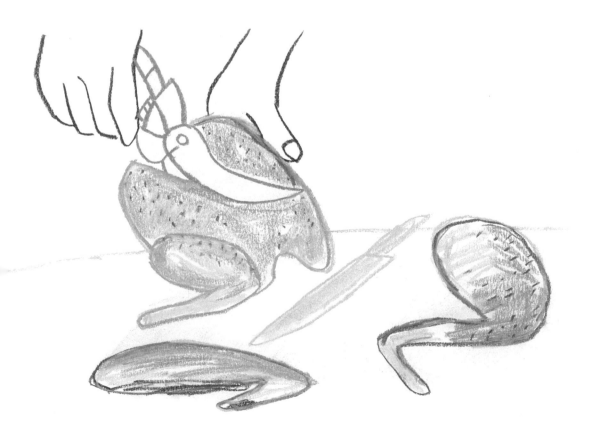

How to truss

Cover the opening at the neck with the overhanging skin. Take quite a long piece of fine kitchen string with both hands. Pass the string under the wings, also catching the neck, then cross it over the central breastbone and fold the wings. Cross it again underneath, bring it back to the top and tie it where the legs join.

How to joint a raw chicken

The most important thing is to find the joints. Put the chicken breast side up, put the knife between the thigh and body, then hold the thigh and dislocate the joint, finally cutting the skin. Repeat on the other side of the bird. Cut the legs in two. Also cut the wings in two, putting the knife in at the joint. Now separate the breast from the back, cutting along the base of the ribs. Pull the chest cavity with your hand. Cut the back section in half by cutting out the backbone. Finally, cut the breasts in half lengthways along the breastbone.

How to carve a roast chicken

This requires a carving board or tray, a carving knife and fork and a warm serving dish. If you're not going to serve the chicken immediately, have some foil ready to cover the dish to prevent it becoming cold. To separate the legs from the body, put the chicken in the centre of the carving board or tray and hold it steady with the carving fork. Then cut through the thigh joints. Next cut off the wings, putting the knife into the joint with the back. Next, separate the breast from the carcass, cutting along the breastbone to separate the breast into two parts. Slip the knife under the breast to separate it from the carcass. Cut the legs in two at the joint. Never cut the cooked chicken on the same board, or with same utensils, that you used to prepare it when raw. Doing so could infect the bird with harmful bacteria that were present in the bird when it was raw. These bacteria are destroyed in cooking, but can be reintroduced if the meat comes into contact with implements used to prepare the raw bird.

803

Chicken cooked in a casserole
POLLO ASADO EN «COCOTTE» O CACEROLA

- 1 chicken, 1.5–2 kg/3¼–4½ lb
- 3 thin rashers of bacon
- 25 g/1 oz lard or butter
- 2 tablespoons sunflower oil
- juice of ½ lemon
- salt

Serves 4–6

Season the chicken with salt and put one bacon rasher over the breast, one over the back and the third inside the chicken. Truss with fine kitchen string as described on page 676. Melt the lard or butter with the oil in a heavy-based saucepan. Add the chicken and cook over a medium heat, turning frequently, for 8–10 minutes, until lightly browned on all sides. Cover the pan and continue to cook over a medium heat, allowing 20 minutes per 500 g/1 lb 2 oz. Check that the chicken is done by piercing the thickest part of the thigh with the point of a sharp knife; if the juices run clear and the meat is no longer pink, the chicken is cooked. Remove the lid from the pan, turn up the heat and brown the chicken, turning frequently. Lift the chicken out of the pan, remove and discard the string and bacon, carve the meat and put it on a warm serving dish. Stir 4–5 tablespoons hot water and lemon juice into the cooking juices and bring to the boil, then pour into a sauce boat and serve with the chicken.

804

Chicken with lemons
POLLO CON LIMONES

- 150 ml/¼ pint olive oil
- 1 chicken, 1.5–2 kg/3¼–4½ lb
- 1 large onion, finely chopped
- 3 lemons, cut into quarters
- 175 ml/6 fl oz white wine
- 250 ml/8 fl oz chicken stock
  (home-made or made
  with a stock cube)
- 1 bay leaf
- 1 tablespoon sugar
- salt

Serves 4

Heat the oil in a heavy-based saucepan or a cocotte. Add the chicken and cook over a medium heat, turning frequently, for 8–10 minutes, until browned all over. Remove from the pan and keep warm. Add the onion to the pan and cook over a low heat, stirring occasionally, for 6–7 minutes, until lightly browned. Put three of the lemon quarters into the cavity of the chicken and return the chicken to the pan. Put the remaining lemon quarters around it. Pour the wine and then the stock into the pan, add the bay leaf, sprinkle in the sugar and season with salt. Cover and simmer for about 45 minutes, until the chicken is cooked through and tender. Check that the chicken is done by piercing the thickest part of the thigh with the point of a sharp knife; if the juices run clear and the meat is no longer pink, the chicken is cooked. Lift the chicken out of the pan, carve the meat and put it on a warm serving dish. Strain the sauce through a coarse sieve into a sauce boat. Serve the chicken with the sauce, accompanied by yellow rice (see recipe 191) or croûtons.

805 Roast chicken with grapefruit or oranges

POLLO ASADO CON POMELOS O NARANJAS

- 1 chicken, 1.5–1.8 kg/3¼–4 lb
- 2 tablespoons brandy
- 2 grapefruit or 4 oranges
- 2 rashers of bacon
- 50 g/2 oz lard or 3 tablespoons sunflower oil
- 4–5 watercress sprigs
- salt and pepper

Serves 6

Preheat the oven to 200°C/400°F/Gas Mark 6. Season the chicken inside and out with salt and pepper and place in a roasting tin. Peel one of the grapefruit or two of the oranges and cut out the segments, discarding the bitter white pith. Heat the brandy in a small saucepan for a few seconds and ignite. When it has burned for a moment, pour it into the chicken and add the citrus segments. Put one of the bacon rashers over the breast of the chicken and the other over the back and spread with the lard. Truss with fine kitchen string as described on page 676. Roast, turning occasionally and basting with the cooking juices, for 30 minutes. Meanwhile, squeeze the juice from the remaining citrus fruit. Add to the cooking juices and continue to roast the chicken, turning occasionally and basting, for a further 30 minutes, until the chicken is cooked through and tender. Check that the chicken is done by piercing the thickest part of the thigh with the point of a sharp knife. Lift out the meat, discard the string and bacon, and carve the meat. Serve with the fruit segments and watercress.

806 Fried poussins

POLLITOS FRITOS

- 2 poussins, 750 g/1 lb 10 oz each
- 4 tablespoons olive oil
- 1 lemon, sliced
- 1 onion, sliced
- 7 sprigs fresh parsley
- sunflower oil, for deep-frying
- 50 g/2 oz plain flour mixed with 3 tablespoons breadcrumbs
- salt and pepper

Tomato sauce:
- 2 tablespoons sunflower oil
- 1 onion, finely chopped
- 750 g/1 lb 10 oz peeled, seeded and chopped tomato
- 1 teaspoon sugar
- salt

Serves 4

Using poultry shears or strong kitchen scissors, cut each poussin in half. Season with salt and pepper, put the halves into a deep dish and pour the olive oil over them. Add the lemon, onion and three of the parsley sprigs. Leave to marinate in the refrigerator, turning occasionally, for 2 hours. Meanwhile, make the tomato sauce as described in recipe 73. Heat the sunflower oil in a deep-fryer or frying pan to 160–170°C/325–340°F or until a cube of day-old bread browns in 45 seconds. Drain the poussin halves, coat them in the flour and breadcrumb mixture and add to the hot oil. Cook for 10 minutes, then increase the temperature to 180–190°C/350–375°F and cook for a further 5 minutes, until the poussins are cooked through and golden brown. Check by piercing the thickest part of the thigh with the point of a sharp knife; if the juices run clear and the meat is no longer pink, the poussins are cooked. Place the poussins on a serving dish and keep warm. Tie the remaining sprigs of parsley together with fine thread, add to the hot oil and fry for 1–2 minutes. Reheat the tomato sauce and pour into a sauce boat. Garnish the poussins with the fried parsley and serve immediately, offering the sauce separately.

807

Stuffed Andalusian chicken

POLLO RELLENO A LA ANDALUZA

- **6 tablespoons olive oil**
- **500 g/1 lb 2 oz tart apples, peeled, cored and chopped**
- **150 g/5 oz Serrano ham, diced**
- **40 g/1½ oz pine nuts**
- **1 tablespoon chopped fresh parsley**
- **¼ teaspoon ground cloves**
- **350 ml/12 fl oz amontillado or other sherry**
- **50 ml/2 fl oz anisette**
- **1 chicken, 1.5 kg/3¼ lb**
- **50 g/2 oz lard or 3 tablespoons sunflower oil**
- **1 large onion, cut into 2–3 pieces**
- **salt and pepper**

Serves 6

Heat the oil in a saucepan. Add the apple and cook over a low heat for 2 minutes. Add the ham, pine nuts, parsley and cloves, season with salt and pepper and cook, stirring occasionally, for 3–4 minutes. Pour in half the sherry and the anisette, stir well, cover and simmer, stirring occasionally, for 30 minutes. Remove from the heat and leave to cool slightly. Preheat the oven to 200°C/400°F/Gas Mark 6. Stuff the chicken with the mixture, reserving any extra cooking liquid. Sew up the opening or secure with skewers. Spread the lard or brush the oil all over the bird and place it in a roasting tin. Pour the reserved apple cooking liquid around the chicken. Season with salt and put the pieces of onion on either side of the chicken. Roast, turning occasionally, for 20 minutes, then pour the remaining sherry over the chicken. (If the tips of the legs, start to brown during cooking, cover them in foil.) Return to the oven and roast, basting occasionally, for about 40 minutes, until the chicken is tender and cooked through. Check that it is done by piercing the thickest part of the thigh with the point of a sharp knife; if the juices run clear and the meat is no longer pink, the chicken is cooked. Carve the chicken and spoon out the stuffing on to a warm serving dish. Serve immediately with the sauce.

Chicken with mushroom sauce

POLLO CON SALSA DE CHAMPIÑON

- 5 tablespoons olive oil
- 2.5 kg/5½ lb chicken pieces
- 1 small onion,
  very finely chopped
- 1 x 900-ml/1½-pint packet of
  dehydrated mushroom soup
- 175 ml/6 fl oz white wine
- 750 ml/1¼ pints hot water
- 1 bouquet garni (1 clove garlic,
  1 bay leaf, 1 sprig fresh thyme
  and 1 sprig fresh parsley tied
  together in muslin)
- 300 g/11 oz mushrooms, sliced
- 25 g/1 oz butter
- juice of ½ lemon
- 175 ml/6 fl oz single cream
  (optional)
- salt

Serves 8

Heat the oil in a saucepan. Add the pieces of chicken, in batches, and cook over a medium heat, turning frequently, for 8–10 minutes, until evenly browned. Remove from the pan and set aside. Add the onion and cook over a low heat, stirring occasionally, for 7–8 minutes, until beginning to brown. Return the chicken pieces to the pan. Mix together the soup, wine and hot water in a bowl and pour the mixture over the chicken. Add the bouquet garni and lightly season with salt. Cover and cook over a medium heat for 35–60 minutes, until the chicken is tender. Check that it is done by piercing the thickest part of the thigh with the point of a sharp knife; if the juices run clear and the meat is no longer pink, the chicken is cooked. Meanwhile, put the mushrooms, butter, lemon juice and a pinch of salt into a saucepan and cook over a low heat for 6 minutes. Just before serving, remove and discard the bouquet garni, add the mushrooms and their cooking juices to the chicken and stir in the cream if using. Mix well and serve in a warm deep dish. The dish may be garnished with triangles of fried bread (see recipe 130) or served with boiled rice (see recipe 173).

809

Chicken with leeks and cream
POLLO CON PUERROS Y NATA

- **8 leeks, trimmed and halved lengthways and rinsed well**
- **175 ml/6 fl oz olive oil**
- **1 chicken, quartered**
- **1 tablespoon plain flour**
- **5 tablespoons white wine**
- **10 black peppercorns**
- **175 ml/6 fl oz single cream**
- **salt**

Serves 4

Cut off the white parts of the leeks, cut them into 2-cm/¾-inch pieces and set aside. Cook the green parts in salted boiling water for about 15 minutes, until tender. Drain well and set aside, covered to prevent them drying out. Heat the oil in a heavy based saucepan or a cocotte. Add the chicken portions and cook over a medium heat, turning frequently, for 8–10 minutes, until evenly browned. Remove from the pan and set aside. Drain off nearly all the oil from the pan, leaving about 4 tablespoons, and reheat. Add the white parts of the leeks and cook over a low heat, stirring occasionally, for 8 minutes. Stir in the flour, return the chicken to the pan and pour in the wine and 175 ml/6 fl oz water. Add the peppercorns, cover the pan and cook for about 30–40 minutes, until the chicken is cooked through and tender. Check that it is done by piercing the thickest part with the point of a sharp knife; if the juices run clear and the meat is no longer pink, the chicken is cooked. Add the reserved leeks and the cream and heat through, shaking the pan gently. Serve immediately.

810

Chicken with dried porcini, shallots, cream and egg

POLLO EN SALSA CON SETAS SECAS, CEBOLLITAS, NATA Y YEMAS

- 50 g/2 oz dried porcini
- 150 ml/¼ pint sunflower oil
- 1.6 kg/3½ lb chicken pieces
- 18 shallots
- 250 ml/8 fl oz white wine
- 1 teaspoon sugar
- 20 g/¾ oz butter
- 175 ml/6 fl oz single cream
- 2 egg yolks
- juice of ½ lemon
- 1 tablespoon cornflour
- 6 triangles of fried bread
  (see recipe 130)
- salt and pepper

Serves 6

Put the dried porcini into a bowl, add warm water to cover and leave to soak for 15 minutes. Drain well. Heat 7 tablespoons of the oil in a saucepan. Add the pieces of chicken, in batches, and cook over a medium heat, turning frequently, for 8–10 minutes, until evenly browned all over. Return all the chicken pieces to the pan, add half of the shallots and cook, occasionally shaking the pan, for 8–10 minutes, until golden brown. Pour in the wine and 150 ml/¼ pint water, add the porcini and season with salt and pepper. Cover and cook over a low heat for 20–30 minutes. Check that it is done by piercing the thickest part of the thigh with the point of a sharp knife; if the juices run clear and the meat is no longer pink, the chicken is cooked. Put the remaining shallots into a saucepan, pour in water to cover and add the sugar, butter and a pinch of salt. Cook over a low heat for about 20 minutes, until tender, then drain. Heat the remaining oil in a frying pan, add the drained shallots and cook over a low heat, stirring occasionally, for 5–8 minutes, until golden brown. Remove the pan of chicken from the heat. Lift out the pieces of chicken, set aside in a serving dish and keep warm. Strain the cooking liquid into a bowl. Beat the cream with the egg yolks and lemon juice in a bowl. Mix the cornflour with 1 tablespoon water in another bowl, then stir in the strained cooking liquid. Pour into a saucepan and bring to the boil, stirring constantly, then gradually stir into the cream and egg yolk mixture, a little at a time. Put the triangles of fried bread and the browned shallots around the edge of the serving dish, pour the sauce over the chicken and serve immediately.

Note: You can use 300 g/11 oz fresh porcini instead of dried mushrooms, if you like. They do not need to be soaked.

811

📷

Braised chicken with pine nuts, green peppers and tomatoes

GUISO DE POLLO CON PIÑONES, PIMIENTOS VERDES Y TOMATES

- 2 onions, chopped
- 1.5–1.8 kg/3¼–4 lb chicken pieces
- 4 tomatoes, peeled, seeded and chopped
- 3 green peppers, seeded and thinly sliced into rings
- 1 tablespoon breadcrumbs
- 50 g/2 oz pine nuts
- ¼ teaspoon mixed dried herbs or 1 bouquet garni (1 sprig fresh thyme, 2 bay leaves and 1 sprig fresh parsley tied together in muslin)
- 2 cloves garlic
- 175 ml/6 fl oz olive oil
- 2 chicken stock cubes
- 175 ml/6 fl oz white wine
- salt and pepper

Serves 6

Preheat the oven to 180°C/350°F/Gas Mark 4. Put the onion into a casserole, place the pieces of chicken on top and add the tomato and green pepper. Sprinkle with the breadcrumbs, pine nuts and dried herbs or bouquet garni, and season with salt and pepper. Put the garlic cloves among the pieces of chicken, pour the oil over the top and mix well. Put the casserole into the oven and cook for 15 minutes. Dissolve the stock cubes in 3 tablespoons hot water. Remove the casserole from the oven, stir well and add the wine and stock. Return to the oven and cook, stirring occasionally, for a further 20–30 minutes. Remove and discard the bouquet garni, if used, and try to put the rings of pepper back on top of the chicken, then check that it is done by piercing the thickest part of the thigh with the point of a sharp knife; if the juices run clear and the meat is no longer pink, the chicken is cooked. Serve immediately, straight from the casserole.

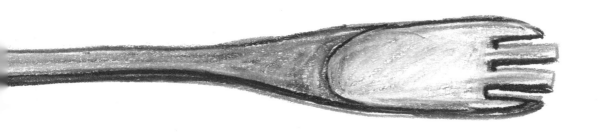

812

Chicken in sauce
POLLO EN SALSA

- 250 ml/8 fl oz sunflower oil
- 1.5–2 kg/3¼–4½ lb chicken pieces
- 2–3 slices of bread, crusts removed
- 1 onion
- 1 small clove garlic
- 2 sprigs fresh parsley
- pinch of saffron powder
- 175 ml/6 fl oz white wine
- 1 teaspoon mixed dried herbs or 1 bouquet garni (1 sprig fresh thyme, 2 bay leaves and 1 sprig fresh parsley tied together in muslin)
- 1 teaspoon very finely chopped parsley
- salt

Serves 6

Heat the oil in a frying pan. Add the pieces of chicken, in batches, and cook over a medium heat, turning fr equently, for 8–10 minutes, until evenly browned. Remove from the pan and set aside. Add the bread to the pan and cook until golden brown on both sides. Remove from the pan and set aside. Drain off and reserve most of the oil from the frying pan, leaving just enough to cover the base, and reheat. Add the onion and cook for 4–6 minutes, until beginning to brown. Remove with a slotted spoon and transfer to a mortar. Add the garlic to the pan and cook for a few minutes, until beginning to brown. Transfer to the mortar along with the parsley sprigs, saffron and fried bread and pound. Put 3 tablespoons of the reserved oil into a large, deep saucepan and heat. Add the chicken pieces and pour the wine over them. Gradually stir 750 ml/1¼ pints water into the mixture in the mortar, then pass it through a food mill or process in a food processor and add to the chicken. Mix well and add the dried herbs or bouquet garni. If necessary, add some water so that the chicken is covered. Season with salt, stir well and bring to a gentle simmer, then cook, partially covered, for 20 minutes. Sprinkle with the chopped parsley and cook for a further 10 minutes, until the chicken is tender but not falling apart. Check that it is done by piercing the thickest part with the point of a sharp knife; if the juices run clear and the meat is no longer pink, the chicken is cooked. Remove the bouquet garni, if used. Serve in a warm deep dish with boiled rice served separately.

813

Chicken casserole

POLLO EN SALSA AL HORNO

- **40 g/1½ oz plain flour**
- **1. 8 kg/4 lb chicken pieces**
- **250 ml/8 fl oz sunflower oil**
- **25 g/1 oz lard or butter**
- **1 small onion,**
  very finely chopped
- **1 clove garlic**
- **2 sprigs fresh parsley**
- **pinch of saffron threads**
- **175 ml/6 fl oz white wine**
- **salt**

Serves 6

Reserve 1 tablespoon of the flour. Season the chicken pieces with salt and coat them in the remaining flour, shaking off any excess. Heat the oil with the lard or butter in a frying pan. Add the pieces of chicken and cook over a medium heat, turning frequently, for 8–10 minutes, until evenly browned. Transfer to a casserole. Preheat the oven to 180°C/350°F/Gas Mark 4. Add the onion to the frying pan and cook over a low heat, stirring occasionally, for about 10 minutes, until golden brown. Stir in the reserved flour and cook, stirring constantly, for 2 minutes, then remove the pan from the heat. Crush the garlic with the parsley and saffron in a mortar and stir in the wine. Return the frying pan to the heat and gradually stir in the wine mixture. Bring to the boil, stirring constantly, then pour the mixture over the pieces of chicken. Put the casserole into the oven and cook for 30–45 minutes, until the chicken is cooked through and tender. Check that it is done by piercing the thickest part with the point of a sharp knife; if the juices run clear and the meat is no longer pink, the chicken is cooked. Serve immediately straight from the casserole.

Note: This dish can be made in advance and refrigerated up to the stage where the chicken goes into the oven.

Roast chicken with orange juice

POLLO ASADO CON SALSA DE ZUMO DE NARANJAS

- **1 chicken, about 1.6 kg / 3 ½ lb**
- **25 g / 1 oz lard or 2 ½ tablespoons sunflower oil**
- **3 thin rashers of bacon**
- **1 orange, sliced**
- **salt**

Sauce:
- **1 ½ tablespoons icing sugar**
- **1 tablespoon white-wine vinegar**
- **juice of 2 large oranges**
- **½ teaspoon meat extract**
- **1 teaspoon potato flour**

Serves 6

Preheat the oven to 200°C/400°F/Gas Mark 6. Season the chicken with salt and spread the lard or brush the oil all over it. Put one of the bacon rashers over the breast, one over the back and the third inside the chicken. Truss the chicken with fine kitchen string as described on page 676, and put into a roasting tin. Roast, turning and basting occasionally with the cooking juices, for about 1 hour, until cooked through and tender. Check that the chicken is done by piercing the thickest part of the thigh with the point of a sharp knife; if the juices run clear and the meat is longer pink, the chicken is cooked. (If the tips of the legs start to brown during cooking, cover them in foil.) Remove the chicken from the roasting tin, cover with foil and keep warm. Skim off the fat from the cooking juices. Stir 3–4 tablespoons hot water into the roasting tin, scraping up any bits from the base. Heat the icing sugar in a frying pan and when it begins to brown, remove the pan from the heat and stir in the vinegar. Immediately add the orange juice, 100 ml / 3 ½ fl oz water and the meat extract. Mix well, return the pan to the heat, cover and simmer gently for 5 minutes. Halve the orange slices. Carve the chicken, place on a warm serving dish and garnish with the half slices of orange and little mounds of mashed potato. Cover and keep warm. Mix the potato flour with a little water in a bowl, then stir into the sauce. Cook over a low heat, stirring constantly, for 2 minutes, then stir in the cooking juices from the roasting tin. Serve the chicken, offering the sauce separately.

Note: When cooking several chickens, it is not necessary to multiply the sauce ingredients by the same amount. Among other things, the cooking juices will not double for each extra chicken. For 3 chickens, use 2 tablespoons sugar, the juice of 3 oranges, 2 tablespoons white-wine vinegar, 1 teaspoon meat extract and 2 teaspoons potato flour.

Chicken cooked with shallots and tomatoes

POLLO GUISADO CON CEBOLLITAS Y TOMATE

- **4 tablespoons olive oil**
- **2.5 kg/5½ lb chicken pieces**
- **100 g/3½ oz streaky bacon, diced**
- **6 small tomatoes, peeled**
- **pinch of mixed dried herbs**
- **120 ml/4 fl oz white wine**
- **8 shallots**
- **15 g/½ oz butter**
- **100 g/3½ oz canned red pepper, drained and cut into thin strips**
- **1 tablespoon chopped fresh parsley**
- **salt**

Serves 6–8

Heat the oil in a saucepan. Add the pieces of chicken, in batches, and cook over a medium heat, turning frequently, for 8–10 minutes, until golden brown all over. Return all the chicken pieces to the pan, add the bacon and cook for a few minutes, then add the tomatoes. Season with salt, add the dried herbs, stir well and pour in the wine and 120 ml/4 fl oz water. Cover the pan and cook over a medium heat for about 45 minutes, until the chicken is tender but not falling apart. Check that it is done by piercing the thickest part of the thigh with the point of a sharp knife; if the juices run clear and the meat is no longer pink, the chicken is cooked. Meanwhile, put the shallots, butter and a pinch of salt into a saucepan and pour in water to cover. Bring to the boil, lower the heat and simmer for about 20 minutes, then drain. When the chicken is done, add the shallots, red pepper and parsley. Stir and heat through briefly, then serve.

Chicken with curry sauce

POLLO CON SALSA AL CURRY

- 1 chicken, 1.8 kg/4 lb
- 3 rashers of bacon
- 25 g/1 oz lard or 2½ tablespoons sunflower oil
- salt

Sauce:
- 25 g/1 oz butter
- 2 tablespoons sunflower oil
- 1 tablespoon plain flour
- 120 ml/4 fl oz milk
- 250 ml/8 fl oz chicken stock (preferably home-made)
- ¼ teaspoon curry powder
- 1 egg yolk
- salt

Rice:
- 500 g/1 lb 2 oz long-grain rice
- 50 g/2 oz butter
- 100 g/3½ oz canned peas, drained
- salt

Serves 6

Season the chicken with salt and put one of the bacon rashers over the breast, one over the back and the third inside the chicken. Truss with fine kitchen string as described on page 676. Melt the lard or heat the oil in a heavy-based saucepan or a cocotte and cook the chicken as described in recipe 803 for about 45 minutes. Check that it is done by piercing the thickest part of the thigh with the point of a sharp knife; if the juices run clear and the meat is no longer pink, the chicken is cooked. Meanwhile, cook the rice as described in the first part of recipe 173. To make the sauce, melt the butter with the oil in a frying pan. Stir in the flour and cook, stirring constantly, for 2 minutes. Gradually stir in the milk and then the stock, a little at a time. Cook, stirring constantly, for about 10 minutes, until thickened. Season to taste with salt and stir in the curry powder. Lightly beat the egg yolk in a bowl, stir in a little of the sauce, then add to the pan. Remove from the heat. Lift out the chicken from the pan, remove and discard the string and bacon and carve the meat. Transfer the meat to a serving dish and keep warm. Skim off the fat from the cooking juices, then stir into the curry sauce and pour it over the chicken. Serve immediately with the rice.

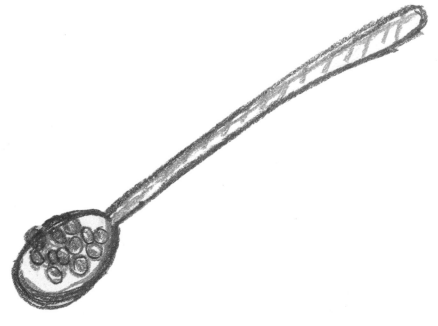

817

Chicken cooked in beer with onions

POLLO GUISADO CON CERVEZA Y CEBOLLAS

- 1 chicken, 1.8 kg/4 lb
- 250 ml/8 fl oz sunflower oil
- 500 g/1 lb 2 oz onions, thinly
  sliced and pushed out into rings
- 350 ml/12 fl oz beer
- 1 teaspoon potato flour
- ½ teaspoon meat extract
- salt

Serves 6

Season the cavity of the chicken with salt and truss with fine kitchen string as described on page 676. Heat the oil in a heavy based sauce-pan or a cocotte. Add the chicken and cook over a medium heat, turning frequently, for 8–10 minutes, until evenly browned all over. Remove from the pan and set aside. Drain off most of the oil from the pan, leaving just enough to cover the base, and reheat. Add the onion and cook over a low heat, stirring occasionally, for about 5 minutes, until softened and translucent. Return the chicken to the pan and pour in the beer. Lightly season with salt, cover and bring to the boil, then lower the heat and simmer, turning and basting the chicken occasionally, for about 45 minutes, until tender. Check that it is done by piercing the thickest part of the thigh with the point of a sharp knife; if the juices run clear and the meat is no longer pink, the chicken is cooked. Lift out the chicken, remove and discard the string, carve the meat and put it on a warm serving dish. Strain the sauce into a clean pan and spoon the onion around the chicken. Mix the potato flour with 1 tablespoon water in a bowl and stir into the cooking liquid. Bring to the boil, stirring constantly, and cook for 2 minutes. Stir in any juices released when the chicken was carved, then pour into a sauce boat and serve with the chicken.

818

Chicken supremes with grapefruit sauce

SUPREMAS DE AVE CON SALSA DE POMELOS

- 2 tablespoons olive oil
- 4 chicken breast quarters
- 2 grapefruit
- 4 tablespoons single cream
- pinch of ground turmeric
- pinch of saffron threads
- salt and pepper

Serves 4

Heat the oil in a frying pan. Add the chicken pieces and cook over a medium heat for 6 minutes, then turn them over, season with salt and cook the other sides for a further 6–10 minutes. Remove from the pan and set aside. Check that it is done by piercing the thickest part of the thigh with the point of a sharp knife; if the juices run clear and the meat is no longer pink, the chicken is cooked. Squeeze the juice from one of the grapefruit. Peel the other grapefruit and cut out the segments from between the membranes discarding the bitter white pith. Drain off nearly all the oil from the pan and reheat. Stir in the grapefruit juice and cream and cook until reduced and thickened, but do not allow to boil. Season with salt and pepper and stir in the turmeric and saffron. Return the chicken to the pan and heat through for a few minutes. Add the grapefruit segments and serve immediately.

819

Chicken breasts with liver and bacon

PECHUGAS DE POLLO ASADAS CON HIGADITOS Y BACON

- 6 boneless chicken breasts
- ½ teaspoon mixed dried herbs
- 6 chicken livers, trimmed
- 6 thin rashers of bacon
- 65g/2½ oz lard or 5 tablespoons sunflower oil
- salt

Serves 6

Preheat the oven to 200°C/400°F/Gas Mark 6. Season the chicken breasts with salt and sprinkle with the dried herbs. Place a chicken liver in the centre of each breast, then roll the breast up. Wrap a rasher of bacon around the roll and tie securely with fine kitchen string. Spread each roll with a little lard or oil and put into a roasting tin. Roast, turning the rolls occasionally and basting them with the cooking juices, for 30 minutes. Lift out the chicken rolls from the roasting tin, remove and discard the string, place on a serving dish and keep warm. Skim off the fat from the cooking juices in the roasting tin, add 4–5 tablespoons hot water and bring to the boil, stirring constantly. Pour over the chicken rolls and serve immediately with straw potatoes (see recipe 243) or Baked Tomatoes with Parsley and Garlic (see recipe 453).

820

Chicken quesadillas

QUESADILLAS DE POLLO

- 1 tablespoon corn oil
- 2 skinless boneless chicken breasts, diced
- 250g/9oz canned sweetcorn, drained
- 4 flour tortillas
- 200g/7oz gruyere cheese, grated

Salsa:
- 3–4 large ripe tomatoes, peeled and chopped
- 10 fresh green chillies, seeded and chopped
- ¼ onion, chopped
- 1 bunch of fresh coriander, chopped
- salt

Serves 4

First make the salsa. Mix together the tomato, chillies, onion and coriander in a bowl. Season to taste with salt, stir in 150ml/¼ pint water and set aside. Heat the oil in a non-stick frying pan. Add the chicken and cook over a low heat, stirring occasionally, for about 5 minutes, until beginning to brown and cooked through. Add the sweetcorn and salsa, mix well and heat through. Warm the tortillas in the microwave or in a heavy-based frying pan, following the instructions on the packet, then place each one on a plate. Spoon the chicken mixture into the middle of each tortilla, sprinkle with some of the gruyere, then roll up the tortilla or fold it into a triangle and serve immediately.

Note: This dish, of Mexican origin, uses tortillas, which are thin, flat, round breads, made from flour or cornmeal.

821

Chicken with cucumber

POLLO CON PEPINO

- 1 cucumber,
  peeled, seeded and diced
- 3 tablespoons olive oil
- 4 skinless boneless chicken
  breasts, cut into strips
- 2 shallots, chopped
- juice of 3 lemons
- 500 ml/18 fl oz chicken stock
  (home-made or made
  with a stock cube)
- 6 fresh mint leaves, chopped
- salt and pepper

Serves 4

Cook the cucumber in salted boiling water for 3 minutes, then drain and set aside. Heat the oil in a deep frying pan. Add the strips of chicken and cook over a medium heat, stirring frequently, for 5 minutes, until golden brown and cooked through. Remove from the pan and set aside. Add the shallots to the pan and cook over a low heat, stirring occasionally, for about 5 minutes, until softened and translucent. Add the lemon juice and stock, return the chicken to the pan, season with salt and pepper and cook over a low heat for 10 minutes. Add the cucumber and cook for a further 5 minutes. Sprinkle with the mint and serve.

822

Chicken supreme

SUPREMA DE POLLO

- 4 chicken breasts
- 2 large carrots,
  cut into large pieces
- 1 large onion, cut into 4 wedges
- 1 chicken stock cube
- truffle slices (optional)
- salt

Supreme sauce:
- 25 g/1 oz butter
- 1½ tablespoons plain flour
- 2 egg yolks
- salt

Serves 4

Put the chicken breasts into a saucepan, pour in water to cover and add the carrot, onion, stock cube and a small pinch of salt. Bring to the boil, then lower the heat and simmer for about 30 minutes, until the chicken is tender and no longer pink when the point of a sharp knife is inserted into the thickest part. Lift out the chicken breasts, remove the skin, place them on a serving dish and leave to cool. Strain and reserve the cooking liquid. For the supreme sauce, melt the butter in a saucepan. Stir in the flour and cook, stirring constantly, for 2 minutes. Gradually stir in 1.5 litres/2½ pints of the reserved cooking liquid, a little at a time. Cook, stirring constantly, for about 5 minutes, until thickened, then remove the pan from the heat and leave to cool slightly. Lightly beat the egg yolks in a bowl, stir in a little of the sauce, then stir into the pan. Pour the sauce over the chicken and leave to cool, then chill in the refrigerator. Serve cold, garnished with slices of truffle, if using.

Chicken terrine with ham and pepper sauce

TERRINA DE POLLO CON JAMON Y SALSA DE PIMIENTO

- **350 g/12 oz skinless boneless chicken breasts, chopped**
- **4 tablespoons dry vermouth**
- **2 egg whites**
- **150 ml/¼ pint double cream**
- **50 g/2 oz ham, chopped**
- **3–4 gherkins, diced**
- **sunflower oil, for brushing**
- **salt and pepper**

Sauce:
- **1 large red pepper**
- **½ chicken stock cube, dissolved in 150 ml/¼ pint warm water**
- **3–4 tablespoons single cream**
- **salt and pepper**

Serves 4

Season the chicken with salt and pepper, put it into a food processor, add the vermouth and process. Transfer to a bowl. Whisk the egg whites in a clean, dry bowl until they form soft peaks, then gently fold them into the chicken mixture. Lightly beat the cream with a fork, then fold into the mixture. Chill in the refrigerator. Meanwhile, preheat the grill. To make the sauce, put the red pepper on a baking sheet and cook under the grill, turning occasionally, for 10–15 minutes, until blistered and charred. Remove with tongs, place in a plastic bag and seal the top. When the pepper is cool enough to handle, peel and seed it and cut the flesh into pieces. Put the pieces of pepper and the stock into a food processor and process until smooth, then pour into a saucepan. the refrigerator and divide it into quarters. Mix one quarter with the ham and gherkin mixture. Brush a healproof mould with oil, cover the base with foil and brush the foil with oil. Tip in the mixture, cover and set the mould over a pan of barely simmering water for about 15–20 minutes, or until thoroughly cooked. Remove the mould from the heat, leave it to cool slightly, then run a knife around the edge of the mould and turn it out. Just before serving, bring the red pepper sauce to the boil, stir in the cream and heat gently, but do not allow to come back to the boil. Season to taste with salt and pepper. Serve the terrine, offering the sauce separately. For the others we suggest a mixture of beef and Serrano ham, carrots and prawns or any other ingredients which go well with chicken, using the same proportions.

Note: The remaining chicken cream can be mixed with chopped mushrooms that have been sautéed with onion.

Blanquette of chicken

BLANQUETA DE GALLINA

- 1 boiling fowl, 1.5 kg/3¼ lb
- 1 bay leaf
- 1 small onion,
  studded with 3 cloves
- 2 carrots, sliced
- 5 tablespoons white wine
- 500 g/1 lb 2 oz long-grain rice
- 80 g/3 oz butter
- 2 tablespoons sunflower oil
- 1½ tablespoons plain flour
- 250 ml/8 fl oz milk
- 2 egg yolks
- juice of ½ lemon
- 1 tablespoon chopped
  fresh parsley
- salt

Serves 6

Put the boiling fowl into a saucepan, pour in water to cover and add the bay leaf, onion, carrot, wine and a pinch of salt. Bring to the boil and skim off the froth that rises to the surface, then lower the heat and simmer for 1½–2 hours, until the boiling fowl is tender. Check that it is done by piercing the thickest part of the thigh with the point of a sharp knife; if the juices run clear and the meat is no longer pink, the chicken is cooked. Meanwhile, cook and rinse the rice as described in recipe 173. Remove the boiling fowl from the pan with a slotted spoon and keep warm. Strain and reserve the cooking liquid. Melt 25 g/1 oz of the butter with the oil in a saucepan. Stir in the flour and cook, stirring constantly, for 2 minutes. Gradually stir in the milk and 500 ml/18 fl oz of the reserved cooking liquid. Beat the egg yolks with the lemon juice and stir in a little of the sauce, then pour into the pan. Sprinkle in the parsley and season to taste with salt. Remove the pan from the heat and keep warm. Season the rice with salt and fry in the remaining butter (see recipe 173). Fill half of a long serving dish with the rice and the other half with the boiling fowl and sauce. Serve immediately.

Note: A regular chicken can be used in place of a boiling fowl.

Chicken roll

PECHUGA DE GALLINA RELLENA

- 1 boneless breast of boiling fowl,
  500 g/1 lb 2 oz
- 250 g/9 oz minced beef
- 250 g/9 oz minced pork
- 1 thick slice of Serrano ham,
  cut widthways into thin strips
- 1 truffle, thinly sliced (optional)
- 175 ml/6 fl oz white wine
- 2 leeks, white parts only, cut into
  short lengths and rinsed well
- 1 stick celery, cut into short
  lengths (optional)
- 2 carrots, cut into short lengths
- pinch of mixed dried herbs
  or 1 bouquet garni
  (1 sprig fresh thyme, 2 bay
  leaves and 1 sprig fresh parsley
  tied together in muslin)
- 4 black peppercorns
- 1 sachet powdered gelatine
  (see Notes)
- salt

Serves 6

Lay the breast of boiling fowl out on a tea towel, skin side down. Mix together the minced beef and pork in a bowl and spread over the breast. Arrange parallel strips of ham on top and add the truffle slices, if using. Roll up the breast, wrap in the tea towel and tie the tea towel at both ends. Put the roll into a saucepan, pour in water to cover and add the wine, leek, celery, if using, carrot, dried herbs or bouquet garni, peppercorns and a pinch of salt. Cover and bring to the boil, then lower the heat and cook for 1½–2 hours, until the breast is tender and no longer pink when the point of a sharp knife is inserted into it. Remove the roll from the pan, weigh it down with a chopping board and leave to cool. Strain and reserve the stock. Once it is cold, unwrap, slice and serve the roll with gelatine (see Notes) and salad.

Notes: Make the gelatine with the strained stock from cooking the boiling fowl and the powdered gelatine, following the instructions on the packet. When it has set, chop it and place it around the meat. Alternatively, use the stock to make a delicious soup. You can use 2 large boneless chicken breasts in place of the boiling fowl.

826

Chicken in red wine
GALLO AL VINO TINTO

- 200 ml/7 fl oz brandy
- 120 ml/4 fl oz chicken's or pig's blood (optional)
- 1 chicken, 2.5 kg/5½ lb
- 100 g/3½ oz streaky bacon, chopped
- 150 g/5 oz butter
- 12 shallots
- 1 bottle (750 ml/1¼ pints) red wine
- 1 teaspoon sugar
- 1 clove garlic, lightly crushed
- 1 bouquet garni (1 sprig fresh thyme, 2 bay leaves and 1 sprig fresh parsley tied together in muslin)
- 250 g/9 oz mushrooms
- 2 tablespoons plain flour
- salt and pepper

Serves 6

Mix together 2 tablespoons of the brandy and the blood, if using, in a bowl and set aside. Cut the chicken into pieces and season with salt and pepper. Blanch the bacon in boiling water for 2 minutes, then drain. Melt 50 g/2 oz of the butter in a saucepan. Add the bacon and shallots and cook over a low heat, stirring occasionally, until lightly browned. Add the pieces of chicken and cook, turning frequently, until evenly browned all over. Drain off the fat released. Heat the remaining brandy in a small saucepan, pour it into the pan with the chicken and ignite. When the flames have died down, add the wine, season with salt and pepper and add the sugar, garlic and bouquet garni. Cover and simmer for 2½ hours. Add the mushrooms and stir well. Reserve 20 g/¾ oz of the remaining butter and mix the rest to a paste with the flour. Add to the pan, in small pieces at a time, and cook, gently shaking the pan until fully incorporated. Cook for a further 15–30 minutes, until the chicken is tender. Check that it is done by piercing the thickest part of the thigh with the point of a sharp knife; if the juices run clear and the meat is no longer pink, the chicken is cooked. Just before serving, remove and discard the bouquet garni and add the brandy and blood mixture, if using, and remaining butter to the sauce. Serve in a warm deep dish, covered with the sauce and garnished with triangles of fried bread (see recipe 130).

Turkey

History and curious facts

Like chicken, turkey is a member of the Gallinacean family. It lives wild in its native North America. Farmed turkeys may grow up to 1 metre/39 inches high and weigh up to 10 kg/25 lb. There are many breeds. The most common is the white-feathered or broad-breasted white, specifically bred to leave smooth, clean-looking skin after plucking. Traditional turkey has thick, dark – almost black – plumage and a speckled skin. Bronze turkeys also have dark plumage with metallic highlights. Turkeys have bald heads and a red wattle. The female of all breeds is smaller than the male. The turkey has long been used for food and remains very popular today. It is highly valued in the United States and is the nearly universal main course for Thanksgiving. It is the traditional Christmas dish in many European countries, including Spain and Britain, but has also increasingly become an everyday option. It has a high nutritional value, being a good source of proteins, B vitamins and some minerals, including phosphorus and iron. It is easily digested and is suitable for people with digestive disorders and growing children. Younger birds have less fat and are good roasted or fried, while older birds are better stewed or braised. Roasting and stewing are the traditional ways to prepare this bird, but nowadays turkey is more often eaten as fillets. In some places, it can be purchased in minced form, as sausages and in deli-style meats.

Nutrition

Turkey is a source of high-quality proteins, vitamins, especially niacin, iron, zinc, phosphorus, potassium and magnesium. There is no difference in the nutritional value of white and dark meat. Turkey contains 21.5 g protein, 19 g fat and 58 g water per 100 g meat. There are no carbohydrates in its composition and it has about 280 calories per 100 g/3 ½ oz.

Value for money

Turkey meat is not a seasonal product and frozen turkey, especially, can be found in shops and supermarkets all year round. Oven-ready fresh birds are more widely available at specific times of the year. Whole birds, fillets, drumsticks, crowns, diced and minced meat are all on sale. Check the quality by looking at the cleanness of the skin and legs, and the texture of the meat in the legs and breast.

Selection

Avoid buying a very heavy turkey. If it weighs more than 4 kg / 8 ¾ lb, its meat will be less tender. If possible, choose a turkey hen which will be both more tender and tastier.

How to clean and prepare

Clean and prepare the turkey in the same way as chicken. When roasting it, put some rashers of bacon over the breast, if you like. To prevent it browning too quickly, cover it with foil.

Roasting times:
1.5–2-kg / 3 ¼ – 4 ½-lb turkey – 1 ¼ hours
2–3-kg / 4 ½ – 6 ½-lb turkey –1 ½ hours
3–5-kg / 6 ½ – 11-lb turkey – 2 – 2 ½ hours.

Fried slices of turkey are delicious with a salad. When preparing stuffed turkey, it is advisable to cook the stuffing separately to ensure that it is cooked through. If you have cooked it inside the bird, the stuffing should reach at least 70°C/160°F (check with a meat thermometre) before you serve it.

Turkey with chestnuts

PAVO CON CASTAÑAS

- 1 turkey, about 3 kg/6½ lb
- 6 rashers of bacon
- dash of lemon juice
- 100 g/3½ oz lard or
  5 tablespoons sunflower oil
- salt and pepper

Stuffing:
- 50 g/2 oz butter
- 200 g/7 oz porcini
- 200 g/7 oz button mushrooms
- 3 skinless boneless chicken
  breasts, coarsely chopped
- 2 eggs
- 200 ml/7 fl oz single cream
- 250 g/9 oz duck foie gras, diced
- 250 g/9 oz canned peeled
  and cooked chestnuts, drained
- 100 g/3½ oz breadcrumbs
- salt and pepper

Serves 6

Preheat the oven to 180°C/350°F/Gas Mark 4. Season the inside of the turkey with salt and pepper. Make the stuffing. Melt the butter in a frying pan. Add the porcini and mushrooms and cook over a low heat, stirring occasionally, for 5 minutes or until much of the liquid has been released and evaporated. Remove the pan from the heat. Put the chicken in a food processor and process until finely chopped. Add the eggs and cream and process again. Then add the porcini and mushrooms, foie gras, chestnuts and breadcrumbs and process again to combine. Season with salt and pepper. Stuff the turkey with the chicken mixture, adding one of the rashers of bacon. Cover the outside of the bird with the remaining rashers of bacon. Place in a roasting tin and cover with foil. Roast for 1 hour, then remove and discard the foil and increase the temperature to 220°C/425°F/Gas Mark 7. Roast, turning and basting occasionally, for a further 1–1½ hours, until the turkey is cooked through and golden brown. Test by piercing the thickest part with the point of a sharp knife; if the juices run clear and the meat is no longer pink, the turkey is cooked. Lift the turkey out of the roasting tin, discard the bacon, carve the meat and put the slices on a warm serving dish. Skim off the fat from the cooking juices, add 4 tablespoons hot water and the lemon juice and cook, stirring and scraping up any bits from the base of the roasting tin, then pour into a sauce boat. Serve immediately.

Capon

A capon is a young cockerel that has been castrated and then fattened on a special diet that makes it especially flavoursome, with a high proportion of white meat. The production of capons is banned in a number of countries including the UK, and Australia (where it is illegal to castrate the birds using chemicals). A large chicken or small turkey may be substituted in traditional recipes for capon.

828 Capon stuffed with pears

CAPON RELLENO DE PERAS

- 2 slices of bread, crusts removed
- 100 ml/3½ fl oz milk
- 1 capon, chicken or turkey, 3–3.5 kg/6½–7¾ lb with giblets
- 10 pears
- 300 g/11 oz sausage meat
- 100 g/3½ oz bacon, diced
- pinch of freshly grated nutmeg
- 1 egg
- 1 egg yolk
- 100 g/3½ oz shelled pistachio nuts, chopped
- 20 g/¾ oz pine nuts
- 1 stick celery, chopped
- 1 onion, chopped
- 2 tablespoons green peppercorns
- 100 g/3½ oz lard or goose fat or 5 tablespoons sunflower oil
- 1 bottle (750 ml/1¼ pints) red wine
- 1½ tablespoons clear honey
- salt and pepper

Serves 6

Put the bread in a bowl, pour in the milk and leave to soak for 10 minutes, then drain. Preheat the oven to 240°C/475°F/Gas Mark 9. Season the inside of the bird with salt and pepper. Chop the liver and heart. Slit the gizzard, remove and discard the gravel sac, then chop. Put the chopped giblets in a bowl. Peel, core and chop two of the pears and add to the bowl along with the sausage meat, bacon, nutmeg, egg, egg yolk, pistachio nuts, pine nuts, celery, onion, half the peppercorns and the soaked bread. Mix well, then stuff the bird with this mixture. Close the cavities with trussing thread. Spread the lard or fat over the bird or brush it with the oil and put into a roasting tin. Roast for 15 minutes, then lower the temperature to 180° C/350°F/Gas Mark 4 and roast, basting frequently, for a further 2 hours. Check that it is done by piercing the thickest part of the thigh with the point of a sharp knife; if the juices run clear and the meat is no longer pink, the chicken is cooked. Meanwhile, peel and core the remaining pears, put them into a saucepan and add the wine, the remaining peppercorns and the honey. Cook over a medium heat for 20 minutes, then remove the pan from the heat and leave to cool. Remove the bird from the roasting tin and cover with foil. Skim off the fat from the cooking juices and add 200 ml/7 fl oz of the cooking liquid from the pears. Cook over a medium heat until reduced by half. Season to taste with salt and pepper. Carve the bird and scoop out the stuffing and place on a warm serving dish. Halve the pears, place a little stuffing in the cavities and put on the dish. Serve immediately, offering the sauce separately.

Duck

Strictly speaking, duckling less than four months old is the bird most commonly found in shops and supermarkets, as the meat will be tender. It is usually sold oven-ready, but if you need to prepare it yourself follow the method for preparing a chicken. In addition, remove the glands from either side of the tail bone. Duck is sold whole or in parts, as breast or legs. A whole duck is cut up slightly differently from a chicken. Cut the skin between the legs and body. Carve the breast into fillets, as shown in the diagram. Carve the legs and wings in the same way as a chicken.

To roast a duck, allow 15–20 minutes per 500 g/1 lb 2 oz. Bear in mind that the duck is a bird with a lot of fat, so only use a little lard or oil when preparing it and do not add bacon.

829

Duckling à l'orange (first version)
PATO A LA NARANJA

- 3 oranges
- 1 duckling, 1.5 kg/3¼ lb
- 50 g/2 oz lard or 3 tablespoons
  sunflower oil
- 1 large carrot, sliced
- 2–3 shallots, sliced
- 175 ml/6 fl oz white wine
- 250 ml/8 fl oz duck
  or chicken stock (home-made
  or made with a stock cube)
- juice of 2 oranges
- 1 tablespoon potato flour
- strip of thinly pared orange rind
- 2 tablespoons Curaçao
- salt

Serves 4–5

Peel one of the oranges and cut out the segments from between the membranes. Slice the remaining oranges and set aside. Put the orange segments inside the duckling and season with salt. Melt the lard or heat the oil in a saucepan. Add the duckling, carrot and shallots and cook over a medium heat, turning the duckling frequently, for about 8 minutes, until evenly browned all over. Pour in the wine, stock and 3 tablespoons of the orange juice. Cover and cook over a medium heat for 45 minutes. Lift out the duckling from the pan. Remove and discard the orange segments. Strain the cooking liquid into a clean pan. Mix the potato flour with 2 tablespoons water and the remaining orange juice in a bowl and add the orange rind. Skim off the fat from the cooking liquid, stir in the potato flour and juice and cook over a low heat, stirring constantly, for 2–3 minutes, until thickened. Stir in the Curaçao. Remove and discard the orange rind and pour the sauce into a sauce boat. Carve the duckling and serve, garnished with the orange slices, offering the sauce separately.

830

Duckling à l'orange (second version)
PATO A LA NARANJA

- 3 oranges
- 1 duckling, 1.5 kg/3¼ lb
- 50 g/2 oz lard or 3 tablespoons
  sunflower oil
- 1 large carrot, sliced
- 2–3 shallots, sliced
- 175 ml/6 fl oz white wine
- 250 ml/8 fl oz duck
  or chicken stock (home-made
  or made with a stock cube)
- juice of 2 large oranges
- 1 duck liver
- 20 g/¾ oz butter
- 1 tablespoon sunflower oil
- 1 tablespoon plain flour
- 2 tablespoons Curaçao
- skimmed duck cooking juices
- salt

Serves 4–5

Peel one of the oranges and cut out the segments from between the membranes. Slice the remaining oranges and set aside. Put the orange segments inside the duckling and season with salt. Melt the lard or heat the oil in a saucepan. Add the duckling, carrot and shallots and cook over a medium heat, turning the duckling frequently, for about 8 minutes, until evenly browned all over. Pour in the wine, stock and 3 tablespoons of the orange juice. Cover and cook over a medium heat for 45 minutes. Lift out the duckling from the pan. Remove and discard the orange segments. Strain the cooking liquid into a clean pan. Lightly fry the duck liver, then pound it well in a mortar. Melt the butter with the oil in a frying pan. Stir in the flour and the liver and cook over a low heat, stirring constantly, for 2 minutes. Stir in the orange juice, Curaçao and cooking liquid and cook over a low heat, stirring constantly, for a few minutes. If the sauce is too thick, stir in 1 tablespoon hot water. Season to taste with salt and strain.

831 Braised duckling with olives

PATO BRASEADO CON ACEITUNAS

- 3–4 tablespoons olive oil
- 1 duckling, 1.5 kg/3¼ lb
- 1 large onion, chopped
- 2 large carrots, sliced
- 2 large, ripe tomatoes,
  peeled, seeded and chopped
- 175 ml/6 fl oz white wine
- 500 ml/18 fl oz duck
  or chicken stock (home-made
  or made with a stock cube)
- 100 g/3½ oz olives, stoned
- 1 heaped teaspoon potato flour
- 6 triangles of fried bread
  (see recipe 130)
- salt and pepper

Serves 6

Heat the oil in a large, heavy based saucepan or a cocotte. Add the duckling and cook over a low heat, turning frequently, for 5 minutes. Add the onion and carrot and cook, turning the duckling frequently, for about 15 minutes, until the vegetables have softened and the duckling is evenly browned all over. Add the tomato and cook for 10 minutes, then pour in the wine and stock and season with salt and pepper. Cover and simmer over a low heat for 1 hour. Meanwhile, put the olives in a small saucepan, pour in cold water to cover and bring to the boil, then lower the heat and simmer for 1 minute. Drain well and cut each into two or three slices. Remove the duckling from the pan and keep warm. Pass the sauce through a food mill or press it through a sieve into a clean pan. Mix the potato flour with 2–3 tablespoons of the sauce in a bowl, then stir into the pan with the olives. Place the duckling into the pan and cook for 8–10 minutes. Lift out the duckling and carve, placing the meat on a warm serving dish. Spoon the sauce over the top and serve garnished with the triangles of fried bread (see recipe 130).

832 Duck fillet

MAGRET DE PATO

- 50 g/2 oz lard or goose fat or
  3 tablespoons sunflower oil
- 1 large duck fillet, 500 g/1 lb 2 oz

Serves 1–2

Grease a flat griddle with lard, goose fat or oil and set over a high heat for 10 minutes to preheat. Add the duck fillet, skin side down, and cook for 8 minutes. Turn the fillet, season with salt and pepper, turn again and cook for 2–3 minutes more, or until done to your liking. Using a very sharp carving knife, cut the fillet diagonally into slices. Collect the cooking juices and serve with any one of several sauces, such as Béarnaise (see recipe 84).

833

Duck salad with pears and raspberries
ENSALADA DE PATO CON PERAS Y FRAMBUESAS

- 1 lettuce
- 40 g/1½ oz butter
- 2 tablespoons olive oil
- 1 duck fillet, thinly sliced
- 2 pears
- 80 g/3 oz raspberries
- 20 g/1¾ oz pine nuts (optional)

Vinaigrette:
- 3 tablespoons olive oil
- 1 tablespoon raspberry vinegar
- salt and pepper

Serves 4

Put the lettuce leaves into a salad bowl. Melt the butter with the oil in a frying pan. Add the slices of duck and cook over a medium heat, turning once, for 2–5 minutes, until done to your liking. Remove with a fish slice and add to the salad bowl. Make the vinaigrette. Whisk together the oil and vinegar, season to taste with salt and pepper. Peel, core and thinly slice the pears and place them on the salad. Add the raspberries and the pine nuts, if using, and pour over the salad. Serve immediately.

834

Stuffed squab with apple compote
PICHONES RELLENOS Y SERVIDOS CON COMPOTA DE MANZANA

- 3 squab, 500 g/1 lb 2 oz each
- 12 sausages, skinned
- 5 tablespoons olive oil
- 175 ml/6 fl oz full-bodied red wine
- salt

Apple compote:
- 500 g/1 lb 2 oz eating apples
- 2 tablespoons sugar
- 1 tablespoon brandy

Serves 6

Lightly season the squab with salt and fill the cavities with the meat from the sausages. Secure the openings with wooden cocktailsticks. Heat the oil in a large, heavy based saucepan or a cocotte. Add the squab and cook over a low heat, turning frequently, for about 8 minutes, until evenly browned all over. Pour in the wine and 250 ml/8 fl oz water, season with salt and cook over a medium heat for about 40 minutes, until tender and cooked through. Meanwhile, make the apple compote. Peel, core and dice the apples, put into a saucepan and pour 3 tablespoons water over them. Mix well, cover and cook over a low heat for about 20 minutes, until most of the liquid has evaporated. If necessary, remove the lid and cook for a little longer. Stir in the sugar. Heat the brandy in a small saucepan, ignite it and carefully pour it into the compote. Mix well, then remove from the heat and keep warm. When the squab are ready, put the compote into the base of a warm serving dish. Remove and discard the cocktail sticks and cut the squab in half lengthways. Put them on top of the compote and arrange the stuffing around the edge of the dish. This dish can also be garnished with triangles of fried bread (see recipe 130) if you like. Serve immediately.

Note: Some people like to pass the compote through a food mill before adding the flaming brandy.

835

- 120 ml / 4 fl oz olive oil
- 2 squab, 500 g / 1 lb 2 oz each
- 1 onion, very finely chopped
- 1 tablespoon plain flour
- 2 tomatoes,
  peeled, seeded and diced
- 1 clove garlic
- 1 chicken stock cube
- 1 large sprig fresh parsley
- 120 m / 4 fl oz white wine
- salt and pepper

Serves 4

Squab in sauce

PICHONES EN SALSA

Heat the oil in a saucepan. Add the squab and cook over a low heat, turning frequently, for about 8 minutes, until evenly browned all over. Remove from the pan and set aside. Add the onion to the pan and cook, stirring occasionally, for about 8 minutes, until beginning to brown. Stir in the flour and cook, stirring constantly, for about 5 minutes, until lightly browned, then add the tomato. Crush the garlic, stock cube and parsley in a mortar and stir in 150 ml / ¼ pint water, then add to the pan. Stir well, return the squab to the pan and season with salt and pepper. Pour in the wine and 500 ml / 18 fl oz water, cover and cook over a very low heat for about 2 hours, until the birds are tender and cooked through. Remove the squab from the pan, halve them lengthways and place on a warm serving dish. Pass the sauce through a food mill or process in a food processor and spoon it over the squab. Serve immediately, garnished with triangles of fried bread (see recipe 130) if you like.

836

- 1 kg / 2 ¼ lb ostrich fillet
- 1 quantity Red Wine Sauce
  (see recipe 88) or Shallot Sauce
  for Fried Meat (see recipe 93)

Serves 6–8

Ostrich

AVESTRUZ

Now that it is quite widely farmed, this bird is becoming increasingly popular. It has a good flavour and is very nutritious. Having very little fat, it is a great ally in the fight against cholesterol and weight gain. It can be cooked in the same ways as steak and can also be roasted, but as the steaks are thinner than beef steaks, they will need less time in the oven. A piece of ostrich weighing 1 kg / 2 ¼ lb will be ready to serve in 17 minutes. It is worth pointing out that ostrich cannot be reheated as it becomes tough. Otherwise it is a delicious meat and compares well with steak.

gAME

Hunting is as old as the human race itself and depictions of hunting appear in even the most primitive art. So far as cooking game is concerned, the first written records of how to prepare it come from the ancient Romans. They developed the technique of hanging game for a few days before eating it, a method of preparation that continues today in many places. There are also extant Roman recipes for marinades that are similar to those of today.

Furred game

Traditionally, furred game meant any fur-bearing animal killed for sport, but it has always been an important source of food. Big game includes wild boar, deer, reindeer, elk, moose and antelope, while small game covers animals such as rabbit and hare. It is becoming increasingly difficult to obtain game directly from hunters. However, meats that were once found only in the wild are now being raised commercially, and they are available from specialist butchers or Internet purveyors. Game bought this way has the advantage of being bred for tenderness and flavour, and having been hung for the appropriate length of time. In addition, the butcher will prepare it for you. Rabbit, wild boar and venison can also be found in some supermarkets, although the meat is more likely to be from farmed rather than wild animals.

Selection and storage
When buying game, check that there are no blue or greenish discolorations. If you're not planning to eat it immediately, it can be frozen. Otherwise it can be stored for several days in foil in the refrigerator.

How to prepare
Marinades were once used to mask unpleasant flavours, but nowadays they are used to tenderize the meat. They also help keep meat succulent during cooking. This is especially important with furred game, which is often very lean and can dry out easily. In general, game should be cooked until well done, but it has become fashionable to serve it almost raw, in a carpaccio for example. In such cases, it is important to know the meat came from a reputable supplier, but even so, there is still risk of infection from foodborne bacteria.

Suggestions

Game is delicious accompanied by both wild and cultivated mushrooms, Brussels sprouts, chestnuts or even a mixture of the latter two. In this case, cook the sprouts and chestnuts separately, and then sauté them together and season. Marinades should always be made with a base of herbs, onion, carrot, celery, wine and vinegar. Preparations called a 'la cazadora' (hunter-style) are usually based on wild mushrooms, onion, thyme, wine and bay leaves. From a nutritional viewpoint, game is typically low in fat and high in protein. The meat also contains minerals such as calcium, phosphorus and iron, as well as B vitamins.

Tricks

• Traditionally, to tenderize game that you or someone you know had shot, you would hang it in a cool place for no more than five or six days, and draw, but not skin it until just before using. Today, many hunters don't hang game at all, both out of concern for foodborne illnesses that come with unrefrigerated meat and because they prefer the flavour.

Rabbit

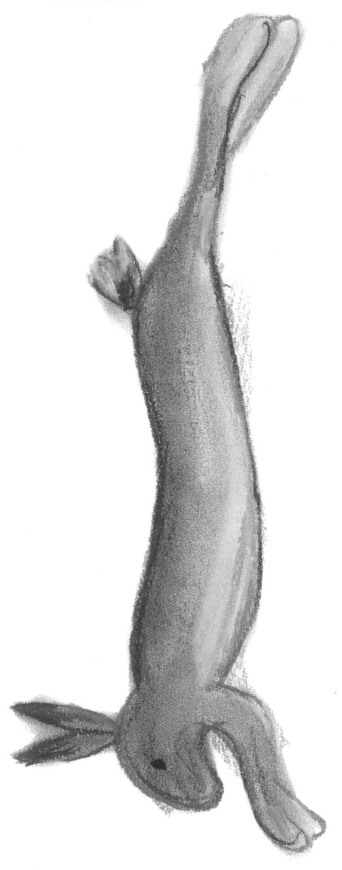

Rabbit with liver, pine nut and pepper sauce

CONEJO CON SALSA DE HIGADITOS, PIÑONES Y PIMIENTOS

- 4 tablespoons olive oil
- 100 g/3½ oz streaky bacon, diced
- 1 small onion, chopped
- 1 large rabbit or 2 small ones, cut into pieces
- 4 tomatoes, peeled, seeded and chopped
- pinch of mixed dried herbs
- 25 g/1 oz pine nuts
- 120 ml/4 fl oz white wine
- 2 rabbit or chicken livers, thawed if frozen, trimmed
- 100 g/3½ oz canned red peppers, drained and cut into strips
- 1 tablespoon chopped fresh parsley
- salt

Serves 4

Heat the oil in a saucepan. Add the bacon and onion and cook over a low heat, stirring occasionally, for 5 minutes, until the onion is soft and translucent. Add the pieces of rabbit and cook over a medium heat, turning frequently, for about 10 minutes, until evenly browned all over. Add the tomato, season with salt and stir in the dried herbs and nearly all the pine nuts. Mix the wine with 120 ml/4 fl oz water and pour it over the rabbit. Cover and cook over a medium heat for about 45 minutes, until the meat is tender but not falling apart. Put the livers, the remaining pine nuts and a strip of red pepper into a mortar and pound, then stir into the pan. Add the remaining red pepper and sprinkle in the parsley. Stir, heat through briefly and serve.

838

Rabbit stewed with onions, tomatoes and carrots
CONEJO GUISADO CON CEBOLLITAS, TOMATES Y ZANAHORIAS

- 6 tablespoons olive oil
- 2 small rabbits, 1.2 kg/2½ lb each, cut into pieces
- 100 g/3½ oz streaky bacon, diced
- 3–4 large, ripe tomatoes, peeled, seeded and quartered
- 3 carrots, thinly sliced
- ½ teaspoon mixed dried herbs or 1 bouquet garni (1 sprig fresh parsley, 2 bay leaves, 1 sprig fresh thyme and 1 clove garlic tied together in muslin)
- 120 ml/4 fl oz white wine
- 8 shallots
- 15 g/½ oz butter
- 100 g/3½ oz canned red peppers, drained and cut into thin strips
- salt

Serves 6–8

Heat the oil in a saucepan. Add the pieces of rabbit and cook over a medium heat, turning frequently, for about 10 minutes, until evenly browned all over. Add the bacon, tomato and carrot, season with salt and sprinkle in the dried herbs or add the bouquet garni. Mix well, pour in the wine and 120 ml/4 fl oz water, cover the pan and bring to the boil. Lower the heat and simmer for about 45 minutes, until the rabbit pieces are tender but not falling apart. Meanwhile, put the shallots, butter and a pinch of salt into a saucepan. Pour in water to cover and cook for 10–15 minutes. Drain the shallots and add to the pan along with the red pepper. Stir well and transfer the rabbit and vegetables to a warm serving dish, removing the bouquet garni, if used. Serve immediately, garnished with triangles of fried bread (see recipe 130), if you like.

839

Rabbit cooked with white wine
CONEJO GUISADO CON VINO BLANCO

- 120 ml/4 fl oz olive oil
- 1 onion, chopped
- 2 small rabbits, about 1.2 kg/2½ lb each, cut into pieces
- 1 tablespoon plain flour
- 175 ml/6 fl oz dry white wine
- ½ teaspoon mixed dried herbs
- 1 tablespoon chopped fresh parsley
- salt

Serves 6–8

Heat the oil in a saucepan. Add the onion and cook over a low heat, stirring occasionally, for about 5 minutes, until softened and translucent. Add the pieces of rabbit and cook over a medium heat, turning frequently, for about 10 minutes, until evenly browned all over. Stir in the flour and cook, stirring constantly, for 2 minutes. Gradually stir in the wine and 120 ml/4 fl oz water. Season with salt and add the dried herbs. Cover and cook over a medium-low heat for about 45 minutes, until the rabbit pieces are tender and cooked through. Serve immediately, sprinkled with the parsley.

Note: This dish can be served with Mashed Potato (see recipe 230) or macaroni tossed in butter and grated cheese.

840 📷 Rabbit cooked with olives and almonds

CONEJO GUISADO CON ACEITUNAS Y ALMENDRAS

- 1 small rabbit, 1.2 kg/2½ lb,
  cut into pieces
- 40 g/1½ oz plain flour
- 5 tablespoons olive oil
- 3 cloves garlic
- 1 large onion, finely chopped
- 175 ml/6 fl oz white wine
- 100 g/3½ oz olives, stoned
- 50 g/2 oz toasted almonds
- salt and pepper

Serves 4

Season the pieces of rabbit with salt, then coat them in the flour, shaking off any excess. Heat the oil in a saucepan. Add the pieces of rabbit, in batches if necessary, and cook over a medium heat, turning frequently, for about 10 minutes, until evenly browned all over. Remove from the pan and set aside. Lightly crush two of the garlic cloves and add to the pan. Cook, stirring occasionally, for a few minutes, until browned, then remove with a slotted spoon. Add the onion to the pan and cook, stirring occasionally, for about 8 minutes, until beginning to brown. Return the rabbit pieces to the pan, pour in the wine and cook for about 10 minutes, until slightly reduced. Season with pepper and add just enough warm water to cover the rabbit. Cover the pan and cook over a medium-low heat for about 30 minutes. Put the olives into another saucepan, pour in water to cover and bring to the boil. Lower the heat and cook for 2 minutes, then drain, pat dry and cut each olive widthways into two or three slices. Stir the olives into the pan. Pound the almonds with the remaining garlic clove in a mortar, then add to the pan. Mix well, re-cover and cook for a further 15 minutes, until the rabbit is tender but not falling apart. Put the rabbit pieces into a warm dish and pour the sauce over them. Serve garnished with Potato Balls (see recipe 231)

841 Saddle of rabbit roasted with mustard

TRASERO DE CONEJO ASADO CON MOSTAZA

- saddle of 1 large or
  2 small rabbits
- 2 tablespoons mustard
- 4 tablespoons olive oil
- 2 onions, coarsely chopped
- 100 g/3½ oz streaky bacon,
  diced
- ½ teaspoon mixed dried herbs
  or 2–3 sprigs fresh thyme
- 4–5 tablespoons boiling water
- 250 ml/8 fl oz double cream
- 1 tablespoon plain flour
- salt

Serves 4

Preheat the oven to 200°C/400°F/Gas Mark 6. Season the rabbit with salt and spread the mustard all over it. Pour the oil into a roasting tin or a deep, ovenproof dish and add the rabbit. Put the onion and bacon around it. Sprinkle with the dried herbs or put the thyme on top of the meat and roast, basting with the cooking juices and gradually adding the boiling water, for 30 minutes. Stir in 7 tablespoons of the cream, lower the temperature to 180°C/350°F/Gas Mark 4 and cook for a further 10 minutes. Mix together the flour and remaining cream in a bowl. Remove the rabbit from the roasting tin, carve the meat and put it on to a warm serving dish. Strain the cooking juices into the flour and cream mixture and mix well. Pour into a saucepan and heat gently, stirring constantly, for a few minutes. Pour the sauce over the rabbit and serve immediately.

842

Jugged rabbit
GUISO DE CONEJO CON SALSA DE SANGRE (CIVET)

- 1 small rabbit, about
  1.2 kg/2½ lb, cut into pieces
- 2 tablespoons white-wine
  vinegar
- 150 g/5 oz lean bacon, diced
- 1 onion, chopped
- 2 tablespoons plain flour
- 250 ml/8 fl oz meat stock
  (home-made or made
  with a stock cube)
- salt and pepper

  Marinade:
- 1 onion, cut into large pieces
- 2 small carrots, cut into
  4 pieces
- 2 cloves garlic
- 1 sprig fresh thyme
- 1 bay leaf
- 2 cloves
- 6 black peppercorns
- 1 litre/1¾ pints red wine
  Serves 4–6

Place the rabbit pieces in a non-metallic dish and season with salt and pepper. To make the marinade, add the onion, carrot, garlic, thyme, bay leaf, cloves and peppercorns and pour the wine over all the ingredients. Cover and leave to marinate overnight in a cool place but not in the refrigerator, stirring three or four times. Drain the pieces of rabbit, reserving the marinade. Heat the bacon in a large, heavy based saucepan or a cocotte until the fat runs, then remove with a slotted spoon. Add the pieces of rabbit and cook over a medium heat, turning frequently, for about 10 minutes, until evenly browned all over. Remove and set aside. Add the onion to the pan and cook over a low heat, stirring occasionally, for about 8 minutes, until beginning to brown. Stir in the flour and cook, stirring constantly, for 2 minutes. Return the pieces of rabbit to the pan and strain the reserved marinade over them, reserving the solids. Tie the reserved thyme sprig, bay leaf and garlic together in a piece of muslin and add to the pan. Cover and bring to the boil, then lower the heat to medium and cook, stirring occasionally and gradually adding the stock, for 45 minutes. The sauce should be rich but, if it is too thin, remove the lid and cook further until it is slightly reduced. Remove and discard the bouquet garni and serve the rabbit in a warm deep dish with the sauce poured over the top.

843

Rabbit in spiced sauce
CONEJO ESCABECHADO

- 250 ml/8 fl oz olive oil
- 1 small rabbit, 1.2 kg/
  2½ lb, cut into pieces
- 3 cloves garlic
- 2 bay leaves
- 6 black peppercorns
- 175 ml/6 fl oz white-wine vinegar
- salt
  Serves 4–5

Heat the oil in a frying pan. Add the pieces of rabbit, in batches, and cook over a medium heat, turning frequently, for about 10 minutes, until evenly browned all over. As each batch is cooked, transfer the meat to a large saucepan. Drain off most of the oil from the frying pan, leaving 5–6 tablespoons to cover the base, and reheat. Add the garlic, bay leaves and peppercorns, remove the pan from the heat and stir in the vinegar and 175 ml/6 fl oz water. Pour the sauce over the rabbit in the saucepan and, if there is not enough to cover it, add more water. Season with salt, cover the pan and cook over a low heat for about 45 minutes, until the rabbit is tender and cooked through. Serve hot or cold.

Hare

The hare is a relative of the rabbit, but is larger, weighing up to 6 kg/
13 lb or 6 ½ kg/ 14 lb. If hare is not available, substitute rabbit in the
following recipes. Handle hare with caution. It can carry a harmful
bacterial infection, so it is best to wear gloves when you prepare it
and wash all utensils used with it separately.

How to prepare

You will need to separate the gall bladder from the liver. To do this,
remove the gall bladder and liver, then cut.

844

Jugged hare

GUISO DE LIEBRE CON SALSA DE SANGRE (CIVET)

- 1 young hare, 1.5–2 kg/
  3 ¼–4 ½ lb, skinned
- 2 tablespoons white-wine
  vinegar
- 150 g/5 oz lean bacon, diced
- 1 onion, chopped
- 2 tablespoons plain flour
- 250 ml/8 fl oz meat stock
  (home-made or made
  with a stock cube)
- salt and pepper

  Marinade:
- 1 onion, cut into large pieces
- 2 small carrots, cut into 4 pieces
- 2 cloves garlic
- 1 sprig fresh thyme
- 1 bay leaf
- 2 cloves
- 6 black peppercorns
- 1 litre/1 ¾ pints red wine

  Serves 4–6

Start the preparation the day before you intend to cook the hare. In order for the civet – also known as jugged hare – to turn out well, the hare must be young and it must have blood. It is necessary to reserve the liver, having carefully removed the gall bladder. To collect the blood, pour the vinegar into the belly of the hare and collect the washed-out blood, including any clots, in a bowl. Set aside in the refrigerator. Cut the hare into medium-sized pieces, put them into a non-metallic dish and season with salt and pepper. To make the marinade, add the onion, carrot, garlic, thyme, bay leaf, cloves and peppercorns and pour the wine over all the ingredients. Cover and leave to marinate overnight in a cool place but not in the refrigerator, stirring three or four times. Drain the pieces of hare, reserving the marinade. Heat the bacon in a large, heavy based saucepan or a cocotte until the fat runs, then remove with a slotted spoon. Add the pieces of hare and cook over a medium heat, turning frequently, for about 10 minutes, until evenly browned all over. Remove and set aside. Add the onion to the pan and cook over a low heat, stirring occasionally, for about 8 minutes, until beginning to brown. Stir in the flour and cook, stirring constantly, for 2 minutes. Return the pieces of hare to the pan and strain the reserved marinade over them, reserving the solids. Tie the reserved thyme sprig, bay leaf and garlic together in a piece of muslin and add to the pan. Cover and bring to the boil, then lower the heat to medium and cook, stirring occasionally and gradually adding the stock, for 1 ½ hours. If the sauce is too thin, remove the lid and cook until slightly reduced. Shortly before serving, pound the liver to a purée in a mortar, add the blood and vinegar mixture and stir in 2 tablespoons of the sauce. Stir the mixture into the sauce and heat through. Remove and discard the bouquet garni and serve the hare in a warm deep dish with the sauce poured over the top.

Note: This stew, which in French is also called a civet, is at its best when reheated, so save some of the stock in case the sauce is too thick. The liver and the blood should be added only just before serving.

Marinated hare stew

GUISO DE LIEBRE ADOBADA

- 1 hare, 1.5 kg/3¼ lb,
  cut into pieces
- 2 onions
- 1 bouquet garni (1 bay leaf,
  2 sprigs fresh parsley, 1 sprig
  fresh thyme and 1 clove garlic
  tied together in muslin)
- 2 tablespoons white-wine
  vinegar
- 500 ml/18 fl oz white wine
- 5 tablespoons olive oil
- 200 g/7 oz streaky bacon, diced
- 40 g/1½ oz plain flour
- 500 ml/18 fl oz meat stock
  (home-made or made
  with a stock cube)
- 1 tablespoon chopped
  fresh parsley
- salt and pepper

Serves 4

The night before you intend to cook the stew, put the pieces of hare into a non-metallic dish and season with salt and pepper. Cut one of the onions into four pieces and add to the dish along with the bouquet garni, vinegar and wine. Mix well and turn the pieces of hare to coat, then leave to marinate in the refrigerator for about 12 hours. The next day, finely chop the remaining onion. Drain the pieces of hare and reserve the marinade. Heat the oil in a large saucepan, add the bacon and chopped onion and cook over a low heat, stirring occasionally, for about 7 minutes, until just beginning to brown. Coat the pieces of hare lightly in the flour, shaking off any excess, and add to the pan. Cook, stirring constantly, for 2 minutes, then gradually stir in the reserved marinade, a little at a time. Cook, stirring constantly, for 5 minutes, then stir in the stock. Cover the pan with brown paper that has been cut in a circle to fit snugly inside the saucepan or a clean tea towel, then seal tightly with the lid. Cook over a low heat, shaking the pan occasionally, for 1½–2 hours, until the hare is tender. Remove and discard the bouquet garni. Put the hare into a warm deep serving dish and pour the sauce over it. Sprinkle with the parsley and serve immediately, garnished with triangles of fried bread (see recipe 130) and with macaroni tossed in butter and grated cheese if you like.

846

Saddle of hare roasted with mustard

TRASERO DE LIEBRE ASADO CON MOSTAZA

- **saddle of 1 hare**
- **2 tablespoons mustard**
- **4 tablespoons olive oil**
- **2 onions, coarsely chopped**
- **100 g/3½ oz streaky bacon, diced**
- **½ teaspoon mixed dried herbs or 2–3 sprigs fresh thyme**
- **4–5 tablespoons boiling water**
- **250 ml/8 fl oz double cream**
- **1 tablespoon plain flour**
- **salt**

Serves 4–6

Preheat the oven to 200°C/400°F/Gas Mark 6. Season the hare with salt and spread the mustard all over it. Pour the oil into a roasting tin or a deep, ovenproof dish and add the hare. Put the onion and bacon around it. Sprinkle with the dried herbs or put the thyme on top of the meat and roast, basting with the cooking juices and gradually adding the boiling water, for 30 minutes. Stir in 7 tablespoons of the cream, lower the temperature to 180°C/350°F/Gas Mark 4 and cook for a further 10 minutes. Mix together the flour and remaining cream in a bowl. Remove the hare from the roasting tin, carve the meat and put it on to a warm serving dish. Strain the cooking juices into the flour and cream mixture and mix well. Pour into a saucepan and heat gently, stirring constantly, for a few minutes. Pour the sauce over the hare and serve immediately.

847

Hare with chestnuts

LIEBRE CON CASTAÑAS

- **1 large hare, 2 kg/4½ lb**
- **2 tablespoons red-wine vinegar**
- **100 g/3½ oz lard or 5 tablespoons sunflower oil**
- **500 g/1 lb 2 oz onions, chopped**
- **1 sprig fresh thyme**
- **¾ teaspoon black peppercorns**
- **150 g/5 oz sausage meat**
- **175 ml/6 fl oz dry sherry**
- **600 g/1 lb 5 oz chestnuts**
- **salt**

Serves 4

In order for this stew to turn out well, the hare needs to be young and must have blood. Reserve the liver, having carefully removed and discarded the gall bladder. Pound the liver to a purée in a mortar. To collect the blood, pour the vinegar into the belly of the hare and collect the washed-out blood, including any clots, in a bowl. Set aside in the refrigerator. Cut the hare into pieces and season with salt. Melt the lard or heat the oil in a flameproof casserole. Add the onion and pieces of hare and cook over a medium heat, stirring and turning frequently, for about 10 minutes, until evenly browned all over. Add the thyme and peppercorns and stir well. Cook the sausage meat in a frying pan until lightly browned, then add to the casserole. Pour in the sherry and add just enough water to cover the hare. Cover and cook over a medium heat for 45 minutes. Add the chestnuts, recover the casserole and cook for a further 40 minutes. Stir 2 tablespoons of the sauce into the blood and vinegar mixture, then stir into the casserole and cook for a further 5 minutes. Taste and adjust the seasoning, if necessary, and serve immediately.

Venison

Tradition says that older deer should be hung for several days or even
several weeks. Unlike most other game, deer are skinned and drawn
before they are hung. Farmed venison is widely available, sold in oven-
ready form and surprisingly inexpensive. 'A la cazadora' (hunter style)
is prepared with mushrooms, Brussels sprouts, turnips and potatoes.
Redcurrant jelly can be served with the sauce. If you want to lard the
venison before roasting, thread the strips of fat along the grain of the
meat. Venison is suitable for most beef recipes, but it is a good idea
to marinate it first. If you buy frozen venison, thaw it in a mari-nade.
Discard this marinade afterwards and then put the thawed meat in a
fresh marinade.

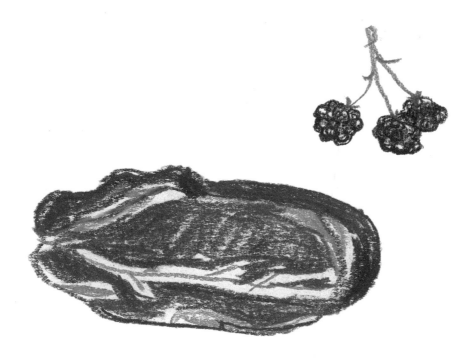

848

- 2 bay leaves
- 1 sprig fresh thyme
- 5 tablespoons olive oil
- 6 black peppercorns
- pinch of freshly grated nutmeg
- 1 leg of venison, 2.5 kg/5 ½ lb
- 150 ml/¼ pint hot water
- salt

Redcurrant sauce:
- 4 tablespoons olive oil
- 2 shallots, chopped
- 1 small stick celery, chopped
- 200 g/7 oz boneless venison, chopped
- 750 ml/1 ¼ pints full-bodied red wine
- 5 tablespoons brandy
- 250 g/9 oz redcurrant jelly
- 1 tablespoon potato flour
- salt and pepper

Serves 8–10

Leg of venison with redcurrant sauce
PIERNA DE CORZO CON SALSA DE GROSELLA

Pound the bay leaves and thyme in a mortar. Add the oil, peppercorns and nutmeg and pound again. Spread this mixture over the leg of venison, put it into a roasting tin and leave to stand in the refrigerator for 3–4 hours. Preheat the oven to 190°C/375°F/Gas Mark 5. Roast the venison for 1 hour, then season with salt and gradually add the hot water. Return to the oven and roast for a further 30 minutes, but do not baste the meat. Meanwhile, make the redcurrant sauce as described in recipe 97. Lift out the leg of venison and carve it like a leg of lamb. Serve immediately, offering the sauce separately.

Pan-cooked venison

CIERVO O CORZO EN CAZUELA

- I venison loin, haunch or fillet,
  2 kg/4½ lb
- 1.5 litres/2½ pints milk
- 4 tablespoons brandy
- 175 ml/6 fl oz olive oil
- 750 g/1 lb 10 oz onions, chopped
- 1 sprig fresh thyme
- 10 black peppercorns
- 5 cloves
- 275 ml/9 fl oz game or beef stock
  (home-made or made
  with a stock cube)
- 80 g/3 oz raisins
- 8 prunes, stoned
- 250 g/9 oz shallots
- 20 g/¾ oz butter
- 1 teaspoon sugar
- salt and pepper

Serves 8–10

The night before you intend to serve, put the venison into a dish and pour in the milk. Leave to soak in the refrigerator, turning occasionally, for 12 hours. Drain the venison and put into a saucepan. Cook over a high heat, turning twice, for 5 minutes. Meanwhile, heat the brandy in a small saucepan. Pour it over the venison and ignite. When the flames have died down, pour in the oil, add the onion, thyme, peppercorns and cloves and season with salt. Cook over a medium heat, gradually adding the stock, a little at a time. Cover the pan and simmer, turning the meat occasionally, for 1 hour. Add the raisins and prunes, re-cover the pan and cook for a further 45 minutes. Put the shallots, butter, sugar and a pinch of salt into a saucepan, add water to cover and cook for 20 minutes. Remove the pan from the heat and set aside. Lift out the venison, carve it into slices, put it on a serving dish and keep warm. Pass the sauce through a food mill or process in a food processor. Drain the shallots and place them around the meat. Serve immediately, offering the sauce separately.

Note: Boiled potatoes or apple compote (see recipe 973) can also be served with this dish.

Feathered game

Game birds have always featured among the most common dishes in the Spanish kitchen and many different birds are popular throughout the world. They may be prepared in many different ways. As some species that were once hunted have become, or are becoming, endangered, wild birds are now protected and many countries have 'closed' seasons when game cannot be shot. 'Open' seasons may vary depending on the type of bird, and differ from country to country. The principle, however, is to give breeding birds an opportunity to recoup their numbers. Fresh game may be sold only during the open season, but in some countries frozen game is available throughout the year.

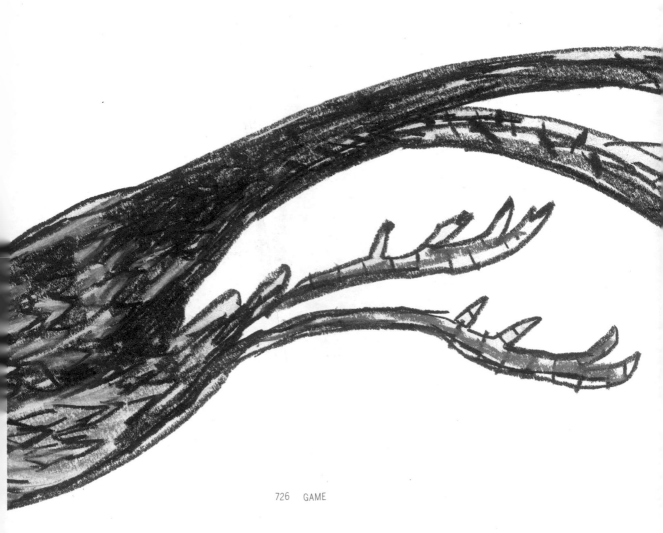

Selection and storage

Shiny feathers are a clear indicator of freshness. Avoid birds with severe injuries, such as broken limbs or badly damaged skin. Although game birds have quite a strong aroma, they should not smell unpleasant. It is best to buy from a specialist butcher or reputable Internet supplier, although supermarkets now stock increasing quantities of oven-ready game birds in season. Keep game in a cool, dry place rather than in the refrigerator. Nowadays, most feathered game is eaten fresh. Quail and other small birds should be drawn as soon as they are killed. Keep them in a cool place and eat within a couple of days. If you choose to hang your game, partridge, pheasant and other large birds are better briefly hung. Hang them by the head in a dry, cool place without plucking or drawing them. Allow about 3 days for partridges and 4–5 for pheasants. Wild duck should be plucked and drawn, then left to stand for a couple of days before being cooked. Always pluck and draw game birds before freezing them and never keep them in the freezer for more than 6 months.

How to prepare

As game is quite expensive, it is usually served as a main course, but it can also be used to make pâté. This is easy to prepare and the meat is usually mixed with pork or other lean meat and with bacon. A slightly more complicated but absolutely delicious way to prepare game birds is to bone them and stuff them with mushrooms, pistachios, etc., or with ham or bacon to make the meat jucier. Doing this changes the flavour slightly which may not be to everyone's taste. Wrap in muslin and poach in flavoured liquid, then put a weight on top to press out all the fat. Remove the muslin and serve cut into slices. Delicious stuffings can be made by mixing meat with breadcrumbs soaked in milk, egg yolks, mushrooms and spices. Game birds should never be frozen after stuffing, as the bacon will become rancid and ruin the meat.

Partridge

Characteristics and curious facts

The French or red-legged partridge can grow to about 40 cm/16 inches in length and has a stout body, short neck, a small head and beak and shiny red feet. Its plumage is varied, being grey-brown on the back with brighter tones on the head and neck. It has a white throat and a reddish-brown breast. The other species of partridge commonly found in Britain is the grey-legged partridge. It is smaller than the French partridge, with a reddish-grey back and an ashy breast with a horseshoe-shaped patch, and is generally considered to have a better flavour and texture. There are a number of other types of partridge. Patridges live in open spaces on moors and arable land. They live in flocks or coveys and have a tendency to burst into flight when flushed. Breeding adults form monogamous pairs in the winter and the hens lay 8–16 eggs in the spring in a rudimentary nest made on the ground. Both parents incubate the eggs and rear the chicks.

How to prepare and cook

Like most game meat, partridge can be hung to make it more tender and tastier. Three to four days are all that is required. Younger birds and hens are usually more tender and can be hung for a shorter time. Partridge has a fine, delicate flavour and a texture similar to that of chicken. It may be roasted, braised or made into pies and pâtés but however it is cooked, it is always tasty. As it has a high calorie content, is packed with protein and contains a lot of mineral salts, partridge was not traditionally recommended for people who are overweight, hypertensive or rheumatic or who have high levels of uric acid. On the other hand, because it contains high-quality protein it is believed to be excellent for children and adolescents, especially during periods of growth and intense physical exercise.

How to pluck and draw

Simply pull the feathers, which will usually come out easily. Hold the bird by the legs and pull out the feathers, starting with the back. Then cut the skin close to the tail end at the back and remove the intestines. Remove the gall bladder from the liver. Singe the remaining feathers over a flame or use cotton wool soaked in alcohol. Cut the legs and the neck towards the middle of their length. Pull the skin towards the wings and then cut the neck down by the wings. Join the skin and sew, it or hold, it in place with a wooden cocktail stick. Rinsing the bird is not recommended, but if you do rinse it, dry it carefully afterwards with a clean tea towel.

Nutrition

Partridge contains all the essential amino acids that form the protein 'building blocks' of the body. Partridge has about 22 g protein, 4 g fat and 0.5 g carbohydrate per 100 g meat. Its calorie content is about 130 calories per 100 g / 3 ½ oz and it is 72 per cent water. It has high quantities of B vitamins and is a good source of potassium, calcium, magnesium and iron.

Partridge meat per 100 g	Calories (Kcal)	Carbohydrates (g)	Fats (g)	Protein (g)
Raw	130	0.5	4	22
Braised	220	0.5	10	36
Roasted	212	0	7	36

Value for money

Fresh partridge is available during the 'open season' in the autumn and winter. In some countries, frozen partridge is available all year round. You can buy it from specialist butchers, Online or from some supermarkets. It is widely available oven-ready. The best way to guarantee the quality of a partridge is to know its origin and when and where it was shot. Otherwise, you must judge by its appearance – the shininess and cleanness of its plumage, the brightness of its eyes and the texture of its muscles. Do not buy birds with severe wounds or obvious deterioration resulting from being stored badly.

Selection

How to choose them: The hen is tastier and more tender than the cock. It can be recognized because it does not have a spur shaped like a button on its foot. To tell if it is tender look at the beak – the lower part a young bird's beak is soft.

850

Partridge with sausages and carrots
PERDICES CON SALCHICHAS Y ZANAHORIAS

- **3 partridges**
- **9 sausages**
- **175 ml/6 fl oz olive oil**
- **1 large onion, chopped**
- **500 g/1 lb 2 oz carrots, thickly sliced**
- **250 ml/8 fl oz white wine**
- **1 bay leaf**
- **salt**

Serves 6

Season the partridges with salt and put one sausage in the cavity of each bird. Cut lengthways along the centre of each remaining sausage, open it out like a book and place one sausage on the breast and one on the back of each partridge. Tie the partridges and the sausages with fine kitchen string. Heat the oil in a large, heavy based saucepan. Add the birds and cook over a medium heat, turning frequently, for 8–10 minutes, until evenly browned all over. Remove from the pan and set aside. Add the onion to the pan and cook over a low heat, stirring occasionally, for about 8 minutes, until beginning to brown. Add the carrot and cook, stirring occasionally, for 5 minutes. Return the partridges to the pan, pour in the wine and 500 ml/18 fl oz water and add the bay leaf. Bring to the boil, lower the heat, cover and simmer for about 1¼ hours, until the partridges are tender and cooked through. Check by piercing the thickest part with the point of a sharp knife; if the juices run clear, the partridge is done. Lift out the partridges from the pan, and remove and discard the string. Remove the sausages from the outsides of the birds and put them in a food processor with the sauce and process until smooth. Return the sauce to the pan and set aside. Cut each bird in half lengthways and place on a warm serving dish. Halve the sausages from the cavities and put them around the dish. Spoon a little of the sauce over the partridges and serve immediately, offering the rest of the sauce in a sauce boat.

Note: Always use good quality butcher's sausages in this recipe. For a particularly attractive presentation, garnish the serving dish with little mounds of Brussels sprouts (500 g/1 lb 2 oz), cooked and then fried in butter, alternated with shallots (500 g/1 lb 2 oz), cooked and then fried in oil until golden brown. The dish could also be garnished with straw potatoes (see recipe 243).

851

Partridge stuffed with raisins and cooked in milk

PERDICES RELLENAS DE PASAS Y GUISADAS CON LECHE

- 100 g/3½ oz raisins
- 2 partridges
- 5 tablespoons olive oil
- 1 onion, chopped
- 1½ tablespoons plain flour
- 3 tablespoons brandy
- 500 ml/18 fl oz warm milk
- salt and pepper

Serves 4

Put the raisins in a bowl, pour in warm water to cover and leave to soak for 20 minutes, then drain. Season the cavities of the partridges with salt and fill them with the raisins. Secure the openings with wooden cocktail sticks. Heat the oil in a large, heavy based saucepan. Add the partridges and cook over a medium heat, turning frequently, for 8–10 minutes, until evenly browned all over. Remove the birds from the pan and set aside in a flameproof dish. Add the onion to the pan and cook over a low heat, stirring occasionally, for about 5 minutes, until translucent. Stir in the flour and cook, stirring constantly, for about 5 minutes, until light golden brown. Remove the pan from the heat. Heat the brandy in a small saucepan, ignite it and carefully pour it over the partridges. When the flames have died down, place the birds into the saucepan together with any cooking juices. Pour in the milk, season and bring to the boil. Lower the heat, cover and simmer for about 1 hour, until the partridges are tender. Lift out the birds, cut them in half lengthways and put them on a warm serving dish. Pass the sauce through a food mill or process and pour it over the birds. Serve garnished with Potato Balls (see recipe 231), if you like.

852

Partridges in cream sauce

PERDICES CON SALSA DE NATA

- 2 partridges
- 4 tablespoons olive oil
- 1 onion, coarsely chopped
- 5 tablespoons white wine
- pinch of mixed dried herbs
  or 1 bouquet garni
  (2 bay leaves, 1 sprig fresh
  thyme and 1 sprig fresh parsley
  tied together in muslin)
- ¼ teaspoon meat extract
- 1 teaspoon potato flour
- juice of ½ lemon
- 250 ml/8 fl oz single cream
- salt and pepper

Serves 4

Season the cavities of the partridges with salt. Heat the oil in a large, heavy based saucepan or a cocotte. Add the birds and the onion and cook over a medium heat, turning and stirring frequently, for 8–10 minutes, until the partridges are evenly browned all over. Pour in 175 ml/6 fl oz water and the wine, season with salt and pepper and add the dried herbs or bouquet garni. Cover and cook over a low heat for about 1 hour, until the partridges are tender. Lift out the birds from the pan, cut them in half lengthways and put them on a serving dish. Keep warm. Remove and discard the bouquet garni, if used. Pass the sauce through a food mill or process in a food processor. Transfer to a clean pan and stir in the meat extract. Mix the potato flour with 1 tablespoon water and the lemon juice in a bowl, stir in a little of the sauce and add to the pan. Heat gently, stirring constantly, then stir in the cream. Heat the sauce for a few minutes more but do not allow to boil. Pour the sauce over the partridges and serve.

853 Partridges with grapes

PERDICES CON UVAS

- **3 partridges**
- **50 g/2 oz lard or 3 tablespoons sunflower oil**
- **400 g/14 oz seedless white grapes, peeled**
- **3 tablespoons olive oil**
- **175 ml/6 fl oz white wine**
- **3 tablespoons brandy**
- **salt and pepper**

Serves 6

Season the cavities of the partridges with salt, spread a little of the lard or the sunflower oil over the outsides, then season the outsides with salt. Put a handful of grapes into the cavity of each bird. Heat the olive oil in a large, heavy based saucepan or a cocotte. Add the birds and cook over a medium heat, turning frequently, for 8–10 minutes, until evenly browned all over. Pour in the wine and 175 ml/6 fl oz water, season with pepper and bring to the boil. Lower the heat, cover and simmer, turning the birds occasionally, for about 1 hour, until the partridges are tender. Add the remaining grapes. Heat the brandy in a small saucepan, ignite it and carefully pour it over the partridges. When the flames have died down, put the lid back on the pan and cook over a medium heat for a further 5 minutes. Lift out the partridges from the pan, cut them in half lengthways and place on a warm serving dish. Spoon the grapes around them and pour the sauce over them. If there is not very much sauce, stir in a few tablespoons of very hot water.

Note: You can use 2-cm/¾-inch cubes of sweet ripe melon in place of the grapes.

854

Stuffed partridge wrapped in cabbage
PERDICES ESTOFADAS Y ENVUELTAS EN REPOLLO

- 2 partridges
- 250 ml/8 fl oz white wine
- 250 ml/8 fl oz olive oil
- 1 bouquet garni (1 clove garlic, 1 bay leaf, 2 sprigs fresh parsley and 1 sprig fresh thyme tied together in muslin)
- 1 onion, cut into 4 wedges
- 2 ripe tomatoes, seeded and cut into quarters
- 6–12 Savoy cabbage leaves
- 20 g/1½ oz butter
- 2 tablespoons sunflower oil
- 1½ tablespoons plain flour
- 250 ml/8 fl oz milk
- 100 g/3½ oz gruyere cheese, grated

Serves 6

Season the cavities of the partridges with salt and put them into a large, heavy based saucepan or a cocotte with the wine, olive oil, bouquet garni, onion, tomatoes and a pinch of salt. Pour in 250 ml/8 fl oz water, cover and cook over a low heat for about 1¼ hours, until the partridges are tender. Meanwhile, bring a large sauce-pan of salted water to the boil. Add the cabbage leaves, pushing them down into the water with a slotted spoon, cover and cook for about 20 minutes. Drain well and set aside. Lift out the partridges from the pan, reserving the cooking liquid, and carve the meat, like chicken. Divide the meat among the cabbage leaves, then fold over the leaves to form parcels. Transfer to an ovenproof dish. Remove and discard the bouquet garni from the reserved cooking liquid and pass the liquid through a food mill or process in a food processor, then set aside. Preheat the oven to 200°C/400°F/Gas Mark 6. Melt the butter with the sunflower oil in a frying pan. Stir in the flour and cook, stirring constantly, for 2 minutes. Gradually stir in the milk, a little at a time. Cook, stirring constantly, for about 6 minutes, until thickened, then add 120 ml/4 fl oz of the cooking liquid. Mix well, cook for a further 5 minutes, season to taste with salt and pour the sauce over the cabbage parcels. Sprinkle with the gruyere and bake for about 15 minutes, until the topping is golden brown. Serve immediately, straight from the dish.

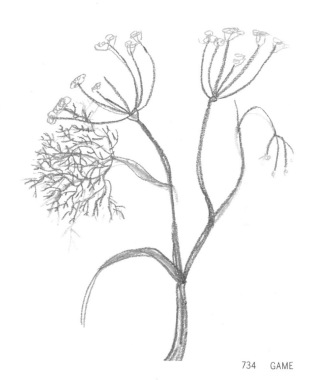

Partridges with orange

PERDICES EN SALSA CON CÁSCARA DE NARANJA

- **5 tablespoons olive oil**
- **2 partridges**
- **2 large onions, chopped**
- **1 heaped tablespoon plain flour**
- **175 ml / 6 fl oz white wine**
- **1 chicken stock cube**
- **finely grated rind of 2 oranges**
- **juice of 1 orange**
- **salt**

Serves 4

Heat the oil in a large, heavy based saucepan. Add the birds and cook over a medium heat, turning frequently, for 8–10 minutes, until evenly browned all over. Remove from the pan and set aside. Add the onion to the pan and cook over a low heat, stirring occasionally, for about 8 minutes, until beginning to brown. Stir in the flour and cook, stirring constantly, for 5 minutes. Return the partridges to the pan, pour the wine over them and add warm water to cover. Crumble the stock cube, mix with a little hot water and add to the pan along with the orange rind. Season to taste with salt, cover and bring to the boil, then lower the heat and simmer gently for 1¼–1½ hours, until the partridges are tender. Remove the birds from the pan, cut them in half lengthways and put on a warm serving dish. Pass the sauce through a food mill or process in a food processor, stir in the orange juice and season to taste with salt. Spoon a little of the sauce over the meat and serve immediately, offering the rest of the sauce separately. The dish can be served with macaroni tossed in butter and grated cheese, Mashed Potato (see recipe 230) or Brussels sprouts sautéed in butter.

Note: If the sauce becomes too thin when the orange juice is added, mix in 1 teaspoon potato flour dissolved in 1 tablespoon water. Cook the sauce over a low heat, stirring constantly, for 2–3 minutes, then serve as above.

856

Partridges with cabbage
PERDICES CON REPOLLO

- 2 partridges
- 4 rashers of lean bacon
- 3 tablespoons olive oil
- 1 tablespoon plain flour
- pinch of mixed dried herbs
  or 1 bouquet garni
  (1 clove garlic, 2 sprigs fresh
  parsley, 1 sprig fresh thyme and
  1 bay leaf tied together in muslin)
- 150 g/5 oz streaky bacon,
  cut into strips
- 1 Savoy cabbage, shredded
- ½ teaspoon meat extract
- salt

Serves 4

Season the cavities of the partridges with salt, put a rasher of lean bacon over the breast and back of each one and tie in place with fine kitchen string. Heat the oil in a large, heavy based saucepan or a cocotte. Add the birds and cook over a medium heat, turning frequently, for 8–10 minutes, until evenly browned all over. Sprinkle the flour into the pan and pour in warm water to come halfway up the partridges. Add the dried herbs or bouquet garni and season with salt. Bring to the boil, lower the heat to medium, cover and cook for about 1¼ hours. Bring a saucepan of salted water to the boil and add the streaky bacon. When it comes back to the boil, add the cabbage, pushing it down into the water with a slotted spoon, and cook for 20 minutes. Drain well and place the cabbage and bacon around the partridges. Cook for a further 10 minutes, until the partridges are tender. Lift the birds out of the pan and remove and discard the bacon and string. Cut the partridges in half lengthways and put on a warm serving dish. Remove and discard the bouquet garni, if used. Drain the cabbage and bacon, reserving the cooking liquid, and place around the partridges. If the cooking liquid is too thin, cook, uncovered, over a high heat, until slightly reduced. Strain, stir in the meat extract and serve in a sauce boat with the partridges.

Partridges cooked with hot vinegar

PERDICES GUISADAS CON VINAGRE CALIENTE

- **3 small partridges**
- **100 g/3½ oz lard or 175 ml/ 6 fl oz olive oil**
- **1 large onion, chopped**
- **3 carrots, sliced**
- **175 ml/6 fl oz white wine**
- **5 tablespoons white-wine vinegar**
- **1 chicken stock cube**
- **pinch of mixed dried herbs or 1 bouquet garni (1 sprig fresh thyme, 2 bay leaves, 1 sprig fresh parsley and 1 clove garlic tied together in muslin)**
- **salt**

Serves 6

Season the cavities of the partridges with salt. Melt the lard or heat the oil in a large, heavy based saucepan or a cocotte. Add the partridges and cook over a medium heat, turning frequently, for 8–10 minutes, until evenly browned all over. Remove from the pan and set aside. Add the onion to the pan and cook over a low heat, stirring occasionally, for about 5 minutes, until softened and translucent. Add the carrot and cook, stirring occasionally, for a further 10 minutes. Return the partridges to the pan and pour in the wine and vinegar. Dissolve the stock cube in a little water in a bowl, add to the pan and pour in just enough hot water to cover the birds completely. Add the dried herbs or bouquet garni, season with salt, cover and cook over a low heat for about 1¼ hours, until the partridges are tender. Lift out the birds from the pan, cut them in half lengthways and put on a warm serving dish. Remove and discard the bouquet garni, if used. Pass the sauce through a food mill or process in a food processor and pour over the partridges. Serve immediately, garnished with triangles of fried bread (see recipe 130), if you like.

858

- **3 small partridges**
- **175 ml/6 fl oz olive oil**
- **1 onion, coarsely chopped**
- **3 carrots, sliced**
- **1 bouquet garni
  (1 sprig fresh thyme, 2 bay
  leaves, 1 sprig fresh parsley,
  1 stick celery and 2 cloves garlic
  tied together in muslin)**
- **6 black peppercorns**
- **175 ml/6 fl oz white wine**
- **175 ml/6 fl oz white-wine vinegar**
- **salt**

Serves 6

Pickled partridges

PERDICES ESCABECHADAS

Season the cavities of the partridges with salt. Heat the oil in a large, heavy based saucepan or a cocotte. Add the birds and cook over a medium heat, turning frequently, for 8–10 minutes, until evenly browned all over. Remove them from the pan and set aside. Drain off nearly all the oil from the pan, leaving just enough to cover the base. Return the birds to the pan, add the onion, carrot, bouquet garni and peppercorns and cook for 5 minutes. Pour in the wine and vinegar, cover and cook over a medium heat for 10 minutes. Pour in just enough water to cover the partridges, season with salt, re-cover the pan, lower the heat and cook for about 1 ½ hours, until the partridges are tender. Remove the pan from the heat and leave the birds to cool in their sauce. If they are to be eaten immediately, lift them out when cold, cut in half lengthways and put on a serving dish. Remove and discard the bouquet garni and pass the sauce through a food mill or process in a food processor. Spoon it over the partridges and serve. If you do not plan to eat them right away, transfer the whole partridges to an earthenware or glass container. Remove and discard the bouquet garni. Ladle in the sauce to cover the partridges completely. Add a few tablespoons of olive oil and seal the container. Store in a cool place. When serving, cut the partridges in half lengthways, garnish with the slices of carrot and strain the sauce before pouring it over the birds. In both cases, serve cold.

Woodcock

How to prepare

Allow 1 woodcock per 2–3 servings. If you hang them, woodcock should be hung by their feet, without plucking, for 4–5 days in the open air in a cool, but not damp place. When ready to cook, pluck them, remove the eyes and gizzards but do not draw them. The innards, called the 'trail', may be spread on toast and eaten. Singe the woodcock over a flame to remove any remaining feathers and season inside and out with salt and pepper. They are then ready to be cooked as preferred. Like most game birds, woodcock are available oven-ready. However, they are rarely sold in any form by commercial butchers. You are more likely to obtain them from friends or acquaintances who shoot or sometimes from online sources.

859

Pan-cooked woodcock
BECADAS EN CACEROLA

- 3 woodcock
- 50 g/2 oz lard or
  4–5 tablespoons olive oil
- 6 rashers of streaky bacon,
  diced
- 250 ml/8 fl oz sherry
- 3–4 tablespoons boiling water
- salt and pepper

Serves 6

Season the woodcock inside and out with salt and pepper. Melt the lard or heat the oil in a large, heavy based saucepan or a cocotte. Add the woodcock and bacon and cook over a medium-high heat, stirring and turning frequently, for about 8 minutes, until evenly browned all over. Cover and cook, turning occasionally, over a medium heat for 10 minutes. Pour in the sherry, re-cover and cook for a further 10–15 minutes, until the birds are tender. Lift out the birds from the pan and cut them in half lengthways. Remove and reserve the intestines. Place the birds on a serving dish and keep warm. Stir the boiling water into the sauce and cook, stirring and scraping up any bits on the base of the pan. Chop the intestines, if using, and stir into the sauce. Pass the sauce through a food mill, pressing down well, or process in a food processor. Pour it over the woodcock and serve with triangles of fried bread (see recipe 130) or Potato Balls (see recipe 231).

860

Woodcock with cognac
BECADAS CON COÑAC

- 3 woodcock
- 100 g/3½ oz lard or
  5 tablespoons sunflower oil
- 175 ml/6 fl oz cognac or
  other brandy
- juice of ½ lemon
- 1 tablespoon chopped
  fresh parsley
- salt and pepper

Serves 6

Preheat the oven to 240°C/475°F/Gas Mark 9. Season the woodcock inside and out with salt and spread some of the lard or brush some of the oil over them. Divide the remaining lard or oil among the cavities and put the birds into a roasting tin. Roast for 12–15 minutes, until tender. Remove the birds from the roasting tin, cut off the breasts and legs and put on a serving dish. Keep warm. Carefully collect the carving juices. Chop the carcass and intestines with a heavy knife or a cleaver. Heat the brandy in a small saucepan and ignite it. When the flames have died down, add the chopped carcass and the carving juices and season with salt and pepper. Cook over a high heat, stirring constantly, for 10 minutes, then pass the sauce through a food mill, pressing down well, or process in a food processor. Taste and adjust the seasoning if necessary, stir in the lemon juice and parsley and pour the sauce over the woodcock. Serve immediately, with triangles of fried bread (see recipe 130) or Potato Balls (see recipe 231).

Quail

These migratory birds which originated in the Middle East, appear in Europe in the spring but are becoming quite rare. The wild common quail is a protected species in Britain. In Spain, quail are often caught alive in order to fatten them up, although these birds have less flavour than wild ones. Some types of quail are also farmed in many different countries, including Britain, and are therefore available all year round. Quail are small birds, 150–200 g / 5–7 oz, and their meat has a delicious flavour. Quails' eggs are also used in cooking. Fresh and frozen oven-ready quail are widely available. Depending on their size, allow 1–2 per serving.

861

- 4 quail
- 1 large onion, finely chopped
- 2 carrots, sliced
- 1 tomato,
  peeled, seeded and chopped
- 3 cloves garlic
- 1 bouquet garni
  (1 sprig fresh marjoram, 1 bay
  leaf and 1 sprig fresh parsley
  tied together in muslin)
- 250 ml/8 fl oz white wine
- ½ game or chicken stock cube
  dissolved in 250 ml/8 fl oz water
- 250 ml/8 fl oz olive oil
- salt and pepper
Serves 4

Stewed quail
CODORNICES ESTOFADAS

Season the cavities of the quail with salt. Put them into a saucepan with the onion, carrot, tomato, garlic and bouquet garni, pour in the wine, stock and oil and bring to the boil. Lower the heat and simmer for 1 hour, until the birds are tender. Transfer the quail to a warm serving dish. Remove and discard the bouquet garni and garlic and process the sauce in a food processor. Pour the sauce over the stewed quail and serve.

862

- 6 vine leaves
- 6 quail
- 50 g/2 oz lard
- 6 thin rashers of bacon
- 6 slices of fried bread
  (see recipe 130)
- dressed watercress
- salt
Serves 6

Roast quail
CODORNICES ASADAS

If using brined vine leaves, soak them in hot water for 20 minutes, then drain, rinse well and pat dry. You do not need to soak fresh vine leaves. Preheat the oven to 220°C/425°F/Gas Mark 7. Season the cavities of the quail with salt. Spread a little of the lard on the vine leaves and stick them on to the birds' breasts. Put the bacon over the birds' backs and spread with the remaining lard. Truss with fine kitchen string, put into a roasting tin and roast for 15–20 minutes, until tender. Lift out the quail from the roasting tin, remove and discard the string and vine leaves and reserve the bacon. Place each quail on a slice of fried bread and top with a bacon rasher. Stir 3–4 tablespoons hot water into the cooking juices and cook over a medium heat, scraping up any bits from the base of the roasting tin, for a few minutes. Pour the sauce over the quail and serve immediately, garnished with the watercress.

Quail in potato nests
CODORNICES EN NIDO DE PATATAS PAJA

- **6 quail**
- **50 g/2 oz lard**
- **6 thin rashers of bacon**
- **500 g/1 lb 2 oz potatoes, thinly sliced then cut into fine straws**
- **sunflower oil, for deep-frying**
- **salt**

Serves 6

Preheat the oven to 220°C/425°F/Gas Mark 7. Season the cavities of the quail with salt. Put the bacon over the birds' backs and spread with a little of the lard. Truss with fine kitchen string, put into a roasting tin and roast for 15–20 minutes, until tender. Meanwhile, heat the sunflower oil in a deep-fryer or saucepan to 180–190°C/350–375°F or until a cube of day-old bread browns in 30 seconds. Divide the potato straws into 6 equal amounts. Spread one amount over the base and slightly up the sides of a wire basket and lower into the hot oil. Cook for about 2 minutes, until golden brown, then remove from the oil and drain. Repeat with the remaining potato straws. Put a roasted quail, breast uppermost, in each potato nest, top with the bacon. Stir 3–4 tablespoons hot water into the roasting tin and cook over a medium heat, scraping up any bits from the base of the roasting tin, for a few minutes. Pour into a sauce boat and serve immediately with the quail.

864

Pan-cooked quail
CODORNICES EN CACEROLA

- 6 vine leaves
- 6 quail
- 50 g/2 oz pork lard
- 6 thin rashers of bacon
- 3 tablespoons olive oil
- 6 slices of fried bread
  (see recipe 130)
- salt

Serves 6

If using brined vine leaves, soak them in hot water for 20 minutes, then drain, rinse well and pat dry. You do not need to soak fresh vine leaves. Season the cavities of the quail with salt. Spread a little of the lard on the vine leaves and stick them on to the birds' breasts. Put the bacon over the birds' backs and spread with the remaining lard. Truss with fine kitchen string. Heat the oil in a large, heavy based saucepan or a cocotte. Add the quail and cook over a medium heat, turning frequently, for about 8 minutes, until evenly browned all over. Lower the heat and cook, uncovered, over a medium heat for 15–20 minutes, until tender. Lift out the quail, remove and discard the string, bacon and vine leaves and put each bird on a slice of the fried bread. Put on a serving dish and keep warm. Stir 4–5 tablespoons hot water into the pan and cook over a medium heat, stirring and scraping up any bits from the base, for a few minutes, then serve the sauce in a sauce boat or poured over the quail.

865

Quail in white-wine sauce
CODORNICES EN SALSA

- 5 tablespoons olive oil
- 12 quail
- 3 large onions, finely chopped
- 175 ml/6 fl oz game or chicken
  stock (home-made or made
  with a stock cube)
- 1 teaspoon mustard powder
- 175 ml/6 fl oz white wine
- pinch of freshly grated nutmeg
- pinch of ground cinnamon
- salt and pepper

Serves 6

Heat the oil in a saucepan. Add the quail and cook over a medium heat, turning frequently, for about 5 minutes but do not allow them to brown. Remove from the pan and set aside. Add the onion to the pan and cook over a low heat, stirring occasionally, for about 5 minutes, until softened and translucent. Put the quail on top of the onion, pressing them down well, and pour in the stock. Stir the mustard into the wine and pour into the pan, then season with salt and pepper and sprinkle in the nutmeg and cinnamon. Cover and bring to the boil, then lower the heat and simmer gently for 1–2 hours, until the birds are tender. Put the quail on a warm serving dish and spoon the sauce over them. Serve immediately, with triangles of fried bread (see recipe 130).

866

Braised quail
CODORNICES GUISADAS

- **5 tablespoons olive oil**
- **1 large onion, chopped**
- **6 fat quail or 12 small quail**
- **40 g/1½ oz plain flour**
- **pinch of freshly grated nutmeg**
- **pinch of ground cinnamon**
- **350–500 ml/12–18 fl oz**
  white wine
- **1 bay leaf**
- **1 sprig fresh thyme**
- **salt and pepper**

Serves 6

Heat the oil in a saucepan. Add the onion and cook over a low heat, stirring occasionally, for about 8 minutes, until beginning to brown. Coat the quail in the flour, shaking off any excess, put them into the pan and cook over a medium heat, turning frequently, for about 8 minutes, until evenly browned all over. Season with salt and pepper, sprinkle in the nutmeg and cinnamon and pour in enough wine to half cover the birds. Add the bay leaf and thyme, cover the pan with brown paper that has been cut in a circle to fit snugly inside the saucepan and put the lid on top. Cook over a medium heat, shaking the pan occasionally, for about 25 minutes, until the quail are tender. Lift out the birds and put them on a warm serving dish. Remove and discard the bay leaf and thyme sprig, pass the sauce through a food mill or process in a food processor and spoon it over the quail. Serve immediately, garnished with triangles of fried bread (see recipe 130).

Pheasant

Selection

Nowadays pheasants are widely available and relatively inexpensive. The best ones are about 12 months old and the hen pheasant has a finer flavour and texture than the cock, although he has the more colourful plumage. A hen and cock are often sold in pairs, called a brace. For tender, tasty meat the pheasant should be hung for at least 3 days and up to 2 weeks in cold weather. Farm-raised birds do not need to be hung. From a dietary point of view, the meat has some similarities to chicken and has about 200 calories per 100 g/3 ½ oz. Young birds, weighing between 800 g/1 ¾ lb and 1 kg/2 ¼ lb, can be roasted and will need to cook for 45–60 minutes. Older birds are better braised and most chicken recipes work well with pheasant.

How to clean

Like most other game birds, pheasants are widely available oven-ready. If you do have to pluck and draw a bird, chill it in the refrigerator for several hours as this will make it easier. First, remove the biggest feathers on the wings, twisting them, then pluck the body, neck and wings in that order. Remove the entrails as you would a chicken and season the cavity with salt. Truss securely with fine kitchen string, especially if the bird is to be roasted.

867

Pheasant with apples
FAISAN CON MANZANAS

- **1 pheasant**
- **100 g / 3 ½ oz goose fat or butter**
- **6 apples**
- **175 ml / 6 fl oz single cream**
- **120 ml / 4 fl oz apple liqueur or Calvados**
- **salt and pepper**

Serves 4

Preheat the oven to 230°C/450°F/Gas Mark 8. Season the pheasant inside and out with salt and truss with fine kitchen string. Melt half the goose fat or butter in a frying pan. Add the pheasant and cook over a medium heat, turning frequently, for about 10 minutes, until evenly browned all over. Meanwhile, peel, core and slice the apples, season with salt and pepper and make a thick layer of about half of them in the base of a casserole. Dot with the remaining goose fat or butter and put the pheasant on top. Put the remaining apples around the bird, season with salt and pepper, cover and roast for about 25 minutes, or until the pheasant is tender. Just before serving, gently heat the cream and apple liqueur or Calvados in a saucepan and pour over the pheasant.

Roast pheasant

FAISANES O POULARDAS ASADOS

- 1 pheasant, 2 kg/4½ lb
- 4 thin rashers of streaky bacon
- 100 g/3½ oz lard or
  5 tablespoons sunflower oil
- 450 ml/¾ pint game or chicken
  stock (home-made or
  made with stock cubes)
- 100 g/3½ oz Serrano ham, diced
- 2 carrots, sliced
- 1 tablespoon breadcrumbs
- 100 g/3½ oz canned peas,
  drained
- salt

Serves 4

Preheat the oven to 180°C/350°F/Gas Mark 4. Season the pheasant inside and out with salt, cover the back and breast with the bacon and truss with fine kitchen string. Spread the lard of brush the oil over the bird and put it into a roasting tin. Roast, turning occasionally, for 45 minutes. Lift out the pheasant, remove and discard the string and bacon and carve the bird, collecting the carving juices. Put the meat into a saucepan with the carving juices, pour in the stock and add the ham, carrot and breadcrumbs. Cook over a medium-low heat for about 30 minutes, until the carrot is tender. Add the peas and cook for a further 5–6 minutes, until heated through. Serve immediately.

Note: This dish can be garnished with raw mushroom salad (see recipe 476) or with artichoke hearts fried in a little oil and sprinkled with chopped fresh parsley.

Terrines and meat loaves

869

Meat and chicken liver terrine
PASTEL-TERRINA DE CARNES VARIADAS E HIGADITOS DE POLLO

- 250 g/9 oz chicken livers, thawed if frozen, trimmed
- 400 g/14 oz skinless boneless chicken breasts
- 150 g/5 oz streaky bacon
- 350 g/12 oz boneless pork
- 3 eggs, lightly beaten
- 4 tablespoons brandy
- 120 ml/4 fl oz double cream
- 300 g/11 oz lean bacon, thinly sliced
- 6 cloves
- 1 sprig fresh thyme
- 2 bay leaves
- salt and pepper

Serves 8

Preheat the oven to 180°C/350°F/Gas Mark 4. Chop the chicken livers, chicken breasts, streaky bacon and pork and mix together in a bowl. Stir in the eggs and brandy. Whisk the cream in another bowl with an electric mixer, then add to the meat mixture. Season with salt and pepper and mix well. Cover the base and sides of a terrine with two-thirds of the slices of lean bacon. Fill the terrine with the meat mixture, pressing it down with a wooden spoon. Cover with the remaining slices of lean bacon and push the cloves into them, then put the thyme and the bay leaves on top. Put the lid on the terrine, stand it in a roasting tin and pour in hot water to come about halfway up the sides. Bake for 1½ hours, then turn off the oven and leave the terrine inside until it has cooled. Remove the terrine from the oven, take off the lid, cover with foil and put something heavy on top, such as an iron. Leave in the refrigerator for 3–4 hours. To serve, remove and discard the thyme, bay leaves, cloves and the top layer of bacon. Invert the terrine on to a serving dish and remove the remaining slices of bacon. Cut into slices and serve cold, garnished with watercress or lettuce.

870

Hare terrine
PASTEL-TERRINA DE LIEBRE

- 1 large boneless saddle of hare
- 400 g/14 oz lean boneless pork spare rib
- 400 g/14 oz boneless breast or leg of veal
- 150 g/5 oz streaky bacon
- 350 g/12 oz lean bacon, thinly sliced
- pinch of freshly grated nutmeg
- pinch of dried tarragon
- 5 tablespoons brandy
- 1 sprig fresh thyme
- salt and pepper

Serves 8–10

Preheat the oven to 180°C/350°F/Gas Mark 4. Cut the saddle of hare, pork, veal and streaky bacon into strips about 1.5 cm/⅝ inch wide, keeping each type of meat separate. Line the base and the sides of a terrine with two-thirds of the slices of lean bacon. Make layers of veal, hare and pork in the terrine, seasoning each layer with salt, pepper, nutmeg and tarragon and separating the layers with strips of streaky bacon. When all the meat has been used up, pour the brandy over the top, cover with the remaining slices of bacon and put the thyme on top. If you have any bones from the saddle of hare, you can add some of them for extra flavour. Cover the terrine, put it into a roasting tin and pour in hot water to come about halfway up the sides. Bake for 3 hours. Remove the terrine from the roasting tin and leave to cool. Take off the lid, remove and discard the bones, if used, and the thyme, and cover the terrine with foil. Place something heavy on top, such as an iron, and leave in the refrigerator for 6–8 hours. This dish is served in the terrine after removing the covering of bacon.

871

Liver terrine
PASTEL-TERRINA DE HÍGADO DE CERDO

- 350 g/12 oz lean bacon, thinly sliced
- 500 g/1 lb 2 oz pig's liver, trimmed and finely chopped
- 500 g/1 lb 2 oz minced pork
- pinch of mixed dried herbs
- 2 eggs, lightly beaten
- 4 tablespoons brandy
- salt and pepper

Serves 8–10

Preheat the oven to 160°C/325°F/Gas Mark 3. Line the base and sides of a terrine with two-thirds of the bacon. Mix together the liver, minced pork and dried herbs in a bowl and season with salt. Stir in the eggs and brandy and spoon the mixture into the terrine, pressing down well with a wooden spoon. Cover the top with the remaining slices of bacon and put the lid on the terrine. Put the terrine into a roasting tin and pour in hot water to come about halfway up the sides. Bake for 3 hours, then remove from the roasting tin and leave to stand in the refrigerator for 48 hours before serving. This dish is usually served in the terrine, after removing the top covering of bacon.

872

Veal loaf
PASTEL DE TERNERA

- 120 g/4 oz breadcrumbs
- 200 ml/7 fl oz boiling milk
- 500 g/1 lb 2 oz boneless middle neck of veal
- 150 g/5 oz boneless ham hock
- 120 g/4 oz mushrooms, finely chopped
- 1 boned breast of veal, 750 g/1 lb 10 oz
- 150 g/5 oz Serrano ham, in a single piece
- 3 tablespoons olive oil
- 1 onion, chopped
- ½ calf's foot, cut into pieces
- 1 teaspoon mixed dried herbs or 1 bouquet garni (2 bay leaves, 1 sprig fresh thyme, 1 sprig fresh parsley and 1 clove garlic tied together in muslin)
- 250 ml/8 fl oz white wine
- salt and pepper

Serves 8–10

Put the breadcrumbs into a bowl, pour in the boiling milk and leave to soak. Meanwhile, mince the middle neck of veal and ham hock together with a meat mincer or in a food processor. Mix together the minced meat, breadcrumbs (if they are too liquid, squeeze gently) and mushrooms in a bowl and season with salt and pepper. Spread this mixture evenly over the breast of veal. Cut the Serrano ham into strips about 5 mm/¼ inch wide and arrange them over the meat. Roll up the breast of veal and wrap it carefully in muslin. Tie the ends with kitchen string and secure the centre of the muslin with a wooden cocktail stick. Heat the oil in a large saucepan. Add the onion and cook over a low heat, stirring occasionally, for 7–8 minutes, until beginning to brown. Add the calf's foot and cook, turning occasionally, for about 8 minutes, until lightly browned. Add the dried herbs or bouquet garni and pour in the wine. Add the rolled breast of veal, pour in water to cover and season with salt. Cover and bring to the boil, then lower the heat and simmer for 3 hours. Remove the rolled breast of veal from the pan and drain it. Reserve the cooking liquid. Put the rolled meat on a work surface, still wrapped in muslin, and place something heavy on top until it has cooled completely. Remove the muslin, wrap the meat in foil and chill in the refrigerator. Meanwhile, bring the cooking liquid back to the boil, then simmer, uncovered, for 1 hour. Strain into a deep dish and chill in the refrigerator until set, then chop. To serve, cut the meat into slices, place on a serving dish and garnish with lettuce, if you like.

873

Chicken, ham and veal loaf

PASTEL DE POLLO, JAMÓN Y TERNERA

- 80 g/3 oz lard,
  plus extra for greasing
- 400 g/14 oz minced veal
- 1 large skinless boneless chicken
  breast, coarsely chopped
- 1 tablespoon breadcrumbs
- 2 eggs, lightly beaten
- 5 tablespoons sherry
- 150 g/5 oz Serrano ham,
  cut into thin strips
- salt and pepper

Serves 4–6

Preheat the oven to 180°C/350°F/Gas Mark 4. Grease a loaf tin with lard. Mix together the lard, veal, chicken, breadcrumbs, eggs and sherry in a bowl and season with salt and pepper. Make alternate layers of the meat mixture and strips of ham in the prepared tin. Cover the tin with foil, put it into a roasting tin and pour in boiling water to come about halfway up the sides. Bake for 2 hours. Remove the loaf tin from the roasting tin and leave to cool slightly, then place something heavy on top, such as an iron, until the loaf has cooled completely. To serve, run a knife around the edge of the loaf tin and turn out on to a serving dish. Garnish with watercress or lettuce, if you like, and serve.

874 📷 Chicken and ham terrine

TERRINA DE POLLO Y JAMÓN

- 1 chicken, 1.2 kg/2½ lb,
  giblets reserved
- 4 tablespoons olive oil
- 1 small onion, cut into 4 wedges
- 150 g/5 oz Serrano ham,
  finely chopped
- 100 g/3½ oz thinly sliced
  lean bacon
- 2 tablespoons brandy
- 1 bay leaf
- 1 sprig fresh thyme
- salt and pepper

  Jelly stock:
- 1 calf's foot, cut into pieces
- 2 carrots, chopped
- 1 leek, trimmed and rinsed well
- 2 sticks celery
- 1 bay leaf
- 5 tablespoons white wine
- salt

Serves 8–10

First, make the stock. Pour 3 litres/5¼ pints water into a saucepan and add the calf's foot, carrot, leek, celery, bay leaf and the chicken giblets. Pour in the wine, season with salt and bring to the boil. Lower the heat to medium and cook for 1½ hours. Remove the pan from the heat and strain the liquid into a bowl. Discard the contents of the strainer. Leave the liquid to cool completely and if a layer of fat forms on top, remove it with a spoon. Cut the chicken in half lengthways. Heat the oil in a saucepan. Add the chicken and onion, season with salt and cook, turning the chicken occasionally, for 20 minutes. Remove the pan from the heat and leave to cool. Remove the skin from the chicken, cut the meat into very small pieces and mix it with the ham in a bowl. Preheat the oven to 180°C/350°F/Gas Mark 4. Line the base of a terrine with the bacon, then make a layer of the chicken and ham mixture and pour in a little of the stock. Continue making layers of chicken and ham, followed by more stock, until the terrine is full. Pour in the brandy and put the bay leaf and thyme sprig on top. Put the lid on the terrine, place it in a roasting tin and pour in boiling water to come about halfway up the sides. Bake for 1 hour. Remove the terrine from the roasting tin, take off the lid and leave to cool. If necessary, add a little more stock. Leave the terrine in the refrigerator for at least 6 hours, until completely set. Remove an discard the bay leaf and thyme. Turn the terrine out on to a serving dish and discard the bacon. The terrine can be served with a salad.

875

Pork loaf
PASTEL DE CABEZA DE CERDO

- 1 onion
- 6 cloves
- olive oil, for drizzling
- 2 carrots, halved lengthways
- 1 bay leaf
- 1 sprig fresh thyme
- 1 small nutmeg, halved
- 250 g/9 oz lean pork
- pig's trotters, ears and snout,
  1 kg/2 ¼ lb total weight
- 5 tablespoons white wine
- salt and pepper

Serves 8–10

Preheat the oven to 180°C/350°F/Gas Mark 4. Stud the onion with the cloves and put into a small, ovenproof dish. Drizzle with oil and roast for 30 minutes. Remove from the oven and set aside. Cut the carrots in half widthways and tie the bay leaf and thyme sprig together with fine kitchen string, then put them into a saucepan with the onion, nutmeg and pork. Singe the pig's trotters, ear and snout, if necessary, wash thoroughly and add to the pan. Season with salt and pepper and pour in the wine and just enough water to cover the ingredients completely. Bring to the boil over a high heat, then lower the heat, cover and simmer gently for 4 hours. Remove the pan from the heat and leave to cool. Lift out the pork and dice finely. Lift out the trotters, cut the meat off the bones and dice finely. Dice the snout and cut the ears into very thin strips with kitchen scissors. Mix all the meats together. Strain the stock into a bowl and pour a little into a loaf tin, then add the meat mixture and cover it with more stock. Stir well with a fork so that the stock penetrates and is evenly distributed. Leave in the refrigerator until set. To serve, run the blade of a knife around the edge of the tin, turn the loaf out on to a serving dish and garnish with watercress or escarole, if you like.

Note: Pig's trotters are widely available, but the snout and ears are less commonly seen and may have to be ordered if you want to make the authentic dish. However, as trotters are very gelatinous, you could simply use 1 kg/2 ¼ lb trotters.

876

Chicken liver mould
GELATINA DE HIGADITOS DE POLLO

- 1 small onion
- 2 cloves
- olive oil, for drizzling
- 1 calf's foot
- 2 veal knuckles
- 1 small leek,
  trimmed and rinsed well
- 1 stick celery
- 2 carrots, cut into short lengths
- 175 ml/6 fl oz sherry
- 500 g/1 lb 2 oz chicken livers,
  thawed if frozen, trimmed and
  coarsely chopped
- pepper

Serves 4–6

Preheat the oven to 180°C/350°F/Gas Mark 4. Stud the onion with the cloves and put it into a small, ovenproof dish. Drizzle with oil and roast for 30 minutes. Remove from the oven and set aside. Put the calf's foot, veal knuckles, onion, leek, celery and carrot into a large saucepan and pour in water to cover. Bring to the boil and skim off any froth that rises to the surface, then lower the heat and simmer gently for 2½–3 hours. Strain the stock into a clean saucepan, discarding the contents of the strainer. Add the sherry and chicken livers to the stock in the pan, season to taste with pepper and cook for a further 10 minutes. Strain a layer of stock about 2 cm/¾ inch deep into a mould or loaf tin. Chill in the refrigerator or freezer until set. Garnish with thin slices of carrot, making an attractive pattern all around the edge of the mould or tin. Using a slotted spoon, transfer the chicken livers to the mould or tin, spreading them out evenly. Pour in stock to cover and fill the mould. (Some stock will be left over and can be used for another recipe as it is delicious.) Chill in the refrigerator for 24 hours, until set. Serve with a salad.

877

'Foie gras'
FOIE-GRAS

- 500 g/1 lb 2 oz pork livers,
  thawed if frozen, trimmed
- 500 g/1 lb 2 oz lard
- 4 tablespoons brandy
- 1 egg, beaten

Serves 4–6

Put the livers and lard through a mincer together in batches. Stir in the brandy and egg. Spoon the mixture into a tart tin with a solid bottom and smooth the surface. Put the tart tin into a roasting tin with a solid bottom and pour in hot water to come about halfway up the sides. Bring to the boil over a medium-low heat and cook for about 1 hour, until the fat comes to the surface. Remove the tart tin from the water and leave the foie gras to cool in it, then turn it out and cover with the lard that has oozed out.

Note: Foie gras is normally made from goose or duck livers and this recipe is not a direct substitute when foie gras is required within another dish.

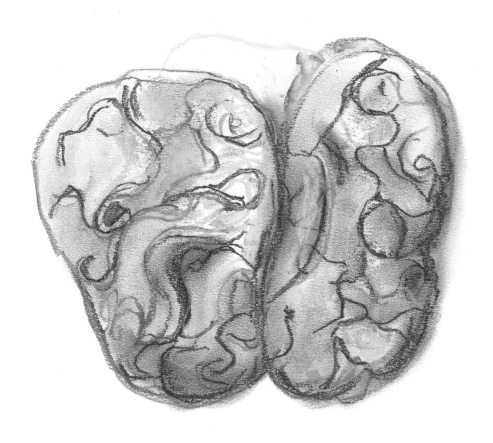

OFFAL

The nobility of offal

Sweetbreads, liver, kidneys, and more – offal is fine food. After all, it often appears on the menus of our best restaurants. It is all a matter of knowing how to get the best out of it. The most important thing when preparing offal is freshness. Always buy from a reliable source. The best criteria for quality is colour – the clearer the better.

Liver

How to cook

Whatever sort of liver you are cooking, from calf's to chicken liver, the oil should not be too hot, especially at the beginning of the process. Liver can be cooked in slices, as kebabs or roasted whole in the case of calf's liver and then cut into slices and served with a sauce.

Tricks

- To tenderize liver, soak it in milk for 1 hour before cooking. Discard the milk and dry the liver before cooking. This is particularly worth-while with coarse-textured liver such as ox liver
- You might have to cut away visible ducts, veins or membrane from the liver before cooking
- If liver is lightly dusted with flour before frying, it will brown better and the oil will splatter less.

878

Simple fried calf's liver
HÍGADO DE TERNERA FRITO SENCILLO

- 6 x 120-g/4-oz slices of
  calf's liver, trimmed
- 175 ml/6 fl oz olive oil
- 1 tablespoon white-wine vinegar
  or lemon juice (optional)
- 1 tablespoon chopped
  fresh parsley
- salt

Serves 6

Season the liver with salt. Heat the oil in a frying pan. Add the slices of liver, in batches, and cook over a medium-high heat for about 2 minutes on each side, until just firm. Transfer to a serving dish and keep warm while cooking the remaining batches. Remove the pan from the heat and stir in the vinegar or lemon juice, if using. Return the pan to the heat and cook, stirring constantly, for a few minutes, then pour the sauce over the liver. Sprinkle with the parsley and serve.

Note: Some people like to add a very finely chopped garlic clove when frying calf's liver. Put this into the frying pan with the parsley and cook for a couple of minutes. Alternatively, substitute 2 tablespoons rinsed and drained capers for the garlic, parsley and vinegar and sauté briefly in the frying pan.

879

Calf's liver marinated in Malaga wine
FILETES DE HÍGADO DE TERNERA MACERADOS CON VINO DE MÁLAGA

- 6 x 120-g/4-oz slices of calf's
  liver, trimmed
- 175 ml/6 fl oz Malaga wine
  or dry sherry
- ½ teaspoon mixed dried herbs
- 275 ml/9 fl oz olive oil
- 1 tablespoon chopped
  fresh parsley
- salt

Serves 6

Put the liver into a fairly deep dish, pour the wine or sherry over it, sprinkle with the dried herbs and leave to marinate in the refrigerator, turning occasionally, for 1 hour. Drain the liver, pat dry and season with salt. Heat the oil in a frying pan. Add the liver and cook over a medium-high heat for about 2 minutes on each side, until just firm. Transfer the liver to a warm serving dish. Sprinkle the parsley over the liver and pour the cooking juices over the top. Serve immediately with Mashed Potato (see recipe 230), Chips (see recipe 242) or seasonal vegetables.

880

Calf's liver in breadcrumbs

FILETES DE HÍGADO DE TERNERA EMPANADOS

- **80 g/3 oz fine breadcrumbs**
- **2 eggs**
- **1 clove garlic**
- **1 sprig fresh parsley**
- **6 thin slices of calf's liver,**
  100–120 g/3½–4 oz each,
  trimmed
- **sunflower oil for deep frying**
- **salt**

Serves 6

Spread out the breadcrumbs in a shallow dish. Lightly beat the eggs in another shallow dish. Pound the garlic with the parsley and a pinch of salt in a mortar. Season the liver with salt and rub in the garlic mixture with your fingertips. Immediately coat the liver first in the breadcrumbs, then in the beaten egg and, finally, in breadcrumbs again, making sure that the breadcrumbs form an even coating. Heat the oil in a deep-fryer or saucepan to 180–190°C/350–375°F or until a cube of day-old bread browns in 30 seconds. Add the liver and cook for few minutes, until golden brown. Remove with a fish slice, drain well and serve immediately.

881

- 6 x 120-g/4-oz slices
  of calf's liver, trimmed
- 1–2 tablespoons Dijon mustard
- 250 ml/8 fl oz olive oil
- 6 thin rashers of bacon
- salt

Serves 6

Liver with mustard and bacon
FILETES DE HÍGADO CON MOSTAZA Y BACON

Season one side of each slice of liver with salt and spread the mustard generously on the other side. Heat the oil in a frying pan. Add the bacon and cook over a medium-high heat for 2–4 minutes on each side, until browned. Remove from the pan and keep warm. Drain off nearly all the oil from the pan, leaving just enough to cover the base. Add the liver, in batches, and cook over a medium-high heat for about 2 minutes on each side, until just firm. Put the slices of liver into a warm serving dish, mustard side uppermost, and top with the bacon. Serve immediately.

882

- 6 tablespoons olive oil
- 2 large onions, cut into
  wedges 2 cm/¾ inch wide
- 2 large green peppers,
  seeded and cut into 2-cm/
  ¾-inch wide strips
- 4 x 120-g/4-oz slices
  of calf's liver, trimmed
- salt

Serves 4

Liver with onions and peppers
FILETES DE HÍGADO CON CEBOLLAS Y PIMIENTOS

Heat the oil in a frying pan. Add the onion and cook over a low heat, stirring occasionally, for about 8 minutes, until beginning to brown. Remove from the pan and keep warm. Add the pepper to the pan, cover and cook over a low heat for 12–15 minutes, until softened. Remove the peppers from the pan and keep warm. Season the liver with salt. Add to the pan and cook over a medium-high heat for about 2 minutes on each side, until just firm. Transfer to a warm serving dish. Return the onion and the pepper back to the pan and heat through. Season them to taste with salt, place around the liver and serve.

883

- 250 ml/8 fl oz olive oil
- 750 g/1 lb 10 oz calf's liver,
  very thinly sliced, trimmed
- 40 g/1½ oz plain flour
- 250 g/8 oz onions,
  very finely chopped
- 175 ml/6 fl oz white wine
- pinch of dried tarragon
- salt

Serves 6

Liver with onions and white wine
ESCALOPINES DE HÍGADO CON CEBOLLA Y VINO BLANCO

Reserve 4 tablespoons of the oil and heat the remainder in a frying pan. Season the liver with salt and dust with the flour, shaking off the excess. Add to the pan, in batches, and cook over a medium-high heat for about 2 minutes on each side, until just firm. Remove from the pan and set aside. Heat the reserved oil in another frying pan. Add the onion and cook over a low heat, stirring occasionally, for 6 minutes, until softened and translucent, then add the wine and cook for a further 5 minutes. Add the liver to the pan, cover and simmer gently for 5 minutes. Serve immediately.

884

Braised calf's liver
HÍGADO DE TERNERA (EN UN TROZO) GUISADO

- **120 g/4 oz bacon,
  cut into thin strips**
- **900-g/2-lb calf's liver
  in a single piece, trimmed**
- **4 tablespoons olive oil**
- **1 onion, chopped**
- **pinch of mixed dried herbs
  or 1 bouquet garni (1 bay leaf,
  1 sprig fresh thyme and 1 sprig
  fresh tarragon tied together
  in muslin)**
- **275 ml/9 fl oz white wine**
- **salt**

Serves 6

Using a larding needle, thread some of the bacon through the liver and put the remainder on top, then tie with fine kitchen string like a roast. Heat the oil in a saucepan. Add the onion and cook over a low heat, stirring occasionally, for about 5 minutes, until softened and translucent. Add the liver and cook, turning frequently, until evenly browned all over. Season with salt and sprinkle with the dried herbs or add the bouquet garni. Pour in the wine and 175 ml/6 fl oz water, cover the pan and cook over a medium heat, turning the liver occasionally, for 25–35 minutes, until the liver is firm. Lift out the liver from the pan, remove and discard the string and the bacon from the top, slice the meat and put the slices on a warm serving dish. Remove and discard the bouquet garni, if used, pour the sauce into a food processor and process or pass through a food mill. Pour the sauce over the liver or serve separately in a sauce boat.

Note: The liver can be served with macaroni tossed in butter and grated cheese, Mashed Potatoes (see recipe 230) or any kind of green vegetable such as Brussels sprouts, peas or green beans.

885

Liver with onion, tomato and cream
FILETES DE HÍGADO CON CEBOLLA, TOMATE Y NATA

- 275 ml/9 fl oz olive oil
- 6 x 120-g/4-oz slices of calf's liver, trimmed
- 40 g/1½ oz plain flour
- 1 large onion, sliced and pushed out into rings
- 4 tomatoes, peeled, seeded and chopped
- ½ teaspoon meat extract
- 1 tablespoon chopped fresh parsley
- 3 tablespoons single cream
- salt

Serves 6

Heat the oil in a large frying pan. Season the liver with salt and dust with the flour, shaking off any excess. Add to the pan, in batches if necessary, and cook for about 2 minutes on each side, until just firm. Remove from the pan and keep warm. Add the onion to the pan and cook over a low heat, stirring occasionally, for about 5 minutes, until softened and translucent. Add the tomato and cook, stirring occasionally and breaking it up with the side of the spoon, for 15 minutes. Stir in the meat extract, return the liver to the frying pan, cover and cook for 3 minutes. Turn the liver and cook for a further 3 minutes. Transfer the liver to a warm serving dish. Sprinkle the parsley into the pan, remove it from the heat and stir in the cream. Season to taste with salt and pour the sauce over the liver. Serve with Mashed Potato (see recipe 230), macaroni tossed with butter and grated cheese or triangles of fried bread (see recipe 130).

886

Calf's liver and bacon brochettes (first version)
PINCHOS DE HÍGADO DE TERNERA CON BACON

- 750 g/1 lb 10 oz calf's liver, trimmed and cut into cubes
- 6 medium-thick rashers of bacon, cut into squares
- olive oil, for brushing
- 6 thin slices of bread
- salt

Serves 6

Preheat the oven to 220°C/425°F/Gas Mark 7. Season the liver with salt, then thread the cubes, alternating with the squares of bacon, on to skewers. Brush the brochettes with oil. Put the slices of bread in a roasting tin and balance the ends of the skewers on the rim. Cook in the oven, turning occasionally, for about 20 minutes, until the liver is just firm and the bacon is brown. Transfer the bread (soaked in the cooking juices) to a serving dish and put the brochettes on top.

887

Calf's liver and bacon brochettes (second version)
PINCHOS DE HÍGADO DE TERNERA CON BACON

- 750 g/1 lb 10 oz calf's liver
- 6 medium-thick rashers of bacon, cut into squares
- 2 eggs, beaten
- 120 g/4 oz breadcrumbs
- sunflower oil, for deep frying

Serves 6

Season the cubed liver with salt, then thread the cubes, alternating with the squares of bacon, onto skewers. Coat first in beaten egg, then breadcrumbs, pressing the crumbs on firmly. Heat the oil in a frying pan to 180-190°C/350-375°F or until a cube of day-old bread browns in 30 seconds. Cook the skewers, turning occasionally, until golden. Serve immediately.

Chicken livers with tomatoes
HIGADITOS CON TOMATE

- **2 tablespoons olive oil**
- **1 onion, chopped**
- **500 g/1 lb 2 oz chicken livers, thawed if frozen, trimmed**
- **3 tomatoes, peeled, seeded and chopped**
- **1 sprig fresh basil, chopped**
- **3 tablespoons white wine**
- **½ chicken stock cube**
- **salt and pepper**

Serves 4–6

Heat the oil in a non-stick frying pan. Add the onion and cook over a low heat, stirring occasionally, for about 5 minutes, until softened and translucent. Add the chicken livers and cook, turning occasionally, for 3 minutes, then add the tomato and basil and cook, stirring occasionally, for a few minutes more. Pour in the wine, crumble in the stock cube and season with salt and pepper. Simmer gently over a low heat for 15 minutes, then serve.

Kidneys

The most delicately flavoured are veal kidneys, although pig's and lamb's kidneys are also delicious. Pig's kidneys have a robust flavour, while ox kidneys are very strongly flavoured and may be quite tough. Lamb's kidneys are smaller and quite tender. They are ideal for kebabs and for grilling or griddling. Whether veal or lamb's kidneys, try to buy the smaller ones – their flavour is more exquisite and their consistency nicer, but they are harder to find. If possible, buy them with their fat intact as they will keep better because they are protected from the air.

How to clean and prepare

Kidneys must be properly prepared, otherwise they will taste bad. Veal and ox kidneys are multi-lobed. Remove the surrounding fat, if necessary, and peel off the membrane. Cut the kidney into small pieces, removing and discarding the core and any ducts or veins. Put the pieces of meat into a coarse sieve, add a handful of salt and turn to coat. Leave to stand for about 2 hours, then rinse under cold running water, shaking the sieve occasionally, for about 10 minutes. Drain well. They will now be ready to cook. Lamb's and pig's kidneys are shaped like a haricot bean. Remove the surrounding fat, if necessary, and peel off the membrane. Cut the kidney in half lengthways with a knife. Use kitchen scissors to cut out the core and any veins.

How to cook

Veal kidneys are delicious cooked in their own fat and are also excellent sautéed. They can be sautéed whole and then sliced before serving or cut into 1-cm/½-inch slices first. Whichever way they are prepared, cook them on all sides over a high heat. If the fat or oil is not hot enough, they will boil, become hard and taste frightful. In fact, you can simply heat kidneys in the sauce that is to accompany them. Prepare the sauce separately and put the two together just before serving.

889

Kidneys with white wine and rice
RIÑONES CON VINO BLANCO Y ARROZ

- 350 g/12 oz onions, finely chopped
- 1 kg/2¼ lb veal kidneys, trimmed and cleaned
- 4 tablespoons olive oil
- 1 clove garlic, coarsely chopped
- 2 sprigs fresh parsley
- 175 ml/6 fl oz white wine
- 1 tablespoon breadcrumbs

Rice:
- 400 g/14 oz long-grain rice
- 50 g/2 oz butter
- salt

Serves 6

Cook and rinse the rice as described in recipe 173, then set aside. Put the onion into a saucepan, put the kidneys on top, pour in the oil and cook over a very low heat for 10 minutes. Pound the garlic with the parsley in a mortar, stir in the wine and pour the mixture over the kidneys. Cook, stirring occasionally, for a further 5 minutes. If the sauce seems thin, stir in the breadcrumbs. Season with salt and cook for 5 minutes more. Season the rice and fry it in the butter as described in recipe 173, then spoon into a ring mould. Turn out on to a warm serving dish and spoon the kidneys and the sauce into the centre. Serve immediately.

890

Veal kidneys in sherry sauce with rice

RIÑONES DE TERNERA CON SALSA DE JEREZ Y ARROZ BLANCO

- **2 tablespoons plain flour**
- **4 tablespoons olive oil**
- **275 ml/9 fl oz sherry**
- **1 kg/2¼ lb veal kidneys, trimmed and cleaned**
- **salt**

Rice:
- **400 g/14 oz long grain-rice**
- **50 g/2 oz butter**
- **salt**

Serves 6

Cook and rinse the rice as described in recipe 173, then set aside. Put the flour into a frying pan and cook over a medium heat, stirring constantly, for about 10 minutes, until beginning to brown. Stir in the oil, then add the sherry, 450 ml/¾ pint water and a pinch of salt. Cook for about 5 minutes. Add the kidneys, lower the heat and cook for about 10 minutes, until firm. Meanwhile, season the rice with salt and fry in the butter as described in recipe 173. Spoon into a ring mould and turn out on to a warm serving dish. Spoon the kidneys and sauce into the centre and serve immediately.

891

Kidneys in tomato sauce, served in bread rolls

RIÑONES CON SALSA DE TOMATE, PRESENTADOS EN PANECILLOS

- 1 tablespoon pine nuts
- 1 hard-boiled egg yolk
- 3 tablespoons sherry
- ½ teaspoon paprika
- 6 round rolls
- sunflower oil for deep frying
- 1 veal kidney, about 750 g/
  1 lb 10 oz, trimmed, cleaned
  and diced
- salt

Tomato sauce:
- 2 tablespoons sunflower oil
- 1 onion, chopped
- 500 g/1 lb 2 oz ripe tomatoes,
  seeded and chopped
- 1 teaspoon sugar
- salt

Serves 6

Make the tomato sauce as described in recipe 73, but do not transfer it to a food processor. Pound half the pine nuts with the egg yolk in a mortar, stir in the sherry, then pour the mixture into the frying pan of tomato sauce. Stir in the paprika, sugar and a pinch of salt. Mix well, then transfer to a food processor and process to a purée. Keep warm. Cut a thin layer off the tops of the rolls and scoop out the middle. Heat the oil in a deep frying pan. Add the rolls upside down, in batches, and cook until golden brown. Remove with a slotted spoon, drain well and keep warm. Transfer about 150 ml/¼ pint of the oil to another frying pan. Add the diced kidney and cook, stirring occasionally, for 5–6 minutes, then drain off the fat. Lightly season the kidney with salt, then stir it into the tomato sauce. Add the remaining pine nuts and divide the mixture among the rolls. Serve immediately.

Note: This recipe can be made with pig's or lamb's kidneys. The individual rolls can be replaced with a large loaf of bread.

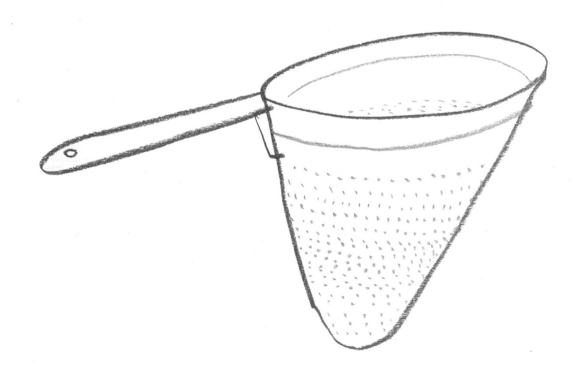

892

- 2 pig's kidneys or 6 lamb's
  kidneys, halved and trimmed
- juice of ½ lemon
- 1 thick rasher of bacon,
  cut into squares
- 120 g/4 oz button mushrooms
- 2 tablespoons olive oil
- salt and pepper

Serves 2

Kidney, bacon and mushroom brochettes

PINCHOS DE RIÑONES DE CERDO O CORDERO, CON TOCINO Y CHAMPIÑONES

Preheat the oven to 230°C/450°F/Gas Mark 8. Put the kidneys into a bowl, pour in water to cover and add the lemon juice. Stir the kidneys around with your hand, then drain and pat dry. Cut the kidneys into large pieces and thread them on to skewers, alternating with the bacon squares and mushrooms. Season with salt and pepper and brush with the oil. Rest the ends of the skewers on the rim of a roasting tin or ovenproof dish. Cook in the oven, turning occasionally, for 15 minutes. Put the skewers on a warm dish and serve with watercress or straw potatoes (see recipe 243)

893

- 3 pig's kidneys or 8 lamb's
  kidneys, halved and trimmed
- juice of ½ lemon
- 2 tablespoons olive oil
- 3 slices of bread
- 1 clove garlic, finely chopped
- 1 teaspoon chopped
  fresh parsley
- salt

Serves 2

Simple kidney brochettes

PINCHOS SIMPLES DE RIÑONES DE CERDO O DE CORDERO

Preheat the oven to 230°C/450°F/Gas Mark 8. Put the kidneys into a bowl, pour in water to cover and add the lemon juice. Stir the kidneys around with your hand, then drain and pat dry. Thread the kidneys lengthways on to skewers. Season with salt and brush with some of the oil. Put the slices of bread in a roasting tin or ovenproof dish and rest the ends of the skewers on the rim with the rounded sides of the kidneys uppermost. Cook in the oven for 5 minutes, turn the skewers and sprinkle with the garlic, parsley and a little more oil. Cook for a further 6 minutes and serve on the slices of bread, with straw potatoes (see recipe 243).

Brains

How to clean and prepare

Both lamb brains and calf brains are cleaned and prepared in the same way, regardless of how they will be cooked later. Put the brains in a colander that just holds them comfortably and place under a gentle flow of cold running water. Continue rinsing until there are no longer any traces of blood. Transfer them to a bowl, pour in water to cover and add 50 ml/2 fl oz vinegar for each calf brain or each pair of lamb brains. Leave to soak for 15–20 minutes, then drain and carefully remove the membrane that covers them, the veins and any remaining blood. Put the brains in a saucepan, pour in water to cover and bring to the boil. Skim off any froth that rises to the surface and simmer gently for a few minutes. Drain and rinse well. The brains are now ready for cooking.

Note: Brains from cattle over six months old may not be sold in Britain as a result of bovine spongiform encephalopathy (BSE).

894

- 1½ calf brains
  or 3 lamb brains
- sunflower oil, for deep frying
- deep-fried parsley sprigs
  (see recipe 918)
- 1 quantity Classic Tomato Sauce
  (see recipe 73)
- 1 quantity batter
  (see recipe 58)

Serves ?

Frittered brains

SESOS HUECOS (O EN BUÑUELOS)

Prepare and blanch the brains as described on page 772. Drain and leave to cool, then cut them into pieces 2–3 cm/¾–1¼ inches long. Make the batter as described in recipe 58. Heat the oil in a deep-fryer or saucepan to 180–190°C/350–375°F or until a cube of day-old bread browns in 30 seconds. Coat the pieces of brain in the batter, add to the hot oil and cook until golden brown all over. Drain well and transfer to a warm serving dish. Garnish with the fried parsley sprigs and serve immediately, offering the tomato sauce separately.

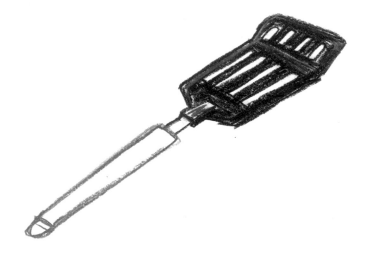

895

- 1½ calf brains
  or 3 lamb's brains
- 2 eggs
- sunflower oil, for deep frying
- 80 g/3 oz breadcrumbs
- salt
- fresh Classic Tomato Sauce
  (see recipe 73)

Serves 6

Coated brains

SESOS EMPANADOS

Prepare and blanch the brains as described on page 772. Leave to cool, then cut them in half lengthways, separating the two lobes, and slice thinly. Beat the eggs with 1 tablespoon of oil and a pinch of salt in a shallow dish. Spread out the breadcrumbs in another shallow dish. Coat the slices of brain first in the beaten egg and then in the breadcrumbs, pressing the crumbs on firmly with your hands. Leave the brains to stand on a work surface or a chopping board. Heat the oil in a deep-fryer or saucepan to 180–190°C/350–375°F or until a cube of day-old bread browns in 30 seconds. Add the brains, in batches, and cook until golden brown. Drain well, put them on to a serving dish and keep warm. Serve with boiled rice, offering the tomato sauce separately.

896

Brains with black butter
SESOS CON MANTEQUILLA NEGRA

- 6 lamb brains
- 40 g/1½ oz plain flour
- 500 g/1 lb 2 oz butter
- 2 tablespoons chopped
  fresh parsley (optional)
- 3 tablespoons
  white-wine vinegar
- salt

Serves 6

Prepare and blanch the brains as described on page 772. Leave to cool, then cut them in half lengthways, separating the two lobes, and dust them with the flour. Melt 225 g/8 oz of the butter in a frying pan. Add the brains, in batches, and cook, turning occasionally, until evenly golden brown all over. Transfer to a warm serving dish and sprinkle with the parsley, if using. Add the remaining butter to the pan and heat until it turns dark brown, then remove the pan from the heat. Stir in the vinegar and return the pan to the heat for a few minutes. Pour the sauce over the brains and serve immediately.

Note: The vinegar can be replaced with rinsed and drained capers.

897

Brains in béchamel sauce
SESOS EN SALSA BECHAMEL CLARITA

- 4 lamb brains
- 25 g/1 oz butter
- 2 tablespoons sunflower oil
- 1 small onion, finely chopped
- 2 tablespoons plain flour
- 175 ml/6 fl oz milk
- 275 ml/9 fl oz chicken stock
  (home-made or made
  with a stock cube)
- 2 egg yolks
- juice of 1 lemon
- 1 tablespoon chopped
  fresh parsley
- salt

Serves 6

Prepare and blanch the brains as described on page 772. Leave to cool, then cut them in half lengthways, separating the two lobes. Cut each lobe in half lengthways and set aside. Melt the butter with the oil in a saucepan. Add the onion and cook over a low heat, stirring occasionally, for 6–8 minutes, until beginning to brown. Stir in the flour and cook, stirring constantly, for 3–4 minutes, until lightly coloured. Gradually stir in the milk, a little at a time, then stir in the stock. Cook, stirring constantly, for 2–3 minutes, until slightly thickened. Remove the pan from the heat and lightly season with salt. Lightly beat the egg yolks with the lemon juice in a bowl, then stir in 2 tablespoons of the sauce, 1 tablespoon at a time. Stir the mixture into the pan of sauce, add the pieces of brain, sprinkle in the parsley and return the pan to a low heat. Heat gently, spooning the sauce over the brains to warm them through. Transfer to a warm serving dish and serve immediately.

898

Gratin of brains, béchamel sauce and mushrooms

SESOS AL GRATÉN, CON BECHAMEL Y CHAMPIÑONES

- 2 calf brains
- 120 g/4 oz button mushrooms
- 50 g/2 oz butter
- juice of ½ lemon
- 2 tablespoons sunflower oil
- 2 tablespoons plain flour
- 350 ml/12 fl oz milk
- 50 g/2 oz gruyere cheese, grated
- salt

Serves 6

Prepare and blanch the brains as described on page 772. Leave to cool, then cut them in half lengthways, separating the two lobes. Slice each lobe into 1-cm/½-inch thick slices and put into a flameproof dish. Preheat the grill. Put the mushrooms, 20 g/¾ oz of the butter, the lemon juice and a pinch of salt into a saucepan. Cover and cook over a medium heat, shaking the pan occasionally, for about 6 minutes. Melt the remaining butter with the oil in a saucepan. Stir in the flour and cook, stirring constantly, for 2 minutes. Gradually stir in the milk, a little at a time. Cook over a medium heat, stirring constantly, for about 6 minutes, until thickened. Drain the mushrooms and add them to the sauce, then season to taste with salt. Pour the béchamel sauce over the brains, sprinkle with the gruyere and cook under the grill for 5–10 minutes, until the topping is golden brown. Serve immediately.

899

Grilled brains with tomato sauce

SESOS CON SALSA DE TOMATE GRATINADOS

- 2 calf brains
  or 4–5 lamb brains
- 3 tablespoons sunflower oil
- 1 onion (optional)
- 1 kg/2¼ lb tomatoes,
  seeded and chopped
- 1 teaspoon sugar
- 3 tablespoons breadcrumbs
- 25 g/1 oz butter
- salt

Serves 6

Prepare and blanch the brains as described on page 772. Leave to cool, then cut into 2-cm/¾-inch thick slices and arrange in a ring in an ovenproof dish. Preheat the oven to 200°C/400°F/Gas Mark 6. Make a very thick tomato sauce with the sunflower oil, onion, if using, tomatoes and sugar as described in recipe 73. Pour the tomato sauce over the brains, sprinkle with the breadcrumbs, dot with the butter and bake for 10–15 minutes, until the top is golden brown. Serve immediately, straight from the dish.

Tongue

How to cook

Allow 1.2 kg/2 ½ lb tongue for 6–8 servings. Tongue is usually sold cleaned and ready to cook. If not, carefully remove any gristle and fat. Put it in cold water to soak in the refrigerator for about 12 hours or overnight, then drain and brush well. Bring a large saucepan of water to the boil, add the tongue and cook at a rolling boil for 10 minutes. Remove the pan from the heat and put it under cold running water. When the tongue has cooled, remove it from the pan and peel off the thick skin with a sharp knife. Some people prefer to remove the skin after the tongue has been braised in stock. It's simply a matter of personal preference. Put 150 g/5 oz pork rind on the base of a large saucepan and put the tongue on top. Add 1 large halved onion, 2 sliced carrots, veal knuckle bones and 1 bouquet garni with 1 sprig fresh parsley, 1 sprig fresh thyme, 1 bay leaf and 1 garlic clove. Season with salt, add some black peppercorns, pour in 175 ml/6 fl oz white wine and add water to cover. Bring to the boil over a high heat, then lower the heat, cover and cook for 2 ½–3 hours, until the tongue is tender. The tongue is now ready to eat and can be accompanied by a variety of sauces or used in a number of different stews. Tongue can also be cooked in a pressure cooker, reducing the cooking time by 1 hour.

900

Tongue with special vinaigrette
LENGUA CON SALSA DE VINAGRETA HISTORIADA

- **1 ox tongue**
- **1 quantity Vinaigrette (see recipes 99 and 100)**

Serves 4

Braise the tongue as described above. Cut it into diagonal slices, and place on a serving dish. Garnish with shredded lettuce and finely chopped hard-boiled egg, offering the vinaigrette separately. This dish can be served hot or cold.

901

Tongue in béchamel sauce with capers

LENGUA CON BECHAMEL Y ALCAPARRAS

- 1 ox tongue
- 1 quantity Béchamel Sauce with capers (see recipe 80)

Serves 4

Braise the tongue as described on page 776. Cut it into diagonal slices and then cook as described in recipe 717.

902

Tongue with onion, tomato and white wine sauce

LENGUA CON SALSA DE CEBOLLA, TOMATE Y VINO BLANCO

- 1 ox tongue
- 6 tablespoons olive oil
- 2 large onions, chopped
- 1 teaspoon plain flour
- 750 g/1 lb 10 oz ripe tomatoes, peeled, seeded and chopped
- 175 ml/6 fl oz white wine
- pinch of mixed dried herbs or 1 bay leaf and 1 sprig fresh thyme
- salt

Serves 4

Braise the tongue as described on page 776, and cut it into diagonal slices. Substituting the tongue for the fish fillets, prepare in the same way as bonito with onion and tomato (see recipe 557). As the tongue is already cooked, it will not release any water, so it may be a good idea to add a few tablespoons of water. This dish can be served with moulded rice.

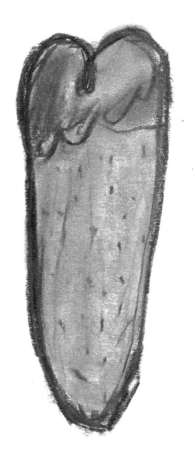

903

Stewed tongue

LENGUA ESTOFADA

- 1 ox tongue, 1–1.2 kg/2¼–2½ lb
- 80 g/3 oz lard
- 2 onions, chopped
- 4 carrots, thickly sliced
- 175 ml/6 fl oz white wine
- 175 ml/6 fl oz, plus
  2 tablespoons cooking liquid
  from braising the tongue
- pinch of mixed dried herbs or
  1 bouquet garni (1 bay leaf and 1
  sprig fresh thyme tied together)
- 1 slice of fried bread
  (see recipe 130)
- 1 clove garlic
- 2–3 black peppercorns
- 1 teaspoon potato flour
  (optional)
- salt

Serves 6

Braise the tongue as described on page 776, but only for 2 hours, and drain well, reserving the cooking liquid. Melt the lard in a large saucepan. Add the onion and cook over a low heat, stirring occasionally, for about 5 minutes, until softened and translucent. Put the tongue on top of the onion and place the carrot around it. Pour in the wine and 175 ml/6 fl oz of the reserved cooking liquid and add the dried herbs or bouquet garni. Pound the fried bread with the garlic in a mortar and stir in the remaining cooking liquid. Pour into the pan, add the peppercorns and lightly season with salt. Bring to the boil over a high heat, then lower the heat, cover the pan with brown wrapping paper that has been cut in a circle to fit inside the pan snugly, put the lid on and cook for 1½ hours. Remove the tongue from the pan and slice it. Put the slices on a warm serving dish and garnish with the carrot. Remove and discard the bouquet garni, if used, and process the sauce in a food processor or pass through a food mill, then pour it over the tongue and serve. If the sauce is too thin, mix 1 teaspoon potato flour with a little of the sauce in a bowl. Return the sauce to the pan, stir in the potato flour mixture and cook, stirring constantly, for 2–3 minutes, until thickened.

904

Breadcrumbed tongue

LENGUA REBOZADA

- 1 ox tongue
- 2 eggs, beaten 80g/3oz
- breadcrumbs
- sunflower oil, for deep frying
- 1 quantity of Classic Tomato
  Sauce (see recipe 73), optional

Serves 4

Braise the tongue as described on page 776, and cut it into thin slices. Coat the slices first in the beaten egg and then in the breadcrumbs, pressing the crumbs on with your fingertips. Heat the oil in a deep-fryer or deep frying pan to 180–190°C/350–375°F or until a cube of day-old bread browns in 30 seconds. Fry the slices in the hot oil, in batches, until golden brown. Remove with a slotted spoon, drain well, and keep warm while you cook the remaining slices. Serve them as they are or with the tomato sauce served separately in a sauce boat.

Sweetbreads

Two kinds of glands are used for Sweetbreads. The thymus gland, from the neck, shrinks as the young animal matures. The pancreas gland, also called belly Sweetbreads, does not shrink with age, but it becomes tougher and not so pleasant to eat. The most commonly eaten sweetbreads are veal and beef, and in Europe, lamb.

How to prepare

Allow 1–1.2 kg/2 ¼ – 2 ½ lb sweetbreads for 6 servings. No matter how they are to be cooked, the sweetbreads should be prepared as follows. Leave to soak in cold water in the refrigerator for about 4 hours, changing the water three or four times. Drain and blanch as described below. The quantities given are sufficient for 1–1.2 kg/2 ¼ – 2 ½ lb sweetbreads.

- 2 carrots, sliced
- 1 leek, halved and rinsed well, or 1 small onion, halved
- 1 stick celery (optional)
- 1 bay leaf
- juice of ½ lemon
- salt

Put the sweetbreads in a saucepan and pour in water to cover. Add the carrot, leek or onion, celery, if using, bay leaf, lemon juice and a pinch of salt. Bring to the boil, lower the heat and simmer gently for 5 minutes. Remove the pan from the heat, drain off the hot water and refresh the sweetbreads in cold water, then drain well. Peel off the membrane, and remove any gristle, fat, ducts, membrane or traces of blood. Place the sweetbreads on a tea towel and fold it back over them so that they are covered, then put something heavy on top, such as a light chopping board. Leave for 1 hour, then slice thickly and cook according to taste.

Note: Calf's sweetbreads may not be sold in Britain as a result of bovine spongiform encephalopathy (BSE). However, lamb's sweetbreads are still available.

905

Sweetbreads with mushrooms and shallots

MOLLEJAS GUISADAS CON CHAMPIÑONES FRESCOS Y CEBOLLITAS

- 1 kg/2¼ lb sweetbreads
- 250 g/9 oz button mushrooms
- 20 g/¾ oz butter
- juice of ½ lemon
- 4 tablespoons olive oil
- 250 g/9 oz shallots
- 40 g/1½ oz plain flour
- 350 ml/12 fl oz white wine
- 120 ml/4 fl oz single cream
  or 2 egg yolks, lightly beaten
- salt

Serves 6

Prepare and blanch the sweetbreads as described on page 779. Put the mushrooms, butter, lemon juice and a pinch of salt into a saucepan. Cover and cook over a low heat for 6 minutes. Set aside and keep warm. Heat the oil in another saucepan. Add the shallots and cook over a low heat, stirring occasionally, for about 10 minutes, until beginning to brown. Slice the sweetbreads and coat in the flour, but do not shake off any excess, as it will serve to thicken the sauce. Add to the pan and cook, turning occasionally, until evenly browned. Pour in the wine and simmer over a low heat, shaking the pan occasionally, for about 15 minutes. Stir in the mushrooms and their cooking juices and season to taste with salt. Remove the pan from the heat. Put the cream or egg yolks into a bowl and stir in a little of the sauce, then pour this mixture into the pan. Stir well and pour the contents of the pan into a warm serving dish. Serve with little mounds of boiled rice.

906

Sweetbreads cooked in sherry

MOLLEJAS GUISADAS AL JEREZ

- 1.2 kg/2½ lb sweetbreads
- 4 tablespoons olive oil
- 1 onion, chopped
- 2 carrots, sliced
- 1 large ripe tomato, seeded
  and cut into 4 wedges
- pinch of mixed dried herbs
  or 1 bouquet garni
  (2 bay leaves, 1 sprig fresh
  thyme and 1 sprig fresh parsley
  tied together in muslin)
- 5 tablespoons sherry
- 250 ml/8 fl oz chicken stock
  (home-made or made
  with a stock cube)
- 1 heaped tablespoon plain flour
- salt and pepper

Serves 6

Prepare and blanch the sweetbreads as described on page 779, and slice. Heat the oil in a saucepan. Add the onion and cook over a low heat, stirring occasionally, for about 5 minutes, until softened and translucent. Add the carrot and cook, stirring occasionally, for a few minutes more, then add the tomato. Add the sweetbreads and cook, turning carefully, until evenly browned all over. Season with salt and pepper, add the dried herbs or bouquet garni and pour in the sherry, followed by the stock. Bring to the boil, then lower the heat, cover and simmer, stirring occasionally, for 30 minutes. Using a slotted spoon or fish slice, transfer the sweetbreads to a warm serving dish. Remove and discard the bouquet garni, if used, and pass the sauce through a food mill or process in a food processor. Pour the sauce over the sweetbreads and serve immediately, with fried bread (see recipe 130) around the dish if you like.

907

Sweetbreads flamed in brandy and served with peas

MOLLEJAS FLAMEADAS CON COÑAC Y SERVIDAS CON GUISANTES

- 1 kg/2¼ lb sweetbreads
- 100 g/3½ oz lard or
  6 tablespoons sunflower oil
- 5 tablespoons brandy
- 1 tablespoon chopped
  fresh parsley
- 500 g/1 lb 2 oz canned peas or
  2 kg/4½ lb fresh peas, shelled
- 50 g/2 oz butter
- salt and pepper

Serves 6

Prepare and blanch the sweetbreads as described on page 779, and slice. Melt the lard or heat the oil in a frying pan. Add the sweetbreads and cook, turning occasionally, until lightly browned all over. Season with salt and pepper. Heat the brandy in a small saucepan, ignite it and carefully pour it into the pan, spooning it over the sweetbreads. When the flames have died down, sprinkle in the parsley and cook over a medium heat for 15 minutes. Meanwhile, open the can of peas, if using, and stand it in a saucepan of hot water set over a medium heat. Cook the fresh peas, if using, in a pan of salted boiling water for about 20 minutes, until tender. Drain the peas, put them into a saucepan, add the butter and cook over a low heat, stirring occasionally, for 5 minutes. Season to taste with salt. Put the sweetbreads on a warm serving dish, pour the sauce over them and put the peas around the edge. Serve immediately.

908

Sweetbreads with spinach

MOLLEJAS CON ESPINACAS

- 1 kg/2¼ lb sweetbreads
- 3 kg/6½ lb spinach,
  coarse stalks removed
- 25 g/1 oz butter
- 50 g/2 oz plain flour
- 250 ml/8 fl oz milk
- 350 ml/12 fl oz sunflower oil
- salt

Serves 6

Prepare and blanch the sweetbreads as described on page 779, and slice. Cook the spinach as described on page 315. Drain well and chop finely or put it through a mincer or food processor. Heat the butter in a saucepan. Stir in 1 tablespoon of the flour and cook, stirring constantly, for 2 minutes. Gradually stir in the milk, a little at a time. Cook, stirring constantly, for about 5 minutes, until thickened, then stir in the spinach and season to taste with salt. Remove the pan from the heat and keep warm. Heat the oil in a frying pan. Coat the sweetbreads in the remaining flour, shaking off any excess. Add them to the pan and cook, turning occasionally, until golden brown. Remove with a fish slice and drain well. Spoon the spinach sauce on to a warm serving dish, place the sweetbreads on top and serve immediately.

909

Coated sweetbreads with tomato sauce
MOLLEJAS EMPANADAS CON SALSA DE TOMATE

- 2 eggs
- 1 tablespoon olive oil
- 80 g/3 oz breadcrumbs
- 1.2 kg/2½ lb sweetbreads
- 250 ml/8 fl oz sunflower oil
- 2 sprigs fresh parsley
- 1 quantity Classic Tomato Sauce
  (see recipe 73)
- salt

Serves 6

Prepare and blanch the sweetbreads as described on page 779, and slice. Beat the eggs with the olive oil and a pinch of salt in a shallow dish. Spread out the breadcrumbs in another shallow dish. Coat the sweetbreads first in the egg mixture and then in the breadcrumbs, pressing the crumbs on with your fingertips. Heat the sunflower oil in a frying pan over a low heat. Add the parsley sprigs and cook for a few minutes, then remove with a slotted spoon and set aside. Increase the heat until the oil is hot enough to brown a cube of day-old bread in 30 seconds. Add the sweetbreads and cook until golden brown. Remove with a fish slice and drain well. Put the sweetbreads on a warm serving dish and garnish with the parsley. Serve immediately, offering the tomato sauce separately.

910

Vol-au-vent with sweetbreads, mushrooms and truffles
VOL-AU-VENT DE MOLLEJAS, CHAMPIÑONES Y TRUFAS

- 500 g/1 lb 2 oz sweetbreads
- 500 g/1 lb 2 oz mushrooms
- 65 g/2½ oz butter
- juice of ½ lemon
- 2 tablespoons sunflower oil
- 2 tablespoons plain flour
- 500 ml/18 fl oz milk
- ½ teaspoon meat extract
- pinch of freshly grated nutmeg
- 1 small can or jar of truffles,
  drained and thinly sliced
- 6 individual vol-au-vent cases
  or one large case, cooked
- salt

Serves 6

Prepare and blanch the sweetbreads as described on page 779. Cut the sweetbreads into 2-cm/¾-inch cubes. If the mushrooms are large, chop them coarsely. Put them mushrooms, 40 g/1½ oz of the butter, the lemon juice and a pinch of salt into a saucepan. Cover and cook over a medium heat, shaking the pan occasionally, for about 6 minutes. Preheat the oven to 180°C/350°F/Gas Mark 4. Melt the remaining butter with the oil in a saucepan. Stir in the flour and cook, stirring constantly, for 2 minutes. Gradually stir in the milk, a little at a time. Cook, stirring constantly, for about 5 minutes, until thickened, then stir in the meat extract and nutmeg and season to taste. Add the sweetbreads to the sauce. Drain the mushrooms and add them to the sauce along with the truffles and stir well. Divide the mixture among the vol-au-vent cases or spoon it into the large case. Place on a baking sheet and heat through in the oven. Serve hot.

Sweetbread croquettes
CROQUETAS DE MOLLEJAS

- 500 g/1 lb 2 oz sweetbreads
- 2 tablespoons sunflower oil
- 40 g/1½ oz butter
- 3–4 tablespoons plain flour
- 750 ml/1¼ pints milk
- 2 eggs
- 120–175 g/4–6 oz breadcrumbs
- vegetable oil, for deep-frying
- salt

Serves 4

Prepare and blanch the sweetbreads as described on page 779. Cut the sweetbreads into small cubes. Then follow the method for making croquettes (see recipe 62).

Tripe

How to prepare

Tripe is the edible lining of the stomachs of cows, pigs or sheep. It is usually sold partly or fully cooked, so cooking times may vary. If you are in doubt, ask your butcher for advice. Uncooked tripe requires repeated and very careful cleaning and will need prolonged simmering – up to 5 hours.

912

Tripe in French sauce
CALLOS EN SALSA A LA FRANCESA

- 100 g/3½ oz streaky bacon, cut into strips
- 2 onions
- 6 cloves
- 3 carrots, sliced
- 1 bouquet garni (2 bay leaves, 1 sprig fresh thyme, 1 clove garlic and 1 sprig fresh parsley tied together in muslin)
- 3 tablespoons brandy
- 1 kg/2¼ lb prepared tripe, cut into large pieces
- 500 g/1 lb 2 oz snout
- 1 calf's or ox foot, 750 g/ 1 lb 10 oz, cut into pieces
- 1 tablespoon chopped fresh parsley
- salt and pepper

French sauce:
- 4 tablespoons sunflower oil
- 2 tablespoons plain flour
- 500 ml/18 fl oz beef stock (home-made or made with stock cubes)
- 3 egg yolks
- juice of 1 lemon
- salt

Serves 6–8

Put the bacon into a large saucepan. Stud the onions with the cloves and add them to the pan with the carrot, bouquet garni, brandy, tripe, snout and calf's or ox foot. Season with salt and pepper and pour in water to cover. Bring to the boil, then lower the heat and simmer for about 1½ hours, until the tripe is tender. Drain off the cooking liquid. Cut the tripe and snout into small pieces and set aside. Remove the meat from the foot and set aside with the tripe. To make the sauce, heat the oil in a saucepan. Stir in the flour and cook, stirring constantly, for 2 minutes. Gradually stir in the stock and season to taste with salt. Add all the meat to the sauce and simmer gently for 30 minutes. Just before serving, beat the egg yolks with the lemon juice in a bowl and stir in a few tablespoons of the sauce, then tip this mixture into the pan. Stir well and pour into a warm deep serving dish. Sprinkle with the parsley and serve immediately.

913

Madrid-style tripe
CALLOS A LA MADRILEÑA

- 2 small onions
- 1.5 kg/3 ¼ lb prepared tripe,
  cut into bite-size pieces
- 150 g/5 oz andouille sausage
  (tripe sausage)
- 500 g/1 lb 2 oz snout
- 1 calf's or ox foot, 750 g/
  1 lb 10 oz
- 1 bay leaf
- ½ chilli, seeded
- 10 black peppercorns
- 4 cloves
- pinch of freshly grated nutmeg
- 2 cloves garlic, chopped
- 2 tomatoes, peeled, seeded
  and chopped
- 4 tablespoons olive oil
- 1 teaspoon paprika
- 2 chorizo sausages, 150 g/5 oz
- 1 tablespoon plain flour
- salt

Serves 6–8

Cut one of the onions into four pieces and chop the other. Put the tripe into a saucepan, pour in water to cover and bring to the boil. When it reaches a rolling boil, drain off the water and add fresh water to cover. Add the andouille, snout, calf's or ox foot, bay leaf, chilli, peppercorns, cloves, nutmeg, the pieces of onion, garlic and tomato. Cook for about 1 ½ hours, until the tripe is tender. Heat the oil in a frying pan. Add the chopped onion, paprika and chorizo. Cook, stirring occasionally, for 10 minutes, then add to the tripe and cook for 1 hour more. Remove the pan from the heat and leave to cool. Cut the andouille into slices and cut the meat off the calf's or ox foot, and return both to the pan. Reheat before serving.

Note: This dish should be prepared a day in advance and refrigerated, as it is much better when reheated. This quantity of tripe listed is the minimum that should be prepared in order for the dish to be tasty.

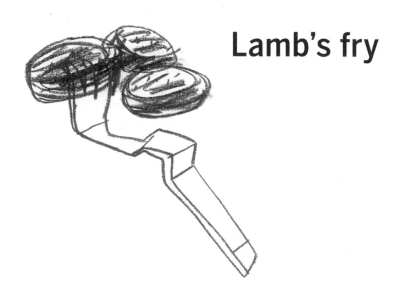

Lamb's fry

Lamb's fry, also known as animelles, are testicles and are not widely available. However, if you are lucky enough to obtain them, here's how they are prepared. If they are not sold ready skinned and sliced, you must blanch them in boiling water for 2 minutes, then drain and re-fresh them under cold running water. Skin them immediately and then leave to soak in cold water for 10 hours. Drain and press between two plates before slicing and cooking.

914

Coated lamb's fry with rice

CRIADILLAS EMPANADAS CON ARROZ BLANCO

- 1 egg
- 80 g/3 oz breadcrumbs
- sunflower oil, for deep frying
- 500–750 g/1 lb 2 oz-1 lb 10 oz prepared and sliced lamb's fry
- salt

Rice:
- 400 g/14 oz long-grain rice
- 50 g/2 oz butter
- salt

Serves 6

Cook and refresh the rice as described in recipe 173, then set aside. Beat the egg with a pinch of salt in a shallow dish. Spread out the breadcrumbs in another shallow dish. Heat the oil in a deep-fryer or saucepan to 180–190°C/350–375°F or until a cube of day-old bread browns in 30 seconds. Cut the slices of lamb's fry into strips and coat first in the beaten egg and then in the breadcrumbs. Add the strips, in batches, to the hot oil and cook until golden brown. Remove with a slotted spoon and drain well. Put them along one side of a serving dish and keep warm. Cook the rice with the butter as described in recipe 173 and season with salt. Spoon it on to the other side of the serving dish or shape it in little mounds. Serve immediately.

Note: This dish can be served with a sauce boat of Classic Tomato Sauce (see recipe 73).

915

Calf's heart in sauce

CORAZÓN DE TERNERA EN SALSA

- 120 ml/4 fl oz olive oil
- 1.2 kg/2 ½ lb veal heart, thickly sliced
- 1 large onion, finely chopped
- 1 clove garlic, lightly crushed
- 4 carrots, sliced
- 1 tablespoon plain flour
- 2 ripe tomatoes, peeled, seeded and chopped
- pinch of mixed dried herbs or 1 bouquet garni (1 sprig fresh thyme, 2 bay leaves and 1 sprig fresh parsley tied together in muslin)
- 120 ml/4 fl oz white wine
- 1 chicken stock cube
- salt

Serves 6

Heat the oil in a heavy-based saucepan or casserole. Add the slices of heart, in batches, and cook, turning occasionally, until evenly browned all over. Remove from the pan and set aside. Add the onion to the pan and cook over a low heat, stirring occasionally, for about 5 minutes, until softened and translucent. Add the garlic and cook, stirring occasionally, for a further 5 minutes. Add the carrot and cook for 2–3 minutes, then stir in the flour and cook, stirring constantly, for 2 minutes. Return the meat to the pan and add the tomato and dried herbs or bouquet garni. Pour in the wine and 120 ml/4 fl oz water, season with salt, cover the pan and bring to the boil. Lower the heat and simmer gently for 45 minutes. Crumble the stock cube into a bowl, stir in a little of the cooking liquid and add to the pan. Stir well and cook for a further 30 minutes, until the heart is tender. Taste and adjust the seasoning, if necessary. Serve immediately with Mashed Potato (see recipe 230) or boiled potatoes cut into large pieces.

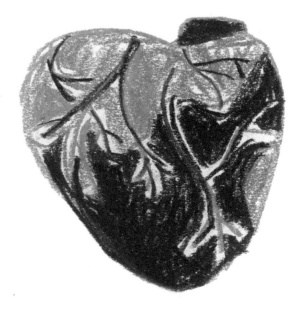

Coated calf's heart
CORAZÓN DE TERNERA EMPANADO

- **1 quantity Classic Tomato Sauce (see recipe 73)**
- **2 eggs**
- **80 g/3 oz breadcrumbs**
- **sunflower oil, for deep frying**
- **1 kg/2¼ lb calf's heart, sliced**
- **salt**

Serves 6

Warm the Tomato Sauce. Beat the eggs in a shallow dish and spread out the breadcrumbs in another shallow dish. Heat the oil in a deep-fryer or saucepan to 180–190°C/350–375°F or until a cube of day-old bread browns in 30 seconds. Season the slices of heart with salt, and coat them first in the beaten egg and then in the breadcrumbs, pressing the crumbs on with your fingers. Add the slices, in batches, to the hot oil and cook until golden brown. Remove with a fish slice, drain well and put into a warm serving dish. Serve immediately with boiled rice or Chips (see recipe 242). Offer the tomato sauce separately.

Feet and trotters

How to cook

If the feet are not already blanched and cleaned, remove any remaining skin and even singe them, over a flame or using cotton wool soaked in alcohol and lit with a match. Put the feet into a saucepan, pour in water to cover and cook over a high heat for 10 minutes. Drain, refresh under cold water and drain again. Fill a large saucepan with water. Stir 2 tablespoons plain flour into a bowl of cold water, then add it to the water in the pan with 1 large onion studded with 3 cloves, 2 bay leaves, a sprig fresh parsley, 1 garlic clove, the juice of ½ lemon, 1 sprig fresh thyme and a pinch of salt. Bring to the boil and add the lamb's feet so that they are completely submerged. Bring back to the boil, cover and cook, occasionally skimming off the froth that rises to the surface, for about 3 hours, until the lamb's feet are tender. Drain the lamb's feet, which are now ready to cook.

917

Lambs' feet stuffed with sausages, coated in breadcrumbs and fried

MANOS DE CORDERO RELLENAS CON SALCHICHAS, EMPANADAS Y FRITAS

- **12 lamb's feet**
- **12 sausages**
- **3 eggs**
- **80 g/3 oz breadcrumbs**
- **sunflower oil, for deep frying**
- **salt**
- **Classic Tomato Sauce (see recipe 73)**

Serves 6

Clean and precook the lamb's feet as described on page 788. When they are cool enough to handle, remove and discard the central bone. (It will come out very easily.) Prick the sausages in several places. Fill the cavities in the lamb's feet with the sausages and secure the opening with a wooden cocktail stick, if necessary. Beat the eggs with a pinch of salt in a shallow dish and spread out the breadcrumbs in another shallow dish. Heat the oil in a deep-fryer or frying pan to 180–190°C/350–375°F or until a cube of day-old bread browns in 30 seconds. Coat each foot first in the beaten egg and then in the breadcrumbs, pressing the crumbs on with your fingertips. Add the feet, in batches, to the hot oil and cook until golden brown all over. Remove and drain, then put on a serving dish and keep warm while you cook the remaining batches. Serve immediately, offering the tomato sauce separately, if using.

Note: You can omit the sausages if you like, but the dish will have less flavour.

918

Lambs' feet fritters
BUÑUELOS DE MANOS DE CORDERO

- **8 lamb's feet**
- **sunflower oil, for deep frying**
- **deep-fried fresh parsley sprigs (see Note)**
- **salt**

Fritter batter:
- **300 g/11 oz plain flour**
- **3 tablespoons white wine**
- **3 tablespoons sunflower oil**
- **350 ml/12 fl oz milk**
- **½ teaspoon baking powder**
- **salt**

Serves 6

Clean and precook the lamb's feet as described on page 788. When they are cool enough to handle, remove the bones. Make the batter for the fritters as described in recipe 58. Heat the oil in a deep-fryer or saucepan to 180–190°C/350–375°F or until a cube of day-old bread browns in 30 seconds. One at a time, coat the lamb's feet in the batter. Add to the hot oil, in batches, and cook until golden brown. Remove from the pan and drain well, then put on a serving dish and keep warm while cooking the remaining batches. Serve imm-ediately garnished with the fried parsley.

Note: Tie parsley sprigs together with thread and fry in moderately hot oil for an attractive garnish.

919

Lambs' feet with tomato

MANOS DE CORDERO CON TOMATE

- **12 lamb's feet**
- **salt**

Tomato sauce:
- **3 tablespoons sunflower oil**
- **1 onion, chopped**
- **1 kg/2¼ lb ripe tomatoes, peeled, seeded and chopped**
- **1 teaspoon sugar**
- **salt**

Serves 6

Ask the butcher to remove the central bones from the feet. Clean them and precook as described on page 788. Meanwhile, make the tomato sauce as described in recipe 73. When the lamb's feet are tender, transfer them to the pan of tomato sauce and simmer gently for 25 minutes. Serve in a warm deep serving dish.

920

Lambs' feet in savoury lemon sauce

MANOS DE CORDERO CON SALSA DE LIMÓN

• 8 lamb's feet

Savoury lemon sauce:
• 60 g/2¼ oz butter
• 1 heaped teaspoon plain flour
• 1 chicken stock cube
• 2 egg yolks
• juice of 1 lemon
• pinch of freshly ground nutmeg
• 1 tablespoon chopped
  fresh parsley
• salt
Serves 4

Clean and precook the lamb's feet as described on page 788. Meanwhile, make the savoury lemon sauce as described in recipe 86. Drain the lamb's feet, put them into a warm serving dish and pour the sauce over them. Serve immediately.

Pig's trotters

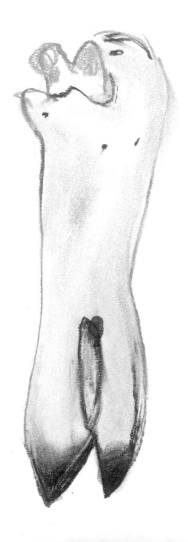

Cooking method for 4 trotters

Pig's trotters are usually sold with the skin cleaned and the hair singed. If not, follow the method for lamb's feet (see page 788). Wash the trotters in several changes of water. Make a cut in them from the hoof upwards. Put them into a saucepan and pour in water to cover, then add 175 ml/6 fl oz white wine, 2 halved onions, 3 carrots, cut into four pieces, 2 cloves garlic, a bay leaf, 1 sprig fresh thyme, 1 sprig fresh parsley, 2 cloves and a pinch of salt. Bring to the boil over a high heat, then lower the heat, cover the pan and simmer gently for about 4 hours, until the trotters are tender. Drain well, then prepare them as preferred.

921

- 8 pig's trotters
- 2 beaten eggs
- 80 g/3 oz breadcrumbs
- sunflower oil

Serves 4

Pig's trotters in breadcrumbs

MANOS DE CERDO EMPANADAS

Prepare and precook the trotters as described on page 792, but before precooking wrap each one in muslin and tie with fine kitchen string so that it does not lose its shape. When the trotters are tender, drain well and remove the muslin. Remove as many bones as possible, then put the trotters on a work surface and place a chopping board on top. Leave for 30 minutes. Coat the trotters first in the beaten egg and then in the breadcrumbs. Heat the oil in frying pan, add the trotters, two at a time, and cook until golden brown. Drain well and serve immediately.

Note: The trotters can be served with Classic Tomato Sauce (see recipe 73), Mayonnaise with Tomato and Brandy (see recipe 108) or Green Mayonnaise (see recipe 107). Offer the sauce separately.

922

- 12 pig's trotters
- salt

Tomato sauce:
- 3 tablespoons sunflower oil
- 1 onion, chopped
- 1 kg/2 ¼ lb ripe tomatoes,
  peeled, seeded and chopped
- 1 teaspoon sugar
- salt

Serves 6

Pig's trotters with tomato

MANOS DE CERDO CON TOMATE

Ask the butcher to remove the central bones from the trotters. Clean them and precook as described on page 792. Meanwhile, make the tomato sauce as described in recipe 73. When the pig's trotters are tender, transfer them to the pan of tomato sauce and simmer gently for 25 minutes. Serve in a warm deep serving dish.

923

- 10 pig's trotters
- sunflower oil for deep frying
- deep-fried fresh parsley sprigs
  (see note)
- salt

  Fritter batter:
- 300 g/11 oz plain flour
- 3 tablespoons white wine
- 3 tablespoons sunflower oil
- 350 ml/12 fl oz milk
- ½ teaspoon baking powder
- salt
  Serves 5

Pig's trotter fritters
BUÑUELOS DE MANOS DE CERDO

Clean and precook the pig's trotters as described on page 792. When they are cool enough to handle, remove the bones. Make the batter for the fritters as described in recipe 58. Heat the oil in a deep-fryer or saucepan to 180–190°C/350–375°F or until a cube of day-old bread browns in 30 seconds. One at a time, coat the pig's trotters in the batter. Add to the hot oil, in batches, and cook until golden brown. Remove from the pan and drain well, then put on a serving dish and keep warm while cooking the remaining batches. Serve immediately garnished with the fried parsley.

Note: Tie parsley sprigs together with thread and fry in moderately hot oil.

924

- 8 pig's trotters
- 1 quantity Spanish Sauce
  (see recipe 82)
  Serves 4

Pig's trotters with Spanish sauce
MANOS DE CERDO CON SALSA ESPAÑOLA

Cook the pig's trotters as described on page 792. When the trotters are cool enough to handle, cut them in half, remove the bones, put the meat into the Spanish sauce and bring to the boil.

Note: This dish is very good with the addition of 2 tablespoons of pine nuts. Add them to the sauce at the same time as the pig's trotters.

Pluck

Lamb's pluck
ASADURA DE CORDERO

- **4 tablespoons olive oil**
- **2 large onions, finely chopped**
- **500 kg/1 lb 2 oz lamb's pluck,**
  cut into 4-cm/1½-inch cubes
- **1 teaspoon paprika**
- **2 tomatoes,**
  peeled, seeded and chopped
- **175 ml/6 fl oz white wine**
- **pinch of mixed dried herbs or**
  1 bouquet garni (2 bay leaves,
  1 sprig fresh thyme and 1 clove
  garlic tied in muslin)
- **1 tablespoon chopped**
  fresh parsley
- **salt**

Serves 4

Heat the oil in a saucepan. Add the onion and cook over a low heat, stirring occasionally, for about 8 minutes, until beginning to brown. Add the lamb's pluck and cook, stirring frequently, until evenly browned. Stir in the paprika and add the tomato, wine, dried herbs or bouquet garni and a pinch of salt. Cover and cook over a very low heat for 45 minutes. Remove and discard the bouquet garni, if used. Sprinkle with the parsley and serve with triangles of fried bread (see recipe 130) or Mashed Potato (see recipe 230).

Note: Pluck is a collective term that refers to the lungs, heart, liver and other offal of lamb. It is often hard to obtain outside the Mediterranean.

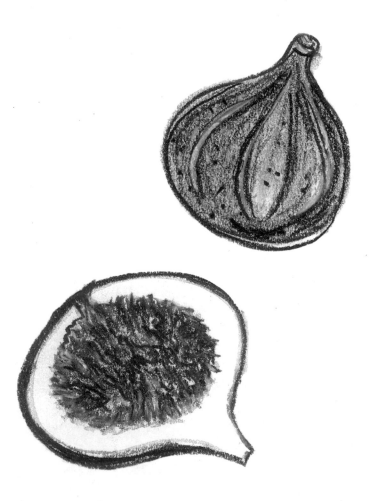

DESSERTS

926

Sponge made with milk and oil
BIZCOCHO CON LECHE Y ACEITE

- 200 ml/7 fl oz sunflower oil,
  plus extra for brushing
- 250 g/9 oz plain flour,
  plus extra for dusting
- 2 eggs
- 200 ml/7 fl oz milk
- 200 g/7 oz caster sugar
- grated rind of 1 lemon, or a pinch
  of vanilla powder or a few drops
  of vanilla extract
- ½ teaspoon baking powder
- pinch of salt

Serves 8

Preheat the oven to 150°C/300°F/Gas Mark 2. Brush a long cake tin with oil and dust with flour, tipping out any excess. Beat the eggs in a bowl and stir in the milk, oil, sugar and lemon rind or vanilla. Mix together the flour, baking powder and salt in another bowl, then sift them into the egg mixture in three batches, mixing well. Pour the sponge mixture into the prepared tin and bake until it starts to rise, then increase the oven temperature to 160°C/325°F/Gas Mark 3. Bake for about 1 hour, until golden brown. Insert a wooden cocktail stick into the centre of the sponge and if it comes out clean, the cake is cooked. Remove the cake from the oven, leave to cool until the tin is cold, then turn out on to a wire rack to cool completely.

Note: All sponges can be kept for a couple of days, wrapped in foil once they are cold.

927

Genoese sponge
BIZCOCHO GENOVESA

- 100 g/3½ oz butter, melted,
  plus extra for greasing
- 50 g/2 oz self-raising flour,
  plus extra for dusting
- 3 eggs, separated
- 80 g/3 oz caster sugar
- grated rind of 1 lemon
- pinch of salt

Serves 8

Preheat the oven to 160°C/325°F/Gas Mark 3. Grease a long cake tin with butter and dust with flour, tipping out any excess. Whisk the egg whites with a pinch of salt in a clean, dry bowl until stiff peaks form. Add the egg yolks and sugar and stir constantly with a wooden spoon and always in the same direction for 10 minutes. Add the flour, 1 tablespoon at a time, the lemon rind and, finally, the melted butter. Pour the mixture into the prepared tin and bake for 45–60 minutes. Insert a wooden cocktail stick into the centre of the sponge and if it comes out clean, the cake is cooked. Remove the cake from the oven and leave to cool until the tin is cold, then turn out on to a wire rack to cool completely.

928 Light orange sponge

BIZCOCHO LIGERO DE NARANJA

- 1 piece of crystallized orange
  rind, chopped
- 2 tablespoons white rum
- margarine, for greasing
- 50 g/2 oz self-raising flour,
  plus extra for dusting
- 120 g/4 oz caster sugar
- grated rind of 1 orange
- 4 egg yolks
- 50 g/2 oz potato flour
- 3 egg whites
- pinch of salt

Serve 6–8

Put the crystallized orange rind in a bowl, pour in the rum and leave to macerate for as long as possible. Grease a 26-cm/10 ¼-inch long cake tin with margarine and dust with flour, tipping out any excess. Put the sugar and grated orange rind into another bowl, add the egg yolks and whisk until pale and fluffy. Add the flour and potato flour sifted together and stir in. Whisk the egg whites with a pinch of salt in a clean, dry bowl until stiff peaks form. Gently fold them into the creamed mixture with a rubber spatula or metal spoon. Put half the sponge mixture into the prepared tin. Drain the crystallized orange rind, pat dry and sprinkle it evenly in the tin. Cover with the remaining sponge mixture. Put the tin into the oven, turn it on to 160°C/325°F/ Gas Mark 3 and bake for 45 minutes. Insert a wooden cocktail stick into the centre of the sponge and if it comes out clean, the cake is cooked. Remove the cake from the oven, leave to cool until the tin is cold, then turn out on to a wire rack to cool completely.

929 Sponge made with egg whites

BIZCOCHO DE CLARAS DE HUEVO

- 100 g/3 ½ oz butter, melted,
  plus extra for greasing
- plain flour, for dusting
- 6 egg whites
- 200 g/7 oz caster sugar
- 150 g/5 oz cornflour
- pinch of vanilla powder or
  a few drops of vanilla extract
- salt

Serves 6–8

Preheat the oven to 180°C/350°F/Gas Mark 4. Grease a cake tin with butter and dust with flour, tipping out any excess. Whisk the egg whites, three at a time, with a pinch of salt in a clean, dry bowl until stiff peaks form, then put them together in another bowl. Add alternate tablespoonfuls of sugar and cornflour until they are used up. Finally, fold in the melted butter. Pour the mixture into the prepared tin and bake for about 50 minutes. Insert a wooden cocktail stick into the centre of the sponge and if it comes out clean, the cake is cooked. Remove the cake from the oven, leave to cool until the tin is cold, then turn out on to a wire rack to cool completely.

930

Chocolate sponge
BIZCOCHO DE CHOCOLATE

- 80 g/3 oz butter,
  plus extra for greasing
- 80 g/3 oz plain flour,
  plus extra for dusting
- 80 g/3 oz plain chocolate,
  broken into pieces
- 80 g/3 oz caster sugar
- 3 eggs, separated
- ¾ teaspoon baking powder
- salt

Serves 6–8

Preheat the oven to 160°C/325°F/Gas Mark 3. Grease a long cake tin with butter and dust with flour, shaking out any excess. Melt the butter in a pan over a low heat, add the chocolate and stir until melted. Remove the pan from the heat and stir in the sugar. Stir in the egg yolks, one at a time. Mix together the flour and baking powder, sift into a bowl and mix well and add the chocolate mixture. Whisk the egg whites with a pinch of salt in a clean, dry bowl until stiff peaks form, then fold into the chocolate mixture. Pour the mixture into the prepared tin and bake for about 50 minutes. Insert a wooden cocktail stick into the centre of the sponge and if it comes out clean, the cake is cooked. Remove the cake from the oven, leave to cool until the tin is cold, then turn out on to a wire rack to cool completely.

931

Rum baba
BIZCOCHO BORRACHO (BABA)

- butter, for greasing
- 3 egg whites
- 3 tablespoons caster sugar
- 2 egg yolks
- 6 tablespoons plain flour
- 1 tablespoon baking powder
- salt
- whipped cream and crystallized
  fruit, to decorate

Syrup:
- 120 g/4 oz caster sugar
- 200 ml/7 fl oz rum

Serves 6–8

Preheat the oven to 180°C/350°F/Gas Mark 4. Grease a ring mould with butter. Whisk the egg whites with a pinch of salt in a clean, dry bowl until stiff peaks form. Fold in the sugar and then the egg yolks. Fold in half the flour, 1 tablespoon at a time, fold in the baking powder and then fold in the remaining flour, 1 tablespoon at a time. Pour the mixture into the prepared mould and bake for about 45 minutes. Insert a wooden cocktail stick into the cake and if it comes out clean, the cake is cooked. Meanwhile, make the syrup. Pour 250 ml/8 fl oz water into a saucepan, add the sugar and rum and heat gently, stirring until the sugar has dissolved, then cook for a further 5 minutes. Remove the pan from the heat but do not allow the syrup to cool. Remove the cake from the oven and while it is still in the tin, pour the hot syrup over it; a little at a time. When it is completely soaked, turn out on to a serving dish. Serve the baba with whipped cream in the middle and decorate it with crystallized fruit.

Rum baba made with breadcrumbs

BIZCOCHO BORRACHO HECHO CON PAN RALLADO (BABA)

- butter, for greasing
- 4 eggs, separated
- 4 tablespoons caster sugar
- 4–5 tablespoons breadcrumbs
- 1 teaspoon baking powder
- salt
- whipped cream and crystallized fruit, to decorate

Syrup:
- 100 g/3½ oz caster sugar
- 275 ml/9 fl oz rum

Serves 8

Preheat the oven to 180°C/350°F/Gas Mark 4. Grease a ring mould with butter. Beat the egg yolks with the sugar until pale and fluffy, then stir in the breadcrumbs and baking powder. Whisk the egg whites with a pinch of salt in a clean, dry bowl until stiff peaks form, then fold into the egg yolk mixture. Pour into the prepared mould and bake for about 45 minutes. Insert a wooden cocktail stick into the cake and if it comes out clean, the cake is cooked. Meanwhile, make the syrup. Put the sugar, rum and 275 ml/9 fl oz water into a sauce-pan and heat, stirring until the sugar has dissolved, then cook for a further 5 minutes. Remove the pan from the heat but do not allow the syrup to cool. Remove the cake from the oven and while it is still in the tin, pour the hot syrup over it, a little at a time. When it is completely soaked, turn out on to a serving dish. Serve it with whipped cream in the middle and decorate it with crystallized fruit.

Note: You could decorate the rum baba with Confectioner's Cream (see recipe 1010).

933

Sponge made with yogurt and lemon
BIZCOCHO CON YOGUR Y LIMÓN

- 50 g/2 oz margarine, softened, plus extra for greasing
- 120 g/4 oz plain flour, sifted, plus extra for dusting
- 130 g/4½ oz caster sugar
- 150 ml/¼ pint lemon yogurt
- 2 eggs
- 1 tablespoon baking powder
- grated rind of 1 lemon

Serves 6

Preheat the oven to 150°C/300°F/Gas Mark 2. Grease a long cake tin with margarine and dust with flour, tipping out any excess. Using an electric mixer, beat the margarine with the sugar, yogurt and eggs. Sift together the flour and baking powder and add to the mixture a spoonful at a time along with the lemon rind. Pour the mixture into the prepared tin and bake until the sponge is beginning to rise, then increase the oven tempera-ture to 160°C/325°F/Gas Mark 3 and bake for 45–60 minutes. Insert a wooden cocktail stick into the centre of the sponge and if it comes out clean, the cake is cooked. Remove the sponge from the oven and turn out on to a wire rack to cool.

934

Fruit cake
PLUM-CAKE

- 200 g/7 oz softened margarine, plus extra for greasing
- 250 g/9 oz caster sugar
- 5 eggs
- 150 g/5 oz crystallized fruit, chopped
- 65 g/2½ oz raisins, soaked in hot water for 15 minutes, drained and dried
- 300 g/11 oz plain flour
- 2 teaspoons baking powder
- 6–7 tablespoons of rum

Serves 6–8

Preheat the oven to 150°C/300°F/Gas Mark 2. Grease a 30-cm/12-inch long cake tin with margarine. Put the margarine and the sugar into a warmed bowl and beat until pale and fluffy. Add the eggs, one at a time. Coat the crystallized fruit and raisins in flour, shake them in a colander with large holes and collect and reserve the excess flour. Set the fruit aside. Sift together all the flour and the baking powder and add to the creamed mixture, a little at a time. Stir in the rum and the coated fruit. Pour the mixture into the prepared tin and bake for 10 minutes, then increase the oven temperature to 160°C/325°F/Gas Mark 3 and bake for about 50 minutes. Insert a wooden cocktail stick into the centre of the cake and if it comes out clean, the cake is cooked. Remove the cake from the oven and leave to cool in the tin for about 10 minutes, then turn out on to a wire rack to cool completely. The cake will keep very well if wrapped in foil.

Orange tart

BIZCOCHO-TARTA DE NARANJA

- butter, for greasing
- grated rind of 2 oranges
- 120 g / 4 oz caster sugar
- 4 eggs, separated
- 50 g / 2 oz self-raising flour
- 50 g / 2 oz potato flour
- ½ jar of orange marmalade
- 50 ml / 2 fl oz Cointreau, Curaçao or other orange-flavoured liqueur

Syrup:
- 200 g / 7 oz caster sugar
- pinch of vanilla powder or a few drops of vanilla extract
- ¼ teaspoon orange essence

Serves 6

Preheat the oven to 160°C/325°F/Gas Mark 3. Grease a 26-cm/10 ¼ inch round cake tin with butter. Put half the orange rind into a bowl, add the sugar and beat in the egg yolks, one at time. Stir with a wooden spoon for 15 minutes, then sift in the flour and potato flour. Finally, stir in the egg whites (not whisked). The mixture will be thick, smooth and pale yellow in colour. Pour the mixture into the prepared tin and bake for about 30 minutes. Insert a wooden cocktail stick into the centre of the sponge and if it comes out clean, the cake is cooked. Remove the cake from the oven, leave to cool until the tin is cold, then turn out on to a wire rack to cool completely. Using a sharp serrated knife, halve the cake horizontally. Mix together the orange marma-ade, the remaining grated orange rind and the liqueur in a bowl and use to sandwich the two halves together. To make the syrup, put the sugar and vanilla into a saucepan, pour in 7 tablespoons water and heat gently, stirring until the sugar has dissolved. Increase the heat to medium and cook for 10 minutes, then stir in 1 tablespoon cold water. Stir until thickened, add the orange essence and pour the syrup over the cake. Leave to cool.

Note: Decorate with glacé cherries or whipped cream.

Sweet walnut bread

PAN DE NUECES

- 20g/¾oz butter, softened,
  plus extra for greasing
- 1 egg
- 200g/7oz caster sugar
- 250g/9oz plain flour,
  plus extra for dusting
- 250ml/8floz milk
- 120g/4oz currants,
  soaked in warm water for
  20 minutes and drained
- 120g/4oz walnuts,
  coarsely chopped
- ½ teaspoon easy-blend dried
  yeast

Makes 1 loaf

Cream the butter with the egg and sugar. Stir in half the flour, in batches alternating with the milk. Add the currants and walnuts. Mix the remaining flour with the yeast and stir in. Turn out the mixture on to a floured work surface and bring it together with your fingertips. Generously grease a long loaf tin with butter and lightly dust with flour, tipping out the excess. Put the mixture into the tin and leave to stand in a warm place for 30 minutes, until risen. Meanwhile, pre-heat the oven to 180°C/350°F/Gas Mark 4. Bake for about 1 hour. If necessary, cover the top of the loaf with foil during the cooking time to prevent it burning. Insert a wooden cocktail stick into the centre of the loaf and if it comes out clean, it is cooked. Remove the loaf from the oven and leave to cool in the tin for about 10 minutes, then turn out on to a wire rack to cool completely. Keep it wrapped in a damp tea towel or foil for 24 hours before slicing and eating, as this will improve the flavour.

937

Fairy cakes
MAGDALENAS

- 3 eggs, separated
- 250 g/9 oz caster sugar
- 250 ml/8 fl oz sunflower oil
- 120 ml/4 fl oz milk
- grated rind of 1 lemon
- 300 g/11 oz self-raising flour
- a pinch of salt

Makes about 50

Preheat the oven
with a pinch of salt to 180°C/350°F/Gas Mark 4. Whisk the egg whites
stir in the yolks, then a clean, dry bowl until stiff peaks form. Gradually
sifted flour. Add these the sugar, oil, milk, lemon rind and, finally, the
well with a wooden spoon ingredients a little at a time, stirring them in
mixture and place them n. Half fill about 50 paper cake cases with the
until golden brown. Remove baking sheets. Bake for 18–25 minutes,
their paper cases, to wire ra from the oven and transfer the cakes, in
days in an airtight containe cks to cool. They can be stored for a 3–4
r.

938

Fairy cakes made with egg whites
MAGDALENAS DE CLARA DE HUEVO

- 165 g/5½ oz butter, softened,
  plus extra for greasing
- 250 g/9 oz caster sugar
- 6 egg whites
- 120 g/4 oz self-raising flour

Makes about 28

Preheat the oven to 1
other cake moulds with 0°C/350°F/Gas Mark 4. Grease dariole or
batches.) Beat the bu butter. (You will have to bake the mixture in
beat in the egg whites ter with the sugar until pale and fluffy, then
at a time, and mix we (not whisked). Gradually sift in the flour, a little
leaving plenty of spa . Spoon the mixture into the prepared moulds,
20–25 minutes, un ace for the cakes to rise during cooking. Bake for
and turn them out til golden brown. Remove the cakes from the oven
batter. They can on to wire racks to cool. Repeat with the remaining
e stored in an airtight container for 3–4 days.

Note: Dariole mo
not available, y ulds are small cylindrical baking moulds. If they are
ou can use a muffin tin.

939

Coconut
ASTAS ... S
TAS DE COCO

- butter, for greasing
- 5 egg whites
- 300 g/11 oz caster sugar
- 250 g/9 oz desiccated coconut
- pinch of vanilla powder or
  a few drops of vanilla extract

Makes about 50

Preheat the oven to 150°C/300°F/Gas Mark 2. Grease two baking
sheets with butter. Put the egg whites and sugar into a saucepan
and whisk together over a medium-low heat until stiff. Whisk in the
coconut and vanilla, then remove the pan from the heat. Using a teaspoon, put mounds of the mixture on to the prepared baking sheets.
Bake for about 30 minutes, until lightly browned. Remove from the
oven and leave to cool for 10–15 minutes, then lift the cakes off the
baking sheets with a palette knife and place on a wire rack to cool.

940

- butter, for greasing
- 5 egg whites
- 300 g/11 oz caster sugar
- 300 g/11 oz desiccated coconut
- pinch of vanilla powder or
  a few drops of vanilla extract

Makes about 50

941

- butter, for greasing
- 3 eggs
- 200 g/7 oz caster sugar
- 250 g/9 oz self-raising flour,
  sifted
- pinch of vanilla powder or
  a few drops of vanilla extract

Makes about 50

942

- 200 g/7 oz butter, softened
- 150 g/5 oz caster sugar
- 1 egg
- 300 g/11 oz plain flour
- 65 g/2½ oz blanched almonds,
  chopped

Makes about 35

ck cakes
Coconut ro

ROCAS DE COCO

same way as coconut cakes (see recipe 939), but spoon Make in tbunds of the mixture on the baking sheets and use a fork, larger mo cold water, to give them an attractive shape before putting dipped ito the oven.
them i

Simple cakes

PASTAS SENCILLAS

F

heat the oven to 180°C/350°F/Gas Mark 4. Grease two or three Prei g sheets with butter. Beat the eggs with the sugar, then stir in bakinour, 2 tablespoons at a time, followed by the vanilla. Using a the floon, put small mounds of the mixture on the prepared baking teasps, spacing them well apart and working in batches if necessary. shee for about 15 minutes, until golden brown. Remove the baking Bakes from the oven and lift off the cakes with a palette knife. Trans- sheet wire racks to cool. These cakes will keep for 2–3 days in an fer to container.
airtight c

sablé biscuits
Almond ENDRAS

SABLÉS DE ALN

en to 200°C/400°F/Gas Mark 6. Cream the butter Preheat the ovntil pale and fluffy. Gently stir in the egg, then the with the sugar Put the mixture into a churro machine, in batches, flour and alm work surace, cutting the lines formed into 4- then spread it out on a wo the biscuits to a baking sheet cm/1½-inch lengths. Carefully transfer utes, until golden brown. with a palette knife. Bake for about 15 m can be stored for 2–3 Remove from the oven and leave to cool. The days in an airtight container.

Note: A machine for making churros (strips of fried dough) has a flat plate on one side and a ridged one on top. However, ou can simply roll out the dough to 5 mm/¼ inch thick and stamp ou the biscuits with a round or oval cutter. Make a ridged pattern on the ps with a fork and bake as described.

943

Langues de chat
LENGUAS DE GATO

- **120 g/4 oz butter, softened**
- **120 g/4 oz caster sugar**
- **4 egg whites**
- **pinch of vanilla powder or
  a few drops of vanilla extract**
- **120 g/4 oz plain flour, sifted**

Makes about 55

Preheat the oven to 180°C/350°F/Gas Mark 4. Beat the butter with the sugar in a bowl. Stir in the egg whites (not whisked), one at a time, and the vanilla, then stir with a wooden spoon for 8–10 minutes. Gradually stir in the flour, 1 tablespoon at a time. Use a spoon or a piping bag to put 2-cm/¾-inch wide strips of the mixture on to a baking sheet, spacing them well apart and working in batches if necessary. Bake for about 10 minutes, until golden brown around the edges but a lighter colour in the centre. Remove the baking sheet from the oven and loosen all the biscuits with a palette knife, then carefully transfer them to a flat work surface to cool. The biscuits can be stored for 2–3 days in an airtight container.

Note: These biscuits are called Langues de chat, or cats' tongues, because of their narrow shape.

944

Almond pastries
PASTAS DE TÉ CON ALMENDRAS RALLADAS

- **80 g/3 oz butter, softened**
- **100 g/3½ oz ground almonds**
- **100 g/3½ oz caster sugar**
- **100 g/3½ oz plain flour**
- **grated rind of 1 lemon**
- **1 egg, lightly beaten**

Decoration:
- **15 glacé cherries, halved,
  or 30 blanched almonds**

Makes about 30

Preheat the oven to 180°C/350°F/Gas Mark 4. Beat the butter with the ground almonds and sugar in a bowl. Gently stir in the flour, lemon rind and half the egg. Form teaspoonfuls of the mixture into balls, place on a baking sheet and flatten them gently, working in batches if necessary. Brush the pastries with the remaining egg. Place a cherry half or an almond on top of each one, then bake for 15–20 minutes, until golden brown. Remove from the oven, lift the pastries off the baking sheet with a palette knife and leave to cool, preferably on a marble slab. These pastries can be stored for up to 2–3 days in an airtight container.

945

- **2 eggs**
- **100 g / 3½ oz butter, softened**
- **120 g / 4 oz caster sugar**
- **250 g / 9 oz plain flour,**
  plus extra for dusting
- **1 tablespoon baking powder**
- **1 tablespoon milk**
- **50 blanched almonds,**
  to decorate

Makes about 50

Teatime pastries

PASTAS DE TÉ

Preheat the oven to 180°C/350°F/Gas Mark 4. Separate one of the eggs. Beat together the butter, sugar, whole egg and the egg yolk in a bowl. Gradually sift in the flour and baking powder together, stirring to mix, and add the milk. Lightly flour your hands. Working in batches, form teaspoonfuls of the mixture into balls, place on a baking sheet and flatten them gently to make 1.5-cm/⅝-inch rounds. Decorate each one with an almond. Beat the egg white in a bowl with a fork, then brush it over the pastries to glaze. Bake for 15–20 minutes, until golden brown. Remove from the oven, lift the pastries off the baking sheet with a palette knife and leave to cool, preferably on a marble slab. Repeat with the remaining batter. These pastries can be stored for 2–3 days in an airtight container.

946

- **3 eggs**
- **150 g / 5 oz lard, melted**
- **250 ml / 8 fl oz milk**
- **grated rind of 1 lemon**
- **3 tablespoons sweet anisette**
- **350 g / 12 oz caster sugar**
- **1 kg / 2¼ lb plain flour,**
  plus extra for dusting
- **½ teaspoon baking powder**
  or bicarbonate of soda
- **sunflower oil, for deep frying**
- **icing sugar, for dusting**

Makes about 35

Lemon doughnuts

ROSQUILLAS DE LIMÓN

Put the eggs, lard, milk, lemon rind, anisette and sugar into a bowl and stir for 15 minutes. Gradually stir in the flour, a little at a time, and the baking powder or bicarbonate of soda, until the mixture comes away from the sides of the bowl. (You may not need all of the flour.) With floured hands, form the dough into little rolls about 1.5 cm/⅝ inch thick. Heat the oil in a deep-fryer or saucepan to 150–160°C/300–325°F or until a cube of day-old bread browns in 45 seconds. Add the doughnuts, in batches, cook until puffed up, then turn up the heat and cook until golden brown. Remove the doughnuts from the oil with a slotted spoon, drain well and dust with icing sugar. Repeat with the remaining batter.

947

Almond doughnuts
ROSQUILLAS ALARGADAS DE ALMENDRAS

- 3 eggs
- 200 g/7 oz caster sugar
- 100 g/3½ oz blanched almonds, chopped
- 1 tablespoon kirsch
- 25 g/1 oz butter
- 300 g/11 oz plain flour, plus extra for dusting
- sunflower oil, for deep frying

Makes about 50

Put the eggs, sugar, almonds and kirsch into a bowl and stir with a wooden spoon for 15 minutes. Melt the butter and stir it into the mixture. Finally, gently stir in the flour, stirring as little as possible. With floured hands, shape the mixture into little rolls, 3–4 cm/1¼–1½ inches long and about 1.5 cm/⅝ inch wide. Heat the oil in a frying pan to 150–160°C/300–325°F or until a cube of day-old bread browns in 45 seconds. Remove the pan from the heat and add the first batch of doughnuts. When they have puffed up, return the pan to the heat and cook until lightly browned. Remove with a slotted spoon and drain well. Repeat with the remaining batter. Once cooled, these doughnuts can be stored for a 2–3 days in an airtight container.

948

Little almond cakes
POLVORONES DE ALMENDRA (MANTECADOS)

- 300 g/11 oz plain flour
- 300 g/11 oz lard
- 300 g/11 oz caster sugar
- 100 g/3½ oz ground toasted almonds
- pinch of ground cinnamon
- 1 egg, lightly beaten
- icing sugar, for dusting
- salt

Makes about 50

Preheat the oven to 150°C/300°F/Gas Mark 2. Heat the flour in a frying pan, stirring constantly, for 7 minutes but do not allow it to brown. Tip the flour on to a marble slab and spread it out into a round. Put the lard, sugar, almonds, cinnamon, a pinch of salt and the egg in the middle and bring the ingredients together with your hands until thoroughly combined. Shape pieces of the dough into balls about the size of a walnut, then flatten them. Working in batches, if necessary, place the little cakes on a baking sheet and bake for about 30 minutes. Remove from the oven and leave on the baking sheet to cool completely, then dust with icing sugar. Store them in an airtight container or wrap individually in tissue paper.

949

Fried bows

LAZOS FRITOS

- **250 g/9 oz self-raising flour, plus extra for dusting**
- **2 eggs, lightly beaten**
- **25 g/1 oz butter**
- **2 tablespoons caster sugar**
- **1 tablespoon eau-de-vie or other fruit brandy**
- **sunflower oil, for deep fryng**
- **icing sugar, for dusting**
- **salt**

Makes about 25

Sift the flour with a pinch of salt into a bowl and add the eggs, butter, sugar and eau-de-vie. Mix well with your hands, then turn out on to a lightly floured marble slab and knead the mixture until smooth. Roll out the dough on a lightly floured work surface and cut it into strips about 2 cm/¾ inch wide and 25 cm/10 inches long. Carefully tie the dough strips into bows.Heat the oil in a deep-fryer or saucepan to 180–190°C/350–375°F or until a cube of day-old bread browns in 30 seconds. Add the bows, four at a time, and cook until golden brown. Remove with a slotted spoon and drain well. Repeat with the remaining batter. Serve sprinkled with plenty of icing sugar.

950

Fried Marie biscuits

GALLETAS «MARÍA» FRITAS

- **4 Marie biscuits per serving**
- **raspberry or redcurrant jam (about ½ teaspoon per biscuit sandwich)**
- **sunflower oil, for deep frying**
- **icing sugar, for coating**

Serves 1

Sandwich the biscuits together in pairs with the jam. Heat the oil in a large frying pan to 150–160°C/300–325°F or until a cube of day-old bread browns in 45 seconds. When it is hot (but not too hot, as these biscuits will burn easily), fry them quickly, about 10–12 seconds. Remove from the pan with a fish slice, drain, coat them in sugar and serve immediately.

Choux puffs

PETITS-CHOUX

Choux pastry:
- 225 g/8 oz plain flour
- 250 ml/8 fl oz milk
- 50 g/2 oz butter
- 50 g/2 oz lard
- ½ teaspoon sugar or
  1 sugar cube
- sunflower oil, for brushing
- 3 eggs
- 2 egg whites
- salt

Custard filling:
- 3 egg yolks
- 2 tablespoons plain flour
- 750 ml/1¼ pints milk
- 150 g/5 oz caster sugar
- thinly pared rind of 1 lemon
- 1 egg white

Caramel topping:
- 3 tablespoons sugar

Makes about 30 large puffs or 70 small puffs

Sift the flour on to a sheet of greaseproof paper. Put the milk, butter, lard, sugar and a pinch of salt into a saucepan and heat gently, stirring with a wooden spoon. When the mixture comes to the boil, tip in the flour all at once and stir rapidly for about 3 minutes. Remove the pan from the heat and leave to cool. Meanwhile, make the cus-tard filling. Beat the egg yolks with the flour and 2 tablespoons of the milk in a bowl, then set aside. Put the remaining milk, the sugar and lemon rind in a saucepan over a medium heat and bring to the boil. Stir a ladleful of the hot milk into the egg yolk mixture, then tip the mixture into the pan and cook, stirring constantly, for a further 3–5 minutes, until thickened. Remove the pan from the heat, strain the custard through a coarse sieve into a bowl and leave to cool, then chill in the refrigerator. Preheat the oven to 200°C/400°F/Gas Mark 6. Brush 2 baking sheets with oil. Add the eggs, one at a time, to the cooled choux paste, making sure each is fully incorporated before adding the next. Finally, stir in the egg whites (not whisked). Using a teaspoon, put small mounds of the mixture, spaced well apart on to the prepared baking sheets, working in batches if necessary. Al-ternatively, spoon the mixture into a piping bag fitted with a plain nozzle and pipe small balls on to the baking sheets, spacing them well apart. Bake for 10 minutes, then lower the oven temperature to 180°C/350°F/Gas Mark 4 and bake for a further 10 minutes for small choux puffs or a further 20–25 minutes for larger choux puffs, until they are golden brown. Remove from the oven. Using kitchen scis-sors, make a slit about 3 cm/1¼ inches long in the side of each puff, then press gently to open it slightly and allow the steam to escape. (Make the slit about halfway up the puff so that the custard does not leak out when it is filled.) Set aside to cool. To finish the custard fill-ing, whisk the egg white in a grease-free bowl until soft peaks form, then gently fold it into the custard. Use a teaspoon to fill the puffs with the custard filling. To make the caramel topping, put the sugar into a saucepan with 1 table-spoon water and heat gently, stirring until the sugar has dissolved. Continue to heat without stirring until the caramel is golden. Remove the pan from the heat and quickly dip the top of each choux puff into the mixture, then remove immediately. Hold the choux puffs carefully to avoid burns.

Roulade
BRAZO DE GITANO

- butter, for greasing
- 4 tablespoons plain flour
- 2 tablespoons potato flour
- 1 teaspoon baking powder
- pinch of vanilla powder or
  a few drops of vanilla extract
- 3 eggs, separated
- 1 egg white
- 5 tablespoons caster sugar
- salt
- icing sugar, to decorate

Serves 8

Preheat the oven to 160°C/325°F/Gas Mark 3. Grease a Swiss roll tin, about 38 x 25 cm/15 x 10 inches, with butter. Line the base with greaseproof paper and grease with butter. Sift together the plain flour, potato flour, baking powder and vanilla powder, if using, into a bowl. Whisk the egg whites with a pinch of salt in a clean, dry bowl until stiff peaks form. Add the egg yolks, and the vanilla extract, if using, then the sugar and, finally, the flour mixture, a spoonful at a time. Spoon the mixture into the prepared tin. Bake for about 35 minutes, until firm but only lightly browned. Insert a wooden cocktail stick into the centre of the sponge and if it comes out clean, the sponge is cooked. Wring out a clean tea towel in warm water, spread it out on a work surface and immediately turn the sponge out on to it. Remove and discard the greaseproof paper, spread your chosen filling over the sponge (see below) and use the tea towel to help roll it up. Transfer to a dish, cover and leave to cool. Before serving, trim off the ends of the roll and sprinkle icing sugar on the top. Once the sponge is on the tea towel, spread a thin layer of jam over it with a knife. Spread the whipped cream on top and quickly roll up. You will need about 500 ml/18 fl oz double cream.

Note: The roulade can be filled with Confectioner's Cream (see recipe 1010) in place of the jam and cream.

Orange roulade

BRAZO DE GITANO DE NARANJA

- butter, for greasing
- 12 eggs, separated
- 250 g/9 oz caster sugar
- 1 tablespoon cornflour
- juice of 2 oranges
- grated rind of 1 orange
- salt
- icing sugar, to decorate

Serves 4–6

Preheat the oven to 150°C/300°F/Gas Mark 2. Line a Swiss roll tin with foil and grease with butter. Beat the egg yolks with the sugar and the cornflour in a bowl. Add the orange juice and rind. Whisk the egg whites with a pinch of salt in a clean, dry bowl until stiff peaks form. Gently fold them into the egg yolk mixture. Pour the mixture into the prepared tin and bake for 30–45 minutes, until firm but only lightly browned. Remove from the oven and turn out on to a clean tea towel. Roll up, using the tea towel to help you, sprinkle icing sugar on top and leave to cool.

954

Walnut log
TRONCO DE NUECES

- butter, for greasing
- 4 tablespoons plain flour
- 2 tablespoons potato flour
- 1 teaspoon baking powder
- pinch of vanilla powder or
  a few drops of vanilla extract
- 3 eggs, separated
- 1 egg white
- 5 tablespoons caster sugar
- 50 g/2 oz chocolate curls
- 100 ml/3½ fl oz freshly brewed
  strong coffee
- salt

Filling:
- 65 g/2½ oz caster sugar
- 150 g/5 oz walnuts,
  peeled and chopped
- 200 ml/7 fl oz milk
- 2 egg yolks
- 1½ teaspoons cornflour
- 150 g/5 oz butter, softened
- dash of walnut liqueur

Serves 6

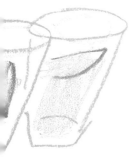

First make the filling. Put the sugar into a saucepan with 2 tablespoons water and heat gently, stirring until the sugar has dissolved. Continue to heat without stirring until the caramel is golden. Stir in the walnuts, remove the pan from the heat and leave to cool. When the caramel has cooled, bring the milk to the boil, then stir it into the mixture. Beat the egg yolks with the cornflour in a bowl and stir into the caramelized milk mixture. Return the pan to a low heat and cook, stirring constantly, for a few minutes. Remove the pan from the heat and leave to cool. Pour the cooled mixture into a bowl, add the butter and beat with an electric mixer on high speed. Stir in the liqueur and set aside. Preheat the oven to 160°C/325°F/Gas Mark 3. Grease a large Swiss roll tin, about 38 x 25 cm/15 x 10 inches, with butter. Line the base with greaseproof paper and grease with butter. To make the sponge, sift together the plain flour, potato flour, baking powder and vanilla powder, if using, into a bowl and set aside. Whisk the egg whites with a pinch of salt in a clean, dry bowl until stiff peaks form. Stir in the yolks and vanilla extract, if using, then the sugar and, finally, the flour mixture, a spoonful at a time. Pour the mixture into the prepared tin and bake for 35 minutes, until just firm but only lightly browned. Wring out a clean tea towel in warm water and spread it out on a work surface. Remove the sponge from the oven and immediately turn it out on to the towel. Remove and discard the greaseproof paper and sprinkle the coffee over the sponge. Spread the filling over the sponge, then roll it up using the tea towel to help. Carefully transfer to a dish, cover and leave to cool. Just before serving, trim off the ends diagonally and decorate the cake with the chocolate curls.

Note: You can make chocolate curls by shaving a bar of chocolate with a swivel-blade vegetable peeler. The cake can be filled with mango cream, creme anglaise with raspberries or chocolate cream.

955

Pastry for tarts
MASAS PARA TARTAS

- **200 g/7 oz plain flour, plus extra for dusting**
- **1 tablespoon caster sugar**
- **80 g/3 oz butter, cut into pieces, plus extra for greasing**
- **1 egg yolk**
- **1 tablespoon groundnut (Aus: peanut) oil**
- **salt**

Makes pastry for 1 tart, 25-cm / 10-inch diameter

Sift the flour with a pinch of salt into a bowl. Sprinkle in the sugar and add the butter, egg yolk and oil. Rub in the butter with your fingertips until the mixture resembles fine breadcrumbs. Gradually stir in about 175 ml/6 fl oz water, a little at a time, until the dough comes together. Turn out on to a lightly floured surface and knead lightly. Shape the dough into a ball, wrap in foil and leave to rest in the refrigerator for at least 3 hours. Preheat the oven to 200°C/400°F/Gas Mark 6. Grease a 25-cm/10-inch tart tin with butter. Roll out the dough on a lightly floured surface, transfer to the prepared tin, trim the edge and prick the base with a fork. Line the pastry case with greaseproof paper and half fill with baking beans. Bake blind for 10–15 minutes. Remove the pastry case from the oven. Remove the beans and paper and fill the case according to your chosen recipe.

Note: If the tart is to be filled with fruit that will release juice, brush the base and sides of the pastry case with lightly beaten egg white before baking blind.

956

Sweet shortcrust pastry for tarts
MASA DULCE PARA TARTAS

- **120 g/4 oz plain flour, plus extra for dusting**
- **65 g/2½ oz butter, softened, plus extra for greasing**
- **2 tablespoons caster sugar**
- **1 egg white**

Makes pastry for 1 tart, 25-cm / 10-inch diameter

Sift the flour on to a marble slab and add the butter, sugar and 2 table-spoons water. Work these ingredients together with your fingertips until combined. Shape the dough into a ball, wrap in foil and leave to rest for about 30 minutes. Preheat the oven to 160°C/325°F/Gas Mark 3. Grease a tart tin with butter. Roll out the dough on a lightly floured surface, transfer to the prepared tin, trim the edge and prick the base with a fork. Lightly beat the egg white with a fork, then brush it over the base and sides of the pastry case. Bake blind for about 15 minutes. Remove the pastry case from the oven, add your chosen filling and bake according to the recipe.

957

Sweet French pastry for tarts
MASA DULCE PARA TARTAS (3)

- 3 tablespoons lukewarm milk
- 20 g / ¾ oz easy-blend dried yeast
- 100 g / 3½ oz butter, softened
- 2 egg yolks
- 250 g / 9 oz plain flour, plus extra for dusting
- 2–3 tablespoons caster sugar
- salt

Makes 1 tart, 25 cm / 10 inch

Put the milk in a bowl, sprinkle the yeast over the surface and leave to stand for about 10 minutes, until frothy. Stir well. Grease a baking sheet with butter. Pour the yeast mixture into a mixing bowl, add the egg yolks and butter and sift in the flour with a pinch of salt. Bring the mixture together with your hands, then roll it out with a rolling pin or pat it out with your hand on a floured surface. Put the dough on to the prepared baking sheet, cover with a clean tea towel and leave to rise for 30 minutes. Prick the dough base all over with a fork, sprinkle with the sugar and fill according to taste.

958

Sablé pastry for tarts
MASA SABLÉ PARA TARTAS

- 120 g / 4 oz butter, softened, plus extra for greasing
- 1 egg
- 3 tablespoons caster sugar
- 250 g / 9 oz plain flour, plus extra for dusting
- grated rind of ½ lemon
- salt

Makes 1 tart, 25 cm / 10 inch

Preheat the oven to 180°C/350°F/Gas Mark 4. Grease a 20-cm/8-inch tart tin with butter. Beat the egg with the sugar and a pinch of salt in a bowl until the sugar and salt have dissolved completely. Sift the flour into a mound on a work surface and make a well in the centre. Pour the egg mixture into the well and dot the flour with the butter. Work the ingredients with your fingertips until combined but still grainy. Roll out the dough on a lightly floured surface, then transfer to the prepared tin and trim the edge. Prick the base with a fork and bake until just dry or golden brown, depending on the recipe.

959

Almond pastry
MASA DE ALMENDRAS PARA TARTAS

- 200 g / 7 oz plain flour, plus extra for dusting
- 100 g / 3½ oz butter, cut into pieces, plus extra for greasing
- 3 tablespoons caster sugar
- 1 small egg, lightly beaten
- 2 tablespoons milk
- 50 g / 2 oz ground almonds
- 3–4 tablespoons fine breadcrumbs

Makes 1 tart, 25 cm / 10 inch

Sift the flour with a pinch of salt into a bowl. Add the butter and rub in with your fingertips. Lightly work in the sugar, egg, milk and almonds until combined. Shape the dough into a ball, cover with a clean tea towel and leave to rest for 1 hour. Preheat the oven to 180°C/350°F/Gas Mark 4. Grease a 25-cm/10-inch tart tin with butter and sprinkle with the breadcrumbs, shaking out the excess. Roll out the dough on a lightly floured work surface, transfer to the prepared tin, trim the edge and prick the base with a fork. Bake blind for 25–30 minutes.

Note: This pastry case can be filled with cream and fresh berries. Brush the pastry case with lightly beaten egg white before baking.

Fruit for filling tarts

How to cook

Make a syrup with 500 ml/18 fl oz water and 100 g/3 ½ oz caster sugar and heat for 10 minutes. Add the fruit – apple wedges, halved and stoned plums, cherries, apricots, etc. Simmer until softened but not falling apart. Drain well, reserving the syrup, and spoon into the prepared pastry case. Mix 2 teaspoons potato flour with a little water, add to the syrup and cook for a few minutes, then pour it over the tart.

960

Strawberries:
- **250 g/9 oz strawberries, hulled**
- **½ leaf gelatine**
- **2 tablespoons redcurrant or apricot jam**
- **3 tablespoons caster sugar**

Serves 4–6

Strawberry tart

TARTA DE FRESA

Put the strawberries in a cooked pastry case (see recipe 956). Pour 3 tablespoons water into a small heatproof bowl, add the gelatine and leave to stand for 5 minutes to soften. Place the bowl over a pan of barely simmering water until the gelatine has dissolved, then remove from the heat. Put the jam into a saucepan, add the sugar, dissolved gelatine and 3 tablespoons water and heat gently. Strain the glaze over the strawberries.

961

- **1 sweet shortcrust pastry tart shell (see recipe 955)**

Filling:
- **1 tablespoon caster sugar**
- **80 g/3 oz currants**
- **3 eating apples**
- **2 tablespoons apricot jam**
- **whipped cream, to decorate (optional)**

Serves 4–6

Apple tart

TARTA DE MANZANA

Preheat the oven to 160°C/325°F/Gas Mark 3. Put the sugar and cur-rants into a saucepan, pour in 120 ml/4 fl oz water and cook over a medium heat for about 10 minutes. Remove the pan from the heat and set aside. Cut the apples into quarters, peel, core and slice thinly. Arrange the slices around the edge of the cooked pastry case, overlapping slightly, then continue making similar concentric circles, until the case is full. Put the tart on to a baking sheet and bake for about 20 minutes. Remove the tart from the oven. Drain the currants, reserv-ng the syrup, and sprinkle them over the tart. Stir the jam into the syrup and cook over a high heat for about 5 minutes. Remove the pan from the heat and allow to cool slightly, then strain the syrup over the tart. Leave to cool. Serve the tart plain or decorated with a little whipped cream.

Fruit tart

TARTA DE FRUTAS

- butter, for greasing
- 1 quantity pastry for tarts
  (see recipe 955)
- plain flour, for dusting
- 1 egg white, lightly beaten

Fruit filling:
- 120 ml/4 oz caster sugar
- 3 large oranges,
  peeled and sliced, or
- 750 g/1 lb 10 oz apricots,
  halved and stoned, or
- 750 g/1 lb 10 oz pears,
  peeled, cored and sliced, or
- 750 g/1 lb 10 oz apples, peeled,
  cored and sliced
- 2 tablespoons cornflour
- 350 ml/12 fl oz milk
- 1 egg, lightly beaten
- 2 tablespoons apricot jam

Serves 6–8

Preheat the oven to 200°C/400°F/Gas Mark 6. Grease a 25-cm/10-inch loose-based tart tin with butter. Roll out the dough on a lightly floured surface, transfer to the prepared tin, trim the edge and brush the base and sides with the egg white. Bake blind for about 25 minutes. Meanwhile, prepare the filling. Put 5 tablespoons of the sugar into a saucepan, pour in 100 ml/3 ½ fl oz water and cook over a medium heat for 5 minutes. Add the fruit and cook in the syrup for about 8 minutes, until softened but not falling apart. Remove the pan from the heat and lift out the fruit with a slotted spoon and reserve. Reserve the syrup. Mix the cornflour to a paste with 4 tablespoons of the milk in a bowl. Pour the remaining milk into a saucepan, add the remaining sugar and bring to the boil. Stir in the cornflour and cook, stirring constantly, for 3 minutes. Remove the pan from the heat. Remove the pastry case from the oven but do not switch off the oven. Gradually stir the egg into the cornflour mixture, a little at a time. Pour the mixture into the pastry case and arrange the fruit on top. Return the tart to the oven for 5 minutes. Remove the tart from the oven and leave to cool. Remove the tart from the tin and place on a serving dish. Stir the jam into the reserved syrup and cook for about 10 minutes. Just before serving, strain the glaze over the tart in a thin layer.

Note: Do not fill the tart more than 30 minutes before serving or the pastry will become very soggy. You can omit the custard if you like, but more fruit will be needed. Sprinkle the base of the pastry case with a little sugar before adding the fruit, then continue as described above.

Linzertorte

TARTA VIENESA CON MERMELADA DE FRAMBUESAS (LINZERTARTE)

- 150 g/5 oz butter, softened, plus extra for greasing
- 200 g/7 oz plain flour
- ½ teaspoon baking powder
- 1 tablespoon cocoa powder
- 150 g/5 oz caster sugar
- 150 g/5 oz ground almonds
- 1 teaspoon ground cinnamon
- 2 eggs, lightly beaten
- 130 g/4 ½ oz raspberry or redcurrant jam

Serves 6

Preheat the oven to 160°C/325°F/Gas Mark 3. Grease a 23-cm/9-inch loose-based tart tin with butter. Sift together the flour, baking powder and cocoa into a bowl and stir in the sugar, almonds and cinnamon. Add the eggs and mix well, then mix in the butter. Reserve a little of the dough for decoration and put the remainder into the prepared tin, gently pressing it out with your hand to spread it all over the base and sides. Spread the jam over the base. Roll the reserved pastry into thin strips between the palms of your hands and lay them over the jam in a diamond-shaped lattice. Put the tart on a baking sheet and bake for 10 minutes, then increase the oven temperature to 180°C/350°F/Gas Mark 4 and bake for a further 10 minutes. Increase the oven temperature to 190°C/375°F/Gas Mark 5 and bake for 10 minutes more, then increase the oven temperature to 200°C/400°F/Gas Mark 6 and bake for a further 15–30 minutes, until the pastry is lightly browned. Remove the tart from the oven and leave to cool in the tin, then remove it and place on a serving plate.

Note: This Austrian pastry, usually made with raspberry jam, originates in Linz, hence its name. It can also be made with cranberries or apricots in the filling.

Lemon tart

TARTA DE LIMÓN

Dough:
- 200g/7oz plain flour, plus extra for dusting
- 1 tablespoon caster sugar
- 80g/3oz butter, cut into pieces, plus extra for greasing
- 1 egg
- 1 tablespoon sunflower oil
- 1 egg white, lightly beaten
- salt

Filling:
- 3 egg yolks
- grated rind of 1 lemon
- 370g/13oz sweetened canned condensed milk
- juice of 2–3 lemons

Meringue topping:
- 3 egg whites
- 2 tablespoons icing sugar, sifted
- 1 teaspoon plain flour, sifted
- salt

Serves 6

Make the dough with the flour, sugar, butter, egg, oil and salt as described in recipe 955. Shape it into a ball, wrap in foil and leave to rest in the refrigerator for a few hours. Preheat the oven to 190°C/375°F/Gas Mark 5. Grease a 25-cm/10-inch tart tin with butter. Roll out the dough on a lightly floured surface, transfer to the prepared tin, trim the edge and prick the base all over with a fork. Line the pastry case with greaseproof paper and half fill with baking beans. Put the tin on a baking sheet and bake for about 30 minutes, until beginning to brown. Remove the pastry case from the oven but do not switch off the oven. Remove the beans and paper. Brush the base and sides of the case with the egg white, return it to the oven and bake for a further 5 minutes. Meanwhile, make the filling. Beat the egg yolks with the lemon rind in a bowl, then gradually beat in the condensed milk, a little at a time, followed by the lemon juice. Remove the pastry case from the oven but do not switch off the oven. Pour the filling into the pastry case. To make the meringue topping, whisk the egg whites with a pinch of salt in a clean, dry bowl until stiff peaks form, then fold in the sugar and flour. Spread the meringue over the tart and return it to the oven. Bake for 10–15 minutes, until the meringue is beginning to brown. Remove the tart from the oven and leave to cool before serving.

Note: The tart can be filled with lemon curd (see recipe 1037).

Tipsy kiwi tart

TARTA BORRACHA DE KIWIS

- **150 g / 5 oz butter, softened, plus extra for greasing**
- **120 g / 4 oz caster sugar**
- **4 eggs**
- **65 g / 2½ oz plain flour, sifted**
- **1 tablespoon baking powder**
- **4–5 kiwi fruits, peeled and sliced**
- **salt**
- **whipped cream, to decorate (optional)**

Glaze:
- **120 g / 4 oz caster sugar**
- **175 ml / 6 fl oz rum**

Serves 6–8

Preheat the oven to 160°C/325°F/Gas Mark 3. Line the base of a loose-based 23-cm/9-inch tart tin with foil and lightly grease the foil with butter. Pour hot water into a saucepan or metal bowl to warm it, tip it out and immediately add the butter, sugar and a pinch of salt. Mix well, then stir in the eggs, one at a time. Finally, sift in the flour and baking powder and mix well. Press the dough into the prepared tin with your fingers and place two sliced kiwis on top. Put the tart on a baking sheet and bake for 15 minutes, then increase the oven temperature to 180°C/350°F/Gas Mark 4 and bake for a further 45 minutes, until the pastry is golden. Meanwhile, prepare the glaze. Pour 175 ml/6 fl oz water into a saucepan, stir in the sugar and cook over a medium heat for 10 minutes. Stir in the rum and cook for a further 5 minutes, then remove the pan from the heat and leave to cool. Remove the tart from the oven and leave to cool in the tin. Remove the tart from the tin and place on a serving plate. Gradually spoon half the glaze over the tart, a little at a time. Put the remaining slices of kiwi on top and pour the rest of the glaze over them. Serve plain or decorated with whipped cream.

966

Grape tart
TARTA DE UVAS

- 120 g/4 oz plain flour, plus extra for dusting
- 2 tablespoons caster sugar
- 65 g/2½ oz butter, plus extra for greasing
- 1 egg white

Filling:
- 1 teaspoon cornflour
- 250 ml/8 fl oz milk
- 3 egg yolks
- 80 g/3 oz icing sugar
- 50 ml/2 fl oz muscatel wine or other sweet white wine
- 2 tablespoons peach jam
- 1 bunch of seedless grapes (this can be a mixture of green and black grapes)

Serves 6

Sift the flour on to a work surface, add the sugar, butter and 2 tablespoons water and mix with your fingertips until combined. Shape the dough into a ball, wrap in foil and leave to rest in the refrigerator for 30 minutes. Grease a 23-cm/9-inch tart tin with butter and lightly dust with flour. Roll out the dough on a lightly floured surface, transfer to the prepared tin, trim the edge and prick the base all over with a fork and brush with beaten egg white. Chill in the refrigerator. Make the filling. Mix the cornflour to a paste with 1 tablespoon of the milk. Pour the remaining milk into a saucepan and bring to the boil. Beat the egg yolks with the sugar in another saucepan and stir in the cornflour and boiling milk. Cook over a low heat, stirring constantly, until thickened. Remove the pan from the heat and leave to cool, then stir in the wine. Preheat the oven to 200°C/400°F/Gas Mark 6. Line the chilled pastry case with greaseproof paper and half fill with baking beans. Place on a baking sheet and bake for 15 minutes. Remove the beans and paper, return to the oven and bake for a further 5 minutes, until lightly browned. Remove the pastry case from the oven and lower the oven temperature to 150°C/300°F/Gas Mark 2. Spread a thin layer of the custard on the base of the pastry case and return to the oven for 15 minutes. Remove the tart from the oven and leave to cool. Heat the jam in a saucepan. Pour the remaining custard into the pastry case and top with the grapes. Pour the jam over them.

967

Egg custard tart
TARTA DE YEMA

- 1 French pastry case (see recipe 957)

Custard:
- 3 eggs
- 80 g/3 oz caster sugar, plus extra for sprinkling
- 2 tablespoons ground almonds (optional)
- 40 g/1½ oz butter

Serves 4–6

Leave the pastry case to rise for 30 minutes then prick with a fork. Preheat the oven to 180°C/350°F/Gas Mark 4. Make the custard. Beat the eggs in a bowl, then stir in the sugar and almonds, if using. Sprinkle the pastry case with sugar and pour in the custard. Dot with the butter, place on a baking sheet and bake for about 20 minutes. Increase the oven tem-perature to 200°C/400°F/Gas Mark 6 and bake until the top is golden brown. Remove the tart from the oven and leave to cool. Turn it out of the tin and place on a plate so the custard is uppermost. This is easiest if you use a loose-based tin.

968

Puff pastry turnovers

HOJALDRE

- 200 g / 7 oz plain flour,
  plus extra for dusting
- 120 g / 4 oz lard, softened
- 120 g / 4 oz margarine, softened
- juice of 1 lemon
- 1 egg, lightly beaten
- salt

Makes 6

Try to prepare the puff pastry in a cool place, particularly in the summer time. Sift together the flour and a pinch of salt into a mound on a marble slab. Dot with the lard and margarine and mix lightly with a knife, then add the lemon juice and a little water (the amount depends on the type of flour, but never very much) and bring together with your fingers. Briefly knead the dough on a lightly floured work surface, then roll out into a rectangle. Fold each of the short sides of the dough into the middle (see drawing). Leave to rest for 15 minutes. Give the dough a quarter turn and roll out again to a rectangle. Fold each of the short sides of the dough into the middle and leave to rest for 15 minutes. Repeat this procedure of turning the dough a quarter turn, rolling out and folding three times, leaving it to rest for 15 minutes each time. Wrap the dough in foil and leave to rest in a cool place for at least 2 hours or overnight. Preheat the oven to 220°C/425°F/Gas Mark 7. Roll out the dough on a lightly floured surface and make a turnover with your chosen filling spooning the filling in the centre of the dough, and folding one side of the dough over the filling to meet the other side. Leave a 2-cm border of pastry around the whole turnover and press to seal it with a fork or your fingertips. Place on a dampened baking sheet. Prick the turnover in several places with a skewer to allow steam to escape during cooking. You can also make a decorative pattern with a knife blade, if you like. Brush with the beaten egg to glaze, and bake for about 30 minutes, until puffed up and golden brown.

Note: To fill the turnovers, you can use a variety of fillings including: custard made with a lot of flour or cornflour to make it very thick (see recipe 1008); Confectioner's Cream (see recipe 1010), without the addition of whisked egg white, and jam; Apple Compote (see recipe 972) which should be mixed with currants and walnuts (drain the purée well to prevent it from spoiling the puff pastry); fruit in syrup, such as pineapple, pears, etc., well drained.

969

Baked apples

MANZANAS ASADAS

- 1 apple per serving
- 1 teaspoon sugar per serving
- 1 knob of butter per serving
- apricot or other jam or custard
  (see recipe 1008)

Serves 1

Preheat the oven to 180°C/350°F/Gas Mark 4. Core the apples with an apple corer or pointed knife, but do not cut right through them. Score a line all the way around each apple, about halfway up, then place them in an ovenproof dish. Put the sugar into the cavities and put the butter on top. Put 3 tablespoons water (for 6 apples) into the base of the dish and bake for about 30 minutes, until the apples are tender. Test by piercing with a wooden cocktail stick. Serve warm or cold, filling the cavity in each apple with any kind of jam, or serve covered with custard.

970

Baked apples with cream and caramel

MANZANAS ASADAS CON NATA Y CARAMELO

- 1 apple per serving
- 1 teaspoon sugar per serving
- 1 knob of butter per serving
- 1 tablespoon sweetened
  whipped cream
- 1 quantity Caramel Sauce
  (see recipe 117)

Serves 1

Bake the apples as described in recipe 969 and leave to cool. Fill them with the sweetened whipped cream and pour the caramel sauce over the top.

971

Baked apples with almonds

MANZANAS ASADAS CON ALMENDRAS

- 2 tablespoons rum
- 50 g/2 oz currants
- 6 large eating apples
- ½ lemon
- 2 egg yolks
- 5 tablespoons caster sugar
- 25 g/1 oz butter, softened
- 50 g/2 oz blanched almonds,
  toasted and chopped
- 6 glacé cherries

Serves 6

Preheat the oven to 180°C/350°F/Gas Mark 4. Warm the rum in a saucepan for a few seconds, then remove from the heat. Add 1 tablespoon water and the currants and leave to soak. Meanwhile, core the apples with an apple corer or a sharp knife, then peel them and rub them all over with the lemon to prevent discoloration. Place them in an ovenproof dish. Beat the egg yolks with the sugar in a small bowl and add the butter and almonds. Drain the currants, reserving the rum, and add to the mixture. Divide the mixture among the cavities in the apples. Stir 2 tablespoons water into the reserved rum and pour it into the dish. Bake for about 30 minutes, until the apples are tender. Remove from the oven and serve warm or cold, decorated with a glacé cherry on top of each one.

928

952

965

1009

972

Apple Compote

COMPOTA DE MANZANAS

- 2 kg/4½ lb eating apples,
  peeled, cored and sliced
- 6 tablespoons caster sugar
- 1 cinnamon stick
- 1 tablespoon rum (optional)

Serves 6

Put the apples into a saucepan, sprinkle the sugar over them and add the cinnamon stick. Cook over a medium heat, stirring occasionally, for about 20 minutes, until tender. Remove the cinnamon stick, pour the compote into a bowl and leave to cool. Stir in the rum, if using. Pass the apples through a food mill of process in a food processor if you prefer a smoother texture.

973

Apple compote to accompany meat

COMPOTA DE MANZANAS PARA ACOMPAÑAR LA CARNE

- 2 kg/4½ lb eating apples,
  peeled, cored and sliced

Serves 4–6

Prepare and cook the apples as described in recipe 972, omitting the cinnamon and sugar. Leave to cool, then pass through a food mill or pulse in a food processor.

974

Apple purée with orange juice

PURÉ DE MANZANAS CON ZUMO DE NARANJA

- 2 kg/4½ lb eating apples,
  peeled, cored and thickly sliced
- thinly pared strip of orange rind
- 6 tablespoons orange juice
- 6 tablespoons caster sugar
- 2 tablespoons rum (optional)

Serves 6

Put the apples into a saucepan with 3 tablespoons water and the orange rind. Cover and cook over a low heat for about 20 minutes, until soft, then add the orange juice and remove and discard the orange rind. Increase the heat to medium and cook for about 8 minutes, until the juice has been absorbed. Remove the pan from the heat and stir in the sugar, beating well with a wooden spoon. Put the apple purée into a glass bowl and leave to cool. Stir in the rum, if using, and serve with Langues de Chat (see recipe 943) or other biscuits.

975

Apple mousse with custard
MOUSSE DE MANZANAS CON NATILLAS

- **8 eating apples,**
  about 1.2 kg/2½ lb,
  peeled, cored and chopped
- **6 tablespoons caster sugar**
- **2 tablespoons rum**
- **4 egg whites**
- **salt**

  Caramel:
- **3 tablespoons caster sugar**

  Custard:
- **750 ml/1¼ pints milk**
- **6 tablespoons caster sugar**
- **3 egg yolks**
- **1 tablespoon cornflour**
- **pinch of vanilla powder or**
  a few drops of vanilla extract

Serves 6

Put the apples into a saucepan, sprinkle with the sugar and cook over a low heat for about 20 minutes, until softened. Drain well, then put the apples on a clean tea towel or square of muslin, gather up the corners and hang over a bowl for about 10 minutes to drain completely. Make the caramel. Put the sugar into a saucepan, add 2 tablespoons water and stir to dissolve, then cook over a low heat until golden. Pour the caramel into a cake tin and tip it back and forth until the tin is completely coated. Make the custard as described in recipe 1008, leave to cool, then chill in the refrigerator. Preheat the oven to 180°C/350°F/Gas Mark 4. Transfer the strained apples to a bowl and stir in the rum. Whisk the egg whites with a pinch of salt in a clean, dry bowl until stiff peaks form and gently fold into the apple mixture. Pour the mixture into the prepared tin. Place it in a roasting tin, pour in boiling water to reach about halfway up the sides of the tin and bake for 1 hour. Remove the mousse from the oven and leave to cool in the tin. Just before serving, turn out on to a serving dish and pour some of the custard over it. Serve, offering the remaining custard separately.

976

Apple fritters
BUÑUELOS DE MANZANA

- **4 eating apples**
- **juice of ½ lemon**
- **3 tablespoons caster sugar,**
  plus extra for coating
- **4 tablespoons rum**
- **sunflower oil, for deep frying**

  Batter:
- **300 g/11 oz plain flour**
- **3 tablespoons white wine**
- **3 tablespoons sunflower oil**
- **1 tablespoon caster sugar**
- **300 ml/½ pint milk**
- **½ teaspoon baking powder**
- **salt**

Serves 4

Peel the apples, core with an apple corer or sharp knife and cut into slices about 5 mm/¼ inch thick. Toss them in the lemon juice to prevent discoloration. Mix together the sugar, rum and 1½ tablespoons water in a shallow dish, add the slices of apple and leave to macerate, stirring occasionally, for 30 minutes. Meanwhile, make the batter. Sift the flour with a pinch of salt into a bowl, make a well in the centre, pour in the wine and oil and add the sugar. Mix well, then stir in the milk. Cover and leave to rest for 30 minutes. Heat the oil in a deep-fryer or large saucepan to 180–190°C/350–375°F or until a cube of day-old bread browns in 30 seconds. Drain the slices of apple and pat dry. Stir the baking powder into the batter. Dip the slices of apple into the batter, one at a time, add to the hot oil, in batches, and cook until golden brown. Remove with a slotted spoon and drain well, then coat the fritters in sugar while they are still hot. Put the fritters on a serving dish and keep warm while cooking the remaining batches. Serve immediately.

977 Cheap-and-cheerful fried apple purée

FRITOS DE PURÉ DE MANZANA, BARATOS Y RÁPIDOS

- 5 tablespoons plain flour
- 6 large eating apples, about 1.2 kg/2½ lb, peeled and grated
- 6 tablespoons caster sugar, plus extra for coating
- sunflower oil, for deep frying

Serves 6

Sift the flour into a bowl, add the apples and sugar and mix well. Heat the oil in a deep-fryer or saucepan to 180–190°C/350–375°F or until a cube of day-old bread browns in 30 seconds. Drop spoonfuls of the apple mixture into the hot oil and cook until golden. Remove with a slotted spoon, one at a time, coat in sugar and place on a warm serving dish. Keep warm until all the purée has been cooked. Serve immediately.

978 Flamed apple omelette

TORTILLA DE MANZANAS FLAMEADA

- 25 g/1 oz butter
- 5–6 tablespoons sunflower oil
- 3 eating apples, peeled, cored and sliced
- 6 eggs
- 5 tablespoons caster sugar
- 5 tablespoons brandy or rum
- salt

Serves 5–6

Melt the butter with 3 tablespoons of the oil in a frying pan. Add the apples and cook, stirring occasionally, until golden brown. Put enough of the remaining oil into another frying pan to cover the base, and heat it. Beat the eggs with a pinch of salt in a bowl, then pour them into the pan. Cook until the omelette is beginning to set, then spoon the apples in a semi-circle on one half and sprinkle 2 tablespoons of the sugar on top. Fold the uncovered half of the omelette over the apples. Slide the omelette on to a warm serving dish and sprinkle with the remaining sugar. Heat the brandy or rum in a small saucepan, ignite it and carefully pour it over the omelette. Serve while it is still burning, spooning the rum or brandy over the omelette so that it is well flamed.

Tarte tatin

TARTA DE MANZANA CALIENTE Y HECHA AL REVÉS (TATIN)

- 200 g/7 oz plain flour,
  plus extra for dusting
- ½ teaspoon salt
- 100 g/3 ½ oz butter,
  softened and cut into pieces
- 1 tablespoon sunflower oil
- 2 teaspoons caster sugar
- whipped or pouring cream,
  to serve

Caramel:
- 100 g/3 ½ oz caster sugar
- 1 teaspoon lemon juice

Apples:
- 500 /1 lb 2 oz eating apples
- 2 tablespoons caster sugar
- 20 g/¾ oz butter

Serves 6

First, make the pastry dough. Sift together the flour and salt on to a work surface and put the pieces of butter on top. Pour on the oil and sprinkle with the sugar. Gently mix together with your fingertips, gradually adding about 5 tablespoons warm water, a little at a time, until a smooth dough forms. Shape the dough into a ball, cover with foil and leave to rest in the refrigerator. Make the caramel. Put the sugar into a saucepan, add 3 tablespoons water and stir to dissolve, then cook over a low heat until golden. Stir in the lemon juice, then pour the caramel into a tarte tatin tin or loose-based tart tin and tip it back and forth until the tin is completely coated. Leave to cool. Peel, core and slice the apples thickly. Arrange them in the prepared tin, bearing in mind that the first layer of apples will be on top when the tart is turned out so they should be placed attractively. Sprinkle the apples with the sugar and dot with the butter. Preheat the oven to 220°C/425°F/Gas Mark 7. Knead the dough, pressing it out with your hands on a lightly floured surface. Fold it into four, then roll it into a round with a rolling pin. Lift the dough on the rolling pin and place it over the apples. Tuck it in around the edge. Bake the tart for about 45 minutes, until golden brown. Remove it from the oven and immediately turn out on to a warm serving dish. (If the caramel is allowed to cool, it is difficult to turn out the tart properly.) This upside-down apple tart is served hot with whipped or pouring cream.

Apple tart with baked custard topping

FLAN-TARTA DE MANZANAS

- **750 g/1 lb 10 oz eating apples,
  peeled, cored and chopped**
- **165 g/5½ oz caster sugar**
- **6 eggs**
- **450 ml/¾ pint milk**
- **2 tablespoons brandy**
- **pinch of vanilla powder or
  a few drops of vanilla extract**
- **grated rind of ½ lemon**
- **3 day-old sugared buns,
  thinly sliced**
- **750 ml/1¼ pints whipped
  cream and crystallized fruit,
  to decorate (optional)**

Serves 6–8

Put the apples into a saucepan, add 2 tablespoons water and 2 tablespoons of the sugar and cook, stirring occasionally, for about 20 minutes, until softened. Drain well, then put the apples on a clean tea towel or square of muslin, gather up the corners and hang over a bowl for about 10 minutes to drain completely. Meanwhile, put 2 tablespoons of the remaining sugar into a saucepan, add 2 tablespoons water and stir to dissolve, then cook over a low heat until golden. Pour the caramel into a tart tin and tip it back and forth until the tin is completely coated. Preheat the oven to 160°C/325°F/Gas Mark 3. Beat the eggs with the remaining sugar in a bowl, then mix in the milk, brandy, vanilla and lemon rind. Arrange a layer of sliced bun over the base of the coated tart tin and cover with a layer of apple purée. Continue making alternate layers until both ingredients are used up. Pour the egg mixture on top, but do not fill the tin completely so that there is room for the filling to rise. Put the tin into a roasting tin and pour in hot water to come about halfway up the sides. Bake for about 45 minutes, until set. Remove from the oven and leave to cool before turning out on to a serving dish. The tart can be covered with whipped cream and decorated with crystallized fruit if you like.

Note: This tart is delicious made with cherries. Stone them before cooking them in the same way as the apples.

Apple charlotte

POSTRE DE COMPOTA DE MANZANAS CON SOLETILLAS Y NATA

- **6 tablespoons caster sugar**
- **15–16 sponge fingers**
- **1.5 kg/3¼ lb eating apples**
- **250 ml/8 fl oz double cream, stiffly whipped**

Serves 6

Trim one end of the sponge fingers so that they will stand upright. Put half the sugar into a saucepan, add 2 tablespoons water and stir to dissolve, then cook over a low heat until golden brown. One at a time, dip the cut ends of the sponge fingers into the caramel to a depth of about 2 cm/¾ inch. Place the sponge fingers upright, side by side, around a charlotte mould or round dish. Leave to cool. Peel, core and dice the apples. Put them into a saucepan with the remaining sugar and 175 ml/6 fl oz water. Cook over a low heat for about 20 minutes, until softened. Drain well, then put the apples on a clean tea towel or square of muslin, gather up the corners and hang over a bowl for about 10 minutes to drain completely. Put the purée into a bowl and chill in the refrigerator. To serve, pour the purée into the centre of the ring of sponge fingers, cover with the cream and serve.

Note: Do not put the purée into the dish too far in advance of serving, as it will soften the sponge fingers and they will fall over. If you like, you can sweeten the cream with sugar before adding it to the charlotte. You could even fold in a whisked egg white. The cream can be decorated with chopped, caramel-coated almonds or with spun caramel, made from caramel beaten with a fork just as it is beginning to brown.

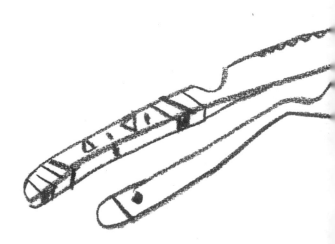

Pears with cream and chocolate

PERAS CON NATA Y CHOCOLATE

- **6 large pears**
- **150 g/5 oz caster sugar**
- **1 small cinnamon stick**
- **250 ml/8 fl oz double cream, stiffly whipped**
- **175 g/6 oz plain chocolate, broken into pieces**
- **25 g/1 oz butter**

Serves 6

Peel and halve the pears and cut out the cores with a pointed knife. Put them in a saucepan in a single layer and sprinkle with 6 tablespoons of the sugar. Add the cinnamon and pour in just enough water to cover the fruit. Cook over a medium heat for about 20 minutes, until softened and translucent but not falling apart. Lift out the pears with a slotted spoon, drain well and leave to cool in a dish. Divide the cream among six glasses or sundae dishes and put two pear halves, cut sides down, on top. Chill in the refrigerator until ready to serve. Pour 350 ml/12 fl oz water into a saucepan, add the remaining sugar and the chocolate and heat gently until the chocolate has melted and the sauce has thickened slightly. Add the butter and stir until it is fully incorporated, then remove the pan from the heat and leave the sauce to cool slightly. Pour the sauce over the pears and serve the fruit immediately.

983

Tipsy cherries
BORRACHOS CON CEREZAS

Dough:
- 8 g/⅓ oz fresh yeast
- 50 ml/2 fl oz lukewarm milk
- 175 g/6 oz plain flour,
  plus extra for dusting
- 80 g/3 oz butter,
  plus extra for greasing
- 20 g/¾ oz icing sugar
- 2 eggs
- salt

Decoration:
- 3 tablespoons peach jam
- 800 g/1¾ lb black cherries,
  stoned
- 2 tablespoons icing sugar
- 1 tablespoon potato flour
- 100 ml/3½ fl oz kirsch

Syrup:
- 300 g/11 oz caster sugar
- 100 ml/3½ fl oz kirsch

Serves 4–6

Cream the yeast in a bowl with the lukewarm milk, mashing it well with a fork. Sift the flour into a bowl, make a well in the centre and pour in the yeast mixture. Mix well, cover with a clean tea towel and leave to rise in a warm place until cracks begin to appear on the surface. Melt the butter in a saucepan and beat in the sugar, a pinch of salt and the eggs. Add the mixture to the dough and knead vigorously. Leave to rise for a further 15 minutes. Grease individual ring moulds with butter and dust them with flour. Divide the dough among the prepared moulds, only half filling them. Leave to stand for about 15 minutes, until the dough has risen to the top of the moulds. Meanwhile, preheat the oven to 220°C/425°F/Gas Mark 7. Put the moulds in the oven and bake for 15–20 minutes, until golden brown. Remove from the oven and turn out on to a wire rack to cool. Meanwhile, make the syrup. Pour 500 ml/18 fl oz water into a saucepan, add the sugar and stir to dissolve, then cook over a low heat for about 6 minutes. Remove from the heat and leave to cool, then stir in the kirsch and pour over the cake rings. Make the decoration. Heat the jam in a saucepan and pour it over the cake rings. Put the cherries and icing sugar into a saucepan and pour in 200 ml/7 fl oz water. Cover and cook for 4 minutes. Meanwhile, mix the potato flour with 2 tablespoons water in a bowl, add to the cherries and cook, stirring constantly, for a few minutes, until the juice has thickened. Put the cake rings on to individual plates and divide the cherries among them, putting some in the centre of the rings and some around the edge. Spoon a little juice over them. Heat the kirsch in a saucepan, ignite it and carefully pour it over the cherries. Serve immediately.

Melon and strawberry brochettes with raspberry sauce

BROCHETASDE MELON Y FRESON CON SALSA DE FRAMBUESAS

- ½ melon, preferably cantaloupe
- 12 strawberries, hulled
- 25 g/1 oz butter
- 50 g/2 oz caster sugar

For the sauce:
- 150 g/5 oz raspberries
- juice of ½ lemon
- 1 tablespoon icing sugar

Serves 2

Soak the wooden skewers in water for 15–20 minutes and pat dry. Meanwhile, remove the seeds from the melon and scoop out the flesh with a melon baller or teaspoon. Halve the strawberries lengthways. Thread the melon balls and strawberry halves alternately on to the skewers. Preheat the grill. Put the raspberries, lemon juice and sugar in a food processor and process to a purée. Pass the purée through a sieve into a bowl and chill in the refrigerator. Melt the butter in a non-stick frying pan over a medium heat. Add the brochettes and cook quickly, turning frequently, until the fruit is lightly browned but remains firm. Sprinkle the sugar on the brochettes, place them on a baking sheet and caramelize them under the grill for a few minutes until they start to brown. Spread a little of the raspberry sauce on a plate and place the brochettes on top. Serve immediately, offering the remaining raspberry sauce separately.

Note: You can use metal skewers if you like. Other fruit, such as slices of banana or pieces of kiwi, can also be included.

985

Crunchy fruit in lemon sauce

CRUJIENTE DE FRUTAS CON SALSA AL LIMON

- juice of 2 green lemons
- 80 g/3 oz brown sugar
- 1 tablespoon chopped fresh mint
- 2 bananas
- 2 mangos
- 2 kiwi fruits
- 15 g/½ oz butter,
  plus extra for greasing
- 8 sheets of filo pastry
- 8 fresh mint leaves

Sauce:
- juice of 5 lemons
- grated rind of 1 lemon
- 2 egg yolks
- 50 g/2 oz icing sugar
- 1 tablespoon potato flour

Serves 4

Mix together the lemon juice, sugar and chopped mint in a shallow dish. Peel and slice the bananas and put them in the dish. Peel, stone and dice the mangos and add to the dish. Peel and dice the kiwis and put them in the dish. Leave the fruit to macerate. Make the sauce. Put the lemon juice and rind in a saucepan and bring to the boil. Beat the egg yolks with the sugar and potato flour in a bowl until light and fluffy. Pour in the boiling lemon juice, stirring constantly. Tip the mixture back into the pan and cook, stirring constantly, for a few minutes, until thickened, but do not allow it to boil. Remove the pan from the heat, leave to cool, then chill in the refrigerator. Preheat the oven to 220°C/425°F/Gas Mark 7. Grease a baking sheet with butter. Melt the butter in a saucepan, then brush it over both sides of the filo pastry sheets. Cut the sheets in half and place two halves on top of each other to form a star shape. Place a mint leaf on each sheet of filo. Drain the fruit, reserving the liquid, and divide it among the pastry sheets. Fold the pastry over and press the edges to seal. Put the parcels on the prepared baking sheet and bake for about 10 minutes, until lightly browned. Meanwhile, stir the reserved liquid into the lemon sauce. Remove the parcels from the oven and serve immediately, offering the sauce separately.

986

Barbecued melon with sesame and honey

MELONES A LA BARBACOA CON SESAMO Y MIEL

- sunflower oil, for brushing
- 2 tablespoons orange blossom
  or other single flower honey
- 4 small melons, such as piel
  de sapo or cantaloupe, halved,
  seeded and cut into wedges
- 2 tablespoons vanilla sugar
- juice of 1 lemon
- 2 tablespoons toasted sesame
  seeds
- 100 g/3½ oz caramelized
  almonds, chopped

Serves 4

Brush the barbecue grill with oil. Pour the honey into a saucepan and place the pan on the side of the barbecue to warm through. Slice the melons and put them on the barbecue. Cook for 3–4 minutes on each side, until lightly marked with the bars of the grill. Transfer to a plate and sprinkle with the vanilla sugar and pour the lemon juice over them. Put the melon slices on individual plates or a serving dish and pour the warm honey over them. Sprinkle with the sesame seeds and almonds and serve.

Note: The melon is good served with raspberry sauce or sorbet. Vanilla sugar is simply vanilla-flavoured sugar. It is available to buy, but to make it yourself, bury a whole vanilla bean in 1 to 2 cups sugar, cover and let sit for several days.

987

Ricotta cheese with peaches in syrup
QUESO FRESCO CON MELOCOTONES EN ALMIBAR

- 400 g/14 oz canned peach halves in syrup
- 100 g/3½ oz caster sugar
- 50 ml/2 fl oz peach liqueur or rum
- 16 sponge fingers
- 250 g/9 oz ricotta cheese
- 4 tablespoons redcurrant jam

Serves 4

Drain the peaches, reserving the syrup. Put the syrup into a saucepan and stir in 4 tablespoons of the sugar. Heat gently until the syrup thickens, then stir in the peach liqueur or rum. Remove the pan from the heat. Lightly coat the sponge fingers in the syrup and divide them among individual dessert plates. Beat the cheese with the remaining sugar. Spread the redcurrant jam on the sponge fingers and cover with the sweetened cheese. Decorate with the peach halves.

Note: The redcurrant jam can be replaced in the recipe with raspberry or blackberry jam.

988

Fresh fruit soup with cava
SOPA DE FRUTA FRESCA AL CAVA

- 1 small pineapple
- 20 lychees
- 300 g/11 oz raspberries
- 80 g/3 oz brown sugar
- 600 ml/1 pint cava or other sparkling white wine, chilled
- 5 fresh mint leaves

To serve:
- juice of ½ lemon
- caster sugar
- marzipan petits fours

Serves 4

Lay the pineapple in a shallow dish to catch the juice and cut off the crown. Cut the pineapple into 1-cm/½-inch slices. Cut off and discard the skin, then stand each slice on its side and cut out the 'eyes' with the point of a sharp knife. Lay each slice flat again and stamp out or cut out the core. Chop the slices and put them into a bowl. Reserve the juice. Peel, halve and stone the lychees and add them to the pineapple with the raspberries. Stir in the sugar and chill in the refrigerator for 35 minutes. Prepare the glasses for serving the fruit soup. Brush the rims of four large goblets or water glasses with the lemon juice, then dip them into a saucer of caster sugar to frost the rims. Set aside. Just before serving, pour the reserved juice and the wine over the fruit. Decorate with the mint leaves and serve in the prepared glasses. Offer the petits fours separately.

Note: The fruit may be varied. Oranges could be substituted for pineapple. Cut off the orange rinds, removing all traces of pith, then cut the segments from between the membranes and chop. Do this over a dish to collect the juice. Squeeze any juice out of the membranes. Pour the reserved juice over the fruit with the wine, just before serving.

989

Chestnut purée with layered sponge fingers

TARTA DE PURÉ DE CASTAÑAS Y SOLETILLAS

- sunflower oil, for brushing
- 2–3 tablespoons rum
- 3 tablespoons caster sugar
- 35 sponge fingers
- 2 egg whites
- 500 g/1 lb 2 oz canned sweet chestnut purée
- salt

- Custard:
- 500 ml/18 fl oz milk
- 3 tablespoons caster sugar
- 2 eggs or 2 egg yolks
- 1 teaspoon cornflour

Serves 6

Brush an 18-cm/7-inch cake tin with oil. Put half the rum, half the sugar and 150 ml/¼ pint water into a shallow dish and mix well. Dip about half the sponge fingers into the mixture. Place a layer of dipped sponge fingers in the base of the prepared tin. Line the sides of the tin with dipped sponge fingers, first cutting off one of the rounded ends, placing them upright side by side. Whisk the egg whites with a pinch of salt in a clean, dry bowl until stiff peaks form and fold into the chestnut purée. Pour half the mixture into the tin. Dip some more sponge fingers into the rum mixture and place them on top of the purée. Mix together the remaining rum and sugar, stir in 150 ml/¼ pint water and dip the remaining sponge fingers into this. Add the remaining chestnut mixture to the tin and finish with a final layer of lightly dampened sponge fingers. Brush foil or greaseproof paper with oil and cover the tin. Put a lid or plate that is slightly smaller than the diameter of the cake tin on top so that it rests inside the tin. Put a light weight on top of the lid or plate and chill in the refrigerator for 6–8 hours. Make the custard as described in recipe 1008. To serve, remove the lid or plate and carefully take off and discard the foil or greasproof paper. Run a round-bladed knife around the edge of the tin and turn out on to a serving dish. Serve with the custard, or cream if preferred.

990

Chestnut dessert

POSTRE DE CASTAÑAS

- 6 gelatine leaves
- 50 g/2 oz caster sugar
- 120 g/4 oz canned sweet chestnut purée
- 200 ml/7 fl oz double cream
- 12 sponge fingers
- 3 marrons glacés and 50 g/2 oz chopped marrons glacés, to decorate

Serves 6

Put the gelatine leaves in a bowl of water and leave to soak for 5 minutes. Meanwhile, pour 50 ml/2 fl oz water into a saucepan, add the sugar and stir until it has dissolved. Bring to the boil and boil for 1 minute, then remove the pan from the heat. Squeeze out the gelatine, add to the pan and stir well to dissolve. Stir this mixture into the chestnut purée. Stiffly whisk the cream and fold it into the chestnut mixture, then pour into a fluted mould. Chill in the refrigerator for 2 hours, until set. Turn out the chestnut mould on to a serving dish and place the sponge fingers around it. Decorate with the whole marrons placed on top and the chopped marrons around the edge.

Notes: To make it easier to turn out the dessert, first dip the mould into hot water for 30 seconds . Marron glacés are chestnuts that have been canned in syrup.

Sponge finger, cream and orange dessert
POSTRE DE SOLETILLAS, CREMA Y NARANJAS

- **5 navel oranges**
- **50 ml/2 fl oz Cointreau, Curaçao or other orange-flavoured liqueur**
- **300 g/11 oz sponge fingers**
- **500 ml/18 fl oz milk**
- **150 g/5 oz caster sugar**
- **4 egg yolks**
- **1 tablespoon plain flour**
- **1 heaped tablespoon cornflour**
- **sunflower oil, for brushing**
- **6 glacé cherries, halved**

Serves 6–8

Prepare this dish the night before you intend to serve it. Peel the oranges, reserving the rind of one of them, then thinly slice on a plate in order to catch the juice. Rinse out a cake tin with water and drain, then arrange the orange slices on the base and around the sides. Pour the juice into a shallow dish and add half the liqueur and 2 tablespoons water. Make a layer of sponge fingers on top of the oranges in the base of the tin, dipping them first in the juice mixture. Line the sides of the tin with sponge fingers, again dipping them first in the juice mixture. Pour the milk into a saucepan and add the reserved orange rind and half the sugar. Heat gently, stirring until the sugar has dissolved, and bring to the boil. Beat the egg yolks with the remaining sugar, the flour, cornflour and the remaining liqueur in a bowl, then stir in a few spoonfuls of the hot milk. Pour the egg yolk mixture into the pan and simmer, stirring constantly, for about 4 minutes, until thickened. Remove the pan from the heat, remove and discard the orange rind and stir until cold. Pour half the custard into the cake tin, make a layer of sponge fingers (not soaked), add the remaining custard and make a final layer of sponge fingers (not soaked). Brush foil or greaseproof paper with oil and cover the tin. Put a lid or plate that is slightly smaller than the diameter of the tin on top so that it rests inside the tin and add a light weight. Chill in the refrigerator for at least 6 hours before serving. To serve, remove the lid or plate and carefully take off the foil or greaseproof paper. Run a round-bladed knife around the edge of the tin and turn out on to a serving dish. Decorate with the cherries.

Note: You can serve this dessert with a thin custard (see recipe 1008) made with orange extract.

Sponge fingers with custard filling

SOLETILLAS RELLENAS DE CREMA

- **24 sponge fingers**
- **sunflower oil, for deep frying**
- **2 eggs**

Custard filling:
- **500 ml/18 fl oz milk**
- **3 tablespoons caster sugar,**
  plus extra for dredging
- **thinly pared rind of 1 lemon**
- **3 egg yolks**
- **2 heaped tablespoons cornflour**
- **1 tablespoon plain flour**

Serves 6

First make the custard filling. Reserve 2 tablespoons of the milk and pour the remainder into a saucepan. Stir in 2 tablespoons of the sugar, add the lemon rind and bring to the boil. Beat the egg yolks with the remaining sugar, the cornflour and flour in a bowl and stir in the reserved milk. Gradually stir in the boiling milk, a little at a time, then pour the custard back into the pan and simmer gently, stirring constantly, for 3–4 minutes, until thickened. Remove the pan from the heat and leave to cool slightly. Cover the flat sides of half the sponge fingers with a generous layer of the warm custard filling. Put the remaining sponge fingers on top, but do not press down or the custard will squirt out. Heat the oil in a deep-fryer or saucepan to 180–190°C/350–375°F or until a cube of day-old bread browns in 30 seconds. Beat the eggs in a shallow dish and coat the filled sponge fingers in them. Add to the hot oil and cook until golden brown. Remove with a fish slice, drain and dredge with sugar while they are hot. Place them in a serving dish and leave to cool before serving.

993

Layered coffee and sponge-finger dessert

TARTA DE MOKA Y SOLETILLAS

- **sunflower oil, for brushing**
- **3 teaspoons instant coffee granules**
- **185 g/6½ oz caster sugar**
- **2 tablespoons rum**
- **35 sponge fingers**
- **2 egg yolks**
- **150 g/5 oz butter, softened**
- **100 g/3½ oz toasted almonds, coarsely chopped**

Serves 6–8

Prepare this dish the night before you intend to serve it. Brush an 18-cm/7-inch cake tin with oil. Mix together 1½ teaspoons of the coffee granules, 1½ tablespoons of the sugar, 1 tablespoon of the rum and 3 tablespoons water in a shallow dish. Quickly dip about half the sponge fingers into the liquid, so that they absorb some flavour but are not sodden. Place a layer of dipped sponge fingers in the base of the prepared tin. Line the sides of the tin with dipped sponge fingers, first cutting off one of the rounded ends, and placing them upright side by side, cut ends down. Mix together the remaining instant coffee, 1½ tablespoons of the remaining sugar, the remaining rum and 3 tablespoons water. Beat the egg yolks with all the remaining sugar in a bowl until pale and fluffy. Gradually beat in the butter, small pieces at a time. Reserve one-third of this creamed mixture and store in the refrigerator until required. Pour half the remaining creamed mixture into the cake tin, cover with a layer of the remaining sponge fingers, first dipping them in the coffee mixture, pour in the other half of the remaining creamed mixture and finish with another layer of lightly dampened sponge fingers. Brush foil or greaseproof paper with oil and cover the tin. Put a lid or plate that is slightly smaller than the diameter of the tin on top so that it rests inside the tin and add a light weight. Chill in the refrigerator for at least 6 hours. Remove the reserved creamed mixture from the refrigerator about 2 hours before serving to soften. About 1–1½ hours before serving, remove the lid or plate and carefully take off the foil or greaseproof paper. Run a round-bladed knife around the edge of the tin and turn out on to a serving dish. Cover the dessert with the reserved creamed mixture, spreading it evenly with a palette knife. Sprinkle the almonds on top and chill in the refrigerator for 1 hour.

994

Layered strawberry dessert
BUDÍN DE SOLETILLAS Y FRESAS

- sunflower oil, for brushing
- 5 tablespoons kirsch
- 2 tablespoons caster sugar
- 36 sponge fingers
- 500 ml/18 fl oz double cream
- 750 g/1 lb 10 oz ripe
  strawberries, hulled

Sauce:
- 4 tablespoons caster sugar
- 500 g/1 lb 2 oz strawberries,
  hulled

Serves 6–8

Prepare this dish the night before it is needed. Brush an 18-cm/7-inch cake tin with oil. Mix together the kirsch, sugar and 175 ml/6 fl oz water in a shallow dish. Dip about half the sponge fingers in the liquid. Line the sides of the prepared tin with dipped sponge fingers, first cutting off one of the rounded ends, placing them upright side by side, cut ends down. Make a layer of dipped sponge fingers over the base. Stiffly whisk the cream and spread half of it over the layer of sponge fingers in the base of the tin. Set six strawberries aside for decoration and halve the remainder. Put half of them on top of the cream, then cover with a layer of the remaining sponge fingers, first dipping them in the kirsch mixture. Add the remaining cream, the remaining strawberries and a final layer of lightly dampened sponge fingers. Brush foil or greaseproof paper with oil and cover the tin. Put a lid or plate that is slightly smaller than the diameter of the tin on top, so that it rests inside the tin and add a light weight. Chill in the refrigerator for at least 8 hours. To make the sauce, pour 175 ml/6 fl oz water into a saucepan, stir in the sugar and bring to the boil. Cook for about 10 minutes, then remove the pan from the heat and leave to cool. Put the strawberries in a food processor and process to a purée, then pass through a sieve into a bowl. Stir in the cooled syrup. Store in the refrigerator until required. To serve, remove the lid or plate and carefully take off the foil or greaseproof paper. Run a round-bladed knife around the edge of the tin and turn out on to a serving dish. Pour the sauce over the top and decorate with the reserved strawberries. Serve this dessert chilled.

Note: The filling can be made by crushing the strawberries with a fork and mixing them with the cream. Alpine strawberries can be used, if available, to make a more delicate pudding.

995

Sponge fingers with jam and chocolate
SOLETILLAS CON MERMELADA Y CHOCOLATE

- **6 tablespoons apricot or raspberry jam**
- **36 sponge fingers**
- **4 tablespoons cold milk**
- **200 g/7 oz chocolate, coarsley grated**

Makes 18

Spread a little jam on the flat side of a sponge finger and place another one on top, pressing them together. Dip them in the milk and then roll them in the chocolate. Repeat with the remaining biscuits. Place each prepared sponge finger 'sandwich' into a paper case.

Tiramisu

TIRAMISÚ

- **3 tablespoons rum**
- **250 ml/8 fl oz very strong coffee**
- **5 tablespoons caster sugar**
- **20 sponge fingers**
- **4 egg yolks**
- **300 g/11 oz mascarpone cheese**
- **3 tablespoons cocoa powder**
- **sunflower oil, for brushing**
- **750 ml/1¼ pints thick custard, to serve (see recipe 1008)**

Serves 4–5

Line a 20-cm/8-inch loose-based cake tin with lightly greased foil. Mix together the rum, coffee and 3 tablespoons of the sugar in a shallow dish. Dip the sponge fingers into the mixture and make a layer of them in the base of the tin. Beat the eggs yolks with the mascarpone in a bowl. Cover the layer of sponge fingers with a layer of the mascarpone mixture, sprinkle with a little of the remaining sugar and make another layer of dipped sponge fingers on top. Continue making layers in this way until the tin is full, finishing with a layer of sponge fingers. Brush foil or greaseproof paper with oil and cover the tin. Put a lid or plate that is slightly smaller than the diameter of the tin on top, so that it rests inside the tin and add a light weight. Chill in the refrigerator for 24 hours. To serve, remove the lid or plate and carefully take off the foil or greaseproof paper. Turn the tiramisu out on to a serving dish, remove the foil and sprinkle cocoa over it. Serve the custard separately in a sauce boat.

Note: The name of this popular dessert of Italian origin means 'pick me up'.

997 Churros

CHURROS

- 175 g/6 oz plain flour
- sunflower oil, for deep frying
- icing sugar, for dredging
- salt

Makes about 25

Pour 350 ml/12 fl oz water into a saucepan, add a pinch of salt and bring to the boil. Tip in the flour all at once and cook, stirring constantly, until the mixture comes away from the sides of the pan. Remove the pan from the heat and leave to cool. Heat the oil in a deep-fryer or saucepan to 180–190°C/350–375°F or until a cube of day-old bread browns in 30 seconds. Put the cooled mixture into a churrera and make the churros, cutting them to the required length with a sharp knife as the dough is pushed out, and adding them immediately to the hot oil. Alternatively, spoon the cooled mixture into a piping bag fitted with a star nozzle and pipe directly into the hot oil, cutting the churros to the required length with a sharp knife and working in batches if necessary. When the strips of fried dough are golden brown all over, remove with a slotted spoon, drain well, dredge with icing sugar and serve immediately.

Note: These sweet, fried pastry strips are extremely popular in Spain, Latin America and the US.

998 Honey coated pastries

PESTIÑOS

- 300 g/11 oz plain flour,
  plus extra for dusting
- 5 tablespoons white wine
- 25 g/1 oz butter
- 25 g/1 oz lard
- sunflower oil , for deep frying
- 275 ml/9 fl oz clear honey
- salt

Makes about 50

Sift the flour with a pinch of salt on to a sheet of greaseproof paper. Pour the wine and 175 ml/6 fl oz water into a saucepan, add the butter and lard and heat until the fat has melted. Tip in the flour all at once, remove the pan from the heat and stir well with a wooden spoon. Turn out the dough on to a work surface and knead well. Shape the dough into a ball, wrap in foil and leave to rest for 1–2 hours. Roll out the dough to a very thin sheet on a lightly floured surface. With a sharp knife, cut it into rectangles, about 15 x 8 cm/6 x 3 ¼ inches. Starting at one corner, roll the rectangles up. Curl each one round like a miniature croissant, dampen one corner and stick it to the other so that the roll does not open when frying. Heat the oil in a deep-fryer or saucepan to 180–190°C/350–375°F or until a cube of day-old bread browns in 30 seconds. Add the pastries, in batches, and cook until golden brown. Remove with a slotted spoon, drain well and leave to cool. Put the pastries on wire racks set over shallow dishes or baking sheets. Spoon the honey over them (if it's not sufficiently runny, stir in a little warm water). Leave to stand until the honey is no longer running off the pastries, then transfer them to a serving dish.

999

Fritters
BUÑUELOS

- 300 g/11 oz plain flour
- 3 tablespoons white wine
- sunflower oil, for deep frying
- 350 ml/12 fl oz milk
- 5 eggs
- ½ teaspoon baking powder
- fresh fruit such as bananas or apples chunks, pineapple slices, figs or cooled rice or semolina pudding
- salt

Serves 4

Sift the flour with a pinch of salt into a bowl, make a well in the centre and pour in the wine and 3 tablespoons of the oil. Mix well with a wooden spoon, then gradually stir in the milk and add the eggs, one at a time. Cover the bowl and leave to stand for at least 30 minutes. Stir in the baking powder when you are ready to start cooking. Use the batter to coat pieces of fresh fruit, such as banana, apple, pineapple and figs, or cooled and set rice or semolina pudding, before deep-frying in oil heated up to 180–190°C/350–375°F or until a cube of day-old bread browns in 30 seconds. Add the fritters, in batches, and cook until golden brown. Remove with a slotted spoon, drain well, and let cool. Repeat with the remaining fritters.

1000

Apricot fritters with raspberry and cinnamon sauce
BUÑUELOS DE ALBARICOQUE CON SALSA DE FRAMBUESA Y CANELA

- 12 apricots, halved and stoned
- 150 g/5 oz icing sugar
- pinch of ground cinnamon
- 1 tablespoon raspberry liqueur
- sunflower oil, for deep frying

  Batter:
- 300 g/11 oz plain flour
- 3 tablespoons beer
- 3 tablespoons sunflower oil
- 1 tablespoon caster sugar
- 300 ml/½ pint milk
- ½ teaspoon baking powder
- salt

  Sauce:
- 100 g/3½ oz raspberries
- juice of ½ lemon
- 20 g/¾ oz caster sugar
- pinch of ground cinnamon

Serves 4

First make the batter. Sift the flour with a pinch of salt into a bowl, make a well in the centre and pour in the beer and oil. Stir in the sugar and mix well with a wooden spoon. Gradually stir in the milk, then cover and leave to rest for at least 30 minutes. Reserve half the apricots, put the rest into a food processor with a little water and process to a purée. Scrape into a saucepan, stir in 50 g/2 oz of the sugar and cook over a low heat, stirring occasionally, for 10 minutes. Remove the pan from the heat and leave to cool. Stir in the cinnamon and the raspberry liqueur. Make the sauce. Put the raspberries, lemon juice and sugar into a food processor. Add the apricot purée and process until smooth. Strain into a bowl and stir in the cinnamon. Heat the oil in a deep-fryer or saucepan to 180–190°C/350–375°F or until a cube of day-old bread browns in 30 seconds. Stir the baking powder into the batter. Dip the remaining apricots into the batter to coat, then add to the hot oil and cook for about 2 minutes, until puffed up and golden brown. Remove with a slotted spoon and drain on kitchen paper, then dredge with the remaining icing sugar. Serve the fritters with the raspberry and apricot sauce offered separately in a sauce boat.

1001

- 250 g/9 oz plain flour
- 1 heaped teaspoon caster sugar
- 2 eggs
- 1 tablespoon sunflower oil,
  plus extra for brushing
- 1 tablespoon rum or brandy
- 120 ml/4 fl oz milk
- salt

Makes 15–20

Pancakes
CRÊPES

Sift the flour with a pinch of salt into a bowl, stir in the sugar and make a well in the centre. Break the eggs into the well and pour in the oil and rum or brandy. Stir well until the mixture is smooth. Mix the milk with 120 ml/4 fl oz water and gradually stir it into the batter, a little at a time. The batter should have the consistency of thick custard and it may be necessary to add a little more liquid, depending on the type of flour. Cover the bowl with a clean tea towel and leave to rest for at least 1 hour, longer if possible. When you are ready to cook, stir the batter. If it has become too thick, stir in a little more mixed milk and water. Brush oil over the bases of two small heavy-based frying pans, about 14 cm/5 ½ inches in diameter. Heat well. Pour a ladleful of the batter into a pan and tilt the pan so that it covers the whole base evenly. Cook, gently shaking the pan to prevent the pancake from sticking or burning, until the underside is golden brown. Toss the pancake to turn, or flip it over with a palette knife, and cook until the second side is lightly browned. Meanwhile, pour a ladleful of batter into the second pan and cook in the same way. It is usual to make pancakes in two pans simultaneously, as it is quicker. Put a saucepan full of very hot water over a low heat, put a flat plate on top like a lid and put a large sheet of foil on the plate. As the pancakes are cooked, transfer them to the foil, then fold it over them to keep them warm while you cook the remaining pancakes.

1002

- 25 g/1 oz butter
- 2 tablespoons Curaçao or
  other orange-flavoured liqueur
- 2 tablespoons caster sugar
- 150 ml/¼ pint orange juice
- ½ quantity Pancakes
  (see recipe 1001)
- 2 tablespoons rum or brandy

For 6–7 pancakes

Sauce for crêpes suzette
SALSA DE CRÊPES SUZETTE

Melt the butter in a frying pan. Add the Curaçao, sugar and orange juice and cook for a few minutes. Add six or seven pancakes, folded into four, to heat through in the sauce. Briefly warm the rum or brandy, ignite it and carefully pour it over the pancakes. Gently shake the pan until the flames die down, then serve the pancakes immediately with the hot sauce on top.

1003

Pancakes with custard filling
CRÊPES RELLENAS DE CREMA

- 1 quantity Pancakes
  (see recipe 1001)
- 5 tablespoons caster sugar
- 2 tablespoons rum or brandy

Custard:
- 500 ml/18 fl oz milk
- 5 tablespoons caster sugar
- pinch of vanilla powder or
  a few drops of vanilla extract,
  or grated rind of 1 lemon
- 3 egg yolks
- 1½ teaspoons plain flour
- 1½ tablespoons cornflour
  Serves 2–4

Make the custard filling as described in recipe 1008, in advance and leave to cool. Fill each pancake with custard and roll up. Place the pancakes next to each other and sprinkle with the sugar or flambé with the rum as described in recipe 1005.

1004

Pancakes filled with cream
CRÊPES RELLENAS DE NATA

- 1 quantity Pancakes
  (see recipe 1001)
- 300 ml/½ pint whipped cream
- 1 quantity Caramel Sauce
  (see recipe 117)
  Makes 15–20

Make the pancakes and, while they are fresh, fill them with whipped cream and pour the caramel sauce over the top.

Note: Pancakes are delicious filled simply with apricot or other jam.

1005

Flambéed pancakes
CRÊPES FLAMEADAS

- 1 quantity Pancakes
  (see recipe 1001)
- 5 tablespoons caster sugar
- 6 tablespoons rum or brandy
  Makes 15–20

Fold the pancakes in four and place them in a dish, then sprinkle the sugar over them. Heat the rum or brandy in a small saucepan, ignite it and carefully pour it straight over the pancakes. Scoop up the spirit from the dish with a tablespoon and pour it back over the pancakes so that the flames do not die down too rapidly.

1006

- **200 g/7 oz plain flour**
- **¾ teaspoon salt**
- **1½ teaspoons baking powder**
- **1 tablespoon caster sugar**
- **2 eggs**
- **1 tablespoon sunflower oil**
- **250 ml/8 fl oz milk**

Makes about 14

Little American pancakes

TORTITAS AMERICANAS

Sift the flour with the salt and baking powder on to a plate and add the sugar. Lightly beat the eggs in a bowl and stir in the oil and milk. Add the dry ingredients and beat briefly (it does not matter if there are lumps as these will dissolve on their own when the pancakes are cooked). Pour the batter into a jug. Heat a flat griddle or stove-top grill pan. Pour about 1 tablespoon of the batter on to it and cook for 2–3 minutes, until bubbles start to rise. Turn the pancake with a spatula and cook until golden brown on the underside. Try to serve these immediately. If they have to wait a while, keep them warm in little piles of no more than four.

Note: Serve these pancakes with Cream and Caramel Sauce (see recipe 117), chocolate sauce or jam. They can also be eaten spread with butter and jam.

1007

- **1 quantity Pastry Dough (see recipe 968)**
- **1 quantity Confectioner's Cream (see recipe 1010)**
- **sunflower oil, for deep frying**
- **icing sugar, for dredging**

Makes about 20

Bartolillos

BARTOLILLOS

Make the pastry dough as described in recipe 968 and leave to rest. Make the confectioners' cream as described in recipe 1010 and leave to cool. Roll out the dough to a thin sheet on a lightly floured surface. Stamp out 10-cm/4-inch rounds with a biscuit cutter. Put 1 tablespoon of the confectioner's cream on each round and fold the bartolillo, pressing down firmly around the edges to seal. (You could use the metal wheel designed for cutting empanadillas, if you have one.) Heat the oil in a deep-fryer or saucepan to 180–190°C/350–375°F or until a cube of day-old bread browns in 30 seconds. Add the bartolillos, in batches, and cook until golden brown. Remove with a slotted spoon and drain well, then transfer to a serving dish and dredge with icing sugar. Serve warm or cold.

Note: Bartolillos are small cream-filled pastries popular in Madrid and throughout Spain.

Custards and creams

Home-made custards and creams are delicious, but there is a trick to making them. From custard to confectioner's cream, many of them are used in the preparation of numerous desserts and also constitute desserts in themselves. They have a common denominator – their extreme fragility. Therefore you should use top quality ingredients for them and eat them within hours of their being made.

Custards:
Making a traditional egg custard requires a little patience and care. It acquires its characteristic consistency because heat causes the egg yolks to coagulate. Therefore, the more egg yolks added, the thicker the custard will be.

- The usual proportion is 8 egg yolks for each 1 litre/1 ¾ pints milk and 250 g/9 oz sugar, but add more yolks for a thicker custard
- Rinse out the saucepan with cold water before pouring in the milk. This prevents the milk sticking to the base and sides of the pan
- It is critical to be thorough when beating the egg yolks with sugar
- Put the sugar in a bowl and make a well in the centre. Add the eggs and beat quickly with a whisk until the mixture is smooth
- Remember to wash your hands after breaking the eggs to avoid bacterial contamination
- Be careful when heating the custard. It should thicken but not cook too much and should never boil, as it would spoil and lumps would form. However, if it doesn't cook enough, it will be too liquid. To find the ideal point, remove a little of the custard with a spatula and draw a line in it with your finger. The mark should be clear – if the sides rejoin, the custard is not yet cooked enough
- If the custard spoils, it may be possible to rescue it. Put a little cold water in a bowl and gradually pour in the custard, a little at a time, stirring vigorously.

Confectioner's cream:
- The base is the same as for custard but it is usual to add flour or cornflour to thicken it
- Add the cornflour very carefully, beating with a whisk, but do not mix too much or the cream will harden
- To prevent a skin forming as the confectioner's cream cools, sprinkle icing sugar over the top or cover it with cling film.

1008

- **1.5 litres/2½ pints milk**
- **6 heaped tablespoons caster sugar**
- **thinly pared rind of 1 lemon or 2 vanilla pods**
- **6 egg yolks**
- **1 tablespoon cornflour**
- **pinch of ground cinnamon (optional)**

Serves 6–8

Custard

NATILLAS

Pour the milk into a saucepan, add 4 tablespoons of the sugar and the lemon rind and bring just to the boil. Meanwhile, beat the egg yolks with the remaining sugar and the cornflour in a bowl. Gradually stir in the hot milk, a little at a time, then pour the custard back into the pan, lower the heat and cook, stirring constantly, for about 5 minutes, until thickened and smooth. Do not allow the mixture to boil. Strain the custard and pour it into a deep dish or individual bowls. Chill in the refrigerator until required. Sprinkle a little ground cinnamon on the top before serving if you like.

1009

- **1 litre/1¾ pints milk**
- **130 g/4½ oz caster sugar**
- **thinly pared rind of 1 lemon**
- **8 egg yolks**
- **1½–2 tablespoons potato flour or cornflour**

Serves 6

Catalan cream

CREMA CATALANA

Pour the milk into a saucepan, add 4 tablespoons of the sugar and the lemon rind and bring just to the boil. Meanwhile, beat the egg yolks with 2 tablespoons of the remaining sugar and the potato flour. Gradually stir in the hot milk then pour the custard into the pan. Lower the heat and cook, stirring con-stantly, for about 5 minutes, until thickened. Strain into a serving dish or individual dishes and leave to cool, then chill in the refrigerator for at least 1 hour. Just before serving, sprinkle the remaining sugar on top and use a kitchen blow torch to caramelize it.

Note: Crema catalana is the best-known Spanish dessert and is said by some to be the predecessor of France's crème brûlée.

Confectioner's cream for fillings

CREMA PASTELERA (PARA RELLENOS)

- 500 ml/18 fl oz milk
- 5 tablespoons caster sugar
- thinly pared rind of 1 lemon or
  pinch of vanilla powder or
  a few drops of vanilla extract
- 3 egg yolks
- 2 tablespoons cornflour
- 1 tablespoon plain flour
- 1 egg white (optional)
- salt (optional)

Serves 4–6

Reserve 3 tablespoons of the milk. Pour the remaining milk into a saucepan, add 3 tablespoons of the sugar and the lemon rind or vanilla and bring just to the boil. Meanwhile beat the egg yolks with the remaining sugar, the cornflour, flour and reserved milk in a bowl. Gradually stir in the hot milk, a little at a time, then pour the custard back into the pan and simmer over a low heat, stirring constantly, for about 5 minutes, until thickened and smooth. Remove the pan from the heat, pour the custard into a dish or a bowl and leave to cool. Remove and discard the lemon rind, if using. If you like, whisk the egg white with a pinch of salt in a clean, dry bowl until stiff peaks form and fold it into the custard.

1011

- **4 egg yolks**
- **9 tablespoons caster sugar**
- **1 teaspoon plain flour**
- **2 heaped tablespoons cornflour**
- **1 litre/1¾ pints milk**
- **1 vanilla pod, or a pinch of vanilla powder or a few drops of vanilla extract**

Serves 6–8

Confectioner's cream

CREMA PASTELERA

Mix together the egg yolks, 3 tablespoons of the sugar, the flour and cornflour in a bowl. Pour the milk into a saucepan, add 3 tablespoons of the remaining sugar and the vanilla and heat, stirring until the sugar has dissolved, then bring to the boil. Stir about 4 tablespoons of the milk into the egg yolk mixture, then pour the mixture into the pan. Cook, stirring constantly, for about 3 minutes, until thickened. Remove the pan from the heat and remove the vanilla pod, if used. Leave to cool, stirring occasionally. When the rum baba is cold and has been turned out on to a serving dish, pour the cooled confectioner's cream into the centre and sprinkle with the remaining sugar. Caramelize the sugar with a kitchen blow torch. Serve immediately.

1012

Custard:
- **750 ml/1¼ pints milk**
- **6 tablespoons sugar**
- **pinch of vanilla powder or a few drops of vanilla extract**
- **4 egg yolks**
- **1 tablespoon cornflour**

Rock:
- **8 egg whites**
- **100 g/3½ oz caster sugar**

Caramel:
- **2 tablespoons caster sugar**

Serves 6

Custard with a floating island

NATILLAS CON ROCA FLOTANTE

First make the caramel. Put the sugar in a saucepan, add 1 tablespoon water and stir to dissolve, then cook over a low heat until golden. Pour the caramel into a cake tin and tip it back and forth until the base is completely coated. Leave to cool. Make the custard. Pour the milk into a saucepan, add half the sugar and the vanilla and bring just to the boil. Meanwhile, beat the egg yolks with the remaining sugar and the cornflour in a bowl. Gradually stir in the hot milk, a little at a time, then pour the custard back into the pan and cook over a medium heat, stirring constantly, for a few minutes, until thickened, but do not allow it to boil. Strain into a deep serving dish, leave to cool and then chill in the refrigerator. Preheat the oven to 150°C/300°F/ Gas Mark 2. To make the island, whisk the egg whites in a clean, dry bowl until stiff peaks form, then whisk in half the sugar. Put the remaining sugar into a saucepan, add 2 tablespoons water and stir to dissolve, then cook over a low heat until a dark golden colour, but do not allow the caramel to burn or it will taste bitter. Gradually pour the caramel on to the egg whites, a little at a time, stirring quickly so that it mixes well and no lumps of caramel form. Pour the mixture into the caramel-lined tin. Put it into a roasting tin, pour in hot water to come about halfway up the sides and bake for about 25 minutes. Remove from the oven and leave to cool. To serve, tip the island out on top of the custard.

Chocolate custard

CREMA DE CHOCOLATE

- **225 g/8 oz dark chocolate**
- **3–4 tablespoons hot water**
- **1 litre/1¾ pints milk**
- **6 tablespoons caster sugar**
- **3 egg yolks**
- **1½ tablespoons cornflour**

Serves 6

Put the chocolate and hot water into a saucepan and melt over a low heat, stirring occasionally. Remove the pan from the heat. Pour the milk into another saucepan, add 4 tablespoons of the sugar and stir to dissolve, then bring just to the boil. Meanwhile, beat the egg yolks with the remaining sugar and the cornflour in a bowl. Gradually stir in the hot milk, a little at a time, then pour the custard back into the pan and cook, stirring constantly, for a few minutes, until thickened. Stir in the melted chocolate mixture and cook, stirring constantly, for a further 3 minutes, but do not allow the mixture to boil. Remove the pan from the heat and leave the custard to cool, then strain into a bowl and chill in the refrigerator until required.

Note: To decorate the custard, whisk 2 egg whites with a pinch of salt in a clean, dry bowl until stiff peaks form, then fold in 2 tablespoons caster sugar. Put spoonfuls of the mixture on top of the custard and sprinkle with 10 chopped toasted almonds.

1014

Sugared bun pudding
BUDÍN CON SUIZOS

- **50 g/2 oz currants**
- **3 tablespoons sherry**
- **5 tablespoons caster sugar**
- **475 ml/16 fl oz milk**
- **3–4 day-old sugared buns,**
  cut into 1-cm/½-inch slices
- **3 eggs**
- **1 quantity Jam Sauce**
  (using redcurrant or apricot jam,
  see recipe 119)

Caramel:
- **3 tablespoons caster sugar**

Serves 6

Put the currants into a saucepan, add 5 tablespoons hot water and the sherry and leave to soak. Make the caramel. Put the sugar into a saucepan, add 2 tablespoons water and stir to dissolve, then cook over a low heat until golden. Pour the caramel into a cake tin and tip it back and forth until the tin is completely coated. Leave to cool. Gently heat the pan of currants and simmer for a few minutes, then remove the pan from the heat. Strain the currants, reserving the liquid if you like (see note). Preheat the oven to 150°C/300°F/Gas Mark 2. Stir 2 tablespoons of the sugar into half the milk in a shallow dish and add the slices of bun. Leave to soak for a few minutes, then turn over and leave to soak for a few minutes more. Remove the slices from the milk, squeeze them out and layer them in the tin alternating with the currants. Beat the eggs in a bowl with the remaining sugar, then beat in the remaining milk. Pour the mixture into the cake tin, shaking the tin gently so that the liquid penetrates. Put the tin into a roasting tin, pour in hot water to come about halfway up the sides and bake for about 45 minutes. Check by inserting a wooden cocktail stick into the centre of the pudding. If it comes out clean, the pudding is cooked. Remove the tin from the roasting tin and leave to cool. Run a round-bladed knife around the edge of the cake tin and turn the pudding out on to a long serving dish. Serve the sauce separately.

Note: If you like, cook the reserved soaking liquid for a further 3 minutes and pour it over the pudding when you remove it from the oven. This makes the pudding softer and some people prefer it. The pudding can also be served flamed with rum, instead of with jam sauce.

1015

Crème caramel with pears
FLAN CON PERAS

- **4 pears**
- **5 tablespoons caster sugar**
- **4 eggs**
- **250 ml/8 fl oz milk**

Caramel:
- **3 tablespoons caster sugar**

Serves 6

Make the caramel. Put the sugar into a saucepan, add 2 tablespoons water and stir to dissolve, then cook over a low heat until golden. Pour the caramel into a cake tin, 25 cm/10 inches in diameter and 5 cm/2 inches deep. Tip it back and forth until the base is completely coated. Leave to cool. Peel, core and dice the pears, put them into a saucepan, pour in 250 ml/8 fl oz water and add 2 tablespoons of the sugar. Cover the pan and cook over a medium heat until the pears are soft but not falling apart. Drain the pears and spoon them into the cake tin in an even layer. Preheat the oven to 150°C/300°F/Gas Mark 2. Beat the eggs with the remaining sugar in a bowl, then beat in the milk. Pour the mixture over the pears. Put the tin into a roasting tin, pour in hot water to come about halfway up the sides and bake for about 40 minutes, until set. Remove from the oven but leave the tin standing in the water. When the water has cooled to warm, remove the cake tin and turn the crème caramel out on to a round serving dish. Serve slightly warm.

Note: The dish can also be made with apples.

1016

Classic crème caramel
FLAN CLÁSICO

- **750 ml/1¼ pints milk**
- **pinch of vanilla powder or**
  a few drops of vanilla extract
  or 1 vanilla pod
- **2 eggs**
- **6 yolks**
- **200 g/7 oz caster sugar**

Caramel:
- **3 tablespoons caster sugar**

Serves 6

Make the caramel. Put the sugar into a saucepan, add 2 tablespoons water and stir to dissolve, then cook over a low heat until golden. Pour the caramel into a cake tin and tip it back and forth until the tin is completely coated. Leave to cool. Preheat the oven to 150°C/300°F/Gas Mark 2. Pour the milk into a pan, add the vanilla and bring just to the boil. Meanwhile, beat the eggs and egg yolks with the sugar in a bowl. Gradually stir in the hot milk, a little at a time. Strain into the cake tin. Put the tin into a roasting tin, pour in hot water to come about halfway up the sides and bake for about 50 minutes, until set. Remove the tin from the oven and leave to cool, then chill in the refrigerator. Turn out on to a round dish and serve.

1017

- 750 ml/1¼ pints milk
- pinch of vanilla powder or
  a few drops of vanilla extract or
  1 vanilla pod
- 2 eggs
- 6 yolks
- 200 g/7 oz caster sugar
- 250 ml/8 fl oz double cream
- 1 egg white
- 1 quantity Jam Sauce
  (using redcurrant or apricot jam,
  see recipe 119)

Caramel:
- 3 tablespoons caster sugar

Serves 6

Crème caramel surprise

FLAN SORPRESA

For crème caramel surprise, make the creme caramel as described in recipe 117. Stiffly whisk the cream. Whisk the egg white in a clean, dry bowl until stiff peaks form, then fold into the cream. Turn out the chilled crème caramel and cover it with the cream mixture, then pour the jam sauce over it.

1018

- 3 eggs
- 1 can sweetened condensed
- milk (370 g/13 oz)
- 750 ml/1¼ pints milk
- pinch of vanilla powder or
  a few drops of vanilla extract

Caramel:
- 3 tablespoons caster sugar

Serves 4

Crème caramel made with condensed milk
FLAN CON LECHE CONDENSADA

Make the caramel. Put the sugar into a saucepan, add 2 tablespoons water and stir to dissolve, then cook over a low heat until golden. Pour the caramel into a cake tin and tip it back and forth until the tin is completely coated. Preheat the oven to 150°C/300°F/Gas Mark 2. Beat the eggs in a bowl, stir in the condensed milk, then stir in the milk and vanilla. Pour the mixture into the tin. Put the tin into a roast-ing tin, pour in hot water to come about halfway up the sides and bake for 30–45 minutes, until set. Remove the tin from the oven and from the water and leave to cool. Do not chill this crème caramel in the refrigerator. Turn out and serve.

1019

- 100 g/3½ oz caster sugar
- 2 tablespoons cornflour
- 1 tablespoon plain flour
- 750 ml/1¼ pints milk
- 100 g/3½ oz desiccated coconut
- 5 eggs

Serves 6–8

Coconut crème caramel
FLAN DE COCO

Put 2 tablespoons of the sugar into a saucepan, add 1½ tablespoons water and stir to dissolve, then cook over a low heat until golden. Pour the caramel into a ring mould and tip it back and fourth until the mould is completely coated. Leave to cool. Preheat the oven to 150°C/300°F/Gas Mark 2. Mix together the cornflour, flour and 3 tablespoons of the milk in a bowl. Pour the remaining milk into a saucepan, stir in the remaining sugar and heat gently. Add the flour mixture and cook, stirring constantly, for 3 minutes. Remove the pan from the heat and stir in the coconut. Beat the eggs in a bowl, then gradually stir in the milk and coconut mixture, a little at a time. Pour the custard into the mould. Put the mould into a roasting tin, pour in hot water to come about halfway up the sides and bake for 35–45 minutes, until set. Remove the mould from the roasting tin and leave to cool, but do not chill in the refrigerator. Turn out and serve.

1020

- **6 sugar cubes**
- **5–6 oranges**
- **275 g/10 oz caster sugar**
- **2 tablespoons cornflour**
- **6 eggs**

Caramel:
- **3 tablespoons caster sugar**

Serves 4

Crème caramel with orange juice

FLAN CON ZUMO DE NARANJA

Make the caramel. Put the sugar into a saucepan, add 1 ½ tablespoons water and stir to dissolve, then cook over a low heat until golden. Pour the caramel into a cake tin and tip it back and forth until the tin is completely coated. Leave to cool. Preheat the oven to 150°C/300°F/Gas Mark 2. Rub the sugar cubes all over the outside of a couple of the oranges, then put them in a saucepan. Squeeze the oranges, measure 500 ml/18 fl oz juice, reserve 2 tablespoons and pour the remainder into the pan. Stir in the caster sugar. Mix together the cornflour and reserved orange juice in a bowl and add to the pan. Bring the mixture to the boil, stirring constantly. Cook, stirring constantly, for 1–2 minutes, until thickened. Remove the pan from the heat and leave to cool slightly. Beat the eggs in a bowl, then gradually stir in the orange juice mixture, a little at a time. Pour the mixture into the cake tin. Put the tin into a roasting tin, pour in hot water to come about halfway up the sides and bake for about 40 minutes. Remove the tin from the water and leave to cool. Turn out on to a serving dish and serve.

1021

- **1 can sweetened condensed milk (370 g/13 oz)**
- **2 eggs, separated**
- **salt**

Serves 6

Argentinean caramel spread

DULCE DE LECHE CONDENSADA ESTILO ARGENTINO

Put the unopened can of condensed milk into a saucepan, pour in water to come about halfway up the sides of the can and bring to the boil. Lower the heat and simmer gently for 3 hours, topping up with hot water as necessary. Remove the can from the water, open it and leave to cool. Spoon the condensed milk into a small bowl or dish. Stir in the egg yolks. Whisk the egg whites with a pinch of salt in a grease-free bowl until soft peaks form, then fold into the mixture. Chill in the refrigerator for 1 hour, then serve, decorated with whipped cream and accompanied by Langues de Chat (see recipe 943) or other biscuits.

Note: This popular caramel spread (most commonly called dulce de leche) is also widely available for purchase ready-made.

1022

- **250 ml/8 fl oz milk**
- **250 g/9 oz caster sugar**
- **5 egg yolks**
- **3 egg whites**
- **salt**

Caramel:
- **3 tablespoons caster sugar**

Serves 6

Chinese-style crème caramel
FLAN CHINO

Make the caramel. Put the sugar and 2 tablespoons water into an 18 cm/7 inch cake tin and cook over a low heat until golden brown. Remove from the heat and tip the tin so that the caramel coats the base and sides evenly. Leave to cool. Pour the milk into a saucepan, stir in the sugar and cook over a low heat, stirring frequently, for about 15 minutes, until thickened. Beat the egg yolks in a bowl and gradually stir in the hot milk, a little at a time. Leave to cool, stirring occasionally with a wooden spoon. Preheat the oven to 150°C/300°F/ Gas Mark 2. Whisk the egg whites with a pinch of salt in a clean, dry bowl until stiff peaks form, then fold into the custard. Pour the mixture into the cake tin, put it into a roasting tin and pour in water to come about halfway up the sides. Cover with a lid and bake for 20 minutes, then remove the lid and cook for a further 15 minutes, until set. Remove from the oven but leave the tin in the roasting tin to cool. Once it is has cooled, transfer the tin to the refrigerator and chill for 30 minutes. Run a round-bladed knife around the edge of the tin, turn the dessert out on to a serving dish and serve.

1023

📷

Custard and syrup dessert
TOCINO DE CIELO

- **290 g/10½ oz caster sugar**
- **2 strips of thinly pared lemon rind**
- **7 egg yolks**
- **1 egg**

Caramel:
- **2 tablespoons caster sugar**

Serves 6

Make the caramel. Put the sugar into a saucepan, add 1 tablespoon water and stir to dissolve, then cook over a low heat until golden. Pour the caramel into a 14-cm/5 ½-inch cake tin and tip it back and forth until the tin is completely coated. Leave to cool. Pour 350 ml/12 fl oz water into a saucepan, stir in the sugar and add the lemon rind. Bring to the boil, then cook over a low heat for 20 minutes. Remove the pan from the heat and leave to cool. Preheat the oven to 150°C/300°F/Gas Mark 2. Beat the egg yolks and egg with 2 tablespoons water in a bowl, then gradually beat in the cooled syrup, a little at a time. Pour into the cake tin, cover with foil and place a well-fitting lid on top. Put the tin into a roasting tin, pour in hot water to come about halfway up the sides and bring to the boil. Lower the heat and simmer for 9 minutes, then transfer the cake tin in the roasting tin to the oven. Bake for 10 minutes. Remove the tin from the oven and leave to cool. Run a round-bladed knife around the edge and turn the dessert out on to a serving dish.

Note: This dessert can be made in individual dishes. In that case they will not need to bake for quite so long.

Quick custard and syrup dessert

TOCINO DE CIELO RAPIDO

- **500 g/1 lb 2 oz caster sugar**
- **strip of thinly pared lemon rind**
- **18 egg yolks**

Serves 6

Pour 50 ml/2 fl oz water glasses into a saucepan, stir in the sugar, add the lemon rind and bring to the boil. Cook for about 5 minutes, until the syrup reaches thread stage and registers 107°C/225°F on a sugar thermometer. Remove the pan from the heat and leave to cool, then use some of the syrup to coat the inside of a mould. Beat the egg yolks in a bowl and stir in the remaining syrup with a wooden spoon until the mixture acquires the consistency of mayonnaise. Strain this mixture into the mould and cover with foil. Fit the trivet into the base of a pressure cooker and pour in enough water to reach the edge. Place the mould on the trivet and put a plate on top of it. Close the pressure cooker, bring to high pressure and cook for 10 minutes. Remove the pressure cooker from the heat and leave to cool with the lid on. When cooled, remove the mould from the pressure cooker, turn out the dessert and serve.

Note: This is delicious with meringue, cream or a raspberry sauce. If you prefer, make the dessert in individual moulds.

1025

- butter, for greasing
- 10 egg yolks
- 1 egg white
- 2 tablespoons cornflour

Syrup:
- 150 g/5 oz caster sugar
- thinly pared rind of 1 lemon

Topping:
- 120 g/4 oz caster sugar
- 3 egg yolks

To decorate:
- 2 egg whites
- 3 tablespoons caster sugar

Serves 8

Capuchina

CAPUCHINA

Preheat the oven to 150°C/300°F/Gas Mark 2. Generously grease a 23-cm/9-inch cake tin with butter, then chill in the refrigerator. Beat the egg yolks and egg white with an electric mixer or by hand for about 20 minutes. Sift the cornflour over the mixture and gently fold it in, then pour into the prepared tin. Put the tin in a roasting tin, pour in hot water to come about halfway up the sides and simmer for 8–10 minutes, until bubbles begin to form on the surface of the mixture. Transfer the cake tin in the roasting tin to the oven and bake for 25–30 minutes, until set. Meanwhile, make a thin syrup. Pour 150 ml/¼ pint water into a saucepan, stir in the sugar, add the lemon rind and bring to a boil. Lower the heat and simmer for 7 minutes. Remove the pan from the heat. Next, make the topping. Pour 100 ml/3 ½ fl oz water into a saucepan, stir in the sugar and bring to the boil, then lower the heat and simmer for 10 minutes, until a thick syrup forms. Remove the pan from the heat. Beat the egg yolks with 1 teaspoon water in a flameproof dish. Gradually stir in the thick syrup, a little at a time. Cook over a low heat, stirring constantly in a figure-of-eight with a whisk, for 3 minutes, until thickened. Remove from the heat and leave to cool. Remove the capuchina from the oven and prick it all over with a wooden cocktail stick without penetrating all the way through to the tin. Pour the thin syrup into these little holes. Run a round-bladed knife around the edge of the tin and turn the capuchina out on to a serving dish. Carefully pour the topping over it and spread it out to the edges with a palette knife. Chill in the refrigerator for at least 6 hours or overnight. Just before serving, whisk the egg whites in a clean, dry bowl until stiff peaks form, then fold in the sugar. Spoon into a piping bag and pipe decorations over the dessert.

Note: Capuchina is a light, pudding-like cake bathed in syrup.

1026

- **80 g/3 oz butter,**
  plus extra for greasing
- **1 tablespoon sunflower oil**
- **4 tablespoons plain flour**
- **4 teaspoons potato flour**
- **500 ml/18 fl oz milk**
- **100–130 g/3½–4½ oz**
  caster sugar
- **pinch of vanilla powder or**
  a few drops of vanilla extract
- **5 eggs, separated**
- **5 egg whites**
- **salt**

Serves 6–8

Sweet soufflé
SOUFFLÉ DULCE

Melt the butter with the oil in a saucepan. Stir in the flour and potato flour and cook, stirring constantly, for 2 minutes. Gradually stir in the milk, a little at a time. Cook, stirring constantly, for about 5 minutes, until thickened, then remove the pan from the heat. Stir in the sugar and vanilla and leave to cool. When the sauce is just warm, beat in the egg yolks. Preheat the oven to 160°C/325°F/Gas Mark 3. Grease a soufflé dish with butter. Whisk all the egg whites with a pinch of salt, in three batches, in a clean, dry bowl until stiff peaks form, then gently fold into the egg yolk mixture. Pour into the prepared dish and bake for 15 minutes, then increase the oven temperature to 180°C/350°F/ Gas Mark 4 and bake for a further 10 minutes. Increase the oven temperature to 190°C/375°F/Gas Mark 5 and bake for 10 minutes more, until risen and golden brown. Serve immediately straight from the dish.

Note: The flavour of the soufflé can easily be altered in a variety of ways: substitute 3 tablespoons Grand Marnier for the same quantity of milk; infuse thinly pared lemon rind in the milk and substitute the grated rind of a lemon for the vanilla powder or extract; stir 2–3 teaspoons instant coffee granules into the milk; or stir 3 tablespoons cocoa powder into the milk.

1027 Orange soufflés

NARANJAS SUFLÉS

- **4 large oranges**
- **100–150 g/3½–5 oz caster sugar**
- **2 heaped tablespoons cornflour**
- **3 tablespoons Cointreau, Curaçao or other orange-flavoured liqueur**
- **2 egg yolks**
- **3 egg whites**
- **salt**

Serves 4

Cut a thin slice off the base of each orange so that it stands flat. Cut a slice off the top and carefully squeeze out the juice without damaging the 'shells'. Scoop out the pulp and reserve the shells. Pour 350 ml/12 fl oz of the orange juice into a saucepan and stir in the sugar to taste. Mix the cornflour to a paste with 5 tablespoons water in a bowl. Heat the orange juice and when bubbles begin to appear around the edge of the pan, stir in the cornflour and cook, stirring constantly, for 3 minutes. Remove the pan from the heat and leave to cool, stirring to prevent a skin forming. Preheat the grill. Stir in the liqueur, then beat in the egg yolks. Whisk the egg whites with a pinch of salt in a clean, dry bowl until stiff peaks form, then gently fold into the egg yolk mixture. Divide the mixture among the orange shells and grill for 1 minute. Serve immediately.

1028 Floating strawberry and raspberry island with sugar-coated brochettes.

ISLA FLOTANTE DE FRESONES Y FRAMBUESA
CON BROCHETAS REBOZADAS EN AZUCAR

- **500 g/1 lb 2 oz strawberries, hulled**
- **100 g/3½ oz icing sugar**
- **juice of ½ lemon**
- **65 g/2½ oz raspberries**
- **250 ml/8 fl oz milk**
- **10 egg whites**
- **1 teaspoon caster sugar**
- **salt**

Brochettes:
- **pineapple cubes**
- **mango cubes**
- **apple cubes**
- **strawberry halves**
- **2 egg whites, lightly beaten**
- **brown sugar**

Serves 4–6

Prepare the brochettes, alternating the fruit. Brush the fruit with the egg whites and coat in brown sugar. Leave the brochettes to dry or caramelize them in a frying pan. Set aside 12 whole strawberries for decoration. Put the remainder in a bowl, sprinkle with the icing sugar and leave to macerate for 30 minutes. Put the strawberry mixture into a food processor, add the lemon juice and raspberries and process to a purée. Scrape into a bowl and chill in the refrigerator. Pour the milk into a saucepan and bring to simmering point. Whisk the egg whites with a pinch of salt in a clean, dry bowl until stiff peaks form. Fold in the caster sugar. Drop large spoonfuls of the meringue into the milk and poach for 3 minutes. Remove with a slotted spoon and drain well. Divide the strawberry and raspberry sauce among individual dishes and place the meringues on top. Thinly slice the reserved strawberries and place them on the meringues. Serve immediately with the brochettes.

1029

- 175 g/6 oz round grain rice
- 475 ml/16 fl oz milk
- 6 tablespoons caster sugar
- 50 g/2 oz toasted almonds, coarsely chopped
- 1 egg white
- 250 ml/8 fl oz double cream
- salt
- canned or bottled morello cherries in syrup, to decorate

Serves 6–8

Rice pudding with cream and almonds

ARROZ CON LECHE, CON NATA Y ALMENDRAS

Bring a large saucepan of water to a rolling boil. Add the rice and cook for 8 minutes, then drain well. Meanwhile, heat the milk in another saucepan. Add the drained rice, bring to the boil and cook over a medium heat for about 20 minutes, until tender. Stir in the sugar and remove the pan from the heat. Leave to cool slightly, then stir in the almonds and leave to cool completely. Whisk the egg whites with a pinch of salt in a clean, dry bowl until stiff peaks form. Stiffly whisk the cream in another bowl. Fold the egg white into the cream, then fold into the rice. Serve cold decorated with a sprinkling of morello cherries in syrup.

1030

- 200 g/7 oz round grain rice
- 1.2 litres/2 pints milk
- 2½ packets of crème caramel powder
- 130 g/4½ oz caster sugar
- 500 g/1 lb 2 oz canned peaches in syrup, drained and diced
- 250 ml/8 fl oz double cream, whipped
- glacé cherries, to decorate

Serves 8–10

Rice dessert

BUDÍN DE ARROZ

Bring a large saucepan of water to the boil. Add the rice and cook for 8 minutes, then drain well. Meanwhile, heat 1 litre/1¾ pints of the milk in another saucepan. Add the drained rice, bring to the boil and cook over a medium heat for about 20 minutes, until tender. Mix the crème caramel powder with the sugar, then stir in the remaining milk. Stir the mixture into the pan of rice and cook over a medium heat, stirring constantly, according to the instructions on the packet. Remove the pan from the heat, add the peaches and mix well. Pour the mixture into a mould and chill in the refrigerator for 3–4 hours. To serve, run a round-bladed knife around the edge of the mould and turn out the dessert. Decorate it with the cream and glacé cherries.

1031

Rice pudding cones
CORNETES DE ARROZ CON LECHE

- 2 litres/3½ pints milk
- 1 small vanilla pod,
  halved lengthways
- 200 g/7 oz round grain rice
- 100 g/3½ oz caster sugar
- 4 ice cream cones
- ground cinnamon, grated lemon
  rind or grated orange rind,
  to decorate

Serves 4

Put the milk and vanilla pod into a saucepan and bring to the boil. Add the rice, cover the pan and cook over a low heat for about 40 minutes. Stir in the sugar and cook for a further 5 minutes, until the rice is tender. Remove the pan from the heat, take out the vanilla pod and leave the rice to cool. Put the rice in a blender and process to a creamy mixture. Fill the ice cream cones with the rice, sprinkle with cinnamon or grated citrus rind and serve.

1032

Chocolate mousse
MOUSSE DE CHOCOLATE

- 120 g/4 oz plain chocolate,
  broken into pieces
- 3 tablespoons milk
- 80 g/3 oz butter, cut into pieces
- 3 egg yolks
- 3 tablespoons caster sugar
- 4 egg whites
- salt
- whipped cream or morello
  cherries, to decorate

Serves 6

Put the chocolate into a saucepan, pour in the milk and heat gently until the chocolate melts. Remove the pan from the heat and stir in the butter, one piece at a time. Beat the egg yolks with the sugar in a bowl, then add the chocolate mixture. Stir well to mix the ingredients and to cool the mixture. Whisk the egg whites with a pinch of salt in a clean, dry bowl until stiff peaks form, then gently fold them into the cooled chocolate mixture. Spoon the mousse into a serving bowl, individual little pots or champagne glasses and chill in the refrigerator for at least 1 hour. Decorate the mousse with a little cream or morello cherries and serve with Langues de Chat (see recipe 943) or other biscuits.

Note: Whipped cream can be mixed into the mousse, but in this case whisk only 3 egg whites.

📷

Chocolate mousse with sponge fingers

MOUSSE DE CHOCOLATE CON SOLETILLAS

- **175 g/6 oz butter, softened, plus extra for greasing**
- **3–4 tablespoons rum**
- **6 tablespoons caster sugar**
- **35 sponge fingers**
- **100 g/3½ oz plain chocolate, broken into pieces**
- **3 tablespoons milk**
- **3 egg yolks**
- **4 egg whites**
- **salt**
- **whipped cream, to decorate (optional)**

Custard (optional):
- **750 ml/1¼ pints milk**
- **5 tablespoons caster sugar**
- **3 egg yolks**
- **1 tablespoon cornflour**

Serves 6–8

Grease a 20-cm/8-inch cake tin with butter. Mix together 175 ml/6 fl oz water, 1½ tablespoons of the rum and 1 tablespoon of the sugar in a shallow dish. Dip about half the sponge fingers in the mixture and make a layer of them in the base of the prepared tin. Line the sides of the tin with dipped sponge fingers, first cutting off one of the rounded ends, placing them upright side by side cut ends down. Make the mousse as described in recipe 1032, but using more butter so that when it is turned out of the tin it can stand up. Mix another batch of the liquid for dipping the sponge fingers. Spoon half the mousse into the tin and cover it with a layer of dipped sponge fingers. Spoon in the remaining mouse and add a final layer of lightly dampened sponge fingers. Put a greased lid or plate that is slightly smaller than the diameter of the tin on top so that it rests inside the tin and add a light weight. Chill in the refrigerator for at least 5 hours. Make the custard, if using, as described in recipe 1008. To serve, remove the lid or plate, then run a round-bladed knife around the edge of the tin and turn the mousse out on to a round serving dish. Decorate with cream or serve with custard poured over the top.

1034

- 50 g/2 oz butter,
  plus extra for greasing
- 150 g/5 oz plain chocolate
- 150 g/5 oz caster sugar
- 2 egg yolks
- 50 g/2 oz ground almonds
- 4 egg whites
- salt
- whipped cream, to decorate
  (optional)

Custard (optional):
- 500 ml/18 fl oz milk
- 2 egg yolks
- 5 tablespoons caster sugar
- 1 tablespoon cornflour
- pinch of vanilla powder or
  a few drops of vanilla extract

Serves 6

Light chocolate crown with custard
CORONA DE CHOCOLATE LIGERA CON NATILLAS

Preheat the oven to 150°C/300°F/Gas Mark 2. Generously grease a ring mould with butter. Break the chocolate into pieces. Pour 5 tablespoons water into a saucepan, add the chocolate and heat gently until the chocolate has melted. Remove the pan from the heat and leave to cool slightly. Stir in the butter, sugar, egg yolks and ground almonds. Whisk the egg whites with a pinch of salt in a clean, dry bowl until stiff peaks form, then gently fold them into the mixture. Pour the mixture into the prepared mould, put it in a roasting tin, pour in boiling water to come halfway up the sides and bake for 45–60 minutes, until set. Remove the mould from the roasting tin and leave to cool. Make the custard, if using, as described in recipe 1008. Turn the dessert out on to a serving dish and decorate with cream or serve with custard.

1035

- 200 g/7 oz dark chocolate,
  broken into pieces
- 150 g/5 oz butter, melted,
  plus extra for greasing
- 200 ml/7 fl oz double cream
- 130 g/4½ oz icing sugar
- 3 eggs, separated
- 1 tablespoon vanilla sugar
- salt
- sliced kumquats, to decorate

Serves 6

Chocolate marquise
MARQUESA DE CHOCOLATE

Melt the chocolate in a heatproof bowl set over a pan of barely simmering water. Remove from the heat, stir in the butter and leave to cool. Beat the cream into the chocolate mixture. Reserve 2 tablespoons of the icing sugar and beat the egg yolks with the remainder and with the vanilla sugar in a bowl, until pale and fluffy. Stir in the chocolate mixture. Whisk the egg whites with a pinch of salt in a clean, dry bowl until stiff peaks form, then whisk in the reserved sugar. Gently fold the egg whites into the chocolate mixture. Grease a long or round mould with butter and pour the mixture into it. Chill in the refrigerator for 12 hours, until set. Turn the dessert out of the mould, decorate with slices of kumquat and serve.

Note: Run the blade of the knife under cold water before slicing the marquise. Vanilla sugar is simply vanilla-flavoured sugar. It is available to buy, but to make it yourself, bury a whole vanilla bean in 1 to 2 cups sugar, cover and let sit for several days.

1036

- **1 tablespoon cornflour**
- **4 eggs**
- **grated rind of 2 lemons**
- **juice of 3 lemons**
- **200 g/7 oz caster sugar**

Serves 5–6

Lemon cream

CREMA CUAJADA DE LIMÓN

Put the cornflour into a bowl and gradually stir in 250 ml/8 fl oz water to make a smooth paste. Beat the eggs in a flameproof dish and add the lemon rind and juice, sugar and the cornflour mixture. Mix well, bring to the boil over a low heat, stirring constantly, and cook, still stirring constantly, for 3 minutes. Remove from the heat and leave to cool, then chill in the refrigerator if you like. Serve with Langues de Chat (see recipe 943) or other biscuits.

1037

- **50 g/2 oz butter**
- **juice of 3 lemons**
- **grated rind of 1 lemon**
- **250 g/9 oz caster sugar**
- **3 eggs, lightly beaten**

Serves 4–6

Lemon curd

CREMA DE LIMÓN

Melt the butter in a saucepan and remove the pan from the heat. Add the lemon juice and rind, stir in the sugar and beat in the eggs. Put the pan in a roasting tin, pour in hot water to come about halfway up the sides and set over a low heat. Cook, stirring constantly, for 15 minutes, until thickened. Remove the pan from the heat and pour the mixture into a sterilized screw-top jar. Seal the lid and store in a cool place, but not the refrigerator. Use to make lemon meringue pie or spread on bread like jam.

1038

- **4 egg yolks**
- **150 g/5 oz caster sugar**
- **juice of 1 lemon**
- **grated rind of ½ lemon**
- **4 egg whites**
- **salt**
- **6 glacé cherries, to decorate**

Serves 5–6

Lemon mousse

MOUSSE DE LIMÓN

Beat the egg yolks with the sugar and lemon juice in a saucepan. Put the pan in a roasting tin, pour in hot water to come about halfway up the sides and cook over a low heat, stirring constantly, for 15–20 minutes, until almost doubled in volume. Remove the pan from the heat and leave to cool. Stir the lemon rind into the mixture. Whisk the egg whites with a pinch of salt in a clean, dry bowl until stiff peaks form, then gently fold them into the egg yolk mixture. Pour the mixture into little bowls or champagne glasses and chill in the refrigerator for about 2 hours. Serve the mousse decorated with glacé cherries and accompanied by home-made biscuits.

1039

Date mousse
MOUSSE DE DÁTILES

- 500 ml/18 fl oz milk
- 5 tablespoons caster sugar
- 1 cinnamon stick
- 3 egg yolks
- 2 tablespoons cornflour
- 1 tablespoon plain flour
- 30 dates
- 1 egg white

Serves 6

Reserve 3 tablespoons of the milk, pour the remainder into a saucepan and add 3 tablespoons of the sugar and the cinnamon. Bring to the boil. Beat the egg yolks with the remaining sugar, the cornflour, flour and reserved milk in a bowl. Gradually stir in the hot milk, a little at a time, then pour the custard back into the pan and simmer over a low heat, stirring constantly, for 7 minutes. Pour the custard into a bowl, remove the cinnamon stick and leave to cool. Set three of the dates aside. If your dates are not ready-to-eat, peel and stone the remaining ones, put them into a food processor, add the cooled custard and process for 5 minutes, until thoroughly combined, then transfer to a bowl. Whisk the egg white in a clean, dry bowl until stiff peaks form, then gently fold into the mousse. Spoon the mousse into individual dishes. Cut the reserved dates in half and remove the stones if necessary. Top each mousse with a date half and chill in the refrigerator.

Note: Ground cinnamon may be sprinkled on top of the mousse. This dessert is also delicious if a vanilla pod is substituted for the cinnamon stick.

1040

Coffee mousse with curd cheese
MOUSSE DE CAFÉ CON REQUESÓN

- 250 g/9 oz curd cheese,
  cut into pieces
- 4 tablespoons caster sugar
- 3–4 tablespoons rum
- 2 tablespoons instant
  coffee granules
- 120 ml/4 fl oz hot milk
- 2 egg whites
- salt

Serves 4

Put the curd cheese into a bowl, sprinkle with the sugar and add the rum. Dissolve the coffee granules in the hot milk, leave to cool slightly, then pour into the bowl. Mix well using a hand-held blender. Whisk the egg whites with a pinch of salt in a clean, dry bowl until stiff peaks form, then carefully fold them into the cheese mixture. Put the mousse into glasses and chill in the refrigerator for several hours. Serve with Langues de Chat (see recipe 943) or other biscuits.

1041

- juice of 3 large oranges
- 100–150 g/3½–5 oz caster sugar
- 2 tablespoons cornflour
- 3 tablespoons Cointreau, Curaçao or other orange-flavoured liqueur
- 2 egg yolks
- 3 egg whites
- salt
- 1 orange, peeled and sliced, to decorate

Serves 6

Orange mousse

MOUSSE DE NARANJA

Put the orange juice into a saucepan and stir in the sugar to taste. Mix the cornflour with 4 tablespoons water in a bowl. Heat the juice and when bubbles begin to appear around the edge of the pan, stir in the cornflour mixture and cook, stirring constantly, for 3 minutes. Remove the pan from the heat and leave to cool, stirring to prevent a skin forming. Stir in the liqueur and beat in the egg yolks. Whisk the egg whites with a pinch of salt in a clean, dry bowl until stiff peaks form, then gently fold them into the mousse. Divide the mixture among individual dishes or champagne glasses and chill in the refrigerator for about 3 hours. Just before serving decorate the mousse with orange slices. Serve with Langues de Chat (see recipe 943) or other biscuits.

1042

- 500 g/1 lb 2 oz mixed fruit, such as bananas, apples, peaches, plums, grapes, strawberries or raspberries
- 3 tablespoons rum or brandy
- 120 g/4 oz caster sugar
- 250 ml/8 fl oz orange juice
- 4 gelatine leaves, cut into pieces

Serves 6

Fruit jelly

GELATINA DE FRUTAS

Make this dessert the night before you intend to serve it. Prepare the fruit in the appropriate way and cut it into pieces. Put them into a bowl, pour the rum or brandy over them and leave to macerate, stirring occasionally. Pour 150 ml/¼ pint water into a saucepan, stir in the sugar and cook for about 4 minutes to make a syrup. Pour the orange juice into a bowl, add the gelatine and leave to soften for 5 minutes. Stir the syrup into the orange juice, mixing until the gelatine has completely dissolved. Line a round or ring mould with foil. Pour in the liquid to a depth of about 2 cm/¾ inch and chill in the refrigerator or freezer until set. Arrange the fruit on top and pour in the remaining liquid. Chill in the refrigerator for several hours until set. Turn the jelly out of the mould to serve.

1043

- 6 gelatine leaves, cut into pieces
- 250 g/9 oz white grapes
- 250 g/9 oz black grapes
- 250 ml/8 fl oz grape juice
- 2 tablespoons lemon juice
- 120 ml/4 fl oz white wine
- 200 g/7 oz caster sugar
- 475 ml/16 fl oz milk
- fresh mint leaves, to decorate

Serves 6–8

Grape jelly
GELATINA DE UVAS

Put the gelatine into a small bowl of water and leave to soften for 5 minutes. Reserve some of the grapes for decoration and halve and seed the remainder. Pour the grape juice, lemon juice and wine into a saucepan, stir in the sugar and cook, stirring until the sugar has dissolved. Drain the gelatine, add it to the pan and stir until it has dissolved. Pour a little of the liquid into a bowl and chill in the refrigerator until set. Add a layer of grapes, pour in a little more liquid and chill in the refrigerator until set. Continue making layers in this way until all the ingredients are used up, then chill in the refrigerator for at least 3 hours. Decorate with the reserved grapes and the mint leaves before serving.

1044

- 500 ml/18 fl oz milk
- 100 g/3½ oz caster sugar
- 2 egg yolks
- 1 tablespoon instant coffee granules
- 1½ tablespoons cornflour
- 3 egg whites
- 50 g/2 oz toasted or caramel-coated almonds, chopped (optional)
- salt

Serves 6

Coffee mousse
MOUSSE DE CAFÉ

Pour nearly all the milk into a saucepan, stir in 50 g/2 oz of the sugar and bring to the boil. Beat the egg yolks with the remaining sugar and the coffee granules in a bowl. Mix the cornflour with the remaining milk in another bowl. Stir the cornflour mixture into the egg yolk mixture. Gradually stir the hot milk into the egg yolk mixture. Pour the custard back into the pan and cook, stirring constantly, for 3–4 minutes, until thickened. Remove the pan from the heat and leave to cool, stirring to prevent a skin forming. Whisk the egg whites with a pinch of salt in a clean, dry bowl until stiff peaks form, then gently fold them into the mixture. Divide the mousse among individual bowls or champagne glasses or pour into a large serving bowl. Chill in the re-frigerator for 2–3 hours but no longer. Just before serving, sprinkle with the almonds, if using.

1045 Small raspberry or strawberry bavarois

BAVAROISES PEQUEÑAS DE FRESAS O FRAMBUESAS

- 300 g/11 oz strawberries, hulled, or 250 g/9 oz raspberries or 4 tablespoons redcurrant jam
- 750 ml/1¼ pints milk
- 4–8 tablespoons caster sugar
- 6 tablespoons cornflour
- 3 gelatine leaves, cut into pieces
- 2 egg whites
- salt
- 120 ml/4 fl oz whipped cream or strawberries or glacé cherries, to decorate

Serves 6–8

Process the fresh fruit, if using, in a food processor. Pour nearly all the milk into a saucepan, stir in 8 tablespoons sugar if using fresh fruit or 4 tablespoons if using jam and bring to the boil. Mix the cornflour with the remaining milk in a bowl. When the milk in the pan is about to boil, stir in the cornflour mixture and cook, stirring constantly, for 3 minutes. Remove the pan from the heat and stir in the strawberries or raspberries or jam. Put the gelatine in a small saucepan of water and leave to soften for 5 minutes, then heat gently untilthe gelatine has completely dissolved. Gradually stir it into the milk mixture, a little at a time. Whisk the egg whites with a pinch of salt in a clean, dry bowl until stiff peaks form, then gently fold them into the milk mixture. Rinse out individual moulds with cold water, divide the ba-varois among them and chill in the refrigerator for 2 hours. Run a knife around the edge of each mould and turn the bavarois out on to a serving dish. If they do not come out easily, use the point of a knife to separate them from the edge a little so that air enters, as this type of dessert sometimes forms a suction seal. Decorate with whipped cream or top each bavarois with a strawberry or glacé cherry.

1046 Praline bavarois

BAVAROISE DE PRALINÉ

- 4 gelatine leaves, cut into pieces
- 500 ml/18 fl oz milk
- 6 tablespoons caster sugar
- pinch of vanilla powder or a few drops of vanilla essence
- 5 egg yolks
- 1 tablespoon cornflour
- 150 g/5 oz caramel-coated almonds, coarsely crushed or 100 g/3½ oz amaretti, coarsely chopped
- 2 egg whites
- 250 ml/8 fl oz double cream
- salt

Serves 6

Pour 120 ml/4 fl oz water into a small saucepan, add the gelatine and leave to soften for 5 minutes, then heat gently, stirring until the gelatine has dissolved. Pour the milk into another pan, stir in half the sugar and the vanilla and bring to the boil over a medium heat. Beat the egg yolks with the cornflour and remaining sugar in a bowl. Gradually stir in the hot milk, a little at a time. Pour the custard back into the pan and cook, stirring constantly, for a few minutes, until thickened. Remove the pan from the heat, leave to cool for about 5 minutes, then stir in the gelatine. Add the almonds or amaretti and mix well. Stand the pan a bowl of cold water and stir the mixture until cold. Whisk the egg whites with a pinch of salt in a clean, dry bowl until stiff peaks form. Stiffly whisk the cream in another bowl, then fold in the egg whites. Gently stir the cream mixture into the custard. Rinse a mould with cold water and spoon the bavarois into it. Chill in the refrigerator for at least 4 hours, until set. Turn the bavarois out of the mould on to a serving dish to serve. If it does not come out easily, use the point of a knife to separate it from the edge a little.

1047

Bavarois with peaches

BAVAROISE DE MELOCOTONES (DE LATA)

- **500 ml/18 fl oz milk**
- **150 g/5 oz caster sugar**
- **4 egg yolks**
- **1 teaspoon cornflour**
- **500 g/1 lb 2 oz canned peaches in syrup**
- **5 gelatine leaves, cut into pieces**
- **4 egg whites**
- **sunflower oil, for brushing**
- **salt**

Serves 6

Pour the milk into a saucepan, stir in half the sugar and bring to the boil. Beat the egg yolks with the remaining sugar and the cornflour in a bowl. Gradually stir in the hot milk, a little at a time, then pour the custard back into the pan and cook over a low heat, stirring constantly, for a few minutes, until thickened. Remove the pan from the heat and leave to cool, stirring occasionally. Drain the peaches, reserving the syrup. Set a peach aside for decoration. Put the remaining peaches in a food processor and process to a purée. Stir the purée into the custard. Put the gelatine into a saucepan, add the reserved syrup and leave to soften for 5 minutes, then heat gently until the gelatine has dissolved completely. Gradually stir it into the custard, a little at a time. Stir the custard until it is almost cold. Whisk the egg whites with a pinch of salt in a clean, dry bowl until stiff peaks form, then gently fold them into the custard. Brush a mould with oil and spoon in the bavarois. Chill in the refrigerator for at least 3 hours. (It can be made a day in advance.) Run a round-bladed knife around the edge of the mould and turn the bavarois out. If it does not come out easily, use the point of a knife to separate it from the edge a little so that air enters, as this type of dessert sometimes forms a suction seal. Decorate with the reserved peach cut into wedges.

Bavarois with pineapple

BAVAROISE DE PIÑA (DE LATA)

- **500 ml/18 fl oz milk**
- **200 g/7 oz caster sugar**
- **4 egg yolks**
- **1 heaped teaspoon cornflour**
- **500 g/1 lb 2 oz canned pineapple in syrup**
- **4 gelatine leaves, cut into pieces**
- **1 egg white**
- **250 ml/8 fl oz double cream**
- **sunflower oil, for brushing**
- **salt**

Serves 6–8

Pour the milk into a saucepan, stir in half the sugar and bring to the boil. Beat the egg yolks with the remaining sugar and the cornflour in a bowl. Gradually stir in the hot milk, a little at a time, then pour the custard back into the pan. Cook over a low heat, stirring constantly, for a few minutes, until thickened. Remove the pan from the heat. Drain the pineapple, reserving the syrup in a saucepan. Add the gelatine to the syrup and leave to soften for 5 minutes, then heat gently, stirring until the gelatine has completely dissolved. Gradually stir the gelatine into the custard, a little at a time, then stand the pan in a bowl of cold water and stir until the custard is almost cold. Chop half the pineapple slices into pieces and add to the custard. Halve the remaining slices and set aside. Whisk the egg whites with a pinch of salt in a clean, dry bowl until stiff peaks form. Stiffly whisk the cream in another bowl, then fold in the egg white. Reserve a little of the mixture for decoration and gently fold the remainder into the custard. Brush a bavarois mould or a cake tin with oil. Spoon the bavarois into the mould or tin and chill in the refrigerator for about 10 hours or overnight. To serve, dip the base of the mould or tin into hot water for a few seconds and then turn out the bavarois. If it does not come out easily, use the point of a knife to separate it from the edge a little so that air enters, as this type of dessert sometimes forms a suction seal. Decorate the bavarois with the reserved cream mixture and the half slices of pineapple.

1049

Orange bavarois
BAVAROISE DE NARANJA

- 3 eggs, separated
- 200 g/7 oz caster sugar
- 4 gelatine leaves, cut into pieces
- 200 ml/7 fl oz orange juice, strained
- 50 ml/2 fl oz Cointreau
- 1 egg white
- sunflower oil, for brushing

Serves 6–8

Beat the egg yolks with the sugar for about 5 minutes, until the mixture is creamy. Put the gelatine into a small saucepan, add 4 tablespoons water and leave to soften for 5 minutes, then heat gently until the gelatine has dissolved completely. Mix together the orange juice and Cointreau and add to the egg yolk mixture, then stir in the gelatine. Whisk the egg whites in a clean, dry bowl until stiff peaks form, then gently fold them into the egg yolk mixture. Brush a cake tin with oil and pour in the bavarois. Chill in the refrigerator for at least 6 hours, until set. (The bavarois will need to be stirred a couple of times to prevent the gelatine sinking to the bottom.) To serve, turn the bavarois out on to a serving dish. If it does not come out easily, use the point of a knife to separate it from the edge a little so that air enters, as this type of dessert sometimes forms a suction seal.

Note: The bavarois can be decorated with a little whipped cream or some thin slices of orange.

1050

Chocolate bavarois
BAVAROISE DE CHOCOLATE

- 150 g/5 oz dark chocolate, broken into pieces
- 250 ml/8 fl oz milk
- 4 gelatine leaves, cut into pieces
- 4 egg yolks
- 150 g/5 oz caster sugar
- 6 egg whites
- salt
- whipped cream or glacé cherries, to decorate (optional)

Serves 6–8

Put the chocolate in a saucepan, pour in the milk and melt the chocolate over a medium heat. Remove the pan from the heat and leave to cool. Pour 4 tablespoons water into a small saucepan, add the gelatine and leave to soften for 5 minutes, then heat gently, stirring constantly, until the gelatine has dissolved completely. Gradually stir the gelatine into the chocolate mixture, a little at a time. Leave to cool, stirring occasionally. Beat the egg yolks with the sugar in a bowl, then stir into the chocolate mixture. Whisk the egg whites with a pinch of salt in a clean, dry bowl until stiff peaks form, then gently fold into the chocolate mixture. Pour the bavarois into a large mould or individual moulds and chill in the refrigerator for at least 5 hours, until set. To serve, turn the bavarois out on to a serving dish. If it does not come out easily, use the point of a knife to separate it from the edge a little so that air enters, as this type of dessert sometimes forms a suction seal. Decorate with whipped cream or glacé cherries if you like.

1051

- 500 g/1 lb 2 oz strawberries, hulled
- 2 tablespoons kirsch
- 3 eggs, separated
- 200 g/7 oz caster sugar
- 4 gelatine leaves, cut into pieces
- 3 drops of red food colouring (optional)
- 250 ml/8 fl oz double cream
- sunflower oil, for brushing
- salt

Serves 6–8

Strawberry bavarois

BAVAROISE DE FRESAS

Reserve a few strawberries for decoration and process the remainder in a food processor. Mix the strawberry purée with the kirsch. Beat the egg yolks with the sugar in a bowl until pale and fluffy. Put the gelatine into a small saucepan, add 4 tablespoons water and leave to soften for 5 minutes, then heat gently, stirring constantly, until the gelatine has dissolved completely. Stir the strawberry purée into the egg yolk mixture, then gradually stir in the gelatine, a little at a time. Stir in the food colouring, if using. Whisk the egg whites with a pinch of salt in a clean, dry bowl until stiff peaks form. Stiffly whisk the cream in another bowl. Fold half the cream into the strawberry mixture and then fold in the egg whites. Brush a cake tin with oil, spoon in the bavarois and chill in the refrigerator for at least 4 hours, until set. To serve, turn the bavarois out on to a serving dish. If it does not come out easily, use the point of a knife to separate it from the edge a little so that air enters, as this type of dessert sometimes forms a suction seal. Pipe the remaining cream over the bavarois and decorate with the reserved strawberries.

1052

- 4 gelatine leaves, cut into pieces
- 250 g/9 oz nougat (see recipe 1080), cut into pieces
- 4 eggs, separated
- 2–3 tablespoons rum
- salt

Serves 6

Bavarois with nougat

BAVAROISE DE TURRÓN DE JIJONA

Put the gelatine in a small saucepan of water and leave to soften for 5 minutes, then heat gently, stirring constantly, until the gelatine has dissolved completely. Remove the pan from the heat. Mash the nougat with a fork, then mix with the egg yolks and rum to make a smooth cream. Gradually stir in the gelatine, a little at a time. Whisk the egg whites with a pinch of salt in a clean, dry bowl until stiff peaks form, then fold them into the nougat cream. Pour the bavarois into a ring mould and chill in the refrigerator for at least 4 hours, until set. (The dish can be made a day in advance.) To serve, turn out the bavarois. If it does not come out easily, use the point of a knife to separate it from the edge a little so that air enters, as this type of dessert sometimes forms a suction seal. Serve with tuiles or Langues de Chat (see recipe 943) or other biscuits.

1053

Raspberry bavarois
BAVAROIS DE FRAMBUESA

- 500 g/1 lb 2 oz raspberries
- 2 tablespoons raspberry liqueur
- 3 eggs, separated
- 200 g/7 oz caster sugar
- 4 gelatine leaves, cut into pieces
- 3 drops of red food colouring (optional)
- 250 ml/8 fl oz double cream
- sunflower oil, for brushing
- salt
- whipped cream, to decorate

Serves 4–6

Set aside a few raspberries for decoration and beat the remainder to a purée with a wooden spoon in a bowl. Stir in the liqueur. Beat the egg yolks with the sugar in a bowl until pale and fluffy, then stir into the raspberry purée. Put the gelatine into a small saucepan, add 4 tablespoons water and leave to soften for 5 minutes, then heat gently, stirring constantly, until the gelatine has dissolved completely. Remove from the heat and stir into the raspberry mixture, then stir in the food colouring, if using. Whisk the egg whites with a pinch of salt in a clean, dry bowl until stiff peaks form. Stiffly whisk the cream in another bowl. Fold the cream into the raspberry mixture, then fold in the egg whites. Brush a mould with oil and spoon in the bavarois. Chill in the refrigerator for at least 4 hours, until set. To serve, turn out the bavarois. If it does not come out easily, use the point of a knife to separate it from the edge a little so that air enters, as this type of dessert sometimes forms a suction seal. Pipe cream over the bavarois and decorate it with the reserved raspberries.

1054

Vanilla ice cream
BISCUIT GLACÉ

- **butter, for greasing**
- **1 tablespoon cornflour**
- **200 ml / 7 fl oz milk**
- **175 g / 6 oz caster sugar**
- **pinch of vanilla powder or**
  a few drops of vanilla extract
- **6 eggs, separated**
- **few drops of yellow food**
  colouring (optional)
- **salt**

Serves 6–8

Grease a metal mould with butter, then chill it in the freezer. Mix the cornflour with 2–3 tablespoons of the milk in a bowl. Pour the remaining milk into a saucepan with 5 tablespoons of the sugar and the vanilla and bring to the boil. Stir in the cornflour and cook, stirring constantly, for 3 minutes. Remove the pan from the heat and leave to cool slightly. Beat the egg yolks with 5 tablespoons of the remaining sugar in a bowl. Gradually stir in the milk mixture, a little at a time, then stir in the food colouring, if using. Whisk the egg whites with a pinch of salt in a clean, dry bowl until stiff peaks form, then fold in the remaining sugar. Gently fold the egg whites into the custard, then pour into the prepared mould and put in the freezer for about 3 hours. Remove the mould from the freezer about 5 minutes before serving. Run a round-bladed knife around the mould and turn the ice cream out on to a serving dish.

Note: The ice cream can be put into individual glass or foil moulds.

1068

Lemon sorbet

SORBETE DE LIMÓN

- **200 g / 7 oz caster sugar**
- **grated rind and juice of 4 large lemons**
- **2 egg whites**
- **salt**

Serves 4

Pour 500 ml / 18 fl oz water into a saucepan, stir in the sugar and bring to a rolling boil, then cook for 10–12 minutes, until syrupy. Re-move the pan from the heat and leave to cool. Stir the lemon rind and juice into the cold syrup, pour into a freezerproof container and put into the freezer. When the mixture begins to freeze, whisk the egg whites with a pinch of salt in a clean, dry bowl until stiff peaks form, then fold them into the mixture. Return to the freezer and freeze until firm. Serve in sundae glasses, accompanied by Langues de Chat (see recipe 943) or other biscuits, if you like.

1056

- **4 oranges, about 1 kg/
  2 ¼ lb, halved**
- **2 lemons, halved**
- **1 kg/2 ¼ lb caster sugar**

Makes 3 large jars

Orange marmalade

MERMELADA DE NARANJA (ESTILO INGLÉS)

Squeeze the oranges and lemons, reserving the pips. Tie the pips in a square of muslin. Cut the rinds into julienne strips, preferably with a mandoline. Mix the rinds with the juice and add the bag of pips. Leave to stand for 24 hours. Pour the mixture into a preserving pan or large saucepan, pour in 1 litre/1 ¾ pints water and bring to the boil. Lower the heat and simmer gently, stirring occasionally, for 1 hour. Remove the pan from the heat and leave to stand for 24 hours. Stir the sugar into the juice mixture and heat, stirring until the sugar has dissolved. Skim off the foam that rises to the surface and simmer for 1 ¼–1 ½ hours, until the temperature measures 105°C/220°F on a sugar thermometer and the marmalade has reached setting point. To test for setting point, put a teaspoon of the marmalade on a cold saucer and cool quickly. When the surface has set, push it with your finger; if it wrinkles, the marmalade is at setting point. Remove the pan from the heat and leave to cool slightly, then remove and discard the bag of pips and ladle the marmalade into sterilized glass jars.

1057

- **1 kg/2 ¼ lb very ripe fleshy
  tomatoes, seeded and cut
  into pieces**
- **500 g/1 lb 2 oz caster sugar**
- **juice of 1 lemon**

Makes 3 large jars

Tomato jam

MERMELADA DE TOMATES

This is an unusual recipe that is ideal for people who have a vegetable garden. Once the jam is made it does not taste like tomato. Put the pieces of tomato into a frying pan and cook over a medium heat, stirring occasionally and breaking them up with the side of the spoon, for 15 minutes. Pass the tomatoes through a food mill or food processor and pour the purée into a saucepan. Stir in the sugar and lemon juice and cook over a low heat for about 30 minutes, depending on how thick you like your jam. Bear in mind it will thicken a little more as it cools.

1058

Quince jelly

MEMBRILLO

• 1.5 kg/3¼ lb ripe quinces,
  cored and cut into pieces
• 1.2 kg/2½ lb caster sugar

Makes 3–4 jars

Put the quinces into a saucepan and add just enough cold water to cover. Cook over a medium heat for about 1 hour, until the quinces have softened. Pass them through a food mill or food processor into a clean saucepan and stir in the sugar. Cook, stirring occasionally, for a further 30 minutes. Pour the quince mixture into a square of muslin or a jelly bag. Bring the corners of the square together and suspend over a bowl to drain. Leave to drain for about 20 minutes, then pour the liquid into glass jars or bowls and leave to cool and set. Run a round-bladed knife around the edge of the container and turn out the jelly once it is cold and set.

1059

Flamed quinces with redcurrant jam

MEMBRILLOS CON JALEA DE GROSELLA Y FLAMEADOS

• 4 quinces,
  peeled, cored and thickly sliced
• 3 tablespoons caster sugar
• 3 tablespoons redcurrant jam
• 120 ml/4 fl oz rum or brandy

Serves 6

Put the quinces into a saucepan, add water to cover, cover the pan with a lid and cook over a medium heat for about 35 minutes, until softened. Drain off some of the water and sprinkle the sugar into the pan. Return it to the heat and cook for a further 10–15 minutes. Remove the fruit from the syrup that will have formed and set aside. Just before serving, put the slices of quince on to a serving dish and put the jam in the centre. Pour the rum or brandy into a saucepan and heat for a few seconds, then ignite it and carefully pour it over the quinces. Spoon the spirit over the fruit while the alcohol is still burning. Serve before the flames die down.

1060

- 1 kg/2¼ lb sweet potatoes, peeled
- 350 g/12 oz caster sugar
- 1 cinnamon stick
- 250 ml/8 fl oz single cream, to serve (optional)

Serves 6

Sweetened sweet potatoes

BATATAS EN DULCE

If the sweet potatoes are fat, halve them lengthways. Put them into a saucepan, pour in just enough water to cover and add the sugar and cinnamon. Cover the pan with brown paper that has been cut in a circle to fit snugly inside the plan, seal with a lid and bring to the boil, then lower the heat, and cook until a thick syrup forms. Tip the mixture into a bowl and leave to cool. Serve immediately with cream, if you like, or keep in the refrigerator for 3–4 days.

1061

- 250 ml/8 fl oz wine
- 120 g/4 oz caster sugar
- 1 cinnamon stick
- 500 g/1 lb 2 oz stoned prunes, soaked in warm water for 3–6 hours and drained

Serves 6

Prunes with red wine

CIRUELAS PASAS CON VINO TINTO

Pour 250 ml/8 fl oz water and the wine into a saucepan, stir in the sugar and add the cinnamon and prunes. There should be enough liquid in the pan to cover the prunes but if not, add a little more wine or a mixture of water and wine. Cook over a medium heat for about 30 minutes. Remove the pan from the heat, remove and discard the cinnamon, put the mixture into a bowl and leave to cool. Serve cold, but do not chill in the refrigerator.

1062

- 9 large pears
- 4 tablespoons caster sugar
- 2 cinnamon sticks
- 750 ml/1¼ pints red wine
- 250 ml/8 fl oz sweetened whipped cream (optional)

Serves 6

Pear compote with red wine

PERAS EN COMPOTA CON VINO TINTO

Peel the pears, then quarter and core them. Put them into a saucepan, sprinkle with the sugar, add the cinnamon and pour in enough wine to cover. Cover and cook over a medium heat for about 20 minutes, until the pears are tender. Tip the pears into a bowl and leave to cool. Serve with sweetened cream, if you like, offered separately.

Note: If the pears are fairly small, leave them whole. Peel them but leave the stalks intact. Allow 2 small pears per serving. The cream can be replaced with custard (see recipe 1008).

1063

Flamed peaches
MELOCOTONES FLAMEADOS

- **2 cylindrical bread rolls**
- **6 canned or bottled peach halves in syrup, drained**
- **6 teaspoons redcurrant or raspberry jam**
- **icing sugar, for sprinkling**
- **175 ml / 6 fl oz rum**

Serves 6

Preheat the grill. Cut the rolls into three and place a peach half on each piece with the cavity uppermost. Press down lightly on the fruit so it is firmly positioned. Fill the cavities in the peaches with redcurrant or raspberry jam and then put them into a flameproof dish. Sprinkle with icing sugar and cook briefly under the grill. Meanwhile, heat the rum in a saucepan for a few seconds. Remove the dish from the grill, ignite the rum and carefully pour it over the peaches. Keep spooning it back over the peaches until the flames die down. If possible, serve while the rum is still burning.

1064

- 6 canned or bottled peach
  halves in syrup, drained
- 350 ml/12 fl oz rum
- 3 cylindrical bread rolls,
  crusts removed
- 500 ml/18 fl oz vanilla ice cream

Serves 6

Flamed peaches with vanilla ice cream

MELOCOTONES FLAMEADOS CON HELADO DE VAINILLA

Put the peach halves into a frying pan. Heat the rum in a saucepan for a few seconds, ignite it and carefully pour it over the peaches. Keep spooning the rum over the fruit. Halve the rolls and scoop out a little of the crumb from each half to make a cavity. When the flames have died down, place a peach half in each piece of roll with the cavity uppermost. Press down gently so the peach is firmly positioned. Fill the cavities with the ice cream and spoon a little of the sauce from the frying pan over the top. Serve immediately.

1065

- 6 large peaches, peeled,
  stoned and quartered
- 200 g/7 oz caster sugar
- 750 ml/1¼ pints white wine
- 3 heaped tablespoons orange
  gelatine

Serves 4–5

Peaches with white wine and orange jelly

MELOCOTONES CON VINO BLANCO Y GELATINA DE NARANJA

It is better to prepare this dish a day in advance. Put the peaches into a saucepan in a single layer. Sprinkle them with the sugar and pour the wine over them. Bring to the boil, lower the heat and simmer gently for about 30 minutes, until softened. Remove the pan from the heat, lift out the peaches with a slotted spoon and put them into a serving bowl. Return the pan to the heat and cook the liquid for about 15 minutes, until syrupy. Transfer 175 ml/6 fl oz of the syrup to a saucepan and dissolve the orange gelatine in it, then cook it for 1 minute. Stir in another 275 ml/9 fl oz of the syrup and mix well. Pour the mixture over the peaches, chill before serving.

1066

Peaches cooked with zabaglione

MELOCOTONES COCIDOS CON SABAYON

• 8 ripe peaches, peeled

Syrup:
• 250 g/9 oz caster sugar
• 1 vanilla pod, halved lengthways

Zabaglione:
• 4 egg yolks
• 3 tablespoons icing sugar
• 200 ml/7 fl oz Madeira wine or
  other fortified wine
• raspberries
• flaked almonds

Serves 4

Make the syrup. Pour 500 ml/18 fl oz water into a saucepan, stir in the sugar, add the vanilla and bring to the boil. Add the peaches, cover and cook for 5 minutes. Remove the pan from the heat and leave the peaches to cool in the syrup. Make the zabaglione. Beat the egg yolks with the sugar and Madeira in a heatproof bowl set over a pan of barely simmering water until thick and creamy. Remove the bowl from the heat and continue to beat until the mixture cools. Drain the peaches and divide them among individual plates. Spoon the zabaglione over them, decorate with raspberries and almonds and serve.

Note: To make the peaches easier to peel, submerge them in boiling water for 8 seconds and then put them into cold water. The skin will then peel off more easily.

1067

Flamed bananas with vanilla ice cream

PLÁTANOS FLAMEADOS CON HELADO DE VAINILLA

• 6 bananas
• juice of 1 lemon
• 500 ml/18 fl oz sunflower oil
• 175 ml/6 fl oz rum
• 500 ml/18 fl oz vanilla ice cream
• icing sugar, for sprinkling

Serves 6

Peel the bananas and cut them in half lengthways. Sprinkle with the lemon juice to prevent discoloration. Heat the oil in a deep-fryer or saucepan to 180–190°C/350–375°F or until a cube of day-old bread browns in 30 seconds. Add the bananas and cook until golden brown, working in batches if necessary. Remove with a slotted spoon, drain well and set aside on a plate. Heat the rum in a small saucepan for a few seconds, ignite it and carefully pour it over the bananas. Spoon the rum back over them until the flames have died down. Working quickly so that neither the rum nor the bananas have time to cool, divide the ice cream among individual plates, top with the banana halves crossed over each other and spoon the rum over them. Sprinkle with icing sugar and serve.

1068 Fig compote with red wine and spices
COMPOTA DE HIGOS CON VINO TINTO Y ESPECIAS

- **3 tablespoons red wine**
- **2 large pieces of thinly pared orange rind**
- **3 tablespoons caster sugar**
- **1 cinnamon stick**
- **6 cloves**
- **1 sprig fresh mint**
- **24 small figs or 12 large figs, peeled**

Serves 4–6

Pour 135 ml / 4 ½ fl oz water and the wine into a saucepan, add the orange rind, sugar, cinnamon, cloves and mint and simmer for 10 minutes. Add the figs and cook over a low heat for 6 minutes. Lift out the figs with a slotted spoon and put them into a serving bowl. Simmer the cooking liquid for a further 15 minutes, then strain it into a dish, reserving the orange rind, and leave to cool. Cut the orange rind into very thin strips and add to the compote. Pour the sauce over the figs and chill in the refrigerator.

1069

Cointreau foam

ESPUMOSO DE COINTREAU

- **4 eggs, separated**
- **130 g/4 ½ oz caster sugar**
- **2 tablespoons Cointreau**
- **100 ml/3 ½ fl oz double cream**

Serves 4

Put the egg yolks and sugar into a saucepan and beat over a low heat until the mixture is smooth and even, but do not allow it to boil. Remove the pan from the heat and add the liqueur; the mixture will thicken immediately. Leave to cool. Whisk the egg whites in a clean, dry bowl until stiff peaks form. Stiffly whisk the cream in another bowl. Fold the egg whites and cream into the egg yolk mixture. Divide the foam among glasses or sundae dishes and chill in the refrigerator.

1070

Caramelized pear compote

COMPOTA DE PERAS CARAMELIZADA

- **25 g/1 oz slivered almonds**
- **juice of ½ lemon**
- **200 g/7 oz icing sugar**
- **4 pears**
- **25 g/1 oz butter,
  cut into small pieces**

Serves 4

Toast the almonds in a small frying pan, stirring frequently, for a few minutes until golden and fragrant, but be careful not to let them burn, then remove from the heat and set aside. Pour 5 tablespoons water and the lemon juice into a saucepan, stir in the sugar and cook over a low heat until golden. Meanwhile, peel, core and dice the pears. Add the pears and butter to the caramel, cover and cook for 15 minutes. Divide the compote among individual pots or dishes and sprinkle with the almonds. Leave to cool slightly before serving.

1071

Green tea custard

NATILLAS AL TÉ VERDE

- **1 litre/1 ¾ pints milk**
- **250 g/9 oz icing sugar**
- **4 teaspoons green tea leaves**
- **8 egg yolks**
- **sponge fingers, to serve**

Serves 4

Reserve 1 tablespoon of the milk. Pour the remainder into a saucepan, stir in the sugar and bring to the boil. Remove the pan from the heat, stir in the tea and leave to infuse for 30 minutes. Strain through a muslin-lined sieve into a bowl and leave to cool completely. Beat the egg yolks with the reserved milk in a heatproof bowl. Add the infused milk and set over a pan of barely simmering water. Cook, whisking constantly, until thickened. Remove the pan from the heat and pour the custard into a mould. Leave to cool, then chill in the refrigerator. Serve with sponge fingers.

1072

Grape and orange compote

COMPOTA DE UVAS Y NARANJAS

- **200 g / 7 oz muscatel grapes, seeded**
- **2 oranges, thinly sliced**
- **100 g / 3 ½ oz caster sugar**
- **100 g / 3 ½ oz raisins**
- **4 individual portions of fromage frais or other fresh cheese, to serve**

Serves 4

Put the grapes and oranges into a heavy-based saucepan, mix well and add the sugar and raisins. Cook over a low heat for about 1 hour, until the compote thickens. Remove the pan from the heat and leave to cool, then serve accompanied by the cheese.

1073

Grilled oranges with zabaglione

GRATINADO DE NARANJAS CON SABAYON

- **4 oranges**
- **4 egg yolks**
- **20 g/¾ oz icing sugar**
- **¼ bottle of cava or other sparkling wine**

Serves 4

Peel the oranges and cut out the segments from the membranes. Put half of them in a decorative shape on individual serving plates. Beat the egg yolks with the sugar in a heatproof bowl until pale and fluffy. Add the cava and cook over a pan of barely simmering water, beating constantly, until thickened. Meanwhile, preheat the grill. Pour the zabaglione over the oranges on the plates and top with the remaining orange segments. Cook under the grill for about 3 minutes, until the tops of the oranges are golden brown. Serve immediately.

Note: Prepare the orange segments a day in advance and leave them on a wire rack in the refrigerator so that they will not release too much juice when they are cooked. This dessert is delicious prepared with pink grapefruit.

1074

Melon and fig aspic

ASPIC DE MELÓN E HIGOS

- **1 sachet gelatine powder**
- **100 ml/3½ f l oz port**
- **4 figs**
- **1 cantaloupe or other melon, halved and seeded**
- **4 sprigs fresh parsley, plus extra to decorate**
- **150 g/5 oz emmenthal cheese, sliced**
- **12 thin slices of Serrano ham**

Serves 4

Prepare 500 ml/18 fl oz gelatine following the instructions on the packet and stir in the port. Pour a 1-cm/½-inch layer of warm gelatine into individual flan tins or dishes and chill in the refrigerator until set. Meanwhile, peel the figs and cut them into pieces. Scoop out balls of the melon flesh with a melon baller or teaspoon. Put pieces of fig, melon balls and a parsley sprig on the set gelatine in each tin or dish. Pour in the remaining gelatine and return to the refrigerator until set. To serve, dip the bases of the tins or dishes into hot water for a few seconds and run a round-bladed knife around the edge of each one, then turn the moulds out on to plates. Place alternating slices of cheese and ham around each mould and decorate with parsley.

1075

Marzipan cake
PONCHE AL ESTILO SEGOVIANO

Sponge:
- 3 eggs
- 25 g/1 oz caster sugar
- 80 g/3 oz self-raising flour
- icing sugar, to decorate

Filling:
- 500 ml/18 fl oz milk
- 3 egg yolks
- 2 tablespoons caster sugar
- 50 g/2 oz plain flour
- pinch of vanilla powder or
  a few drops of vanilla extract
- pinch of ground cinnamon

Marzipan:
- 40 g/1½ oz caster sugar
- 4 egg whites
- 50 g/2 oz ground almonds

Serves 4–6

Preheat the oven to 180°C/350°F/Gas Mark 4. Grease a Swiss roll tin with butter. line the base with greaseproof paper and grease with butter. First, make the sponge. Beat together the eggs, sugar and flour in a bowl. Spoon the mixture into the prepared tin and bake for 10 minutes. Remove from the oven, remove and discard the greaseproof paper and transfer to a wire rack to cool. Meanwhile, prepare the filling. Heat the milk in a saucepan. Beat the egg yolks with the sugar, flour, vanilla and cinnamon in a bowl. Gradually stir in the hot milk, a little at a time, then return the custard to the saucepan and cook, stirring constantly, for a few minutes until thickened. Remove the pan from the heat and set aside. Prepare the marzipan. Mix together the sugar and 1 tablespoon water in a saucepan and heat gently for a few minutes to make a syrup, then remove the pan from the heat. Whisk the egg whites in a clean, dry bowl until stiff peaks form, then add the almonds, then add the syrup. Mix well until firm, then heat gently in a saucepan, working the mixture until it acquires the desired consistency. To serve, cut the sponge into three long rectangles and pour the syrup over them. Spread half the filling on one sponge rectangle, put another sponge rectangle on top. Spread the remaining filling on top and add the remaining sponge rectangle. Cover with a layer of marzipan and sprinkle with icing sugar. Caramelize the marzipan with a salamander or kitchen blow torch.

1076

Santiago torte
TARTA DE SANTIAGO

- 250 g/9 oz butter, softened,
  plus extra for greasing
- 8 eggs
- 500 g/1 lb 2 oz caster sugar
- 400 g/14 oz plain flour
- 500 g/1 lb 2 oz ground almonds
- grated rind of 1 lemon
- icing sugar, to decorate

Serves 4–6

Preheat the oven to 180°C/350°F/Gas Mark 4. Grease a cake tin with butter. Beat the eggs with the sugar in a bowl until pale and fluffy, then add the flour, butter and 250 ml/8 fl oz water. Mix well, then stir in the ground almonds and lemon rind. Pour the mixture into the prepared tin and bake for about 30 minutes, until cooked through. Insert a wooden cocktail stick into the centre of the torte and if it comes out clean, the pie is cooked. Remove from the oven and leave the torte to cool in the tin, then turn it out. Sprinkle with icing sugar. For an attractive effect, cut out a simple cardboard stencil, such as a star, and hold this over the pie when you sprinkle it with the sugar.

Note: The torte can also be sprinkled with cocoa powder.

1077

Traditional Christmas biscuits

MANTECADAS

- butter, for greasing
- 750 g/1 lb 10 oz plain flour, plus extra for dusting
- 3 tablespoons caster sugar
- 400 g/14 oz lard
- juice of ½ lemon
- icing sugar and ground cinnamon, to decorate

Makes 8–9 dozen

Preheat the oven to 150°C/350°F/Gas Mark 2. Grease a baking sheet with butter. Sift the flour on to a marble slab, make a well in the centre and add the sugar, lard and lemon juice. Knead together until the dough is smooth, then leave to rest for 10 minutes. Using a floured rolling pin, roll out the dough on a lightly floured surface to about 8 mm/³⁄₈ inch thick. Stamp out small rounds or ovals with a 5-cm biscuit cutter. Put the little biscuits on to the pre-pared baking sheet (some people prefer to make a hole in the middle of each one). Bake for about 15 minutes, but do not allow them to brown. Remove the biscuits from the oven and sprinkle with icing sugar and ground cinnamon.

1078

French toasts in wine

TORRIJAS AL VINO

- 1 day-old white bread loaf, cut into 2-cm/¾-inch thick slices
- 500 ml/18 fl oz milk
- 3 tablespoons caster sugar
- 500 ml/18 fl oz red wine
- 3 eggs
- 500 ml/18 fl oz sunflower oil
- sugar and ground cinnamon, for sprinkling

Makes 20 slices

Put the slices of bread into a deep dish. Pour the milk into a saucepan, stir in the sugar and bring just to the boil. Remove the pan from the heat and pour the sweetened milk over the bread together with the wine. Leave to soak. Beat the eggs in a shallow dish. Heat the oil in a frying pan. One at a time, lift a slice of bread with a slotted spoon or tongs, coat it in the beaten eggs and add to the hot oil. Cook until golden brown on both sides, then remove from the pan and drain. Sprinkle the toasts with sugar and ground cinnamon and leave to cool. Serve warm or cold.

1079

Filled walnuts

NUECES RELLENAS

- 150 g/5 oz ground almonds
- 1 egg white
- 100 g/3½ oz icing sugar
- 65 g/2½ oz plain chocolate, grated
- 12 walnuts, halved and peeled

Makes 24 petits fours

Mix together the ground almonds, sugar and chocolate in a bowl until thoroughly combined. Shape the mixture into small balls. Place a walnut half on top of each ball and leave to harden in the refrigerator. Serve in petit four cases.

Note: Vary the flavour of these sweet treats by adding a spoonful of strong coffee or a favourite liqueur.

Nougat

TURRON DE JIJONA

- **250 g / 9 oz toasted almonds, chopped**
- **2 egg whites**
- **100 g / 3 ½ oz set honey**
- **500 g / 1 lb 2 oz caster sugar**
- **4–8 sheets of rice paper**

Serves 8–10

Pound the almonds to a paste in a mortar. Stir in the egg whites. Put the honey and sugar into a saucepan and bring to the boil, then remove the pan from the heat and stir them into the almond paste. Continue to stir without stopping for 10 minutes. Line two baking sheets with rice paper. Shape the mixture into bars and place them on the prepared baking sheets. Cover with rice paper and place a weight on top. Leave to dry out for at least 8 days.

Note: Instead of only almonds, you could use 150 g / 5 oz almonds and 100 g / 3 ½ oz hazelnuts.

MENUS
FROM
CELEBRATED
SPANISH CHEFS

The following pages contain menus from some of the world's favourite chefs cooking Spanish or Spanish-influenced food. From Spain to the United States, these chefs celebrate the best of Spanish cuisine — its simplicity and emphasis on the finest of ingredients — but offer that little extra genius in the kitchen that has made these chefs acknowledged across the world

1080 guest chefs

José Andrés	Washington, DC, USA
Pepe Balaguer	Valencia, Spain
Sam & Sam Clark	London, UK
Ramón Freixa	Barcelona, Spain
Andy Nusser	New York, USA
José Manuel Pizarro	London, UK
Alexandra Raij	New York, USA
Joan, Jordi & Joseph Roca	Gerona, Spain
Carme Ruscalleda	Sant Pol de Mar, Barcelona, Spain
Santi Santamaría	Sant Celoni, Barcelona, Spain

José Andrés

Restaurants: Zaytinya, Washington, DC; Jaleo, Maryland; Jaleo, Washington, DC; Minibar at Café Atlantico, Washington, DC

José Andrés is a multi-award winning Spanish chef. Early in his career he trained under Ferran Adrià at the famous restaurant El Bulli in Spain, and now he and his partners own several successful restaurants in Washington, DC. He has written a cookbook and produces and hosts a popular food programme on Spanish television.

Chilled tomato soup with garlic langoustines
GAZPACHO CONGAMAS AL AJILLO

- 900 g/2 lb ripe red tomatoes
- 1 medium cucumber
- ½ green pepper
- 1 clove garlic, peeled
- 1 tablespoon sherry vinegar
- 175 ml/6 fl oz Spanish extra-virgin olive oil
- sea salt
- finely chopped chives, to garnish

Garnish:
- 1 medium cucumber
- 4 plum tomatoes
- 1 red pepper
- 1 green pepper
- 2 shallots
- 4 slices of rustic bread

Langoustines:
- 4 tablespoons Spanish extra-virgin olive oil
- 6 cloves garlic, thinly sliced
- 20 large langoustines
- 1 dried chille
- 1 teaspoon brandy
- 1 teaspoon chopped parsley
- sea salt

Serves 5–6

To make the gazpacho, chop the tomatoes into quarters roughly and place in a food processor. Peel the cucumber, cut the flesh into chunks. Halve and deseed the pepper, and cut into large pieces. Transfer both to the food processor. Add the garlic and vinegar and blend. Add the oil and season with salt to taste. Pour the gazpacho through a strainer into a jug. Place in the refrigerator to cool for at least half an hour. Next, prepare the garnish. Cut the cucumber in half lengthways and remove the seeds. Sprinkle the flesh with salt and set aside for an hour to allow it to release its water. Rinse the cucumber well and dice into small pieces. Slice the ends off each tomato. Locate the fleshy dividing wall of one segment inside the tomato. Slice into the dividing wall and peel back the skin and flesh to expose the seeds. Remove the seeds taking care to keep the mass of seeds whole. (The point here is to extract the tomato seeds and their surrounding gel intact.) Repeat the process with the remaining tomatoes and set aside. Seed and dice the peppers. Dice the shallots. Combine the cucumber, pepper and shallots. Cut the bread into 1 cm/½-inch cubes and fry in olive oil over a medium heat until golden. When the soup is chilled, prepare the langoustines. In a medium sauté pan, heat the olive oil over a medium-high heat. Sauté the garlic for 2 minutes, or until browned. Add the langoustines and chilli and cook for 2 minutes each side. Pour in the brandy and cook for another minute. Sprinkle in the parsley and season. To serve, remove the gazpacho from the refrigerator. Place 3–4 langoustines and one tomato seed' fillet' in the middle of each bowl. Arrange the cucumber mixture around the edge and sprinkle the chives on top. Place four croûtons on the cucumber. Drizzle a little extra olive oil over the langoustines and add a few flakes of sea salt. Serve the gazpacho on the side.

Veal cheeks with La Serena mashed potatoes

CARRILLERAS DE TERNERA CON PURE DE PATATAS Y QUESO LA SERENA

- **4 cloves garlic,**
  whole and unpeeled
- **10 veal cheeks (cleaned)**
- **1 litre/1¾ pints Spanish**
  red wine, such as a Rioja
- **1 Spanish onion,**
  coarsely chopped
- **1 leek, outer leaves removed,**
  coarsely chopped
- **1 medium carrot,**
  coarsely chopped
- **3 sprig fresh rosemary**
- **4 sprigs fresh thyme**
- **3 teaspoons caster sugar**
- **50 ml/2 fl oz Spanish**
  extra-virgin olive oil
- **plain flour, for dusting**
- **veal stock**
- **1 black truffle**
- **1 tablespoon fresh chervil,**
  chopped
- **1 tablespoon fresh tarragon,**
  chopped
- **sea salt and black pepper**

  Potatoes:
- **450 g/1 lb potatoes**
  (we recommend Idaho potatoes),
  peeled and cut into chunks
- **120 ml/4 fl oz double cream**
- **80 g/3 oz La Serena cheese, rind**
  removed, cut into small cubes
- **50 ml/2 fl oz Spanish**
  extra-virgin olive oil
- **sea salt**

Serves 5

Split open the garlic cloves by placing them on a chopping board and pressing down on them hard with the flat side of a paring knife. In a mixing bowl, combine the veal cheeks with the wine, crushed garlic, onion, leek, carrot, rosemary and thyme. Cover and marinate in the refrigerator overnight. Preheat the oven to 150°C/300°F/Gas Mark 2. Remove the meat from the marinade and pat dry. Strain the marinade into another bowl, reserving the vegetables. Combine the sugar and reserved marinade in a small saucepan over a low heat. Cook until the wine reduces by half. Skim off any foam that appears on the surface. Set the pan aside to cool. Drain the vegetables well. Heat 1 tablespoon of the olive oil in a large sauté pan over a medium heat. When the oil is hot, add the vegetables and cook until soft and lightly browned. Add 2 tablespoons of olive oil to a saucepan and heat over a medium heat. Season the veal cheeks with salt and pepper and dip both sides in flour, shaking off any excess. Place the meat in the saucepan and cook for 1–2 minutes each side until the meat is brown. Set on paper towel to drain and discard the oil from the pan. Place the vegetables in a deep roasting pan. Lay the veal cheeks on top, without overlapping. Pour the reduced wine and sugar mixture over the top and add enough veal stock to cover. Place kitchen foil on top of the pan, and press down until it touches the contents. Transfer to the oven and cook for 2 ½–3 hours, until the meat is tender. Remove the pan from the oven carefully and, using a slotted spoon, place the veal pieces on a warm serving plate. Strain the remaining sauce through a fine sieve, into a bowl. Discard the vegetables and let the sauce sit for 5 minutes until the fat separates. Remove the fat. Place the veal cheeks and the strained sauce in a clean saucepan over a low heat. Cook until the sauce thickens and add salt to taste. Bring a large pot of water to the boil, add the potatoes and cook for 20 minutes until soft. Drain and mash thoroughly. In a small saucepan, heat the cream to boiling point. Set aside 1 tablespoon and add the rest to the potatoes. Mix with a wooden spoon until thoroughly combined, then add the cheese mixing vigorously until the cheese is fully incorporated. Gradually add the oil, stirring constantly until thoroughly combined. To serve, place a spoonful of mashed potato in the centre of each plate and top with two veal cheeks and a little of the veal-cheek sauce. Shave black truffle sparingly over the top and drizzle with a little truffle oil. Add a few flakes of sea salt, some chervil and tarragon to garnish.

Homestyle flan with crema catalana foam

FLAN CASERO CON ESPUMA DE CREMA CATALANA

- 120 ml/4 fl oz full-fat Jersey milk
- 120 ml/4 fl oz double cream
- 1 vanilla bean, split
- peel of 1 lemon
- 1 stick cinnamon
- 250 g/9 oz caster sugar
- 3 large eggs
- 2 large egg yolks
- orange supremes (see Note)
- mint

Caramel:
- 150 g/5 oz caster sugar

Espuma de crema catalana:
- 1 litre/1 ¾ pints full-fat
  Jersey milk
- 300 ml/½ pint double cream
- 250 g/9 oz sugar
- 12 egg yolks

Serves 4

Preheat the oven to 140°C/275°F/Gas Mark 1. To make the caramel, put the sugar in a small saucepan and cook over a low heat. After 5–6 minutes, the sugar will start to turn light brown. Cook for another 7–8 minutes until it becomes dark brown. Be careful to watch the mixture carefully as you don't want it to burn. Remove the pan from the heat and carefully add 120 ml/4 fl oz water. The caramel will spit and release steam as it hardens. Return the pan to the heat and, after about 5 minutes, the caramel will become thick and syrupy. Remove from the heat and allow to cool a little. Coat the bottom and sides of 4 small ramekins with the caramel, using your fingers or a spatula. Next, make the flan. In a medium saucepan, combine the Jersey milk and the cream. Add the vanilla bean and seeds, along with the lemon peel, cinnamon, and the sugar. Bring to the boil over a medium-high heat, removing the pan from the heat just as the liquid reaches boiling point. In a large bowl, whisk together the eggs and egg yolks. Carefully pour the hot cream mixture into the eggs, whisking vigorously. Strain the mixture into another bowl then fill the ramekins. Set the ramekins in a deep roasting pan. Carefully pour hot water into the pan to come halfway up the sides of the ramekins. Transfer to the oven and bake for 45 minutes. Remove and let the ramekins cool. (The flans can be stored in the refrigerator overnight.) While the flans are cooling, prepare the espuma. Combine the Jersey milk, cream and sugar in a small saucepan and bring to the boil. Gradually mix the eggs with about half the hot liquid, then add the remaining liquid, return the mixture to the pan and cook over a low heat for about 5 minutes, until thick. Remove the pan from the heat and allow the mixture to cool. Place in an iSi bottle or soda siphon with 2 charges of gas and charge. To serve, place a ramekin in the middle of a serving plate. Garnish with some of the espuma, and the orange supremes and mint leaves.

Note: To make orange supremes, remove the skin, pith, membranes and seeds of the fruit and separate into wedges.

Pepe Balaguer
Restaurant: La Pepica, Valencia

The restaurant La Pepica was a favourite of Ernest Hemingway, and has been popular with Spanish royalty and the food-loving public since it opened in 1898. La Pepica is widely credited with serving the best paella in Valencia.

Lobster paella
PAELLA DE BOGAVANTE

- ½ kg/1 lb white fish
  (croaker, haddock, grouper or
  any available white fish),
  cut into small chunks
- 1 carrot, finely chopped
- 1 onion, finely chopped
- 1 tomato,
  peeled and coarsely chopped
- 2 cloves garlic
- 2 sprigs fresh flat-leaf parsley,
  finely chopped
- 1 tablespoon olive oil
- 1 large live male lobster
- 1 teaspoon smoked paprika
- 1 tomato, peeled, de-seeded
  and cut into thin julienne strips
- 400 g/14 oz paella or risotto rice
  (such as Calaspara or canaroni)
- a few strands saffron
- salt

Serves 4–6

To prepare the stock:
Heat 3 litres/5 pints water in a large Dutch oven or stock pot and, when simmering, add the fish, carrot, onion and chopped tomato and cook for 45 minutes. Remove from the heat and pass through a sieve or vegetable mill into a large bowl. Crush 1 of the cloves of garlic with the parsley and olive oil in a mortar and set aside.

To prepare the rice:
Cut the lobster in half. Place a paella pan, measuring 40 cm/17 inches in diameter, over a medium heat and pour in a dash of olive oil. Add the halves of lobster and sauté them with the second, chopped, clove of garlic, the smoked paprika and the julienne strips of tomato. Add the rice and sauté. Next, pour in the stock, using two measures of liquid to one of rice (to a total volume of approximately 1 litre/ 1 ¾ pints). Stir, then add the saffron and salt to taste. Bring to the boil and cook for 10 minutes over a high heat, then add a spoonful of the garlic and parsley mixture from the mortar, reduce the heat to low and continue to boil for a further 10 minutes. Remove the paella pan from the heat and let stand for 5 minutes (if you can resist that long!) Serve this special paella straight from the pan.

Sam & Sam Clark

Restaurant: Moro, London

Sam and Sam Clark, business partners and husband and wife, opened the award-winning southern Mediterranean restaurant Moro in 1997, after spending three months travelling through Spain, Morocco and the Sahara. They were inspired by the local ingredients and regional cooking they had experienced and their passion and ideas can be seen in the Moorish cuisine and in the tapas they serve.

Grilled chicory with sherry vinegar and jamon

ENDIBIAS CON VINAIGRE DE JEREZ Y JAMON

- 2 large white chicory heads
- ½ small bunch flat-leaf parsley, roughly chopped
- 150 g/5 oz jamon pata negra or Serrano ham, thinly sliced

Dressing:
- 6 tablespoons sherry vinegar
- ½ clove garlic
- ½ teaspoon fresh thyme leaves
- 3 tablespoons extra-virgin olive oil
- salt and black pepper

Serves 4

To make the dressing, put the sherry vinegar into a small saucepan and place over a low heat until reduced to about 2 tablespoons (be careful not to let it cook for too long as it reduces very quickly). Crush the garlic and thyme with a good pinch of salt, preferably in a mortar with a pestle, to a smooth paste. Transfer to a bowl, add the reduced vinegar, some freshly ground black pepper and the olive oil. Set aside. To prepare the chicory, cut off the very end and remove any old, discoloured leaves, but keep the head intact. Cut the chicory heads in half lengthways and cut each length into thirds. Place the chicory on a hot griddle pan, barbecue or grill over medium heat, and, when one side is slightly charred, carefully turn the chicory and grill the other side (this will not take very long). Add the dressing immediately, along with the parsley. To serve, fan the chicory out on a serving plate, and serve the jamon alongside.

Note: This recipe balances the rich, salty jamon with the nutty sherry vinegar and bitter chicory.

Whole baked sea bass with roast beetroot and almond and sherry-vinegar sauce

LUBINA RELLENA AL HORNO

- 1 large (1.5 kg/3¼ lb) sea bass, scaled and gutted
- 1½ teaspoons Maldon sea salt
- ½ teaspoon coarsely ground black pepper
- 4 flat-leaf parsley stems

Preheat the oven to 230°C/450°F/Gas 8. Rinse the fish inside and out, pat dry, then season inside and out with the sea salt and pepper. Stuff the cavity with the parsley stems, lemon slices, fennel stalks, fennel seeds and bay leaves. Toss the sliced fennel bulb and red onion with 4 tablespoons of the olive oil, the white wine, and a little salt and pepper. Spread the sliced vegetables in a thin layer to cover

- **4 thin slices lemon**
- **2 medium fennel bulbs,**
  stalks removed and reserved,
  bulb sliced into
  ½ cm-/¼ inch- thick wedges
- **1 teaspoon whole fennel seeds**
- **2 bay leaves**
- **1 red onion, thinly sliced**
- **6 tablespoons extra-virgin**
  olive oil
- **6 tablespoons white wine**
- **salt and black pepper**
  Serves 4

the base of a large roasting pan, then place the fish on top. Drizzle the fish with the remaining oil, and transfer to the oven. Bake until just cooked through (this will take about 35 – 40 minutes). Remove from the oven and set aside to rest for 5 minutes before serving, either in the roasting pan or on a serving dish with the fennel on the side.

Note: A whole baked fish is perfect for a dinner or lunch party, hot or at room temperature. In the summer when fennel is at its peak, it is a great way to use up a glut of this delicious vegetable.

Roast beetroot:
- **1 kg/2¼ lb young beetroot,**
  washed carefully and halved
- **3 sprigs fresh thyme,**
  leaves picked
- **½ clove garlic crushed with salt**
- **5 tablespoons olive oil**
- **1 tablespoon red-wine vinegar**
- **salt and pepper**
  Serves 4

Roast beetroot with thyme
Place the washed beetroot in a mixing bowl. Sprinkle over the thyme, add the garlic, olive oil, vinegar and a little salt and pepper and toss well. Transfer to a roasting pan and cover tightly with kitchen foil. Place in the preheated oven and cook for 30 minutes (see recipe above), then remove the foil and continue roasting for a further 20–30 minutes or until the beetroot are tender. Serve as a side dish with the Whole baked sea bass and the Almond and sherry-vinegar sauce (see above and below).

Almond and sherry-vinegar
sauce:
- **150 g/5 oz whole**
  blanched almonds
- **25 g/1 oz stale white bread,**
  crusts removed, soaked in water
- **1 clove garlic, crushed with salt**
- **½–¾ tablespoon sherry vinegar**
- **1½ tablespoons capers,**
  soaked in water, squeezed and
  finely chopped (optional)
- **sea salt**
  Serves 4

Almond and sherry-vinegar sauce
In a food processor, grind the almonds to as fine a consistency as possible. Add 3 tablespoons water and process until the almonds form a paste. Squeeze the bread of excess water and add to the almonds along with the garlic. Combine until smooth. Mix together 5 tablespoons water with the sherry, then slowly add the almond mixture, until you end up with a thick cream with a smooth consistency similar to mayonnaise. Transfer to a bowl, add the capers, if using, and season with salt to taste.

Malaga raisin ice cream

HELADO DE PASAS DE MALAGA

- **600 ml/1 pint double cream**
- **300 ml/½ pint milk**
- **1 small cinnamon stick**
- **1 vanilla pod**
- **7 egg yolks**
- **85 g/3 oz caster sugar**
- **100 g/3½ oz raisins covered with 100 ml/3½ fl oz Pedro Ximenez sherry or Pedro Ximinez Malaga wine**

Serves 8 (makes just over 1 litre)

Place the cream, milk and cinnamon stick in a large saucepan. Split the vanilla pod in half lengthways and scrape the tiny seeds into the pan, discarding the pod. Heat until just below boiling point, then remove the pan from the stove. In a bowl, beat the egg yolks and sugar together for 5–10 minutes until the mixture is pale and thick. Loosen the egg mixture by stirring in a little of the cream and milk mixture, then pour the egg mixture into the saucepan, scraping the bowl out with a spatula. Whisk well to mix everything properly and return to a low heat, stirring constantly. Heat gently but be careful not to curdle the mixture. When it thickens and just before it bubbles, remove from the heat, pour into a bowl and place over ice water to cool. Churn in an ice cream machine, in batches if necessary, adding the raisins and sherry towards the end of the churning. (For those without an ice cream machine, you can freeze the ice cream by hand, but remember to stir every half-hour to prevent ice crystals forming. Stirring will also help to distribute the raisins evenly as they tend to sink to the bottom before the ice cream is hard enough to suspend them.) The churning process will take about 2 hours, depending on the temperature of your freezer or the specification of your ice cream maker. Serve the ice cream with a chilled glass of Pedro Ximenez on the side or poured over the top.

Note: Although this is a very simple recipe (using a basic custard for the ice cream) complexity and flavour is provided by the sherry. The raisins are soaked in Pedro Ximenez sherry, a treacly, sweet, raisiny sherry made from Pedro Ximenez grapes, that have been first dried in the sun to concentrate their sugar and taste.

Ramón Freixa

Restaurant: El Raco d'en Freixa, Barcelona

Ramón Freixa's passion for cooking began in his grandparents' bakery. He has worked in some of the best kitchens of Europe, and in 1998, after four years at his father's restaurant, Ramón was given control of the kitchen. From this point, he has continued to create award-winning food at El Racó d'en Freixa – and also finds time to promote Spanish cuisine in newspapers, radio, television and in three cookbooks, making him a worthy winner of many awards.

Minted baby beans with cucumber and algae ice-cream
BOCADILLO DE HABITAS A LA MENTA CON COHOMBROS Y HELADO DE ALGAS

- 500 ml/18 fl oz single cream
- 500 ml/18 fl oz full-cream milk
- 400 g/14 oz fresh algae (such as sea lettuce or laver bread)
- 20 g/¾ oz ice cream stabilizer
- 12 egg yolks
- 300 ml/½ pint mint water
- 10 g/¼ oz xantana gum
- 500 g/1 lb 2 oz broad beans, cooked
- 1 clove garlic, finely chopped
- 100 ml/3½ fl oz olive oil
- 1 loaf rustic bread, thinly sliced
- 1 handful ficoide glacial (ice plant)
- 1 handful Ceylon spinach
- 1 handful mitzuna
- 1 handful frisee
- 1 head chicory
- 'Picada Catalana' oil, for drizzling
- 1 tablespoon chervil, chopped
- 400 g/14 oz cucumber
- 1 tablespoon groundnut oil

Serves 8–10

To make the algae ice cream, put the cream, milk, algae, ice cream stabilizer and egg yolks into a blender and pulse until thoroughly combined. Strain the mixture and set aside in the refrigerator for 12 hours. Pour into an ice cream maker and follow the manufacturer's instructions. (If an ice cream maker is unavailable, place the mixture in a deep dish and freeze, stirring every 20 minutes to prevent ice crystals from forming.) To make the mint jelly, bring the mint water to the boil and add the xantana gum. Leave to set in a shallow tray or pan and when solid, cut into cubes. Once the ice cream and the mint jelly have been made, you can start to make the other components of the recipe. Rinse the broad beans, blanch them, then remove their pale skins. Mix the chopped garlic with the olive oil. Preheat the oven to 170°C/340°F/Gas Mark 3. Cut the bread into long, thin slices and brush with the garlic-infused oil. Bake the coated bread slices for 10 minute, then, set aside and keep warm until ready to serve. Dress the salad leaves with the Picada Catalana oil, and add a little chopped chervil. Set aside until ready to serve. Peel the cucumber and cut off the ends. Slice lengthways and scoop out the seeds. Cut the flesh into slices 1 cm/¼ inch thick. Heat the groundnut oil in a frying pan and add the cucumber. Cook over a medium heat until begining to shine. Remove from the pan and keep warm. To serve, place several slices of warm garlic bread on a plate and top with the beans, then add another slice of bread, the cucumber and salad leaves. Place a spoonful of the mint jelly and a ball of algae ice cream to the side.

Note: To make mint water, twist or bruise 1 handful mint leaves, place in a clean 1½ litre/2½ pint container and fill with still mineral water.

Chill in the refrigerator for 24 hours, strain and use. Xantana gum is available from online retailers but, if not available, subtitute gelatine leaves. The 'picada' oil, which is a Catalan speciality is made with olive oil, raisins, pine nuts and hazelnuts and is available from online suppliers. Ice plant, Ceylon spinach, mitzuna, frisee and chicory may be hard to obtain. If so, try substituting a different selection of salad leaves and experiment until you find a combination you like.

Hazelnut cream with pheasant and truffle ravioli
CREMA DE AVELLANAS CON RAVIOLI DE FAISAN I TRUFA

- 200 g/7 oz pumpkin
- 2 tablespoons groundnut oil
- 1 shallot, chopped
- 200 g/7 oz roast pheasant,
  finely chopped
- 1 semi-sweet biscuit, crushed
- 1 black truffle (melanosporum),
  very finely chopped
- 12 sheets ravioli pasta
- 1 egg, lightly beaten
- salt and pepper

Smoked milk foam:
- 4 sheets gelatine
- 2 teaspoons smoked salt
- 1 litre/1¾ pints milk

Cream of hazelnut :
- 500 g/1 lb 2 oz hazelnuts,
  toasted in their skins
- 1 litre/1¾ pints chicken stock
- 400 ml/14 fl oz of single cream

Contrasting Garnishes:
- alpine or wild strawberries
- quince jelly
- enoki or other fresh mushrooms,
  raw or lightly fried
- toasted pine nuts
- black truffle, thinly sliced

Serves 6

First, make the filling for the ravioli. Roast the pumpkin in the groundnut oil for 30 minutes in a hot oven. Fry the shallot until transluscent and add the roast pumpkin and the pheasant. Mix in the crushed biscuit and the truffle, season to taste with salt and pepper and set aside. Next, assemble the ravioli. Lay out half the pasta sheets and place generous teaspoons of the pheasant mixture at regular spaced intervals on the pasta. Add the pasta 'lids', seal with the beaten egg, cut and set aside. To make the smoked milk foam, first soak the sheets of gelatine in warm water until spongy. Add the smoked salt to the milk and bring to the boil. When the milk is boiling, add the sheets of gelatine and leave the mixture to thicken. Place in a soda siphon with 2 charges of gas and set aside. To make the cream of hazelnut, finely chop the hazelnuts. Pour the chicken stock and cream into a deep saucepan and heat gently. When the milk and stock mixture is hot, add the hazelnuts and strain. Add salt and pepper to taste and strain again. Place the pan over a bowl of hot water to keep it warm. Bring a large saucepan of water to the boil and cook the ravioli until al dente. When cooked remove from the saucepan and transfer to a ridged frying pan coated with a little groundnut oil to 'mark' them. To serve, arrange a selection of the contrasting garnishes in an irregular pattern on each plate alongside the pheasant and pumpkin ravioli. Top with the smoked milk froth and serve the cream of hazelnut separately in a soup tureen.

Note: To prepare roast pheasant, first ensure it is clean and free from feathers. Preheat the oven to 170°C/340°F/Gas Mark 3 and truss the bird(s) as you would a chicken. Rub the skin with half a tablespoon goose fat and roast breast-side down in a deep pan for 40 minutes, covered with foil. Then turn the bird over and cook for 20 minutes at 200°C/400°F/Gas 6 with the breasts covered with bacon if you like. Smoked sea salt is available from specialist retailers.

Chocolate mousse tartlets

TARTALETA DE MOUSSE COCIDA

Pastry:
- **750 g/1 lb 7 oz butter**
- **350 g/12 oz caster sugar**
- **400 g/14 oz ground almonds**
- **1.3 kg/1 lb 14 oz plain flour**
- **300 g/11 oz unsweetened cocoa**
- **20 g/¾ oz salt**
- **450 g/1 lb eggs**

Filling:
- **250 g/9 oz gianduja chocolate (70 % cocoa solids)**
- **100 g/3½ oz butter**
- **120 g/4 oz egg yolks**
- **80 g/3 oz caster sugar**
- **160 g/5½ oz egg whites**

Serves 8–10

To make the pastry, cut the butter into cubes, place in a food processor with a mixing blade and add the caster sugar, ground almonds and 400 g/14 oz of the flour. When the mixture is smooth, sift the remaining flour with the cocoa and salt into a clean bowl and add the eggs, mixing well until fully incorporated. Let the dough rest in a cool place until needed. Preheat the oven to 170°C/340°F/Gas Mark 3. To make the mousse filling, melt the gianduja chocolate with the butter in a double-boiler. In a large bowl, whisk the egg yolks with half the sugar until fully incorporated. In another bowl, whisk the egg whites until they form peaks. Pour the melted chocolate into the egg yolks and mix until combined, then carefully fold in the whites. Roll out the pastry and use it to line 7 cm/2 ¾ inch tartlet tins. Add baking beans or pastry weights and bake 'blind' for 10 minutes. Remove the baking beans or pastry weights and fill the pastry cases with the mousse mixture. Increase the oven temperature to 180°C/360°F/Gas Mark 4, return the tartlets to the oven and cook for 8 minutes.

Andy Nusser

Restaurant: Casa Mono, New York

Andy Nusser grew up in Spain in the 1970s, where he began his career in food as a dish washer at Casa Nun restaurant in the village of Cadaques. Andy went on to New York where he cooked with Mario Batali in the tiny kitchen of Po before becoming executive chef of the award-winning Babbo. Nusser and partners opened the popular Casa Mono and Bar Jamon in 2003, which has gone on to be the number one Zagat-rated Spanish restaurant in New York City.

Langoustines with Gazpacho Salad

LANGOSTINOS CON GAZPACHO ENSALADA

- 8 large langoustines or Dublin Bay prawns
- ½ loaf baguette, cut in 1¼ cm / ½ inch dice
- 180 ml / 6 fl oz olive oil
- 1 red onion, sliced into 6 wedges
- 4 piquillo peppers
- 6 tablespoons red-wine vinegar
- salt and pepper

Spicy Candied Tomatoes:
- 1 pint cherry tomatoes
- 2 cups sugar
- 1 tablespoon kosher salt
- 1 tablespoon crushed red pepper
- 1 cinnamon stick

Gazpacho salad:
- 120 g / ¼ lb sea beans
- 1 cucumber, peeled and cubed
- 8 piquillo peppers, sliced into 1¼ cm / ½ inch strips
- salt and pepper

Serves 4

Cut the langoustines from head to tail down both sides with kitchen scissors. Peel off their shells and drop them into boiling salted water and cook for two minutes. Plunge the cooked langoustines into a bowl of ice water and then dry on a clean towel. Next make the spicy candied tomatoes. Bring a medium saucepan of water to the boil and blanch the tomatoes for 15 seconds each before plunging them into a bowl of ice water to cool. In the same saucepan, combine 1 cup water with the sugar, salt, red pepper and the cinnamon stick, sim-mering over a medium heat until the sugar has dissolved. Drain and peel the tomatoes, then place them in a dry bowl. Strain the sugar syrup over the tomatoes and let stand until cool. To make the croûtons, preheat the oven to 180°C/350°F/Gas Mark 4 and toss the diced bread on a baking tray with 2 tablespoons of the olive oil. Season to taste and bake for about 10 minutes until golden brown. On another baking tray, toss the onion wedges with 2 tablespoons of the red-wine vine-gar and the 2 tablespoons of the remaining olive oil. Season with salt and pepper and add to the oven to bake for 20 minutes. After the onions are cooked, cool and separate 4 of the wedges into 'petals'. To make the gazpacho salad, bring a medium saucepan of water to the boil. Add the sea beans and blanch for 15 seconds. Plunge the beans into ice water to cool and then drain on a clean towel. Add the cucum-ber and pepper strips. Finally, to prepare the gazpacho vinaigrette, combine the 2 whole wedges of the roasted onion, 4 spicy candied tomatoes and four piquillo peppers with the remaining red-wine vine-gar and the remaining olive oil in a blender or food processor and pulse until fully combined. To serve, toss the different elements of the dish in the gazpacho vinaigrette, top with the langoustines and dress with more vinaigrette.

Note: Sea beans are also known in the US as marsh samphire, salicornia, sea pickle or glasswort. They are available fresh along the atlantic and pacific coasts but can also be bought pickled and in jars. In north-western Europe, a very similar plant called samphire is more common, though not commonly available. Both varieties of plant have a salty or even fishy taste and are prized among gourmands.

Sweetbreads with Fennel al Mono
MOLLEJAS CON FENNEL AL MONO

- **1 kg/2¼ lb sweetbreads**
- **12 baby fennel bulbs,**
  fronds attached
- **500 ml/18 fl oz olive oil**
- **1 tablespoon anchovy paste**
- **120 ml/4 fl oz Anis del Mono**
- **50 ml/2 fl oz white-wine vinegar**
- **250 g/9 oz ground almonds**
- **250 g/9 oz Wondra flour**
  or plain flour
- **salt and pepper**

Almond vinaigrette:
- **250 g/9 oz salted and**
  fried marcona almonds
- **250 ml/8 fl oz almond oil**
- **50 ml/2 fl oz sherry vinegar**

Serves 6–8

Rinse the sweetbreads under cold running water and then soak them overnight in 1 litre/1 ¾ pints of cold water combined with 50 ml/2 fl oz white-wine vinegar. The next day, blanch them in boiling seasoned water for 1–2 minutes before plunging them into ice water and laying them out to drain on a towel-covered tray. Remove the membranes and divide the sweetbreads into portions, each made up of 3 pieces and weighing 150–175 g/5–6 oz. Trim the baby fennel bulbs, reserving the fennel fronds, then blanch in seasoned boiling water for 5 minutes, before plunging into ice water to stop the cooking process. Dry on clean towels, then cut the bulbs in half lengthwise. Heat 100 ml/3 ½ fl oz of the olive oil in a frying pan and cook the baby fennel until golden. Add the anchovy paste and the Anis del Mono, stirring until combined. Remove from the heat and set aside to cool. To make the almond vinaigrette, first grind the marcona almonds coarsely in a food processor. Transfer to a clean bowl and fold in the almond oil and sherry vinegar with a spoon. Heat the remaining olive oil in a frying pan over a medium-high heat. Prepare a dusting mixture by combining the ground almonds and flour in a bowl. Season the sweetbread portions, dust them thoroughly in the almond mixture and pan fry in the olive oil until golden brown and crispy. Remove from the pan and drain on paper towels, seasoning again to taste. To serve, place three pieces of fennel al mono on each plate, top them with 3 fried sweetbreads and add the almond vinaigrette. Garnish with the reserved fennel fronds.

Note: Marcona almonds are native only to Spain. They are large and flat in shape and have a more delicate and sweet flavour than other almonds. Wondra flour is a variety of wheat flour to which some malted barley flour has been added; if it is not available, you can substitute Instant Flour or plain flour.

Rhubarb Flan

RUIBARTO FLAN

- 1 litre/1¾ pints double cream
- 1 cinnamon stick
- 1 vanilla bean
- 3 sheets gelatine, softened in warm water until spongy
- 8 egg yolks
- 200g/7oz caster sugar

Rhubarb Marmalade:
- 50ml/2floz grenadine
- 2 tablespoons brown sugar
- 4 stalks rhubarb (including whites), cut into small dice
- 2 sheets gelatine, softened in water until spongy

Serves 6–8

Preheat the oven to 160°C/325°F/Gas Mark 3. Place the cream, cinnamon stick and vanilla bean in a large saucepan and heat gently. When the cream is almost boiling, add the sheets of softened gelatine to the cream, one sheet at a time, stirring constantly. Whisk the egg yolks and the sugar in a large bowl until smooth and then whisk in half of the hot cream. Pour back into the large saucepan and heat, stirring the mixture with a wooden spoon, to a point at which the back of the spoon is coated with the custard when stirring. Ensure the ingredients are incorporated thoroughly but be careful not to overcook the mixture and remove the pan from the heat if necessary. Strain the mixture through a cone shaped strainer, pressing the vanilla pod against it to ensure you extract as much flavour as possible. Pour the mixture into a heatproof jug and then three-quarter fill 6–8 ramekins or individual cocottes. Place these in a roasting pan and add cold water to the pan to come halfway up the sides of the ramekins. Cover the roasting pan with kitchen foil, transfer to the oven and bake for 35 minutes. To make the rhubarb marmalade, bring the grenadine and brown sugar to a boil over a medium heat. Add the rhubarb, stirring constantly. Do not look away at this point as the rhubarb cooks in less than 5 minutes. Process the mixture in a blender or food proc-essor. Add the softened gelatine sheets. Top each flan with one tablespoon of the rhubarb mixture. Remove the foil carefully from the roasting pan and check that the custard has set. Place the ramekins in the refrigerator to cool.

José Manuel Pizarro

Restaurant: Tapas Brindisa, London

José Manuel Pizarro spent his early years working in a number of Spain's best restaurants and has been cooking in London since 2002. He is currently the head chef at Tapas Brindisa, the restaurant named after and supplied by the much-loved Brindisa shops owned by Monika Linton, who has been sourcing the best Spanish produce for her shops in Exmouth and Borough markets for years. Her specialist knowledge of local Spanish producers means Tapas Brindisa is able to source ingredients, such as cheeses, charcuterie and store-cupboard provisions from local producers all over Spain. José then uses his flair and imagination to turn them into a delicious range of tapas.

Cecina with Pomegranate and Endive Salad

ENSALADA DE CECINA CON GRANADA Y ENDIVIAS

- **200 g/7 oz cecina**
- **3 tablespoons olive oil**
- **1½ tablespoons moscatel vinegar**
- **1½ tablespoons orange blossom honey**
- **seeds of one small pomegranate**
- **1 small endive**
- **1 tablespoon chopped fresh parsley**
- **salt and pepper**

Serves 4

Divide the cecina among 4 plates and season with black pepper to taste. In a bowl, mix the oil, vinegar and honey until well combined and then add the pomegranate seeds. Place the endive and parsley in another bowl, dress with the vinaigrette and season to taste. Arrange the endive on top of the cecina and serve.

Note: Cecina is similar to the Italian cured meat bresaola in texture and appearance. The best-known cecina is Cecina de Leon, which is Spanish air-dried and smoked cured beef made from the hind legs of cattle. Moscatel vinegar is a pale amber vinegar made from moscatel grapes, which is much prized for its bittersweet flavour.

Pan-fried chicken with Romesco sauce

POLLO CON SALSA ROMESCO

- **2 whole baby chickens (poussins), deboned**
- **2 tablespoons olive oil**
- **1 tablespoon chopped parsley**
- **salt and pepper**

  Romesco sauce:
- **1 ñora (dried red pepper)**
- **80 ml/3 fl oz olive oil**
- **1 clove garlic, chopped**
- **1 small slice rustic bread**
- **200 g/7 oz roasted tomatoes**
- **25 g/1 oz toasted almonds**
- **1 teaspoon sherry vinegar**
- **salt and pepper**

  Serves 2

First make the Romesco sauce. Leave the ñora to soak overnight before you begin cooking, then scoop out its centre. Heat 2 tablespoons of the olive oil in a frying pan and cook the garlic and the slice of bread until golden, then remove and leave to cool. Put the pepper, garlic and bread mixture into a food processor or blender. Add the roasted tomatoes, toasted almonds and vinegar and mix until smooth. Season with salt and pepper to taste. Heat the olive oil in a frying pan. Season the chickens and fry until golden brown all over. To serve, place a tablespoon of Romesco sauce in the centre of two dinner plates and position the baby chickens on top. Sprinkle with a little olive oil and add the chopped parsley before serving.

Note: Instead of the ñora, peppers of varying sweetness or hotness can be used, depending on taste. A teaspoon of pepper flesh is sufficient for this recipe.

Fillet steak on toast with caramelized onion and torta de barros

FILETES DE SOLOMILLO CON CEBOLLA CARAMELIZADA Y TORTA DE BARROS

- **1 tablespoon olive oil**
- **4 fillet steaks (approx. 200 g/7 oz each)**
- **200 g/7 oz torta de barros cheese, cut into 4 pieces**
- **4 slices of rustic bread, toasted**
- **salt and pepper**
- **1 tablespoon fresh oregano, chopped**

  Caramelized onion:
- **6 tablespoons olive oil**
- **750 g/1 lb 9 oz onions, finely sliced**
- **1 teaspoon caster sugar**
- **1 small bay leaf**

  Serves 4

To make the caramelized onion, heat the oil in a large saucepan with a lid and then add the onion, sugar and bay leaf. Cover and cook over a low heat, stirring occasionally, until the onion turns a deep brown. This will take approximately 60 minutes. Heat the oil in a frying pan, add the steaks and cook to taste. Season and add the cheese to one side of the pan so that it begins to melt. To serve, put a spoonful of caramelized onion on each slice of the toasted bread, add the steaks on top and then sprinkle with the oregano.

Alexandra Raij

Restaurant: Tia Pol, New York

Alexandra Raij is the chef and partner of two Manhattan tapas bars, Tia Pol, and El Quinto Pino. She cooks alongside her Basque husband Eder Montero, who is a native of Bilbao. Together the two have set a new standard for Spanish food and the tapas tradition in New York. Alex's preoccupation with good cooking and eating was cultivated at home where her food-passionate parents exposed her to the pleasures of cooking, eating and gathering around the table. Her parents, originally from Argentina, embraced the diversity of cuisines available in the US. This encouraged her deep interest in new flavours and ways of eating and gave her an enduring love of cookbooks.

Baby romaine hearts with Spanish anchovy vinaigrette

COGOLLITOS CON VINAGRETA DE ANCHOAS

- **12 baby romaine heads or 6 commercially-grown romaine hearts**
- **18 Spanish or other mild anchovies, packed in oil**
- **250 ml/8 fl oz extra-virgin olive oil**
- **2 cloves garlic, minced**
- **80 g/3 oz Panko breadcrumbs**
- **1½ tablespoons Smoked Pimenton de la Vera**
- **50 ml/2 fl oz seasoned rice wine vinegar**
- **¼ teaspoon salt**

Serves 6

Trim the ends of each lettuce without detaching the leaves from the stalk. Cut each lettuce head in half, vertically through the stem end, and submerge in cool water shaking off any dirt or sand (if using commercial romaine hearts cut them in quarters lengthways). Pat the lettuces dry and set aside, cut side down, on paper towels until ready to use (in the refrigerator if cleaning ahead). To make the vinaigrette, heat a small saucepan over a medium heat with 12 of the anchovies (the best anchovies are from Ondaorroa), breaking them up with a spoon as they 'melt'. Add half of the oil, and the garlic and breadcrumbs and stir until both are brown and you have a paste. Remove from the heat and add the paprika. Stir to combine and add the vinegar. Add the salt and 2 tablespoons water to a blender or processor, turn the motor to its lowest setting and slowly add ½ the anchovy paste. Add the remaining oil in a thin stream and follow with the rest of the anchovy paste. Season to taste and adjust the salt or acidity as needed, remembering that vinegars have different acid values and you want the vinaigrette to be slightly acidic. Set aside in the refrigerator if not using immediately. To serve, place 2 baby romaine heads (4 halves), cut side up on each plate. Spoon the thick vinaigrette over the lettuces. Cut the remaining anchovies into long slices and drape over the lettuce, drizzling with extra olive oil, if you like.

Note: The vinaigrette can be made a day ahead of serving. You can substitute the seasoned rice wine vinegar with sherry vinegar with

1 tsp sugar dissolved in it. This recipe is wonderful in the summer when the farmers' markets are full of the small baby lettuce heads that are so prized in Spain. However, if you are not lucky enough to find them, commercially grown romaine hearts can be substituted.

Salt-baked sea bream with green olive and pinenut vinaigrette

DORADA A LA SAL CON SALSA MARIANITO

- 3 sea bream (700 g/1½ lb each), filleted, skin on
- 500 g/1 lb 2 oz kosher salt

Vinaigrette:
- 4 tablespoons pinenuts, toasted
- 4 tablespoons pitted and chopped green manzanilla olives
- 3 tablespoons minced red onion
- 3 tablespoons thinly sliced spring onion (light green and white parts only)
- 4 tablespoons Spanish pickled green guindilla pepper
- 1 teaspoon sugar
- 250 ml/8 fl oz best-quality Spanish extra-virgin olive oil
- 3 tablespoons rice wine vinegar
- 1 tablespoon sherry vinegar
- salt, to taste

Serves 6

To make the vinaigrette, mix all the ingredients together in a bowl and reserve until the fish is ready. To prepare the fish, first remove the pin bones and pat dry. Lightly oil a baking sheet with olive oil and place the fillets on it, skin side up. Mix the salt and 250 ml/8 fl oz water to make a rough paste and divide among the fillets, making sure the salt mixture stays only on the skin and does not touch the flesh. Place under a pre-heated grill about 10 cm/4 inches from the heat for approximately 5–7 minutes. The salt will form a hard crust and promote an even cooking. When the fish is ready, remove the salt crust carefully by lifting it off each fillet with the help of a small spatula. Carefully pull back the skin, which should come off without resistance. Discard the skin, transfer the fillets to individual plates and top with 2–3 teaspoons of the vinaigrette.

Note: If Spanish pickled green guindilla pepper is not available, you can substitute mild pepperoncini. The vinaigrette may be made up to one day ahead, but make sure that you bring it back to room temperature 1 hour before serving.

Orange flan

FLAN DE NARANJA

- **400 g/14 oz sugar**
- **400 ml/14 fl oz orange juice**
- **120 ml/4 fl oz cold water**
- **2 whole eggs**
- **8 egg yolks**
- **juice of 1 lemon**
- **1 teaspoon cornflour**

Serves 6

First, place half the sugar in a small saucepan and add water to cover. Heat the mixture without stirring until the sugar dissolves and turns medium-dark amber in colour. When it reaches this stage, quickly pour this mixture into the bottom of 6 (120 g/4 oz) ramekins and set aside to cool completely. Preheat the oven to 150°C/300°F/Gas Mark 2. Bring the orange juice and half of the remaining sugar to the boil and then cool slightly by adding 120 ml/4 fl oz cold water. In a medium bowl, whisk the eggs, extra yolks, remaining sugar, lemon juice and cornflour. Slowly add the orange juice mixture to the egg mixture, whisking constantly until combined. Pass the mixture through a fine sieve to remove the fruit pulp and egg membranes. Place the sugared ramekins in a roasting pan and fill them with the custard mixture. Pour hot water into the roasting pan to come three-quarters of the way up the sides of the ramekins and cover the roasting pan with kitchen foil. Pierce the foil many times to allow steam to escape during cooking. Carefully place the pan on the middle shelf of the oven and bake for 20 minutes. Lift the foil to let more steam escape and continue baking until the custard is set, which should be approximately another 10–15 minutes. Allow the custards to cool at room temperature then cover and chill in the refrigerator. To serve, run a warmed knife around the inside edges of the ramekins and tip the custards out onto individual plates.

Note: This is a very fresh and light flan due to the absence of cream.

The Roca Brothers

Restaurant: El Celler de Can Roca, Gerona

Joan, Joseph and Jordi are the third generation of a family that has been dedicated to the restaurant business since the 1920s. Since 1986, they have run El Celler de Can Roca, in Gerona, near Barcelona, where Joseph is in charge of the dining room and wines, Jordi the baking, and Joan is the chef. The three, who are noted exponents of the art of 'Molecular Gastronomy', have won international recognition and awards for everything from their food to the wine, cigars and baking of their restaurant.

Asparagus with Viognier

ESPARRAGOS CON VIOGNIER

- 500 g/1 lb 2 oz asparagus
- 200 ml/7 fl oz single cream at room temperature
- 40 g/1½ oz powdered egg white
- 2 g xantana
- truffle oil
- crystallised lemon peel, to garnish
- powdered holm oak, to burn

Metil celulosa:
- 150 ml/5 fl oz mineral water
- 5 g metil

Viognier:
- 200 ml/7 fl oz Viognier
- 1 g xantana

Serves 4–6

Cut off and reserve the tips of the asparagus spears. Heat a grill plate or barbecue grill to hot and cook the asparagus. When cool enough to handle, peel the asparagus and mix them in a bowl with the cream. Add the egg white and xantana. Chop and strain. Put into a soda siphon with two charges of gas and keep in a bain marie (we use a Roner) at 62°C/143°F. To prepare the metil celulosa, mix the mineral water with the metil and leave to stand at 3°C/37°F for approximately 12 hours. Mix the Viognier and the xantana and leave to stand. Preheat the oven to 150°C/300°F/Gas Mark 2. Cut the asparagus tips into thin slices and blanch in boiling water. Cut strips of paper to line the inside of metal cooking rings of 10 cm/4 inch diameter. Place the paper flat on a chopping board, putting the asparagus slices, overlapping, along the length of the paper, like a picket fence. Pour the metil through a sieve to cover the asparagus. Carefully line each ring with a strip of paper and asparagus and bake for 5 minutes to allow the metil to solidify. Move the rings to individual serving plates and fill the centres with the asparagus froth from the soda siphon. Carefully remove the ring and the paper. Finish the dish with the Viognier, peel and truffle oil. Cover each round with a glass dome, place the powdered holm oak in a specialist culinary pipe, burn it and introduce the smoke into the dome. Take the dome off the dish at the table.

Note: Xantana is used to thicken sauces and soups and is available from online retailers. Mentil is a form of gelatine (available as a powder), extracted from the cellulose of vegetables. When used cold, it acts as a thickener but jellifies when heat is added. Powdered egg white is available from online retailers.

Oyster in cava

OSTRA AL CAVA

- **4 oysters**
- **1 Royal Gala apple, cored**
- **1g agar agar**
- **1.6 g xanatana**
- **400 g Cava, or other sparking**
  white wine
- **toasted, sliced almonds**
- **breadcrumbs made with**
  spiced bread
- **curry powder**
- **crystallised lemon**

  Serves 4

Make an apple compote by liquidizing the apple. Cool and decant the liquid, eliminating the pulp and leaving a clear, transparent water. Measure 100 ml/3 ½ fl oz apple water and add the agar agar. Leave to set, then blend to form a purée. For the Cava soda, mix the xantana and Cava in a blender, then place into a soda siphon with 2 charges of gas. To serve, line the individual dishes with the apple and agar purée. Place an oyster in each dish and surround with the Cava soda. Garnish with the other ingredients and serve.

Note: Agar agar is a form of gelatine derived from sea vegetables. It is also known by its Japanese name, Kanten. See note on opposite page for information regarding xanatana.

White Cromaticism

CROMATISMO BLANCO

Crema de Haba Tonka:
- **10 g sugar**
- **0.5 g salt**
- **1 g agar agar**
- **100 ml/3 ½ fl oz distilled Haba Tonka**

Coffee gelatine:
- **10 g sugar**
- **0.5 g de agar agar**
- **100 ml/3 ½ fl oz distilled coffee**
  (made from 250 ml/8 ½ fl oz
  coffee and 50 g coffee beans)

Iced passion fruit drink:
- **0.5 g gelatine**
- **15 g dextrose**
- **100 ml/3 ½ fl oz distilled passion**
  fruit (made from 250 ml/
  8 ½ fl oz passion fruit juice)

Cocoa sorbet:
- **100 ml/3 ½ oz distilled Haba Tonka**
- **25 g sprayed glucose**
- **15 g dextrose**
- **0.6 g stabiliser**

Make the following elements of this dessert separately, then arrange a small amount of each on individual serving plates. To mke the crema de Haba Tonka, mix the sugar, salt and agar agar in a small saucepan and add half the distilled Haba Tonka. Bring to the boil before mixing in the other half of the Haba Tonka. Cool and then emulsify in blender. To make the coffee gelatine, mix the sugar and agar agar in a small saucepan and add half the distilled coffee. Bring to the boil and then add the other half of the coffee. Leave to set in a medium sized container and once cold, cut into cubes measuring 0.5 x 0.5 cm/⅕ x ⅕ inch. To make the iced passion fruit drink, dissolve the dextrose and gelatine with half the distilled passion fruit juice and then mix in the rest. Put into a container and place in the freezer. To make the cocoa sorbet, mix the glucose, dextrose and stabiliser in a small saucepan with 30 ml water and heat to 85ºC/185ºF. Mix in the distilled Haba Tonka and put into an ice cream maker (we use the glass of a paco jet). Freeze, and just before serving, mix with an electric whisk.

Notes: Only metric measurements have been supplied for the ingredients in this recipe due to the exact quantities required. Distilled Haba Tonka can be made from 250 ml/7 fl oz water and 50 g/1 ¾ oz Haba Tonka cocoa beans.

Carme Ruscalleda

Restaurant: Carme Ruscalleda – Sant Pau, Sant Pol de Mar

Carme Ruscalleda and her husband Toni Balam grew up in Sant Pol de Mar, near Barcelona, where they now own and run Carme Ruscalleda – Sant Pau. This award-winning restaurant is a favourite amongst media, gastronomic guides and the public. Carme's cooking is inspired by seasonal products and by the reinterpretation of traditional Catalan cooking. She has received numerous awards and published a number of cookbooks.

Green noodles

FIDEUÁ VERDE

- 50 g/2 oz green garlic
- 250 g/9 oz very fine fresh noodles (n° 0)
- 100 g/3½ oz fresh spinach, cut into julienne strips
- 100 g/3½ oz courgettes, green part only, cut into julienne strips
- 100 g/3½ oz tender green beans, cut into julienne strips
- 50 g/2 oz very tender peas
- 50 g/2 oz baby broad beans
- 50 g/2 oz parmesan cheese, grated
- olive oil, for frying
- salt and white pepper

Vegetable stock:
- 2 litres/3 ½ pints still mineral water
- 1 onion, finely chopped
- 2 carrots, finely chopped
- 2 leeks, finely chopped
- 2 cloves garlic, chopped
- 1 stick celery, finely chopped
- ¼ bay leaf

Serves 4

To prepare the stock, heat the mineral water in a large saucepan over a medium heat and, when boiling, add the vegetables and bay leaf. Cook for 20 minutes. Add salt and pepper to taste, then strain and set back on the heat to keep warm. Cut the green garlic into julienne strips, then blanch in boiling water with a little salt for just 15 seconds. Drain, rinse and set aside. Preheat the oven to 190°C/380°F/Gas Mark 5. Brown the noodles in a little oil in a non-stick paella pan or frying pan. When they are golden brown, but before they start to burn, add the courgette strips and the green beans. As soon as the vegetables begin to fry lightly, add the strips of fresh spinach leaves, the green garlic, and the peas and beans. Season with salt and white pepper. Just cover with the very hot vegetable stock, bring to the boil and leave to cook over a high heat for 1 minute. Sprinkle the grated parmesan cheese over the top of the noodles and vegetables and then finish cooking the dish in the hot oven for 5 minutes. Serve immediately.

Note: Green garlic is unripe garlic and has a mild and delicate flavour. It is difficult to obtain commercially but is sometimes available in spring from farmers' markets. Perhaps the best solution, however, is to grow your own supply by planting separated unpeeled cloves of garlic, pointed side up, in a shallow bed or pot. Green garlic is ready to harvest when the stalks are tender and have reached the length of an average spring onion.

Quick prawn soup

SUQUET RÁPIDO DE GAMBAS

- 16 large Mediterranean prawns,
  unpeeled
- 1½ kg/3¼ lb waxy potatoes
  (such as Charlotte or BF 15),
  cut into regular sized pieces
- olive oil
- salt and white pepper

Stock:
- 6 cloves garlic
- 1 small slice fried bread
- 20 fried parsley sprigs
- 2 small dried red peppers,
  soaked to rehydrate
- 50 g/2 oz almonds,
  peeled and toasted
- 75 ml/3 fl oz dry sherry
- 2 litres/3½ pints mineral water

Serves 4

Peel the prawns and remove their heads, reserving the peeled tails in a cool place. Sauté the heads in a saucepan with a little oil until they are golden brown, then add the stock ingredients except for the mineral water and leave to cook over a high heat for 2 minutes. Heat the mineral water in another saucepan until boiling point, then add to the pan with the prawn heads. Season to taste, and leave to cook for 15 minutes over a medium heat. Pass the mixture through a vegetable mill and pour the stock into a large saucepan. Add the potatoes and cook for 15 minutes over a medium heat, until cooked. Add salt to taste and leave to stand, with the heat turned off, for 4 minutes. Dress the prawn tails with a little oil and salt and fry them lightly in a non-stick frying pan. Add them to the saucepan just before taking the soup to the table to serve.

Apricot sponge

BIZCOCHO DE ALBARICOQUE

- 15 fresh apricots
- 30 ml/2 fl oz of apricot liqueur
  (which can be substituted
  by Kirsh)
- 4 eggs
- 125 g/4½ oz plain flour
- 1 teaspoon baking powder
- 20 g/¾ oz brown sugar
- 250 g/9 oz caster sugar
- 10 g/¼ oz sifted chemical yeast

Makes 1 cake to serve 6–8

Put the apricots into a bowl, cover with the liqueur and leave to marinate. Preheat the oven to 190°C/380°F/Gas Mark 5. Put the eggs into a large bowl with the sugar and beat the mixture with an electric mixer or a hand whisk until frothy and firm. Sift the flour and baking powder into the mixture a little at a time and stir in carefully. Line a rectangular baking tray (approximately 30 cm x 25 cm/12 inches x 8 inches) with baking paper suitable for use in the oven. Pour in the mixture and arrange the marinated quarters of apricot over the top. Sprinkle with the brown sugar. Transfer to the oven and cook for 20 minutes. Leave to cool before turning out; the baking paper will make the sponge easy to remove from the tin. Serve freshly baked.

Santi Santamaría

Restaurant: El Raco de Can Fabes, Sant Celoni, Barcelona

Santi Santamaría was born in Sant Celoni, where in 1981 he opened El Raco de Can Fabes with his wife Àngels Serra. Countless awards later, El Raco continues to evolve and is one of Spain's favourite restaurants. Santi has published a number of cookbooks, writes for newspapers, and contributes to television, championing the bridge from classical to modern food, and in his own words 'creating a cuisine that weds craft and art'.

Sautéed clams and Swiss chard

SALTEADO DE ALMEJAS Y ACELGAS

- 1 tablespoon olive oil
- 1 clove garlic, chopped
- ½ kg/1 lb 2 oz Swiss chard
- 6 slices Serrano ham
- 16 good quality clams from Carril
- 1 small teaspoon chopped
  fresh parsley

Serves 4

Heat the oil in a frying pan over a medium heat. Add the garlic and cook for 5 minutes until brown. Add the Swiss chard, sauté and add salt and pepper to taste. Set aside a couple of slices of ham, chop the remainder, and add to the Swiss chard. Sauté until brown. Transfer the Swiss chard and ham to a serving plate. Cook the clams in the same frying pan until they open. Remove them from their shells and add them to the serving plate, along with the cooking juices from the frying pan and the chopped parsley.

Charcoal grilled duck foie gras with endives

FOIE GRAS DE PATO A LA BRASA CON ENDIVIAS

- 500 g/16 oz foie gras,
  cut into four slices
- 2 endives
- 200 g/7 oz Brussels sprouts
- 2 mandarin oranges, segmented
- sugar, to taste
- 60 ml/2 fl oz brandy
- juice of one mandarin orange
- 10 g/¼ oz butter
- grating of mandarin orange peel
- 1 teaspoon grey salt
- pepper

Serves 4

Preheat the oven to 180ºC/360ºF/Gas Mark 4. Season the foie gras to taste, then char quickly over a hot barbeque or charcoal grill before transfering to the oven for 5 minutes. Cut the endives down the middle lengthways and sauté, along with the sprouts. Saute the mandarin-orange segments in a separate pan, then add to the sprouts with a little sugar. Pour in the brandy, add the extra mandarin-orange juice and leave to reduce until the segments are almost caramelized. Add the butter and continue to cook until the sauce is sticky and glutinous. Arrange the vegetables on a serving plate and very finely grate a little of the mandarin peel over the top. Add freshly ground pepper and grey salt on top of the foie gras.

Note: Grey salt, which is also referred to as sel gris or Celtic sea salt, is a 'moist' and unrefined sea salt usually found on the coastal areas of France. If it is unavailable, you can substitute sea salt.

Angel hair tart with fruit

TARTA DE CABELLO DE ÁNGEL CON FRUTAS

- 225 g/8 oz angel hair or kadaif
- 100 g/3½ oz butter, plus extra, melted, for brushing
- caster sugar, for sprinkling
- 4 Calanda peaches
- 1 vanilla pod
- 125 ml/5 fl oz muscatel wine

Serves 4

Preheat the oven to 180°C/360°F/Gas Mark 4. Spread the angel hair on a baking tray, brush with a little melted butter and sprinkle with the sugar. Spread the mixture out to make a circle, creating a hollow in the centre. Transfer to the oven and cook for 7 minutes, until golden brown and crispy. Peel the peaches and cut into wedges. Sauté in the butter in a small saucepan over a medium heat and add the seeds from the vanilla pod. Add the muscatel and reduce until the peach juice thickens. Add the hot fruit to the angel-hair base and serve immediately.

Note: Angel hair is a type of fine vermicelli-like pastry made from Malabar gourd and sugar syrup. If you cannot find it, you may be able to find kadaif, which is similar in appearance to angel hair and is often used in middle-eastern pastry making. If Calanda peaches are not available, you can substitute apples, mangoes, pineapples or pears.

COOKING
INFORMATION

Tips

Aluminium To prevent aluminium saucepans and pots turning black when something is cooked in them, put half a slice of lemon or a piece of lemon rind into the water during cooking.

Baking tins and moulds, sticking To prevent pastry dough or cake mixture sticking, never wash baking tins and moulds with detergent. Clean them as thoroughly as possible with kitchen paper or cloth, then rinse them in clean water and dry thoroughly.

Baking tins and moulds, greasing When greasing tins and moulds with butter, put a knob of butter into the tin or mould and stand it somewhere warm, near the hob for example. When it has melted, use a brush to spread it all over the base and sides, then leave to cool. Unsalted butter is best for greasing as it is less likely to burn.

Beetroot This will retain its colour if cooked with its stalk intact.

Burnt stews If a stew burns and sticks to the base of the pan, put the pan into a container with vinegar and leave to stand for a while. Then transfer the stew to a clean saucepan, without scraping in the burnt part.

Cauliflower To make sure cauliflower stays very white, add a generous dash of milk to the cooking water. To prevent it from disintegrating, add salt only at the last minute.

Chickpeas To ensure chickpeas remain tender, put them into warm water to cook. If more water has to be added during cooking, make sure that it is hot.

Chips When making chips, once the potatoes have been peeled and cut, leave them to soak in plenty of cold water for 30 minutes to allow them to release their starch.

Custard If custard curdles during cooking, pour it into another saucepan or bowl and beat vigorously with a balloon whisk until cold. The liquid will once again come together and be smooth.

Eggs, boiling To prevent eggs from cracking when they are boiled, pierce the shell with a needle or pin at the round end.

Eggs, peeling To make hard-boiled eggs easier to shell, add 1–2 tablespoons salt to cooking water.

Eggs, storing The refrigerator is the best place to store eggs. This ensures that they will be firm when beaten or whisked.

Eggs, whisking When whisking egg whites, add a pinch of salt or 3 drops of lemon juice before you start. Use a ceramic, glass or metal bowl (not plastic) and make sure it is completely grease-free.

Fruit tarts Once the pastry has been layed in the tin, use a flat brush to glaze the base with a little lightly beaten egg white, then leave it to dry for 15–20 minutes. When completely dry, fill it with fruit and cook in the usual way.

Garlic To crush garlic more easily in a mortar, add a little salt.

Garlic and shallots To prevent indigestion, cut garlic and shallots in half lengthways and remove the green shoot from the middle before cooking.

Mayonnaise It is important to remember mayonnaise is made from raw eggs, which can contain harmful bacteria. Use the freshest eggs and consume the sauce as soon as possible. If you do not have time to make your own mayonnaise, use good quality bottled.

Mayonnaise, making If mayonnaise separates while you are making it, there are three ways to solve the problem: 1. Put an egg yolk into a bowl and gradually beat in spoonfuls of the curdled mayonnaise, a little at a time. When this is done, add salt, vinegar or lemon juice etc. to taste. 2. Mash a piece of boiled potato about 2 cm/¾ inch thick, then gradually stir in the curdled mayonnaise, a little at a time. 3. Put a piece of bread, without crusts and about the size of a walnut, into a bowl, soak it in vinegar or lemon juice and beat in the mayonnaise.

Meat If it seems that stewed meat is going to be tough, add a large, clean cork (kept solely for this purpose) to the sauce while it is cooking. This helps tenderize it.

Meat, cooking To avoid foodborne illness caused by bacterial contamination, cook meat to the temperature at which the bacteria are destroyed. Use an instant-read thermometer to check the temperature. Minced beef should be cooked to an internal temperature of 155ºF. Other cuts of beef can be cooked to 120–145ºF for medium-rare, 140–145ºF for medium, 155–165ºF for medium-well and 170–180ºF for well done. Lamb tends to favour slightly lower internal temperatures and can be cooked to 125–130ºF for medium-rare, 135–145ºF for medium or 165ºF for well done. Pork does well at no more than 155ºF for boneless loin, 160ºF for bone-in loin, and 185ºF for the roasted leg and shoulder.

Meat, marinating Prepare the meat for cooking before you marinate; meat should not be trimmed after marinating. Make sure the marinade completely covers the meat and turn every half hour to ensure the flavour is absorbed. Use glass, ceramic or plastic containers for marinating, and avoid aluminium or metal containers altogether as this can affect the taste. Always store raw meat in a sealed container away from cooked meat or other food to avoid cross-contamination. Though some marinades and spices keep the levels of bacteria down, it is still advisable to marinate in the refrigerator. Do not re-use marinades that have been used with raw meat, fish or poultry.

Milk To prevent milk from acquiring an unpleasant flavour when it is boiled, rinse out the pan with cold water first.

Odours When cooking brassicas (cabbage, Brussels sprouts or cauliflower) put a piece of lemon, squeezed gently to remove the juice, into the cooking water. Alternatively, add a piece of day-old bread, soaked in vinegar and wrapped in muslin, to the cooking water. To remove the smell of onion or fish on the hands, dampen them and rub in 2 tablespoons salt. Rinse well.

Oil Which cooking oil to use is often a matter of personal taste, but some are better than others. Sunflower oil is a near flavourless oil made from sunflower seeds. It is a good all-purpose oil, suitable for frying and deep-frying, though care must be taken as it can burn at high temperatures. Vegetable oil is a bend of different refined oils extracted from a number of sources, such as sunflower seeds, rapeseeds, cottonseeds, safflower seeds, corn, soybeans, and peanuts. It is often the cheapest oil, good for frying and deep-frying, but not the healthiest. Olive oil is a healthy oil, high in monounsaturated fats and polyphenols, and is good for sautéing and stir-frying. It is available in a variety of different flavours, colours, textures and aromas, from mild to strong. Extra-virgin olive oil comes from the first pressing of the olives and is considered to have a superior flavour to other olive oil, though it's distinctive taste can be very strong. It is best for salads, pastas and marinades. Peanut or groundnut oil is made from pressed peanuts to produce a clear, mild oil that does not absorb or transfer flavours. It is good for salads.

Oil, cooking To prevent oil foaming too much when deep-frying put a large, brand new iron nail (kept solely for this purpose) into the pan; or add some half egg shells to the pan. To prevent it from splattering when heated, sprinkle in a little salt.

Onions To prevent onions from making your eyes water when you're peeling and chopping them, first put them into the freezer for 10 minutes or into the refrigerator for 1 hour.

Paella Valencia rice This rice is the ideal choice for traditional Spanish paella but it can be difficult to find outside Spain. It is a short-to-medium grain rice and Italian risotto rice is not a suitable substitute as paella should not have a creamy texture and is not cooked in the same way. If you can't get Valencia rice, your usual type of long-grain rice is probably best.

Paprika To retain the lovely red colour, remove the pan from the heat when adding paprika to a dish.

Pastry for little tarts Add a dash of groundnut (peanut) oil to the dough to make the tarts crustier.

Pressure cookers Times for pressure cookers are about one-third of conventional cooking times. For example, potatoes which take 30 minutes cooked conventionally will be done

in about 10 minutes in the pressure cooker once it comes to pressure.

Pulses All pulses apart from chickpeas should be put into cold water to cook. If water has to be added during the cooking time, it should always be cold. When cooking dried beans, stop them from boiling on three separate occasions by adding some cold water, even if extra liquid is not required. This way they will have a softer texture.

Raw eggs These can carry harmful bacteria, such as salmonella and other foodborne illnesses. To avoid food-poisoning, it is important to handle, cook and store eggs properly, especially where young children, the elderly or pregnant women are concerned. Eggs that have the British Lion Quality stamp will be from flocks vaccinated against salmonella, but they are still not risk-free from other contamination. Always use the freshest eggs available and discard any cracked or broken ones. Many of the recipes in this book use raw egg as an ingredient. If concerned about the health implications of this, please contact your doctor for advice.

Refrigerator, cleaning Wash the lining well with a damp cloth and a little bicarbonate of soda, then rinse it with another damp cloth well wrung out in warm water. The refrigerator will then be perfectly clean with no detergent smells to taint the food.

Rice To ensure grains stay separate during cooking, add 3–4 drops lemon juice to each 1 litre/1¾ pints cooking water.

Salty stews If you have added too much salt to a stew, add a couple of slices of peeled raw potato, about 2 cm/¾ inch thick. Leave the stew over a low heat for 30 minutes, then remove and discard the potato slices, as they will have absorbed the excess salt. Another method is to add 1 teaspoon sugar, stirring it into the sauce until dissolved. It will improve the flavour noticeably.

Sponge cake Leave sponge cakes to cool in their tin until just warm or almost cold. Then turn out on to a wire rack to cool completely.

Strawberries If you have to wash strawberries, do it quickly and hull them afterwards to prevent water from

getting into the fruit and destroying its delicate flavour. To enhance their flavour, put the strawberries into a glass or china bowl, sprinkle them with a little sugar and pour in 1 tablespoon balsamic or sherry vinegar for each 1 kg/2 ¼ lb strawberries. Chill in the refrigerator, stirring occasionally.

Sautéing vegetables If vegetables (peas, beans, pieces of carrot, etc.) are to be cooked in butter, put them into the frying pan first and put the butter on top. If they are to be cooked in oil, put the oil in first, heat it a little and then add the vegetables.

Sweetening desserts For rice pudding, add sugar to the rice after it has been cooked. For puréed compotes, add sugar to the fruit after has been cooked and passed through a food mill.

Tea towels For recipes that use teatowels to wrap and submerge meat, etc., it is important to use a flour-sack-style tea towel or several layers of muslin as towels made of terry cloth or similar will shed fibres on the food.

Tomatoes To make tomatoes easier to peel, use a very sharp knife to make a cross in the end opposite the stalk, then put them into vigorously boiling water and leave for 1 minute. Drain and immediately refresh under cold water so the flesh remains firm.

Yeast Three main types of yeast are used as raising agents in baking. To prepare fresh yeast, cream it in a bowl with the lukewarm liquid specified in the recipe, then mash well with a fork to make a paste. Fresh yeast is available from health food shops and bakers' supply stores, but may be difficult to obtain elsewhere. To prepare dried yeast, dissolve a teaspoon of sugar in the amount of lukewarm liquid specified in the recipe in a bowl, then sprinkle the dried yeast on the surface. Leave to stand for 10–15 minutes, until frothy, then stir well to make a paste. Easy-blend dried yeast can be added with the flour; there is no need to mix it with liquid first. Dried yeast and easy-blend dried yeast are both widely available from supermarkets. The equivalents are: 15–25 g/½–1 oz fresh yeast = 2 teaspoons dried yeast = 1 sachet easy-blend dried yeast.

Glossary

Aspic A cold dish of cooked ham, poultry, foie gras, seafood or vegetables set in flavoured gelatine.

Bain marie Also known as a double-boilder, this is a water bath that allows food to be cooked slowly and gently. To use a bain marie in the oven, put the mixture into an ovenproof dish, place the dish in a roasting tin and pour in boiling water to come about halfway up the sides. Bake for the specified time. A roasting tin, double saucepan, or a heatproof bowl placed over a pan of barely simmering water, may be used on the hob. A bain marie is also a convenient way of keeping delicate foods, particularly sauces, warm.

Bake blind This technique of partially cooking prevents a pastry case from becoming soggy when a filling, such as fresh berries or eggs and cream, is added. Once the pastry case has been put into the tin, prick the base all over with a fork to prevent it from rising, then line with greaseproof paper, foil or baking parchment and half fill with baking beans. Ceramic and metal baking beans are available from kitchenware shops or you can use uncooked rice or dried beans kept solely for the purpose. Bake the pastry case for the time specified in the recipe, then remove the beans and lining. For some recipes the pastry case is then returned to the oven and baked until golden brown.

Beards The wiry tuft that protrudes from the hinge of mussel shells is known as the beard and should be pulled off before cooking.

Blanch To cook briefly in boiling water to remove salt or bitterness, or to soften or to firm up vegetables. Blanching also means to soak briefly in boiling water to make it easier to peel off skins from ingredients, such as tomatoes and nuts.

Bouquet garni An aromatic mixture of fresh herbs tied together and added to stocks, soups and casseroles to provide added flavour. A classic combination is 3 fresh parsley sprigs, 2 fresh thyme sprigs and 1 bay leaf tied together with a strip of leek or celery. Sachets of dried bouquet garni herbs, rather like tea bags, are available.

Whether fresh or dried, the bouquet garni should be removed and discarded at the end of cooking and before a mixture is puréed or served.

Braise To cook slowly in a small amount of liquid at a low temperature on the hob or in the oven.

Brochettes Long metal or wooden skewers on to which all kinds of ingredients may be threaded.

Brown To let food acquire a pleasing golden colour when cooked in oil or melted fat, such as butter. In the oven this is achieved by glazing the top with egg or milk or by sprinkling cheese or breadcrumbs over the top.

Carpaccio An Italian appetizer of meat or fish, originally beef, cut into wafer-thin slices and marinated in lemon juice or vinegar.

Chinois sieve This conical sieve with an ultra-fine mesh is used with a tapered wooden pestle to strain and press down ingredients to make a very smooth purée. It is often used for making sauces.

Cocotte Sometimes called a Dutch oven, this is a cast-iron pan with straight sides, a heavy base and a very well fitting lid and is used for cooking stews. The recipe œufs en cocottes is cooked in individual ramekins, also sometimes called cocotte.

Croûtons You can buy these in packets in your local supermarket, but it is better to make them yourself. Cube some day-old French bread and toss the cubes in a generous quantity of olive oil. Then either bake in a preheated oven, turning once, or fry them until golden brown and crispy. For additional flavour toss the croûtons afterwards in Parmesan and chopped fresh herbs such as oregano or basil, or cook with garlic to make garlic croûtons. You can also add a few drops of chilli sauce to the oil to make spicy croûtons.

Dress To season salad leaves with a dressing, such as vinaigrette or mayonnaise.

Fumet A concentrated aromatic stock, usually made from fish but sometimes from poultry, used to flavour other stocks and sauces.

Gelatine This is available in powdered form or as leaves. To use powdered gelatine, pour the liquid into a heatproof bowl and sprinkle the gelatine over the surface. Leave to sponge, that is, soften, for 5 minutes, then place over a pan of barely simmering water until dissolved. To use leaf gelatine, put the required number of leaves in a bowl of cold water and leave to soak for 5 minutes. Squeeze out the excess water, place in a bain marie and heat until the gelatine has dissolved. It is best not to stir gelatine with a spoon, but simply to swirl the bowl a few times, if necessary.

Julienne Very thin strips or sticks of vegetables, most easily cut with a mandoline.

Lard To thread strips of fat through lean meat to keep it moist during cooking.

Macédoine A mixture of diced vegetables or fruits.

Marinate To put raw meat or fish into a mixture of wine, vinegar, citrus juice or oil, together with vegetables, such as carrots and onions, and aromatics, such as garlic, bay leaves and spices, so that it absorbs flavours before being cooked. Marinades also often help to tenderize meat. *See also* Tips

Meat extract This is a seasoning that can add a meaty, salty flavour to sauces, soups and stews. One popular brand is Bovril. If you can't find it, use Maggi Seasoning or some crumbled beef stock cubes.

Mixed herbs A collection of commercially available dried herbs.

Papillote To make a parcel of meat, poultry or fish with other ingredients in foil, baking parchment or greaseproof paper and cook it.

Pinch The quantity of a solid ingredient, such as salt or saffron threads, that can be held between the tips of the thumb and forefinger or on the point of a knife.

Poach To simmer very gently in water without any large bubbles breaking the surface.

Roll out To smooth out pastry dough to an even thickness with a rolling pin. Always roll in one direction, not backwards and forwards, turning the dough frequently.

Salpicon Very finely diced ingredients bound with a sauce or, in the case of fruit, a syrup. A salpicon is eaten cold.

Sauté To fry lightly in a frying pan or sauté pan, sometimes covered, other times not. The process may involve shaking the pan to prevent the food from sticking.

Scald To dip food into boiling water to remove impurities or sharpness.

Set To make a delicately textured mixture or a liquid thicken or solidify.

Singe Briefly to pass poultry, game birds, sucking pigs, kids or animals' legs through a flame to remove the remains of feathers or hairs that may still be on the meat.

Skim To remove scum or foam that rises to the surface of liquid when cooking meat or jam. Use a skimmer or a slotted spoon.

Stew To cook slowly in plenty of liquid at a low temperature on the hob or in the oven.

Thicken To augment or thicken a liquid by stirring it with a wooden spoon over a low heat and/or adding plain flour, cornflour, potato flour or egg yolks.

Tomato sauce This is a versatile sauce made with fresh tomatoes that is delicious as a pouring sauce or with pasta and can be used as a base for a number of different recipes.
If you do not have time to make your own tomato sauce you can use good quality bottled. Tomato passata is readily available in most supermarkets along with a huge variety of other tomato sauces.

Vegetable mill Sometimes also called a food mill, this consists of a container with a selection of metal sieving discs. As you turn the handle, a metal blade forces the food through to produce a coarse, medium or fine texture purée.

Vinegar There are a number of types of vinegar. Red-wine vinegar has quite a strong taste and is perfect for vegetable salads, marinades for meat or game, or for some strong sauces. Two are particularly famous: Jerez vinegar, made from the wine of the same name, and balsamic, a concentrated vinegar produced in the region of Modena in Italy. White-wine vinegar is perfect as an accompaniment to fish. Aromatic vinegars are usually wine vinegars to which herbs, spices, fruits or condiments with aromas have been added. Cider vinegar has a milder taste than white wine vinegar, it can be served to season a fruit compôte or liven up some strawberries, as well as adding it to concentrated fish stocks. Vinegar with alcohol is colourless and without aroma, and is mostly used for conserves.

Vinegar, making To make vinegar with aromatic herbs the herbs should be cleaned well with paper but not washed. Pound them lightly in a mortar and put them into a sterilised jar. Fill the jar about ¾ full and then pour previously warmed vinegar (which should not have reached a boil) over the herbs.

Directory

The following sources specialise in high-quality Spanish products such as chorizo, Serrano ham, olive oil, cheese and other items used in these recipes and will ship directly to your home. Additionally, most specialty food stores carry or will order the items for you as well.

London

Bayley & Sage
60 High Street
Wimbledon Village
London SW19 5EE
020 8946 9904

Brindisa
32 Exmouth Market
Clerkenwell
London EC1R 4QE
020 7713 1666

Brindisa at Borough Market
The Floral Hall
Stoney Street
Borough Market
London SE1
020 7407 1036

East Dulwich Deli
15–17 Lordship Lane
London SE22 8EW
020 8693 2525

R Garcia & Sons
248–250 Portobello Road
London W11 1LL
020 7923 0600

Jeroboams W11
96 Holland Park Avenue
London W11 3RB
020 7727 9359

Lisboa
54 Goldborne Road
London W10 5NR
020 8969 1052

Mortimer & Bennett
33 Turnham Green Terrace
London W4 1RG
020 8995 4145

Raoul's Deli
8–10 Clifton Road
London W9 1SS
020 7289 6649

The South

Bill's Produce Store
56 Cliffe High Street
Lewes
East Sussex BN7 2AN
01273 476 918

Ceci Paolo
21 High Street
Ledbury
Herefordshire HR8 2DS
01531 632 976

Chandos Deli
6 Princess Victoria Street
Clifton
Bristol BS8 4BP
01179 743 275

Effings
74 Queen Street
Exeter
Devon EX4 3RX
01392 211 888

Humble Pie
Market Place
Burnham Market, King's Lynn
Norfolk PE31 8HS
01328 738 581

Real Eating Company
86–87 Western Road
Hove
Sussex BN3 1JB
01273 221 444

Williams & Brown
28a Harbour Street
Whitstable
Kent CT5 1AH
01227 274 507

The North

Appleyards
85 Wyle Cop
Shrewsbury
Shropshire SY1 1UT
01743 240 180

Define Food & Wine
Chester Road
Sandiway
Cheshire CW8 2NH
01606 882 101

The Olive Store
12 Church View
Maften
Newcastle Upon Tyne
NE20 0RP
01661 886 755

Roberts & Speight
40 Norwood
Beverley
East Yorkshire HU17 9EY
01482 870 717

Online

www.delicioso.co.uk
info@delicioso.co.uk
www.spanishhampers.co.uk

INDEX

Indian rice with raisins and pine
nuts 194
*isla flotante de fresones y frambuesa con
brochetas rebozadas en
azucar* 1028

J

jam
jam sauce 119
linzertorte 963
orange marmalade 1056
sponge fingers with jam and chocolate
995
tomato jam 1057
jamón Californiano con piña 779
jamón Californiano en cerveza 780
jamón con espárragos 387
*jamón de York con bechamel y
champiñones* 778
*jamón de York con espinacas y salsa de
vino Madeira* 777
jelly
eggs in port jelly 489
fruit jelly **896–7**, 1042
grape jelly 1043
peaches with white wine and orange
jelly 1065
poached eggs in jelly 494
quince jelly 1058
tomato jelly 72
jointing chicken 676
judías blancas con costra 219
*judías blancas con salchichas y
bacon* 222
judías blancas de adorno 221
judías blancas en ensalada 218
*judías blancas guisada con
morcillas* 220
judías blancas guisadas 217
judías pintas con arroz 226
judías pintas o encarnadas con vino tinto
225
judías verdes con mayonesa 415
judías verdes con salsa de tomate 411
*judías verdes con salsa de vinagre y
yemas* 412
judías verdes con vinagreta 413
judías verdes rebozadas 414
judías verdes rehogados con tocino 409
*judías verdes rehogados solo con aceite
y ajos* 408
*judías verdes salteadas con mantequilla,
perejil y limón* 407
jugged hare 844
jugged rabbit 842

K

kidney beans
kidney bean, bacon and red pepper
rice 200
kidney beans with red wine 225
kidneys *767–8*
eggs en cocotte with kidneys in
sherry 495

kidney, bacon and mushroom
brochettes 892
kidneys in tomato sauce, served in
bread rolls 891
kidneys with white wine and rice 889
lamb chops with kidneys 802
rice with kidneys 190
simple kidney brochettes 893
veal kidneys in sherry sauce with rice
890

L

lamb *651–2*
boned shoulder of lamb 792
braised lamb 796
braised shoulder of lamb 794
English-style leg of lamb 790
lamb chops with kidneys 802
lamb cutlets with béchamel
sauce 801
lamb stew with carrots and
turnips 799
lamb stew with courgettes 798
lamb stew with peas, artichokes and
potatoes 797
lamb with garlic and tomato 800
lamb with quinces 795
leg of lamb with pea sauce 791
roast lamb in a salt and rosemary crust
789
roast lamb with egg and tomato sauce
787
roast leg of spring lamb 785
roast milk lamb 784
Sepulvedana roast lamb **608–9**, 786
shoulder of lamb with potato and onion
793
stuffed leg of lamb 788
lamb brains
brains in béchamel sauce 897
brains with black butter 896
cannelloni 297
coated brains 895
frittered brains 894
grilled brains with tomato sauce 899
lambs' feet
lambs' feet fritters 918
lambs' feet in savoury lemon
sauce 920
lambs' feet stuffed with sausages,
coated in breadcrumbs and
fried 917
lambs' feet with tomato 919
lamb's fry *786*
coated lamb's fry with rice 914
lamb's kidneys *767, 768*
kidney, bacon and mushroom
brochettes 892
kidneys in sherry sauce with rice 890
kidneys in tomato sauce, served in
bread rolls 891
kidneys with white wine and rice 889
lamb chops with kidneys 802
simple kidney brochettes 893

lamb's pluck 925
langosta cocida, servida con salsa 660
langosta con bechamel al horno 663
*langostinos con salsa Americana y arroz
blanco* 665
langostinos empanados y fritos 664
langostinos en salsa 666
langoustines *552*
breaded scampi **544–5**, 664
langoustines in sauce 666
langoustines with American sauce and
rice 665
seafood cocktail 667
seafood noodles **192–3**, 280
sole fillets with spinach, béchamel
sauce and langoustines 576
langues de chat 943
lasagne 303
salmon lasagne with ratatouille 302
lasaña 303
lasaña de salmón con pisto 302
layered coffee and sponge-finger dessert
993
layered strawberry dessert 994
lazos fritos 949
lean pork and black pudding puff-pastry
pie 48
lechugas al jugo 416
lechugas guisadas 417
lechugas rellenas 418
leeks *346*
chicken with leeks and cream 809
curried leeks 439
leek and potato soup 134
leek mousse 70
leek soup with milk 136
leek tart with rice 440
leeks au gratin 437
leeks with béchamel sauce 438
leeks with vinaigrette or
mayonnaise 436
lobster mousse with leek fondue 662
porcini ravioli in leek sauce 294
'porrusalda' **128–9**, 133
ravioli filling 291
veal stew with leeks 744
vichyssoise 172
watercress soup 141
lemon
baked cauliflower with butter, lemon,
parsley and hard-boiled egg 378
chicken with lemons 804
crunchy fruit in lemon sauce 985
lambs' feet in savoury lemon
sauce 920
lemon cream 1036
lemon curd 1037
lemon doughnuts **832–3**, 946
lemon mousse 1038
lemon sorbet 1055
lemon tart 964
mackerel with garlic sauce and lemon
juice 566
pork chops with honey, lemon and
curry powder **608–9**, 769
savoury lemon sauce 86

Simone Ortega has been writing about food for over fifty years and has become the foremost authority on traditional Spanish cooking. Generations of Spaniards have learned to cook through her books. Her daughter **Inés Ortega** has collaborated with her mother from a young age.

Javier Mariscal is one of the most highly respected illustrators and designers working in Spain today. His work covers a multitude of disciplines, from graphic and industrial design to textiles, furniture, interiors, animation and multi-media projects. In this, his first cookbook, he celebrates the vibrancy of the Mediterranean with an explosion of colour and exuberance.

Phaidon Press Limited
Regent's Wharf
All Saints Street
London N1 9PA

www.phaidon.com

First published in 2007
© 2007 Phaidon Press Limited

ISBN 978 0 7148 4783 2
(UK edition)

Text first published in Spanish
as *1080 Recetas de Cocina*
by Alianza Editorial, S.A.

A CIP catalogue record for
this book is available from
the British Library.

Designed by Estudio Mariscal
Illustrated by Javier Mariscal
Photographs by Jason Lowe
Translated from the Spanish
by Equipo d'Edición
Printed in China

Note

Unless otherwise stated, milk is assumed to be full fat.

Unless otherwise stated, eggs and individual vegetables and fruits, such as onions and apples, are assumed to be medium.

Unless otherwise stated, pepper is freshly ground black pepper.

Cooking times are for guidance only, as individual ovens vary.

If using a fan oven, follow the manufacturer's instructions concerning oven temperatures.

Some recipes include raw or very lightly cooked eggs. These should be avoided particularly by the elderly, infants, pregnant women, convalescents and anyone with an impaired immune system.

Both metric and imperial measures are used in this book. Follow one set of measurements throughout, not a mixture, as they are not interchangeable.

All spoon measurements are level.
1 teaspoon = 5 ml; 1 tablespoon = 15 ml.

Australian standard tablespoons are 20 ml, so Australian readers are advised to use 3 teaspoons in place of 1 tablespoon when measuring small quantities of flour, cornflour, etc.